STAY AHEAD OF THE PACK

Your Comprehensive Guide to the Upper Level Curriculum

Robert Glicksman

J.B. & Maurice C. Shapiro Professor of Environmental Law
The George Washington University Law School

David Gray

Professor of Law
University of Maryland, Frances King Carey School of Law

Andrew Lund

Professor of Law
Faculty Director, John F. Scarpa Center for Law and Entrepreneurship
Villanova University Charles Widger School of Law

Eric Miller

Professor of Law
Loyola Los Angeles School of Law

Gregg Polsky

Francis Shackelford Distinguished Professor in Taxation Law
University of Georgia School of Law

W. Bradley Wendel

Professor of Law
Cornell Law School

WEST ACADEMIC PUBLISHING

444 Cedar Street, Suite 700
St. Paul, MN 55101
1-877-888-1330

Printed in the United States of America

ISBN: 978-1-68328-337-9

FOREWORD

Welcome back! For our law student readers, welcome back to law school. For our non-law student readers, welcome back to your continuing legal education. Like the first book in this series, *Get a Running Start: Your Comprehensive Guide to the First Year Curriculum*, this book is written for law students, lawyers, and interested citizens. It is designed to provide you with a platform for adding to your legal knowledge. The substantive chapters in this volume offer overviews of the main "bar" courses many law students take in their second and third years: Administrative Law, Business Associations/Corporations, Criminal Procedure, Evidence, Income Tax, and Professional Responsibility. The individual lessons cover core concepts, rules, and areas of doctrine that students in these courses are expected to learn. The lessons themselves are brief and designed to be read in ten minutes. Although they cannot provide a substitute for rigorous study of these topics; they offer a basic introduction that will provide you with a foundation for further exploration.

Any engaged citizen has much to gain by reading the lessons in this book, but our principal audience is law students. In these courses and lessons, we aim to offer students a resource they can use to give them a jump start on their classes and a competitive advantage over their peers. Our experience with *Get a Running Start* has shown that students who use that book as it is designed have had better learning and performance outcomes than students who do not. We therefore have every confidence that if you use this book as part of a thoughtful preview, study, and review process, then you will get ahead and stay ahead.

TABLE OF CONTENTS

STAY AHEAD OF THE PACK

Your Comprehensive Guide to the Upper Level Curriculum

CHAPTER 1

HOW TO USE THIS BOOK

By now you know there are no short cuts in law school. That is fair. After all, there are no shortcuts in the practice of law. Successful law students and successful attorneys are diligent, disciplined, attentive to details, and have a demonstrated capacity for hard work. Although we think this book is a remarkably effective tool for law students, it offers no substitutes for careful and thoughtful preparation for your classes. What we offer is a leg up. If you use this book as it is designed to be used, then you will have a clear and comprehensive overview of your courses before the first day. You will also be able to prime yourself for your weekly class preparations, enhancing your ability to identify issues, understand legal rules, and apply those rules when analyzing legal problems. And you will have guidance ready-to-hand when the time comes to prepare for exams. This book is designed to facilitate your learning, not to substitute for careful study and preparation.

In our experience, students who excel in law school commit themselves to process. They create multiple opportunities to cover and review class materials in different ways many times over the course of the semester. The materials in this book are designed to be part of that process, adding more opportunities to work through the concepts and rules central to each of the courses covered. What should that process look like? This is what we suggest:

1. A week or so before classes start, make time to read each of the chapters covering the courses you will be taking that semester. If you are taking Personal Income Tax and Business Associations (sometimes called "Corporations"), then reserve two afternoons, one for each of these chapters. By design, reading a full chapter should only take a few hours, but we think they will be among the most valuable hours you will spend. That is because reading the full

chapter for a course will provide you with a comprehensive overview of the main concepts, giving you a view of the whole forest before you embark on your journey. Take your time with this first read, but do not get hung-up trying to remember every detail. The idea is to begin to build a conceptual framework. You will spend the rest of the semester doing the detail work.

Based on our experience with *Get a Running Start* this first step is critical. ***Do not cheat yourself by putting this one off for later***. Later is just not as useful. The real value in this step is having a conceptual framework in place before classes start. And, at any rate, "later" seldom happens. Once the semester starts, time becomes very short and the focus is naturally and necessarily on the day-to-day and week-to-week demands of your classes and extra-curricular activities. In the midst of all those commitments, tasks left for "later" seldom get done.

2. During the semester, reread the relevant lessons before doing your assigned course reading. Although your professors may present material in a slightly different order, the chapters in this book are organized in a way that should line-up with most course syllabi. Where the order of things is different, you should be able to match the lessons in this book to the topics on the syllabi. Before sitting down to read the cases and materials assigned by your professor, reread the relevant lesson or lessons in this book. For example, if you are assigned to read materials relating to *Terry v. Ohio* in your criminal procedure course, then reread the Stop & Frisk lesson first. This will put you in a better position to spot the major arguments and understand the central concepts in your reading. Do not make the mistake of substituting the lessons in this book for your assigned readings, however. Priming yourself by reading the lessons in this book will dramatically improve your learning and

comprehension but cannot provide you with the detail and nuance you will be expected to glean from the cases and other materials assigned.

3. Before class, skim the relevant lessons in this book and review the "What You Need to Know" sections for those lessons. Memory is a tricky thing. Based on our personal experiences and our observations of students, it is very easy to prepare carefully in the days before class and then blank when the professor calls on you. Taking five or ten minutes before class to refresh your memory makes a tremendous difference, even if you are not on call that day. As part of this pre-class review, you should also look over notes you took on the readings.

4. Periodically, over the course of the semester, take a few minutes to reread the lessons you have already covered and review the "What You Need to Know" sections for those lessons. Professors incorporate reviews into their lectures at different points over the semester. And for good reasons. These reviews reinforce learning and show students how material from different parts of the course interact. For example, when working through a privilege problem in Evidence, your professor may ask whether the testimony sought is relevant and whether it is hearsay. If you make a practice of reviewing lessons covered, then you will be ready for these moments when they come. More importantly, you will start to see these connections yourself, assisting in your mastery of the material.

5. When it comes time to work on your outline for a class, reread the entire chapter for that course. This will help refresh your memories of material covered earlier in the semester while also bringing to the fore of your mind the broad themes of the course. This should put you in a much better position to structure your outline. It may also direct you to

areas that remain unclear, which will help to focus your final preparations.

If you have been counting, then you will have realized that, if you follow these recommendations, then you will cover the lessons in this course at least five times. Add to that your weekly course preparations, attending lectures, consolidating your reading and class notes every week, outlining, and studying for the exam, and your total rises to ten. That may seem like a lot, but our decades of combined experience as law students and professors has proven to us that there is simply no substitute for process throughout the semester. Covering concepts and material multiple times at different times from various perspectives is what generates mastery.

Many students make the mistake of thinking that learning is a goal. That often leads them to believe they can coast through the semester and then cram what they need to know into their heads when exams loom. That is a strategy guaranteed to fail in law school and the practice of law. You should instead think of learning as a process that takes place over a period of time through exposure, repetition, manipulation, and application. More mechanically, it is the process of developing and reinforcing durable neural pathways. It just cannot be done overnight. This book is designed to help you through that process while also providing a basic structure. If you use it wisely, this book will help you to get ahead and stay ahead in your second- and third-year courses.

CHAPTER 2

ADMINISTRATIVE LAW

LESSON 1: INTRODUCTION AND OVERVIEW

Administrative law focuses on the "ground rules" for decision-making by administrative agencies. These include constitutional provisions, statutes, regulations, and judicial doctrines governing the creation, structure, delegation of authority to, and operation of agencies. Administrative law addresses the procedural rules by which agencies make decisions and the rules under which courts review those decisions, which may be derived from the same sources.

Agencies operate at all levels of government. This chapter only covers federal administrative law. The concepts and issues may be similar to those governing state or local agencies, but the details almost certainly differ, requiring inquiry into those other bodies of law.

Federal agencies have no inherent authority, deriving their authority to act from legislation. They are literally agents of the legislatures that create them. They are also answerable to Executive Branch officials, including the President. The statutes that create agencies and provide their decision-making authority are referred to as their organic statutes or enabling acts. These statutes also may dictate the procedural requirements for agency action and the applicability of and standards for judicial review. Other statutes specifying procedures for agency action and governing judicial review apply to all or most agencies unless displaced by an organic statute. The federal Administrative Procedure Act (APA) is the best example.

The balance of legislative and executive branch control of an agency depends on whether it is an executive or independent agency. Executive agencies tend to be federal departments or bodies within a department headed by a single individual appointed by the President (often subject to Senate confirmation) and subject to dismissal by the President at will. Independent agencies are more shielded from presidential influence. They tend to be multi-member commissions or boards whose members serve fixed (and often staggered) terms and may be fired by the President only for statutorily specified causes.

Administrative law disputes present recurring issues. Sometimes the issue is whether agency action conflicts with the Constitution's allocation of authority among the branches of the federal government or infringes on constitutionally protected individual rights. In other instances, the issue is whether an agency's decision exceeded the authority delegated to it under its organic statute, was not supported by an adequate explanation, or was inconsistent with the evidence in the record. In still others, the question is whether an agency complied with applicable procedural requirements.

Resolution of these disputes often turns on how courts regard agencies and the work they do. Federal agencies have existed since the founding, but their number and the scope of their activities grew significantly in response to the Progressive movement of the 19th century, the New Deal, and the civil rights and environmental movements of the 1960s and 1970s. Because the Constitution, for the most part, fails to address explicitly how agencies should operate, the manner in which they interact with the three branches of government is unclear. Although the administrative state is well entrenched, some continue to contest its validity and value, arguing that agencies improperly usurp legislative, executive, and judicial power.

In a capitalist society with a free market economy, agency intervention in the market in the form of regulation or the administration of public benefits programs requires justification. Although Congress often creates agencies to address "market failures" (such as inadequate information, imperfect competition, externalities, or public goods) not everyone agrees that markets are defective or that the creation of agency programs is the best way to fix them. Agency intervention in private affairs also may be perceived of as a threat to individual liberty.

Those seeking to justify the operation of agencies have long relied on three principal arguments. First, agency decision-making is efficient. Congress lacks the time or capacity to legislate in the detail needed to advance its policy goals. It often couches statutory standards broadly and delegates to agencies authority to fill in the details. Similarly, the federal courts would be overwhelmed if they had to resolve thousands of public benefits and other disputes each year. Congress has created adjudicatory programs within agencies to reduce that burden. Second, agencies enjoy an expertise advantage over legislatures and courts. Third, at least in theory, agency officials are less subject to political pressures than elected officials, making them better able to base decisions on neutral application of legal principles instead of raw politics.

We may express the essential conflict reflected in these opposing arguments as one between those who favor maximizing agency autonomy so that agencies may pursue legislative policies efficiently and based on their expertise, and those who are suspicious of agencies and seek to rein them in to prevent abuses of power and protect individual liberty. These broad themes surface in administrative law cases. Pro-agency litigants (including the agencies) may argue that to promote agency autonomy and expertise, courts should apply constitutional doctrines in ways that empower agencies, interpret statutory delegations of authority broadly (and defer to agency interpretations of that authority), and refuse to overturn agency actions based on minor procedural mistakes. Litigants contesting agency action may argue that agency action conflicts with constitutional separation of powers or rule of law principles, that courts should construe statutory delegations narrowly, or that strict adherence to procedural requirements is critical. This clash of conceptions recurs throughout administrative law.

What You Need to Know:

1. Administrative law deals with the ground rules governing how agencies created by the legislature operate.
2. These rules are derived from the Constitution, organic statutes, cross-cutting legislation, agency regulations, and judicial decisions, including judge-made doctrines.

3. An agency has no inherent authority; anything it does must be rooted in authority derived from its organic statute.
4. Executive agencies are subject to greater presidential control than independent agencies.
5. Many administrative law issues reflect a conflict between promoting agency autonomy and expertise and constraining agencies to prevent abuses of power and protect individual liberties.

LESSON 2: INTRODUCTION TO THE ADMINISTRATIVE PROCEDURE ACT

The most important federal administrative law statute is the APA, which Congress passed in 1946 in response to concerns that pre-existing administrative law did not sufficiently constrain agencies or provide safeguards against arbitrary or erroneous action. The statute strikes a balance, recognizing both the benefits of taking advantage of agency expertise and efficiency and the need to prevent abuses of the authority delegated to agencies in their organic statutes. With few exceptions, the APA is essentially the same statute today as it was in 1946. It is important to understand the APA's scope, its rules for agency operation, and how it interacts with other sources of administrative law.

The APA has two main sets of provisions. First, it specifies the procedures governing exercise of the authority delegated to agencies under their organic statutes, such as when they adopt regulations or adjudicate cases. These procedural "rules of the road" appear in Chapter 5, 5 U.S.C. §§ 551 to 559. Second, it governs judicial review of agency action (and inaction), addressing both when judicial review is available and the standards of review that apply when it is. These provisions appear in Chapter 7, 5 U.S.C. §§ 701 to 706.

Both sets of provisions apply to "agencies." The APA defines an "agency" as "each authority of the Government of the United States, whether or not it is within or subject to review by another agency," with several exceptions. § 551(1). Congress and the federal courts are not agencies, and neither is the President. Franklin v. Massachusetts, 505 U.S. 788 (1992).

Identification of applicable APA procedures requires understanding the distinction between two key procedural vehicles by which agencies make decisions—rulemaking and adjudication. The Supreme Court addressed that basic distinction decades before the APA's adoption in addressing whether the Fourteenth Amendment's Due Process Clause required state and local governments to afford notice and an opportunity to be heard to those affected by property tax increases. In *Londoner v. City and County of Denver*, 210 U.S. 373 (1908), the Court held that due process required an adjudicatory hearing before a locality could assess taxes on landowners who would benefit from a local street paving project. But in *Bi-Metallic Inv. Co. v. State Bd. of Equalization*, 239 U.S. 441 (1915), it held that the state need not conduct an adjudicatory hearing before imposing an across-the-board increase in property valuations. It reasoned that due process requires an adjudicatory hearing when a few people are especially affected on individualized grounds, as in *Londoner*, but not when many people are affected in the same way on policy grounds, as in *Bi-Metallic*.

The APA defines both rulemaking and adjudication, but courts continue to rely on *Londoner* and *Bi-Metallic* to differentiate the two when the application of the APA's definitions is unclear. Rulemaking typically is a process for adopting a general policy that governs conduct prospectively. Adjudication typically is a process for making an individualized decision in which an agency makes determinations of legal consequences based on past events. The APA defines rulemaking as "agency process for formulating, amending, or repealing a rule," and defines a rule, in part, as "an agency statement of general or particular applicability and future effect designed to implement, interpret, or prescribe law or policy." § 551(5), (4). The APA defines adjudication as "agency process for the formulation of an order," which it defines in part as "a final disposition . . . in a matter other than rule making but including licensing." § 551(6), (7). If an agency action is not rulemaking, it qualifies as adjudication.

The APA divides rulemakings into several categories. The first includes those exempt from all APA rulemaking requirements, including matters relating to military or foreign affairs functions or public property, loans, grants, benefits, or contracts. § 553(a). The second, which encompasses most agency rulemakings, is known as informal, or notice and comment rulemaking. Subsections 553(b) and (c) require agencies to publish notice of a proposed rule in the Federal Register, provide an opportunity for public comment, and accompany publication of the final rule with a concise statement of basis and purpose. The third category includes several kinds of rules that are exempt from notice and comment procedures, but not publication requirements. These include interpretive rules, policy statements, and rules of agency organization and procedure, and rules for which there is good cause to forego notice and comment procedures. § 553(b). Finally, when an agency organic statute requires that a rule "be made on the record after opportunity for an agency hearing," formal rulemaking procedures specified in APA §§ 556 and 557 apply. § 553(c). Formal rulemaking procedures are essentially the same as those for formal adjudication, discussed below.

The APA also divides adjudications into three categories. First, some are exempt from all APA procedures. § 554(a)(1)–(6). Second, if an agency's organic statute requires that an adjudication "be determined on the record after an opportunity for an agency hearing," the procedures for formal adjudication found in §§ 554, 556, and 557 apply. Agencies engaged in formal adjudication must provide parties personal notice and afford them participatory rights that includes presentation of oral or documentary evidence and, at times, opportunity for witness cross-examination. The adjudication must be presided over by an administrative law judge (ALJ) with some independence from the agency for which the adjudication is conducted, and the decision must be based exclusively on evidence introduced at the hearing. Third, for adjudications not required to be on the record after opportunity for hearing, the APA has little to say. Their procedures are dictated by other sources of law, including organic statutes, agency regulations and, in some cases, the Due Process Clause.

The Supreme Court has interpreted the APA's judicial review provisions as creating a presumption that agency decisions are judicially reviewable. Section 702 creates a cause of action for those suffering legal wrong or adversely affected or aggrieved by agency action and waives sovereign immunity. Section 701(a) shields from review actions for which statutes preclude review and actions committed to agency discretion by law. The APA also addresses the timing of judicial review, making only final agency action subject to review and requiring exhaustion of administrative remedies in some cases. § 704. Assuming review is available, § 706 provides the applicable standard of review. It directs reviewing courts to "decide all relevant questions of law [and] interpret constitutional and statutory provisions," although courts may review agency statutory interpretations deferentially. A reviewing court may compel agency action unlawfully withheld or unreasonably delayed. § 706(1). Section 706(2) directs courts to hold unlawful and set aside agency action found to violate one of six standards. Courts can invalidate agency action that violates the Constitution, exceeds the agency's statutory authority, fails to conform to procedures required by law, is "arbitrary, capricious, and abuse of discretion, or otherwise not in accordance with law," or is not supported by substantial evidence.

An important question is how other sources of federal administrative law interact with the APA. Agency action that violates the Constitution is invalid even if it complies with the APA. Organic statutes and the APA interact in various ways. For example, organic statute provisions determine whether formal rulemaking or formal adjudication is triggered under §§ 553(c) and 554(a), respectively. That determination may affect whether the arbitrary and capricious or substantial evidence standard of review applies to agency factual determinations.

Section 559 provides that the APA does "not limit or repeal additional requirements imposed by statute or otherwise recognized by law." As a result, other statutes may impose procedural requirements more rigorous than the APA's. Likewise, some pre-APA judicial doctrines survived the APA's enactment, such as the principle that courts may only uphold agency decisions on grounds the agency itself advanced at the time of its decision. SEC v. Chenery Corp. (I), 318 U.S. 80 (1943). Section 559 also provides, however, that a "[s]ubsequent statute may not be held to supersede or modify" the APA's procedural or judicial review provisions. Although the relationship between those two provisions of § 559 is not entirely clear, under the latter sentence, courts should not interpret an organic statute as allowing an agency to conform to procedures less rigorous than APA procedures unless it expressly overrides the APA.

What You Need to Know:

1. The APA is the principal source of federal administrative law, providing rules for conducting rulemakings and adjudications and addressing when judicial review of a final agency action is available and what standard of review a court should apply.
2. The distinction between rulemaking and adjudication is critical to determining which APA procedures apply. The former is typically a process for adopting a general policy that governs conduct prospectively. The latter entails an individualized determination of legal consequences based on past events.
3. The APA dictates different procedures for formal and informal rulemaking and adjudication. Whether formal procedures are required depends on the interaction of an agency's organic statute and the APA.
4. Judicial review of final agency action is generally available if a litigant has suffered legal wrong or been adversely affected or aggrieved by it. Among the grounds for invalidating agency action are findings that it is arbitrary and capricious, unconstitutional, in excess of statutory authority, violates applicable procedural requirements, or not supported by substantial evidence.

LESSON 3: SEPARATION OF POWERS: BASICS

The separation of powers is an important aspect of administrative law's effort to balance effective implementation of regulatory and public benefit programs with the need to protect against abuse of delegated authority and infringement on individual rights. By giving each branch of government a different power, the Framers sought to prevent excessive accumulation of power in the same hands, a constraint which Montesquieu, Locke, and others regarded as critical to the preservation of liberty. Separation of powers also preserves liberty by subjecting governmental actors to the rule of law (the duty to exercise power consistent with legal rules enforceable in the courts by an independent judiciary).

Separation of powers principles are central to administrative law because they constrain the permissible structure and operation of agencies and define the roles of the three branches in relation to agencies. The Constitution, however, does little to clarify these relationships. "[T]he amorphous character of the administrative agency in the constitutional system escapes simple explanation." FCC v. Fox Television Stations, Inc., 556 U.S. 502 (2009) (Kennedy, J., concurring).

That lack of clarity is problematic because the tension between separation of powers principles and the administrative state is evident. Agencies adopt binding rules that look like "laws" without complying with the bicameralism and presentment procedures that apply to the adoption of legislation. Agency adjudicators find facts and apply laws to resolve disputes, but they lack the life tenure or salary protections that protect the independence of federal judges. Many agencies appear to exercise legislative, executive, and judicial power notwithstanding the Constitution's allocation of those powers to discrete branches of the government. For these reasons, some question the legitimacy of the administrative state. *See, e.g.*, Perez v. Mortgage Bankers Ass'n, 135 S.Ct. 1199 (2015) (Alito, J., concurring in part and concurring in the judgment) (noting "an understandable concern about the aggrandizement of the power of administrative agencies"); City of Arlington v. FCC, 569

U.S. 290 (2013) (Roberts, C.J., dissenting) (expressing concern that the accumulation of legislative, executive, and judicial powers in the same hands "is a central feature of modern American government").

Because the Constitution vests all legislative power in Congress and judicial power in the federal judiciary, agencies may exercise neither of those kinds of power. Accordingly, agencies are confined to the exercise of executive power, and are part of the Executive Branch. Agency exercise of executive power is constrained, however, by separation of powers and rule of law principles. Agencies can only exercise authority delegated to them by statutes, which are binding both on agencies and the President. *See* Kendall v. United States ex rel. Stokes, 37 U.S. (12 Pet.) 524 (1838). Because Article II vests executive power in the President, who has a duty to "take Care" that the laws are faithfully executed, agency execution of the laws is subject to presidential supervision, at least to some extent. Finally, the federal courts have authority to review executive action for compliance with the law. Marbury v. Madison, 5 U.S. (1 Cranch) 137 (1803).

Judicial concern over the separation of powers implications of the operation of administrative agencies has waxed and waned. Early cases approved of the delegation to the President and other executive officials of powers that appeared analogous to the power to legislate and adjudicate. *See* Brig Aurora v. United States, 11 U.S. (7 Cranch) 382 (1813); Murray's Lessee v. Hoboken Land & Improvement Co., 59 U.S. (18 How.) 272 (1855). Later, the Supreme Court struck down New Deal legislation on separation of powers grounds, concluding that Congress had improperly delegated legislative power to agencies. *See* A.L.A. Schechter Poultry Corp. v. United States, 295 U.S. 495 (1935); Panama Refining Co. v. Ryan, 293 U.S. 388 (1935). It also recognized constraints on agency adjudicatory authority. *See* Crowell v. Benson, 285 U.S. 22 (1932). Since 1937, the Court has generally accommodated the administrative state, although it has invalidated particular arrangements as separation of powers violations.

The Court's treatment of separation of powers issues in administrative law cases has reflected two approaches. First, the

Court has resolved some cases using a "formalistic" approach that appears to regard the legislative, executive, and judicial powers as distinct and for the most part mutually exclusive. Each power may only be exercised by the appropriate branch. When the Court applies this model, it tends to find separation of powers violations. In *Immigration and Naturalization Serv. v. Chadha*, 462 U.S. 919 (1983), for example, it invalidated the exercise of a legislative veto of the Attorney General's grant of asylum to an alien because Congress exercised "legislative" power without complying with Article I's bicameralism and presentment requirements. In *Northern Pipeline Constr. Co. v. Marathon Pipe Line Co.*, 458 U.S. 50 (1982), the Court invalidated a delegation of judicial power to non-Article III courts under the Bankruptcy Code. In *Bowsher v. Synar*, 478 U.S. 714 (1986), it struck down a delegation of executive power to a legislative officer who was removable by the President only for cause.

Second, the Court has applied a "functional" approach whose application typically results in rejection of separation of powers challenges. Under this conception, an agency's "quasi-legislative" or "quasi-judicial" authority is executive in character because it is exercised pursuant to statutes delegating authority and defining its limits (thus providing a legislative check on agency power) and courts usually can review the exercise of delegated power to ensure its consistency with the law (thus providing a judicial check). From a functional perspective, agencies conform to separation of powers norms because each branch has some measure of control over them. Under this model, a separation of powers violation is likely to occur only when an agency's exercise of delegated authority interferes with or usurps the "essential functions" of one of the three branches. The Court has endorsed broad delegations of rulemaking authority, *e.g.*, Whitman v. Am. Trucking Ass'ns, 531 U.S. 457 (2001), and an agency's authority to resolve common law counterclaims to an individual's alleged statutory or regulatory violation. Commodity Futures Trading Comm'n v Schor, 478 U.S. 833 (1986).

What You Need to Know:

1. The separation of powers is designed to preserve liberty by establishing political checks against the accumulation of power by any one branch of the government and by subjecting governmental officials to the rule of law.
2. The Supreme Court has vacillated between applying formalistic and functional approaches to the application of separation of powers doctrine to administrative agencies. The former regards legislative, executive, and judicial power as discrete and mutually exclusive.
3. The functional approach is more accommodating to agencies, viewing agency activities that appear to resemble exercises of legislative or judicial power as "execution" of the law. Its application tends to result in invalidation of administrative arrangements only when agency action usurps the essential functions of one of the three branches.

LESSON 4: SEPARATION OF POWERS: LEGISLATIVE POWER

The dividing line between legislative power, which only Congress may exercise, and executive power, which agencies may exercise, is not always clear. When agencies adopt binding legislative rules whose violation triggers sanctions, for example, they appear to be exercising legislative power. The adoption of binding regulations, however, can be characterized as the execution of a statute from which an agency derives its authority and to which its action must conform. Under this conception, such agency exercises of "quasi-legislative" authority present no separation of powers problems.

The Supreme Court has generally accommodated delegation to agencies of the authority to adopt legislative rules that create binding standards of conduct. In *J.W. Hampton, Jr. & Co. v. United States*, 276 U.S. 394 (1928), the Court held that delegation to agencies of authority to adopt legislative rules is not an improper delegation (or abdication) of Congress's core legislative authority, so long as the statute contains an "intelligible principle." Such a principle ensures that basic policy decisions are made by the elected branch of government, guides agencies in the exercise of the delegated authority, and creates standards for the courts to apply in assessing whether the agency exceeded its delegated authority. *See* Ind'l Union Dep't, AFL-CIO v. Am. Petroleum Inst., 448 U.S. 607 (1980) (Rehnquist, J., concurring).

The Court held that two New Deal-era statutes violated the nondelegation doctrine in *A.L.A. Schechter Poultry Corp. v. United States*, 295 U.S. 495 (1935), and *Panama Refining Co. v. Ryan*, 293 U.S. 388 (1935). It has not invoked the nondelegation doctrine to strike down a federal statute since the mid-1930s, but it has not overruled those two cases. Instead, it has distinguished them by identifying an intelligible principle, even in statutes with broad and general delegations of rulemaking power. For example, in *Whitman v. Am. Trucking Ass'ns, Inc.*, 531 U.S. 457 (2001), the Court upheld a provision of the Clean Air Act vesting in the Environmental Protection Agency (EPA) the authority to adopt air quality standards that are "requisite to protect the public health." It construed that provision as requiring EPA to adopt standards that are neither more nor less than necessary to protect the public health. But the Court noted that "the degree of agency discretion that is acceptable varies according to the scope of the power congressionally conferred." The broader the scope of the delegated power, the more specific the statutory intelligible principle must be to satisfy the nondelegation doctrine.

Other factors may influence the fate of nondelegation challenges. One is the subject matter of the delegation. Some congressional powers are so central to the exercise of legislative authority that they may not be delegated, or may only be delegated pursuant to a narrowly defined intelligible principle. Another factor is the identity of the recipient of the delegation. Delegations to private entities are suspect because they may be self-interested and are not subject to constraints such as presidential oversight that apply to agencies. *See* Carter v. Carter Coal Co., 298 U.S. 238 (1936); *Schechter Poultry*, *supra*. On the other hand, delegations to the President, the states, or tribal governments, who have independent constitutional or sovereign authority, are less likely to be problematic. Thus, the President's powers in military matters and foreign affairs justified delegation to the President or executive officials of the power to define court martial offenses and to activate a statutory arms embargo. Loving v. United States, 517 U.S. 748 (1996); United States v. Curtiss-Wright Corp., 299 U.S. 304 (1936). Whether the statute conditions exercise of the delegated power on compliance with procedural constraints such as mandatory public participation, or provides for judicial review that can promote accountability by providing a check on exercise of delegated authority by an independent judiciary, also may be relevant.

Although invalidation of a grant of rulemaking authority to an agency is unlikely today, courts continue to use the nondelegation doctrine as a tool in statutory construction. Under the doctrine of constitutional avoidance, courts often construe statutes to avoid raising constitutional problems. If the scope of a statutory intelligible principle may be interpreted broadly or narrowly, the court is likely to adopt the narrower construction if a broader one gives rise to nondelegation concerns. *See, e.g., Ind'l Union Dep't, supra.*

The need to identify the dividing line between legislative and executive power has arisen outside the nondelegation context. Some statutes purport to vest in Congress, one House of Congress, or a congressional committee a "legislative veto" over executive action. In *Immigration and Naturalization Serv. v. Chadha*, 462 U.S. 919 (1983), the Court invalidated the House of Representatives' veto of the Attorney General's grant of asylum to an alien. The veto was an exercise of legislative power that did not comply with Article I's mandatory procedures for bicameralism (the veto was exercised by only one House of Congress) or presentment (the veto was not presented to the President for his signature or veto). The veto qualified as a legislative act because an act is presumptively an exercise of the power vested in the branch that took it (here, the legislature), the veto altered the legal rights of both the Attorney General (by limiting his authority to grant asylum under the statute) and Chadha (by subjecting him to deportation), and the veto effectively revoked authority delegated to the executive branch by statute. The most salient remaining questions about the legislative veto are how to sever unconstitutional veto provisions from the statutes in which they appear. *See, e.g.*, Nat'l Mining Ass'n v. Zinke, 877 F.3d 845 (9th Cir. 2017); Alabama Power Co. v. U.S. Dep't of Energy, 307 F.3d 1300 (11th Cir. 2002).

In the wake of *Chadha*, Congress has turned to alternative methods of constraining the exercise of delegated discretion, such as report-and-wait provisions that defer the effective date of agency action to afford Congress an opportunity to pass a statute blocking the action and secure presidential signature of the legislation. The Congressional Review Act (CRA), adopted in 1996, allows Congress to adopt a joint resolution of disapproval of any regulation adopted within the previous 60 days of legislative session using expedited procedures. If the President signs the resolution, the regulation is nullified. In addition, the agency may not reissue the rejected rule "in substantially the same form, and a new rule that is substantially the same as such a rule may not be issued, unless the reissued or new rule is specifically authorized by a law enacted after the date of the joint resolution disapproving the original rule." 5 U.S.C. § 801(b)(2). Congress invoked the CRA only once between 1996 and 2016. In a flurry of activity, it rejected a host of Obama Administration regulations at the beginning of the Trump Administration. *See, e.g.*, Pub. L. No. 115–5, 113 Stat. 10 (2017) (repealing Interior Department regulation restricting disposal in streams of debris caused by mountaintop removal mining).

The validity of the line-item veto, pursuant to which the President attempts to excise statutory provisions such as line item appropriations, also turned on demarcation of the boundaries of legislative and executive power. Although some state Constitutions explicitly grant line-item veto authority to the Governor, the U.S. Constitution does not grant the President such power. In *Clinton v. City of New York*, 524 U.S. 417 (1998), the Court declared the line-item veto unconstitutional. The exercise of the veto was a legislative act that failed to conform to bicameralism and presentment procedures because "[i]n both legal and practical effect, the President has amended two Acts of Congress by repealing a portion of each," and repeal of statutes, as well as enactment, must comply with Article I procedures.

What You Need to Know:

1. Agencies may exercise only executive power, but exercises of quasi-legislative authority, such as the adoption of binding legislative rules, may be regarded as execution of statutes.
2. Congress may not forfeit its core legislative authority to make public policy determinations, but it may delegate to agencies the power to enact legislative rules if it supplies an intelligible principle to guide the exercise of the delegated power and to enable courts to determine whether the agency acted within the confines of the delegation.
3. The constitutionality of a delegation of rulemaking or other discretionary authority may turn on the subject matter of the delegation, the identity of the recipient of the delegated authority, and the presence or absence of accountability mechanisms such as mandatory procedures or judicial review.
4. The nondelegation doctrine is most likely to be invoked to support narrow judicial constructions of the scope of delegated statutory discretion.
5. Both the legislative veto and the line-item veto are invalid exercises of legislative authority that do not conform to Article I's bicameralism or presentment procedures.

LESSON 5: SEPARATION OF POWERS: JUDICIAL POWER

Although the exercise of judicial power is confined to the Article III judiciary, agency adjudications are often regarded as legitimate exercises of quasi-adjudicatory authority that qualify as execution of the laws. As long as agency adjudication does not infringe on the core judicial power vested by Article III in the federal courts, agency resolution of disputes through interpretation and application of law to facts is not likely to amount to the forbidden exercise of judicial power. But agency adjudication is constrained by Article III, the Seventh Amendment, and the Fifth Amendment's Due Process Clause. Under both Article III and the Seventh Amendment, the constitutionality of agency adjudication turns largely on whether the dispute being adjudicated implicates public or private rights.

The Supreme Court has long accepted the legality of some exercises of agency adjudicatory authority. In *Murray's Lessee v. Hoboken Land & Improvement Co.*, 59 U.S. (18 How.) 272 (1855), it recognized that many executive functions "involve an inquiry into the existence of facts and the application to them of rules of law." It held that Congress may allow executive officials to adjudicate matters involving "public rights" without improperly delegating Article III judicial power, even though those matters are capable of judicial determination. The Court initially defined public rights to be those implicated in a case in which the government is a party. The justification for allowing agency adjudication of public rights was that sovereign immunity precludes suits against the government without its consent. If the government consents to be sued, it may attach conditions, such as requiring a litigant to pursue its case before an agency instead of in an Article III court. *Crowell v. Benson*, 285 U.S. 22 (1932), upheld a statute that delegated to an agency the power to decide whether an employer had to compensate injured workers, even though such disputes involve the potential liability of one private party to another. The Court declared agency adjudication of private rights to be valid as long as the legislation provides for meaningful review in an Article III court. The statute in *Crowell* did that because the courts could review questions of law, even though agency factual findings were conclusive.

The Court expanded the definition of public rights in *Thomas v. Union Carbide Prods. Co.*, 473 U.S. 568 (1985). It upheld a statute requiring registered pesticide manufacturers unable to agree on the extent of compensation owed by one to another to resolve their disputes in binding arbitration before EPA. Although the dispute was between two private entities, the right to compensation bore many of the characteristics of a public right because it "serves a public purpose as an integral part of a program safeguarding the public health."

Similarly, in *Granfinanciera, S.A. v. Nordberg*, 492 U.S. 33 (1989), the Court declared that a public right includes a right "so closely integrated into a pubic regulatory scheme as to be appropriate for agency resolution with limited involvement by the Article III judiciary." *Granfinanciera* involved the constitutionality of agency adjudication under the Seventh Amendment, but the Court indicated that the same definition of public rights applies for purposes of Article III. This expanded definition as it applies to disputes between private parties divorces the legitimacy of agency adjudication from its original sovereign immunity rationale. The Court also ruled that administrative adjudication of public rights is per se constitutional. It did not make it clear, however, whether that position applies only to the Seventh Amendment, which was the context in which the case was decided, or also to Article III. Most observers seem to interpret *Granfinanciera* as confining that statement to Seventh Amendment issues.

Assuming that agency adjudication of public rights is not per se constitutional for Article III purposes, *Commodity Futures Trading Comm'n v. Schor*, 478 U.S. 833 (1986), identifies three factors relevant to the constitutionality of a delegation of adjudicatory authority to agencies (whether it involves public or private rights). *Schor* involved the submission to the Commodity Futures Trading Commission (CFTC) of an individual's claim that his commodities broker had violated the agency's anti-fraud rules. The broker filed a counterclaim, alleging that the customer had not paid the broker's fees—a breach of contract claim. The Supreme Court had always treated the power to resolve common law claims between private parties as a core Article III judicial function, but it ruled that the CFTC's resolution of the counterclaim complied with Article III.

The Court enunciated a three-part test for evaluating the legality of agency adjudication under Article III. First, a court must determine the extent to which the "essential attributes of judicial power" are reserved to Article III courts. This factor weighed in favor of constitutionality because the scope of the

CFTC's adjudicatory authority was narrow (*compare* Northern Pipeline Constr. Co. v. Marathon Pipe Line Co., 458 U.S. 50 (1982), invalidating the broad jurisdiction granted Article I bankruptcy courts under the Bankruptcy Code), CFTC decisions were subject to non-deferential judicial review (legal rulings were subject to de novo review), and the CFTC did not exercise all "ordinary powers" of federal district courts, such as the power to preside over jury trials or issue writs of habeas corpus.

Second, the "origins and importance of the right to be adjudicated" are relevant. Even if agency adjudication of public rights is not per se constitutional under Article III, it is less likely to infringe on federal judicial power. In *Schor*, the counterclaim appeared to implicate only private rights, but the Court reasoned that the public-private rights distinction is only designed to reflect a "pragmatic understanding" that when, as in *Schor*, agencies adjudicate matters that could constitutionally be determined by the Executive or Legislative Branches, there is less danger of encroachment on judicial power than when the authority to adjudicate private rights is "relegated as an initial matter to administrative adjudication."

Third, courts must consider the "concerns that drove Congress to depart from the requirements of Article III" in delegating adjudicatory power to an agency. If Congress created adjudicatory authority in an agency for the purpose of withdrawing a class of cases from the jurisdiction of the federal courts, this factor would cut strongly against the constitutionality of the delegation. A statute foreclosing judicial review in a category of cases arising under federal law may conflict with Article III's vesting of "the judicial power" in the federal courts. In *Schor*, however, Congress had the legitimate purpose of creating a quick, alternative dispute resolution forum of limited jurisdiction.

Most delegations of administrative adjudicatory power are likely to pass muster under the *Schor* test, especially given the expanded definition of public rights reflected in *Thomas* and *Granfinanciera* and the Court's willingness in *Schor* to allow CFTC adjudication of a counterclaim grounded in a traditional common law cause of action.

The Seventh Amendment creates a right to a jury trial for actions that triggered such a right in 1789. Because there was no equivalent of a right to a jury trial for matters involving public rights in 1789, administrative adjudication of those rights is per se constitutional. *See* Atlas Roofing Co. v. Occupational Safety and Health Review Comm'n, 430 U.S. 442 (1977). Likewise, agencies can adjudicate matters in which equitable relief is sought because such relief was not within the purview of common law courts in 1789. But the Seventh Amendment forbids agency adjudication of a claim for which a jury trial would have been available in 1789, unless the litigant has waived his right to a jury trial (as the brokerage customer in *Schor* did by submitting his fraud claim to the agency). Agency adjudications are not conducted before a jury. Indeed, if an agency tried to use a jury in adjudicating a case, it would likely run afoul of Article III under the first *Schor* factor by infringing on one of the essential attributes of judicial power.

A third set of constraints on agency adjudication derives from the Due Process Clause. Procedural due process rights—notice, an opportunity to participate, and a decision by a neutral decision maker—are addressed in Lessons 29–30. For now, what is relevant is the possibility that foreclosure of review of an agency's adjudicatory decision, especially of constitutional issues, will raise due process concerns. *See, e.g.*, Tenn. Valley Auth. v. Whitman, 336 F.3d 1236 (11th Cir. 2003) (declaring statute authorizing EPA to issue administrative compliance orders unconstitutional because it deprived the defendant of "meaningful judicial review").

What You Need to Know:

1. Agencies may exercise delegated adjudicatory authority, but they must do so in a manner consistent with Article III, the Seventh Amendment, and the Due Process Clause.

2. The application of Article III and the Seventh Amendment turns largely on the distinction between public and private rights. A case involves public rights if the government is a party or the rights at issue are so closely integrated into a public regulatory scheme as to be appropriate for agency

resolution with limited involvement by the Article III judiciary.

3. If an agency adjudicates a case involving public rights, it is per se constitutional under the Seventh Amendment and may be so under Article III. If the per se rule does not govern Article III's application, then the validity of the delegation of adjudicatory power to the agency turns on (1) the extent to which the "essential attributes of judicial power" are reserved to Article III courts, (2) the "origins and importance of the right to be adjudicated," and (3) the "concerns that drove Congress to depart from the requirements of Article III" in delegating adjudicatory power to an agency.

4. An assessment of agency adjudicatory authority in a case involving private rights is also governed by those factors. The private nature of the right cuts against constitutionality to a greater extent than in a public rights case under the second *Schor* factor.

5. The Seventh Amendment guarantees a right to a jury trial in any case for which such a right existed at common law in 1789, unless the litigant has waived the right. Agencies may not adjudicate cases using juries.

LESSON 6: SEPARATION OF POWERS: EXECUTIVE POWER

Article II, § 1 of the Constitution vests "[t]he Executive power" in the President. Article II, § 3 provides that the President "shall take Care that the Laws be faithfully executed." These provisions envision presidential supervision of the Executive Branch, but the scope of that authority and the manner in which it may be exercised are not clear.

Some judges and scholars construe Article II as creating a "unitary executive" that is headed by the President, and argue that any interference with the President's authority to control subordinate officials within that branch whose acts conform to the law violates separation of powers. This strong version of the unitary executive theory casts doubt on the constitutionality of independent agencies, which are shielded to some degree from presidential control. Others respond that limits on presidential control over subordinate officials within the Executive Branch is consistent with the Framers' desire to check the accumulation of power in that branch and facilitate apolitical policy decisions based on the expertise of agency officials.

Questions concerning the President's relationship to subordinate officials within the Executive Branch, and the authority of the other two branches to check the exercise of presidential power, tend to arise in three contexts, each representing a different method of presidential control over agencies. First, who is responsible for appointing agency officials? Second, to what extent may the President supervise the exercise of delegated agency policy discretion? Third, who controls the removal of agency officials?

The first question is governed by the Appointments Clause, Article II, § 2. It provides that the President, with the advice and consent of the Senate, "shall appoint . . . Officers of the United States" other than those whose appointment is governed by other constitutional provisions. It also provides that "the Congress may by Law vest the Appointment of such inferior Officers as they think proper, in the President alone, in the Courts of Law, or in the Heads of Departments." Appointments Clause issues fall into three categories: (1) whether the employee whose method of appointment is in question is an "Officer of the United States"; (2) if so, whether that officer is a principal or an inferior officer; and (3) whether the method of appointment of an inferior officer was appropriate.

The Appointments Clause applies to officers of the United States, but not to so-called "lesser functionaries." The Supreme Court has defined an officer of the United States as "any appointee exercising significant authority pursuant to the laws of the United States." Buckley v. Valeo, 424 U.S. 1 (1976).

Morrison v. Olson, 487 U.S. 654 (1988), crafted a four-factor test for determining whether an officer of the United States is a principal or inferior officer: whether the officer is removable by an officer beneath the President; has significant policymaking discretion or authority; has limited jurisdiction; and has a limited tenure of office. The Court held that independent counsels appointed by federal appellate court judges to investigate and prosecute wrongdoing within the Executive Branch were inferior officers because they were removable by the Attorney General, had no policymaking authority, had jurisdiction to investigate and prosecute only cases for which they were specifically appointed, and had terms of office that ended when the case for which they were appointed did. In *Edmond v. United States*, 520 U.S. 651 (1997), the Court, without overruling *Morrison*, identified a single factor as the controlling characteristic of an inferior officer—having a superior in the Executive Branch other than the President. If an officer's work is directed and supervised at some level by other officers appointed by the President with the Senate's consent, the officer is an inferior officer. The Court confirmed that approach in *Free Enter. Fund v. Pub. Co. Accounting Oversight Bd.*, 561 U.S. 477 (2010), holding that members of the Board were inferior officers because they were removable (after the Court struck down certain statutory restrictions on their removal as unconstitutional) at will by the Securities and Exchange Commission (SEC), an independent agency whose members are appointed by the President.

The circuit courts have split on the question of whether federal administrative law judges are officers of the United States subject to the Appointments Clause. *Bandimere v. SEC*, 844 F.3d 1168 (10th Cir. 2016), held that ALJs who work for the SEC are because their office was "established by law"; federal statutes set forth their duties, salaries, and means of appointment; and they exercise significant discretion in performing their functions. That decision conflicts with *Raymond J. Lucia Cos. v. SEC*, 832 F.3d 277 (D.C. Cir. 2016), *aff'd by an equally divided court on reh'g en banc*, 868 F.3d 1021 (D.C. Cir. 2017), *cert. granted*, 138 S.Ct. 736 (2018), which held that SEC ALJs are not officers of the United States. The court found it determinative that the decisions of SEC ALJs are merely recommendations to the Commission which bind neither third parties nor the government. The ALJs lack significant authority because only the SEC has the power to issue final decisions.

The third Appointments Clause issue concerns the method of appointment of inferior officers. In *Freytag v. Comm'r of Internal Revenue*, 501 U.S. 868 (1991), the issue was whether the appointment by the Chief Judge of the Tax Court of special tax judges, which the Court held were inferior officers, conformed to the Appointments Clause. The Court held that the Tax Court is not a "department," which it appeared to confine to cabinet-level departments. It then held that the Tax Court is a "Court of Law" for purposes of Article II, § 2 even though it is a court created by Congress pursuant to its Article I tax power rather than its Article III authority to create inferior federal courts. Accordingly, the Chief Judge could appoint the tax judges. In *Free Enter. Fund, supra*, the Court held that "departments" are not confined to cabinet-level agencies. Rather, they include any freestanding component of the Executive Branch subordinate to or contained within any other such component, including independent agencies such as the SEC. The Court also held that the "Head of a Department" may be an entire multi-member commission or board, rather than its individual chair. The SEC Commissioners qualified as the head of a department empowered to appoint members of the Board, who were inferior officers.

The Court addressed the constitutionality of presidential recess appointments—appointments made while the Senate is in recess—in *NLRB v. Noel Canning*, 134 S.Ct. 2550 (2014). Article II, § 2, cl. 2 vests in the President the power to "fill up all Vacancies that may happen during the Recess of the Senate," although a recess appointment expires at the end of the next legislative session. The Court held that a "recess" is not limited to formal recesses, but includes intrasession adjournments in which the Senate is incapable of conducting business. It also held that an adjournment "happens" not only if it first arises during an adjournment, but also if it occurs during a session and continues into a recess.

The Court has provided limited guidance on the scope of the President's authority to control an agency's exercise of delegated policy discretion. Lower courts have ruled that the President may not order an agency official to violate a statute. *See, e.g.*, Chamber of Commerce of U.S. v. Reich, 74 F.3d 1322 (D.C. Cir.

1996); *see also* In re Aiken County, 725 F.3d 255 (D.C. Cir. 2013) ("[T]he President may not decline to follow a statutory mandate or prohibition simply because of policy objections"). Presidents routinely issue executive orders directing agency operations, such as orders requiring agencies to prepare a cost-benefit analysis on major regulations. These directives usually apply only "to the extent permitted by law," and only to executive agencies. If a President directed an independent agency to follow an executive order, the courts might weigh in on the validity of various versions of the unitary executive theory.

A third method of presidential oversight is removal of agency officials. Article II is silent on removal authority, other than to authorize impeachment by Congress and removal from office for "Treason, Bribery, or other high Crimes and Misdemeanors." Art. II, § 4. In *Myers v. United States*, 272 U.S. 52 (1926), the Supreme Court held that the President has inherent power to remove executive officials, whose exercise Congress cannot condition on its own consent. *Humphrey's Executor v. United States*, 295 U.S. 602 (1935), upheld statutory provisions limiting the President's authority to remove members of the Federal Trade Commission to specified causes such as misconduct or incapacity, reasoning that, unlike the Postmaster General removed in *Myers*, who performs purely executive functions, the FTC is a "quasi-legislative" or "quasi-judicial" agency because it issues rules and adjudicates cases.

Those cases did not resolve whether Congress may impose "for cause" removal restrictions on purely executive officials. In *Morrison v. Olson*, *supra*, the Court upheld a statute allowing the Attorney General to remove independent counsels only for cause. The fact that the counsels perform "quintessential executive functions" (investigation and prosecution) was not dispositive. The restrictions on removal authority did not impermissibly interfere with the exercise of executive power by impairing the President's ability to take care that the laws are faithfully executed because independent counsels are not policymaking officials.

The D.C. Circuit in *PHH Corp. v. Consumer Financial Prot. Bureau*, 881 F.3d 75 (D.C. Cir. 2018), upheld a statute imposing for cause removal restrictions on the Director of the CFPB. The court couched the constitutional challenge that it rejected as "a wholesale attack on independent agencies" that, if successful, would have "broadly transform[ed] modern government." The court found untenable the contention that Congress may not impose for cause removal restrictions on an agency headed by a single leader, even if it may do so on multi-member commissions. It reasoned that the presence or absence of "internal checks" on agency authority are irrelevant to removal-power doctrine, which "focuses on executive control and accountability to the public, not the competing virtues of various internal agency design choices."

The Court struck down a double for cause removal provision in *Free Enter. Fund, supra.* The Sarbanes-Oxley Act of 2002 created the Public Company Accounting Oversight Board, whose members were appointed by the SEC and removable only for cause. The members of the SEC are removable by the President only for cause. Over a strong dissent, the Court found the restrictions on the SEC's authority to remove Board members unconstitutional because disagreement with the SEC on whether there was good cause to remove a Board member might not provide good cause to remove SEC members. The removal restrictions therefore interfered with the President's authority to ensure faithful execution of the law under Article II, § 3. The Court did not use the occasion to invalidate independent agencies such as the SEC, as some had speculated it might, instead converting the SEC's power to remove Board members to at will removal authority.

What You Need to Know:

1. Article II vests in the President the executive power and the duty to ensure that the laws are faithfully executed by Executive Branch officials. The President's influence over those officials takes the form of the power to appoint and remove them and to supervise their implementation of statutory authority.

2. The Appointment Clause applies to officers of the United States, who exercise significant authority pursuant to the laws of the United States. The method of appointment depends on whether an

officer is a principal or inferior officer, which turns on whether the officer's work is supervised by other officials appointed by the President with Senate consent.

3. The President appoints principal officers with Senate consent, while Congress may delegate the authority to appoint inferior officers to the President alone, the courts of law, or the heads of departments. Departments include any freestanding entity within the Executive Branch, including independent agencies.

4. The President may not order an agency to violate a statute, but may issue executive orders directing operation of the executive branch. Whether the President may order independent agencies to comply with executive orders is unclear.

5. Congress may not condition the President's inherent removal authority on its own consent, but it may impose for cause restrictions on removal, at least if an official exercises quasi-legislative or quasi-judicial authority. For cause removal restrictions for officials exercising purely executive power are more likely to be valid if the official is an inferior officer. A statute that imposes two levels of for cause removal restrictions is unconstitutional because it infringes on the President's duty to take care that the laws are faithfully executed.

LESSON 7: OVERVIEW OF JUDICIAL REVIEW

Judicial review plays an essential role in promoting the rule of law. Congress delegates authority to agencies to implement statutes through the exercise of quasi-legislative (rulemaking) and quasi-judicial (adjudication) authority that is nevertheless executive in character. Such agency actions are usually subject to review by the courts, which have the power to determine whether the actions conformed to constitutional, statutory, or regulatory provisions.

One question when a litigant challenges agency action is whether the court has the authority to hear the dispute and is willing to exercise it. Lessons 12–18 address these threshold justiciability questions. A second set of questions implicates both the scope and standard of judicial review. Scope of review refers to the range of issues subject to review. Standard of review refers to the degree of deference a court affords an agency in determining whether it acted lawfully. The term standard of review is sometimes used to cover both sets of issues, and references to standard of review in this book are also meant to include scope of review. Lessons 8–11 address the standards of review that apply to different kinds or aspects of agency decisions.

The choice of the standard of review reflects the essential administrative law conflict between allowing agencies to exercise sufficient discretion to enable them to operate effectively and providing a judicial check to ensure that agencies do not infringe on individual rights or abuse their delegated powers. Deferential review is supported by Congress's decision to delegate the authority to implement statutes, and make the policy choices needed to do that, to agencies, not courts. Deference is also justified by the comparative institutional competence of agencies and courts in the areas of agency expertise, by the agency's greater familiarity with the administrative record (especially when the record contains the testimony of witnesses that appeared before the agency but not the reviewing court), and by the desire to avoid inefficiencies resulting from duplicative agency and judicial decision-making processes.

Meaningful judicial review is supported by the need for an independent review of whether the agency's decision was within the scope of its delegated authority and consistent with applicable procedures, without which agencies could evade the rule of law. Judicial review also protects against capture of agencies by special interests whose agendas may diverge from those Congress sought to pursue. Agencies do not necessarily have greater competence to decide all questions than courts. Courts are more experienced at deciding constitutional questions, and may be more adept at the process of statutory construction. Familiarity with the record is less salient when the decision being reviewed is not based on witness testimony, or witness demeanor or credibility is not at issue. *See generally* Ethyl Corp. v. EPA, 541 F.2d 1 (D.C. Cir. 1976) (several opinions by judges who agreed that the role of the courts is to promote agency accountability, but disagreed on the most effective means of doing so).

Section 706 of the APA authorizes courts to (1) "compel agency action unlawfully withheld or unreasonably delayed," and (2) "hold unlawful and set aside agency action, findings, and conclusions" found to violate any one of six standards. Although an agency's organic statute may apply a standard of review other than the one triggered by § 706(2), these six standards usually govern. Each reflects a different balance between preserving agency autonomy and promoting agency accountability.

Agency decisions are comprised of factual, legal, and policy components. Factual determinations are reviewed under one of two standards. Under § 706(2)(E), a court reviewing agency factual determinations reached in formal rulemaking or adjudication must reverse an agency decision that is not supported by substantial evidence. An agency's organic statute may subject factual determinations in other kinds of agency proceedings to substantial evidence review. Assuming the organic statute does not do so, § 706(2)(A) provides that factual determinations reached in non-formal proceedings are reversible if they are "arbitrary, capricious, an abuse of discretion, or otherwise not in accordance with law" (a standard that is usually regarded as a single standard called the arbitrary and capricious standard).

Agencies make legal determinations when they interpret their organic statutes or agency regulations, among other things. The introductory language of § 706 provides that:

> To the extent necessary to decision and when presented, the reviewing court shall decide all relevant questions of law, interpret constitutional and statutory provisions, and determine the meaning or applicability of the terms of an agency action.

This provision appears to dictate de novo judicial review of agency resolution of questions of law. Arguably, so does § 706(2)(C), which directs reviewing courts to set aside agency action and conclusions found to be "in excess of statutory jurisdiction, authority, or limitations, or short of statutory right." As Lessons 9 and 10 indicate, however, courts in some contexts defer to agency statutory interpretations. *See* Chevron U.S.A. Inc. v. Natural Res. Def. Council, Inc., 467 U.S. 837 (1984). The degree to which such deference is appropriate is a hotly contested question, and the doctrines governing its resolution are less than clear.

Finally, an agency must apply the law, as it has construed it, to the facts it has found to reach an ultimate determination. This process is sometimes referred to as resolution of a mixed question of fact and law, but it essentially involves the exercise of the policy discretion delegated to the agency by its organic statute. Courts apply § 706(2)(A)'s arbitrary and capricious standard in reviewing such determinations. Unless an organic statute provides otherwise, that standard applies to policy determinations reached in formal proceedings, even though factual determinations in those proceedings are subject to substantial evidence review.

The arbitrary and capricious test traditionally was regarded as more deferential than the substantial evidence test, though the difference has narrowed if not disappeared. *Citizens to Preserve Overton Park, Inc. v. Volpe*, 401 U.S. 402 (1971), a leading case on the application of the arbitrary and capricious test, stated that the Secretary of Transportation's decision to approve construction of a highway through a city park was entitled to "a presumption of regularity," but that the reviewing court was obliged to conduct "a thorough, probing, in-depth review." Courts applying the arbitrary and capricious test must inquire whether the agency based its decision on consideration of the relevant statutory factors and whether it made a "clear error of judgment."

When a court reviews an agency's ultimate policy determination the question is not whether the agency reached the correct decision, or one with which the court agrees. The question is whether the agency provided adequate reasons for its determinations. Litigants identifying gaps or flaws in agency reasoning have the best chance of prevailing. The agency's decision stands or falls on the basis of the reasons it gave when it made its decision. Courts may not uphold an agency's decision on alternate grounds, even if they would have sufficed to support the agency's decision had it relied on them at the time of decision. *Chenery I*, 318 U.S. 80 (1943).

The APA specifies three other standards. Section 706(2)(B) authorizes courts to hold unlawful agency actions that violate the Constitution, which courts have independent authority to do anyway. Section 706(2)(D) authorizes courts to invalidate agency actions that violate applicable procedural requirements. Because courts frequently defer to agency procedural choices, they sometimes inquire whether those choices were arbitrary and capricious. *Vermont Yankee Nuclear Power Corp. v. Natural Res. Def. Council, Inc.*, 467 U.S. 837 (1984), bars courts from imposing on agencies procedures not required by statute, regulation, or due process.

Under § 706(2)(F), courts may reverse agency action found to be "unwarranted by the facts to the extent that the facts are subject to trial de novo by the reviewing court." In *Overton Park*, the Court limited the applicability of this standard to cases in which fact-finding procedures in an informal adjudication are deemed inadequate or factual issues not addressed by the agency are raised in an enforcement proceeding. Although *Overton Park* seemed to involve inadequate fact-finding, the Court held that § 706(2)(F) did not apply. Following this narrow interpretation of the scope of de novo review, lower courts almost never apply § 706(2)(F).

The final sentence of § 706 provides that in reviewing the validity of agency action under any of the standards in § 706, "the court shall review the whole record." The Supreme Court has interpreted that provision, consistent with pre-APA doctrine, to require that judicial review of challenged agency decisions be conducted exclusively on the basis of the administrative record compiled by the agency. *See* Camp v. Pitts, 411 U.S. 138 (1973). Unless an organic statute provides otherwise, reviewing courts typically do not allow the introduction of new evidence, although in limited situations they grant motions to complete or supplement the record. Conducting review solely on the basis of the administrative record is consistent with the judicial role of determining whether the agency provided a reasonable explanation for its decision.

What You Need to Know:

1. APA § 706 provides standards for judicial review of agency action, authorizing courts to compel agency action unlawfully withheld or unreasonably delayed, and to hold unlawful and set aside agency action that violates one of the six standards specified in § 706(2).
2. Judicial review of agency fact-finding in proceedings subject to the APA's procedures for formal rulemaking or adjudication is conducted under § 706(2)(E)'s substantial evidence test.. Agency organic statutes may trigger substantial evidence review in other contexts.
3. Judicial review of agency statutory interpretations is subject to § 706(2)(C), which, along with the introductory language of § 706, appears to provide for de novo review. Courts often defer to reasonable agency statutory interpretations, however, as explored further in Lesson 9.
4. Judicial review of an agency's application of law to facts involves an inquiry into the reasonableness of the agency's policy choices and is conducted under § 706(2)(A)'s arbitrary and capricious test. Courts may not uphold an agency decision on the basis of reasons not given by the agency when it made the decision.
5. Judicial review is usually limited to the administrative record compiled by the agency.

LESSON 8: JUDICIAL REVIEW OF AGENCY FACT-FINDING

The substantial evidence test applies to judicial review of facts found in formal rulemaking or adjudication governed by

§§ 556 and 557 of the APA. The arbitrary and capricious test (covered in Lesson 11) is the default standard that applies to agency fact-finding when the substantial evidence standard does not apply, unless the organic statute provides otherwise. Occasionally, the organic statute will allow judicial reversal of agency factual determinations only if they are clearly erroneous. On a spectrum, the clearly erroneous standard is the least deferential, the arbitrary and capricious test is the most deferential, and the substantial evidence standard probably falls somewhere in between.

Universal Camera Corp. v. NLRB, 340 U.S. 474 (1951), made two points about application of the substantial evidence test under the National Labor Relations Act that apply more broadly. First, it described substantial evidence as "such relevant evidence as a reasonable mind might accept as adequate to support a conclusion." The question is not whether the court would reach the same conclusion as the agency, but whether the evidence might have persuaded a reasonable fact-finder. Second, in applying the test, a court must review the record as a whole, including not only evidence that supports the agency's decision, but also contrary evidence.

This second point is implicated when the ALJ or other official who presides over a formal rulemaking or adjudication and the agency reviewing the ALJ's determinations reach different factual conclusions. An ALJ's decision is usually not the final decision of the agency, unless the agency adopts it as its own. Therefore, the decision reviewed by a court is the agency's, not the ALJ's. In *Universal Camera*, the Court concluded that because the ALJ's decision is part of the "whole record," a court must consider it. An agency must be careful to explain why it disagrees with an ALJ's factual findings. The importance of doing so is heightened when the disagreement concerns witness testimony, and especially when the divergence relates to testimonial as opposed to derivative inferences.

Testimonial inferences are based on witness demeanor (e.g., we find that this event occurred because X testified at the hearing that it did, and we find X to be more credible than Y, who testified that it did not). Derivative inferences are those based on other aspects of witness testimony (e.g., we find that this event occurred because Y's testimony that it did not conflicts with the physical evidence introduced at the hearing). Courts are likely to review an agency's disagreement with an ALJ's testimonial inference carefully because the ALJ has a comparative advantage over the agency—the ALJ, unlike the agency, was present when the witness testified and could assess his or her demeanor. *See, e.g.*, Penasquitos Village, Inc. v. NLRB, 565 F.2d 1074 (9th Cir. 1977) (overturning agency decision that rejected ALJ's credibility determinations). Agencies must have cogent reasons for rejecting an ALJ's testimonial inferences.

What You Need to Know:

1. The substantial evidence test applies when courts review factual determinations reached in formal rulemaking or adjudication, or when an organic statute otherwise requires.
2. Substantial evidence is "such relevant evidence as a reasonable mind might accept as adequate to support a conclusion."
3. Courts applying the substantial evidence test must review the entire administrative record, not just the evidence that supports the agency's determination. The record includes the decision of an ALJ who presided over a formal hearing, even if the agency, not the ALJ, made the final decision.
4. It is typically harder for an agency to justify overturning an ALJ's testimonial inferences, such as determinations of witness credibility, than an ALJ's derivative inferences.

LESSON 9: JUDICIAL REVIEW OF STATUTORY INTERPRETATION UNDER *CHEVRON*

Section 706 of the APA directs the federal courts to "interpret constitutional and statutory provisions and determine the meaning and applicability of the terms of an agency action." Section 706(2)(C) authorizes reversal of an agency action which a court finds to be "in excess of statutory jurisdiction, authority, or limitations, or short of statutory right." Finally, *Marbury v. Madison*, 5 U.S. (1 Cranch) 137 (1803), established that "[i]t is emphatically the province and duty of the judicial department to say what the law is." All these point toward de novo judicial review of agency interpretations of the meaning of statutes, regulations, or other sources of law.

Several factors, however, support judicial cognizance of—and perhaps deference to—agency statutory interpretations. First, Congress delegates policymaking discretion to an agency, not the courts. *See* Morton v. Ruiz, 415 U.S. 199 (1974) (noting that statutory administration requires the formulation of policy to fill statutory gaps). Selection among competing statutory interpretations has policy implications. Second, the agency's experience in administering its organic statute gives it more expertise than courts have in understanding the impact of adopting competing interpretations. Third, although agency officials are not elected, they are appointed and can be removed by officials accountable to the electorate. Federal judges are intentionally shielded from public accountability. To the extent that statutory interpretation has policy implications, allocation of decision-making authority to agencies is more consistent with democratic values than allocation of exclusive authority in the courts.

The leading case on judicial review of agency statutory interpretations is *Chevron U.S.A. Inc. v. Natural Res. Def. Council, Inc.*, 467 U.S. 837 (1984). The Court enunciated a two-step inquiry. The first question is whether the statute is clear on the precise question at issue. If so, the reviewing court applies the statute as written and owes no deference to the agency's views. In answering this question, courts use "traditional tools of statutory construction," which include statutory text, dictionary definitions, canons of statutory construction, and legislative history. Courts and scholars have debated which "tools of statutory construction," especially legislative history, are appropriate at Step One, and how to apply them.

If the statute is not clear, the second question is whether the agency's interpretation of the ambiguous provision is "permissible," or reasonable. If so, the court must defer to it. *Chevron* treats statutory ambiguity as an implicit delegation to the agency of authority to fill statutory gaps through its interpretive choices. *City of Chicago v. Envtl. Def. Fund*, 511 U.S. 328 (1994), indicated that an agency interpretation that goes "beyond the scope of whatever ambiguity" the statute contained is impermissible for purposes of Step Two. In other cases, the Court has equated the Step Two inquiry with arbitrary and capricious review under § 706(2)(A). *See, e.g.*, Judulang v. Holder, 565 U.S. 42, 52 n.7 (2011). In still other cases, the Court has described the task at Step Two as inquiring whether the agency's interpretation is "arbitrary and capricious in substance, or manifestly contrary to the statute." *E.g.*, Astrue v. Capato ex rel. B.N.C., 566 U.S. 541 (2012). It is not clear why a court could not determine that an agency interpretation is manifestly contrary to the statute at Step One. Agencies prevail in a higher percentage of cases decided at *Chevron* Step Two than Step One.

The Supreme Court has indicated that courts should uphold an agency's interpretations of its own regulations unless they are "plainly erroneous or inconsistent with the regulation." Auer v. Robbins, 519 U.S. 452, 461 (1997); Bowles v. Seminole Rock & Sand Co., 325 U.S. 410 (1945). The rationale for this "super deference" is that, the agency, in addition to its comparative expertise advantage, drafted the regulations and knows what it intended in doing so.

Some oppose *Auer* deference based on separation of powers and other concerns. An agency's interpretation of an ambiguous regulation entails a combination of lawmaking and interpretive authority in a single body. *Auer* deference also may create incentives for agencies to draft ambiguous regulations intentionally so that when the regulation's meaning arises in a specific context, the agency can adopt the interpretation that favors its interests. *See* Christopher v. Smithkline Beecham Corp., 567 U.S. 142 (2012) (Scalia, J., dissenting) (urging that *Auer* be overruled). Justice Thomas regards *Auer* deference as an erosion of the judicial check on the political branches. Perez v. Mortgage Bankers Ass'n, 135 S.Ct. 1199 (2015) (Thomas, J., concurring). Some observers think the Court will either eliminate or narrow the scope of *Auer* deference.

What You Need to Know:

1. Both Article III and the APA's judicial review provisions delegate the authority to interpret statutes to the federal courts. Yet, congressional delegation of policymaking authority, agency expertise, and democratic accountability considerations support deference to agency statutory interpretations in at least some contexts.
2. *Chevron* established a two-step framework for judicial review of agency statutory interpretations. Under Step One, courts interpret statutes whose meaning is clear de novo. Under Step Two, courts must defer to any permissible agency interpretation of an ambiguous statute. The Supreme Court has acknowledged overlap between *Chevron* Step Two and the arbitrary and capricious test.
3. The courts have long afforded considerable deference to an agency's interpretation of its own regulations, but judges and scholars have increasingly questioned the rationale for doing so and invited reconsideration of so-called *Auer* deference.

LESSON 10: JUDICIAL REVIEW OF STATUTORY INTERPRETATION UNDER ALTERNATIVES TO *CHEVRON*

The Supreme Court had reviewed agency statutory interpretations long before *Chevron*. Two cases dominated the pre-*Chevron* landscape. First, in *NLRB v. Hearst Publ'ns*, 332 U.S. 111 (1944), the Court held that "pure questions of law" (those that can be resolved without reference to facts) are subject to de novo review, while mixed questions of law and fact whose resolution involves application of law to facts in light of statutory policies are subject to more deferential review. Courts must uphold agency determinations of such mixed questions if they have "warrant in the record" and "a reasonable basis in law."

Second, in *Skidmore v. Swift & Co.*, 323 U.S. 134 (1944), the Court deferred to an agency's interpretation in non-binding guidance documents, even though such interpretations did not bind the courts. The Court declared that "[t]he weight of an agency's judgment in a particular case [involving review of agency statutory interpretations] will depend upon the thoroughness evident in its consideration, the validity of its reasoning, its consistency with earlier and later pronouncements, and all those factors which give it the power to persuade, if lacking the power to control." *Chevron* Step Two review is more deferential than *Skidmore* deference.

Many assumed that *Chevron* displaced both *Hearst* and *Skidmore* as the universally applicable framework for judicial review of agency statutory interpretations, but the Supreme Court has since recognized exceptions to *Chevron*'s applicability. The analysis is often referred to as *Chevron* "Step Zero" because it precedes application of *Chevron*'s two steps by inquiring whether *Chevron* applies at all. If not, one must identify the alternative standard of review.

Christensen v. Harris County, 529 U.S. 576 (2000), held that interpretations in documents that "lack the force of law"—such as opinion letters, non-binding policy statements, agency manuals, and enforcement guidelines—do not trigger *Chevron* review. Instead, *Skidmore* applies. In *United States v. Mead Corp.*, 533 U.S. 218 (2001), the Court declared that an agency interpretation qualifies for *Chevron* deference "when it appears that Congress delegated authority to the agency to make rules carrying the force of law, and the agency interpretation claiming deference was promulgated in the exercise of that authority." Such authority exists when Congress authorizes an agency to engage in adjudication or notice and comment rulemaking, or when there is "some other indication of a comparable congressional intent."

Finally, in *Barnhart v. Walton*, 535 U.S. 212 (2002), the Court deferred to the Social Security Administration's interpretation of a provision establishing the eligibility criteria for disability benefits. The interpretation was reflected in both a regulation adopted using notice and comment procedures (triggering *Chevron*'s applicability under *Mead*) and a Social

Security Ruling and Disability Insurance Letter, both of which were non-binding. The claimant alleged that the Court should ignore the regulation because the agency had adopted it recently, perhaps in response to the suit in which the claimant challenged SSA's denial of benefits. The Court stated that the fact that the Ruling and Letter were not adopted using notice and comment rulemaking procedures did not "automatically deprive" them of eligibility for *Chevron* deference. It disavowed any suggestion in *Christensen* to the contrary. It concluded that *Chevron* applied given "the interstitial nature of the legal question, the related expertise of the Agency, the importance of the question to administration of the statute, the complexity of that administration, and the careful consideration the Agency had given the question over a long period of time."

Most lower courts have applied *Mead*'s two-part test in determining *Chevron*'s applicability, although the factors identified in *Barnhart* sometimes also bear on the analysis. One wrinkle emerged from *Encino Motorcars, LLC v. Navarro*, 136 S.Ct. 2117 (2016), in which the Court refused to apply *Chevron* to an interpretation issued in the course of issuing a procedurally defective regulation (which the court also characterized as arbitrary and capricious). The procedural flaw may have meant that, even though the agency had delegated rulemaking authority, its interpretation was not a proper exercise of that authority under *Mead*. When the application of Step Zero makes *Chevron* inapplicable, courts tend to apply *Skidmore*. *See, e.g.*, Hagans v. Comm'r of Social Security, 694 F.3d 287 (3d Cir. 2012). *Skidmore* deference remains weaker than *Chevron* Step Two deference.

The Supreme Court has also created exceptions to *Chevron*'s applicability based on the nature of the issues raised by the agency's interpretation. In *Immigration and Naturalization Serv. v. Cardoza-Fonseca*, 480 U.S. 421 (1987), Justice Stevens, *Chevron*'s author, declined to apply *Chevron* to a pure question of statutory construction, which is subject to de novo review. *Cardoza-Fonseca* involved an interpretation issued during a formal adjudication. In *Negusie v. Holder*, 555 U.S. 511 (2009), Justice Stevens, writing separately, took the position that the "pure question of statutory construction" exception also applies to interpretations issued during notice and comment rulemaking. The status and scope of the *Cardoza-Fonseca* exception is unclear, as it is not frequently applied but has not been disavowed. The exception echoes *Hearst*'s enunciation of a de novo review test for pure questions of law.

What happens if a court construes a statute in the absence of an agency interpretation? Is the court's interpretation binding on the agency? *Nat'l Cable & Telecommc'ns Ass'n v. Brand X Internet Serv.*, 545 U.S. 967 (2005), held that the judicial interpretation binds the agency only if it was based on a determination that the statute was clear (i.e., the issue would have been decided at *Chevron* Step One had the court been reviewing an agency interpretation). If the court did not regard the statute as clear, the agency may provide a different interpretation, which will trigger review under *Chevron* Step Two.

Courts may refuse to apply *Chevron* if the agency's interpretation raises constitutional questions. In *Solid Waste Agency of N. Cook County v. U.S. Army Corps of Eng'rs*, 531 U.S. 159 (2001), the Court applied the canon of construction that courts should interpret statutes narrowly to avoid having to address constitutional (in that case, federalism) issues instead of applying *Chevron* to the agency's interpretation of the scope of a Clean Water Act permit program. Courts have also eschewed *Chevron* when applying other strong statutory interpretive canons, such as the canon against extraterritorial application of statutes. *See* Validus Reins., Ltd. v. United States, 786 F.3d 1039 (D.C. Cir. 2015). It is not clear why courts do not regard these canons as traditional tools of statutory construction to be used in applying *Chevron* Step One. *Chevron* also may not apply to agency statutory interpretations that do not implicate agency expertise, undercutting one rationale for deference. *See, e.g.*, Bamidele v. Immigration and Naturalization Serv., 99 F.3d 557 (3d Cir. 1996) (Chevron not applicable to agency interpretation of statute of limitations).

The Court recognized another exception in *King v. Burwell*, 135 S.Ct. 2480 (2015). The issue was whether the Affordable Care Act's penalty for failure to buy health insurance applies only to individuals covered by state exchanges or also to those covered by the federal exchange. Although the Court ultimately agreed with the IRS that the penalty applied to both state and federal exchanges, it addressed the question de novo, refusing to apply *Chevron*. The interpretive question was one of "deep 'economic and political significance' " that was so central to the statutory regime that if Congress had wanted to assign resolution of the question to the agency, it would have done so expressly, which it did not. Future cases will presumably flesh out the scope of this "major questions" exception to *Chevron*.

The Court refused to recognize an exception to *Chevron* for an agency's interpretation of the scope of its own jurisdiction. In *City of Arlington v. FCC*, 569 U.S. 290 (2013), the Court reasoned that the distinction between jurisdictional and interpretive questions is "a mirage." Recognition of the exception would have vitiated *Chevron* because every statutory authority issue may be characterized as a jurisdictional question.

What You Need to Know:

1. *Chevron* is not the universally applicable test for judicial review of agency statutory interpretations. Review of pure questions of law may trigger de novo review under *Hearst* and *Cardoza-Fonseca* (at least in adjudications).

2. Pursuant to *Chevron* Step Zero, as enunciated in *Mead*, *Chevron* provides the applicable review framework if Congress has delegated to the agency the authority to make rules carrying the force of law and the agency issued its interpretation in the exercise of that authority.

3. If *Chevron* does not apply under *Mead*, the less deferential *Skidmore* review framework applies. The question is whether the agency's interpretation has "the power to persuade."

4. Agency jurisdictional determinations are not exempt from *Chevron* review, but agency interpretations on questions of "deep economic and political significance" are, absent an express delegation to the agency of the power to resolve such important issues.

LESSON 11: JUDICIAL REVIEW UNDER THE ARBITRARY AND CAPRICIOUS STANDARD

Section 706(2)(A) of the APA directs courts to hold unlawful agency action found to be "arbitrary, capricious, an abuse of discretion, or otherwise not in accordance with law." This "arbitrary and capricious" standard applies under the APA to review of factual findings made in proceedings other than formal rulemaking and adjudication governed by §§ 556 and 557. Factual findings in formal proceedings are subject to substantial evidence review. The arbitrary and capricious standard also applies to agency determinations resulting from the application of law to agency factual findings in light of statutory policies. Some courts apply the arbitrary and capricious test to factual inferences drawn by agencies from other facts in the record, even in formal proceedings, on the ground that such inferences are part of the reasoning process that supports the agency's ultimate determination, while other courts review such inferences under the substantial evidence test. Finally, as Lesson 9 explains, the arbitrary and capricious standard may be implicated even in judicial review of statutory construction at Step Two of *Chevron*.

Overton Park, discussed in Lesson 7, simultaneously described arbitrary and capricious review as "probing" and "narrow." Lower courts tended to regard *Overton Park* as a signal to engage in more rigorous review under the arbitrary and capricious test, an approach that became known as "hard look" review. Nevertheless, the standard remains relatively deferential. *Overton Park* described the task of a court engaged in arbitrary and capricious review as determining whether the agency's decision was based on consideration of the relevant factors and whether the agency made "a clear error of judgment." The Court remanded the Secretary of Transportation's decision to approve of an interstate highway through a city park because the inadequacy of the record prevented the Court from applying the arbitrary and capricious standard.

The court's function in applying that standard is "ensuring that agencies have engaged in reasoned decision-making." Judulang v. Holder, 565 U.S. 42 (2011). Litigants challenging decisions as arbitrary and capricious typically seek to identify gaps or flaws in agency reasoning. *See* FCC v. Fox Television Stations, Inc., 556 U.S. 502, 548 (2009) (Breyer, J., dissenting) (describing "a process of learning through reasoned argument" as "the antithesis of the 'arbitrary' "). One example is internal inconsistency.

The Court decided two important cases applying the arbitrary and capricious standard in 1983. In *Baltimore Gas & Elec. Co. v. Natural Res. Def. Council, Inc.*, 462 U.S. 87 (1983), it upheld the Nuclear Regulatory Commission's decision not to consider the environmental impacts created by storage of high-level nuclear waste in licensing nuclear reactors because they were insignificant. The Court indicated that a court must uphold an agency's decision if it considered the relevant factors and "articulated a rational connection between the facts found and the choice made." It also warned courts to be at their "most deferential" when reviewing technical matters, such as the determinations within an agency's "area of special expertise, at the frontiers of science." Courts tend to cite *Baltimore Gas & Elec.* when they review agency decisions on scientific and technical matters, and they usually uphold the agency in doing so.

Motor Vehicle Mfrs. Ass'n v. State Farm Mut. Auto. Ins. Co., 463 U.S. 29 (1983), involved a challenge to the Department of Transportation's rescission of a recently adopted regulation requiring new vehicles to be equipped with "passive restraints," either automatic seat belts or airbags. The Court remanded the rescission, concluding that DOT failed to provide a reasoned explanation of why passive restraints would be ineffective at improving safety. After repeating *Overton Park*'s formulation of the arbitrary and capricious test, the Court added:

> Normally, an agency rule would be arbitrary and capricious if the agency has relied on factors which Congress has not intended it to consider, entirely failed to consider an important aspect of the problem, offered an explanation that runs counter to the evidence before the agency, or is so implausible that it could not be ascribed to a difference in view or the product of agency expertise.

Litigants challenging agency action as arbitrary and capricious often seek to identify one or more of the flaws enumerated in *State Farm* to demonstrate the lack of reasoned decision-making. This aspect of *State Farm* often provides the key framework for arbitrary and capricious review, but courts continue to cite the versions of the test enunciated in *Overton Park* and *Baltimore Gas & Elec.*

The Court in *State Farm* stated that if an agency changes course, it must "supply a reasoned analysis for change beyond that which may be required when an agency does not act in the first instance." The Court has since struggled with application of the arbitrary and capricious standard to agency policy changes. *See, e.g.*, *Fox Television*, 556 U.S. at 535 (Kennedy, J., concurring) (concluding that whether a change in policy requires "a more-reasoned explanation" than an initial policy determination is context-specific).

Encino Motorcars, LLC v. Navarro, 136 S.Ct. 2117 (2016), acknowledged that agencies are free to change policies if they provide a reasoned explanation for doing so. Although the explanation need not always be more detailed than if the agency were writing on a clean slate, the agency must display awareness that it is changing its position and be cognizant of reliance on its previous policy. An agency must supply a reasoned explanation if it disregards facts or circumstances underlying the prior policy. *See also* Perez v. Mortgage Bankers Ass'n, 135 S.Ct. 1199 (2015) (stating that the APA requires a "more substantial justification" if a new policy rests on factual findings that contradict those on which the earlier policy was based).

What You Need to Know:

1. Under the APA, the arbitrary and capricious standard applies to agency factual findings in informal proceedings. It is also the default standard that applies to agency policy determinations reflecting the application of the organic statute to the facts in the record, even in formal proceedings (unless the organic statute provides otherwise). Courts have even applied it to resolve *Chevron* Step Two issues.

2. The arbitrary and capricious test focuses on the agency's reasoning process. A decision is arbitrary and capricious if it is not based on relevant factors, reflects a clear error of judgment, or lacks a rational connection between the facts found and the choice made.

3. *State Farm* identified four indicia of arbitrary and capricious decision-making: reliance on irrelevant statutory factors, failure to consider an important aspect of the problem, an explanation that runs counter to the evidence, or sufficient implausibility that it cannot be attributed to a difference in view or the product of agency expertise.

4. Agencies may change existing policies, but must provide a reasoned explanation for doing so, including an awareness that a change is being made and consideration of potential reliance on the existing policy.

LESSON 12: STATUTORY PRECLUSION OF JUDICIAL REVIEW

The question of what standard of review to apply only arises if a court reaches the merits of a challenge to agency action. Several reasons may prevent a court from doing so, including the absence of a cause of action, lack of standing, and the filing of the lawsuit at an improper time. As this lesson and the next indicate, § 701(a)(2) of the APA provides another obstacle, stating that the Act's judicial review provisions apply "except to the extent that—(1) statutes preclude judicial review; or (2) agency action is committed to agency discretion by law."

The Supreme Court has recognized a rebuttable presumption that judicial review of agency action is available. The inability to challenge agency action may raise constitutional concerns. While preclusion of review of agency factual findings would be appear to be permissible, preclusion of review of constitutional challenges would not. The difficult question is whether Congress may bar suits alleging that an agency has exceeded its delegated authority. The Court has avoided due process concerns that might arise if a statute precluded such challenges to agency action affecting a protected property or liberty interest by interpreting organic statutes to allow review. *See* Leedom v. Kyne, 358 U.S. 184 (1958); Am. School of Magnetic Healing v. McAnnulty, 187 U.S. 94 (1902).

The statutory foundation for the presumption is the APA. Section 701(a) provides that the Act's judicial review provisions "apply," subject to the two stated exceptions. Section 702 states that "[a] person suffering legal wrong because of agency action, or adversely affected or aggrieved by agency action within the meaning of a relevant statute, is entitled to judicial review thereof." Under § 704, "[a]gency action reviewable by statute and final agency action for which there is no other adequate remedy in a court are subject to judicial review." Based on the APA's history and purposes, the Court has characterized these provisions as "generous," to be given a 'hospitable interpretation.' " Abbott Labs. v. Gardner, 387 U.S. 136 (1967). An agency may rebut the presumption by showing "clear and convincing evidence" of congressional intent to preclude review. The Court later insisted that it did not use that standard in *Abbott Labs.* "in the strict evidentiary sense," and that the presumption may be rebutted "whenever the congressional intent to preclude judicial review is 'fairly discernible in the statutory scheme.' " Block v. Cmty. Nutrition Inst., 467 U.S. 340 (1984). But in *Cuozzo Speed Tech., LLC v. Lee*, 136 S.Ct. 2131 (2016), the Court dubbed the presumption in favor of review a "strong" one, which may be overcome "by clear and convincing indications, drawn from specific language, specific legislative history, and inferences of intent drawn from the statutory scheme as a whole, that Congress intended to bar review."

In applying § 701(a)(1), courts focus on the judicial review provisions of the organic statute to determine if they reflect an intent to preclude review of decisions taken under it. A statute may preclude judicial challenges explicitly, in which case the question is whether a particular challenge falls within the scope of the statutory preclusion. In light of the presumption, the Court has construed provisions that appeared to preclude judicial review as not doing so. *See, e.g.*, Bowen v. Michigan Acad. of Family Physicians, 476 U.S. 667 (1986); Johnson v.

Robison, 415 U.S. 361 (1974). Even if an organic statute does not preclude review explicitly, it may do so implicitly. A question of implicit preclusion may arise if a statute allows review of certain kinds of actions or at the behest of certain classes of litigants.

Ordinarily, the mere presence of a provision allowing certain kinds of suits does not support a finding that others are precluded. But the structure and history of a statute may support a finding of implicit preclusion. In *Block*, *supra*, for example, the Court held that consumers could not obtain judicial review of milk marketing orders approved by the Department of Agriculture. The organic statute allowed suits challenging such orders by milk handlers, but required them to exhaust administrative remedies as a prerequisite to suit. Because the statute's review provision only applied to handlers, consumers could not rely on it to challenge a marketing order. The issue was whether they could nevertheless challenge such orders under the APA. The Court held that they could not and that suit was precluded by § 701(a)(2). Allowing consumers to sue under the APA would allow them to avoid the statutory exhaustion requirement, which would "severely disrupt" the statutory scheme and require a court to review the action without the full benefit of the agency's expertise.

More recently, *Sackett v. EPA*, 566 U.S. 120 (2012), held that the Clean Water Act did not preclude review of EPA's issuance of an administrative compliance order, even though EPA had not yet sought to enforce it in federal court. The Act provides for judicial review of an EPA decision imposing penalties after an administrative hearing. The Court refused to infer from that authorization an intent to preclude review of a compliance order. It stated that "if the express provision of judicial review . . . were alone enough to overcome the APA's presumption of reviewability for all final agency action, it would not be much of a presumption at all." The property owners who received the order did not have an alternative "adequate remedy" for purposes of § 704 of the APA. Civil penalties accrue beginning when EPA issues a compliance order, so its recipient may incur substantial liability if it must wait to contest its liability until EPA sues it and the court finds that the defendant is indeed liable.

What You Need to Know:

1. The Supreme Court has recognized a presumption that judicial review of agency action is available based on the due process implications of barring review and the APA's judicial review provisions.
2. The standard for rebutting the presumption has wavered, with the Court alternating between requiring clear and convincing evidence of congressional intent to preclude review and a more modest showing of fairly discernible evidence of such intent.
3. Section 701(a)(1) provides that judicial review is unavailable under the APA if an organic statute's judicial review provisions "preclude judicial review."
4. An organic statute may preclude review explicitly or implicitly. If a statute's judicial review provisions preclude certain kinds of challenges, the issue is whether a challenge falls within the purview of that provision. Absent explicit preclusion, an organic statute may nevertheless implicitly preclude review under the APA. The Court has been reluctant to infer intent to preclude review of a particular kind of challenge merely because an organic statute provides for judicial review of other kinds of challenges, absent further evidence of preclusive intent in the statute's structure or history.

LESSON 13: REVIEWABILITY OF ACTION COMMITTED TO AGENCY DISCRETION BY LAW

Under § 701(a)(2), judicial review under the APA is unavailable if "agency action is committed to agency discretion by law." Whereas application of § 701(a)(1)'s statutory preclusion exception turns on interpretation of an organic statute's judicial review provisions, application of § 701(a)(2) requires analysis of the organic statute's substantive grants of authority. The mere delegation of discretionary decision-making authority is insufficient to trigger the exception, as § 706(2)(A)'s mandate that reviewing courts set aside agency action found to be an abuse of discretion makes clear. The presumption in favor of reviewability discussed in Lesson 12 also supports a narrow reading of § 701(a)(2)'s exception.

In *Citizens to Preserve Overton Park, Inc. v. Volpe*, 401 U.S. 402 (1971), the Court characterized the "committed to agency discretion by law" exception as "very narrow," barring review only "in those rare instances where 'statutes are drawn in such broad terms that in a given case there is no law to apply.'" Section 701(a)(2) applies if only there is "no meaningful standard against which to judge the agency's exercise of discretion." Heckler v. Chaney, 470 U.S. 821 (1985).

Two decisions illustrate the kinds of delegations that create unreviewable discretion. In *Webster v. Doe*, 486 U.S. 592 (1988), the CIA Director's decision to terminate an employee satisfied *Overton Park*'s "no law to apply" test. The decision implicated national security considerations and the courts lacked competence to review the Director's determinations, although the bar to review did not extend to constitutional challenges to termination decisions. In *Lincoln v. Vigil*, 508 U.S. 182 (1993), the Court held that a discretionary allocation of a lump sum appropriation was committed to agency discretion because allocation decisions require "a complicated balancing of a number of factors which are peculiarly within [the agency's] expertise."

Pragmatic considerations may be relevant to § 701(a)(2)'s applicability. The concerns include the nature of the agency action (*e.g.*, an action bearing on national security matters as in *Webster*); the nature of the issue (*e.g.*, the exception is less likely to apply to constitutional or other purely legal questions); the need for unreviewable discretion; judicial competence; whether review would interfere with agency administration of statutory programs; and the nature and importance of the individual interest affected by the agency decision.

What You Need to Know:

1. The applicability of the APA's bar on judicial review of actions "committed to agency discretion by law" turns on the breadth of an organic statute's substantive grant of discretionary authority, not on its judicial review provisions.
2. The "committed to agency discretion by law" exception is narrow, shielding agencies from judicial challenges only if there is "no law to apply" or "no meaningful standard against which to judge the agency's exercise of discretion."
3. Courts may take pragmatic considerations into account in applying § 701(a)(2), including the nature of the agency action, the nature of the issue, the need for unreviewable discretion, judicial competence to review the challenged decision, the extent to which review would interfere with statutory programs, and the nature and importance of the individual interest affected by the agency's decision.

LESSON 14: JUDICIAL REVIEW OF PROGRAMMATIC ACTION AND INACTION

Sections 701(a), 702, 704, and 706 of the APA all use the term "agency action" in delineating when and how those provisions apply. The APA defines "agency action" in § 551(13) as "the whole or part of an agency rule, order, license, sanction, relief, or the equivalent or denial thereof, or failure to act." In construing that term, the Court has restricted review of programmatic actions and of inaction.

The Court imposed restrictions on review of programmatic action in *Lujan v. Nat'l Wildlife Fed'n*, 497 U.S. 871 (1990). Environmental groups sued the Interior Department's Bureau of Land Management (BLM), alleging that it violated its organic statute, the Federal Land Policy and Management Act (FLPMA), by implementing a program to review, and in some cases repeal, previous withdrawals of public lands from mineral extraction. The Court held that the groups failed to identify any reviewable "agency action." It construed the challenge as an attack on "the continuing (and thus constantly changing) operations of the BLM in reviewing withdrawal revocation actions." The groups could challenge individual revocations, but litigants are not entitled to review of broader regulatory or management programs unless Congress explicitly endorses review "at a higher level of generality." These limits on the reviewability of programmatic actions stemmed from concern that courts not become embroiled in supervision of day-to-day agency activities and a conviction that complaints about general government operations should be addressed to the political branches.

The APA defines "agency action" to include a failure to act. Yet, it is often more difficult to secure judicial review of inaction than action. The leading case is *Heckler v. Chaney*, 470 U.S. 821 (1985). The suit was a challenge to the Food and Drug Administration (FDA)'s refusal to take enforcement action against prisons administering lethal injections of drugs not authorized for that use. The agency's failure to prosecute was unreviewable because it was committed to agency discretion by law. The Court not only refused to apply the normal presumption of reviewability; it recognized a presumption that an agency's failure to enforce is *unreviewable*. First, a decision not to enforce reflects a balancing of factors peculiarly within the agency's expertise, such as how best to allocate limited resources and whether enforcement is consistent with statutory policies. Second, a refusal to act generally is not an exercise of the agency's coercive power over liberty or property interests. Third, a refusal to enforce is analogous to the core exercise of prosecutorial discretion, whose review by the courts would create separation of powers concerns. The presumption may be rebutted if an organic statute mandates the exercise of agency enforcement powers, but courts are reluctant to interpret statutes that way.

The Court refused to extend the reverse presumption to challenges to a denial of a rulemaking petition. *See* Massachusetts v. EPA, 549 U.S. 497 (2007). Such a denial is action, not inaction. Moreover, denials of rulemaking petitions are less frequent than refusals to enforce, more likely to turn on legal than factual analysis, and subject to special formalities such as the requirement in § 553(e) of the APA to provide an explanation of the denial.

Section 706(1) authorizes the courts to "compel agency action unlawfully withheld or unreasonably delayed." The Supreme Court has interpreted this authorization to challenge agency action "unlawfully withheld" narrowly. In *Norton v. Southern Utah Wilderness Alliance*, 542 U.S. 55 (2004) (*SUWA*), the Court held that a claim under § 706(1) may proceed only where a plaintiff asserts that an agency failed to take "a *discrete* action that it is *required to take*." It refused to hear three claims in which environmental groups asserted that the BLM's failure to restrict off-road vehicle use violated a FLPMA provision requiring the agency to "prevent unnecessary or undue degradation" of public lands, a BLM land use plan provision requiring monitoring of ORV use, and a requirement under the National Environmental Policy Act to prepare a supplemental environmental impact statement. Together, *Heckler* and *SUWA* create significant obstacles to litigants' ability to challenge agency inaction.

SUWA did not address judicial authority under § 706(1) to direct agencies to take action "unreasonably delayed." *Telecmmc'ns Research & Action Ctr. v. FCC*, 750 F.2d 70 (D.C. Cir. 1984) (*TRAC*)'s test for deciding whether such delay has occurred identifies relevant factors:

> (1) the time agencies take to make decisions must be governed by a "rule of reason"; (2) where Congress has provided a timetable or other indication of the speed with which it expects the agency to proceed in the enabling statute, that statutory scheme may supply content for this rule of reason; (3) delays that might be reasonable in the sphere of economic regulation are less tolerable when human health and welfare are at stake; (4) the court should consider the effect of expediting delayed action on agency activities of a higher or competing priority; (5) the court should also take into account the nature and extent of the interests prejudiced by delay; and (6) the court need not "find any

> impropriety lurking behind agency lassitude in order to hold that agency action is 'unreasonably delayed.' "

See, e.g., Solenex LLC v. Jewell, 156 F. Supp. 3d 83 (D.D.C. 2015) (finding unreasonable delay in the BLM's failure to rule on a request to renew a natural gas exploration permit for 29 years).

What You Need to Know:

1. Despite the presumption in favor of reviewability, judicial review of programmatic actions may not be available because courts are reluctant to supervise ongoing agency operations and political remedies may be available.
2. The APA defines "agency action" to include a failure to act, but *Heckler v. Chaney* created a strong presumption that judicial review of an agency's decision not to enforce is unreviewable.
3. Section 706(1) authorizes reviewing courts to compel agency action unlawfully withheld or unreasonably delayed. A remedy for unlawful withholding is available only if an agency failed to take a discrete action that it was required to take. *TRAC*'s multi-factor test often governs whether an agency has engaged in unreasonable delay.

LESSON 15: OVERVIEW OF STANDING

If a plaintiff lacks standing to sue, the court lacks subject matter jurisdiction of the dispute and must dismiss it. Standing rules arise from a mix of constitutional, statutory, and court-created sources. Standing restrictions seek to ensure that the plaintiff has a sufficient interest in the outcome of a dispute to allow the issues to be "presented in an adversary context and in a form viewed as capable of resolution through the judicial process." Sprint Commc'ns Co., L.P. v. APCC Servs., Inc., 544 U.S. 269 (2008). They promote the separation of powers by ensuring that courts act within the confines of Article III's delegation of the judicial power and by "prevent[ing] the judicial process from being used to usurp the powers of the political branches." Clapper v. Amnesty Int'l USA, 568 U.S. 398 (2013). *See also* Allen v. Wright, 468 U.S. 737 (1984) (stating that "the law of Art. III standing is built on a single idea—the idea of separation of powers").

The constitutional component of standing derives primarily from Article III, § 2, which limits the federal courts' jurisdiction to "cases" and "controversies." If the plaintiff cannot meet constitutional standing requirements, there is no case or controversy. The Supreme Court identified the "irreducible constitutional minimum" for standing in *Lujan v. Defenders of Wildlife*, 504 U.S. 555 (1992): (1) an injury in fact that is concrete and particularized, actual or imminent, and not conjectural or hypothetical; (2) a causal connection between the alleged injury and the conduct complained of, such that the injury is "fairly traceable" to the defendant's challenged action; and (3) a likelihood that the injury would be redressed by a favorable decision. Congress is not free to dispense with these requirements by statute, although some members of the Court have recognized Congress's authority to define new types of injury.

At one time, proof of injury in fact depended on demonstration of injury to a legal right derived from the Constitution, a statute, or common law doctrines. In *Sierra Club v. Morton*, 405 U.S. 727 (1972), the Court disavowed this narrow conception of injury, holding that aesthetic, recreational, or environmental injury could qualify, as long as the plaintiff could show use of the affected resource. A "particularized" injury is one that affects the plaintiff in a personal and individual way. An injury is "concrete" if it actually exists. An intangible injury can qualify, but among the factors relevant to determining whether it is concrete is whether it has "a close relationship to harm that has traditionally been regarded as providing a basis for a lawsuit in English or American courts." Spokeo v. Robins, 136 S.Ct. 1540 (2016).

In two cases, the Supreme Court elaborated on when an alleged injury qualifies as actual or imminent. In *Lujan v. Nat'l Wildlife Fed'n*, 497 U.S. 871 (1990), discussed in Lesson 14, it held that an environmental group lacked standing to challenge the BLM's program to revoke withdrawals that had made public lands off limits to mineral extraction. The group's member affidavits failed to establish actual or imminent injury because they alleged use of "unspecified portions of an immense tract of territory," on some portions of which mining might occur. Plaintiffs in environmental cases thus must establish a "geographic nexus" between resources they use or imminently will use and the alleged harms they seek to avert.

In *Defenders of Wildlife, supra*, the Court held that an environmental group lacked standing to challenge an Interior Department regulation limiting the applicability of Endangered Species Act (ESA) restrictions on development to projects located within the United States. The group's members alleged that, absent compliance with the ESA, U.S. financial assistance to projects in Egypt and Sri Lanka would result in the eradication of protected species that the members had sought to view in prior visits to those countries and that they planned to try to view in future visits. Those allegations did not suffice because they did not specify when the intended visits would take place—"such 'someday' intentions—without any description of concrete plans, or indeed even any specification of when the someday will be—do not support a finding of the 'actual or imminent' injury that our cases require." There must be a "temporal nexus" between the alleged harm and the challenged action.

Causation and redressability are related, *see* Allen v. Wright, 468 U.S. 737 (1984) (noting that they are often "two facets of a single causation requirement"), but distinct. Causation addresses the connection between the defendant's conduct and the alleged injury in fact. Redressability involves the connection between the alleged injury and the relief sought. Neither requirement tends to present significant obstacles when the challenger is the subject of agency action (such as the denial of a permit or a refusal to award public benefits). *See, e.g.*, Nat'l Ass'n of Home Builders v. EPA, 786 F.3d 34 (D.C. Cir. 2015) (Silberman, J., concurring) ("And the law is rather clear; *any* party covered by an agency's regulatory action has standing to challenge a rule when it issues. . . . It is only necessary for a potential litigant to show that it is part of the regulated class and its behavior is likely affected by the government's action.").

Establishing causation and redressability is more problematic for parties challenging an agency's failure to regulate or inadequate regulation of someone else, especially if the agency lacks control over the conduct of that third party. The Court has declared that "when the plaintiff is not himself the object of the government action or inaction he challenges, standing is not precluded, but it is ordinarily 'substantially more difficult' to establish." *Defenders of Wildlife, supra.* A plurality of the Court in that case concluded that the environmental groups failed to show redressability because even if the Fish and Wildlife Service (FWS), which administers the ESA, were to agree that the statute applies to agency action occurring in foreign countries, the agencies funding the foreign projects would not be bound by any FWS regulation to that effect, and even if the funding agencies complied and withdrew their funding, the foreign governments might proceed with the projects anyway using alternative funding sources.

Congress and the courts have imposed additional standing restrictions. These restrictions were traditionally referred to as "prudential" standing limits. That term lacked clarity because it sometimes referred to any standing restrictions of nonconstitutional origin, and at other times included only limits created and imposed by the courts. To avoid confusion, this Chapter will refer to these as nonconstitutional standing restrictions. The Supreme Court has identified three: (1) a prohibition on third party standing; (2) a prohibition on the assertion of generalized grievances; and (3) a requirement that the plaintiff fall arguably within the zone of interests that a relevant statute was designed to protect. Lesson 17 explores these restrictions, considering, among other things, whether some have gained constitutional status. For now, it is important to know that while Congress cannot eliminate constitutional standing requirements, it can preclude the courts from applying nonconstitutional standing restrictions.

What You Need to Know:

1. Article III's case or controversy requirement precludes federal courts from resolving a suit brought by a litigant who lacks standing to sue. Standing doctrine promotes separation of powers by limiting courts to their assigned constitutional role and preventing them from infringing on the authority of the political branches.

2. A litigant seeking to establish Article III standing must allege an injury in fact which is causally linked ("fairly traceable") to the challenged action of the defendant and likely to be redressable by the court if it provides the relief sought.

3. Injury in fact must be concrete and particularized, actual or imminent, and not conjectural or hypothetical. In contexts such as environmental law, the alleged injury must have both a geographic and temporal nexus with the defendant's challenged action.

4. Statutes or court-created doctrines may impose additional, nonconstitutional requirements. The Supreme Court has recognized a prohibition on third party standing, a prohibition on the assertion of generalized grievances, and a requirement that the plaintiff fall arguably within the zone of interests that a relevant statute was designed to protect.

LESSON 16: ADDITIONAL CONSTITUTIONAL STANDING CONSIDERATIONS

Some important questions about the nature of constitutional standing restrictions remain unresolved. As indicated in Lesson 15, the injury in fact required by Article III, § 2 must be "actual or imminent." It may be difficult to distinguish imminent future injury from conjectural allegations of harm. In *Clapper v. Amnesty Int'l*, 568 U.S. 398 (2013), the Court referred to "the well-established requirement that the threatened injury must be 'certainly impending.' " In the same opinion, however, the Court stated that its cases "do not uniformly require the plaintiffs to demonstrate that it is literally certain that the harms they identify will come about. In some cases, we have found standing based on a 'substantial risk' that the harm will occur." The Court's other cases addressing whether a risk of future injury qualified as injury in fact appear difficult to reconcile. *Compare* Summers v. Earth Island Inst., 555 U.S. 488 (2009) (claim that statistical likelihood that environmental group's members would experience reduced enjoyment of the national forests because of timber harvests appoved by the Forest Service insufficient) *with* Monsanto v. Geertson Seed Farms, 561 U.S. 139 (2010) (farmer's claim that agency decision to deregulate genetically engineered alfalfa *could* contaminate his traditional alfalfa crops sufficed).

Procedural and informational injury can qualify as injury in fact. A litigant can demonstrate standing based on an alleged procedural injury only if the failure to follow the procedures in question "could impair a separate concrete interest." An "abstract, self-contained, noninstrumental 'right' to have the Executive observe the procedures required by law" is insufficient. Lujan v. Defenders of Wildlife, 504 U.S. 555 (1992). *See also Summers, supra* (violation of a procedural right "*in vacuo*" does not suffice). Thus, denial of procedural rights generally confers standing only if the plaintiff would have had standing to challenge the substantive outcome reached using the allegedly defective procedures.

Those asserting a procedural injury linked to a separate concrete interest need not meet "all the normal requirements for redressability and immediacy." *Defenders of Wildlife*, 504 U.S. at 572 n.7. They need not show that the agency would have reached a different result absent its procedural mistakes, or that requiring it to remedy such mistakes would necessarily eliminate the alleged harm. It is enough if the agency might have come out the other way. This loosened burden of proof is necessary to avoid making it impossible for a litigant claiming procedural injury to meet standing requirements. Procedural mandates do not dictate substantive results, so the agency is always capable of reaching the same substantive result even using proper procedures. What is important is preservation of the litigant's opportunity to convince the agency to change its mind.

The circumstances in which informational injury can qualify as injury in fact are less clear. *Federal Election Comm'n v. Akin*, 524 U.S. 11 (1998), held that voters had standing to challenge the FEC's decision that a lobbying group was exempt from statutory reporting requirements. The voters were injured because they were deprived of information from the group that would have helped them evaluate candidates for public office.

The injury was concrete because it was directly related to the exercise of the right to vote. In other contexts, the absence of a statutory right of access to information has defeated attempts to rely on informational injury. *Cf.* Bensman v. U.S. Forest Serv., 408 F.3d 945 (7th Cir. 2005) (alleged informational injury was non-justiciable generalized grievance).

Another important question is whether statutes can create interests that, if adversely affected by agency action, can qualify as injury in fact. Concurring in *Defenders of Wildlife*, Justice Kennedy urged his colleagues to:

> be sensitive to the articulation of new rights of action that do not have clear analogs in our common-law tradition. . . . In my view, Congress has the power to define injuries and articulate chains of causation that will give rise to a case or controversy where none existed before . . . . In exercising this power, however, Congress must at the very least identify the injury it seeks to vindicate and relate the injury to the class of persons entitled to bring suit.

Statutory procedural rights and rights of access to information may be examples. *See* Spokeo v. Robins, 136 S.Ct. 1540 (2016) (stating that "the violation of a procedural right granted by statute can be sufficient in some circumstances to constitute injury in fact"). The Court also stated in *Spokeo*, however, that "Congress's role in identifying and elevating intangible harm does not mean that a plaintiff automatically satisfies the injury-in-fact requirement whenever a statute grants a person a statutory right and purports to authorize that person to sue to vindicate that right." It is necessary to show that the challenged action impaired that right.

What You Need to Know:

1. To meet Article III standing requirements, an alleged injury must be actual or imminent. Threatened injury can qualify if it is not speculative or conjectural.
2. Procedural injury may qualify as injury in fact, provided procedural violations "could impair a separate concrete interest" whose injury would

have provided a basis for standing. A litigant relying on procedural injury need not meet normal redressability or imminence requirements. It suffices to show that the agency might have reached a different substantive result if it complied with applicable procedures.

3. Congress may create new interests whose impairment creates injury in fact, but the scope of that authority remains unclear.

LESSON 17: NONCONSTITUTIONAL STANDING RESTRICTIONS

Nonconstitutional standing rules cannot expand standing beyond what the Constitution allows, but they can restrict it. Nonconstitutional restrictions of judicial origin are "essentially matters of judicial self-governance—the courts would be called upon to decide abstract questions of wide public significance even though other governmental institutions may be more competent to address the questions and even though judicial intervention may be unnecessary to protect individual rights." Warth v. Seldin, 422 U.S. 490 (1975).

Traditionally, nonconstitutional standing limits have been referred to as "prudential." These included (1) a requirement that an alleged injury fall within the zone of interests of the statute or other source of law allegedly violated; (2) a prohibition on standing to assert generalized grievances; and (3) a prohibition on third party standing. The Court has "not exhaustively defined the prudential dimensions of the standing doctrine." Elk Grove Unified School Dist. v. Newdow, 542 U.S. 1 (2004). Since then, however, the Court has narrowed the range of standing restrictions that qualify as prudential. Indeed, the Court has confirmed that "a federal court's obligation to hear and decide cases within its jurisdiction 'is virtually unflagging,'" Susan B. Anthony List v. Driehaus, 134 S.Ct. 2334 (2014), casting doubt on the courts' authority to impose standing restrictions that are not constitutional or statutory.

A statute cannot authorize standing when constitutional rules prohibit it. Similarly, a federal court must apply constitutional standing limits, and courts assess standing even if the defendant fails to raise a standing defense. Congress can limit or repeal application of statutory standing limits, expanding standing to the extent the Constitution permits. It may be able to preclude application of judicially created standing restrictions (although not if doing so infringes on the judicial power created by Article III), and the courts can choose not to apply standing restrictions that they have created as a matter of judicial self-governance.

The zone of interests test originated as a gloss on § 702 of the APA, which state that a person who is "adversely affected or aggrieved by agency action *within the meaning of a relevant statute*, is entitled to judicial review thereof." *See* Ass'n of Data Processing Serv. Orgs. v. Camp, 397 U.S. 150 (1970). In *Lexmark Int'l, Inc. v. Static Control Components, Inc.*, 134 S.Ct. 1377 (2014), the Court declared that "Congress is presumed to 'legislat[e] against the background of the zone-of-interests limitation," which therefore applies to a statutory cause of action "unless it is expressly negated." Thus, the test takes the form of a rebuttable presumption of statutory construction. *See* Bennett v. Spear, 520 U.S. 154 (1997) (holding that the ESA's citizen suit provision, which authorizes suit by "any person," waived zone of interest restrictions). *Lexmark* also confirmed that the test is statutory, not a "prudential" limit derived from judicial self-restraint.

The zone of interests test is not demanding. *See* Clarke v. Securities Ind. Ass'n, 479 U.S. 388 (1987) (a plaintiff fails the test only if his or her interests "are so marginally related to or inconsistent with the purposes implicit in the statute that it cannot reasonably be assumed that Congress intended to permit the suit"). The issue is whether the interest a litigant seeks to protect "is arguably within the zone of interest to be protected or regulated by the statute or constitutional guarantee in question." *Data Processing, supra*. The zone of interests is defined by the substantive organic statute provisions allegedly violated. The test nevertheless blocks access to the courts in some cases. *See, e.g.*, Air Courier Conf. v. Am. Postal Workers, 498 U.S. 517 (1991) (postal workers were not within the zone of interests protected by a statute prohibiting private companies from competing with the Postal Service because the statute was intended to protect the Service, not to preserve workers' jobs).

Generalized grievances do not support standing because "the political process, rather than the judicial process, may provide the more appropriate remedy for a widely shared grievance." Federal Election Comm'n v. Akins, 524 U.S. 11 (1998). The fact that an injury is widely shared, however, is insufficient to render it a nonjusticiable generalized grievance. A concrete and particularized injury is not a generalized grievance, but an interest that is not only widely shared but also abstract, such as the interest in assuring that agencies obey the law, is. *Akins, supra.* Dictum in *Lexmark* treated the generalized grievance test as constitutional, even though the test has "at times been grounded" in prudential considerations. The generalized grievance prohibition may be the flip side of Article III's requirement that the plaintiff show "particularized injury." A generalized injury is not particularized.

The third standing restriction traditionally regarded as prudential is the prohibition on third party standing. *Lexmark* expressed uncertainty about this characterization, but found it unnecessary to resolve the issue. The rule requires that litigants assert their own rights, not those of third parties not before the court. It is designed to protect control over the assertion of rights by persons to whom those rights belong. Duke Power v. Carolina Envtl. Study Group, 438 U.S. 59 (1978) (the prohibition assures "that the most effective advocate of the rights at issue is present to champion them"). It also seeks to foster "concrete and sharp" presentation of issues. Secretary of State of Md. v. Joseph H. Munson Co., 467 U.S. 947 (1984).

Courts have recognized exceptions to third party standing restrictions. Courts may allow organizations to sue on behalf of their members. "Associational standing" exists if (1) one or more individual members would have been able to establish their own standing, (2) the interests at stake are germane to the organization's purpose, and (3) neither the claim asserted nor the relief sought requires the participation of individual members in the lawsuit. Hunt v. Washington State Apple Advertising Comm'n, 432 U.S. 333 (1977). Courts also have allowed parents to assert their children's rights and, in some cases, doctors to assert their patients' rights. A litigant may bring an action on behalf of third parties if (1) the litigant has suffered an injury in fact that qualifies as a "sufficiently concrete interest" in the outcome of the suit; (2) the litigant has a close relation to the third party; and (3) there is some hindrance to the third party's ability to protect his or her own interests. Powers v. Ohio, 499 U.S. 400 (1991).

What You Need to Know:

1. Traditionally, three restrictions on standing were regarded as prudential doctrines: (1) the requirement that an alleged injury fall within the zone of interests of the statute allegedly violated; (2) a prohibition on standing to assert generalized grievances; and (3) a prohibition on third party standing.
2. The zone of interests test is statutory. It is a gloss on § 702 of the APA, which provides that any person adversely affected or aggrieved by agency action "within the meaning of a relevant statute" is entitled to judicial review. The litigant must show that its interests "arguably" fall within the zone that the statute allegedly violated was designed to protect.
3. The generalized grievance rule is linked to Article III's injury in fact requirement in that a generalized grievance is not particularized. An injury is not necessarily generalized simply because it is widely shared. As long as it is concrete, rather than abstract, it may provide the basis for standing.
4. The prohibition on third party standing requires litigants to assert their own rights, not those of third parties. The prohibition does not prevent associational standing, and courts may allow third parties (such as parents or doctors) to sue on behalf of those unable to protect their own interests.

LESSON 18: TIMING RESTRICTIONS ON THE AVAILABILITY OF JUDICIAL REVIEW

Several doctrines limit a litigant's ability to challenge agency action based on the timing of the suit. These doctrines all serve the same core function: deferring judicial review until the agency has had a chance to resolve the matter in a way that avoids the need for judicial review or apply its expertise in developing an administrative record that will facilitate judicial review. The doctrines, which reflect a different mix of constitutional, statutory, and court-created limits on judicial review, are finality, exhaustion, ripeness, and primary jurisdiction.

Finality

Typically, only final agency action is judicially reviewable. Section 704 of the APA provides that "[a]gency action made reviewable by statute and final agency action for which there is no adequate remedy in a court are subject to judicial review." Agency organic statutes may authorize review of non-final action, but they rarely do so. If the organic statute does not provide for judicial review or is silent on whether finality is a prerequisite to review, § 704's finality requirement applies.

In *Franklin v. Massachusetts*, 505 U.S. 788 (1992), the Supreme Court explained that the "core question" in applying the finality requirement is whether the agency has completed its decision-making process and the result will directly affect the parties. Although there is disagreement on whether there is a definitive test for finality, *see* U.S. Army Corps of Eng'rs v. Hawkes Co., 136 S.Ct. 1807, 1818 n.* (2016) (Ginsburg, J., concurring), the test that courts appear to apply most frequently was enunciated in *Bennett v. Spear*, 520 U.S. 154 (1997):

> First, the action must mark the "consummation" of the agency's decision-making process—it must not be of a merely tentative or interlocutory nature. And second, the action must be one by which "rights or obligations have been determined" or from which "legal consequences will flow."

Applying this test, the Court held in *Sackett v. EPA*, 566 U.S. 120 (2012), that an administrative compliance order issued by EPA under the Clean Water Act was final for purposes of § 704 even though EPA had to bring a separate proceeding to enforce it. The order represented the consummation of EPA's decision-making process because its determination that the recipients' property contained wetlands that triggered a permit requirement was not subject to further review. It affected the property owners' obligations and had legal consequences because it required them to rehabilitate their property, exposed them to civil penalties for noncompliance, and limited their ability to acquire a permit from the Army Corps of Engineers under the same regulatory program.

The status of nonlegislative rules for finality purposes is unclear. *See, e.g.*, Nat'l Mining Ass'n v. McCarthy, 758 F.3d 243 (D.C. Cir. 2014) (concluding that that while legislative rules and some interpretive rules may be subject to pre-enforcement review, general statements of policy are not because they fail the second part of the *Bennett* test).

Exhaustion of Administrative Remedies

The requirement that litigants pursue available administrative remedies has statutory and prudential elements. Exhaustion requirements take three forms. First, a litigant who failed to present a claim to the agency at all may not be able to challenge agency action in court. Second, litigants may need to pursue available internal agency appeals processes. Third, under the "issue exhaustion" doctrine, a court may refuse to hear an argument that a litigant could have but failed to present to the agency, even if the litigant meets the first two exhaustion components.

The first exhaustion component is designed to assure that the agency has an opportunity to correct problems, avoiding the need for judicial challenges altogether. Even if the agency's resolution of an issue does not remove the basis for a judicial challenge, the agency will have had a chance to address the issue, provide the benefit of its expertise, and create an administrative record for judicial review. Some organic statutes require parties to present claims to the agency before going to court. The APA does not include a general exhaustion requirement of this kind.

The second exhaustion component originated as a court-created limit on reviewability, but § 704 of the APA limits judicial authority to dismiss claims based on a litigant's failure to exhaust internal administrative remedies. It provides:

> Except as otherwise expressly required by statute, agency action otherwise final is final for purposes of this section whether or not there has been presented or determined an application for a declaratory order, for any form of reconsideration, or, unless the agency otherwise requires by rule and provides that the action meanwhile is inoperative, for an appeal to superior agency authority.

Darby v. Cisneros, 509 U.S. 137 (1993), interpreted § 704 as precluding a court from requiring internal exhaustion in a case brought under §§ 702 and 704 of the APA unless either the organic statute does so or an agency regulation does so and stays the operation of the agency's action pending completion of the administrative appeal or reconsideration process.

Some organic statutes and agency regulations explicitly require issue exhaustion. Courts may do so even if a statute or regulation does not, but in *Sims v. Apfel*, 530 U.S. 103 (2000), the Court concluded that a judicial requirement of issue exhaustion is inappropriate in an "inquisitorial" adjudicatory process (such as SSA disability benefit adjudications) even if it is appropriate in an adversarial agency adjudication. The courts have disagreed on whether issue exhaustion applies in the context of rulemaking.

Courts have refused to require exhaustion when "the interest of the individual in retaining prompt access to a federal judicial forum [outweighs] countervailing institutional interests favoring exhaustion." McCarthy v. Madigan, 503 U.S. 140 (1992). *McCarthy* provided three examples: (1) when the resulting delay would cause irreparable harm; (2) when the agency lacks the authority or competence to resolve the issue or grant the relief requested, such as when a litigant's challenge raises constitutional questions; or (3) when exhaustion would be futile because the agency is biased or has predetermined the issue. *See, e.g.*, Bowen v. City of New York, 476 U.S. 467 (1986) (refusing to require exhaustion because delay in addressing challenge to SSA policy restricting eligibility for disability benefits would cause irreparable injury). Whether courts may still apply these exceptions after *Darby*'s interpretation of § 704 is unclear.

Ripeness

An agency action may not be judicially reviewable even if it is final because it is not ripe for review. Ripeness is primarily a doctrine of judicial self-restraint, but an issue may be so inchoate that it does not present a case or controversy within the judicial power under Article III. A recurring issue is whether a litigant may challenge a regulation immediately upon its issuance or must await its application. Allowing pre-enforcement review may produce unnecessary judicial review because the agency may not apply the rule to a litigant or may apply it in a way that eliminates the basis for the challenge. But refusing to allow such review may be unfair if it forces a regulated party to choose between investing in compliance with a rule it believes is invalid or foregoing compliance and risking penalties if its challenge after application of the rule (e.g., as a defense in an enforcement action) is unsuccessful.

The Supreme Court allowed pre-enforcement review in *Abbott Labs. v. Gardner*, 387 U.S. 136 (1967), because a drug manufacturer faced that kind of Hobson's choice in deciding whether to change its product labeling to comply with a regulation requiring manufacturers of brand name drugs to include the names of generic alternatives on their labels. In *Toilet Goods Ass'n, Inc. v. Gardner*, 387 U.S. 158 (1967), it precluded pre-enforcement review of a regulation authorizing suspension of a drug company's license if it refused access to FDA inspectors. Assessment of the rule's validity depended on how it was applied in particular cases and the company would not suffer irreparable harm if forced to delay its challenge.

Abbott Labs. applied a two-part test for determining whether a case is ripe: whether the issues are fit for review and whether the party challenging agency action would suffer hardship if judicial review were withheld. *Ohio Forestry Ass'n, Inc. v. Sierra Club*, 523 U.S. 726 (1998), considered three factors: (1) whether delayed review would cause hardship to the plaintiffs; (2) whether judicial intervention would inappropriately interfere with further administrative action; and (3) whether the courts would benefit from further factual development of the issues. In that case, the Court held that a challenge to a Forest Service land use plan that allegedly allowed too much logging was not ripe because the plaintiffs would have an opportunity to challenge timber sales at specific sites in the future, immediate review might hinder the Forest Service's efforts to refine its policies through decisions on reviewable site-specific projects, and review at the plan stage would require judicial resolution of the kind of "abstract disagreements over administrative policies" that the ripeness doctrine is meant to avoid.

Purely legal questions that do not require individualized factual development ordinarily are fit for review, but remote or abstract issues tend not to be. Uncertainty about a litigant's legal rights and obligations may qualify as hardship resulting from delayed review, but not if the uncertainty does not affect the plaintiff's primary conduct in a way analogous to the dilemma facing the drug manufacturer in *Abbott Labs*. See Nat'l Park Hospitality Ass'n v. Dep't of the Interior, 538 U.S. 803 (2003) (mere uncertainty about the validity of a rule does not suffice).

Primary Jurisdiction

Primary jurisdiction is a discretionary judicial doctrine. It permits a court to stay or dismiss a challenge to agency action that is properly before it to allow an agency with concurrent jurisdiction over the issues to address them first. Among the relevant considerations are the scope of agency discretion, the benefits to affected interests of uniformity resulting from initial agency resolution of the issues, and the benefits to reviewing courts of access to agency expertise. *United States v. W. Pac. R. Co.*, 352 U.S. 59 (1956). Courts are free to dismiss or stay if an issue is within an agency's primary jurisdiction. They usually stay the judicial challenge and retain jurisdiction to allow resumption of review after the agency has ruled.

What You Need to Know:

1. Section 704 of the APA authorizes judicial review only of final agency action (unless an organic statute provides otherwise). An action is final if it marks the "consummation" of the agency's decision-making process and is one by which "rights or obligations have been determined" or from which "legal consequences will flow."

2. Litigants may be required to exhaust internal administrative remedies before seeking judicial review. Organic statutes may preclude judicial review if a litigant bypasses the agency entirely. They also may require exhaustion of appeals and kindred processes. Section 704 of the APA precludes dismissal for failure to exhaust unless the organic statute requires exhaustion or an agency regulation does so and stays the agency's decision pending resolution of administrative appeals. Under the "issue exhaustion" doctrine, a litigant may waive its right to raise an issue it could have but failed to raise before the agency.

3. Ripeness is primarily a doctrine of judicial self-restraint. Ripeness issues turn on the fitness of the issue for judicial resolution (purely legal issues are likely to be fit), the hardship that delayed review will impose on litigants, and the degree to which judicial review will interfere with further administrative action. Challenges to agency rules upon adoption and before their application and enforcement (pre-enforcement review) may or may not be ripe, depending on the consequences for those affected if review is delayed.

4. Courts may dismiss or stay challenges under the primary jurisdiction doctrine, which is a court-created prudential doctrine. Among the factors for consideration are the comparative expertise of agency and court, the scope of agency discretion, and the risk of inconsistent rulings by courts absent a prior agency determination.

LESSON 19: OVERVIEW OF RULEMAKING

Rulemaking and adjudication are different procedural mechanisms for agency policymaking. As Lesson 2 indicates, both APA definitions and the decisions in *Londoner v. City and County of Denver*, 210 U.S. 373 (1908), and *Bi-Metallic Inv. Co. v. State Bd. of Equalization*, 239 U.S. 441 (1915), address the difference between the two. Agencies engaged in adjudication make findings of adjudicative (or historical) facts, which are the kind typically resolved by a jury in a jury trial. Agencies usually adopt rules based on findings of legislative fact, which are general facts that help resolve questions of law, policy, and discretion. The advantages of rulemaking as a policymaking mechanism include cost-effectiveness, capacity to solicit broad public input from affected interests, and uniform application, which prevents singling out particular parties to bear regulatory burdens not yet imposed on similarly situated entities. *See* Nat'l Petroleum Refiners Ass'n v. Federal Trade Comm'n, 482 F.2d 672 (D.C. Cir. 1973).

The authority to adopt binding rules must be derived from an agency's organic statute. Some statutory grants are framed in general terms, such as authority to prescribe such regulations as the agency determines are necessary to carry out its functions. Others are more confined and specific. Many courts interpret grants of rulemaking authority expansively. *See, e.g.*, E.I. du Pont de Nemours & Co. v. Train, 430 U.S. 112 (1977) (EPA may limit pollution through industrywide regulations); *Nat'l Petroleum Refiners, supra* (the FTC may define unfair trade practices by regulation). *Chamber of Commerce v. NLRB*, 721 F.3d 152 (4th Cir. 2007), however, held that a statutory grant of authority to the Board to issue "necessary" regulations did not authorize rules requiring employers to post notices advising employees of their rights, given the absence of any provision giving the Board the substantive duty to inform employees of their rights.

Agency rulemaking authority has limits. *Bowen v. Georgetown Univ. Hosp.*, 488 U.S. 204 (1988), prohibits courts from construing statutes to authorize adoption of rules that apply retroactively to past conduct absent an explicit authorization. This constraint applies only to rules that are "primarily" retroactive in the sense that they impose sanctions based on conduct that predated adoption of the rule. It does not apply to rules that merely have "secondary retroactive effects" by altering future regulation in a manner that upsets expectations arising from past investments made in reliance on prior law. It is sometimes difficult to distinguish between primary and secondary retroactivity. *See, e.g.*, Arkema Inc. v. EPA, 618 F.3d 1 (D.C. Cir. 2010).

The APA provides two grounds for challenging an agency's choice to adopt policy through rulemaking. First, litigants can argue that the agency inappropriately used APA rulemaking procedures, especially those for informal rulemaking, to take an action that does not qualify as a rule. The APA defines a rule as "an agency statement of . . . *future effect* designed to implement, interpret, or prescribe law or policy." 5 U.S.C. § 551(4) (emphasis added). If a rule applies retroactively, it has past effect, at least in part, and arguably does not qualify as a rule whose adoption is subject to § 553 procedures. *See Bowen*, 488 U.S. at 216–17 (Scalia, J., concurring). This argument is most forceful if the APA would have required the use of formal adjudicatory procedures if the action qualified as an order instead of a rule.

Second, an agency's choice of rulemaking may be arbitrary and capricious under § 706(2)(A). A rule may be arbitrary and capricious because it operates in unreasonable retroactive fashion, even if only secondarily. *Id.* at 220. Use of rulemaking procedures also may be arbitrary and capricious if the agency should have resorted to adjudication. The argument, which applies to both prospective and retroactive rules, is that the proceeding's characteristics seem more suitable for adjudication than rulemaking based on the APA's definitions of those terms and *Londoner* and *Bi-Metallic*. This argument rarely succeeds, partly because the APA's definition of a rule includes an "agency statement of . . . particular applicability." *See, e.g.*, Am. Hosp. Ass'n v. NLRB, 499 U.S. 606 (1991) (use of rulemaking to define bargaining units of hospital employees was not improper because of the individualized nature of the issues).

Unreasonably retroactive rules may violate substantive due process under a test formulated in the context of retroactive adjudication. *Securities and Exchange Comm'n v. Chenery (II)*,

332 U.S. 194 (1947), concluded that retroactivity is not improper if the "mischief" to statutory policies resulting from failure to apply a policy retroactively outweighs the unfairness of retroactive application. An agency's choice of rulemaking to make policy may violate procedural due process if the matter fits the adjudicatory model better than it does rulemaking, such as if the policy determination rests primarily on adjudicative, not legislative facts. These constitutional constraints on rulemaking mirror those derived from the APA, and the courts do not always carefully differentiate between the two sources of limits on rulemaking authority.

What You Need to Know:

1. An agency may adopt binding legislative rules only to the extent that its organic statute authorizes it to do so.
2. Agencies may not adopt rules with primary retroactive effects (imposition of sanctions for conduct that predated adoption of the rule) unless the organic statute explicitly authorizes retroactive regulation. This constraint does not apply to rules that have only secondary retroactive effects (by interfering going forward with expectations arising from transactions that occurred before the rule's adoption).
3. Unreasonably retroactive rules may be arbitrary and capricious or violate substantive due process. Courts determine whether retroactivity is unreasonable by balancing the subversion of statutory policies resulting from a failure to regulate retroactively against the unfairness of retroactive application.
4. A court may invalidate a rule if an agency uses informal rulemaking procedures to make policy through an action that does not qualify as a "rule" under the APA. Use of rulemaking to resolve issues that better fit the characteristics of adjudication (*e.g.*, because resolution of the issues turned on adjudicative factual determinations) may render

the rule arbitrary and capricious or a violation of procedural due process.

LESSON 20: RULEMAKING PETITIONS

Agencies may begin a rulemaking proceeding on their own initiative or in response to a petition for rulemaking. Some organic statutes authorize members of the public to file such petitions. Even if they do not, § 553(e) of the APA provides that "[e]ach agency shall give an interested person the right to petition for the issuance, amendment, or repeal of a rule." Section 555(e) requires agencies to give "a brief statement of reasons for the denial of a petition." An agency's denial of a rulemaking petition is immediately reviewable because it represents the agency's final determination not to issue the requested rule.

Judicial review of a denial of a rulemaking petition is "extremely limited" and "highly deferential" because courts are reluctant to interfere with agency resource allocation priorities. Massachusetts v. EPA, 549 U.S. 497 (2007). Nevertheless, courts can reverse a denial based on any of the standards in § 706(2) of the APA. Judicial reversals are rare, but in *Massachusetts*, the Court remanded EPA's denial of a petition by environmental groups to regulate greenhouse gas (GHG) emissions from motor vehicles. It held that EPA erroneously determined that GHGs do not qualify as "air pollutants" that the agency is authorized to regulate under the Clean Air Act. It also rejected the policy reasons EPA gave for its denial because they were not relevant under the statutory provision authorizing regulation of GHGs. When courts reverse denial of a petition, the normal remedy is remand to the agency to reconsider the denial or provide a better explanation.

Judicial review also may be available of an agency's delay in responding to a rulemaking petition. Section 706(1) of the APA authorizes courts to "compel agency action unlawfully withheld or unreasonably delayed." An agency's failure to issue a regulation in the face of a statutory deadline is an example of "unlawful withholding." Absent a missed deadline or other directive to begin a rulemaking proceeding, the issue is whether a failure to respond to a rulemaking petition amounts to unreasonable delay. Courts address that question under the framework from the *TRAC* case discussed in Lesson 14. Courts apply a "rule of reason" in addressing § 706(1) unreasonable delay claims.

What You Need to Know:

1. The APA creates a right to petition an agency for issuance or repeal of a rule, and demands a statement of reasons for denial of such a petition.
2. A grant of a petition for rulemaking is not reviewable final agency action, but a denial is immediately reviewable. Courts tend to review a denial deferentially when determining whether it was arbitrary and capricious.
3. Section 706(1) of the APA authorizes courts to compel agency action unlawfully withheld or unreasonably delayed. A missed statutory deadline is an example of unlawful withholding, while unreasonable delay claims are governed by a "rule of reason" and application of the *TRAC* factors.

LESSON 21: OVERVIEW OF RULEMAKING PROCEDURES

The APA governs rulemaking procedures unless its provisions are displaced by other statutes or regulations or unless the application of APA procedures violates the Constitution (such as the Due Process Clause). Statutes other than the APA may reduce the procedural burdens for the adoption of rules. More commonly, they impose additional procedural requirements (as may agency regulations). Some organic statutes require compliance with "hybrid" procedures that are more rigorous than the APA's informal rulemaking procedures described below but less rigorous than APA formal rulemaking procedures.

Other statutes may require agencies to accompany their regulations with documents in which they analyze the impact of regulation on matters such as the environment, small businesses, state and local governments, or compliance burdens. They also often require the promulgating agency to consult with constituencies most likely to be affected by a rule. Presidential executive orders also may dictate rulemaking procedures. The most prominent of these have required agencies proposing to adopt "significant regulations" (those with an annual effect on the economy of $100 million or more) to conduct cost-benefit analyses. *See, e.g.*, Exec. Order No. 13,563, 76 Fed. Reg. 3821 (Jan. 18, 2011); Exec. Order No. 12,866, 58 Fed. Reg. 51,735 (Oct. 4, 1993). An order issued by President Trump requires any agency that adopts a new regulation to identify two regulations for repeal and to offset the cost of the new regulation by eliminating regulations that impose costs of the same magnitude. Exec. Order No. 13,771, 82 Fed. Reg. 9339 (Feb. 3, 2017).

Absent application of these other sources of law, the APA dictates the applicability and nature of rulemaking procedures. Section 553 exempts from all procedures otherwise dictated by the rest of § 553 any rules relating to military or foreign affairs functions or to "agency management or personnel or to public property, loans, grants, benefits, or contracts." Section 552(a) still requires an agency adopting such a rule to publish it in the Federal Register. No person lacking actual notice of a rule not so published may be adversely affected by it.

Section 553(b) excuses agencies adopting "interpretative rules, general statements of policy, or rules of agency organization, procedure, or practice" from complying with the notice and comment requirements described below. These are often referred to as nonlegislative rules. As further discussed in Lesson 31, interpretive rules and policy statements are not binding on the agency or outside parties, reducing the need for the public input that APA rulemaking procedures otherwise enables. Agencies adopting nonlegislative rules must still comply with § 552(a)'s publication requirement and with § 553(d), which, with some exceptions, precludes a rule from going into effect sooner than thirty days after its publication.

Section 553(b) also exempts from notice and comment procedures any rules for which the agency at the time of rule issuance "for good cause finds . . . that notice and public procedure thereon are impracticable, unnecessary, or contrary to the public interest." Courts tend to afford little or no deference to agency good cause findings and have construed each of this good cause exemption's prongs narrowly. Compliance with APA rulemaking procedures is impracticable only if failure to accelerate adoption would pose an imminent health or safety threat or some other emergency. Compliance is unnecessary only if the rule involves a routine determination that is insignificant in nature and impact. It is contrary to the public interest only if compliance with ordinary procedures would harm rather than promote the public interest, such as by allowing the targets of regulation extra time to engage in the conduct the regulation is designed to prevent. *See* Mack Trucks, Inc. v. EPA, 682 F.3d 87 (D.C. Cir. 2012).

If a rule is not exempt from APA procedures, the next question is whether APA procedures for formal or informal rulemaking apply. Section 553(c) provides that "[w]hen rules are required by [the organic] statute to be made on the record after opportunity for an agency hearing, sections 556 and 557 . . . apply instead of this subsection." Sections 556 and 557 set forth the requirements for formal rulemaking. The courts have interpreted this trigger for formal rulemaking narrowly. Mere reference in the organic statute to a "hearing" requirement is insufficient. The organic statute must explicitly require that the hearing be conducted "on the record" or provide some other clear indication that Congress intended such a hearing. *See* United States v. Florida E. Coast Ry. Co., 410 U.S. 224 (1973); United States v. Allegheny-Ludlum Steel Corp., 406 U.S. 742 (1972). If formal procedures are required, they are the same as those that govern formal adjudication, with some exceptions (§ 554 applies only to formal adjudication). Lesson 26 explores the requirements for formal adjudication.

If the organic statute does not trigger formal adjudication under § 553(c), APA informal rulemaking or "notice and comment" procedures governed by § 553(b) and (c) apply by default. Lesson 22 describes those procedures in more detail. The adopting agency must (1) publish a notice of proposed rulemaking in the Federal Register to inform interested persons of the proposal's terms or substance; (2) provide an opportunity for interested persons to participate in the rulemaking, usually through the submission of written comments on the proposal;

and (3) issue a "concise general statement of [the final rule's] basis and purpose."

Courts have interpreted § 553(b) and (c) to create a kind of "paper hearing," requiring agencies, for example, to include important data in the rulemaking record so that interested persons may comment on these matters and to respond to significant comments. To the extent these requirements are rooted in judicial interpretations of § 553(b) and (c), they are valid. *Vermont Yankee Nuclear Power Corp. v. Natural Res. Def. Council, Inc.*, 435 U.S. 519 (1978), held, however, that, "[a]bsent constitutional constraints or extremely compelling circumstances," a court may not impose procedural requirements beyond those specified by statute or regulation.

The most likely source of constitutional constraints is the Due Process Clause. If an agency uses informal rulemaking in a context that seems to demand the greater participatory rights that accompany formal adjudication, there may be a due process violation. Based on *Londoner* and *Bi-Metallic*, that may be the result if the proceeding affects few people especially on individualized grounds, such that the issues presented turn on determinations of adjudicative rather than legislative fact.

What You Need to Know:

1. APA rulemaking procedures apply unless they are displaced by some other source of law, such as an organic statute, a cross-cutting statute that requires preparation of analytical documents, or agency regulations.
2. In rare instances, due process may require procedures more rigorous than the APA. This result is most likely when a rulemaking affects few people especially on individualized grounds, such that the issues turn on determinations of adjudicative fact.
3. Even if the APA applies, § 553(a) exempts rules relating to military or foreign affairs or public property, loans, grants, benefits, or contracts from all APA procedures except a requirement of publication in the Federal Register. Section 553(b) exempts from notice and comment procedures

interpretive rules, policy statements, and rules of agency procedure and practice, as well as rules for which the agency has good cause to avoid those procedures. Courts construe the good cause exception narrowly.

4. Pursuant to § 553(c), formal rulemaking procedures apply only when the organic statute requires that rules be adopted on the record after opportunity for an agency hearing. If formal procedures do not apply, informal (or notice and comment) rulemaking procedures apply. Agencies must publish a proposed rule in the Federal Register, provide an opportunity for interested persons to comment, and accompany the final rule with a concise statement of basis and purpose.

5. *Vermont Yankee* prohibits courts from supplementing applicable statutory procedures.

LESSON 22: INFORMAL RULEMAKING PROCEDURES

Lesson 21 lists the three main components of informal rulemaking required by § 553(b) and (c) of the APA. The notice and comment requirements serve three functions: (1) improving the quality of rulemaking by exposing the agency to diverse public comment, (2) assuring fairness to affected parties, and (3) enhancing the quality of judicial review by expanding the administrative record to include information and arguments submitted in response to the proposal. Small Refiners Lead Phase-Down Task Force v. EPA, 705 F.2d 506 (D.C. Cir. 1987).

A recurring issue is whether an agency that decides to alter its proposal in response to public comments must provide another round of notice and comment before adopting a final rule. An agency need not do so every time it changes its proposal. Such a requirement would create incentives to ignore public comments to avoid delaying the promulgation of final rules.

The courts require a second round of notice and comment if the final rule is not a "logical outgrowth" of the proposal. South Terminal Corp. v. EPA, 504 F.2d 646 (1st Cir. 1974). The issue is whether the notice was "sufficiently descriptive to provide interested persons with a fair opportunity to comment and to participate in the rulemaking." Chocolate Mfrs. Ass'n v. Block, 755 F.2d 1098 (4th Cir. 1985). Essentially, courts inquire whether, in light of any changes made, the original notice served the functions of the notice requirement. If the final rule relies on new information that merely confirms and expands on information available in the proposal or addresses deficiencies in existing data, an additional round of notice and comment is not likely to be required. Courts are likely to require an additional round if the agency's reliance on new information prejudiced affected interests who could not comment on it, especially if those alleging procedural violations contest the accuracy of the information and the information was supplied by someone with conflicting interests.

Section 553(c) does not specify the required content of the "concise statement of basis and purpose." Agencies almost always accompany publication of the text of a final rule in the Federal Register with a "preamble," which is the regulatory equivalent of legislative history. The preamble typically discusses the agency's authority to adopt the rule, explains how the rule promotes statutory purposes and how the final rule differs (if at all) from the proposed rule, and responds to significant public comments. The statement of basis and purpose must be sufficient for a reviewing court to "see what major issues of policy were ventilated by the . . . proceedings and why the agency reacted to them as it did." Citizens to Save Spencer County v. EPA, 600 F.2d 844 (D.C. Cir. 1979).

If an agency fails to supply an adequate statement of basis and purpose, a court can set aside the rule under § 706(2)(D) because it was adopted "without observance of procedure required by law." *See, e.g.*, Northeast Md. Waste Disposal Auth. v. EPA, 358 F.3d 936 (D.C. Cir. 2004). *Cf.* Encino Motorcars, LLC v. Navarro, 136 S.Ct. 2117 (2016) ("One of the basic procedural requirements of administrative rulemaking is that an agency must give adequate reasons for its decisions."). A challenge to the agency's explanation may also be substantive, however; it may reflect arbitrary and capricious decision-making. If an agency fails to respond to significant comments, for example, a court may conclude that it failed to consider an important aspect of the problem. Procedural and substantive challenges to statements of basis and purpose may be difficult to distinguish, and the arguments to support each kind of challenge often overlap.

The normal remedy for a violation of notice and comment procedures is to vacate the rule and remand to the agency for further consideration, such as by conducting another round of notice and comment. Courts also have the power to remand without vacating the rule. Under the approach in a leading case, the decision whether to remand with or without vacatur depends on the seriousness of the deficiencies identified by the court (and thus the likelihood that the agency will be able to correct them quickly) and the disruptive consequences of vacatur. Allied-Signal, Inc. v. Nuclear Regulatory Comm'n, 988 F.2d 146 (D.C. Cir. 1993).

What You Need to Know:

1. APA § 553(b) requires an agency engaged in informal rulemaking to publish a notice of proposed rulemaking in the Federal Register. Section 553(c) requires an opportunity for public participation through the submission of written or oral input, and publication of a concise statement of basis and purpose to accompany the final rule.
2. The notice required by § 553(b) must be sufficient to fairly apprise interested persons of the issues involved. The functions of both the notice and comment requirements are to improve the quality of rulemaking, assure fairness to affected parties, and enhance the quality of judicial review.
3. If an agency changes its approach in response to public comments, it must engage in an additional round of notice and comment if the final rule is not a logical outgrowth of the proposal.
4. The statement of basis and purpose provides a justification for the policy decisions reflected in the rule, including an explanation of how the final rule differs from the proposed rule and responses to

significant public comments. Attacks on the statement of basis and purpose can be couched in procedural terms (violation of § 553(c) publication procedures) or substantive terms (arbitrary and capricious decision-making).

LESSON 23: *EX PARTE* COMMUNICATIONS IN INFORMAL RULEMAKING

The functions of § 553's notice and comment requirements may be subverted if agencies engage in *ex parte* communications (EPCs). The APA defines an EPC as "an oral or written communication not on the public record with respect to which reasonable prior notice to all parties is not given, but it shall not include requests for status reports on any matter or proceeding . . . ." EPCs may create an unfair advantage by depriving interested persons not involved in them of the opportunity to respond. They also may create two administrative records, one that the agency makes publicly available and that a court addressing regulatory challenges reviews, and another that it actually relied on in making its decision.

Whether EPCs are permissible is context-dependent. As Lesson 27 indicates, §§ 554(d) and 557(d) of the APA impose strict limits on EPCs in both formal rulemaking and adjudication. The APA is silent, however, on the propriety of EPCs in informal rulemaking. *Sangamon Valley Television Corp. v. United States*, 269 F.2d 221 (D.C. Cir. 1959), barred EPCs in rulemakings involving "conflicting claims to a valuable privilege" (in that case, the award of an exclusive broadcasting license to one of two competing applicants), reasoning that "basic fairness requires such a proceeding to be carried out in the open." The D.C. Circuit later explained that *Sangamon Valley*'s holding only applies to rulemakings involving conflicting claims to a valuable privilege in proceedings that are "similar functionally to licensing via adjudication," rather than policy determinations of general applicability. Action for Children's Television v. FCC, 564 F.2d 458 (D.C. Cir. 1977). EPCs may vitiate the notice and opportunity to be heard that due process guarantees. Such concerns are not salient in most informal rulemakings.

The leading case on EPCs in informal rulemaking is *Sierra Club v. Costle*, 657 F.2d 298 (D.C. Cir. 1981), which involved a challenge to standards adopted by EPA under the Clean Air Act to limit air pollution from power plants. The Act contains hybrid procedures not required by the APA, such as a requirement to establish a rulemaking docket and place in it important documents which become available after publication of a proposed rule. The courts disagree on whether *Costle*'s holdings apply to rulemakings conducted under APA § 553, rather than just the Clean Air Act hybrid procedures, but at least some are likely to apply under the APA.

Costle took an accommodating view of EPCs in informal rulemaking, recognizing that Congress implicitly endorsed the lobbying of agencies by interested persons throughout the rulemaking process. It identified beneficial aspects of EPCs, including making agency decision makers more accessible, mustering support for agency initiatives, helping affected persons avoid compliance difficulties, and expanding the information on which agencies base their rules. *Costle* nevertheless precludes agencies from relying on EPCs which it has not docketed in time for others to have a meaningful opportunity to respond. Agency EPCs with executive branch officials, including the President, are not likely to be problematic given the President's need to oversee agency exercise of delegated policymaking discretion.

Finally, the court in *Costle* refused to invalidate EPA's rule on the basis of meetings between the agency and members of Congress. It relied on *D.C. Fed'n of Civil Ass'ns v. Volpe*, 459 F.2d 1231 (D.C. Cir. 1971), which established that communications during a rulemaking between an agency and legislative officials are inappropriate only if the purpose of the meeting is to pressure the agency to base its decision on factors that are not relevant under the organic statute and the agency's decision was actually affected by those extraneous considerations.

What You Need to Know:

1. The APA is silent on whether EPCs may occur in informal rulemaking. An EPC is "an oral or written communication not on the public record with

respect to which reasonable prior notice to all parties is not given."

2. EPCs are prohibited in rulemakings that involve conflicting claims to a valuable privilege or that are otherwise similar functionally to licensing via adjudication. They are less likely to be problematic in informal rulemakings, where lobbying is an accepted practice.

3. Even in informal rulemaking, a rule may be invalid if the agency relied on information in an EPC that was central to the issues and to which other interested parties lacked a meaningful opportunity to respond.

4. EPCs between agencies and other Executive Branch officials are generally proper. EPCs between an agency and legislative officials are inappropriate only if those officials pressure the agency to base its decision on irrelevant factors and the agency's decision was actually affected by those extraneous considerations.

LESSON 24: INTRODUCTION TO AGENCY ADJUDICATORY AUTHORITY

An agency may adjudicate only if its organic statute allows it do so. Most organic statutes delegate the power to adopt policy and resolve disputes through adjudicatory procedures. If a statute grants to an agency the discretion to make policy through either rulemaking or adjudication, courts tend to defer to the exercise of that discretion. Adjudication tends to be more flexible, allowing policy development on a case-by-case basis. Adjudication may be attractive for resolution of issues that are highly fact-specific, that turn on historic facts for which witness testimony may be illuminating, or whose implications the agency does not yet fully understand. Adjudication may be quicker than rulemaking, which can be protracted even when it is informal. If agencies must base adjudicatory decisions exclusively on evidence adduced at a hearing, the process may be less susceptible to lobbying and politicization than rulemaking.

Organic statutes, the APA, or due process may constrain adjudicatory authority. An agency purporting to issue an order may violate the APA if the action qualifies as a rule under § 551(4) and it failed to comply with APA rulemaking procedures. If it uses adjudication to resolve an issue that turns largely on legislative facts or otherwise fits the characteristics of rulemaking under *Londoner* and *Bi-Metallic*, a court may conclude that the action was a rule adopted in violation of applicable rulemaking procedures. Similarly, an agency's use of adjudication to address issues better suited to resolution in rulemaking may be arbitrary and capricious.

The leading case is *NLRB v. Wyman-Gordon*, 394 U.S. 759 (1969), where a Supreme Court plurality determined that an agency may not issue an order but refuse to apply it to the parties in that adjudication. A decision with purely prospective effect qualifies as a "rule," not an "order," for APA purposes, and is invalid if the agency did not comply with APA rulemaking procedures in issuing it. The Court upheld the order in the unfair labor practice proceeding conducted in *Wyman-Gordon* even though NLRB relied on an order in a previous case which was invalid for that reason. The NLRB could rely on the reasoning of the invalid order because it applied the policy enunciated in that order to the parties in *Wyman-Gordon* itself.

A decision reached in an adjudication is not a "rule" just because it announces new principles with broad policy implications. *See, e.g.*, NLRB v. Bell Aerospace Co., Div. of Textron, Inc., 416 U.S. 267 (1974). Indeed, the Court in *Bell Aerospace*, relying on *SEC v. Chenery Corp. (II)*, 332 U.S. 194 (1947), recognized that an agency may appropriately prefer adjudication to rulemaking as a mechanism to promote statutory policies if the agency could not reasonably have foreseen the issue so that no relevant rule exists to resolve it, the agency lacks sufficient experience to warrant issuance of a "hard and fast" rule, or the problem is so specialized and varying that it would be impossible to capture within the bounds of a general rule.

What You Need to Know:

1. An agency may use adjudication only if its organic statute authorizes it to do so and subject to whatever constraints that statute provides.
2. The APA also may constrain adjudicatory authority. If the action an agency takes at the end of an adjudication qualifies as a rule under the APA rather than an order, the action is procedurally defective if the agency failed to follow statutory rulemaking procedures. An action may qualify as a rule if it has wholly prospective effect or is based on legislative facts. The fact that a decision announces new principles with broad policy implications is not enough to make it a rule instead of an order.
3. Agency adjudication may violate the APA if the choice of adjudication instead of rulemaking is arbitrary and capricious, such as when the issues are better suited to resolution through rulemaking based on the *Londoner* and *Bi-Metallic* factors.

LESSON 25: RETROACTIVE ADJUDICATION

Adjudication is inherently retroactive in ways that rulemaking is not. Although retroactivity is a well-accepted aspect of judicial decision-making, agencies typically have an option for making policy that courts lack—rulemaking with purely prospective effect. As a result, courts may take issue with retroactive adjudication which unnecessarily upsets the legitimate expectations of parties that relied on prior law. Retroactive adjudication may be reversible under the APA's arbitrary and capricious standard or as a violation of due process.

The *Chenery II* decision referred to in Lessons 19 and 24 provides a test for assessing the legality of an order with retroactive effects:

> Retroactivity must be balanced against the mischief of producing a result which is contrary to a statutory design or to legal and equitable principles. If

> that mischief is greater than the ill effects of the retroactive application of a new standard, it is not the type of retroactivity which is condemned by the law.

Courts apply this test in addressing both arbitrary and capricious and due process challenges, without always clearly distinguishing between the two. Determinations that retroactive adjudication was arbitrary and capricious are more common.

The D.C. Circuit adopted an influential test for assessing the legality of retroactive adjudication in *Retail, Wholesale and Dep't Store Union, AFL-CIO v. NLRB*, 466 F.2d 380 (D.C. Cir. 1972). It identified these factors as relevant to the legality of retroactive adjudication:

> (1) whether the particular case is one of first impression, (2) whether the new rule represents an abrupt departure from well-established practice or merely attempts to fill a void in an unsettled area of law, (3) the extent to which the party against whom the new rule is applied relied on the former rule, (4) the degree of the burden which a retroactive order imposes on a party, and (5) the statutory interest in applying a new rule despite the reliance of a party on the old standard.

The second through fourth factors reflect *Chenery II*'s reference to the "ill effects" of retroactivity. The fifth factor corresponds to the other half of the *Chenery* balance——the damage to statutory purposes of a failure to apply a newly enunciated policy retroactively.

Retail, Wholesale distinguished between cases of first and subsequent impression. In a case of first impression, an agency announces a new policy or principle. In a case of subsequent impression, the agency applies to the parties a doctrine announced in a previous adjudication. In both contexts, the agency applies a policy to a factual situation that arose before the first enunciation of the doctrine. The court nevertheless regarded retroactive adjudication as more objectionable in a case of second impression. First, parties to the first adjudication have a better opportunity to contest the adoption of the new doctrine, as litigants in subsequent cases must convince the agency to repudiate a doctrine it has already adopted. Second, under *Wyman-Gordon*, an agency must apply a doctrine to the parties in a case of first impression or it will be deemed to have adopted a rule in violation of statutory rulemaking procedures. In subsequent cases, the agency can choose not to apply a previously announced policy to avoid unfairness. Third, failure to apply a new doctrine in a case of first impression may dissuade litigants from advancing novel arguments because they will not directly benefit even if the agency accepts those arguments.

In subsequently upholding retroactive adjudication, the D.C. Circuit singled out one particularly important factor—whether retroactivity represents an abrupt break with well-settled policy (which cuts against allowing retroactive application to protect reliance interests of affected parties) or is designed to fill a void in an unsettled area of the law (which does not implicate reliance interests in the same way). United Food and Commercial Workers Int'l Union, AFL-CIO, Local No. 150–A v. NLRB, 1 F.3d 24 (D.C. Cir. 1993).

What You Need to Know:

1. Retroactive adjudication may violate the Due Process Clause or amount to arbitrary and capricious decision-making.
2. *Chenery II*'s test for the validity of retroactive adjudication applies to both due process and arbitrary and capricious challenges. It is unlawful if the unfairness to parties affected by retroactive application of legal principles outweighs the damage to the statutory scheme that would result absent retroactivity.
3. Courts are more likely to object to retroactivity in a case of second or subsequent impression, even though cases of both first and subsequent impression entail application of legal rules adopted in an adjudication to conduct that predated the adjudication.
4. Retroactive adjudication is more likely to be problematic if an agency announces a new rule of

law that disrupts settled expectations than if it clarifies uncertainty or fills a void in preexisting law.

LESSON 26: PROCEDURES FOR FORMAL AND INFORMAL ADJUDICATION

APA §§ 554, 556, and 557 specify procedures governing formal adjudication. The procedures for informal adjudication are mostly dictated by organic statutes and agency regulations. Due process may require more than organic statutes or agency regulations do for adjudications that adversely affect protected property or liberty interests. Lessons 29 and 30 address procedural due process doctrines. Formal adjudication conducted under the APA (or, simply, APA adjudication) normally satisfies due process, although particular adjudications can be problematic if they contravene guarantees such as the right to an unbiased decision maker.

Whether the procedures for formal or informal adjudication apply depends on the interplay of organic statutes and the APA. Under § 554(a), the APA's formal adjudicatory procedures apply "in every case of adjudication required by statute to be determined on the record after opportunity for an agency hearing," with six exceptions. Formal adjudication is triggered only if the organic statute requires (1) an adjudication (2) with a hearing (3) conducted "on the record." Some decisions indicate that while the precise "magic words"—"on the record"—are not required, there must be some other clear indication that Congress intended APA adjudication to apply. City of W. Chicago v. U.S. Nuclear Regulatory Comm'n, 701 F.2d 632 (7th Cir. 1983). Others have reasoned that when the organic statute is ambiguous on whether formal adjudication is required, courts should defer to reasonable agency interpretations under *Chevron* Step Two. Chemical Waste Mgmt., Inc. v. EPA, 873 F.2d 1477 (D.C. Cir. 1989). Some older decisions relied on the organic statute's judicial review provisions—a requirement that *judicial review* be conducted "on the record" or that review proceed under the substantial evidence test—to satisfy § 554(a)'s trigger. The continuing validity of these decisions is questionable.

Section 554(c)(2) requires an agency to give interested parties "opportunity for . . . hearing and decision on notice and in accordance with sections 556 and 557." Thus, if § 554(a)'s trigger is met, the procedural requirements of the rest of § 554 and of §§ 556 and 557 apply. Under § 554(b), an agency must give personal notice to parties of the time, place, and nature of the hearing it intends to conduct, the legal authority for the hearing, and the matters of fact and law asserted. Section 556(a) requires that the agency, one or more of its members, or an ALJ appointed under 5 U.S.C. § 3105 preside at the hearing. Section 556(c) lists the powers of presiding officials, including the power to subpoena witnesses, rule on offers of proof, take depositions, "regulate the course of the hearing," and make recommended decisions.

Section 556(d) imposes the burden of proof on the proponent of a rule or order. It entitles a party "to present his case or defense by oral or documentary evidence, to submit rebuttal evidence, and to conduct such cross-examination as may be required for a full and true disclosure of the facts." EPCs are significantly restricted (*see* Lesson 27). Section 556(e) makes the transcript of the hearing and all submitted papers the exclusive record for decision.

Section 554(d) requires separation of prosecutorial and adjudicative functions, providing a measure of ALJ independence from the agency whose cases are being adjudicated. ALJs may only be removed for cause after a hearing before the Merit System Protection Board. 5 U.S.C. § 7521. Under some organic statutes, an ALJ's decision only goes into effect if the agency adopts it. Under others, it goes into effect if the agency fails to reverse it within a specified time. In either event, the agency conducts de novo review and may take additional evidence.

Depending on the organic statute, informal adjudication may closely resemble an APA adjudication or entail little process. APA § 555(e) requires that notice of a decision after an informal adjudication be provided to the parties. But an organic statute or agency regulation may not require the pre-hearing notice required for formal adjudication. Informal adjudications may be presided over by hearing officers who lack the protections of ALJ independence. The right to call and cross-examine witnesses may be more limited, the APA's restrictions on EPCs do not apply (and may not be replicated in organic statutes or agency regulations), and the agency may be entitled to base its decision on matters outside the hearing record.

What You Need to Know:

1. The APA specifies procedures for formal adjudication (also known as APA adjudication) in §§ 554, 556, and 557, but says little about informal adjudicatory procedures.
2. APA adjudication applies only if an organic statute requires the adjudication to be conducted "on the record after opportunity for an agency hearing." If that statute does not specify that a hearing be conducted "on the record" or otherwise indicate that Congress intended formal procedures, courts may defer under *Chevron* to the agency's interpretation of whether its organic statute triggers formal procedures.
3. Formal adjudicatory procedures are designed to provide participatory opportunities and ensure fairness. Section 554(d) requires separation of prosecutorial and adjudicatory functions and § 557(d) restricts EPCs. APA adjudications are presided over by ALJs with some independence from the agency for whom they adjudicate. Parties may present oral or documentary evidence. The agency's decision must be based exclusively on the hearing transcript and documents submitted during the hearing.
4. Informal adjudicatory procedures, derived from organic statutes and agency regulations, may be less rigorous than formal procedures. Due process may require more process than organic statutes or agency regulations.

LESSON 27: *EX PARTE* COMMUNICATIONS IN ADJUDICATION

The APA restricts *ex parte* communications (EPCs) in formal proceedings to prevent agencies from being "influenced by private, off-the-record communications from those personally interested in the outcome." *See* H.R. Rep. No. 94–880, pt. 1, at 3 (1976). Section 554(d) bars those presiding at a formal adjudication from consulting a person or party on a "fact in issue," unless all parties are notified and allowed to participate. It also bars a presiding official from "be[ing] responsible to or subject to the supervision or direction of an employee or agency engaged in the performance of investigative or prosecuting functions for an agency." Investigatory or prosecutorial officials may not in a case or a factually related case "participate or advise in the decision," except as witness or counsel. *Id.* While these provisions are designed to prevent unfairness resulting from combining prosecutorial and decisional functions in a single person, their practical effect is to restrict EPCs between prosecutorial and adjudicatory officials.

Section 557(d) imposes additional restrictions on EPCs in both formal adjudication and formal rulemaking. Unless an organic statute provides otherwise, no "interested person" outside an agency may make or knowingly cause to be made to any member of the agency, ALJ, or other employee involved in the decisional process an EPC "relevant to the merits of the proceeding." The prohibition also applies to EPCs initiated by agency officials to an interested person outside the agency.

"Interested person" is a "wide, inclusive term covering any . . . person with an interest in an agency proceeding that is greater than the general interest the public as a whole may have." H.R. Rep. No. 94–880, *supra*, at 19–20. *See also* Professional Air Traffic Controllers Org. v. Federal Labor Relations Auth., 685 F.2d 547 (D.C. Cir. 1982) (the *PATCO* case). Section 557(d)'s prohibition is broader than § 554(d)'s; it covers any communication "relevant to the merits of the proceeding," not just those on "facts in issue." But § 557(d), unlike § 554(d), does not apply to communications wholly internal to the agency. Section 551(14) also excludes from the definition of an EPC "requests for status reports." A communication couched as a request for a status report may qualify as an EPC if it amounts to "an indirect or subtle effort to influence the substantive outcome of the proceedings." H.R. Rep. No. 94–880, *supra*, at 20.

The APA's restrictions on EPCs may apply to executive branch officials, despite the President's Article II duty to see that the laws are faithfully executed. *Portland Audubon Soc'y v. Endangered Species Comm.*, 984 F.2d 1534 (9th Cir. 1993), vacated the Committee's decision after a formal adjudication to grant an exemption from a statutory prohibition on the taking of endangered species based on EPCs between the Committee and the President and his staff. The court reasoned that the President is an "interested person," that the President and his staffers were persons from "outside the agency," and that the application of the APA's ban on EPCs did not violate separation of powers because presidential prerogatives do not extend to influencing quasi-judicial administrative proceedings through behind-the-scenes lobbying.

Although § 554(d) is silent on the consequences of engaging in EPCs, § 557(d) specifies both mandatory and discretionary remedies. An agency official involved in a formal proceeding who discovers that an EPC has occurred must place on the public record written EPCs, written summaries of oral EPCs, and all written responses to those materials. Under § 557(d)(1)(D), an ALJ or other presiding official "may," to promote the interests of justice and statutory policies, "require the party [involved in the EPC] to show cause why his claim or interest in the proceeding should not be dismissed, denied, disregarded, or otherwise adversely affected."

APA § 706(2)(D) authorizes courts to set aside agency action taken in violation of the APA's restriction on EPCs. Courts will not necessarily do so, even if an EPC is discovered after agency proceedings have concluded or the agency did not provide relief under § 557(d)(1). *PATCO* lists five factors relevant to deciding what relief, if any, to grant: the EPC's gravity, whether it may have influenced the agency's decision, whether the party making it benefited from the decision, whether opposing parties knew about the EPC and had an opportunity to rebut it, and whether vacatur and remand would serve a useful purpose. In that case, the court did not vacate the agency's decision because the EPC did not influence the agency's decision, no one benefited from it, and no one was deprived of the opportunity to refute it.

The APA is silent on EPCs in informal adjudication. Organic statutes or agency regulations may impose such restrictions. Even if they do not, EPCs in informal adjudication may violate due process if they deprive a party of meaningful opportunity to participate in the proceeding. *See, e.g.*, Morgan v. United States, 304 U.S. 1 (1938) (concluding that the right to a hearing includes a reasonable opportunity to know and meet the claims of the opposing party). Such a result is particularly likely in a proceeding involving conflicting claims to a valuable privilege. Sangamon Valley Television Corp. v. United States, 269 F.2d 221 (D.C. Cir. 1959).

What You Need to Know:

1. APA § 554(d) prohibits an official presiding at a formal adjudication from consulting a party on a "fact in issue" unless all parties have notice and an opportunity to participate. It prohibits agency officials engaged in investigation or prosecution from participating or advising in that or a factually related case, in effect barring those kinds of internal agency communications.
2. Section 557(d) prohibits an interested person outside the agency from engaging in EPCs (defined in § 551(14) as off-the-record communications about which some parties lack notice) "relevant to the merits" with agency officials involved in the decisional process of a formal adjudication or rulemaking.
3. An agency that discovers that an EPC has occurred in a formal proceeding must place it (or a summary of an oral communication) in the public record and provide an opportunity for others to respond. It may dismiss the claim or interest of the party making the EPC if doing so is consistent with the interests of justice. Courts may vacate decisions when EPCs have occurred. *PATCO* identified five factors relevant to deciding whether to do so.

4. The APA does not address EPCs in informal adjudication, but they may violate the due process rights of parties not involved in the EPCs.

LESSON 28: USE OF RULEMAKING AND OTHER MECHANISMS TO NARROW ISSUES IN SUBSEQUENT ADJUDICATION

Agencies sometimes seek to expedite adjudications and dispose of cases efficiently by adopting a regulation and then precluding parties to a subsequent adjudication from raising issues resolved in the rulemaking. *United States v. Storer Broadcasting Co.*, 351 U.S. 192 (1956), endorsed the practice. The Court upheld the FCC's denial of a broadcast license without convening a hearing because the applicant already held the maximum number of licenses allowed under a previously adopted regulation.

The issue also arose in *Heckler v. Campbell*, 461 U.S. 458 (1983). The Social Security Administration (SSA) adopted regulations (called "the grids"), using notice and comment procedures, that established whether sufficient jobs were available to preclude an award of disability benefits to an individual with a particular combination of age, education, and prior work qualifications (the claimant's residual functional capacity). SSA used the grids to avoid the need to call vocational experts as witnesses at a hearing to opine on the range of jobs available to an applicant whose circumstances matched those in one of the grid categories.

The Court upheld this practice, distinguishing between two key determinations in disability adjudications. First, SSA must assess a claimant's capabilities in light of the alleged impairment. Second, it must determine whether jobs exist that a person with the claimant's residual functional capacity is able to perform. SSA must resolve the first inquiry, which turns on historical facts, solely on the basis of evidence adduced at the hearing. SSA regulations allowed claimants to introduce evidence concerning the impact of their impairments and to demonstrate that the grids did not apply to them. The second determination turns on legislative facts that are not unique to individual claimants—the types and number of jobs that exist in the national economy. SSA could resolve that issue through rulemaking in lieu of introduction of the testimony of vocational experts at a disability hearing because those who might be affected had an opportunity to participate and contest SSA's legislative fact determinations during the rulemaking. It reasoned that "when the accuracy of those facts has already been tested fairly during rulemaking, the rulemaking proceeding itself provides sufficient procedural protection." Some courts have refused to extend *Heckler* to factual determinations reflected in nonlegislative rules adopted without resort to notice and comment procedures. *See, e.g.*, Sykes v. Apfel, 228 F.3d 259 (3d Cir. 2000) (expressing skepticism about SSA's ability to rely on Social Security Rulings to foreclose issues concerning residual functional capacity in disability adjudications).

ALJs may narrow the issues in an adjudication by taking official (or administrative) notice of commonly acknowledged facts instead of taking evidence. APA § 556(e) requires that an adjudicator that intends to rely on official notice to assist in fact-finding give prior notice to parties to the adjudication and provide an opportunity to present contrary facts.

What You Need to Know:

1. An agency may resolve issues of legislative fact in rulemaking proceedings and then preclude parties to an adjudication from relitigating those issues. The agency must provide some opportunity for public participation in the initial resolution of the issues, such as by complying with notice and comment procedures. For that reason, an agency may not be able to rely on nonlegislative rules such as policy statements to narrow factual issues in subsequent adjudications.

2. An agency may take official notice of commonly acknowledged facts or facts within its area of expertise, but it must provide prior notice to parties to an adjudication and an opportunity for them to contest the facts.

LESSON 29: PROCEDURAL DUE PROCESS: PROTECTED INTERESTS

The Fifth and Fourteenth Amendments prohibit the deprivation of life, liberty, or property without due process of law. The Due Process Clauses have both a substantive and procedural component. Procedural due process protects against deprivations that occur in the absence of appropriate procedures. Substantive due process prevents deprivations affecting a fundamental right or lacking any rational relation to a legitimate governmental interest, regardless of the process used. Our concern in this lesson and the next is with procedural due process.

At one time, the Supreme Court applied a balancing test to determine both whether due process protections applied and, if so, whether the government used proper procedures in taking the action resulting in the alleged unlawful deprivation. In *Board of Regents v. Roth*, 408 U.S. 564 (1972), the Court bifurcated due process analysis. The threshold question is whether the party claiming a violation has a protected interest to which due process guarantees apply. That inquiry turns on the nature of the interest, not its weight. If a protected interest is present, the second question is what process was due and whether the government supplied it.

The Constitution does not create property interests whose deprivation triggers due process protections. Such interests must derive from an independent source of law, such as a statute, a regulation, or common law. Traditional property interests usually do not pose problematic conceptual questions. Determining whether the holder of a governmental benefit has such an interest may be more difficult. At one time, the Supreme Court seemed to distinguish between rights, which triggered due process protections, and privileges, which did not. Government benefits appeared to qualify as privileges. The Court disavowed that approach in *Goldberg v. Kelly*, 397 U.S. 254 (1970), holding that government welfare benefits qualify as property interests for due process purposes because they are "statutory entitlements"—an applicant meeting statutory or regulatory eligibility criteria is entitled to benefits.

Goldberg endorsed a category of "new property" that, under appropriate circumstances, includes not only benefits under entitlement programs, but also licenses or permits issued by the government and government employment. In *Roth*, the Court ruled that a person has a property interest in a benefit if he or she has "more than an abstract need or desire" for it or "unilateral expectation" of it. Due process protections apply only if the individual has a "legitimate claim of entitlement" to the benefit. In that case, an untenured professor terminated by a state university lacked a protected property interest in his job because the terms of his employment contract did not provide him with a legitimate claim of entitlement to contract renewal.

Government benefits should qualify as protected property interests if the government lacks discretion to deny them if eligibility criteria are met. A government license or permit does not qualify as a property interest for due process purposes if the government has discretionary denial or revocation authority. Similarly, those who work for the government have a property interest in continued employment if a contract provision, statute, or regulation restricts termination to good cause. An individual typically has no property right in being awarded a government job simply by meeting minimal eligibility requirements.

Unlike property interests, protected liberty interests derive directly from the Constitution and its judicial interpretation. In *Meyer v. Nebraska*, 262 U.S. 390 (1923), the Court identified several forms of protected liberty interests:

> Without doubt, it denotes not merely freedom from bodily restraint but also the right of the individual to contract, to engage in any of the common occupations of life, to acquire useful knowledge, to marry, establish a home and bring up children, to worship God according to the dictates of his own conscience, and generally to enjoy those privileges long recognized . . . as essential to the orderly pursuit of happiness by free men.

Reasonable regulation of access to a profession is unlikely to trigger due process concerns. Complete deprivation of access to an occupation might. Government action may implicate a liberty interest if it results in a "stigma plus"—a loss of reputation plus some other tangible adverse impact. *Compare* Paul v. Davis, 424 U.S. 693 (1976) (characterization as a habitual shoplifter did not affect a liberty interest because it did not affect an additional tangible element such as employability) *with* Wisconsin v. Constantineau, 400 U.S. 433 (1971) (designation as habitual drunkard implicated liberty interest because it resulted in both a "badge of disgrace" and inability to purchase alcoholic beverages).

Restrictions on access to elementary and secondary education are more likely to involve due process protections than to post-secondary education. It is not always clear whether a case restricting access to education turns on a liberty interest (the right to acquire useful knowledge) or a property interest (an entitlement to a free public education). Imposition of discipline by a public educational institution may raise due process issues. *See* Goss v. Lopez, 419 U.S. 565 (1975) (discipline implicated property interest in education and liberty interest in reputation).

What You Need to Know:

1. A violation of procedural due process rights occurs if a government action deprives a person of a protected property or liberty interest without appropriate procedural protections.
2. A government benefit can qualify as a protected property interest if its holder has a legitimate claim of entitlement to the benefit. Protected property interests derive from a source independent of the Constitution, such as a statute, regulation, or common law.
3. Protected liberty interests, which derive directly from the Constitution, include the right to freedom of movement, bodily integrity, the pursuit of a calling, and to acquire useful knowledge. Government action that adversely affects reputation also implicates a protected liberty interest under the "stigma plus" test, but only if the loss of reputation is accompanied by adverse effects

on some other tangible element, such as employment.

LESSON 30: PROCEDURAL DUE PROCESS: PROCESS DUE

A litigant asserting a procedural due process claim must identify a defect in the process the government used in taking action alleged to amount to a deprivation of a protected interest. Procedural due process requires a meaningful opportunity to contest the alleged deprivation in the form of notice, an opportunity to be heard, and access to a neutral decision maker.

The government must provide notice that an adjudicatory proceeding will be held, including the time and place of the hearing and the issues to be addressed. The notice must be "reasonably calculated, under all the circumstances, to apprise interested parties of the pendency of the action and afford them an opportunity to present their objections." Mullane v. Central Hanover Bank & Trust Co., 339 U.S. 306 (1950). Due process also may require notice of the means to appeal an adverse agency decision.

Mathews v. Eldridge, 424 U.S. 319 (1976), identified three factors for determining what kind of hearing due process requires (how much process is "due"):

> First, the private interest that will be affected by the official action; second, the risk of an erroneous deprivation of such interest through the procedures used, and the probable value if any, of additional substitute procedural safeguards; and, finally, the Government's interest, including the function involved and the fiscal and administrative burdens that the additional or substitute procedural requirements would entail.

A mathematical formula represents the relationship among these factors: due process is violated if the importance of the interest, multiplied (or discounted) by the probability that additional procedures would have avoided an erroneous deprivation, is greater than the cost to the government of the additional procedures. The test is designed to promote increased accuracy. The issue in *Mathews* was whether due process required SSA to provide a hearing before terminating disability benefits. In *Goldberg v. Kelly*, 397 U.S. 254 (1970), the Court had held that a pre-deprivation hearing is required before the government may terminate welfare benefits. *Mathews* held that a post-deprivation hearing sufficed, distinguishing *Goldberg*.

On the first factor, eligibility for welfare assistance, but not disability benefits, is based on financial need, and benefits recipients are persons "on the very margin of subsistence." Thus, the interest in the continued flow of benefits pending a final decision on continued eligibility was greater in *Goldberg* than in *Mathews*. On the second factor, disability eligibility depends on the extent of the claimant's impairment and its impact on ability to work, issues that are "sharply focused and easily documented" and that will usually turn, according to the Court, on routine, standard, and unbiased reports by expert medical specialists. The disability issue is less likely than the issues bearing on entitlement to welfare benefits to turn on witness credibility and veracity, so there is less need for the procedures that a pre-deprivation evidentiary hearing provides, such as witness cross-examination. With respect to the third factor, the *Mathews* court reasoned that the government has an interest in conserving scarce fiscal and administrative resources. Requiring an evidentiary hearing every time SSA wants to terminate disability benefits would increase the costs of those proceedings, potentially reducing the money available to deserving benefits claimants. Because these same points apply in a welfare benefits case, the Court may have placed more emphasis on this factor than it did in *Goldberg*.

Application of the first *Mathews* factor involves a different inquiry than the threshold question whether a litigant has a protected property or liberty interest, which does not turn on the strength of the interest. The more important a court considers the protected interest to be, the greater the loss suffered through wrongful deprivation, and the greater the need for procedural safeguards. Due process safeguards are triggered by the existence of protected property or liberty interests, not interests in the procedures themselves. Access to adjudicatory procedures is afforded to protect the underlying legal claims. Analyzing whether a party to an adjudication has an interest in fair procedures conflates the issues separated in *Roth*—(1) whether the party has the required protected property or liberty interests and, if so, (2) what procedures were due.

Even if the interest is very important, *Mathews* does not require additional procedures if they would not be likely to reduce the risk of inaccurate adjudication resulting in an erroneous deprivation. The costs to the government of additional procedures include not only out-of-pocket expenses, but also the impact of procedural formality on the character of the underlying program or activity. *Walters v. Nat'l Ass'n of Radiation Survivors*, 473 U.S. 305 (1985), reasoned that extensive use of attorneys in veterans benefit cases would frustrate Congress's goal of keeping the hearings nonadversarial. *See also* Board of Curators v. Horowitz, 435 U.S. 78 (1978) (due process does not require a formal hearing before a student's dismissal from medical school because overformalization would risk deterioration in student-faculty relationships).

Due process may affect the government's burden of proof and persuasion. It may be higher in situations involving interests of great importance. *See, e.g.*, Santosky v. Kramer, 455 U.S. 745 (1982) (requiring state to prove basis for terminating parental rights by clear and convincing evidence). Due process may prohibit *ex parte* communications, which can frustrate a meaningful opportunity to be heard. Litigants alleging that denial of a right to cross-examine adverse witnesses violated due process have had mixed success. *Compare* Richardson v. Perales, 402 U.S. 389 (1971) (due process not violated by SSA's reliance on hearsay at a disability hearing) *with* Yount v. Barnhart, 416 F.3d 1233 (10th Cir. 2005) (due process violated when ALJ relied on report from physician submitted after close of disability hearing, with no opportunity to cross-examine the author or otherwise rebut the report's contents).

Due process provides a right to a neutral decision maker. Schweiker v. McClure, 456 U.S. 188 (1982) ("[D]ue process demands impartiality on the part of those who function in judicial or quasi-judicial capacities."). Parties alleging impartiality may rely on personal or systemic (or institutional) bias. *Withrow v. Larkin*, 421 U.S. 35 (1975), recognized a "presumption of honesty and integrity in those serving as adjudicators." Proof of actual personal bias (such as a financial stake in the outcome or personal animus against a party) is normally required to rebut the presumption, but a showing of a high probability of actual bias may suffice. Lack of agency independence may qualify as systemic bias where adjudicators have incentives to rule in favor of the agency. Subjecting ALJs in disability cases who rule in favor of claimants in a high proportion of cases to special job performance reviews, for example, may be problematic.

What You Need to Know:

1. Procedural due process requires a meaningful opportunity to contest an alleged deprivation of a protected property or liberty interest in the form of notice, an opportunity to be heard, and a neutral decision maker.

2. An agency must provide notice that is "reasonably calculated, under all the circumstances, to apprise interested parties of the pendency of [an adjudicatory] action and afford them an opportunity to present their objections."

3. Under *Mathews v. Eldridge*, three factors determine what kind of hearing due process demands—the importance of the private interest affected by adjudicatory action; the risk of an erroneous deprivation of that interest if the agency does not use particular requested procedures, and the probable value, if any, of those procedures in increasing decisional accuracy; and the government's fiscal and administrative burdens resulting from additional or substitute procedures.

4. Due process provides a right to a neutral decision maker. There is a presumption that adjudicators are unbiased, which may be rebutted by proof of actual bias, personal or systemic. Claims of bias are generally hard to substantiate.

LESSON 31: NONLEGISLATIVE RULES

Previous lessons have distinguished between legislative and nonlegislative rules. Both qualify as "rules" under § 551(4) of the APA. Characterization of a rule as legislative or nonlegislative may matter for three reasons: it may determine what procedures apply to its adoption, whether it is binding, and what degree of deference courts will afford to statutory interpretations reflected in the rule.

Section 553(b)(A) of the APA exempts three forms of nonlegislative rules from notice and comment procedures—interpretative (or interpretive) rules, policy statements, and rules of agency organization, procedure, or practice. The rationale for exempting the first two categories is that they are not binding, reducing the need for the public input assured by notice and comment procedures. Rules of agency organization, procedure, or practice may bind the agency, especially if they provide participatory rights to those affected by agency decisions. Nevertheless, Congress decided that it is more important to assure flexibility and efficiency in agency adoption of procedural or organizational rules that do not affect substantive rights than to require public participation in their adoption.

Courts may apply different standards in reviewing agency statutory interpretations reflected in legislative or nonlegislative rules. *United States v. Mead*, 533 U.S. 218 (2001), subjects agency statutory interpretations to review under *Chevron U.S.A. Inc. v. Natural Res. Def. Council, Inc.*, 467 U.S. 837 (1984), if (1) Congress delegated authority to the agency to make rules carrying the force of law, and (2) the agency adopted its interpretation pursuant to the exercise of that authority. *Chevron* clearly applies to interpretations rendered in notice and comment rulemaking. *See also* Mayo Found. for Med. Educ. and Research v. United States, 562 U.S. 44 (2011) (affording Step Two *Chevron* deference to IRS interpretations reflected in regulation adopted using notice and comment procedures). Nonlegislative rules, especially nonbinding interpretive rules and policy statements, do not meet the second part of the *Mead* test, even if the agency has authority to make binding rules that carry the force of law. Interpretations reflected in those rules tend to be analyzed under the less deferential framework set forth in *Skidmore v. Swift & Co.*, 323 U.S. 134 (1944).

Does one aspect of a rule's characterization necessarily dictate other aspects? Although the Supreme Court has not provided a definitive answer, courts are likely to be skeptical if an agency seeks to take advantage of the benefits of adopting a legislative rule (such as *Chevron* deference) while avoiding some of the disadvantages of its adoption (such as the duty to abide by notice and comment procedures).

Because so much rides on whether a rule is legislative or nonlegislative, it is important to be able to distinguish between them. At one time, courts sought to do so generically. Some cases reasoned, for example, that if a rule had a "substantial impact" on those outside the agency it was legislative, and notice and comment procedures applied. Because of difficulties in applying tests based on the "substantiality" of a rule's impact, courts began applying distinct tests to define each category of nonlegislative rules.

An ***interpretive rule*** advises the public of the agency's construction of the statutes and rules it administers. Courts tend to distinguish between legislative and interpretive rules by inquiring whether a rule imposes a "new duty" on affected parties (making it legislative) or merely clarifies a pre-existing duty imposed by statute or regulation or reminds affected parties of such pre-existing duties. *See, e.g.*, *Iowa League of Cities v. EPA*, 711 F.3d 844 (8th Cir. 2013). One court has reasoned that an interpretive rule "must be derivable from the statute that it implements by a process fairly to be described as interpretive." Ballesteros v. Ashcroft, 452 F.3d 1153 (10th Cir. 2006). Am. Mining Cong. v. Mine Safety and Health Admin., 995 F.2d 1106 (D.C. Cir. 1993), distinguishes legislative and interpretive rules based on several factors:

> (1) whether in the absence of the rule there would not be an adequate legislative basis for enforcement action or other agency action to confer benefits or ensure the performance of duties, (2) whether the agency has published the rule in the Code of Federal Regulations, (3) whether the agency has explicitly invoked its

general legislative authority, or (4) whether the rule effectively amends a prior legislative rule.

If the answer to any of these questions is affirmative, a rule is legislative, not interpretive.

A ***policy statement*** advises the public prospectively of the manner in which the agency proposes to exercise a discretionary power. Courts distinguish legislative rules from policy statements by inquiring whether the agency intended a rule to be binding. If not, it is a policy statement. *See, e.g.*, Nw. Ecosystem Alliance v. U.S. Fish and Wildlife Serv., 475 F.3d 1136 (9th Cir. 2007) (guidance document was not a policy statement because the agency treated it as binding).

Because ***rules of agency organization, procedure, or practice*** often bind the agency, that characteristic cannot distinguish them from legislative rules. Some cases inquire whether a rule alters the rights or interests of parties (legislative rules) or merely alters the manner in which parties present themselves or their viewpoints to the agency (procedural rules). Nat'l Mining Ass'n v. McCarthy, 758 F.3d 243 (D.C. Cir. 2014). Others inquire whether a rule affects "primary conduct" (substantive) or "secondary conduct" (procedural). Primary conduct governs the rights and duties of parties in their relations with other parties, including the agency. Secondary conduct involves the manner in which parties assert those rights before the agency.

What You Need to Know:

1. Whether a rule is legislative or nonlegislative may affect whether it is binding, the procedures that apply to its adoption, and the degree of deference courts afford the statutory interpretations it reflects. Interpretive rules and policy statements are not binding. The APA exempts all three kinds of nonlegislative rules (which also include rules of agency organization, procedure, or practice) from notice and comment procedures. Interpretations contained in legislative rules trigger review under *Chevron*, while interpretations found in nonbinding nonlegislative rules adopted without public

participation are normally subject to less deferential review under *Skidmore*.

2. An interpretive rule advises the public of the agency's construction of the statutes and rules it administers. If a rule imposes a "new duty" on affected parties, it is likely to be a legislative rule. If it clarifies a pre-existing duty imposed by statute or regulation or reminds affected parties of such pre-existing duties, it is interpretive.
3. A policy statement advises the public prospectively of the manner in which the agency proposes to exercise a discretionary power. If the agency intended a rule to be binding, it is a legislative rule, not a policy statement.
4. A rule that alters the rights or interests of parties is legislative, while one that alters the manner in which parties present themselves or their viewpoints to the agency is procedural. Courts may distinguish legislative from procedural rules by inquiring whether the rule affects primary or secondary conduct.

LESSON 32: CONSTRAINTS ON AGENCY CHANGES TO INFORMAL ADVICE

An agency's attempt to repudiate its own informal advice may be prevented from doing so based on the doctrine of estoppel or the application of the arbitrary and capricious standard. In a dispute between non-governmental parties, a successful estoppel argument requires proof of a misrepresentation, reasonable reliance by the party claiming estoppel, and detrimental consequences of that reliance. The United States has argued that it is never subject to estoppel for two reasons. First, estoppel against the government is barred by sovereign immunity. The government has never agreed to be sued to force it to violate a statute simply because an agency official provided erroneous advice. Second, estopping the government would violate separation of powers by providing court-approved force of law to an official's improper conduct, infringing on Congress's exclusive responsibility to make the law. The Supreme Court has refused to rule that estoppel against the government is never appropriate, but it has always concluded that litigants have not met the requirements for estoppel.

It has also concluded that the government may not be estopped on the same terms as other litigants. *See, e.g.*, Federal Crop Ins. Corp. v. Merrill, 332 U.S. 380 (1947) (explaining that those who deal with the government accept the risk that one who purports to act on its behalf lacks authority to do so). Several principles make it difficult to estop the government. First, misrepresentation is not enough; proof of affirmative misconduct is necessary. Such a showing is typically difficult to make, but not impossible. *See, e.g.*, Fredericks v. Comm'r of Internal Revenue, 126 F.3d 433 (3d Cir. 1997) (finding affirmative misconduct when the IRS failed to inform taxpayer that it had erroneously informed him that it never received his revocable agreement to suspend the statute of limitations applicable to the recovery of tax underpayments). Second, reliance is not likely to be reasonable when advice conflicts with a statute or regulation because those who deal with the government are presumed to know the law. Reliance on mistakes of fact is more likely to be reasonable than reliance on mistakes of law. Third, reliance on erroneous advice only qualifies as a detriment if it causes harm other than being required to comply with a legal obligation that would have applied in the absence of erroneous advice. *See* Morgan v. Comm'r of Internal Revenue, 345 F.3d 563 (8th Cir. 2003) (no detriment when taxpayer was subject to tax levy on amount it owed under proper reading of the law).

The Supreme Court has prohibited estoppel if its consequence would be to require monetary payments not authorized by statute. Such a result would violate the Appropriations Clause, U.S. Const., art. I, § 9, cl. 7, which prohibits money from being drawn from the Treasury absent statutory appropriation. *See* Office of Personnel Mgmt. v. Richmond, 496 U.S. 414 (1990).

Courts may prevent agencies from changing course to avoid differential treatment of similarly situated entities, such as when an agency repudiates past positions. Such inconsistent treatment may violate equal protection, but it is more likely to be regarded as arbitrary and capricious decision-making. Courts also may refuse to defer to inconsistent statutory interpretations. *See* Skidmore v. Swift & Co., 323 U.S. 134 (1944) (identifying interpretive consistency as relevant to whether an agency's interpretation has the power to persuade).

One constraint on agency reversals of informal advice no longer applies. In *Paralyzed Veterans of Am. v. D.C. Arena L.P.*, 117 F.3d 579 (D.C. Cir. 1997), and *Alaska Professional Hunters Ass'n Inc. v. FAA*, 177 F.3d 1030 (D.C. Cir. 1999), the D.C. Circuit reasoned that when affected interests rely on an agency's authoritative interpretation of its own legislative regulation, the interpretation gets incorporated into the rule and may only be changed through notice and comment procedures. The Supreme Court repudiated those decisions in *Perez v. Mortgage Bankers Ass'n*, 135 S.Ct. 1199 (2015), finding them to be inconsistent with the APA's explicit exemption from notice and comment procedures for the adoption or repeal of interpretive rules.

What You Need to Know:

1. It may be possible to estop the government from repudiating erroneous informal advice, but litigants seeking to do so must satisfy a more demanding test than the one applicable in cases involving private parties. The government may not be estopped absent affirmative misconduct, and reliance on mistakes of law is not likely to be reasonable.
2. The Appropriations Clause bars courts from requiring the government to make monetary payments not authorized by statute, even if its officials have mistakenly promised to do so.
3. Repudiation of previous informal advice may be arbitrary and capricious if it results in inconsistent treatment of similarly situated entities, and changes in statutory interpretations may trigger less deferential judicial review.
4. An agency need not use notice and comment procedures in issuing an interpretive rule that differs from an earlier such interpretation.

CHAPTER 3

BUSINESS ASSOCIATIONS/ CORPORATIONS

LESSON 1: INTRODUCTION

Many law students who want to be "corporate lawyers" after graduation find their way into the basic Business Organizations course during their second year in law school. Others take the course in their second or third years because the subject may be on the bar exam and they wish to gain some familiarity with the material before taking it. Sometimes this course is titled Corporations and Partnerships or Business Associations, but the subject matter is generally the same—a dash of agency, a smidgen of partnership, a brush with other unincorporated entities, and a load of corporations. The material in the basic course, however, will often have very little to do with the practice of "corporate lawyers" and may or may not cover the subjects tested by a bar exam. Being a corporate lawyer means simply that your practice deals with corporations on one side or another of a transactional, litigation or advisory matter. That matter could be negotiating or litigating a commercial agreement entered into by a corporation. It could involve advising a corporation regarding compliance with federal regulations. But these ways in which business entities interact with the world—entering (or not) into contracts, committing (or not) torts, violating (or not) laws—are not the stuff of the basic Business Organizations course.

The course, instead, is mostly about the relationships of people and entities *within* the firm, from a sole proprietorship with one employee to a large public corporation with thousands of shareholders and dozens of executives. So one organizing choice has to be made at the start: what relationships are inside the firm (and therefore included in the course) and what relationships are outside the firm (and therefore excluded)? There are no hard and fast rules. Much ink has been spilled among legal and finance academics as to why firms exist instead of individual entrepreneurs simply relying on markets to find goods and services when they need them. Ronald Coase suggested that firms materialize where the transaction costs of finding and negotiating with different people exceed the costs incurred by bringing various factors under a hierarchy governed by a person or small group of people.[1] Oliver Williamson added that certain people's talents or assets may become more valuable in certain uses than in others over time, opening those people up to exploitation by less locked-in, "asset specific" constituents and pushing toward *ex ante* commitment rather than *ex post* bargaining.[2]

Business Organizations is about the governance of the relationships among people within the hierarchies that are created whatever the reason. But not even all such relationships are covered! The course touches on some issues of creditor protection, but the vast majority of creditor protection is effected through contracting rather than corporate law and those contracts are not covered in the course. The course touches on the relationship between principals and agents, but employment law more generally is not covered and is instead left to the aptly titled "Employment Law" course. Rather, the course focuses on the relationships between (1) the people in control of business organizations and (2) their agents (in the agency material), their co-controllers and third parties (in the partnership material), and their shareholders *and* agents (in the corporations material). The essential question in each instance is who has power over the operation of a business and what, if any, are the checks on that power?

The basic tension should be becoming clear: business organizations bring many people together in pursuit of some profit or other motive, but those people are of course different and have different desires, talents, interests, etc. How can law affect the relationships between these people in the socially optimal way? The question turns out to be governed by law—statutes, common law opinions, regulations and contract—as well as market forces, each of which we will discuss.

---

1 Ronald H. Coase, *The Nature of the Firm*, 4 ECONOMICA 386 (1937).

2 *See, e.g.*, Oliver Williamson, *Markets and Hierarchies: Analysis and Antitrust Implications*, New York: Free Press (1975).

One final point is worth considering before we jump into the material. What do the people who "do" business organizations take to be the goal of the law in this area? To what end, if any, are we consciously shaping the relationships between all of these people within firms?

The answer is hardly settled, and in different circumstances certain ends will be emphasized differently. However, it is undoubtedly the case that business organizations is one of the areas of law most concerned with efficiency. By "efficiency", scholars are generally talking about behavior that maximizes social wealth, with questions of distribution largely left to other regulations and the tax-and-transfer system. Take the issue of mandatory versus default rules. There may be a rule regarding the relationship among partners that 95% of all partners in the world would value more highly than the alternative rule. We could make that a mandatory rule or a default rule, meaning that people could pick the alternative if they wanted. Absent problems of market failure, a default rule will be more valuable to society as a whole because the 5% of idiosyncratic partners will be able to opt for their preferred alternative which they could not do under a mandatory regime. Thus it is more efficient because it increases the wealth of this small sliver of the population and we will see that, indeed, most rules of business organizations are default rules rather than mandatory ones. But note that the rule in question may have consequences for fairness or justice or some other concern. Perhaps the 5% of partners who prefer the alternative do so for offensive or mistaken reasons that worry us. Efficiency might thus clash with these other concerns. The law of business organizations does not always choose efficiency in such conflicts, but it you may find it far less susceptible to claims of fairness or justice than the law in other areas you have studied.

What You Need to Know:

1. The law of business organizations generally concerns the relationships of people within firms.
2. In particular, we are concerned with the allocation of decision-making power and the establishment of checks and balances on those who are given such power.

3. More often than not, the accepted goal of the law of business organizations is the maximization of social wealth, as opposed to other potential ends.

LESSON 2: THE PRINCIPAL/AGENT RELATIONSHIP AND AN AGENT'S FIDUCIARY DUTIES

Oftentimes we can accomplish important tasks by ourselves. Perhaps you have painted a room in your apartment or moved your furniture from one residence to another. In other cases, there may be others who are better situated to complete the task for us. Sometimes, others are more skilled at the work than we are. Beyond that, it may be cheaper to hire someone to do the work than to do it ourselves, particularly when we consider the opportunity cost of doing something else with our time.

In those cases in which we decide to hire someone else to do the work, we become a principal and the person we hire becomes our agent. To one extent or another we give the agent control over assets or a project that otherwise belongs to us. This relationship is extremely important—it forms a foundational element of a market economy and is the seed from which the material in this chapter grows.

Immediately issues present themselves however. Under what terms (scope of work, duration, compensation, etc.) will the agent perform the services? Many of these types of questions can be solved via tools you acquired in your Contracts class. But still others will be harder, if not impossible, to resolve via contract. When exactly has a principal/agent relationship been created? How can the principal be protected from exploitation by an agent who now exerts substantial control over the project? What is the legal relationship between the principal and third parties whom the agent affects during the course of her agency? These are the basic questions addressed by agency law, some of which we will cover in the remainder of this lesson and some of which we will cover in the following one.

When a principal/agent relationship is formed, it brings with it certain consequences that one or the other party may not like. For instance, as will be discussed in the next lesson, principals may be liable to third parties for actions taken by their agents. Because of that, principals and agents might try to strategically avoid some of these consequences by calling their relationship something else in the underlying contract or even expressly stating the agent was NOT an agent. The law steps in at this point to disallow such gamesmanship. A principal/agent relationship may be created even if the parties call the relationship something different.[3] According to the Restatement (Third) Agency, courts will instead look to the substance of the relationship to determine whether "one person (the 'principal') manifests to assent to another person (the 'agent') that the agent shall act on the principal's behalf and subject to the principal's control" and the agent agrees to do so. Whether someone is acting on someone else's behalf and subject to their control, though, is often a murky question.

If a principal/agent relationship exists, the agent will often be in a position to exploit the principal even though the agent is supposed to be working on the principal's behalf and under the principal's control. In practice, the principal's control will be less than perfect and the agent's interests may diverge from the principal's. Consider the moving example from above. You, the principal, want your belongings moved as safely and quickly as possible within your budget constraints. The mover does not necessarily share your interests. He may wish to take his time transporting the items to enjoy sightseeing along the way. He may not want to spend all of the time necessary to ensure your items remain intact. At the most extreme, he may wish to take some of your items for himself. Of course, you may anticipate some of these divergences and invest in monitoring mechanisms or require the mover to bond himself to the safe and speedy transport (by, say, giving you a discount if he fails to deliver in an appropriate fashion). The sum of these monitoring and bonding costs, together with the remaining costs created by the difference in interests among principal and agent are termed "agency costs." When those costs outweigh the benefits that led you to hire an agent in the first place, you are better off doing the job yourself. If those costs are consistently high, therefore,

[3] We will see this sort of substance-over-form choice again when we get to partnerships in Lesson 4.

certain relationships that would otherwise benefit both parties may not be entered into.

The law steps in to ameliorate these costs in certain ways. Criminal law and tort law deter outright theft, for example. More importantly for our purposes, agency law establishes fiduciary duties that are owed by agents to principals. If the agent fails to abide by those duties, the principal may sue them and recover damages (or disgorgement in certain cases). Fiduciary duties are not unique to agency law—they arise in financial advisory contracts, trusts and estates, and other contexts as well—but agency law, as supplemented by partnership law and corporate law, perhaps provides their most full treatment. The most important fiduciary duties for purposes of this lesson and this chapter more generally are the duties of care and loyalty. The duty of care requires the agent to act as a reasonable person would act in the exercise of her authority granted via the agency relationship. The duty of loyalty requires the agent to pursue the interests of the principal rather than any personal benefit. While these duties are easy enough to state, we shall see throughout this chapter that enforcing them is a complicated matter.

What You Need to Know:

1. Agency is the simplest form of relationship we will study in this chapter and forms the basis for most of the others we will study.
2. A principal/agent relationship will be recognized regardless of what the parties call themselves if one person assents to another that the other shall work on the person's behalf and subject to her control.
3. If an agency relationship exists, the law establishes fiduciary duties owed by the agent to the principal because of the ability of the agent to exploit the principal otherwise.
4. The most important fiduciary duties are the duties of care and loyalty.

LESSON 3: PRINCIPAL'S RESPONSIBILITY FOR AGENT'S ACTIONS

In your first-year torts class, you may have studied the an employer's vicarious liability for the torts of its employee. If so, you already know that a principal may be liable to third parties for acts committed by her agent depending upon the circumstances. In this lesson, we'll delve into principals' liability for the actions of their agents more generally.

First, it will be helpful to divide potential principal liability into tort liability and contract liability, because the rules are different regarding each. A principal is responsible for torts committed by her "employee" within the employee's "scope of employment." We wind up with a seemingly simple two-part test: was the agent an "employee" and, if so, was the agent acting within the scope of his employment. Regarding the first part, while all employees are agents, not all agents are employees. Depending upon the level of control exercised by the principal, the agent may be characterized as an employee (high principal control) or an independent contractor (low principal control). If the agent is an independent contractor, then generally the principal will not be liable in tort for the agent's actions.[4] This distinction raises difficult questions regarding the level of control that must exist for a court to find an agent is an employee—in many cases the principal will disclaim the employer/employee relationship and the employee has little interest in pushing the point, requiring the court to make its own determination. That determination will necessarily be fact-specific and is difficult to reduce to a bright-line rule. The key will normally be to look for indicia of control, whether direct or circumstantial.

Secondly, in order for an employer to be liable for the employee's tort, the employee must commit the tort while in the scope of his employment. Obviously, a pizza delivery man who negligently causes a car accident while on the way to deliver a pizza is acting in the scope of his employment. On the other hand, the employer will not be liable when the pizza delivery man commits a tort while on a tropical vacation. The cases in

---

[4] There are some exceptions for inherently dangerous activities.

between these two extremes are harder, though the thrust of modern practice is to define scope of employment broadly.

For contract liability, the inquiry is different. The question here turns on questions of authority. A principal will be bound to a contract entered into by her agent with a third party when the agent had *actual* authority granted by the principal to enter into the contract. That authority can be granted expressly ("Go enter into that contract on my behalf") or implicitly if a reasonable agent would have understood any expressly granted authority to include the authority to enter into the particular contract. In short, actual authority depends on the content of communication between the principal and the agent.

Alternatively, a principal may be obligated under a contract entered into by her agent even if the principal never gave the agent authority to enter into the contract or even if the "agent" was not an agent of the principal at all! Under the doctrine of *apparent* authority, a principal will be bound if her actions or statements led a third party to reasonably believe that the purported agent had authority to enter into the contract on the principal's behalf. So a person will be bound to a contract with a third party when she tells the third party "That's my representative, he negotiates all my deals" and the purported representative enters into a contract with the third party, even though the principal has told the agent to not enter into the contract thereby destroying actual authority. Apparent authority sensibly protects third parties' reliance interests and encourages third parties to contract without having to go through the costly process of confirming an agent's authority every time.

Finally, there are a grab bag of lesser doctrines under which principals may be bound to a contract even in the absence of actual or apparent authority. These occur more rarely. First, a party may be *estopped* from disclaiming contract liability when she knew or should have known that a third party believed someone was acting on the party's behalf in entering into the contract and the third part reasonably so believed. Second, even in the absence of any authority, a party may *ratify* a contract after the fact and thereby become bound under it. Third, a curious doctrine called *inherent authority* or *inherent agency power* provides that a principal may be liable for an agent's actions even without actual authority (because, say, the principal told the agent not to enter into a particular contract) where an agent in his position would normally have the authority to enter into a contract and the third party reasonably believes that state of affairs to exist. You might think this sounds like apparent authority, but this doctrine applies even (or maybe only) when the third party does not know that the principal exists or, if one does, who the principal is. In such circumstances it is harder to make the case that the principal communicated the agent's "authority" to the third party. Nevertheless, the principal will be bound, though the most recent iterations of the Restatement (Agency) talks less of inherent agency power and more of the special case of an undisclosed principal.

What You Need to Know:

1. Principals may be liable for their agents' actions.
2. In tort, a principal is liable if the agent is an employee and commits the tort in the scope of his employment.
3. Not all agents are employees, as principals exercise more control over employees than they do over independent contractors.
4. In contract, a principal is liable on a contract entered into by her agent if the agent had been given that authority, expressly or implicitly, by the agent herself (Actual Authority).
5. She may also be liable on a contract entered into by her "agent," even if the "agent" hadn't been given that authority, so long as the principal expressed to a third party that the agent did, in fact, have such authority (Apparent Authority).

LESSON 4: PARTNERSHIP AND ITS FORMATION

As we have seen, a sole proprietorship with a principal and a number of agents raises significant legal questions. But those questions grow significantly once joint ownership of the enterprise arises. How is authority allocated among the joint owners? Profits? Losses? How do third parties deal with a jointly-owned entity and its individual owners?

The oldest and most common type of jointly-owned organization is the general partnership. The law of partnerships was almost entirely based on common law until the beginning of the 20th century. Then, in 1914, the Uniform Partnership Act was drafted and ultimately adopted by almost every state. The UPA codified much of the common law surrounding partnerships. But new issues arose over time, and the UPA began to fall out of favor in some precincts. A Revised Uniform Partnership Act was drafted in 1997 and has been adopted by a majority of states, the non-adopters retaining the UPA. Arguably, the two most significant changes between UPA and RUPA are (1) RUPA's commitment to the partnership as a distinct legal entity rather than merely an aggregation of individual partners and (2) RUPA's more laissez-faire attitude toward fiduciary duties among partners. These adopted Uniform Acts, along with the state common law flowing therefrom forms the backbone of partnership law today.

The general partnership is the simplest type of jointly-owned organization to form. No paper work need be filed with a governmental entity nor fees paid in order to form a partnership. All that is needed is an agreement, even oral or tacit, by two or more people to carry on as co-owners of a business for profit.[5]

Sometimes it will be easy, after the fact, to determine whether a general partnership was formed. Individuals may enter into a written partnership agreement or may hold themselves out to others as a partnership in very clear ways. In other cases, however, there may be controversy over partnership formation. As we will discover below, partners owe each other fiduciary duties and third parties may obtain certain advantages in litigation if a partnership is found. So, after the fact, various parties may claim that a partnership existed between two or more people while others will want to make the opposite claim.

5 UPA 6.1 (1914).

In this way, the stakes for partnership formation mimic those surrounding the agent/principal relationship from Lesson 2.

The UPA and RUPA offer some (not terribly clear) guidance regarding the matter. If two people share profits, that arrangement is prima facie evidence of a partnership. But that presumption is rebutted if the profit sharing is better characterized as debt repayment (i.e. the lender shares in the profit of a borrower to the extent that the borrower is able to repay a debt) or wages. Unfortunately, many partnership arrangements also share common features of debt or employment arrangements, so the question of partnership formation will be an intensely factual one. For instance, courts will often look beyond profit sharing to see whether both parties share a level of control appropriate for a finding of partnership.

As suggested earlier, a number of consequences follow from a finding of general partnership. If a partnership is formed, partners will share profits, losses and authority equally as a default rule. However, partnership agreements—both formal and informal ones—may deviate substantially from the default rules. Some partners may have more control than others or be entitled to more profits than others. Also, the potential for "partnership property" arises, with such property being available to partnership creditors with priority over any personal creditors of partners. Sometimes you will read or hear about the "entity theory" of partnership and it is on the question of partnership property that the entity theory has its greatest impact since the property may be disposed or encumbered by the organization more than by one or a subset of the partners.

Perhaps the most significant consequence of partnership formation, though, is that each partner will be personally liable for the partnership's debts. One might expect that the pool of assets held by the partnership is available to partnership creditors, and, indeed, that is the case. In fact, the need for an isolated base of partnership property has led to severe restrictions on individual partners' abilities to dispose of that property. But the general partnership offers even more support to partnership creditors by allowing them to pursue partners' personal assets to satisfy claims they might have against the partnership. In fact, this "unlimited liability" aspect of general partnerships will often frighten your future clients into considering a corporate or alternative-entity structure, rather than exposing their homes or cars to potential business creditors.

A corollary to the rule of unlimited liability is that the acts of a partner performed on behalf of the partnership in the ordinary course of business are binding on other partners. In this way, the law of partnership adopts principles similar to actual and apparent authority (for contract) and vicarious liability (for tort) in the law of agency. A partner's authority to contract on behalf of the partnership is derived from the partnership agreement or majority status as a default, so it is possible for partners in certain circumstances to restrict the authority of other partners to enter into contracts on behalf of the partnership (and therefore subject individual partners to potential liability). But not only must that stripping action be rightfully taken, the absence of authority must be communicated to third parties, hence the analogy to apparent authority.

What You Need to Know:

1. Joint ownership of a business brings additional questions to bear involving the allocation of authority, profit and responsibility among the joint owners.
2. The general partnership is the oldest and simplest form of joint ownership.
3. Partnerships can be formed informally without anything other than a tacit agreement, when profit sharing and control rights will be the most important indications.
4. Partnership property is dedicated to partnership creditors, while partners' personal property may be available to partnership creditors (i.e. unlimited liability) if partnership property is exhausted.
5. Partners have the right to bind the partnership and therefore other partners unless that authority is taken away consistent with the partnership agreement and communicated to third parties.

LESSON 5: PARTNERS' DUTIES AND ENDING THE PARTNERSHIP

Once a partnership is formed, the partners become fiduciaries of each other. They owe each other a number of duties, most significantly a duty of loyalty. The contours of this duty, like most fiduciary duties, are sometimes ill-defined but commonly include prohibitions on stealing and taking partnership opportunities. Most of you will read the famous case *Meinhard v. Salmon* in which soon-to-be-Justice Cardozo colorfully described the relationship between joint venturers. That language suggests a very strictly enforced duty of loyalty among partners. However, the move toward private ordering in business law has suggested a relaxing of partners' loyalty duties, and RUPA 103(b)(3) offers drafters the ability to limit loyalty obligations among partners in a partnership agreement.

The most fraught loyalty questions among partners will often arise when the partners wish to end their relationship. Before moving to that question, one must understand the basic rules regarding partnership dissolution and winding up. Dissolution occurs when any partner ceases to be associated with the partnership. Under RUPA, this is termed "dissociation." In many cases, the business will remain viable without the departing partner, so dissolution (or dissociation) does not necessarily mean the end of the business organization.

But what happens to the partner that leaves? If the partnership agreement specifies the treatment upon dissolution/dissociation, then it controls. Often, though, the partnership agreement will not specify what is to happen in these circumstances. If the business is to continue, the departing partner must be bought out either by the remaining partners or by a third party. The price at which she is to be bought out may be adjusted for damages payable by her if her dissolution/dissociation was "wrongful." It is wrongful if it violates a term of the partnership agreement, usually that the partnership was to continue for a term or for a particular undertaking, neither of which is yet fulfilled.

There exists the possibility of opportunistic dissolution by one or more of the partners. Consider an at-will partnership such that no dissolution can be technically "wrongful." Two partners wish to take future partnership opportunities from a third. Under the relevant partnership, perhaps they can expel the minority partner from the partnership and buy out his interest. Alternatively, they can dissolve the partnership and buy out the third partner's interest in the partnership during the winding up when they reacquire the business. Courts will examine these decisions to determine whether the partners are violating their duty of loyalty or are acting in bad faith. But there may not be a vibrant market for the partnership interests, so the third partner's interest may be tricky for a court to value and may thus present the other partners with an opportunity to buy them out cheaply and still escape liability.

What You Need to Know:

1. Partners owe each other fiduciary duties of care and loyalty.
2. The duty of loyalty requires partners to not misappropriate partnership opportunities or property, though the specific contours of the duty may be delineated via the partnership contract.
3. When one partner leaves the partnership, it is called dissolution (or, under RUPA, dissociation).
4. Dissolution may be wrongful, in which case the dissolving partner will owe damages.
5. Dissolution and dissociation lead to winding up which may mean an end to the business or may simply mean the business is acquired by different people, often the remaining partners.

LESSON 6: CORPORATE FORMATION AND CONSTITUENCIES

Forming a corporation is a much more formalized process than forming a partnership. In the latter, as we have seen, no written agreement is even necessary. To form a corporation on the other hand, one must draft a charter (sometimes called the articles of incorporation or certificate of incorporation) and file it with the appropriate official of the particular state in which one is incorporating along with a fee. In Delaware (which we shall see is the most important state for incorporations), the corporation is a viable legal entity once the charter is filed with the Division of Corporations in the Department of State.

The charter lays out a number of features of the corporation and is discussed further in Lesson 8. But at this point it is worth considering that a Delaware charter will establish at least one class of "common" shares of stock that carry rights to vote on certain matters related to the new corporation. If desired, the charter may establish multiple classes of shareholders each with different or similar voting rights (some of these classes may be called "preferred" shareholders if their voting and economic rights grant them a preference over the common in some way). Common shareholders, in addition to voting rights, must hold a residual claim on the corporation's assets. Another way of putting this is that these shareholders stand last in line should the corporation dissolve and wind up, receiving whatever assets are left over after all creditors and any more senior shareholders of the corporation are paid. This puts them in a relatively risky position vis-a-vis the others as there may not be any money left for shareholders after those other constituencies are paid. On the other hand, because the other claims are fixed (always in the case of debt and sometimes in the case of preferred stock), common shareholders of a profitable company may find their residual claim to be very valuable. And, of course, common shareholders may receive distributions during the life of the corporation in the form or dividends and/or repurchases of shares by the corporation.

One of the most important voting rights that shareholders have is the right to vote for members of the board of directors. Directors, and not the shareholders who elect them, have ultimate authority over the corporation while they serve. This holds out the advantage of allowing a small, nimble body of experts to direct the corporation rather than leaving it up to the larger group of dispersed shareholders. The directors are subject to reelection discipline from shareholders and, as we will discuss later, fiduciary duties owed to the corporation itself. Boards will often be divided into subgroups or committees which specialize in certain functions, e.g. auditing the corporation's finances, awarding executive compensation, etc.

In fact, directors of many larger corporations often have full-time jobs elsewhere and themselves delegate authority over most day-to-day corporate decisions to a set of executives. Such part-time directors are called "outside" or "independent" directors while those who are also employed by the corporation (usually as an executive) are called "inside" directors. The most senior executive appointed by the directors is usually called the Chief Executive Officer. He or she (or his or her delegates) will be in control of most choices the business must make. However, the Chief Executive Officer (and any other executives) are always subject to removal by the board. Questions often arise regarding a part-time board's ability to effectively monitor a full-time executive, and the executive will often have contractual protections that entitle him or her to significant compensation in the event of an employment termination. But, legally, the executives serve at the will of the board and will need board approval to accomplish certain tasks.

Other constituencies of the corporation are crucial to its success. Employees perform the work of the corporation, financial creditors supply needed capital beyond that provided by shareholders, vendors provide materials and services, customers pay for the corporation's products and services, etc. Nevertheless, the bulk of "corporate law," excepting limited liability and other specific issues of creditors' rights, consists of outlining the relationship between shareholders on the one hand and the board and executives on the other.

What You Need to Know:

1. A corporation is formed by drafting and filing a charter with the relevant state authority.
2. A corporation has shareholders who hold voting rights and the residual claim to corporate assets.
3. Shareholders elect the board of directors which wields ultimate control, for any given period, over the corporation.

4. The board hires (and fires) executives who make the vast majority of day-to-day business decisions for the corporation.
5. "Corporate law" is mostly about the law governing the relationship between shareholders, the board and the corporation.

LESSON 7: SEPARATION OF OWNERSHIP AND CONTROL

In a general partnership, the partners are the residual claimants and, as a general matter, also exert a significant amount of control over the enterprise. As just discussed, shareholders give up short term and even medium-term control of the corporation to elected directors while retaining the residual claim on corporate assets. This arrangement is commonly called the "separation of ownership and control" and was most famously noted by Adolf Berle and Gardiner Means in the first part of the twentieth century.

The advantage of this arrangement is that it opens up share ownership to a much larger group of people who might not otherwise have the time or talent for running a business. Moreover, it allows people who have that time and talent to run businesses even if they do not have enough money to invest a substantial amount of equity capital. The corporation permits specialization in potentially very helpful ways.

The disadvantage of this specialization is that the two groups—shareholders and managers—may have very different interests in how the company should be run. Shareholders will usually want their shares' value, i.e. residual claim plus distributions, maximized. That, in turn, gives shareholders an interest in managers working hard and intelligently and for as little money as possible. It may also mean that diversified shareholders will want the corporation taking on risky but valuable projects. Shareholders with investments in many companies are "diversified" and will want each corporation to make the most value-increasing moves it can, since any single firm-specific risk is unlikely to sink the shareholder's whole portfolio. Finally, shareholders will often be happy to accept an offer from a third party to buy or cash out their shares if the offer is at a high enough price.

The directors and executives of a corporation may have different views on each of these issues and others. Usually, they will want to work less hard than shareholders would want and to be paid more than shareholders would want. Because it is hard for executives to diversify their investment in the corporation—it may be hard to find another job—they may want to avoid having the company take on too much risk and thereby fail. Finally, the prospect of a third-party purchaser of the corporation's shares may frighten directors and executives who might lose their positions as part of the transfer.

All of these divergences in interests and others fall into the category of "agency costs." As a technical matter, directors are hard to classify as purely "agents" of the shareholders, but they have enough in common with traditional agents for the term to suit our purposes. Agency costs include the costs of shareholders monitoring directors and executives, the costs that directors and executives expend to bond themselves to performance promises and any remaining differences in director/executive behavior from the behavior shareholders would prefer. Agency costs are more than a mere transfer of wealth from shareholders to managers because shareholders will anticipate those costs and either not invest in shares in the first place or discount the price they are willing to pay. This will lead to less money being available to corporations and create a drag on economic activity.

The central aim of modern corporate law in many ways is to reduce agency costs occasioned by the separation of ownership and control. Those costs are believed to be highest at large, mature public corporations where shareholders are more dispersed and the businesses generate enough money to allow greater managerial discretion. As you move through the rest of the material on corporations, keep this central tension in mind as it will explain many of the issues you will face. As you do, consider how the law does or does not effectively answer the problem. You may also want to consider whether the problem of agency costs is resolved differently based on the kind of corporation one is addressing.

What You Need to Know:

1. Corporations (other than close corporations) tend to separate owners of residual claims (shareholders) from controllers of the business (managers).
2. That separation occurs because it permits valuable specialization by labor and capital providers.
3. The separation also imposes agency costs because the interests of the managers may diverge from those of the shareholders.
4. If agency costs grow too high, it would reduce investment and limit economic activity.
5. One central theme of corporate law is efficiently reducing agency costs.

LESSON 8: CONSTITUTIVE DOCUMENTS

Modern corporation law is largely "enabling." That means that it consists of mostly default rules governing the corporation from which shareholders and directors may deviate if they wish. This means that the agreements entered into by shareholders and/or directors—the charter, bylaws, shareholder agreements, and perhaps others—are incredibly important.

We have already seen the charter, which lays out the basic equity capital structure of the corporation—how many shares of each class, voting rights of each class, any liquidation or dividend provisions related to each class and other features. The charter will also include a statement of corporate purpose, though this is almost uniformly drafted in an open-ended fashion to permit the corporation to pursue "all lawful" purposes. And, because corporation laws are enabling, the charter may also include any provision the drafters wish that is not against the law.

Nevertheless, certain provisions, if the parties agree to them at all, are normally found in the charter. The reason for this is because of the rules regarding the amendment of the charter. Under Delaware law, a charter amendment must be first proposed and approved by the board of directors and then approved in a separate vote by shareholders. We will discuss shareholder voting later, but it should be clear that the structure of the charter amendment process means disagreements between shareholders and directors over provisions will result in a stalemate. The resulting bias in favor of the *status quo* means that it is crucial for a provision to be in the charter in order to prevent another group from unilaterally changing it. Terms commonly found in the charter include classified boards which divide the board into groups that are elected every few years like the U.S. senate, requirements for director removal, special shareholder vote requirements or limitations, the board's power to issue preferred stock, and a broad exculpation provision protecting directors from monetary damages for certain fiduciary duty breaches.

The importance of putting some of these terms in the charter is heightened by the ease with which a corporation's bylaws may be amended unilaterally by shareholders and/or the board. The bylaws will often fix the size of the board, board committees, corporate officials, and other important matters, but may not conflict with the state's corporate law or the corporation's charter. Otherwise, under Delaware law, shareholders may amend the bylaws with or without director approval and directors may amend bylaws with or without shareholder approval. This raises the obvious question of what is to happen when directors' bylaw wishes diverge from shareholders'. The Delaware statute is famously unclear on this point. In answer to a question certified to it by a federal court, the Delaware Supreme Court[6] suggested that shareholders have bylaw primacy over "procedural" issues while boards have bylaw primacy over "substantive" ones. Consider how easy or difficult it is to draw these distinctions.

Finally, in closely-held corporations—corporations with relatively few shareholders—there will often be agreements among the various shareholders. We will discuss particular issues that arise with respect to closely-held corporations, but one way of controlling unique governance problems facing these organizations is for shareholders to precommit to behaving in certain ways. Most commonly, these agreements will bind shareholders to vote in certain ways, restrict their ability to

---

[6] CA, Inc. v. AFSCME Employees Pension Plan, 953 A.2d 227 (2008).

freely sell their shares, or commit to employing the shareholders for some period of time.

What You Need to Know:

1. Corporations will have certificates of incorporation or charters that serve as a "constitution" of the corporation.
2. Charters must have certain information in them and, otherwise, and may have anything in them the incorporators wish as long as not contrary to state law.
3. Both boards and shareholders must approve any charter amendments, creating a powerful status quo bias.
4. Bylaws may be amended by either group and, to the extent there is a conflict over bylaw provisions between the board and shareholders, Delaware has suggested a preference along the procedural/substantive divide.
5. Particularly in close corporations, essential governance terms may be found in shareholders' agreements.

LESSON 9: THE INTERNAL AFFAIRS DOCTRINE AND STATE INCORPORATION CHOICES

Returning to the charter, one of the incorporators' first decisions to make is picking the state in which they wish to incorporate. This is consequential because the chosen state becomes the state whose laws govern the internal arrangements between the corporation, managers, and shareholders. This magic comes about because of something called the internal affairs doctrine that has been universally adopted by courts. The internal affairs doctrine relates to choice of law, not jurisdiction over internal disputes. Thus, other state and federal courts may hear cases about the internal affairs of a corporation, but they will apply the law of the state of incorporation. Moreover, the internal affairs doctrine necessarily does not apply to "external" affairs, such as controversies between a corporation and creditors, customers, employees, etc. or securities law issues.

Just as the enabling nature of state corporate law makes decisions in a corporation's constitutive documents more important, the internal affairs doctrine makes the choice of state of incorporation important. Beginning in the early part of the twentieth century, Delaware began to take a dominant position in incorporations. At that point, New Jersey, which had been the leading state for incorporations, began to regulate corporations more heavily. Delaware, on the other hand, retained a relatively laissez-faire approach to corporate regulation and soon attracted a plurality of incorporations. That leading position has only increased over time, such that today the vast majority of corporations are incorporated either in Delaware or in their home state.

There has been a substantial academic debate over whether in so doing Delaware has won a "race to the top" or a "race to the bottom." The optimistic "race to the top" view is that Delaware has gained supremacy by adopting the most valuable corporate laws both in its statutes and in its common law decisions. It is commonly claimed that Delaware judges are more sophisticated than their counterparts in other state courts when it comes to matters of corporate law and that Delaware law, because it has had so many published decisions, offers a level of clarity and predictability unmatched anywhere else. A more agnostic view is that lawyers advising incorporators and investors considering buying shares in the corporation are most familiar with Delaware law and are therefore attracted to a relatively known quantity. Finally, pessimists suggest Delaware has won a "race to the bottom" by offering excessively management-friendly laws, betting that managers (to-be-directors and -officers) will push to incorporate in the state most friendly to them with little penalty exacted by disempowered shareholders.

Whatever the view of the process by which Delaware became dominant, it is certainly the case that *it is dominant*, particularly among large, public corporations. Given that state of affairs, our focus in the remainder of this chapter will be on Delaware law. Even if you find yourself working in the context of a corporation incorporated in another state, you are likely to find that the relevant state may adopt certain Delaware precedents to inform the state's corporate law.

What You Need to Know:

1. The internal affairs doctrine means that disputes between shareholders and corporations or managers over governance matters will be judged by the law of the state of incorporation, no matter the court in which the case is brought.
2. Delaware dominates the market for incorporations, making Delaware law the most important corporate law.
3. There remains controversy over whether Delaware has achieved this position by offering valuable laws and dispute resolution mechanisms or by pandering to self-interested incorporators and managers.

LESSON 10: LIMITED LIABILITY

One of the distinctive features of corporations as opposed to general partnerships is the limited liability shareholders enjoy. Tort and contract creditors are generally unable to satisfy a judgment against the corporation by grabbing the personal assets of shareholders. Simply filing incorporation papers with the state therefore radically alters the relationship between the residual claimants of a business and its creditors. Of course contract creditors may demand shareholders become personally responsible for corporate debts before entering into the contract with the corporation, thus overcoming any credit problems that limited liability creates. But often they will not, and, in any event, tort creditors will not be able to engage in that sort of self-help. Consider the famous *Walkovsky v. Carlton* case many of you will study: the victim of the negligent taxi driver there cannot pause the impending collision in order to negotiate for a personal guaranty from the taxi company's shareholder.

There are some limitations to this protection afforded shareholders. The most famous exception to the rule of limited liability is the doctrine under which courts *pierce the corporate veil*. Under certain circumstances, courts will find shareholders personally liable for tort or contract claims against the corporation. Those circumstances will be highly fact-specific and the doctrine is famously vague. In general, cases in which the veil is pierced involve controlling shareholders of non-public corporations. The primary question that drives these "PCV" analyses centers on whether the shareholder observed corporate formalities when running the corporation: regular board meetings, keeping corporate records, segregated bank accounts, etc. This focus on corporate formalities strikes many as odd since their observation will have little relationship to the creditor's claim against the corporation. Thus, whether the creditor is able to collect from the shareholder may appear random from the creditor's perspective.

If those formalities are observed, it is extremely unlikely that limited liability will be cast aside. If they are not observed, state courts differ as to whether some other showing is necessary to pierce the corporate veil. Some states require an additional level of "injustice" or "unfairness" to be occasioned by limited liability. But, again, decisions in this area can fairly be characterized as *ad hoc* and difficult to extend beyond the facts of the particular case.

Leaving aside questions about the exception to the rule, why does the law permit shareholders to avoid corporate creditors? Obviously the rule benefits shareholders at the expense of third parties dealing with the corporation. The primary justification given for limited liability is that it permits passive investing in businesses by ensuring that equity investors only risk the money they initially invested in the corporation to buy shares. This significantly expands the pools of equity capital from which corporations can draw and makes equity capital that much cheaper. Without limited liability, shareholders would have to watch corporations they invested in much more closely,[7] making it incredibly unlikely that shareholders would ever invest small sums in corporations—the monitoring costs would swamp whatever investment gains you could expect.

[7] Note that shareholders might also be forced to monitor their fellow shareholders' wealth to determine how "deep" their own pockets were relative to other potential defendants.

Limited liability is a significant departure from the normal partnership rule of partners' liability for the organization's debts. While shareholders will expend less on monitoring the corporation, perhaps they will monitor too little. What is more, to the extent shareholders are able to influence corporate behavior, limited liability skews their interests by insulating shareholders from downside risks—after all, they can lose no more than the money they invested. This skew may encourage overly risky behavior by corporations to the extent they are influenced by shareholders. The shareholders' preference for risk may be curtailed by executives who generally prefer to avoid risk and contract creditors who may negotiate for protection from excessive risk-taking. Still, limited liability may allow shareholders to *externalize* corporate risks, perhaps requiring more robust regulation in order to optimize social welfare.

What You Need to Know:

1. Unlike general partners who hold the residual claim and control in partnerships and face unlimited personal liability, shareholders hold the residual claim and voting control over boards in corporations and face no personal liability.
2. Limited liability may be overcome by self-help when creditors negotiate for personal guaranties from shareholders or by judicial action via piercing of the corporate veil.
3. Piercing the corporate veil, at a minimum, requires that shareholders disregard corporate formalities.
4. The argument in favor of limited liability turns on the desire to open equity markets to large numbers of people.
5. The argument against limited liability turns on concerns that corporations will engage in riskier behavior than they might otherwise.

LESSON 11: CREDITOR PROTECTION

Once a creditor interacts with a firm—whether by lending money to it, being a victim of the corporation's tort, or otherwise—its interests diverge from those of the shareholders and, often, the managers. Yet the creditors will often have little control over the decisions made by the corporation while the managers (and perhaps shareholders) will exercise greater control. We have already seen one way in which corporate law limits the rights of creditors of corporations as limited liability restricts creditors to corporate assets rather than the personal assets of shareholders. This rule increases the cost of debt, i.e. the price creditors charge the corporation to lend it money increases because it is less likely that the debt will be repaid. Think of all of the things the people in charge of a corporation can do to make repayment less likely, all at no risk to their personal assets!

The primary tool that creditors use to control corporate behavior so as to protect themselves is contract.[8] Moreover, state laws may also protect tort creditors by requiring corporations to carry liability insurance at certain levels. At the same time, corporate law attempts to protect creditors from certain moves that shareholders and/or boards might make to harm them. Chief among these protections are rules that restrict the ability of a corporation to distribute assets to shareholders. Recall that corporations may pay their shareholders dividends and/or buy shares back from them. But when money is sent to shareholders in either way, it becomes part of their personal assets and therefore unreachable by creditors under the rule of limited liability. What if that outflow means that the corporate creditors can no longer have their claims satisfied?

So corporate law (Section 170(a) in the Delaware General Corporation Law) requires the corporation to have sufficient assets compared to liabilities (i.e. creditors' claims) and "legal capital" before it can distribute anything to shareholders.[9] This is the so-called balance sheet test and the amount by which assets exceed liabilities is often called "surplus" and becomes the

---

[8] This topic is covered in greater detail in most Corporate Finance courses in law schools' upper-level curricula.

[9] In many states other than Delaware there is also an "insolvency" test which restricts distributions when they would lead to the corporation being unable to pay its debts as they come due.

amount available to be sent out to shareholders.[10] The determination of asset and liability values and, therefore, surplus is subject to the rules of accounting. Accounting rules for calculating balance sheet amounts were traditionally based on historical valuations of both assets and liabilities. Thus, it was often the case that a corporation's assets increased in value but its balance sheet did not take this into account. This mismatch was not terribly important to most market participants because they understood the limitations of the balance sheet when valuing a corporation. However, because shareholder distribution constraints were keyed off of the balance sheet by statute, this accounting quirk had real world effects. Of late, both Delaware and the Model Business Corporations Act have recognized the ability of corporations to "fairly" value the business using up-to-date market values and finance methodologies when faced with statutory surplus tests.

As a result, much of the work of protecting creditors from distributions by the corporation to shareholders comes from the law of fraudulent conveyance. States have adopted one of the Uniform Fraudulent Conveyance Act or the Uniform Fraudulent Transfer Act and many questions of fraudulent conveyance wind up being resolved under the federal Bankruptcy Code. Each of these protects creditors from corporate transfers if the corporation (1) actually intended to hinder the interests of creditors or (2) did not receive "reasonably equivalent value" in exchange for the distributed assets when the corporation was in the zone of insolvency.

One final way in which shareholders may exploit creditors is by converting their equity position into a debt position when the corporation is in trouble and unlikely to have any money left over to pay shareholders. The shareholders loan the corporation a sum of money, thus becoming creditors. The corporation takes the money and buys back their shares at presumably excessive, i.e. non-zero, values. The shareholder/creditor thus transforms an equity claim for a more valuable debt claim. This gives the former shareholder an advantage as he now stands in line with

[10] Corporations may also distribute assets to shareholders if they've had a particularly successful past year, even if there is not enough surplus to otherwise permit the distribution.

other creditors (rather than shareholders) should the company become insolvent. The remedy for this exploitation is "equitable subordination," by which the former shareholder's claim as a creditor is subordinated or put behind the other creditors' claims and thus paid only if the other creditors are paid in full. *Costello v. Fazio* is the case most casebooks use to demonstrate the doctrine which requires a showing that the shareholders (in that case, partners in a partnership that was reorganizing as a corporation) pull equity capital from the corporation for personal gain, thereby endangering both the corporation's viability and creditor interests.

What You Need to Know:

1. Corporate law has specific rules intended to protect creditors, even beyond piercing the corporate veil.
2. Distributions of corporate assets to shareholders, which could harm creditors, are limited by rules requiring enough assets remain in the corporation.
3. In addition, bankruptcy law recognizes fraudulent conveyances and which can be clawed back in the event of corporate bankruptcy and equitable subordination which prevents shareholders from disguising themselves as creditors.

LESSON 12: SHAREHOLDER VOTING AND PROXIES

We now move from the relationship between creditors and the corporation to the relationship between shareholders and management which will be our focus for the remainder of the Chapter. This relationship raises the central question of agency costs (discussed above) that are created when shareholders invest money in the corporation in the hope of profits when the corporation is controlled by a board and executives. How do shareholders ensure that management will run the corporation in line with their expectations and in their interests? We have seen that creditors generally protect their investment via contract. That is more difficult for shareholders to do since their claims are less defined than creditors. Creditors are to be paid certain amounts at certain times and deviations from those terms are easily contractible. Shareholders' claims are for "whatever's left over" at some uncertain point in the future. How can they write an enforceable contract around those terms?

Corporate law establishes a number of mechanisms through which shareholders may nevertheless constrain the behavior of managers. The primary one of these is shareholder voting. Shareholders vote on a number of matters. Most significantly, they vote on board elections, amendments to the charter and significant transactions like merging the company with another or selling substantially all its assets. Regarding board elections, there are a constellation of rules surrounding these votes. In Delaware, there must be an annual meeting at which directors are elected, although the directors may be staggered or "classified" so that only a portion of them (usually 1/3) are up for election in a given year. The statute also establishes rules about the annual meeting which may be tailored by the corporation through the charter or bylaws. So, for instance, there must be a minimum number of shares present to count as a quorum. Director elections are contested under a plurality rule so that the highest vote-getter, even if not garnering a majority, will be seated.[11] Complicating matters further, different classes of stock may be afforded different voting rights in the charter (more votes per share, less votes per share, class veto rights over certain decisions, etc.).

The main problem with director elections is getting shareholders to vote. The problem is partially alleviated by law which permits proxy voting so that shareholders can vote without showing up to the annual meeting in person, thereby lowering the costs to shareholders of voting. In practice, this means that the corporation (i.e. the current board) will solicit proxies from shareholders who may grant the proxy either generally, with specific instructions, or not at all. If the corporation receives sufficient proxies, the shareholder meeting can occur and business can be conducted. The proxy machinery has two notable features. First, the proxy solicitation brings with it federal regulation under the securities laws. If you solicit

---

[11] There has been a trend toward firms adopting "majority voting" provisions which establish consequences in case the winning director does not receive a majority of votes. The effect of these provisions remains the subject of much debate.

proxies there are certain rules (discussed further in the next lesson) that you must follow including the disclosure of information and exposure to antifraud rules. Second, a host of secondary actors arise as assistants in the proxy process. The corporation and anyone attempting to contest a matter at the meeting will hire proxy solicitors. All sides will hire lawyers to draft proxy language. Finally, and for reasons related to shareholders' collective action problems discussed next, proxy advisory firms have grown up to offer guidance to shareholders as to how to vote their shares.

As with our political process, there are even more significant roadblocks to effective voting. For shareholders with relatively small holdings, there is little incentive to invest the time to inform themselves regarding director elections or, perhaps, even fill out the proxy cards. The shareholder will recognize that their limited voting power will unlikely be the difference in any election. What is more, even if their vote mattered, the advantages gained by a "good" result will be shared among all shareholders equally. When compared with the cost of becoming informed, the benefits for small shareholders will often appear very small.

This passivity is concerning if shareholder voting for directors is relied on to check agency costs. Recent trends have made the collective action problem less daunting, however. As mentioned above, proxy advisor firms have served to coordinate some shareholder action by making voting recommendations. Whether those recommendations are well-reasoned or not is up for some debate, but proxy advisors have surely reduced information costs for dispersed shareholders. More than that, shareholdings are more concentrated in institutional investors than ever before. These money managers arguably have better incentives to take voting seriously since they hold significant numbers of shares. On the other hand, it may be the case that institutional investors are better served selling underperforming stocks than attempting to reform those companies. Most importantly, the last decade has seen the rise of shareholder activists who seek out arguably lagging corporations, take large positions in them, and advocate for changes. This new breed of shareholder activism is extremely controversial, but we see, at the very least, the partial erosion of the collective action problem. These trends have strengthened shareholder power via threats to vote out directors to a point never seen before.

What You Need to Know:

1. Shareholders vote on a number of important matters with respect to the corporation, most significantly director elections, charter amendments, and fundamental transactions.
2. In order to encourage shareholders to vote, state corporate law permits them to send in a proxy authorizing others to vote for them.
3. Nevertheless, shareholders face significant collective action problems with voting because the personal benefits to small shareholders of informing themselves and voting will almost always be outweighed by the personal costs.
4. Various actors help ameliorate this collective action problem—proxy advisors, institutional investors serving as intermediaries, and activist investors—though there is a raging debate as to how much of the problem has been solved and at what cost.

LESSON 13: FEDERAL PROXY RULES

Under Section 14(a) of the Securities Exchange Act of 1934, those who solicit proxies via interstate commerce or a facility of a national securities exchange—always the corporation and sometimes shareholders who wish to challenge management via a shareholder vote—must comply with rules promulgated by the Securities Exchange Commission (the SEC). The SEC has taken up that charge and laid out a significant regulatory regime centered on disclosures that those soliciting proxies must make to shareholders. In addition to these disclosure requirements, the SEC's proxy rules also specify the circumstances under which corporations must allow shareholders to make proposals for votes *using the company's proxy solicitation* and establish an anti-fraud rule governing communications related to proxy solicitations.

Disclosure Rules

If the corporation is soliciting proxies for a shareholder meeting at which directors will be elected, it must provide the solicited shareholders with a proxy statement using Schedule 14A. That Schedule 14A will contain a number of items of required disclosures including, among others: the date and place of the shareholder meeting; identity of the persons soliciting the proxies; identity of director nominees and information about those nominees; interests of any solicitor in the votes; and extensive information related to director and executive compensation. If it is someone other than the corporation who is soliciting the proxies, less extensive company-specific information is required.

Shareholder Proposals

The solicitation of proxies carries with it substantial costs. When the corporation solicits proxies from shareholders, the corporation itself bears those costs. Yet shareholders themselves may hope to solicit proxies from other shareholders to vote for various proposals they want adopted. As a way of lowering those costs which might otherwise be prohibitive to shareholders making such proposals, the SEC adopted Rule 14a–8 which requires corporations to place shareholder proposals onto the corporation's proxy solicitation as long as the proposing shareholders held the lesser of $2,000 or 1% of the corporation's voting shares for one year.

The corporation may, of course, recommend in its proxy solicitation that other shareholders vote against the shareholder proposal. Still, the shareholder proposal rule is a departure from the normal rule that the board makes corporate decisions. The SEC rule compromises by allowing the corporation to reject placing shareholder proposals on the corporation's proxy if it meets one of a handful of criteria. Importantly, one (or two) of these exceptions allow the exclusion of proposals that direct management to run the business in particular ways. Some shareholder proposals are not related to the ordinary course of business—proposals related to the governance mechanisms of the corporation, for example, are ok—while others clearly are. As a way around this SEC exclusion, then, proposing shareholders will often phrase the proposal as a recommendation to consider or study the issue rather than a specific directive.

Anti-Fraud

Rule 14a–9 provides an anti-fraud rule for proxy solicitations. The SEC can enforce the rule against solicitors, but shareholders have been held to have a private right of action to police proxy fraud. In order for plaintiffs to prevail, they must show a material misstatement or omission along with a handful of other elements. We will discuss other species of shareholder-enforced antifraud securities law rules in Lesson 24.

What You Need to Know:

1. In most cases, solicitation of proxies will trigger proxy rules promulgated by the SEC under securities law.
2. The lion's share of federal proxy regulation involves disclosure obligations placed on proxy solicitors.
3. Additionally, solicitors will face antifraud enforcement under federal law and corporations must permit certain shareholders to place their proposals onto the company's proxy statement unless one of a handful of exceptions is satisfied.

LESSON 14: DUTY OF CARE AND THE BUSINESS JUDGMENT RULE

Voting for directors and other significant matters is one means by which shareholders may hold directors accountable for their decisions. Directors and officers also owe the corporation fiduciary duties, so, in certain circumstances, shareholders may also use courts to sue them. In Lesson 18 we will discuss the derivative suit mechanism by which shareholders are permitted to stand in the place of the corporation. For now, however, it is enough to discuss the specific fiduciary duties that directors and officers owe the corporation. In the next section, we will discuss the duty of loyalty which is already familiar to us from both agency and partnership.

The first fiduciary duty discussed in most casebooks is the duty of care. The duty of care is not more important than the duty of loyalty and, indeed, a strong case could be made that it is far less important in practice. The duty of care comes first instead because it introduces the business judgment rule, a crucial part of corporate law. The duty of care itself is familiar from negligence concepts in torts and relatively simple to state: directors are required to behave as a reasonably prudent person in their position would. As in torts, there may be arguments about what similarly-situated reasonably prudent person would do, but the standard of conduct is otherwise fairly straightforward.

Corporate law, however, does not simply apply common law negligence to corporate directors. Instead, corporate law interposes a doctrine known as the "business judgment rule," which serves as a standard of liability distinct from the common negligence standard of care. That is, the duty of care tells directors to not be negligent but then corporate law pulls back, via the business judgment rule, from actually holding directors liable for that negligence.

The business judgment rule is judicially, rather than statutorily, crafted. In the famous case *Smith v. Van Gorkom* the Delaware Supreme Court stated it as follows: "The business judgment rule is a presumption that in making a business decision, the directors of a corporation acted on an informed basis, in good faith and in the honest belief that the action taken was in the best interests of the company." The presumption is rebuttable and the court has given a road map towards overcoming it. First, were the directors informed when they made the relevant decision? Second, did they make the decision in "good faith?" Finally, did the directors believe the decision was in the best interests of the corporation? What the business judgment rule crucially does, then, is preclude cases *based on other kinds of complaints*, most importantly the complaint of director stupidity or garden-variety negligence. It makes liability turn on procedural questions—were you informed? were you conflicted in your loyalties?—rather than substantive ones such as whether the decision was wise given the circumstances. The business judgment rule creates a space between the standard of care (reasonable prudence) and the standard of liability, and most duty-of-care claims fall into that space.

Obviously, the business judgment rule makes it less likely that corporate directors will be held liable for breaching their duty of care than they would under a straight negligence standard. One might wonder why courts created this liability-reducing doctrine. Perhaps it is because courts are concerned that standard negligence doctrines are too prone to mistake, meaning that informed, good faith decisions are nevertheless found to be negligent by courts. The hindsight bias of the litigation context is commonly cited as a reason for the business judgment rule since decisions that may not have been negligent at the time they were made appear to be negligent years later after unfortunate events intervened. Of course, this problem, if it exists, also plagues negligence litigation in non-corporate contexts. It is also often suggested that the business judgment rule is a manifestation of judicial modesty with judges admitting that they are not experts in business. Again, however, this explanation fails to explain straight negligence analyses common in complicated contexts like medical malpractice.

The most satisfying explanation for the business judgment rule appears to be that directors prefer it and, in general, shareholders themselves prefer it. This may strike you as counterintuitive since fiduciary duty suits are supposed to be a way for shareholders to discipline directors. Why would shareholders want fewer disciplinary tools? The economic argument begins with the proposition that shareholders want directors to be risk-neutral, i.e. to make the highest value choices possible irrespective of risk. Most shareholders are diversified in their holdings, so that even if they lose on one firm that takes on risk and loses, they will gain on all of the firms that take on risk and win. But directors faced with being second-guessed after the fact and having to potentially pay out of pocket millions or billions of dollars in "loss" situations would avoid taking risk at the margin because they would worry about the potential for courts to make mistakes when determining negligence. Shareholders and corporations could help reduce this risk aversion by providing directors with corporation-paid indemnification agreements and/or insurance. In fact, they do this all the time and these will be discussed in Lesson 17. But indemnification and insurance are not costless to corporations and, by extension, shareholders. Better, so the thinking goes, to avoid the problems of a negligence-based liability in the first instance except in the most egregious cases that involve some easily observable failure of process.

A subset of duty of care cases involve complaints by shareholders that directors failed to monitor the corporation appropriately. The modern public corporation is a massive beast incapable of being fully understood and watched by any person or small group at any given time. Nevertheless, reasonably prudent people in charge of such an organization would certainly be expected to develop ways of keeping track of much of the business. Note that the business judgment rule is a presumption that applies to business *judgments*. Claims of failing to monitor the business are often claims that no judgments were made at all. Most often they arise after crises (e.g. the financial crisis or Enron-era fraud cases) or in the compliance context. In *Stone v. Ritter*, the Delaware Supreme Court clarified that directors violated their monitoring duty in such situations when either "directors utterly failed to implement any reporting or information system or controls [or] having implemented such a system or controls, consciously failed to monitor or oversee its operations."[12]

The only exception to the process-over-substance distinction drawn by the business judgment rule is the so-called "waste" doctrine. Under that doctrine, directors may be liable notwithstanding the business judgment rule if they approve "an exchange of corporate assets for consideration so disproportionately small as to lie beyond the range at which any reasonable person might be willing to trade." Needless to say, waste is extremely rarely found by courts.

What You Need to Know:

1. Directors and officers owe the corporation fiduciary duties, including the duty of care.

[12] Be careful about characterizing these sort of claims as duty of care claims. In *Stone v. Ritter*, for example, this seemingly obvious care claim was characterized as a violation of the board's duty of good faith. Whichever bucket Delaware doctrine places these claims, the fundamental error by the board is one of care as commonly understood.

2. The duty of care imposes a negligence standard on managers.
3. However, the business judgment rule limits that standard by establishing a separate standard of liability precluding liability absent a board's failure to inform itself, bad faith or conflict of interest.
4. The business judgment rule may be preferred by shareholders because it provides less disincentive for directors and officers to take on risk.
5. Directors also have a duty to monitor the corporation but will only be liable if they utterly fail to implement a monitoring system or consciously fail to monitor thereafter.
6. Directors may also be liable for waste if they make a decision that is so bad for the corporation that a court can find that no reasonable person would have been willing to make it but such cases are exceptionally rare.

LESSON 15: DUTY OF LOYALTY AND CLEANSING VOTES

Directors and officers also owe the corporation a duty of loyalty. The business judgment rule is less help in shielding directors and officers from loyalty claims than it is for care claims. Remember that the business judgment rule presumes that the directors acted in the best interest of the company. Sufficient evidence (or allegations, at the motion to dismiss stage) of conflicted loyalties will tend to show that directors acted in their own best interests rather than the company's.

Those allegations and/or evidence of disloyalty rarely consist of emails or eyewitness testimony showing directors trying to intentionally harm the company. The vast majority of disloyalty claims instead center on matters in which the director's or officer's financial interest simply runs counter to that of the corporation. Consider self-dealing in which two of three corporate directors are brothers and they vote to award a vendor contract from the corporation in question to their separately-run family business. The brothers stand to gain personally if the contract is more favorable to the family business than the corporation. The whiff of disloyalty that such an arrangement produces will usually be enough to overcome the business judgment rule.

Rebutting the business judgment rule does not end the case. Delaware courts move on to determine whether or not the conflicted transaction was nevertheless "entirely fair" to the corporation. To continue the example from above, the court will look at evidence of the process by which the contract was awarded to the family business and the economic terms of the deal. This kind of searching review of director decision making is in stark contrast to the deferential approach courts take to duty of care cases.

Naturally, potentially conflicted directors will be reluctant to enter into conflicted transactions with the specter of entire fairness review looming. This is precisely the sort of deterrent effect that the duty of loyalty is meant to create. However, corporate law recognizes that there may be cases in which the best opportunity for the corporation involves dealing with its own directors or officers in a potentially conflicted situation. Delaware law offers a mechanism by which business judgment rule deference can be recovered. Section 144(a) of the DGCL provides that a self-dealing transaction will not be void or voidable solely because of the conflict if the transaction was approved by (1) a majority of disinterested directors; (2) a majority of disinterested shareholders;[13] or (3) fair to the corporation. The statute is unclear on the point but later judicial decisions have clarified that the effect of either cleansing vote under (1) or (2) is to reactivate the business judgment rule, a much more director-friendly posture than entire fairness review.[14]

---

[13] The statute actually does not specify that the majority of shareholders approving the deal must be independent, leaving open the possibility that a majority shareholder could "cleanse" a self-dealing transaction simply by voting for it. Later, courts foreclosed this option by requiring the shareholder majority approving the deal to be disinterested.

[14] A different result sometimes holds in the case of a conflicted controlling shareholder. As discussed later, controlling shareholders owe fiduciary duties to minority shareholders. Their power is believed to be so great, that Delaware courts will often continue to apply entire fairness review even after one of the cleansing votes by disinterested directors or disinterested shareholders, i.e. shareholders other than themselves.

A particularly troublesome subset of conflicted director transactions led courts to develop the corporate opportunity doctrine. When the director or officer stands on the other side of a transaction with the corporation, the problem of conflicted loyalties is easy to see. But what if the director or officer is transacting with a third party and the loyalty question centers on whether that business opportunity belonged to the corporation in the first place rather than the director or officer? Before advancing to the entire fairness/cleansing vote stage, courts must first determine whether the director or officer took something that belonged to the corporation. Courts may look at a number of factors, including whether the corporation was able to take advantage of the opportunity, the manner in which the opportunity was presented to the director or officer, and whether the opportunity was in the general line of business of the corporation.

What You Need to Know:

1. Sufficiently pleaded duty of loyalty claims are not subject to the business judgment rule.
2. Instead, the burden is on the interested director or officer to demonstrate that the transaction was "entirely fair" to the corporation.
3. The director or officer can regain the business judgment rule protection under Delaware law by disclosing the transaction and receiving a cleansing vote from a majority of disinterested directors or a majority of disinterested shareholders.

LESSON 16: CORPORATE PURPOSE AND CORPORATE SOCIAL RESPONSIBILITY

The duty of loyalty raises an interesting question separate and apart from policing self-dealing transactions by management. Beyond those easy cases where directors and officers are lining their own pockets, it is not clear what it means for a director or officer to *loyally* direct the corporation. Loyalty to whom? If the corporation, what are the corporation's interests that demand loyalty exactly? What corporate goals are permissible for directors to pursue assuming they are not enriching themselves? Is director discretion in this regard broadly or narrowly cabined?

The question is conceptually difficult, but practically simple. First, the hard part: it is hard to discern what interests a corporation has because it is not a person. A corporation consists of many different people who have invested their time, money and other assets and these people certainly have interests. But, at least sometimes and perhaps more often than that, those interests will conflict. For instance, a corporation may decide to allocate more money to employee salaries than is strictly necessary to maximize shareholder profit, opening up a fault line between shareholders and employees. Similar cleavages among shareholder, debtholder, employee, and community interests are easy enough to imagine.

In such cases, what decision is "loyal" to the corporation? This is a hugely controversial question. For some time, the dominant view has been that the interests of common shareholders serve as a useful proxy for corporate interests such that directors fulfill their duty of loyalty to the corporation by being loyal to shareholders, i.e. maximizing shareholder wealth. A famous case from Michigan, *Dodge v. Ford Motor Co.*, most clearly expresses the view that shareholders are the ultimate beneficiaries of the duty of loyalty and other Delaware cases—most notable the *Revlon* decision discussed in Lesson 23—do the same. The theoretical argument underlying this view is generally that (1) shareholders as residual claimants are the closest stand-ins for the corporation outside of the insolvency context and (2) other constituencies (creditors, employees, the public) are better able to protect themselves via contract and regulation than shareholders for whom corporate law fiduciary duties are one of the only effective ways of self-protection.

On the other hand, the rule of shareholder wealth maximization is not found in the DGCL nor is it found in many Delaware decisions. Shareholders do not appear to contract for this sort of duty in charters, though that may perhaps be due to an assumption, erroneous or not, that Delaware law does in fact sufficiently call for a shareholder wealth maximization rule. As Lynn Stout and Margaret Blair have pointed out, the theoretical argument for elevating obligations to shareholders may be on shaky ground: (1) the corporation's total value may be maximized when other constituencies do not fear being dominated by shareholders and therefore might invest more freely; and (2) many non-shareholder constituencies are, in fact, unable to protect themselves via contract or regulation putting them in the same tough spot in which shareholders find themselves.

These difficult issues will often be less intractable than it initially appears, at least in terms of director liability for breaching the duty of loyalty. Most decisions that appear to benefit non-shareholder constituencies can be argued with a straight face to increase long-term corporate profitability and thus improve shareholders' positions. The *Dodge* opinion itself points in this direction as the court was unwilling to second-guess a decision by Henry Ford to reduce shareholder dividends in order to invest in a manufacturing plant. Even more egregious (depending upon your point of view), is the consistent line of cases (*A.P. Smith Manufacturing Co. v. Barlow* is the most popular one in Business Organization casebooks) permitting directors to give corporate money to charity. The reason for these seeming departures is once again the business judgment rule and the reluctance of courts to second guess directors when they do not have obviously self-interested motivations. The result is that fiduciary duty liability is effectively a nullity when directors can at least claim that their actions benefitting non-shareholders do in fact benefit shareholders in the long run. "To whom do directors owe loyalty?" is thus less important as a legal question than as an ethical or economic one.

Despite the weak enforcement of any duty to maximize shareholder wealth, recently some corporations have made explicit that they do not want shareholders to be the exclusive object of directors' loyalty. Delaware recently adopted a provision in the DGCL permitting the incorporation of "benefit corporations." These corporations' charters will state a corporate purpose or purposes that are to be balanced by directors with maximizing corporate profit. Thus, shareholders are unable, later on, to state a successful loyalty claim based on directors pursuing the other purpose in tandem (or even above) maximizing shareholder wealth.

What You Need to Know:

1. Directors owe a duty of loyalty to the corporation, but that leaves unspoken the particular corporate constituency whose interests are to be primary.
2. The majority view among corporate law experts is that directors and officers have a fiduciary obligation to advance shareholder interests, though this view is far from unanimous.
3. In any event, courts are loath to actively enforce this shareholder-centric version of the duty of loyalty for the same reasons that underlie the business judgment rule.
4. Of late, some states, including Delaware, have allowed corporations to specify in their charter that directors will corporate interests other than shareholder wealth maximization.

LESSON 17: EXCULPATION, INDEMNIFICATION, AND INSURANCE

Directors at corporations are extremely unlikely to be personally liable for breaches of fiduciary duties, particularly if they avoid self-dealing. Nevertheless, some risk remains or is believed to remain by potential directors. For example, directors who are sued may face litigation costs even if the underlying suit is unsuccessful. Moreover, the damages directors might owe in the unlikely event of a successful claim are apt to be ruinous given the economic consequences of corporate decisions. Unsurprisingly, directors seek further protection before agreeing to take a place on a corporation's board.

Exculpation

After the *Smith v. Van Gorkom* decision holding outside directors liable for breaching their duty of care, Delaware adopted Section 102(b)(7) of the DGCL. 102(b)(7) permits corporations to include a clause in their charters exculpating directors from monetary damages in fiduciary duty suits. Three important caveats are in order. First, only directors may be exculpated—not officers. Second, the exculpation clause only protects against monetary damages and not injunctive relief. Third, directors may not be exculpated for breaches of the duty of loyalty or for "acts or omissions not in good faith or which involve intentional misconduct or a knowing violation of law." The vast majority of public Delaware corporations have adopted these clauses either by amending their charters or by initially going public with the clause in their charters. The fact that so many charters were successfully amended (which you'll recall requires shareholders to have voted for the amendment) at least suggests that shareholders do not place a high value on their ability to enforce care claims via monetary liability.

Indemnification

Many corporations promise to indemnify their directors and officers for costs related to lawsuits they face in their capacities as managers. These promises are often found in either the charter or the corporation's bylaws. Section 145 of the DGCL permits indemnification under certain circumstances and 145(c) even requires it to the extent a director or officer is "successful on the merits." Indemnification is only permissible if the indemnified party "acted in good faith and in a manner the person reasonably believed to be in or not opposed to the best interests of the corporation." In the case of derivative suits, this requirement can only be met by a judicial determination once there is a finding of liability. Because this raises the stakes to directors and officers of completing a trial, it creates substantial incentives to settle claims.

Insurance

If a director is in serious jeopardy of facing monetary damages, it may be the case that the corporation has faced a cataclysmic event. Therefore, the corporation's promise of indemnification may be of little value. In fact, corporations regularly purchase directors' and officers' insurance policies to cover expenses that indemnification programs otherwise might. In fact, one portion of the standard insurance policy covers the corporation for costs expended to defend the director or officer under an indemnification arrangement. The other part directly compensates directors and officers and again typically excludes costs upon a final finding of fraud or self-dealing, thus again offering incentives to settle such cases before a final decision.

What You Need to Know:

1. In addition to the business judgment rule, directors and officers are able to protect themselves from litigation risk in other ways.
2. 102(b)(7) clauses in charters prevent shareholders from successfully suing directors for monetary damages for breaches of the duty of care.
3. Corporations often indemnify their directors and officers for litigation expenses and often purchase insurance to cover the same.

LESSON 18: THE DERIVATIVE SUIT AND SHAREHOLDER LITIGATION

Suppose a majority of directors breach one of their fiduciary duties to the corporation. The corporation should sue the directors since the violated duties were owed to it. But the directors control the corporation. How likely is it that the directors will have the corporation sue themselves? An alternative mechanism for disciplining directors is obviously necessary. The answer that corporate law gave was the derivative suit.[15] In a derivative suit, a shareholder or group of shareholders sue the directors for an injunction forcing the directors to have the corporation sue the original wrongdoers. Thus, there are two acts or omissions about which shareholders are complaining: the underlying breach of fiduciary duty and the directors' subsequent failure to have the company sue on that breach.

The derivative suit is quite remarkable in some ways. Normally, shareholders cannot force directors to do anything. They have the ability to periodically remove them via election, but they cannot demand the directors make particularly

---

[15] Alternatively, directors and officers may breach fiduciary duties owed directly to shareholders. The most common sort of "direct suit" involves claims relating to directors' selling the corporation for too little consideration. The derivative suit mechanism is not appropriate in these cases and, instead, these claims are usually brought as class actions by a shareholder class.

business decisions while in office. The decision to sue is very much a business decision made by the corporation, so it seems strange to allow shareholders to push directors aside in this case. Nevertheless, taking fiduciary duties seriously requires something like the derivative suit. A balance must be struck.

Most states strike that balance via the so-called "demand" requirement. Shareholders are required to make a demand on the board that the board pursue the underlying claim. Of course, this just pushes things back to where they were when we were concerned that the board would not have the corporation sue themselves. Courts could nevertheless force shareholders to make demand and then judge whether the demand was refused for good (selfless) or bad (selfish) reasons. Instead, the common practice is for shareholders to make their derivative claim and simultaneously claim that demand would be futile.

In Delaware, the test for "demand futility" is admittedly somewhat Byzantine. The classic formulation comes from *Aronson v. Lewis* and requires demand unless "under the particularized facts alleged, a reasonable doubt is created that: (1) the directors are disinterested; and (2) the challenged transaction was otherwise the product of a valid exercise of business judgment." In later cases the "and" was changed to the disjunctive "or" so that satisfying either prong of the *Aronson* test will suffice to excuse demand. The strange part of the *Aronson* test is that, on the one hand, it addresses current directors' conflicts of interest and, on the other, the quality of the past, complained-of decision. If a past board breached its fiduciary duty (thus qualifying under (2)), should a new board not be able to make an independent decision as to whether to pursue a suit? Later cases held that the case of a turned-over board will be decided outside of the *Aronson* test and demand will be excused only if "the particularized factual allegations. . . create a reasonable doubt that, as of the time the complaint is filed, the [current] board of directors could have properly exercised its independent and disinterested business judgment in responding to a demand. . ." In either case, the demand futility test creates a mini-trial without discovery at the beginning of each case.

Corporate law goes even further in protecting boards' prerogatives regarding shareholder suits. Even if demand is excused and the derivative suit proceeds, the board may recover some control over the process by establishing a special litigation committee of the board. The members of the committee need to satisfy a court of their ability to independently evaluate the merits of pursuing the action. Moreover, courts will examine those merits if the committee recommends cutting off the litigation without giving the committee the benefit of the business judgment rule.

Shareholder litigation is a very contentious topic in corporate and securities law. At times litigation may be frivolous, driven by plaintiff attorney interests and settlement incentives. Or it may be necessary to police fiduciary duties (and anti-fraud protections in the securities law context). There is an ongoing push and pull within courts and legislatures as to how to handle these matters. Of late, skeptics of shareholder litigation have argued for a number of changes meant to curb vexatious suits. "Disclosure-only" settlements—in which plaintiffs receive only revised disclsoures by the corporation and plaintiff attorneys receive fees—are now reviewed more carefully by courts out of a concern that such settlements were harmful to shareholder interests in the aggregate. Boards also began to adopt "exclusive forum" bylaws that require suits be brought exclusively in certain courts and Delaware has since blessed such provisions as long as the chosen courts are in Delaware. Finally, boards attempted to adopt fee-shifting provisions that required shareholder plaintiffs to bear the litigation costs of corporations in the event the claims were unsuccessful, but the Delaware legislature adopted Section 109(b) of the DGCL to prevent such bylaws.

What You Need to Know:

1. Because the directors control the corporation, we should expect to see systematic under-enforcement of director fiduciary duties owed to the corporation.
2. The derivative suit reinvigorates fiduciary duty enforcement by permitting the shareholders to push past the directors and force the corporation to sue those directors.

3. This is a substantial departure from normal corporate governance, so corporate law requires shareholders to make a demand on directors or otherwise show that the demand would be futile.

4. If demand is deemed futile, a board may regain control of the lawsuit by establishing an independent special litigation committee, but any decision by the committee to halt the litigation will be looked at closely by courts.

5. Delaware has recently sanctioned exclusive forum provisions in bylaws and charters but has prohibited fee-shifting bylaws.

LESSON 19: THE SPECIAL CASE OF CLOSE CORPORATIONS

Not all corporations are created equal. To this point we've mainly focused on public corporations with dispersed, diversified shareholders who are easily able to sell their shares in established public markets. The risks to these shareholders posed by agency costs are relatively low and their incentives to monitor managers are correspondingly low. But many corporations do not fit that model. Instead, these corporations have relatively few shareholders who tend not to be diversified and often rely on dividends and/or wages from the corporation for a return on their investment. What is more, the market for shares of these corporations are imperfect or even non-existent. Shareholders may even face explicit transfer restrictions, effectively locking them into the corporation. The risks to these shareholders posed by managers, i.e. other shareholders holding a majority of control personally or as a group, are therefore high.

To make it more concrete, consider a common fact pattern. A group of four friends start a business, each contributing $100,000 and each expecting return on her investment either via cash dividends distributed to shareholders or salaries paid to them through their employment by the corporation. Suppose there is a falling out and three of the shareholders use their voting power to exclude the fourth. The three form a majority of the board and control the corporation's business decisions. These include, among other things, the hiring and firing of employees and the declaration of dividends. The board thus fires the fourth shareholder from her position as an employee (for plausible business reasons) and declines to declare dividends (again for plausible business reasons). If she can't sell her shares at anything other than a significant discount, what is the fourth shareholder to do?

We have seen that Delaware courts offer relatively weak protection to shareholders in the form of fiduciary suits. Under the facts above, the business judgment rule would seemingly protect the majority's decisions. Given the differences in risks faced by shareholders in public corporations and closely-held corporations, should this approach shift? Delaware's answer has generally been "no." In *Nixon v. Blackwell*, the Delaware Supreme Court observed: "A stockholder who bargains for stock in a closely-held corporation. . . can make a business judgment whether to buy into such a minority position, and if so on what terms." Essentially, Delaware's view of minority shareholders in closely-held corporations is *caveat emptor*.

That is not necessarily the case in other states. The most famous alternative approach to fiduciary duties in close corporation comes from Massachusetts and most casebooks discuss the Massachusetts approach at least to contrast Delaware's. Massachusetts' Supreme Judicial Court once held that majority shareholders owed minority shareholders partner-like loyalty/good faith duties. This helps to solve some of the problems of exploitation inherent in closely-held corporations, but creates different ones for efficiently running the business. In light of those concerns, even Massachusetts courts have noted that the majority must have broad discretion to control decisions but that the minority may be given the opportunity to show a less exploitative alternative approach that would achieve similar ends.

What You Need to Know:

1. Close corporations present different issues than do large, public corporations because there is not often a ready market to sell shares into and shareholders of close corporations are usually not diversified.

2. This creates opportunities for majority shareholders to exploit minority shareholders by withholding dividends and/or wages.

3. Delaware law does not give shareholders in close corporations special protection, though other states may by creating partnership-like fiduciary duties.

LESSON 20: EXECUTIVE COMPENSATION

Executive compensation is highly salient because of the political and moral questions involved. But it also stands out because it so clearly highlights the agency cost concerns we have discussed. On the one hand, executive compensation may be a potentially useful tool for reducing agency costs by bonding executives' pay to their performance, as is commonly done with salespeople On the other hand, the process by which executive pay is awarded is itself subject to significant agency problems. When we observe the resulting pay amounts and structures, what are we seeing exactly?

Bonding via Pay

Recall that directors hire and pay executives who do most of the day-to-day work in running corporations. For most of the twentieth century, executives could fairly be characterized as bureaucrats. For the most part, they were lifelong employees of the corporation who had made it to the top of the ladder through hard work and luck within the organization. They tended not to move between corporations and developed significant firm-specific human capital. This attachment to the firm plausibly led executives to be risk averse since their well-being was tied up with the corporation's survival. Pay was structured accordingly, with most pay coming in the form of salaries and perks like company planes and golf club memberships.

Beginning in the 1970s, critics began to worry that the bureaucratic tendencies of executives were reducing the value or corporations, and in particular shareholder wealth. How to encourage executives to work harder and take more risks? Derivative suits would inevitably run into the business judgment rule and shareholder voting (to bring in new directors who would presumably bring in new executives) faced serious collective action problems discussed earlier. The market for corporate control discussed in the remaining sections proved an important corrective, as did changes to the way executives were paid.

Salaries, while still large, are no longer the main way in which public company executives are compensated. Many perks have been cut back. Bonus plans proliferate, but the most important change in compensation practice has been skyrocketing levels of equity compensation. Shareholders successfully pushed for executives to be paid in shares so that their thinking would be more in line with shareholders'. Executives "bonded" themselves to shareholder-friendly outcomes by making their pay contingent on share prices: if share prices go up, executives' bank accounts get fatter.

The shift to equity compensation was accomplished in part by awarding executives restricted stock—shares that would become vested (and therefore sellable) over time or upon the accomplishment of certain corporate goals. More important, however, was the introduction of enormous amounts of stock options. Stock options give the holder the right to buy shares at some point in the future for a price fixed today. For accounting (historically) and tax (historically and currently) reasons, that price tends to be the value of the share on the date of the option grant. So if the share price goes up, the option becomes "in-the-money" since the holder can exercise it and buy the now-higher-valued share for the original price. If the share price remains the same or declines, the holder simply refuses to exercise the option and loses nothing. Obviously, options give executives serious reason to try and increase share price at all costs, precisely what the shareholders prefer.

Arms'-Length Bargaining?

Partially because options appear costless—for years at-the-money options were not treated as an expense in the corporation's accounting statements—total pay to executives soared beginning in the 1980s reaching new heights each year with only minor hiccups for serious economic downturns. In theory, it makes sense for executive pay level to rise as executives took on more risk that they would be paid very little (if share prices did not increase). But it is difficult to tell now whether the dramatic increase in executive pay is the result of a functioning labor market coming to terms with new understandings of managerial talent and pay structures or something else.

Lucian Bebchuk and Jesse Fried (along with David Walker in the first instance) forcefully argued that observed pay was not the natural outcome of treating executives more like shareholders and less like bureaucrats. They contended that executives were able to influence their own pay because boards had ceded control over almost everything related to the corporation to the executives. Directors' reputations and jobs, they argued, depended on the good graces of the executives and the pay levels and structures we see at large public companies reflect that dynamic—its own kind of agency cost—rather than any arms'-length bargain between the executives and the corporation.

Thousands of academics' hours have been spent researching and debating the new world of executive compensation. Some have claimed that shareholders should be relatively indifferent to executive pay levels as long as the pay is structured properly since the financial effect a properly incentivized executive can have on shareholder wealth dwarfs whatever value is actually leaving the corporation in executive pay. Others have argued that the nature of being an executive has changed, leading to higher pay being required. Still others have suggested that current executive pay is the result of a market failure, but not so much the one Bebchuk and Fried claim. Rather, directors, shareholders and the public generally may simply overestimate the marginal difference that an executive can make and that overestimation often leads to overpayment.

What You Need to Know:

1. Executive compensation is a corporate decision that highlights the agency problem.
2. Executive compensation has increased dramatically in recent decades, driven mostly by significant equity awards.

3. Those equity awards included stock options which give the holder the right (but not the obligation) to pay a fixed price for a company's share for a specified period into the future.
4. Serious debate exists over whether observed compensation patterns represent a properly functioning market, managerial power, or something else.

LESSON 21: INTRODUCTION TO MERGERS AND ACQUISITIONS AND APPRAISAL RIGHTS

Sometimes it will be better (or at least sometimes some important people believe it will be better) for a corporation to acquire the whole or part of another corporation's business. How these combinations are effected drives much of the high-end corporate law practice at large law firms. Moreover, the mergers and acquisition process highlights many of the tensions we've discussed up until this point.

In general, there are three methods by which these deals take place: asset purchases, stock purchases, and mergers. Each of these methods will have different consequences with respect to required third-party approvals, tax, retained liabilities and other matters.

Asset Purchases

Perhaps the simplest form of combination to understand is the asset purchase. One corporation offers consideration (cash, shares, anything else) for assets of another. The acquiring corporation must approve the transaction in the normal course which could require board approval or approval at a lower level depending on the size of the deal. Acquiring corporations' shareholders will usually have no say in the transaction unless the corporation has to issue 20% or more of its common stock to the target corporation as part of the deal consideration.[16] Shareholders at the target corporation, on the other hand, will have a veto right under Delaware law over the sale if the assets

[16] This voting right comes from stock exchange rules rather than Delaware.

to be sold make up "all or substantially all" of the target corporation's assets.

The acquirer can pick which assets it wants to buy and can even pick which of target's liabilities it wants to take on. This specificity comes with costs, as the acquirer has to identify which pieces it wants and then negotiate with the target over pricing.

Stock Purchases

The acquirer can also gain control of the target's business by gaining control of a majority of the target's stock. Once they gain control of the shares, they'll control the election of directors who control the way the target's business is run. The acquirer's shareholders again have no say over the deal unless the consideration going over to the target's shareholders involves issuing 20% of the acquiring corporation's stock. Because the deal is a sale of shares by shareholders, it implicitly requires approval by the target shareholders who voluntarily agree to sell. The acquired shares continue to be affected by any liabilities of the target as they were before.

For publicly-held targets, however, it will be very difficult to negotiate individually with enough target shareholders in order to acquire voting control. Instead, acquirers who wish to purchase the stock of such targets generally rely on the tender offer. The tender offer allows an acquirer to announce that it is accepting shares if tendered to it by the public. The acquirer will state a price it is willing to pay and the length of time the offer will remain open, along with any conditions it has to completing the tender offer. Since the 1960s, the tender offer process has been regulated under a federal law, the Williams Act. The Williams Act requires, among other things, that (1) tender offers remain open for twenty business days, (2) later increases in offer price redound to the benefit of early tenderers, and (3) the target board state its opinion regarding the offer. Often the tender offers will be conditioned on a sufficient number of shares being tendered by shareholders so that the acquirer is not stuck acquiring a large but not majority position in the corporation's equity. Also, the acquirer may only wish to acquire a certain amount of shares, and if the tender offer is oversubscribed, the Williams Act requires the acquired shares to be apportioned proportionately among the tendering shareholders. Tender offers play a crucial role in contests for corporate control because they permit acquirers to negotiate directly with target shareholders rather than the target board who may be more reluctant than the shareholders to accept a deal.

Mergers

The final method for transferring control is the statutory merger and it is perhaps the most challenging to understand. When the appropriate approvals are gained, one corporation ceases to exist independently and is subsumed within the other or both cease to exist only to reappear in a newly formed entity. Those approvals, unsurprisingly, include ones from the target corporation's board and shareholders (tracking similar requirements for a sale of all or substantially all of the target's assets) and the surviving corporation's board. In general, the surviving corporation's shareholders will also get the ability to veto the deal unless their charter is *not* amended or they are *not* heavily diluted by the deal, i.e. substantial surviving corporation's shares are *not* sent to the other corporation's shareholders as consideration in the deal. The "magic" of the merger happens and all of the target corporation's assets and liabilities carry over to the surviving corporation. If the surviving corporation wishes to avoid the target corporation's liabilities from infecting it, the merger can be structured as a triangular merger. In a triangular merger, the acquiring corporation creates a wholly-owned subsidiary and merges that subsidiary (rather than itself) with the target, thus becoming the owner of the shares of the subsidiary/target combination. Of course, if there are substantial unknown liabilities at the target, the subsidiary/target merged entity may become insolvent, but the effect on the acquirer is limited by the rule of limited liability to the loss of whatever consideration it paid to target shareholders in the merger.

Appraisal Rights

In each of the above cases, target shareholders have an explicit (mergers, asset sales) or implicit (stock sales) veto right as a class. Of course, a majority of shareholders may approve a merger or asset sale while a minority dissents. In the case of mergers and asset sales, the transaction would go through and the minority would be forced to have its shares in the going concern converted into either shares of a smaller concern and consideration (asset sale) or whatever consideration the majority agreed upon in exchange for their shares (merger).

Corporate law gives these dissenting shareholders the right to seek judicial appraisal of the fair value of their shares in certain circumstances. In Delaware, appraisal rights are only available for mergers, not asset sales, and why they remain for those is a difficult question to answer. The best argument for appraisal rights may be that they are necessary to protect shareholders when there are reasons to think a deal approved by a majority of shareholders is nevertheless a bad one. This is most likely when a controlling shareholder (including a corporation) wants to buy out minority shareholders. We will discuss those transactions in Lesson 22.

Delaware's appraisal rights regime permits appraisal but then precludes it for target shareholders when their shares had been publicly traded. But then, in an exception to the exception, appraisal rights become available again if those shareholders receive anything other than stock in the surviving corporation or other stock that is publicly traded. For those of you confused at this point, don't worry: few think any of the distinctions drawn above make any sense from a policy perspective!

What You Need to Know:

1. Corporations often acquire other corporations or are acquired by other corporations via merger, asset sale or stock purchase.
2. The various methods of combining firms carry with them unique shareholder approval requirements, transaction costs, liability carry-overs, tax implications and appraisal right consequences.
3. In a stock purchase related to a public company target, acquirers will usually use a tender offer strategy which will be regulated by the Williams Act.

4. In a merger, two previously separate entities are legally transformed into one, with the merger agreement specifying what happens to the shares of the original corporations.

5. Appraisal rights, which grant the right to have a court determine the fair value of one's shares, may be granted to dissenting shareholders of a merged corporation depending on whether the original corporation was public and the consideration to be received.

LESSON 22: CONTROLLING SHAREHOLDER DUTIES

We have already discussed the duty of loyalty owed by directors and officers to the corporation and the processes by which one may "cleanse" conflicted transactions. A similar set of concerns and mechanisms exist with respect to transactions between the corporation and controlling shareholders. While these shareholders do not technically have control over the corporation (the board does), their position often gives them de facto control or, at the very least, significant leverage in negotiations with the board. That gives them the ability to enrich themselves in much the same way as directors and officers might and so the law imposes fiduciary duties on controlling shareholders.

Recall that conflicted directors and officers had a number of options by which they could obtain business judgment review treatment of the relevant transaction should a lawsuit arise—approval by a majority of disinterested directors or approval by majority of disinterested shareholders. Until recently, those options do not revive the business judgment rule in conflicted controlling shareholder situations. Those transactions were always subject to "entire fairness" review—a searching inquiry into the fairness of the process by which the transaction was effected and the consideration received—no matter what disinterested approvals are gained. Why the historically different treatment of directors and controlling shareholders? Courts believed that disinterested directors and shareholders could stand up to interested directors and officers (who may be removed in subsequent periods, after all) more so than interested controlling shareholders (who cannot be).

Despite the fact that entire fairness was going to be the standard of review no matter what, many controlling shareholders structured their interested transactions by obtaining "cleansing" votes by disinterested directors and/or shareholders. Why? Technically, these votes shifted the burden of proof to the plaintiff challenging the transaction. More importantly, these sort of disinterested approvals were *evidence of a fair process* within the entire fairness inquiry.

The issue of controlling shareholder transactions is most commonly litigated in the context of parent/subsidiary consolidations—the parent of a partially-owned subsidiary is trying to buy out the shares of the subsidiary's minority shareholders—but the same issues arise in any interested controlling shareholder situations. And it is in this context that the Delaware Supreme Court appears to have pulled back on its concern for latent coercion. In *Kahn v. M&F Worldwide Corp.*, the Court said that the business judgment rule would apply to a controlling shareholder transaction, at least where the deal was conditioned from the start on (1) the approval of an independent special committee and (2) the uncoerced vote of the majority of the minority shareholders. Perhaps this decision is specific to the parent/subsidiary merger context, but it suggests that Delaware is beginning to treat controlling shareholders like directors and officers.[17]

What You Need to Know:

1. Controlling shareholders owe the corporation and minority shareholders a duty of loyalty.
2. Historically, cleansing votes commonly used by interested directors and officers merely served as evidence of fairness and a burden-shifting device

[17] Even before *Kahn v. M&F Worldwide*, Delaware offered controlling shareholders a way around fairness review if they structured their takeover not as a merger, but rather as a share purchase via tender offer. This led to an unresolved split in Chancery Court decisions, though the availability of the business judgment rule in merger cases after *Kahn* may make the distinction less important, i.e. the absence of fairness review for tender offers less advantageous.

for controlling shareholders rather than bring back generous business judgment rule review.

3. More recently, Delaware courts have liberalized review of controlling shareholder transactions in which thy cash out minority shareholders by awarding them the business judgment rule if the deal is conditioned, from the start, on approval by an independent board and the majority of uncoerced minority shareholders.

LESSON 23: DEFENSIVE TACTICS IN M&A

Potential acquirers are constantly looking for undervalued corporations to buy and shareholders are generally excited about receiving offers—often at a premium to the current share price—from those acquirers. Target boards and executives are often another story, however. They may resist offers because they believe the deal is not in the best interests of the shareholders, i.e. the offer price is too low when compared to the true value of the corporation's shares. A disconnect may exist between the board's perception and shareholders' perceptions because the boards have more information about that true value. Alternatively, target boards and executives may dislike offers for fear that they will lose their positions when the new owners replace them with different (better?) managers. The first rationale is seemingly squarely within the board's wheelhouse. The second rationale, on the other hand, suggests a clear breach of the duty of loyalty—the board and executives are putting their interests ahead of shareholders'. But if courts see target management resisting an offer, how can they tell which rationale is truly driving the board's behavior?

Before addressing that question, we have to understand the ways in which target boards and executives can "play defense" against an unwanted offer. Recall that for mergers and asset sales, the target board must approve the deal. So in those cases it is very easy for a board to stand in the way of an offer. Acquirers who meet resistance from target management may go "hostile." They could simply run a proxy contest at the next director election seeking to change the board to a group more willing to negotiate. In fact, hostile takeovers generally involve a proxy contest to replace the target board and a simultaneous tender offer for at least a majority of the target's outstanding shares. The reason behind the tender offer is easy enough to understand—if target management will not negotiate, the acquirer can go directly to the target shareholders to acquire control.

But why worry about the proxy fight if you are going straight to the shareholders to acquire their shares? The reason is that, in the face of hostile tender offers, target management has developed a range of defenses to stall even tender offers. The most popular and important defense, by far, is the poison pill. The poison pill is triggered by an individual or group's acquisition of a certain percentage of the target corporation's stock. When triggered, "rights" attach to each share of outstanding stock to purchase new stock of the target at a steep discount. However, the triggering party is not allowed to participate, so it will be heavily diluted by everyone else acquiring cheap shares. The pill makes it economically suicidal for anyone to acquire the threshold level of target shares in the first place. The target board retains the ability to redeem the rights (cancel them for negligible or no compensation) if it chooses, so this forces the acquirer to come back to the target board to get it to agree to redeem before pursuing the tender offer. Presumably the target board will refuse to redeem the pill unless the terms of the deal are changed (and maybe even then!), so the acquirer will pair its tender offer with a proxy fight to replace target boards with new directors who will redeem the pill. Well-advised targets may anticipate this and may seek, for example, a staggered board provision in the charter, making it difficult and time-consuming to replace the board with directors more favorably disposed to the deal on the table.

Other defenses are available. For instance, a target's board may try and find an alternative deal to the hostile one, the contours of which strategy will be discussed below. In any event, the question will be what to make of the board's decision to put obstacles in front of its shareholders' ability to say yes or no to a sale of their shares. Recognizing the "omnipresent specter" of board self-interest, Delaware courts established an intermediate level of scrutiny for defensive maneuvers in the face of a takeover bid. Under the *Unocal* test, courts look to see whether there is a reasonably perceived danger to corporate policy and effectiveness that led to the defensive maneuver *and* whether the defensive response was "proportionate" to the threat.

What counts as a threat? The *Unocal* case suggested somewhat controversially that potential harms to non-shareholder constituencies could count as potential threats. That dicta in *Unocal* reopens the question discussed in Lesson 16 regarding corporate purpose and which constituency's interests govern. Obviously, however, the primary instance of a threat to corporate policy is the case in which the target board believes the offer undervalues the corporation. It may seem a bit strange to view the shareholders as being "threatened" by a lowball offer requiring that they be defended by their board from their own choices. Delaware courts have consistently adopted the view—unfortunately called "substantive coercion"—that shareholders may make significant mistakes by tendering their shares too cheaply to acquirers. Academics have been relatively suspicious of this line of thinking since it appears to permit boards to adopt a "just say no" defense without much evidence that the board has better information about the target's value than the shareholders.[18] And, in fact, in the recent *Airgas* case, a board that refused to redeem its pill in the face of an all-cash tender offer and a staggered board structure that required multiple elections before installing a new board to so redeem was deemed to have not acted disproportionately, i.e. preclusively.

This broad discretion to defend the corporation and shareholders from unwanted takeovers does have a limit. According to the *Revlon* decision, if a board has committed to sell the corporation in a cash deal, then its only goal becomes getting the best deal possible for shareholders. The "better deal" may not necessarily be the highest priced deal if, for instance, competing offers have different likelihoods of passing regulatory muster. But the range of considerations open to selling boards becomes extremely limited and entirely shareholder-focused. Indeed, *Revlon* is perhaps the clearest precedent in Delaware

---

[18] The best work on this issue and something that is worth your time to read is Bernie Black and Reinier Kraakman's *Delaware's Takeover Law; The Uncertain Search for Hidden Value*, 96 NW. U. L. REV. 521 (2002).

suggesting the board should be pursuing shareholder interests above all else. The more rigorous examination of board decision-making suggested by the *Revlon* decision has been somewhat tempered by the relatively limited context in which the *Revlon* rule applies. For instance, Revlon does not apply when a board has agreed to merge with another company in a stock-for-stock deal. According to the *Time-Warner* decision, Time's board had no obligation to sell the company to the highest bidder when Paramount jumped in and offered to buy Time. *Revlon* duties were not triggered because the company was not up for sale in the original merger. Rather, the Time board's decision to adjust the Warner deal to ensure its completion as opposed to Paramount's bid was judged under Unocal as an appropriate (i.e. reasonably perceived as a proportionate response to a threat) defensive measure even though the Paramount bid was plainly more valuable to the Time shareholders.

What You Need to Know:

1. Target boards may block an acquirer from taking over the corporation and paying off shareholders.
2. The most common way boards block acquirers is by adopting a poison pill which makes buying shares directly from target shareholders economically unattractive.
3. Courts review pills and other defensive moves under a test of intermediate scrutiny commonly referred to as the *Unocal* test that requires reasonable perception of a threat and a proportionate response.
4. If a board has decided to put the corporation up for sale (generally when the shareholders are expected to receive cash in consideration for their interests in the corporation), the board must negotiate the deal with a sole focus on maximizing shareholder return.

LESSON 24: A BRIEF INTRODUCTION TO SECURITIES LAW

Alongside state corporate law sits a substantial body of federal law regulating the capital markets in which corporate securities (think shares and most debt) are sold. Securities laws have already played a role in this chapter as it relates to proxy solicitation. Recall that federal law lays out a set of rules by which corporations must abide when they solicit proxies for shareholder votes. Those rules are promulgated under the Securities Exchange Act of 1934, one of the two main securities law statutes. The other, the Securities Act of 1933, governs how securities are initially sold by corporations and other business organizations to purchasers. It sets forth an elaborate disclosure scheme required of all primary securities issues as well as a set of exemptions through which companies may avoid the disclosure requirements. In addition, the '33 Act establishes heightened antifraud rules applicable to those disclosures in the primary market, enabling defrauded purchasers of securities to more easily sue issuers.

The '34 Act, on the other hand, governs subsequent "secondary" sales in public markets and, consequently, certain aspects of public corporations' behavior (e.g. proxy solicitation). Public corporations are subject to a complicated continuous disclosure regime. Perhaps most importantly, the '34 Act proscribes fraud in connection with the purchase or sale of securities (including in the primary market) under Section 10(b) and Rule 10b–5. The Rule states that it is unlawful, among other things, to "make any untrue statement of a material fact or omit to state a material fact necessary in order to make the statements made. . . not misleading. . ." Note that this antifraud rule stands entirely separate from the state law fiduciary duty of care and somewhat at a distance from the duty of loyalty which has generally been confined to matters of director or officer self-dealing.[19] 10b–5 is about lying, whatever the motivating factor.

---

[19] Recent Delaware case law has described a duty of candor, a subset of the duty of loyalty, that directors owe to shareholders.

Corporations (and other businesses) often communicate with the public and therefore people who might sue them afterwards for any lies or actionable omissions. Sometimes those communications are mandated by the continuous disclosure rules promulgated under the '34 Act. On the other hand, businesses may voluntarily disclose information to the public. In either case 10b–5's antifraud rule applies and opens up the possibility of class action suits.

Defrauded security holders must prove a number of elements to succeed on a 10b–5 claim: materiality of the misstatement, scienter (something more than negligence is required), reliance, and loss causation. The specific elements are covered perfunctorily if at all in a Business Organizations class and are dealt with in more detail in the traditional Securities Regulation course.

What the securities statutes and rules did not historically do, however, was explicitly prohibit insider trading—trading of securities by corporate insiders who have material non-public information. The ability to use that information to buy undervalued shares or sell overvalued shares before the market learns what the insider knows can be very lucrative. At common law, the question of fiduciary duties owed by insiders to those with whom they traded was a relatively murky one, particularly if shares were traded over an impersonal market as they are today. The '34 Act moves against insider trading in Section 16(b) by requiring corporate managers to disclose trades in corporation securities and disgorge profits gained from "short-swing" transactions. But deterring insider trading is mostly done through 10b–5 fraud cases, despite the absence of a clear connection in the statute. Fraud requires a misstatement or omission where a duty exists. In most insider trading cases there is no misstatement made to counterparties. Instead, the SEC and federal courts have grounded much of the so-called "classical theory" of insider trading under 10b–5 in a duty to disclose material nonpublic information owed by the insider to the counterparty. The insider trader's failure to disclose the information that he has thus is an "omission" that forms the basis for the fraud.

The limitation on the classical theory comes when we consider those holding material nonpublic information but having no fiduciary duty to disclose to the relevant counterparty. In the seminal *Chiarella* case, this meant a printer working for the acquiring company in a merger who discovered that the target company's shares would shoot up in value when the merger was announced. He bought a number of shares from target shareholders with whom he had no relationship. Was that fraudulent? The Supreme Court didn't think so. The SEC pushed for, and the Supreme Court ultimately accepted in the later *O'Hagan* case, an alternative path to insider trading liability termed the "misappropriation theory." Under that theory a trader is liable when he misappropriates confidential information in breach of a duty owed to the source of the information and then trades *with someone else.*

What You Need to Know:

1. Securities law is a set of federal statutes and rules that sits alongside state business organizations law and helps shape those organizations' behavior.
2. The '33 Act governs initial sales from the issuer to the market, mandating detailed disclosures and creating heightened antifraud liability.
3. The '34 Act governs subsequent sales, a/k/a the secondary market, and creates proxy regulations, continuous disclosure obligations for public companies and general antifraud liability under Section 10(b) and Rule 10b–5.
4. Insider trading is not mentioned directly in the securities laws but subsequent SEC rulemaking and case law have treated insider trading as actionable fraud.

LESSON 25: ALTERNATIVE ENTITIES

Up until now we have only discussed sole proprietorships (in the context of agency law), general partnerships, and corporations (both public and close). For newly-formed small businesses, as between the two, corporations hold out the advantage of limited liability and partnerships offer a way to avoid double taxation. S Corporations combine both attractive features, albeit with significant restrictions that make S Corporation status unworkable for many.

Limited partnerships (LPs) and limited liability partnerships (LLPs) arose to fill niches in the market for business organizations. Limited partnerships take the partnership form and divide the partner class into (1) general partners who retain control and unlimited liability and (2) limited partners who exercise minimal control and have limited liability. If the general partner in an LP is a corporation, then unlimited individual shareholder liability ensues. And, even if not, the limited liability limited partnership (LLLP) has been created permitting general partners in a limited partnership to limit their personal liability. That limitation tracks the limitation on liability available to LLP partners. LLPs tend to exist in the professional service market (lawyers, accountants, etc.).

As complicated as that is, the majority of newly formed business organizations in Delaware and other jurisdictions are neither general partnerships nor corporations nor LP/LLP/LLLPs, but rather limited liability companies (LLCs). Like corporations for liability purposes yet a pass-through entity for tax purposes, LLCs have exploded on the scene over the past twenty years. LLC members file a certificate of organization with the state and otherwise govern themselves via an operating agreement that specifies the bulk of their relationship. The background default rules (management rights, fiduciary duties, dissolution provisions) for LLCs often track partnership antecedents, though operating agreements provide the ultimate degree of flexibility in contracting around these defaults.

What You Need to Know:

1. For small businesses, a range of other organizational forms exists.
2. The limited partnership creates a class of limited partners without control rights who are afforded limited liability.
3. The limited liability company has come to dominate entity selection for newly-formed entities and

provides the advantages of limited liability and pass-through entity tax treatment, while affording members significant freedom to tailor their operating agreement.

CHAPTER 4

CRIMINAL PROCEDURE (INVESTIGATIONS)

LESSON 1: INTRODUCTION

Criminal procedure courses generally fall into one of three categories. Most courses titled "Criminal Procedure" cover the constitutional rules governing police investigations. You may see these courses described as "Criminal Procedure I," "Criminal Procedure: Police," or "Criminal Procedure: Investigations." These courses usually cover the Fourth Amendment, Fifth and Fourteenth Amendment due process clauses as they relate to the conduct of law enforcement agents during investigations, the Fifth Amendment privilege against compelled self-incrimination, and the Sixth Amendment right to counsel as it relates to interrogations. Most law schools also offer a course covering the constitutional rules governing prosecution and sentencing. You may see these courses described as "Criminal Procedure II," "Criminal Procedure: Adjudication," or "Criminal Procedure: Bail to Jail." Students in these courses learn about rules governing charging, pre-trial detention, discovery, plea bargaining, jury selection, trial, and sentencing. Some law schools also offer a nuts-and-bolts course designed to familiarize students with the practical tasks performed by criminal lawyers such as drafting indictments, conducting discovery, negotiating plea agreements, and basic trial practice. In addition to these core criminal procedure courses, many law schools offer courses covering closely related topics such as post-conviction practice and civil rights litigation.

The lessons comprising this chapter address the main topics and concepts covered in "Criminal Procedure I." Our primary focus will be on constitutional rules governing the conduct of government agents during the investigative phase of the criminal process. The bulk of that work will happen within the four corners of the Fourth Amendment. In full, the Fourth Amendment provides that:

> The right of the people to be secure in their persons, houses, papers, and effects, against unreasonable searches and seizures, shall not be violated, and no Warrants shall issue, but upon probable cause, supported by Oath or affirmation, and particularly describing the place to be searched, and the persons or things to be seized.

The Fourth Amendment is the primary source of constitutional regulation of police engaged in detecting criminality and gathering evidence. Although seemingly straightforward, we will discover that Fourth Amendment doctrine is complicated. Many of those complications trace to *Katz v. United States*, 389 U.S. 347 (1967). The *Katz* decision, and particularly a concurring opinion written by Justice John M. Harlan II, dramatically changed the landscape of Fourth Amendment law by promoting a definition of search focused on "reasonable expectations of privacy." *Katz* and many of the doctrinal rules based on *Katz* have come under considerable pressure in recent years with the advent of new surveillance technologies. We will also discuss rules governing the exclusionary rule, which is the primary remedy available to criminal defendants who have suffered violations of their Fourth Amendment rights.

In addition to the Fourth Amendment, we will discuss limitations on interrogations derived from the Fifth, Sixth, and Fourteenth Amendments. The Fifth and Fourteenth Amendments prohibit the federal government and state authorities, respectively, from depriving "any person" of "life, liberty, or property, without due process of law." These due process protections bar officers from engaging in conduct that produces "involuntary" confessions. The Fifth Amendment also provides that no person "shall be compelled in any criminal case to be a witness against himself." Although initially conceived as a trial right, the Supreme Court in *Miranda v. Arizona*, 384 U.S. 436 (1966), famously extended the prohibition on compelled self-incrimination to cover police interrogations. We will discuss both the *Miranda* decision and difficult questions relating to its application and constitutional status. We will also engage complementary and sometimes overlapping constraints on police interrogations derived from the Sixth Amendment right to counsel.

Criminal Procedure I is a constitutional law course. In fact, it is often described as "Constitutional Law III," reflecting its place in a series that includes courses covering the structure of our constitutional system and courses covering rights embedded in the First, Second, Fifth, and Fourteenth Amendments. As a result, many of the topics of concern in other constitutional law courses including textual interpretation, historical context, constitutional politics, policy, and the dynamics of the Supreme Court will be front-and-center in your criminal procedure course. Your criminal procedure course will also focus extensively on particular cases and often will entail close reading of those cases. In keeping with these features of your criminal procedure course, the lessons in this chapter will identify and highlight major cases while offering a range of contextual considerations helpful in understanding and applying these cases. Although these lessons cannot replace the materials in your textbook or forgive you the responsibility to read and think carefully about the cases and materials therein, they will provide you with invaluable guidance that will make your class preparation more efficient and effective.

What You Need to Know:

1. The lessons in this chapter review materials covered in criminal procedure courses engaging constitutional rules governing police investigations including detecting criminal activity, gathering evidence, and interrogations.
2. The primary sources of constitutional constraints on police investigations are the Fourth Amendment, which governs searches and seizures, the due process clauses of the Fifth and Fourteenth Amendments, the Fifth Amendment's prohibition on compelled self-incrimination, and the Sixth Amendment right to counsel.
3. The text of the Constitution and major Supreme Court cases play a central role in criminal procedure courses.

LESSON 2: FOUNDATIONS

There are three basic questions and concepts that underlie all the materials in this course. The first is whether the proceeding in question is criminal or civil in nature. That distinction is important because many of the protections in the Fifth and Sixth Amendments apply only in criminal cases. Notably, protections afforded by the Fourth Amendment are not limited to criminal cases and apply to all governmental searches and seizures. *See* Grady v. North Carolina, 135 S.Ct. 1368 (2015). The second question is whether the constitutional right in question protects individuals from federal agents only or from state agents as well. When they were adopted, the protections embedded in the Bill of Rights—inclusive of the Fourth, Fifth, and Sixth Amendments—applied only to the federal government. They did not bind state governments or their agents. Many of these protections have since been incorporated through the Fourteenth Amendment, which means they now bind state as well as federal agents. Finally, the vast majority of criminal investigations and prosecutions occur at the state and local levels where state and local laws apply. State and local rules, including state constitutions, provide important protections, some of which parallel federal rules and some of which provide additional protections beyond those embedded in the Bill of Rights. It is therefore important to keep in mind the role of federalism in our criminal justice system and particularly the relationships between rights afforded by federal, state, and local laws.

Is This a "Criminal" Process?

The Fifth Amendment prohibition on compelled self-incrimination and the Sixth Amendment right to counsel only apply in criminal cases. It is therefore important to know whether a particular legal process is criminal or civil. One obvious place to look might be the potential consequences. For example, if a legal process exposes a person to threats of fines or involuntary incarceration then it is tempting to think it is a criminal process. After all, fines and incarceration are the paradigmatic examples of criminal punishment in our system. There are, however, many civil and regulatory procedures that can also result in fines, incarceration, and other deprivations of liberty. For example, we are subject to civil fines if we violate traffic laws. Corporations are subject to civil fines if they violate environmental or securities regulations. An individual can be subject to civil incarceration if he suffers from a mental disease or disorder and poses a threat to himself or others. Individuals who are critical to ongoing investigations can be held against their wills under material witness orders. But none of these are "criminal" consequences.

So how do we distinguish between criminal procedures and civil or regulatory procedures? The Supreme Court answered that question in *Kansas v. Hendricks*, 521 U.S. 346 (1997). *Hendricks* tested the status of a Kansas law called the Sexually Violent Predator Act, which provided for the indefinite civil commitment of convicted sex offenders. Mr. Hendricks had served the full term of his prison sentence for child molestation. Instead of releasing him, Kansas officials secured an order under the Act providing for his continued incarceration in light of the danger he posed to the public. Mr. Hendricks argued that this continuing incarceration constituted criminal punishment and ran afoul of the Fifth Amendment prohibition on double jeopardy, Fourteenth Amendment due process, and the Article I prohibition on *ex post facto* lawmaking.

In an opinion written by Justice Clarence Thomas, the Court rejected all these claims on grounds that the Kansas law provided only for civil incarceration, not criminal incarceration, and that constitutional rules governing criminal procedures therefore did not apply.[1] According to the Court, whether a statute threatens criminal or civil sanctions is determined first by looking to the legislature's stated purpose. If a legislature designates a penalty or consequence as civil rather than criminal, then courts should presume that it is civil. That presumption can only be overcome on "the clearest proof that the statutory scheme is so punitive either in purpose or effect to negate the State's intention to deem it civil." In determining the

---

1 This may seem obvious on the face of the Fifth and Sixth Amendments, which refer to "criminal cases," but less so Article I, Sections 9 and 10. The Supreme Court has held that the ex post facto clauses of Article I, Sections 9 and 10 only apply in criminal cases or where the law reflects "punitive intent." *See, e.g.*, California Dept. of Corrections v. Morales, 514 U.S. 499 (1995).

punitive purpose or effect of the Sexually Violent Predator Act, the *Hendricks* Court found that the law served neither of the "primary objectives of criminal punishment: retribution or deterrence." It instead operated as a tool for protecting the public from dangerous predators. The Court therefore upheld the Kansas legislature's designation of the Act as civil in nature despite the fact that a criminal conviction was a virtual prerequisite for incarceration under the Act.

Does the Federal Constitutional Protection Apply to the States?

When they were ratified in 1791, the Fourth, Fifth, and Sixth Amendments purported to bind only the federal government and its agents. The Court confirmed that view in *Barron v. Baltimore*, 32 U.S. 243 (1833), holding that the Bill of Rights, inclusive of the Fourth, Fifth, and Sixth Amendments, did not apply to the states. State governments and their agents were bound by their own state laws and constitutions, but those documents did not bind the federal government or its agents. As a result, individual persons and the peoples of the various states enjoyed different rights and protections in relation to the federal government and their state governments. All that seemed to change with ratification of the Fourteenth Amendment in 1868.

Section 1 of the Fourteenth Amendment provides that:

> All persons born or naturalized in the United States, and subject to the jurisdiction thereof, are citizens of the United States and of the state wherein they reside. No state shall make or enforce any law which shall abridge the privileges or immunities of citizens of the United States; nor shall any state deprive any person of life, liberty, or property, without due process of law; nor deny to any person within its jurisdiction the equal protection of the laws.

On its face, the provision commanding that "No state shall make or enforce any law which shall abridge the privileges or immunities of citizens of the United States," referred to as the "Privileges or Immunities Clause," appears to bring all rights prescribed in the Bill of Rights to bear on state governments and their agents. Those who read the Privileges or Immunities

Clause in this way, including Justice Hugo Black[2] and Justice Clarence Thomas,[3] endorse the view that the Fourteenth Amendment "incorporates" the Bill of Rights in its entirety. Since the *Slaughter-House Cases*,[4] however, a sustained majority of the Supreme Court has held that the Privileges or Immunities Clause sweeps more narrowly, addressing only those rights directly related to citizenship functions, such as the right to vote.[5]

Although the doctrine of "full incorporation" has been rejected by the Court, it has nevertheless been willing to selectively incorporate different rights guaranteed in the Bill of Rights under the Due Process Clause of the Fourteenth Amendment. That approach is explained in *Duncan v. Louisiana*, 391 U.S. 145 (1968). The question in *Duncan* was whether the Sixth Amendment right to a jury trial in criminal cases applied in state courts. Writing for the Court, Justice Byron White held that it does because this right is, 1) a "fundamental principle[ ] of liberty and justice which [lies] at the base of our civil and political institutions"; 2) "basic to our system of jurisprudence"; and 3) "a fundamental right, essential to fair trial." Notably, Justice John Harlan II dissented in *Duncan*, favoring latitude for states to serve as criminal procedure laboratories.

Through the process of selective incorporation the vast bulk of protections guaranteed in the Bill of Rights have been enforced against the states. The three notable exceptions are the grand jury clause of the Sixth Amendment,[6] the Seventh

---

2 *See* Adamson v. California, 332 U.S. 46 (1947) (Black, J., dissenting) (arguing that "the language of the first section of the Fourteenth Amendment, taken as a whole, was thought by those responsible for its submission to the people, and by those who opposed its submission, sufficiently explicit to guarantee that, thereafter, no state could deprive its citizens of the privileges and protections of the Bill of Rights.").

3 *See* McDonald v. City of Chicago, 561 U.S. 742 (2010) (Thomas, J., concurring) (arguing that the Second Amendment right to bear arms "applies to the states through the Fourteenth Amendment's Privileges or Immunities Clause.").

4 83 U.S. (16 Wall.) 36, 1872.

5 *See* Palko v. Connecticut, 302 U.S. 319 (1937) (holding that some aspects of the Fifth Amendment's prohibition on Double Jeopardy do not apply in state courts); Twining v. State, 211 U.S. 78 (1908) (holding that the Fifth Amendment privilege against compelled self-incrimination did not apply to the states); Hurtado v. California, 110 U.S. 516 (1884) (holding that the Grand Jury clause of the Fifth Amendment does not apply to the states).

6 Hurtado v. California, 110 U.S. 516 (1884).

Amendment right to jury trials in civil cases, and the Eighth Amendment prohibition on "excessive bail."

What Role Does State Law Play?

The doctrine of incorporation highlights the role of federalism in our criminal justice system. Most criminal investigations and prosecutions are conducted by state and local agents. State and local laws, including state constitutions, therefore play a central role in elaborating the rights of criminal defendants and setting constraints on law enforcement.

The relationships between federal, state, and local rules is complex, but there are several aspects of this federal system that are important to keep in mind.

First and foremost, provisions of the Bill of Rights that have been incorporated to the states set a constitutional floor below which state and local laws cannot descend. This means that state governments cannot use their legislative powers to reduce or diminish rights afforded to criminal defendants by the United States Constitution. Through much of the mid-twentieth century, the Supreme Court wielded this power to promote and protect criminal procedure rights.

Second, state governments have broad authority to grant greater rights to criminal defendants in state courts than those provided for criminal defendants in federal courts. State governments can likewise set more stringent restraints on state and local law enforcement officials. In the late twentieth and early twenty-first centuries, as the Court took a more conservative approach to many constitutional questions, some state courts and state legislatures used this authority to promote more protective criminal procedure rights. This phenomenon is sometimes referred to as "New Federalism."

Third, state courts have final authority over the interpretation and application of their state constitutions. Thus, if a state court interprets its own constitution in a way that provides more rights than are guaranteed by the United States Constitution, then that holding is immune from review by the United States Supreme Court. By contrast, if a state court interprets and applies the United States Constitution, then that decision is reviewable by the Supreme Court. Likewise, if a state court interprets its own constitution in a way that impinges on rights guaranteed by the United States Constitution, then that decision is subject to review by the Supreme Court. State courts seeking a progressive agenda are therefore well-advised to limit themselves to the interpretation and application of their own constitutions.

What You Need to Know:

1. Whether a legal process is "criminal," "civil," or "regulatory" in nature is determined first by considering legislative designation. Legislative designation of a process as "civil" or "regulatory" can be overcome only on "the clearest proof that the statutory scheme is so punitive either in purpose or effect to negate the State's intention to deem it civil." Determining whether a scheme is punitive is a function of whether it serves traditional goals of criminal punishment such as retribution or deterrence.
2. Although the Bill of Rights does not, by its text, bind state and local governments and their agents, the bulk of those rights have been "incorporated" to the states through the Due Process Clause of the Fourteenth Amendment. The only rights that have not yet been incorporated are the grand jury clause of the Sixth Amendment, the Seventh Amendment right to jury trials in civil cases, and the Eighth Amendment prohibition on "excessive bail."
3. Federalism plays an important role in criminal procedure because most criminal investigations and prosecutions are carried out at the state and local levels. State and local law enforcement agents are bound by provisions of the Bill of Rights that have been incorporated. They are also bound by state and local law, including state constitutions, which may provide additional rights but cannot infringe upon rights guaranteed by the United States Constitution.

LESSON 3: FOURTH AMENDMENT BASICS

The heartland of criminal procedure courses is the Fourth Amendment, which provides that:

> The right of the people to be secure in their persons, houses, papers, and effects, against unreasonable searches and seizures, shall not be violated, and no Warrants shall issue, but upon probable cause, supported by Oath or affirmation, and particularly describing the place to be searched, and the persons or things to be seized.

You will spend the majority of your criminal procedure course discussing Fourth Amendment doctrine and its consequences for government investigations. The lessons in this chapter reflect that emphasis. Before digging in to that discussion, however, there are a few preliminary matters relating to the structure, history, and basic understanding of the Fourth Amendment that deserve our attention.

Incorporation

The Fourth Amendment has been incorporated in its entirety. *See* Wolf v. Colorado, 338 U.S. 25 (1949). This means that it is a fundamental principle of liberty and justice that lies at the base of our civil and political institutions, that it is basic to our system of jurisprudence, and that it is a fundamental right, essential to a fair trial, which binds federal, state, and local governments and their agents.

The Historical Context of the Fourth Amendment

The provisions of the Bill of Rights were adopted in response to various governmental practices the founding generation found objectionable. The primary targets for the Fourth Amendment were searches conducted pursuant to general warrants and writs of assistance. General warrants and writs of assistance granted executive agents broad discretion and authority to conduct searches "without evidence of a fact committed, or to seize any person or persons not named, or whose offense is not particularly described and supported by evidence." Virginia Declaration of Rights, Art. X (1776). They amounted to unlimited licenses for government agents to conduct searches and seizures without fear of being held accountable for their conduct, no matter how oppressive or overreaching. *See* Carpenter v. United States, 585 U.S. ___, ___ S.Ct. ___, 2018 WL 3073916 (June 22, 2018).

General warrants were held unlawful in a series of English cases decided in the early 1760s. Commonly called the "general warrants cases," they involved the use of general warrants to target a group of pamphleteers critical of King George III. One of these, *Entick v. Carrington*, (1765) 95 Eng. Rep. 807 (KB), has been "described as a monument in English freedom undoubtedly familiar to every American statesman at the time the Constitution was adopted, and considered to be the true and ultimate expression of constitutional law with regard to search and seizure." United States v. Jones, 565 U.S. 400 (2012). At about the same time, a group of colonists led by former Advocate General of the Admiralty James Otis challenged the legality of writs of assistance. In the course of this litigation, Otis delivered an hours-long oration later described by John Adams as "the first scene of the first act of opposition to the arbitrary claims of Great Britain." "Then and there," Adams recalled, "the child of Independence was born." Riley v. California, 134 S.Ct. 2473 (2014).

During the revolutionary period, many states adopted provisions in their constitutions banning general warrants and writs of assistance. During the ratification debates, prominent commentators expressed concerns that the newly created federal government might override or simply ignore these state constitutional rights by adopting legislation reviving general warrants and writs of assistance. In order to quiet these concerns, proponents of the Constitution agreed that the First Congress would draft and pass an amendment setting limits on the authority of federal agents to conduct searches and seizures. The Fourth Amendment fulfills that promise.

The Two Clauses of the Fourth Amendment

The Fourth Amendment is comprised of two clauses. The "Reasonableness Clause" declares that "[t]he right of the people to be secure in their persons, houses, papers, and effects, against unreasonable searches and seizures, shall not be violated." The "Warrant Clause" specifies that "no Warrants shall issue, but upon probable cause, supported by Oath or affirmation, and particularly describing the place to be searched, and the persons or things to be seized."

The relationship between these two clauses is controversial, but the contemporary Supreme Court has consistently held that reasonableness is the "touchstone" of the Fourth Amendment. That view makes sense given the text and history of the Fourth Amendment. The Reasonableness Clause is broader than the Warrant Clause insofar as it applies to all searches and seizures, and not just searches and seizures conducted pursuant to warrants. Moreover, the original draft of the Fourth Amendment submitted to the First Congress suggested a much narrower role for the Reasonableness Clause. It read:

> The rights of the people to be secured in their persons, their houses, their papers, and their other property, from all unreasonable searches and seizures, shall not be violated by warrants issued without probable cause, supported by oath or affirmation, or not particularly describing the places to be searched, or the persons or things to be seized.

Like similar provisions in many state constitutions, this first draft targeted general warrants and writs of assistance. But some members of the First Congress worried that simply barring general warrants and writs of assistance was not enough. The First Congress ultimately elected to divide the text into the two separate clauses we have today. This suggests that the contemporary Court is right to interpret the Reasonableness Clause as the predominate clause of the Fourth Amendment. More specifically, the Warrant Clause can be read as banning general warrants and writs of assistance by setting strict limits on the conduct of warranted searches. The Reasonableness Clause provides broader protection by targeting all "unreasonable searches and seizures," including the kinds of broad and indiscriminate searches licensed by general warrants and writs of assistance. In so doing, it "seeks to secure the privacies of life against arbitrary power" and "to place obstacles in the way of a too permeating police surveillance." Carpenter v.

United States, 585 U.S. ___, ___ S.Ct. ___, 2018 WL 3073916 (June 22, 2018).

What You Need to Know:

1. The Fourth Amendment has been incorporated in its entirety through the Due Process Clause of the Fourteenth Amendment. It therefore applies equally to federal, state, and local governments and their agents.
2. The Fourth Amendment was adopted in response to controversies in England and the colonies relating to general warrants and writs of assistance.
3. The Fourth Amendment includes two clauses. The Warrant Clause sets rules specific to warranted searches and therefore bans general warrants and writs of assistance. The Reasonableness Clause, which is regarded as "the touchstone" of the Fourth Amendment, provides more general protection against "unreasonable" searches and seizures by "secur[ing] the privacies of life against arbitrary power" and "plac[ing] obstacles in the way of a too permeating police surveillance."

LESSON 4: GOVERNMENT ACTION, "SEARCH," AND SEIZURE

The Fourth Amendment only regulates government actions that constitute "searches" or "seizures." The threshold questions for any Fourth Amendment analysis are therefore whether there is a government action and whether that action is a "search" or "seizure."

Government Action

The Fourth Amendment regulates only government actions and government agents. It does not reach private actors such as corporations and private citizens or searches and seizures conducted by private actors such as private investigators. It is therefore important to understand who is and who is not a government agent.

Government agents include government employees acting in their official roles such as police officers, but may also include private persons acting at the behest or direction of a government agent. In order to determine whether a private party is acting as a government agent, courts generally ask whether that person:

1. Acted at the direction or request of a government agent;
2. Was incentivized by a government agent;
3. Reasonably believed she was acting at the behest or under the authority of a government agent; and
4. Whether a government agent knew or had reason to know that the person was acting on governmental authority.[7]

Applying this framework in *Skinner v. Railway Labor Executives' Ass'n*, 489 U.S. 602 (1989), the Court held that drug testing of railroad employees, who were involved in accidents, by their private employers, constituted government action because the drug testing was mandated by federal regulations. Likewise, the Court has held that the government action requirement is fulfilled when law enforcement "leverages the technology of a wireless carrier" by requesting historical cell site location information from a cellular service provider. Carpenter v. United States, 585 U.S. ___, ___ S.Ct. ___, 2018 WL 3073916 (June 22, 2018). The Court reached a different result in *Burdeau v. McDowell*, 256 U.S. 465 (1921), where it held that there was no government action when an employer searched for and seized documents from an employee's office, including papers housed in a locked safe.

What Is a "Search"?

Most people would define "search" as "looking into," "looking for," "examining," or "trying to find" something or someone. That is more-or-less how search was defined in 1791 when the Fourth Amendment was ratified.[8] Nevertheless, the Supreme Court has

---

[7] Skinner v. Railway Labor Executives' Ass'n, 489 U.S. 602 (1989).

[8] *See* Samuel Johnson's 1792 DICTIONARY OF THE ENGLISH LANGUAGE defining "search" as "To examine; to try; to explore; to look through" and, "To make inquiry" or "To seek; to try to find."

adopted a series of more technical definitions of "search" that have given birth to a very complex body of doctrine.

In *Olmstead v. United States*, 277 U.S. 438 (1928), the Court held that, in order to constitute a "search," governmental action must entail a physical intrusion into a "person, house, paper, or effect." In that case, federal agents investigating a bootlegging conspiracy installed a wiretap device in order to eavesdrop on Olmstead's telephone conversations. At trial, Olmstead objected to the admission of evidence gathered with that device because the agents did not secure a warrant authorizing its installation and use. Writing for a five-justice majority, Chief Justice William Howard Taft held that intercepting Olmstead's telephone conversations was not a "search" under the Fourth Amendment because the investigators did not physically intrude into Olmstead's home. Instead, their device had been installed on telephone lines owned and operated by the telephone company and located in public space. Absent some kind of physical intrusion into Olmstead's property, the Court held that the Fourth Amendment provided no protection because there was no "search."

Justice Louis Brandeis wrote a spirited dissent in *Olmstead* that would eventually provide a blueprint for contemporary Fourth Amendment law. Brandeis worried about the ability of new technologies, including photography, eavesdropping devices, and wiretapping, to compromise citizens' quietude and privacy. Although these technologies do not require the "force and violence" necessary to invade property, Justice Brandeis argued that they compromise the sanctity of the people's thoughts, beliefs, and emotions as well as the "individual security" they invest in private activities such as talking on the telephone. Justice Brandeis therefore would have held that the Fourth Amendment protects against unreasonable government intrusions on privacy, whether by physical invasion or more modern means.

In 1967, the Court picked up Justice Brandeis's torch in *Katz v. United States*, 389 U.S. 347 (1967), holding that "the Fourth Amendment protects people, not places." In that case, investigators installed a listening device on the outside of a public telephone booth in order to eavesdrop on Katz, who used the phone to conduct an illegal sports betting business. Although it was not his telephone booth, and the eavesdropping device did not physically intrude into Katz's person, house, papers, or effects, the Court held that the "Government's activities in electronically listening to and recording the petitioner's words violated the privacy upon which he justifiably relied while using the telephone booth, and thus constituted a 'search and seizure' within the meaning of the Fourth Amendment."

Although Justice Potter Stewart wrote the majority opinion in *Katz*, Justice John Marshall Harlan II wrote a concurring opinion reciting what would become the standard definition of "search" in Fourth Amendment cases. Under Harlan's test, there is a "twofold requirement" that must be met in order for government action to constitute a search. First, that action must invade "an actual (subjective) expectation of privacy." Second, that expectation must be "one that society is prepared to recognize as 'reasonable.'" As we shall see, this reasonable expectation of privacy test has yielded a number of doctrines that have left a wide range of government activities most people would regard as "searches" beyond the scope of Fourth Amendment review and regulation.

Many commentators assumed that *Katz* displaced the *Olmstead* physical intrusion test, but the Supreme Court made clear in 2012 that *Katz* was instead a supplement. In *United States v. Jones*, 565 U.S. 400 (2012), the Court was asked to consider the government's installation and use of a GPS-enabled tracking device. Writing for the majority, Justice Antonin Scalia focused on the fact that agents physically intruded onto Mr. Jones's vehicle in order to install the device. Because this physical intrusion onto Jones's "effect" was for the purposes of gathering information, the Court held that *installing* the device constituted a "search" regardless of whether *use* of the device might also have intruded upon his subjectively manifested and reasonable expectations of privacy. The Court reaffirmed its continued commitment to the physical intrusion test a year later in *Florida v. Jardines*, 569 U.S. 1 (2013), while adding an important qualification: a physical intrusion into a constitutionally protected area for the purpose of gathering information is not a search if officers had explicit or implied permission to make that entry. In *Jardines*, the Court indicated that common practice and widespread norms provide officers implied permission to approach and knock on a front door in order to determine whether someone is home. The Court then held that there is no such implied permission for agents to linger too long at a front door if nobody comes to answer their knocks or to allow a drug-sniffing dog to engage in vigorous and extended sniffing around the exterior of a house.

What Is a "Seizure"?

In contrast to "search," the Supreme Court has adopted a consistent and relatively straightforward definition of "seizure." The Court regards government conduct as a "seizure" if it entails a meaningful interference with possessory rights in a house, paper, or effect, or meaningful interference with the liberty rights of a person. *See, e.g.*, United States v. Jacobsen, 466 U.S. 109 (1984). More specifically, the Court has held that a person is "seized" for purposes of the Fourth Amendment when "in view of all the circumstances surrounding the incident, a reasonable person would have believed that he was not free to leave." United States v. Mendenhall, 446 U.S. 544 (1980).

What You Need to Know:

1. In order to come under Fourth Amendment regulation, a search or seizure must be conducted by a government agent acting in her official capacity or by a private person acting as a government agent.
2. Government action constitutes a "search" if
   a. It entails a physical intrusion into a person, house, paper, or effect with the purpose of gathering information, unless the agents had explicit or implied permission to enter; or
   b. If it intrudes upon a subjectively manifested expectation of privacy that society is prepared to recognize as reasonable.
3. Government action constitutes a "seizure" if it entails a meaningful interference with possessory

rights in a house, paper, or effect, or the liberty interests of a person.

LESSON 5: THE THIRD PARTY DOCTRINE

Although the *Katz* Court imagined that the reasonable expectation of privacy test would expand the scope of Fourth Amendment protections, that expansion has proven to be relatively modest. This is due to the emergence of several important doctrines. One of these is the third party doctrine.

The third party doctrine provides that the Fourth Amendment has no role to play in cases where government agents gain access to information or evidence through third parties with whom that information has been voluntarily shared. The first cases leading to the third party doctrine predate *Katz*. For example, in *Lopez v. United States*, 373 U.S. 427 (1963), the defendant was charged with attempting to bribe an Internal Revenue Agent. The agent surreptitiously recorded several of these conversations. Over objection, those recordings were admitted at trial. The Court upheld the trial court's decision because the case "involve[d] no 'eavesdropping' whatever in any proper sense of the term." Rather, "the device was used only to obtain the most reliable evidence possible of a conversation in which the Government's own agent was a participant, and which that agent was fully entitled to disclose." Because "the device was not planted by means of an unlawful physical invasion of petitioner's premises" but was "carried in and out by an agent who was there with petitioner's assent, and it neither saw nor heard more than the agent himself," the Court saw no grounds for any Fourth Amendment complaint. Rather, the Court suggested, Lopez just chose to place his trust in the wrong person, which essentially voided any claim based on the Fourth Amendment.

It is hard to have too much sympathy for the defendant in *Lopez*. After all, he knew he was talking to a government agent. But what if someone believes he is speaking in private to a confidant? That question was posed to the Court in *Lewis v. United States*, 385 U.S. 206 (1966), and *Hoffa v. United States*, 385 U.S. 293 (1966). The defendants in *Lewis* and *Hoffa* thought they were talking to friends and co-conspirators when they made incriminatory statements. They later discovered that these "friends" were an undercover law enforcement agent (*Lewis*) and a cooperating witness (*Hoffa*). Despite this trickery, the Court followed its holding in *Lopez*. In the Court's view, Lewis and Hoffa just chose to trust the wrong people. The Court declined to extend any Fourth Amendment protection when that trust was violated.

In *United States v. White*, 401 U.S. 745 (1971), the Court merged the misplaced trust rationale from *Lopez*, *Lewis*, and *Hoffa* with the *Katz* definition of "search." In that case, a police informant wore a body wire that transmitted his conversations with the defendant to law enforcement officers in real time. Although the Court allowed that White may well "have relied on the discretion" of his compatriot, it held that this expectation was not "constitutionally justifiable." The Fourth Amendment would not bar that person from testifying about those conversations in open court and the justices saw no difference in terms of reasonable expectations of privacy if those conversations were surreptitiously recorded or broadcast by "the agent to whom the defendant is talking and whose trustworthiness the defendant necessarily risks." Thus, after *White*, the use of undercover agents and confidential informants is not a "search" at all. Neither is it a "search" if government agents induce confidants to disclose secrets or information entrusted to them.

The misplaced trust rationale underlying *Lopez*, *Lewis*, *Hoffa*, and *White* makes intuitive sense. These cases have a sort of "make your own bed" quality and the situations a "no honor among thieves" character. But what about situations that involve third parties who not only deserve trust but are objectively worthy of trust such as banks and telephone companies? In *California Bankers Ass'n v. Shultz*, 416 U.S. 21 (1974), and *United States v. Miller*, 425 U.S. 435 (1976), the Court held that there is no "search" if government agents subpoena or otherwise demand transaction records from a customer's bank even if the bank is required by federal law to maintain those records, thereby making it a government agent. By definition, these records document transactions to which banks are parties and contain information "voluntarily conveyed to the banks and exposed to their employees in the ordinary course of business." By engaging in those transactions a "depositor takes the risk, in revealing his affairs to another, that the information will be conveyed by that person to the Government . . . even if the information is revealed on the assumption that it will be used only for a limited purpose and the confidence placed in the third party will not be betrayed." One might maintain a subjective expectation of privacy in bank records, but, under the third party doctrine, that expectation is not reasonable. Obtaining those records by lawful means and looking through them for information is therefore not a "search" for purposes of the Fourth Amendment.

In *Smith v. Maryland*, 442 U.S. 735 (1979), the Court applied the third party doctrine to telephone records. Although a customer might hope that who he calls, when, and how long he talks is a private matter, the *Smith* Court held that such an expectation is unreasonable. That is because, in the course of their ordinary business, telephone companies must gather basic information about all calls such as the originating number, the number called, the time of day, and duration. By availing himself of this service, a customer "assume[s] the risk that the [telephone] company [will] reveal to the police the numbers he dialed." Thus, there is no "search" if a telephone company installs a device to record this basic call information and passes that information on to law enforcement.

The third party doctrine is sometimes described as "the premise that an individual has no reasonable expectation of privacy in information voluntarily disclosed to third parties." That probably overstates it somewhat. After all, Katz shared with third parties (the people to whom he was talking on the phone) everything picked up by the eavesdropping device used in that case. Nevertheless, the Court held that this eavesdropping was a "search." The third party doctrine is therefore better understood as withdrawing Fourth Amendment limitations on efforts by government agents to obtain information from third parties with whom that information has been shared.

Congress has stepped in to provide enhanced legislative protections for some information shared with some third parties.

For example, the Right to Financial Privacy Act of 1978 provides important protections for banking and other financial information. The Pen Register Act limits government access to telephone records. The Electronic Communications Privacy Act provides protection more broadly for a range of communications information and contents. The Video Privacy Protection Act guards information relating to video rentals. Many states also protect information shared with third parties under state law. Although these legislative efforts provide important *legal* protections, they do not create *constitutional* rights. Even if there is a law guaranteeing privacy in information shared with a third party, a subjective expectation of privacy grounded in that law is not necessarily "reasonable" for purposes of the Fourth Amendment.[9]

In her concurring opinion in *United States v. Jones*, 565 U.S. 400 (2012), Justice Sonia Sotomayor suggested that it may be time to rethink the third party doctrine. The Court had that opportunity during the October 2017 when it decided *Carpenter v. United States*, 585 U.S. ___, ___ S.Ct. ___, 2018 WL 3073916 (June 22, 2018). The question presented to the Court in *Carpenter* was whether a government agent's accessing and looking through historical cell site location information gathered and stored by a cellular service provider is a "search" for purposes of the Fourth Amendment.

Cellular service providers maintain networks of cellular base stations through which they receive and transmit users' voice and data communications. Cellular phones and other user devices are in regular contact with these networks. As a consequence, cellular service providers know the locations of their customers' devices, and therefore the locations of their customers, anytime those devices are turned on. Although there is no federal law requiring them to do so, cellular phone companies record and store this cell site location information. As a consequence, they have a fairly precise historical record of

---

[9] Writing for himself in *Carpenter v. United States,* 585 U.S. ___, ___ S.Ct. ___, 2018 WL 3073916 (June 22, 2018), Justice Neil Gorsuch indicated that the result might be different if a statute created a property right in information held by third parties. While stopping short of endorsing a "positive law" approach to the Fourth Amendment, Justice Gorsuch suggested that government requests to review third party records in which a citizen has a statutory property right might constitute an intrusion upon that citizen's "papers."

where their customers were on a minute-by-minute basis going back months or years.

In many ways, historical cell site location information is similar to the telephone call data at issue in *Smith*. It is information that users share voluntarily with third parties. It is also information that cellular service providers must have in order to provide voice and data services, to properly bill customers, and to monitor, maintain, and upgrade their networks. Despite these similarities, Chief Justice John Roberts, writing for the Court in *Carpenter*, held that government requests for historical cell site location information are searches that require a warrant.[10]

In reaching this result, Chief Justice Roberts declined to overrule or fundamentally rethink the third party doctrine. He instead focused on the unique features of cellular tracking as a surveillance technology. In contrast with traditional means of conducting physical surveillance, cell site location information provides law enforcement with an "easy, cheap, and efficient" means to track individuals. It provides "a detailed chronicle of a person's physical presence compiled every day, every moment, over several years" revealing intimate details of their activities and associations. Cellular devices are also ubiquitous, making "possible the tracking not only of Carpenter's location, but also everyone else's, not for a short period but for years and years." In the Court's view, these qualitative differences provided sufficient grounds to extend full Fourth Amendment protection to historical cell site location information.

The Court was careful to limit the scope of its holding in *Carpenter* to the specific technology at issue: historical cell site location information. Chief Justice Roberts emphasized that the Court was not abandoning the third party doctrine. The Court also did not reach questions relating to data surveillance, national security surveillance, "real-time" cellular tracking, or "tower dumps," by which law enforcement gains access to

---

[10] The facts in *Carpenter* only required the Court to consider requests covering periods of at least seven days. The Court declined to clarify whether requests for data covering periods of less than seven days would also constitute a "search" or require a warrant.

information documenting the presence of all devices in contact with a particular cellular base station at a specific time.

What You Need to Know:

1. Before *Katz*, the Court decided several cases withholding Fourth Amendment protection in cases where undercover agents and confidential informants surreptitiously recorded their conversations with suspects on the grounds that making these recordings did not involve a physical intrusion and that the suspects should suffer the consequences of misplaced trust.
2. After *Katz*, the Court merged this rationale into its new definition of search, holding that there is no "search" where government agents gain access to information through third parties with whom that information had been shared.
3. The Court has extended the third party doctrine to cover individuals and entities who act as trusted fiduciaries such as banks and telephone companies, holding that government efforts to gain access to financial records and call records through lawful means is not a "search."
4. The third party doctrine does not apply to historical cell site location information. Accessing this information is a "search" under the Fourth Amendment and requires a warrant.
5. Congress and many state legislatures have passed laws providing statutory protections for some information excluded from Fourth Amendment protection by the third party doctrine. These efforts do not create and cannot diminish Fourth Amendment rights.

LESSON 6: THE OPEN FIELDS DOCTRINE

A second important line of cases applying the *Katz* definition of "search" is the open fields doctrine. The open fields doctrine is grounded in the common law of trespass. Although it is a trespass under the common law to enter upon privately owned land, allowances are made. One such exception is when entry is made in the pursuit of noxious animals such as wolves and foxes. If a farmer or hunter is in pursuit of a fox, he does not need to stop at his neighbor's fence, but can continue his pursuit through any open fields without committing a trespass.

During the *Olmstead* era, the Court borrowed the concept of open fields to clarify Fourth Amendment protections for "houses" and "effects." *Hester v. United States*, 265 U.S. 57 (1924), is the case on point. There, revenue officers were investigating an illegal moonshine operation. They took up a surveillance position "fifty to one hundred yards" away from Hester's house. From that vantage, they observed Hester as he delivered a jug of what they suspected was illegal whiskey to a man named Henderson. At that point, Hester and Henderson, alerted to the officers' presence, tried to flee and attempted to destroy the evidence by throwing away and breaking their jugs. Officers pursued them and recovered the jugs and residue of "what the officers, being experts, recognized as moonshine whiskey." Hester later argued that the officers came upon his property without a warrant in order to retrieve the broken jugs. The officers may also have been on his property when conducting their initial surveillance. Writing for the Court, Justice Oliver Wendell Holmes held that neither the surveillance nor the agents' pursuit of Hester implicated the Fourth Amendment, which protects only "persons, houses, papers, and effects." Although the agents may have intruded upon "open fields," they did not invade any of these constitutionally protected areas. The Court therefore held that the Fourth Amendment had no role to play.

The Court reaffirmed its commitment to the open fields doctrine in *Oliver v. United States*, 466 U.S. 170 (1984). The petitioners in *Oliver* were growing marijuana on their lands. Their property was fenced and posted with "No Trespassing" signs. Officers ignored those signs and fences, knowingly ventured onto private land, and discovered the marijuana patches. Despite the obvious subjective intentions of the petitioners to assert privacy interests in their property and their activities, the Court held that their expectations were unreasonable. That is because the areas searched by the officers were sufficiently remote from the petitioners' homes to be regarded as "open fields." Harkening back to *Hester*, the Court held that "an individual may not legitimately demand privacy for activities conducted out of doors in fields, except in the area immediately surrounding the home." "In contrast [with houses]," the Court reasoned, "open fields do not provide the setting for those intimate activities that the Amendment is intended to shelter from government interference or surveillance. There is no societal interest in protecting the privacy of those activities, such as the cultivation of crops, that occur in open fields." Any "asserted expectation of privacy in open fields is [therefore] not an expectation that 'society recognizes as reasonable.'" The Court reaffirmed its commitment to the open fields doctrine in *United States v. Jones*, 565 U.S. 400 (2012).

The open fields doctrine rests on a distinction between open fields and "houses." For purposes of the Fourth Amendment "houses" include not only the physical structure of the home, but also "the area to which extends the intimate activity associated with the 'sanctity of a man's home and the privacies of life.'" *Oliver*, 466 U.S. at 180 (quoting Boyd v. United States, 116 U.S. 616 (1886)). This area is commonly referred to as the "curtilage" when describing outdoor areas or the "messuage" when describing structures such as outbuildings. The test applied for determining whether an area is part of the curtilage or messuage attached to a home is set forth in *United States v. Dunn*, 480 U.S. 294 (1987). There, the Court identified four factors relevant to determining whether an area is "so intimately tied to the home" that "it should be placed under the home's 'umbrella' of protection":

1. The proximity of the area to the home;
2. Whether the area is within an enclosure surrounding the home;
3. The nature and uses to which the area is put; and
4. Steps taken by the resident to protect the area from observation by passersby.

Applying those factors in *Dunn*, the Court held that a barn located sixty yards away from a suspect's house and outside the fence immediately surrounding the home that was used for commercial and criminal activities was not part of the messuage.

As the Court pointed out in *Hester* and again in *Dunn*, "An open field need be neither 'open' nor a 'field.'" For Fourth Amendment purposes, "open fields" are instead defined in the negative as privately owned lands lying outside the home, inclusive of its curtilage and messuage. Traversing these areas, no matter the reason, is not a "search" for purposes of the Fourth Amendment.

The open fields doctrine raises questions not only about where we draw the line between "houses" and open spaces, but also what might constitute a "house" in the first place. This is an important question because "houses" are traditionally afforded the highest levels of Fourth Amendment protection. Any private residence, including single-family homes, apartments, fixed trailer homes, and the like are "houses" for purposes of the Fourth Amendment. That is true whether the resident owns the home, or merely rents. During the term of lawful rental, hotel rooms also count as "houses" under the Fourth Amendment. *See* Johnson v. United States, 333 U.S. 10 (1948). Less well-settled is the status of tents, shanties, and recreational vehicles, particularly when pitched or parked on public property.

What You Need to Know:

1. The Fourth Amendment protects "persons, houses, papers, and effects," but does not protect "open fields."
2. "Open fields" are privately owned lands lying outside of the home, curtilage, and messuage.
3. To determine whether an area or a building is part of the curtilage or messuage associated with a home, the Court looks at four factors:
    a. The proximity of the area to the home;
    b. Whether the area is within an enclosure surrounding the home;
    c. The nature and uses to which the area is put; and

d. Steps taken by the resident to protect the area from observation by passersby.

4. No matter how vigorously a landowner might manifest her expectations of privacy in open fields using fences and signs, those expectations are not objectively reasonable. Traversing open fields is therefore not a "search" for purposes of the Fourth Amendment.

LESSON 7: THE PUBLIC OBSERVATION DOCTRINE

A third important line of cases governing the meaning of "search" after *Katz* is the public observation doctrine. Closely related to the open fields doctrine, the public observation doctrine holds that we have no reasonable expectations of privacy in anything exposed to public view. It therefore allows officers to look for, look into, or try to find anything without implicating the Fourth Amendment so long as they do so from a lawful vantage point.

The modern public observation doctrine traces to *United States v. Knotts*, 460 U.S. 276 (1983). The officers in *Knotts* were investigating a methamphetamine ring. They arranged with a local chemical distributor to hide a radio transmitter in a drum of chloroform. When suspects later came to purchase chloroform, the distributor sold to them the "bugged" drum. Officers then used a receiver to monitor signals broadcast by the transmitter, allowing them to more easily track the drum. This technological enhancement turned out to be essential when visual surveillance failed. By deploying their receiver on a helicopter, officers eventually relocated the drum near Knotts's cabin. After conducting additional surveillance, officers secured a warrant for the cabin where they discovered facilities for the manufacture of amphetamine and methamphetamine.

The *Knotts* Court held that the government's use of the tracking device did not constitute a "search" for purposes of the Fourth Amendment because "[a] person traveling in an automobile on public thoroughfares has no reasonable expectation of privacy in his movements from one place to another." "Visual surveillance from public places," it continued, "would have sufficed to reveal" everything disclosed by the tracking device. Although the device may have made the officers' job easier, the Court held that:

> Nothing in the Fourth Amendment prohibited the police from augmenting the sensory faculties bestowed upon them at birth with such enhancement as science and technology afforded them in this case. . . . Insofar as respondent's complaint appears to be simply that scientific devices such as the beeper enabled the police to be more effective in detecting crime, it simply has no constitutional foundation. We have never equated police efficiency with unconstitutionality, and we decline to do so now.

Knotts argued before the Court that granting unfettered access to beeper tracking technologies would open the door to "twenty-four hour surveillance of any citizen of this country . . . without judicial knowledge or supervision." The *Knotts* Court did not see an immediate danger, but promised that "if such dragnet-type law enforcement practices as respondent envisions should eventually occur, there will be time enough then to determine whether different constitutional principles may be applicable." The Court began to outline some of those new principles in *Carpenter v. United States*, 585 U.S. ___, ___ S.Ct. ___, 2018 WL 3073916 (June 22, 2018). There, the Court noted that new tracking technologies like "GPS monitoring" and "cell phone tracking" are so "remarkably easy, cheap, and efficient compared to traditional investigative tools" that they make possible the tracking of everyone's location for long periods of time revealing intimate information about individuals' activities and associations. On this basis, the Court held that accessing historical cell site location information is a search and requires a warrant.

In *United States v. Karo*, 468 U.S. 705 (1984), the Court drew a distinction between the use of beeper tracking technologies to monitor movements in public and the use of those technologies to gather information about the interiors of homes and other constitutionally protected spaces. As was the case in *Knotts*, the officers in *Karo* installed a radio beeper in a container of chemicals, which was then sold to suspected drug manufacturers. Officers used that device to track the container through public spaces and to repeatedly confirm its location inside a private residence, the interior of which was not otherwise open to visual surveillance from a public place. The Court regarded this as a step too far, holding that the use of a tracking device to gather information about the interior of a home violates reasonable expectations of privacy and is therefore a "search" subject to Fourth Amendment regulation.

The Court has applied the public observation doctrine to allow government agents to search areas and even containers exposed to public view. For example, in *California v. Greenwood*, 486 U.S. 35 (1988), the Court held that law enforcement agents may search through garbage cans left out on the street for collection. That is because any member of the public—dumpster divers, say—might be expected to go through garbage that has been set out for collection. Although we might hope that nobody will go through our garbage, the fact that they can, and sometimes do, means that this expectation is unreasonable.

The Court has also applied the public observation doctrine to allow officers to engage in surveillance of private areas associated with the home so long as they do so from a lawful vantage. *Florida v. Riley*, 488 U.S. 445 (1989), and *California v. Ciraolo*, 476 U.S. 207 (1986), are the most important cases on point. In both cases the homeowners had erected fences or outbuildings to hide their marijuana growing operations from public view. Officers defeated those efforts by flying a helicopter (*Riley*) and an airplane (*Ciraolo*) over their suspects' homes, which allowed ready visual inspections of marijuana plants growing in the curtilages and messuages of those homes. Despite the clear manifestations of expectations of privacy, the Court held in both cases that the agents did not violate reasonable expectations of privacy. That is because they were operating in navigable airspace through which aircraft did or could pass. In *Dow Chemical Co. v. United States*, 476 U.S. 227 (1986), the Court held that the use of a powerful telescope mounted on an overflying aircraft does not change the Fourth Amendment calculus.

The Court left a potentially important question open in *Riley*. In that case, officers flew their helicopter at very low altitude, sometimes skimming just 400 feet above Riley's greenhouse. There was no dispute that this was within Federal Aviation Authority rules. The officers were therefore lawfully in a place where they had a right to be. But the record was largely silent as to whether that airspace was *in fact* used with sufficient frequency by civilian or government aircraft to put Riley on notice that otherwise private areas of his messuage were open to public view. Writing for a plurality of four justices, Justice Byron White regarded the legal license as sufficient to render Riley's subjective expectations of privacy unreasonable. Writing in concurrence, Justice Sandra Day O'Connor would have allowed Riley to demonstrate the reasonableness of his subjective expectation of privacy against aerial surveillance by offering evidence that the airspace from which the officers made their observations was little used by civilian or government aircraft.

The difference of opinion among the plurality and Justice O'Connor in *Riley* raises a related question: What is the Fourth Amendment significance of positive law? For example, imagine that a local ordinance provides criminal liability for "peeping toms" who peer into homes from public spaces. Would such a law make expectations of privacy against government agents peering into private homes from public spaces "reasonable"? The question is not settled, but the Court has suggested that positive laws such as these cannot create reasonable expectations of privacy where they otherwise do not exist. The Court's reasoning is that Fourth Amendment rights need to be the same everywhere. If positive law could create reasonable expectations of privacy, then citizens living in some localities or states might have different Fourth Amendment rights than those living in others. *See, e.g.*, Virginia v. Moore, 553 U.S. 164 (2008). There is also an important interest in maintaining the Fourth Amendment as a stable source of protections, immune from the vagaries of the political process. If legislation can create reasonable expectations of privacy, and therefore Fourth Amendment rights, then subsequent changes in that legislation reducing expectations of privacy would also have the function of degrading Fourth Amendment rights.

Despite these reservations, Justice Neil Gorsuch has indicated some sympathy with the proposition that positive law can create property rights in information held by third parties. *See* Carpenter v. United States, 585 U.S. ___, ___ S.Ct. ___, 2018 WL 3073916 (June 22, 2018) (Gorsuch, J., concurring). Where this is the case, Justice Gorsuch suggests, government requests to review records in which a citizen has a statutory property right might constitute an intrusion upon that citizen's "papers," and, therefore, a search.

What You Need to Know:

1. The public observation doctrine allows officers to conduct visual inspections of otherwise protected spaces, including homes, so long as they do so from a lawful vantage.
2. Under the public observation doctrine, officers can look into homes, yards, and outbuildings from public airspace.
3. The public observation doctrine allows officers to look through containers, such as garbage cans, that are left in places where a member of the public might be expected to look through them.
4. The Fourth Amendment does not limit the use of beeper tracking devices to conduct public surveillance, but does limit government access to historical cell site location information and may also limit access to other precise, detailed, cheap, and efficient tracking technologies such as GPS monitoring.
5. Local laws that limit the ability of private citizens to make visual inspections from public places, such as peeping tom laws, probably do not create constitutional reasonable expectations of privacy.

LESSON 8: DETECTION OF CRIMINALITY

A fourth important line of cases governing the meaning of "search" after *Katz* applies to means and methods that can detect only illegal activities. *United States v. Place*, 462 U.S. 696

(1983), is the seminal case. There, law enforcement agents suspected that Raymond Place was transporting narcotics in his luggage on a flight from Miami to New York. Drug Enforcement Administration (DEA) agents confronted Place when he landed at La Guardia Airport. He refused their request to search the interior of his bags at which point the officers seized those bags, transported them to John F. Kennedy airport, and allowed a specially trained dog to sniff the exterior of the bags. The dog "alerted" to one of Place's bags, indicating the presence of olfactory emanations from illegal narcotics. Agents then sought a warrant to search the bag whereupon they discovered more than a kilogram of cocaine.

The Court held that Place and his bags had been unreasonably seized. Although that probably resolved the case, Justice Sandra Day O'Connor, writing for the Court, used the opportunity to clarify the constitutional status of drug detection dogs, which had become an increasingly common law enforcement tool. The Court viewed canine sniffs as "*sui generis*." Well-trained drug detection dogs alert only to the presence of contraband. They therefore do not "expose noncontraband items that otherwise would remain hidden from public view, as does, for example, an officers' rummaging through the contents of the luggage." Moreover, because the dogs just sniff the outsides of containers, "the owner of the property is not subjected to the embarrassment and inconvenience entailed in less discriminate and more intrusive investigative methods." In light of these factors, the Court held that allowing trained dogs to sniff property located in a public place is not a "search" for purposes of the Fourth Amendment. That is because, as the Court put the point later in *Illinois v. Caballes*, 543 U.S. 405 (2005), "any interest in possessing contraband cannot be deemed 'legitimate' and, thus, governmental conduct that only reveals the possession of contraband compromises no legitimate privacy interest." In *Florida v. Harris*, 568 U.S. 237 (2013), the Court held that defendants may challenge the reliability of drug detection dogs in the context of suppression hearings.

As it turns out, drug detection dogs are not *sui generis* after all. For example, law enforcement officers have at their disposal chemical tests capable of determining whether a suspicious looking substance is an illegal narcotic. The Court addressed the constitutional status of these "field tests" in *United States v. Jacobsen*, 466 U.S. 109 (1984), holding that a "chemical test that merely discloses whether or not a particular substance is cocaine does not compromise any legitimate interest in privacy" and therefore does not constitute a "search" for purposes of the Fourth Amendment.

In *Kyllo v. United States*, 533 U.S. 27 (2001), the Court guarded the outer limits of this line of cases. In that case, federal agents suspected that Kyllo was illegally growing marijuana in his home. In order to secure additional evidence confirming their suspicions, the agents pointed an "Agema Thermovision 210 thermal imager" at Kyllo's home. Capable of detecting infrared radiation invisible to the human eye, the device allowed agents to identify heat sources inside Kyllo's home consistent with the use of the halide lights sometimes used to grow marijuana indoors. Based in part on that evidence, agents secured a warrant to search Kyllo's home. During that search, they found a substantial "indoor growing operation involving more than 100 plants."

Writing for the Court, Justice Antonin Scalia worried about the ability of new and emerging technologies "to erode the privacy guaranteed by the Fourth Amendment." He was particularly concerned with the ability of new technologies to see into homes, which have long enjoyed the most stringent Fourth Amendment protection. The Court therefore held that "[w]here, as here, the Government uses a device that is not in general public use, to explore details of the home that would previously have been unknowable without physical intrusion, the surveillance is a 'search' and is presumptively unreasonable without a warrant."

Heat detection devices differ from drug detection dogs on the basis of what they can detect. While drug dogs detect only evidence of crime, in which there is no reason to expect privacy, heat detection devices detect all heat-generating activities in the home, including "at what hour each night the lady of the house takes her daily sauna and bath." Although some of these innocent activities may also be very personal or intimate, Justice

Scalia was careful not to tie the Court's holding to "the quality or quantity of information obtained." What mattered was that the technology was indiscriminate in gathering information about both legal and illegal activity and that it gathered that information from the interior of a closely protected place: the home.

The Court further clarified the limits of *Place* and its progeny in *Florida v. Jardines*, 569 U.S. 1 (2013). There, officers brought a drug detection dog onto the front porch of a suspect's home where it signaled the presence of narcotics. A subsequent search of the home led to the discovery of marijuana plants. In an opinion by Justice Scalia, the Court held that bringing the dog onto the curtilage of Jardines's home and allowing it to conduct an extensive sniff entailed a physical intrusion for the purpose of gathering information and therefore constituted a "search" for purposes of the Fourth Amendment. The Court allowed that there is an implied license for members of the public and officers alike to approach a front door and knock in the hopes of speaking with a resident, but held that lingering too long after nobody answers and bringing a drug detection dog along in order to conduct a careful sniff for drugs is a step too far.

Place is also notable for its definition of "reasonableness." Specifically, when asked to determine the reasonableness of government action under the Fourth Amendment, Justice O'Connor wrote that the Court "must balance the nature and quality of the intrusion on the individual's Fourth Amendment interests against the importance of the governmental interests alleged to justify the intrusion." The "Fourth Amendment interests" at stake in most searches and seizures arise from the individual's interests in privacy, bodily security, and protection of property. Governmental interests usually relate to detection of crime, preservation of evidence, protection of officers, and protection of the public. As we shall see in subsequent lessons, this balancing test pervades Fourth Amendment analysis.

What You Need to Know:

1. There is no reasonable expectation of privacy in illegal activity.

2. The use of means and methods that can detect only illegal activities is not a "search" for purposes of the Fourth Amendment.

3. The use of a device that detects both legal and illegal activity that otherwise could not be discovered without entering a constitutionally protected area is a "search" for purposes of the Fourth Amendment.

4. Physically entering a constitutionally protected area to deploy and use a device that can detect only illegal activities is a "search" for purposes of the Fourth Amendment unless that entry is pursuant to an actual or implied license.

LESSON 9: THE CHALLENGE OF NEW TECHNOLOGIES

The viability and constitutional statuses of the third party and public observation doctrines have been tested in recent years by contemporary and emerging technologies such as GPS-enabled tracking, drones, networked surveillance cameras, license-plate readers, cell-site location, cell site simulators, and "Big Data" systems capable of aggregating and analyzing large volumes of information ranging from consumer transactions to social network activities. Because they are highly scalable and increasingly inexpensive, these technologies challenge common assumptions regarding privacy and anonymity. They also raise dystopian specters of a surveillance state similar to those depicted in literature, such as George Orwell's *1984*, science fiction films, such as *Minority Report*, and fantasy novels, such as J.R.R. Tolkien's *Lord of the Rings* trilogy.

The potential for modern surveillance technologies to facilitate programs of broad and indiscriminate surveillance came to the fore in 2013 when documents leaked by former government contractor Edward Snowden revealed numerous large-scale surveillance programs administered by the National Security Agency, the Federal Bureau of Investigation, and the Central Intelligence Agency. Among these was the now-famous Section 215 telephony metadata program, which gathered, stored, and made available for analysis non-content information about telephone calls handled by United States carriers.

Most of the new and emerging surveillance technologies that have come under recent scrutiny appear to operate outside of Fourth Amendment regulations by virtue of the public observation doctrine, the third party doctrine, or both. For example, the Section 215 telephonic metadata program only involved information shared by customers with their telephone carriers. Under the third party doctrine, customers had no reasonable expectation of privacy in those records, which means that no search occurred when those records were shared with, stored by, and searched by government agencies. Similarly, Big Data technologies gather, aggregate, store, and analyze information shared with third parties. Technologies like New York's Domain Awareness System, which deploy and use vast networks of surveillance cameras, are not subject to Fourth Amendment regulation because they only monitor activities conducted in public spaces.

This state of affairs was foretold in *United States v. Knotts*, 460 U.S. 276 (1983). In answer to concerns about the potential for "twenty-four hour surveillance of any citizen of this country . . . without judicial knowledge or supervision" the Court promised that "if such dragnet-type law enforcement practices . . . should eventually occur, there will be time enough then to determine whether different constitutional principles may be applicable." In *United States v. Jones*, 565 U.S. 400 (2012), the Court suggested that the time is nigh to elaborate new constitutional principles capable of setting limits on the deployment and use of modern surveillance technologies. In that case, officers installed GPS-enabled tracking devices on cars belonging to suspects in a drug conspiracy. The officers then used those devices to monitor the suspects' movements over the course of twenty-eight days, generating thousands of pages of data in the process.

The trial court in *Jones* found that use of GPS-enabled tracking devices falls outside the scope of Fourth Amendment review because the officers were only monitoring Jones's movements through public spaces. On appeal, a panel of the United States Circuit Court of Appeals for the District of

Columbia disagreed. Writing for the panel, Judge Douglas Ginsburg argued that *Knotts* does not stand for the proposition that a person traveling on public roads "has no reasonable expectation of privacy in his movements whatsoever, world without end." Although we may reasonably expect that people will observe us in public spaces, Judge Ginsburg pointed out that we do not expect that anyone is monitoring all of our movements all of the time. That is important because:

> Prolonged surveillance reveals types of information not revealed by short-term surveillance, such as what a person does repeatedly, what he does not do, and what he does ensemble. These types of information can each reveal more about a person than does any individual trip viewed in isolation. Repeated visits to a church, a gym, a bar, or a bookie tell a story not told by any single visit, as does one's not visiting any of these places over the course of a month. The sequence of a person's movements can reveal still more; a single trip to a gynecologist's office tells little about a woman, but that trip followed a few weeks later by a visit to a baby supply store tells a different story. A person who knows all of another's travels can deduce whether he is a weekly church goer, a heavy drinker, a regular at the gym, an unfaithful husband, an outpatient receiving medical treatment, an associate of particular individuals or political groups—and not just one such fact about a person, but all such facts.

This approach to describing Fourth Amendment interests threatened by modern surveillance technologies has been described as the "mosaic theory."

In *Jones*, the Supreme Court declined to address the question whether modern surveillance technologies implicate the Fourth Amendment. In a majority opinion written by Justice Antonin Scalia, the Court focused on the fact that installing the devices required a physical intrusion. Because that physical intrusion was for the purpose of gathering information and did not come with explicit or implied permission, the Court held that installing the tracking devices on private "effects" was a "search." That development came as a surprise to some commentators, including Justice Samuel Alito, who thought that *Katz* had displaced tests focused on physical intrusion or trespass. In response, Justice Scalia made clear that the reasonable expectation of privacy test provided additional protections, but did not replace traditional definitions of search based on the common law of trespass.

Although *Jones* was resolved on narrow grounds, concurring opinions by Justice Sonia Sotomayor and Justice Samuel Alito, who was joined by Justices Ruth Bader Ginsburg, Stephen Breyer, and Elena Kagan, indicated a "shadow majority" of justices was ready to reconsider or limit the public observation doctrine and the third party doctrine. For example, Justice Sotomayor worried about the ability of modern tracking technologies to generate "a precise, comprehensive record of a person's public movements that reflects a wealth of detail about her familial, political, professional, religious, and sexual associations." Justice Sotomayor also expressed concern about the chilling effect this kind of surveillance might have, its susceptibility to abuse, and the potential that "unfettered discretion" to deploy and use these technologies might " 'alter the relationship between citizen and government in a way that is inimical to democratic society.' " Based on similar concerns, Justice Alito would have held that "long-term monitoring" with a GPS-enabled tracking device violates reasonable expectations of privacy, and therefore constitutes a "search" for purposes of the Fourth Amendment.

The Court adopted these concerns as its own in *Carpenter v. United States*, 585 U.S. ___, ___ S.Ct. ___, 2018 WL 3073916 (June 22, 2018). *Carpenter* addressed the Fourth Amendment status of historical cell site location information (CSLI), which is gathered and stored by cellular telephone providers in the normal course of their business. This information can provide a precise, detailed, and extensive record of where a customer has been going back months or years. In *Carpenter*, the United States Court of Appeals for the Sixth Circuit relied on *Smith v. Maryland*, 442 U.S. 735 (1979), to hold that this information is not subject to Fourth Amendment regulation, including the warrant requirement. That decision was in-line with similar decisions by the Fourth and Eleventh Circuit Courts of Appeals. Writing for the Court, Chief Justice John Roberts reversed.

Chief Justice Roberts distinguished CSLI and GPS tracking from traditional investigative methods by focusing on their capacity to facilitate programs of broad and indiscriminate surveillance. The Fourth Amendment, he pointed out, "seeks to secure the privacies of life against arbitrary power" and "to place obstacles in the way of a too permeating police surveillance." Granting unfettered access to technologies like CSLI and GPS tracking threatens that security by lowering those obstacles.

As the *Carpenter* Court recognized, CSLI effectively allows government agents to tail everyone "every moment of the day" "for years and years" and then "call upon the results of that surveillance without regard to the constraints of the Fourth Amendment." In the Court's view, this kind of "detailed chronicle of a person's physical presence compiled every day, every moment, over several years . . . implicates privacy concerns far beyond those considered in" third party doctrine cases. The Court therefore put historical CSLI tracking in a different constitutional category where it is subject to full Fourth Amendment regulation, including the warrant requirement.

Although the *Carpenter* Court declared that its holding was narrow, and addressed only historical CSLI, it repeatedly endorsed the "shadow majority" in *Jones*, indicating that the use of GPS tracking technology is also a "search" subject to Fourth Amendment regulation. More importantly, it signaled the Court's willingness to take a hard look at new and emerging surveillance technologies in order to protect core Fourth Amendment interests in privacy and security from overreaching government power.

What You Need to Know:

1. New tracking and surveillance technologies have put some strain on Fourth Amendment doctrine, including the public observation and third party doctrines.
2. The Supreme Court has begun to elaborate "different constitutional principles" in order to

bring some of these technologies within the compass of Fourth Amendment regulation.

3. These new principles focus on the capacity of new technologies to facilitate broad and indiscriminate surveillance that reveals intimate details about individuals' lives and associations.
4. The Court has applied these new principles to hold that access to historical cell site location information requires a warrant.

LESSON 10: THE WARRANT REQUIREMENT

Recall that the Fourth Amendment contains two clauses. So far, our attention has focused on the first clause, often called the "reasonableness clause," which reads:

> The right of the people to be secure in their persons, houses, papers, and effects, against unreasonable searches and seizures, shall not be violated,

For the next several lessons we will focus on the "warrant clause," which reads:

> and no Warrants shall issue, but upon probable cause, supported by Oath or affirmation, and particularly describing the place to be searched, and the persons or things to be seized.

The warrant clause describes requirements that must be met when searches or seizures are conducted under the authority of warrants. These requirements are demanding. So why would officers ever submit themselves to these demands by obtaining a warrant? Why not just search or seize and then reserve for later the task of demonstrating that their conduct was "reasonable"?

There are two reasons why an officer might secure a warrant before conducting a search or seizure. First, searches and seizures conducted pursuant to lawful warrants are afforded a presumption of reasonableness. Officers might therefore seek a warrant in order to secure themselves against the potential of suppression or civil liability. Second, some searches and seizures are subject to a warrant requirement. In cases governed by this warrant requirement, officers face a strong presumption of unreasonableness if they conduct a search or seizure without first securing a lawful warrant.

The source and scope of the warrant requirement is a subject of considerable controversy. It has been described as providing that "searches conducted outside the judicial process, without prior approval by judge or magistrate, are *per se* unreasonable under the Fourth Amendment." Katz v. United States, 389 U.S. 347, 357 (1967). This is far too broad. For example, warrants are not required for searches of cars or for regulatory inspections and other "special needs" searches. Even where it applies, the warrant requirement is subject to "exceptions," such as in cases of emergency or when incident to arrest. These exceptions have led some members of the Supreme Court to wonder whether there is, in fact, a warrant requirement at all.[11] Their doubts reflect long-standing debates about the constitutional status and practical value of the warrant requirement.

The conventional understanding of the warrant requirement holds that it is implied by the warrant clause. The Court has never explicitly grounded the warrant requirement in the warrant clause, however. Rather, going back to *Agnello v. United States*, 269 U.S. 20 (1925), the Court has treated the warrant requirement as "assumed." Without clarifying the textual or historical basis for that assumption, the Court provided its clearest justification of the warrant requirement in *Johnson v. United States*, 333 U.S. 10 (1948).

In *Johnson*, officers smelled emanations of burning opium while standing outside a hotel room. After knocking, they ordered the occupants to open the door, entered, conducted a search, and found opium and related paraphernalia. There was no doubt that the officers had probable cause to enter and conduct their search. In fact, it was evident from the record that any reasonable magistrate would have granted them a warrant to search the room. But, as Justice Robert Jackson pointed out for the Court, the warrant requirement holds that it is not for

[11] *See* Transcript of Oral Argument at 4, 20, 42–43, Riley v. California, 134 S.Ct. 2473 (2014) (No. 13–132).

"zealous officers" to make determinations of probable cause and reasonableness in the first instance. Instead, the primary "protection" guaranteed by the warrant requirement "consists in requiring that those inferences be drawn by a neutral and detached magistrate, instead of being judged by the officer engaged in the often competitive enterprise of ferreting out crime." Allowing officers to make that determination "would reduce the Amendment to a nullity, and leave the people's homes secure only in the discretion of police officers." That is of concern, Justice Jackson continued, "not only to the individual, but to a society which chooses to dwell in reasonable security and freedom from surveillance." Thus, the Court concluded, "When the right of privacy must reasonably yield to the right of search is, as a rule, to be decided by a judicial officer, not by a policeman or government enforcement agent."

According to the Court's reasoning in *Johnson*, the warrant requirement serves as a constraint on the discretionary use of search and seizure powers. Where it applies, the requirement guarantees "the right of the people to be secure in their persons, houses, papers, and effects against unreasonable searches and seizures" by commanding officers to secure a warrant pursuant to the process and limitations prescribed in the warrant clause. In particular, officers must appear before a **detached and neutral magistrate** and offer, **under oath**, evidence sufficient to show **probable cause** to believe that **specific evidence** will be found in a **particular place** at the time of the search. In concert, these requirements set limits on the discretionary use of search and seizure powers and thereby provide for the general security of the people in their persons, houses, papers, and effects against unreasonable searches and seizures guaranteed by the Fourth Amendment.

What You Need to Know:

1. The Supreme Court has long "assumed" that executive agents must secure warrants before engaging in searches and seizures.
2. The textual and historical foundations for this assumption are subjects of considerable controversy.

3. This warrant requirement is limited by a number of important exceptions.

4. Where it applies, the warrant requirement limits the discretion of law enforcement officers by requiring that they meet the demands set forth in the warrant clause including:

    a. The probable cause requirement;

    b. The oath and affirmation requirement;

    c. The detached and neutral magistrate requirement; and the

    d. Particularity requirement.

LESSON 11: PROBABLE CAUSE

The concept of "probable cause" plays a central role in Fourth Amendment law. When applying for a warrant, officers must provide sufficient evidence that, in combination with reasonable inferences, shows that there is probable cause to believe that evidence of a crime will be found in the place to be searched at the time of the search. Even outside the warrant context, the Court generally requires that searches conducted for purposes of criminal law enforcement must be based on probable cause in order to be deemed reasonable. The notable exceptions to this rule are stops and frisks, which we will discuss in Lesson 19.

A precise definition of "probable cause" is elusive—seemingly by design. For example, in *Illinois v. Gates*, 462 U.S. 213 (1983), Chief Justice William Rehnquist, writing for the Court, opined that "probable cause is a practical, nontechnical standard." It is, he continued, "a fluid concept—turning on the assessment of probability in particular factual contexts—not readily, or even usefully, reduced to a neat set of rules." Probable cause also does not admit of a clear quantitative measure. The question is not whether there is sufficient evidence to support, say, fifty percent certainty. The question instead is whether, on a totality of facts and circumstances, combined with reasonable inferences therefrom, there is reason to believe that evidence of a crime will be found in the place to be searched or, in the case of arrests, that the person arrested has committed a crime.

Assessments of probable cause are objective, not subjective. *Devenpeck v. Alford*, 543 U.S. 146 (2004), provides a useful example. There, the arresting officer believed that he had probable cause to arrest Alford for recording their conversation. As it turned out, making that recording was not a crime. Writing for the Court, Justice Antonin Scalia nevertheless upheld the arrest because evidence readily observable at the time of the arrest provided sufficient grounds for a reasonable officer to conclude that there was probable cause to believe that Alford had committed the crime of impersonating a police officer. It therefore does not matter why a police officer makes an arrest or why a magistrate issues a search warrant. What matters is whether it was reasonable, based on a totality of the facts and evidence observable to the officer or presented to the magistrate, to believe that there was probable cause to justify the arrest or to sustain the warrant.

In order to better understand probable cause, it is important to have a basic understanding of the warrant process. Warrant applications are *ex parte* proceedings. This means that the suspect is not present or represented. Depending on local rules and practices, a prosecutor may be present, but many warrant applications involve only a police officer and a judge or magistrate. Pursuant to the warrant clause, warrant applications must be supported by oath or affirmation. In most cases, the affiant who gives sworn testimony in support of a warrant application is a police officer. The officer may have direct knowledge relating to the application based on her participation in an investigation, but she can also testify based on what she has learned from civilian witnesses or other investigating officers. That is because the rules against hearsay do not apply in warrant application proceedings. It then falls to the judge or magistrate to determine whether the facts and evidence offered by the affiant, in combination with reasonable inferences based on those facts, are sufficient to show that there is probable cause to believe that the evidence sought will be found in the place to be searched at the time of the search.

Although rules governing hearsay do not apply in warrant proceedings, more fundamental rules regarding relevance and weight do apply. Judges reviewing warrant applications must therefore determine whether evidence offered by an affiant is relevant and reliable. Assessing reliability is fairly straightforward if the affiant is testifying to her personal experiences and observations. It can sometimes be more difficult when her testimony is based on the experiences and observations of those not present, including other officers, civilian witnesses, and confidential informants. The Court has addressed some of these issues in cases involving anonymous tips.

In *Aguilar v. Texas*, 378 U.S. 108 (1964), the Court held that warrants cannot issue based solely on an affiant's belief that evidence will be found in the areas to be searched. The affiant must instead provide specific information and facts sufficient to allow the reviewing magistrate to conclude that there is probable cause to believe that evidence will be found. The Court further held that, where the evidentiary foundation for a search warrant includes out-of-court statements by others, the affiant must provide sufficient grounds for the reviewing magistrate to assess the reliability and credibility of those witnesses. In *Spinelli v. United States*, 393 U.S. 410 (1969), the Court emphasized that, in order for a magistrate to assess the reliability and credibility of any witness's testimony, including hearsay statements, the magistrate must have grounds to assess both the witness's basis of knowledge and his veracity. The Court allowed that these assessments can be made in a variety of ways. For example, identified witnesses may be regarded as more likely to tell the truth because they can be held responsible for their lies or misstatements. Confidential informants who have a record of providing reliable information may be regarded as more reliable given their histories. Magistrates should also ask how witnesses know what they claim to know.

After *Spinelli*, lower courts generated an increasingly complex and arcane body of case law delving into the intricacies of veracity and reliability, particularly with respect to anonymous or confidential informants. In *Illinois v. Gates*, the Court cast a dim view on these efforts, emphasizing that warrant applications must be assessed on a "totality of the circumstances." On this approach, potential weakness in the evidence supporting an informant's basis of knowledge or veracity need not doom a warrant application if other facts and evidence gathered by law enforcement provide sufficient certainty that evidence will be found. But where probable cause is based solely or almost exclusively on an informant the *Spinelli* factors still play an important role. For example, as the Court held in *Florida v. J.L.*, 529 U.S. 266 (2000), an anonymous report that someone standing on a street corner is carrying a gun is insufficient to support a finding of probable cause absent additional evidence of the witness's basis of knowledge or veracity. And, as the Court held in *Florida v. Harris*, 568 U.S. 237 (2013), the same considerations apply when officers or magistrates rely on evidence provided by drug detection dogs, whose reliability can be established by training, certification, and experience.

What You Need to Know:

1. Warrant applications are conducted *ex parte.*
2. When adjudicating warrant applications, magistrates may consider all relevant evidence, including hearsay evidence and evidence from anonymous sources.
3. When weighing testimony, hearsay evidence, or statements from anonymous sources, magistrates must consider the witness's credibility and basis of knowledge.
4. When deciding whether to grant a warrant, a magistrate should consider all the evidence offered to determine whether, based on a totality of the circumstances, there is probable cause to believe that evidence will be found in the place to be searched at the time of the search.

LESSON 12: WARRANTLESS SEARCHES: CHALLENGING THE PRESUMPTION OF UNREASONABLENESS

Where the warrant requirement applies, failure to secure a warrant results in a presumption that the subsequent search is unreasonable, and therefore violates the Fourth Amendment. That presumption can be overcome, however, by appeal to what are often referred to as "exceptions" to the warrant requirement. If a prosecutor can show that officers acted within the bounds of an exception to the warrant requirement, then she avoids a presumption of unreasonableness. She nevertheless must still show that officers had probable cause and that they otherwise acted reasonably in that their conduct effected a reasonable balance between law enforcement interests in securing evidence, protecting police officers, and protecting the public and the subject's interests in privacy, bodily security, and protection of their property.

Exigency

One of the most common grounds for claiming an "exception" to the warrant requirement is exigency. Exigency applies when one or more of the law enforcement interests at stake in a search would be unreasonably compromised if officers delayed action in order to seek and secure a warrant. For example, the Court has held that officers may be forgiven from seeking a warrant if they are presented with an emergent threat to public safety, *see* Brigham City, Utah v. Stuart, 547 U.S. 398 (2006) (officers may enter a private home in order to break-up a physical altercation), or even the suspect himself, *see* Michigan v. Fisher, 558 U.S. 45 (2009) (officers may enter a private residence when they have reason to believe that a suspect's life is in danger).

Exigency also covers cases of hot pursuit, where officers chase a suspect into a home and reasonably fear that he might escape, destroy evidence, or pose a danger to others if they do not follow. *See* United States v. Santana, 427 U.S. 38 (1976); Warden, Md. Penitentiary v. Hayden, 387 U.S. 294 (1967). Importantly, the Court held in *Welsh v. Wisconsin*, 466 U.S. 740 (1984), that these threats are unlikely to be present if the suspect does not know he is being pursued. Exigency can justify temporary seizures in order to provide officers a chance to seek a warrant. For example, in *Illinois v. McArthur*, 531 U.S. 326 (2001), the Court held that it was reasonable for officers temporarily to prevent entry by an owner into his home where they had reason to believe there was evidence in the home that the owner might destroy.

Claims of exigency are endemic in narcotics cases where waiting to get a warrant may provide suspects with ample time to flush drugs away or arm themselves to repel police. Nevertheless, the Court has declined to endorse a bright line rule sanctioning exigency claims in all narcotics investigations. *See* Richards v. Wisconsin, 520 U.S. 385 (1997). But it has allowed officers to claim exigency when they initiate the events leading to a crisis. For example, in *Kentucky v. King*, 563 U.S. 452 (2011), officers were trying to locate a suspect who had just purchased illegal drugs. The suspect entered an apartment complex and turned into a breezeway housing two apartments. The officers did not see which apartment the suspect entered, so decided to knock on each of the two doors. Nobody answered when the officers knocked on the first door and announced themselves, but they heard sounds from inside indicating that someone was in the apartment. Fearing the destruction of evidence, the officers effected a forcible entry. They did not find their suspect, who was in the other apartment, but the officers did discover evidence of illegal narcotics. Despite the fact that the officers initiated the potential exigency by knocking on the door and announcing themselves, Justice Samuel Alito, writing for the Court, pointed out that the officers acted within the bounds of the Fourth Amendment at every point in time as the situation evolved. Given this, he saw no reason to deny them a claim of exigency to justify their forcible entry.

Plain View Searches

Another important "exception" to the warrant requirement allows officers to search and, in some cases, seize evidence when they are lawfully in a constitutionally protected area such as a home. Plain view searches often occur in the course of warranted searches, as was the case in *Horton v. California*, 496 U.S. 128 (1990). There, officers sought a warrant to search for the proceeds of an armed robbery as well as the weapon used. The court granted a warrant only as to the proceeds, which included several pieces of jewelry. While searching for the jewelry, officers found and seized a gun used in the robbery. The Court held that this was reasonable because 1) the officers were in a place where they lawfully had a right to be because they had a warrant to search the home; 2) the gun was plainly visible from that vantage because the officers were looking in a place that could reasonably contain items named in the warrant; 3) the incriminating nature of the gun was immediately apparent; and 4) seizing the gun did not require an additional Fourth Amendment intrusion. Applying these factors in *Arizona v. Hicks*, 480 U.S. 321 (1987), the Court held that moving a piece of stereo equipment even slightly in order to see a serial number did not fall under the protections of plain view because the serial numbers were not plainly visible and moving the equipment entailed an additional intrusion upon an "effect." Plain view searches may also occur in the context of exigent entries. For example, the officers in *Kentucky v. King* observed evidence of illegal narcotics in plain view when they entered Mr. King's apartment under a claim of emergency.

Searches Incident to Arrest

In *United States v. Rabinowitz*, 339 U.S. 56 (1950), the Court held that officers who have effected a lawful arrest may conduct a search incident to that arrest of the arrestee and the area within "his immediate possession and control." In order to justify a search under this rule, officers must effect a custodial arrest. *See* Knowles v. Iowa, 525 U.S. 113 (1998). But, so long as the decision to arrest is made before the search, the Court has held that officers may conduct a search incident to arrest before fully perfecting an arrest. *See* Rawlings v. Kentucky, 448 U.S. 98 (1980).

In *Chimel v. California*, 395 U.S. 752 (1969), the Court provided additional explanation for the search incident to arrest rule, opining that officers effecting arrests must always be concerned that the arrestee may be in possession of a weapon, readily access a weapon, destroy evidence in his possession, or destroy evidence within his easy reach. The *Chimel* Court also clarified the physical limits on searches incident to arrest, allowing officers to search readily accessible areas in the room where an arrest takes place but pointing out that searching other rooms, "desk drawers," and "other concealed areas" will usually require separate justification.

Payton v. New York, 445 U.S. 573 (1980), and *Steagald v. United States*, 451 U.S. 204 (1981) set limits on searches incident to arrest conducted in homes. Under *Payton*, if officers want to arrest someone in their home and conduct a search incident to that arrest, then, absent exigency or some other "exception" to the warrant requirement, they must secure an arrest warrant for the arrestee or a search warrant for the arrestee's home. *Steagald* holds that, if officers want to arrest someone in the home of another person and conduct a search incident to that arrest, then, absent exigency or some other "exception" to the warrant requirement, they must secure a search warrant for that home.

The Court limited the search incident to arrest rule in *Arizona v. Gant*, 556 U.S. 332 (2009). In that case, officers arrested Gant for driving without a valid license, handcuffed him, secured him in the back of their patrol car, and then conducted a search incident to arrest of Gant's car during which they discovered drug paraphernalia. Writing for the Court, Justice John Paul Stevens held that because Gant was handcuffed and secured in the back of a patrol car at the time of the search he could not have accessed the interior of his car to secure a weapon or destroy evidence. The officers therefore could not justify their search under *Rabinowitz* and *Chimel*, but needed instead to appeal to another "exception" to the warrant requirement.

The Court limited the search incident to arrest rule further in *Riley v. California*, 134 S.Ct. 2473 (2014). Writing for eight justices in that case (Justice Samuel Alito concurred), Chief Justice John Roberts held that officers do not have an automatic right to search cellular phones seized incident to a lawful arrest but must, instead, seek and secure a separate warrant or rely on another "exception" to the warrant requirement. The Court's reasoning in *Riley* sheds important light on the direction its jurisprudence is likely to take in coming years as it confronts new technologies. Specifically, the Court pointed to the ubiquity of cellular phones, the wide variety of sensitive data stored on phones (including location histories, email correspondence, pictures, etc.), and the fact that phones frequently provide access points to even more data stored on third party servers. In light of these features, the Court held that cellular devices are materially different from their analog analogues, such as wallets and notebooks, both of which may be searched incident to arrest. This, along with the Court's holding in *Carpenter v. United States*, 585 U.S. ___, ___ S.Ct. ___, 2018 WL 3073916 (June 22, 2018), suggests that the Court is willing to take a fresh look at its doctrine as twentieth century rules confront twenty-first century technologies.

Buie Sweeps

In *Maryland v. Buie*, 494 U.S. 325 (1990), the Court applied the exigency rationale to allow officers lawfully present in a home to conduct a cursory sweep of the house in search of potential allies or confederates who might destroy evidence or pose a risk to officers. To justify a *Buie* sweep, officers must point to specific facts giving rise to a belief that such persons are present.

What You Need to Know:

1. Prosecutors may avoid the presumption of unreasonableness that attaches to warrantless searches subject to the warrant requirement by appealing to an "exception."
2. Pursuant to the "emergency exception," officers may forgo getting a warrant where the delay entailed would unreasonably compromise interests in protecting officers, protecting the public, or securing evidence.
3. Pursuant to the "plain view exception," officers do not need a warrant to conduct visual searches from a lawful vantage or to seize items they see so long as their incriminating nature is immediately evident and such seizures do not entail an additional Fourth Amendment intrusion.
4. Pursuant to the "search incident to arrest exception," officers can conduct searches incident to

arrest of an arrestee and areas and objects within his immediate reach and control. The right to conduct a search incident to arrest dissipates after an arrestee has been secured and removed from the scene.

5. Pursuant to the *Buie* rule, if officers lawfully present in a home believe that there are confederates on the premises who may pose a danger to the officers or potential evidence, then the officers may conduct a cursory inspection of areas in the home where those confederates might reasonably be found.

LESSON 13: WARRANTED SEARCHES: CHALLENGING THE PRESUMPTION OF REASONABLENESS

Searches conducted pursuant to a warrant are afforded a presumption of reasonableness. That presumption can be challenged in a number of ways, however.

Insufficient Grounds to Establish Probable Cause

All warrants must be based on specific and articulable facts sufficient to provide probable cause to believe that evidence will be found in the place to be searched at the time of the search. In the event a warrant is granted based on facts insufficient to establish probable cause, any search conducted under authority of that warrant cannot be presumed reasonable. Importantly, this does not necessarily mean that evidence seized during such a search will be excluded at trial. Pursuant to the good faith exception to the exclusionary rule, discussed in Lesson 23, officers are entitled in most circumstances to rely on the legal judgment of the issuing magistrate.

The Warrant Is Not Sufficiently Particular

The warrant clause requires that warrants "particularly describe[ ] the place to be searched, and the persons or things to be seized." Warrants that are insufficiently particular raise the specter of general warrants by failing to limit the discretion of executing officers. Searches conducted pursuant to warrants that are insufficiently particular may therefore be deemed unreasonable.

In cases of searches conducted pursuant to vague or overbroad warrants, the doctrine of severability may allow government agents to argue that their search was reasonable despite defects in their warrant. For example, officers may have a warrant granting them authority to search a specific home for "stolen televisions" and "any other evidence of criminal activity." In such a case, a court might find that officers acted reasonably when searching areas of the home where stolen televisions might be found, but acted unreasonably when searching a desk drawer in an effort to find "other evidence of criminal activity." *See* Andresen v. Maryland, 427 U.S. 463 (1976).

The Search Licensed by a Warrant Is Overly Intrusive

In *Winston v. Lee*, 470 U.S. 753 (1985), the Court held that some searches may be so intrusive in relation to the law enforcement interests at stake that they are "unreasonable" even if there was probable cause to believe that evidence would be found. There, government agents sought a warrant allowing them to remove a bullet from Lee's clavicle in order to help prove his role in an attempted armed robbery. Weighing the risk to Lee against the law enforcement interests at stake, the Court held that forcing Lee to undergo surgery to remove the bullet would constitute an unreasonable search. In reaching this result, the Court pointed out that the government had already amassed considerable evidence against Lee, including eyewitness testimony, suggesting that the actual law enforcement interests at stake were relatively slight.

Staleness

In many cases, assessments of probable cause are time sensitive. For example, facts establishing that there is probable cause to believe that a particular house contained illegal drugs six months ago may not provide probable cause to believe that the house contains drugs today. Where a warrant is granted on stale facts or where the warrant itself has gone stale, a subsequent search based on that warrant may be deemed unreasonable.

Warrant Not Issued by a Detached and Neutral Magistrate

The Court has interpreted the warrant clause as requiring that warrants be issued by detached and neutral magistrates. *See* Johnson v. United States, 333 U.S. 10 (1948). To be "detached," a magistrate need not necessarily be a member of the judicial branch, but must be institutionally insulated from law enforcement. *See* Coolidge v. New Hampshire, 403 U.S. 443 (1971). To be "neutral," a magistrate must not have a financial, professional, or personal interest at stake in the search. *See* Lo-Ji Sales, Inc. v. New York, 442 U.S. 319 (1979) (magistrate showed personal interest by participating in the warranted search); Connally v. Georgia, 429 U.S. 245 (1977) (magistrate was compensated, in part, based on the number of warrants granted). Finally, "magistrates" must be competent and have the expertise necessary to make assessments of probable cause, but need not be judges or even lawyers. *See* Shadwick v. City of Tampa, 407 U.S. 345 (1972).

Officers Search in Areas Not Covered by the Warrant

The principal role of the particularity requirement is to limit the discretion of government agents when conducting searches. Searches conducted in areas not described in a search warrant or in areas where things specified in the warrant cannot reasonably be found do not enjoy the presumption of reasonableness afforded to warranted searches. So, a warrant granting authority to search a home would most likely allow officers to search the main structure, but might not provide authority to search separate and discrete living areas, such as a basement rental apartment or outbuildings. Similarly, a warrant to search for stolen televisions would provide authority to search in rooms and closets, but not in jewelry boxes. Judge Richard Posner made these points in a vivid passage from *United States v. Evans*, 92 F.3d 540 (7th Cir. 1996):

> If [officers] are looking for a canary's corpse, they can search a cupboard, but not a locket. If they are looking for an adolescent hippopotamus, they can search the living room or garage but not the microwave oven. If

they are searching for cocaine, they can search a container large enough to hold a gram, or perhaps less.

Finally, searches that continue after all evidence named in the warrant has been found and secured are not afforded a presumption of reasonableness because they exceed the scope of the warrant.

Failure to Knock and Announce

As the Court held in *Wilson v. Arkansas*, 514 U.S. 927 (1995), officers conducting a warranted search normally must knock, identify themselves, announce their intentions, and provide those on the premises a reasonable period of time to cooperate. Writing for the Court in *Wilson*, Justice Clarence Thomas pointed out that this knock and announce requirement was well-established in eighteenth century common law, in large part because it protects the privacy, safety, and property interests of those on the premises by allowing them time to collect themselves, respond appropriately, and open the door. This requirement is not absolute, however. In some cases, knocking and announcing may unreasonably threaten government agents' interests in securing evidence or protecting their own safety by providing an opportunity for those on a premises to destroy evidence or arm themselves in an effort to resist. Where there is reason to suspect that governmental interests in securing evidence or protecting officers would be unreasonably compromised by knocking and announcing, officers may forgo knocking and announcing. Importantly, violations of the knock and announce requirement do not result in suppression of evidence. *See* Hudson v. Michigan, 547 U.S. 586 (2006). The only remedy for knock and announce violations is a civil action for damages.

Unreasonable Conduct

Officers involved in warranted searches must conduct themselves reasonably. If they use more force than is reasonably necessary to effect an entry, use excessive force in their engagements with those on the premises, linger for an unreasonable amount of time, or otherwise invade the privacy, safety, and property interests of those subject to search more than is reasonably necessary to vindicate their interests in securing evidence and protecting their own safety, then the mere fact that they have a warrant will not immunize that unreasonable conduct from Fourth Amendment challenge. As with knock and announce violations, these Fourth Amendment violations seldom result in the suppression of evidence but can provide grounds for civil actions.

Officers serving valid warrants have authority to detain persons found on the premises during the pendency of the search in order to guarantee their own security and the security of evidence. *See* Muehler v. Mena, 544 U.S. 93 (2005); Michigan v. Summers, 452 U.S. 692 (1981). This authority is limited, however. For example, as the Court held in *Bailey v. United States*, 516 U.S. 137 (2013), persons who are no longer on the premises when a warrant is served do not pose a threat to the security of law enforcement or evidence on the scene and therefore cannot be seized absent independent grounds to do so under the Fourth Amendment.

Involvement of Unnecessary Third Parties

In *United States v. New York Tel. Co.*, 434 U.S. 159 (1977), the Court held that officers may involve third parties in warranted searches if those third parties are necessary to vindicate the government's interests in finding and securing evidence named in the warrant. In that case, officers needed the expertise of the telephone company to install and monitor a pen register device. But in *Wilson v. Layne*, 526 U.S. 603 (1999), the Court made clear that officers may not involve extraneous parties in a warranted search. In that case, officers invited members of the press to accompany them on a search. Although Chief Justice William Rehnquist, writing for the Court, allowed that having members of the press on the scene might help with the public image of law enforcement, assist in deterring officers from engaging in unreasonable behaviors, and provide a means to monitor and document law enforcement procedures, he pointed out that all of those goals could be equally served by in-house monitors without unreasonably compromising the privacy interests of the homeowner and those on the premises during the search.

What You Need to Know:

1. Although warranted searches enjoy a presumption of reasonableness, that presumption can be challenged in a number of ways. Among the most common are:
   a. There was not probable cause to issue the warrant.
   b. The warrant was not sufficiently particular as to the place to be searched.
   c. The warrant was not sufficiently particular as to the things to be seized.
   d. The search endorsed by the warrant was overly intrusive.
   e. The probable cause underlying the warrant was stale.
   f. The warrant itself was stale.
   g. The warrant was issued by a magistrate who was not detached from law enforcement.
   h. The warrant was issued by a magistrate who was not a neutral arbiter.
   i. The warrant was issued by someone who is not designated and qualified to act as a "magistrate."
   j. The officers searched in areas not identified in the warrant.
   k. The officers searched in areas that could not reasonably hold things specified in the warrant.
   l. The officers continued their search even after finding and seizing all items named in the warrant.
   m. The officers failed to knock, identify themselves, announce their intentions, and provide a reasonable opportunity for those on the premises to comply.

n. The officers used excessive force when effecting the search.

o. The officers lingered on the premises longer than was reasonably necessary to effectuate the warranted search.

p. The officers involved unnecessary third parties in the search.

2. Although any of these may provide grounds to argue that a warranted search was not "reasonable," it does not necessarily follow that the Fourth Amendment violation would result in the suppression of evidence. Whether evidence seized in violation of the Fourth Amendment will be excluded from the prosecutor's case in chief at trial entails a separate inquiry.

LESSON 14: SEIZING AND SEARCHING CARS AND DRIVERS

Automobiles are among the "effects" most frequently targeted for seizures and searches. The Supreme Court has therefore had occasion to elaborate a number of rules governing searches and seizures of cars.

Car "Frisks"[12]

In *Michigan v. Long*, 463 U.S. 1032 (1983), the Court granted authority for law enforcement officers to conduct cursory searches of the passenger areas of cars for weapons in the context of lawful stops if they have reason to suspect that there is a weapon present to which a suspect might gain access to threaten the safety of officers or the public. In that case, officers stopped Long on suspicion of impaired driving. Long exited his car, engaged in a verbal exchange with the officers, and then made a move to return to his car. Concerned that he might try to access a weapon, the officers looked into the passenger area where they saw a large hunting knife. They seized the knife and conducted a cursory search of the passenger area to determine whether additional weapons were present.

[12] We will discuss frisks more broadly in Lesson 19.

While conducting that protective search, they discovered illegal drugs in plain view. The Court held that the officers' conduct at each moment of Fourth Amendment significance was reasonable.

Car frisks are limited to the passenger areas of cars. For purposes of the Fourth Amendment, "passenger areas" are defined as those areas of a car that are readily accessible to the driver or passengers. That includes seats, areas under seats, glove compartments, and consoles, but does not include trunks. The cargo areas of hatchbacks, vans, station wagons, and the like may well be regarded as part of the passenger area if a weapon in one of these areas would be readily accessible to a driver or passenger.

Searches Incident to Arrest of Cars

In *New York v. Belton*, 453 U.S. 454 (1981), the Court held that when the driver of a car is arrested, the passenger area of the car is within the driver's area of reach and control and is therefore subject to a search incident to arrest. *Belton* appeared to provide a bright line rule, allowing officers to conduct a search incident to arrest of the passenger area of a car any time the driver is arrested. In *Thornton v. United States*, 541 U.S. 615 (2004), the Court extended the *Belton* rule to allow the search incident to arrest of a car when the driver had stopped, parked, exited the car, and walked away before being arrested. But, as the Court made clear in *Chambers v. Maroney*, 399 U.S. 42 (1970), timing matters. There, officers arrested the occupants in a car, took them into custody, impounded the car, drove it to the police station, and then conducted a search of the car that produced evidence implicating the suspects in a robbery. On these facts, the Court held that the search of the car could not be justified by the search incident to arrest rule because "the reasons that have been thought sufficient to justify warrantless searches carried out in connection with an arrest no longer obtain when the accused is safely in custody at the station house."

The Court further limited searches incident to arrest of cars in *Arizona v. Gant*, 556 U.S. 332 (2009). There, officers arrested Gant for driving without a license, placed him in handcuffs, secured him in the back of their patrol car, and then searched his car. Extending its reasoning from *Chambers*, the Court held that the search of Gant's car could not be justified as a search incident to arrest because Gant was handcuffed, secured, and otherwise could not gain access to the interior of his car at the time of the search. In distinguishing *Belton*, the *Gant* Court pointed out that the defendants in *Belton* were unsecured and relatively close to the car when the officers in that case conducted their search. Given those circumstances, the concerns that underwrite the search incident to arrest rule—that the arrestee might access a weapon or attempt to destroy evidence—were salient on the facts in *Belton* but not in *Gant*.

Drivers are also subject to searches of their persons incident to a lawful arrest. In *Birchfield v. North Dakota*, 136 S.Ct. 2160 (2016), the Court was asked whether the search incident to arrest rule would license compelling drivers arrested on suspicion of drunk driving to submit to a breathalyzer or blood test to determine their levels of intoxication. Citing the different degrees of physical intrusion entailed by these two methods, and the unique potential for blood tests to reveal a variety of personal information not ascertainable from a breathalyzer, the Court held that the Fourth Amendment permits warrantless breath tests incident to arrests for drunk driving but not warrantless blood tests.

The Car Exception to the Warrant Requirement

In *Carroll v. United States*, 267 U.S. 132 (1925), the Court held that it is reasonable for officers to search an automobile where they have probable cause to believe that evidence of a crime will be found therein and that no presumption of unreasonableness would attach if they failed to secure a warrant in advance of that search. The Court's reasoning in *Carroll* focused on the fact that cars are highly mobile, raising concerns about the potential loss or destruction of evidence if officers are forced to delay action.

The Court upheld the *Carroll* rule in *California v. Carney*, 471 U.S. 386 (1985), but on different grounds. Writing for the Court, Chief Justice William Rehnquist pointed out that cars are far more visible than homes and other constitutionally protected areas. They are also subject to a host of regulations, which render them vulnerable to inspection and search. In light of these features, the Court held that our reasonable expectations of privacy in cars are substantially diminished. In the *Carney* Court's view, the *Carroll* rule is justified in light of the diminished expectations of privacy we have in our cars and not the potential exigency that inheres in cars by virtue of their movability. *See also* Maryland v. Dyson, 527 U.S. 465 (1999); Pennsylvania v. Labron, 518 U.S. 938 (1996). That clarification is important because it preserves full reasonable expectations of privacy in other movable effects such as briefcases, backpacks, and luggage. *See* United States v. Chadwick, 433 U.S. 1 (1977).

One might argue that where officers have probable cause to believe that evidence will be found in a car the more reasonable option would be to seize the car while officers seek and secure a warrant. Weighing this option in *Chambers v. Maroney*, 399 U.S. 42 (1970), the Court pointed out that seizing a car pending efforts to secure a warrant is more intrusive and entails a greater infringement upon expectations of privacy than the alternative approach under the *Carroll* rule. That may seem counter-intuitive, but remember that officers searching a car under *Carroll* must have probable cause. Furthermore, the grounds cited for probable cause can be tested before a detached and neutral magistrate, either in a suppression hearing or civil action. Requiring officers to seize a car while they seek a warrant is therefore an additional intrusion both of property interests in the car and liberty interests of the driver and passengers, who often are forced to wait as well.

Given that we have diminished reasonable expectations of privacy in cars, but retain full expectations of privacy in other effects such as bags and luggage, one might wonder about the constitutional status of bags and other personal effects located in cars. The Court answered that question in *California v. Acevedo*, 500 U.S. 565 (1991), holding that containers located in cars are subject to search under the *Carroll* rule, at least where they could contain the evidence officers have probable cause to believe is located in the car. In *Wyoming v. Houghton*, 526 U.S. 295 (1999), the Court held that bags and other effects that belong to passengers rather than drivers are also subject to search under the *Carroll* rule. By contrast, the *Carroll* rule does not automatically justify the search of persons, including drivers and passengers. *See* United States v. Di Re, 332 U.S. 581 (1948). Moreover, cars located on the curtilage of a home enjoy the full Fourth Amendment protection afforded to homes. To search an automobile parked on the curtilage or messuage of a home therefore requires a warrant. *See* Collins v. Virginia, 584 U.S. ___, 138 S.Ct. 1663 (2018).

Establishing probable cause to justify the search of a car usually requires officers to point to objective facts and reasonable inferences from those facts. In *Arizona v. Gant*, the Court pointed out, if a driver has been arrested, then the nature of the crime for which he was arrested may provide probable cause to search his car. For example, if a driver is arrested for drug distribution, then officers might have probable cause to search the car for narcotics based on the crime of arrest. *See* Thornton v. United States, 541 U.S. 615 (2004) (Scalia, J., concurring). Contrariwise, as the Court held in *Gant*, if a driver is arrested for driving on a suspended license, then officers usually do not have probable cause to search the car based on the crime of arrest.

Car Stops

Car stops are among the most dangerous situations faced by police officers. Out of concern for those dangers, the Court permits officers to order a driver to exit his car during a lawful traffic stop. *See* Pennsylvania v. Mimms, 434 U.S. 106 (1977). They may also order any passengers out of the car. *See* Maryland v. Wilson, 519 U.S. 408 (1997).

Dog Sniffs and Cars

In *United States v. Place*, 462 U.S. 696 (1983), the Court held that allowing a drug detection dog to sniff the outside of a bag is not a "search" for purposes of the Fourth Amendment because these dogs only alert to the presence of illegal substances and there is no reasonable expectation of privacy in illegal activity. In *Illinois v. Caballes*, 543 U.S. 405 (2005), the Court extended that rule to cars holding that allowing a drug detection dog to sniff the outside of a car during a lawful traffic stop is not a "search." As the Court made clear in *Rodriguez v. United States*, 135 S.Ct. 1609 (2015), however, the sniff must take place *during* a lawful stop. If officers unreasonably extend a stop past the time necessary to effectuate the purpose of the stop (e.g. checking license, registration, insurance, issuing a ticket, etc.) while waiting for the dog to arrive, then that additional time is a "seizure" that requires adequate Fourth Amendment justification.

What You Need to Know:

1. Officers may conduct cursory searches of the passenger areas of cars if they have reason to suspect there is a weapon present and that a driver or passenger might access that weapon and threaten the safety of officers or the public.
2. Whenever the occupant of a car is arrested, officers may conduct a search incident to arrest of the passenger area of the car as long as it is reasonable to believe that the arrestee might access the vehicle at the time of the search.
3. Secondary to an arrest for drunk driving, officers may compel a driver to submit to a breathalyzer test to determine his level of intoxication, but need a warrant in order to compel submission to a blood test.
4. An officer may search the entirety of a car if he has probable cause to believe that evidence of a crime is in the car. One way an officer may establish probable cause for a car search is when an occupant has been arrested and the nature of that offense suggests the likely presence of evidence in the car.
5. During the course of a lawful traffic stop, officers may allow a drug detection dog to sniff the outside of a car.

LESSON 15: CONSENT SEARCHES

Searches conducted pursuant to lawful consent are generally "reasonable" and do not require any particular level of justification or prior judicial review. Claims of authority to search pursuant to consent do, however, raise important questions including whether consent was given, whether it was given voluntarily, whether the person granting consent had authority to do so, and the scope of consent given.

Was Consent Given?

Explicit verbal consent is sufficient but not necessary to establish the reasonableness of a consent search. Depending on the circumstance, it may be reasonable for an officer to interpret physical cues as consent. For example, in *United States v. Drayton*, 536 U.S. 194 (2002), officers suspected that Drayton was transporting drugs on his person. In order to confirm their suspicions, they asked to pat him down. Drayton did not respond verbally, but instead lifted his hands off his legs and leaned forward in his seat. The Court held that it was reasonable in these circumstances for the officers to interpret Drayton's actions as granting consent to search.

As is the case in other social interactions, mistakes and miscommunications can occur when officers seek and receive consent to search. For example, an officer may believe that she has received consent when, in fact, her suspect did not intend to grant consent. In such cases, the question whether consent was granted is determined from the point of view of a reasonable officer rather than the suspect. Thus, if a reasonable officer would have interpreted the suspect's words or conduct as granting consent to search, then consent was given for purposes of assessing Fourth Amendment reasonableness even if the suspect later claims he did not intend to grant consent.

Was Consent Voluntary?

Consent to search must be given voluntarily, which is assessed on the totality of the circumstances. Among the factors courts can consider when assessing voluntariness are 1) whether the suspect was in custody; 2) the coercive conduct of the officers; 3) whether the suspect demonstrated a willingness to cooperate; and 4) the suspect's intelligence and level of sophistication. Critically, consent to search is not a waiver of Fourth Amendment rights. *See* Illinois v. Rodriguez, 497 U.S. 177

(1990). Consent therefore does not require knowledge of the Fourth Amendment right to refuse or intelligent awareness of the consequences. *See* Schneckloth v. Bustamonte, 412 U.S. 218 (1973). Moreover, officers have no obligation to advise suspects of their right to refuse consent. Nevertheless, awareness of the right to refuse is a factor to consider when assessing voluntariness.

Did the Grantor of Consent Have Authority?

Only those with lawful authority to do so may grant consent to search. Authority to search is determined by the same standards governing Fourth Amendment search. That is, individuals may consent to intrusions upon their reasonable expectations of privacy and to searches of their persons houses, papers, and effects. *See* United States v. Matlock, 415 U.S. 164 (1974). Ownership is neither necessary nor sufficient to establish authority to consent to a search. For example, landlords do not have authority to consent to the search of a lawfully rented residence but tenants do.

Reasonable mistakes of fact as to authority to consent will not necessarily render a search unreasonable. For example, in *Illinois v. Rodriguez*, 497 U.S. 177 (1990), officers received consent to search an apartment from a woman who presented herself as a co-tenant. She then used her keys to let them inside. It turned out that she had moved out weeks earlier, and therefore did not have lawful authority to consent to the search. Nevertheless, the Court held that the officers reasonably believed that she had authority to grant consent, which rendered the subsequent search reasonable for purposes of the Fourth Amendment. Mistakes of law are a different matter. For example, it would be unreasonable for officers to rely on consent from a landlord to search a lawfully leased apartment. *See* Stoner v. California, 376 U.S. 483 (1964).

Searches of residences occupied by multiple parties may present special problems for consent searches. For example, do co-tenants in an apartment have equal and independent authority to consent to a search of the apartment, or must officers receive consent from both of them? Do co-tenants have equal authority to consent to a search of all areas on the premises? What if one co-tenant grants consent, but the other refuses? Must consent be granted by adults, or can a minor child grant consent to search? When answering these questions the Court has assessed the reasonableness of officers' actions by referring to familiar social experiences where requests for permission and grants of consent are commonplace. For example, in *Georgia v. Randolph*, 547 U.S. 103 (2006), the Court held that it is unreasonable for officers to act on the consent of one co-tenant in a premises if the other tenant is on the scene and actively refusing consent because no reasonable visitor would enter in such circumstances. As another example, if officers seek consent to search an apartment occupied by two roommates who have separate bedrooms, then it would probably be unreasonable for officers to rely on consent by one tenant to search his co-tenant's bedroom barring some evidence of authority to do so.

What Was the Scope of Consent?

Citizens are free to grant consent, decline consent, or grant partial consent. Likewise, consent can be withdrawn at any time. Where partial consent is granted, officers are obliged to respect the limits of that consent. Once engaged in a consent search, however, officers may search any areas or items that fall reasonably within the scope of the consent granted. *See* Florida v. Jimeno, 500 U.S. 248 (1991).

Consent Searches and Evolving Encounters

Consent searches are a powerful tool for law enforcement. Officers often seek consent to search during their evolving encounters with citizens. This is particularly true in the context of car stops. Secondary to a lawful traffic stop, officers who begin to suspect more serious criminality may seek consent to search the car. If they receive consent, then any evidence they find will be admissible at trial. It may seem unbelievable that anyone would consent to the search of a car knowing that it contains evidence of a crime. But police officers can be highly skilled in persuading suspects to grant consent in these cases.

What You Need to Know:

1. Searches conducted pursuant to lawful consent are "reasonable" for purposes of the Fourth Amendment.
2. Whether consent has been granted is assessed objectively from the point of view of a reasonable officer.
3. To be valid, consent must be voluntary.
4. Only those with legal authority to do so may grant consent to search.
5. Consent may be granted, granted in part, and withdrawn.

LESSON 16: SPECIAL NEEDS SEARCHES

Government agents often need to conduct searches in service of administrative and regulatory regimes. These "special needs" searches are regulated by the Fourth Amendment, but do not require probable cause, particularized suspicion, or a warrant. They are, instead, governed entirely by the reasonableness clause, which requires 1) striking a balance among the competing interests of targets in their privacy and security and government interests in public policy and effective regulation, and 2) procedural safeguards sufficient to limit the discretion of government agents and to guarantee that searches are conducted only for good and sufficient reasons.

Many businesses are subject to close regulation and are therefore subject to regulatory or administrative searches. *See* See v. City of Seattle, 387 U.S. 541 (1967). So too are some homes, which may be subject to regulatory codes relating to public safety, health, hygiene, and environmental protection. *See* Camara v. Municipal Court of City and County of San Francisco, 387 U.S. 523 (1967). Of course, government agents may enter and inspect any publicly accessible areas of a business during normal business hours without being subject to Fourth Amendment constraints because, pursuant to the public observation doctrine, these inspections are not "searches" at all. *See* Donovan v. Lone Steer, 464 U.S. 408 (1984). But in order to enter and inspect less accessible areas of businesses or homes pursuant to the special needs doctrine agents must show that:

1. There is a substantial government interest at stake that is separate from normal crime control.
2. Warrantless searches are reasonably necessary to vindicate those government interests.
3. The target of the search is on notice that they are subject to the regulatory or administrative regime.
4. There is an established, pre-existing scheme that:
    a. Determines when and in what circumstances searches will be conducted; and
    b. Limits the discretion of agents when conducting searches.
5. The search itself was pursuant to the pre-existing scheme and was otherwise reasonably tied to the government's interests.

Although the government interests at stake must be separate from normal crime control, special needs searches often intersect with efforts to detect and prosecute crime. For example, in *New York v. Burger*, 482 U.S. 691 (1967), the New York legislature passed regulations governing scrap metal and salvage businesses that required keeping records of car parts bought and sold and rendering these businesses vulnerable to warrantless inspections. As the Court recognized, these regulations served a substantial governmental interest in limiting the market for stolen car parts. In *Burger*, police officers arrived at a salvage yard and asked to see the required records. When Burger could not produce his records, the officers examined some of his stock to determine whether it had been stolen. In the course of that search they identified stolen items on the premises, including cars and car parts. Burger was later charged with possession of stolen property. Despite the close relationship between the regulatory and crime control interests at stake, and the fact that the search was conducted by police officers, the Court held that both the statute licensing the search and the search itself were reasonable.

As the Court maintained in *Fergusen v. City of Charleston*, 532 U.S. 67 (2001), regulatory searches may not serve as mere pretexts for advancing criminal law enforcement goals. In that case, the Charleston police entered into agreements with local hospitals to identify pregnant women who were using illegal drugs in an effort to reduce the incidence of health problems associated with exposing babies to drugs in utero. Under these agreements, hospital officials would take urine samples from pregnant women during their prenatal visits, test that urine for illegal substances, and report positive results to law enforcement. Women testing positive were warned that a subsequent positive test would expose them to criminal charges for possession or distribution of illegal narcotics, depending upon the age of the fetus. Despite the compelling public health interests at stake, Justice John Paul Stevens held for the Court that the overall scheme was clearly aimed at serving law enforcement interests, and that the drug tests, which constituted "searches" for purposes of the Fourth Amendment, therefore could not be justified by the special needs doctrine.

The special needs doctrine has also been used to justify searches of school children, their lockers, and their bags. *See* New Jersey v. T.L.O., 469 U.S. 325 (1985). Children do not lose reasonable expectations of privacy in their persons or effects by entering onto school grounds, but those expectations are diminished by the compelling interest schools have in guaranteeing the safety and security of minors in their care. Schools may therefore require those entering their buildings to pass through metal detectors in order to keep weapons off their premises. As the Court held in *T.L.O.*, teachers and administrators may also search students' effects based on reasonable suspicion that they contain contraband. But these searches must strike a reasonable balance between intrusiveness and government interests. Applying these standards, the Court held in *Safford Unified School Dist. No. 1 v. Redding*, 577 U.S. 364 (2009), that forcing a middle school student to submit to a strip search on suspicion that she possessed unauthorized ibuprofen tablets was unconstitutional.

The special needs doctrine is deployed routinely to justify mandatory drug screening programs. For example, in *Skinner v.*

Railway Labor Executives' Ass'n, 489 U.S. 602 (1989), the Court upheld a mandatory drug screening program for railroad workers who were involved in accidents. In that case, there was a demonstrated drug problem among railroad workers, which made the program responsive to a pressing need. But in *National Treasury Employees Union v. Von Raab*, 489 U.S. 656 (1989), the Court held that it was not necessary to establish the existence of a drug problem among Customs agents in order to justify mandatory drug screening if proponents could identify unique security concerns that might be at stake. Those liberal limits were pressed too far in *Chandler v. Miller*, 520 U.S. 305 (1997), where Justice Ruth Bader Ginsburg, writing for the Court, held that a Georgia statute requiring that aspirants to public office submit to drug testing was unconstitutional both because there was no demonstrated drug problem among Georgia politicians and because the program itself was so easy to circumnavigate that it was clearly nothing more than a symbolic exercise. But, citing the special vulnerability of children, the Court has upheld mandatory drug testing of high school athletes, *see* Vernonia School Dist. 47J v. Acton, 515 U.S. 646 (1995), and participants in extracurricular activities more generally, *see* Board of Education of Independent School District No. 92 of Pottawatomie County et al. v. Earls, 536 U.S. 822 (2002).

The Court has long held that parolees and prisoners have diminished expectations of privacy. *See* Samson v. California, 547 U.S. 843 (2006); Griffin v. Wisconsin, 483 U.S. 868 (1987). On the other hand, as the Court found in *Florence v. Board of Chosen Freeholders of City of Burlington*, 566 U.S. 318 (2012), prisons and jails have serious and weighty interests in safety, security, and preventing the smuggling of illegal drugs into their facilities. Given the balance of interests, the Court in that case upheld a blanket policy mandating strip searches of all prisoners entering a jail facility. Relying on a similar balancing analysis, the Court upheld a law mandating DNA testing of persons indicted of violent crimes in *Maryland v. King*, 569 U.S. 435 (2013). Under that program, DNA profiles were compared against the Federal Bureau of Investigation's Combined DNA Index System to identify any matches to unsolved crimes. Writing for the Court, Justice Anthony Kennedy held that establishing an indictee's past crimes was an essential part of the identification process that also provided courts and prison officials with information relevant to bail determinations and custody arrangements.

The special needs doctrine has also been applied to justify inventory searches of cars and other effects lawfully seized by law enforcement. *See* Illinois v. Lafayette, 462 U.S. 640 (1983); Cady v. Dombrowski, 413 U.S. 433 (1973). As the Court pointed out in *Colorado v. Bertine*, 479 U.S. 367 (1987), law enforcement agencies that have taken custody of personal property have an interest in protecting the property, protecting themselves against accusations of theft, and protecting their agents from any contents that might pose a danger. Inventory searches can help secure these interests by identifying and cataloguing the contents of personal property seized by law enforcement. In order to limit the discretion of officers, the Court requires that inventory searches be conducted subject to a preexisting policy. For example, in *Florida v. Wells*, 495 U.S. 1 (1990), the Court found unreasonable the search of a locked suitcase found in an impounded car because the relevant regulations did not provide sufficient guidance.

The special needs doctrine affords authority for officers to deploy checkpoints as a means of promoting non-criminal law enforcement interests. For example, officers may use a checkpoint to stop and screen drivers in an effort to prevent drunk driving. Importantly, checkpoints must be aimed at serving purposes other than the detection and prosecution of crime. For example, the Court in *City of Indianapolis v. Edmond*, 531 U.S. 32 (2000), held that a police checkpoint meant to screen for the presence of drugs could not be defended under the special needs doctrine because the objective purpose of the program was normal crime control rather than public safety on the roads.

Customs and border agents have broad authority under the special needs doctrine to conduct searches at international borders to vindicate weighty public interests in preventing the importation of dangerous or illegal persons and contraband. *See* United States v. Ramsey, 431 U.S. 606 (1997). These searches can be quite invasive, such as in *United States v. Flores-*

Montano, 541 U.S. 149 (2004), where officers removed the gas tank of a car looking for illegal drugs. For similar reasons, the Court has sanctioned the close scrutiny of international mail, *see* United States v. Ramsey, 431 U.S. 606 (1997), as well as the detention of individuals at the border, *see* United States v. Montoya de Hernandez, 473 U.S. 531 (1985).

What You Need to Know:

1. Searches for purposes other than criminal law enforcement are governed by the special needs doctrine.
2. To justify searches under the special needs doctrine, the government must identify compelling interests, show that warrantless searches are necessary to vindicate those interests, provide notice to those subject to potential search, and establish a preexisting scheme sufficient to limit the discretion of government agents.
3. Applying the special needs doctrine, the Court has allowed searches of closely regulated businesses like salvage yards, school children, drug testing, DNA testing of those indicted for violent crimes, inventory searches, DUI checkpoints, and border searches.

LESSON 17: ARRESTS

Arrests are paradigmatic seizures of persons under the Fourth Amendment. To meet constitutional standards, uses of arrest powers must be reasonable. Although many searches face a presumption of unreasonableness when conducted without a warrant, arrests in public do not. Officers may effect a full custodial arrest any time they have probable cause to believe that the arrestee has committed or is committing a crime. Officers are not constitutionally required to seek prior approval from a detached and neutral magistrate. But, as we saw in Lesson 12, arrests in homes require either an arrest warrant or a search warrant in order to vindicate the Fourth Amendment interests of those with a reasonable expectation of privacy in the premises.

In order to establish probable cause for arrest, officers must identify specific, articulable facts, which, in combination with reasonable inferences drawn from those facts, provide reason to believe that the arrestee has engaged or is engaging in a crime. When assessing probable cause, officers may draw on their experience and training. As in the search context, probable cause assessments are based on a totality of the circumstances. In many cases, individual facts may have perfectly innocent explanations, but, when considered in context, and in combination with other facts, they may provide ample grounds for probable cause.

Some law enforcement officers operate under common law, legislative, or administrative rules that limit their arrest powers. For example, the common law granted unfettered discretion for officers to arrest felons, but required warrants to arrest misdemeanants unless the crime was perpetrated in the officer's presence. These rules have no constitutional force under the Fourth Amendment. Although laws limiting the arrest power may create rights under state law, they do not create rights under the Fourth Amendment. It is therefore reasonable under the Fourth Amendment for an officer to effect a full custodial arrest for any offense, no matter how minor, as long as the officer has probable cause. *See* Atwater v. City of Lago Vista, 532 U.S. 318 (2001) (not unreasonable to arrest a defendant for violation of seatbelt law); Hedgepeth v. Washington Metro Area Transit Authority, 386 F.3d 1148 (D.C. Cir. 2004) (not unreasonable to arrest a 12 year-old girl for eating on a Metro train). That is true even if state or local laws specifically prohibit arrests for certain offenses. *See* Virginia v. Moore, 553 U.S. 164 (2008).

The reasonableness of arrests is measured objectively. The subjective beliefs or motivations of officers who conduct arrests are not relevant to assessments of Fourth Amendment reasonableness. This means that motivation is irrelevant when assessing the reasonableness of an arrest—even where those motives may be malignant or reflective of bias. *See* Whren v. United States, 517 U.S. 806 (1996). But it also means that courts will overlook many mistakes officers might make in the field. For example, in *Devenpeck v. Alford*, 543 U.S. 146 (2004), an officer arrested Jerome Alford for recording his conversation with an officer despite Alford's protestations that this recording was entirely legal (Alford even produced a recent court decision confirming the legality of his conduct). Alford turned out to be correct on the law, but Justice Antonin Scalia, writing for the Court, held that the arrest was reasonable because there was ample evidence available to the officer at the time of the arrest to provide probable cause to believe that Alford had illegally impersonated a police officer. In a similar vein, courts have forgiven officers' reasonable mistakes of fact, such as in *United States v. Flores-Sandoval*, 366 F.3d 961 (8th Cir. 2004), where the officer stopped a motorist on suspicion that his car did not have the front license plate required by state law only to discover during the stop that, in fact, the required plate was present. The Court went a step further in *Heien v. North Carolina*, 135 S.Ct. 530 (2014), holding that seizures based on objectively reasonable mistakes of law are not unreasonable for purposes of the Fourth Amendment.

Allegations of pretext are not cognizable under the Fourth Amendment. This means that an officer's true motivations in effecting an arrest, whether noble or malignant, are irrelevant in assessing the reasonableness of that arrest. What matters is whether the totality of the facts and circumstances established probable cause. In *Whren*, this meant that the Court declined to consider allegations that officers engaged in a traffic stop as a pretext when their true motivation was to investigate potential drug crimes. There were also suggestions in that case that racial bias may have played a role in the officers' decision to stop Whren. Although the Court made clear that these concerns had no Fourth Amendment salience, Justice Scalia noted that allegations of racial bias or discrimination might give rise to claims based on the Equal Protection Clause of the Fourteenth Amendment.

Although officers do not need a warrant to effect arrests in public, this does not mean magistrates have no role to play. As the Court held in *Gerstein v. Pugh*, 420 U.S. 103 (1975), arrestees have a Fourth Amendment right to "prompt" review by a detached and neutral magistrate to determine whether there was probable cause for arrest. In the years after *Gerstein*, there was considerable controversy over the meaning of "prompt." Although the Court has declined to issue a bright line rule, it offered some basic parameters in *County of Riverside v. McLaughlin*, 500 U.S. 44 (1991). There, writing for the Court, Justice Sandra Day O'Connor held that, as a general rule, hearings held within 48 hours of arrest are "prompt," while hearings held later are not. The Court's focus in *County of Riverside* was on policies and practices. As the Court made clear, the facts in any particular case may reveal that a hearing 24 hours after arrest may not be "prompt," while a hearing after 60 hours may be "prompt" under different circumstances. Of particular importance to determining promptness is the objective purpose of the delay. Delaying a *Gerstein* hearing primarily to conduct further investigation is generally unreasonable. And, of course, lying or presenting false evidence in a *Gerstein* hearing may render subsequent detention unreasonable under the Fourth Amendment. *See* Manuel v. City of Joliet, 137 S.Ct. 911 (2017).

We will discuss the remedies for unlawful arrest in Lessons 20 through 23. The Court has not addressed squarely the remedy for *Gerstein* violations. In *Powell v. Nevada*, 511 U.S. 79 (1994), Justice Clarence Thomas, writing in concurrence with Chief Justice William Rehnquist, indicated that *Gerstein* violations could only lead to suppression of evidence if the *Gerstein* violation caused the discovery of evidence.

What You Need to Know:

1. Arrests are seizures of persons.
2. To justify an arrest, officers must point to specific facts and circumstances, which, in combination with reasonable inferences based on the officer's experience and training, provide probable cause to believe that the arrestee is committing or has committed a crime.
3. The subjective motivations of officers are irrelevant when assessing the reasonableness of an arrest under the Fourth Amendment. All that matters is whether there was objective probable cause.

4. Claims of racial discrimination or bias on the part of officers are not relevant to determining the lawfulness of arrests under the Fourth Amendment, although those concerns may provide grounds for Equal Protection challenges.
5. Although warrants are not required for arrests in public, arrestees are entitled to a "prompt" review before a detached and neutral magistrate, usually within 48 hours.

LESSON 18: USE OF FORCE

Searches and seizures entail the use of force. The Fourth Amendment bars the use of unreasonable force by officers effecting a search or seizure.

The knock and announce requirement discussed in Lesson 13 sets limits on when officers may reasonably use force to effect entry into a premises subject to search. As the Court held in *Wilson v. Arkansas*, 514 U.S. 927 (1995), it is generally unreasonable for officers to effect a forceful entry before knocking, announcing themselves, and providing a reasonable opportunity for those on the premises to respond. As the Court recognized, however, it may sometimes be unreasonable to require that officers abide the knock and announce rule where doing so would unreasonably compromise law enforcement interests in securing evidence, the security of officers, or public safety. This same balance of interests approach determines the reasonableness of the use of force during a search. For example, it may sometimes be reasonable for officers to employ paramilitary tactics when conducting a search if there is good reason to believe that those on the premises may be armed and pose a danger to officers.

Use of force questions arise most frequently in the context of seizures of persons, including stops and arrests. These are fraught situations in which officers, those seized, and the public may be at substantial risk of physical harm. When officers use force to seize a person, the Fourth Amendment question is whether, on a totality of the circumstances, the officers' use of force reflected a reasonable balance between the safety and security interests of the person seized, the safety and security interests of law enforcement, and the safety and security interests of the public. *See* Scott v. Harris, 550 U.S. 372 (2007). In order to defend themselves and the public, officers may sometimes resort to the use of deadly force. The Fourth Amendment is particularly concerned with these cases. In determining whether officers' use of deadly force is reasonable, traditional rules governing self-defense and defense of others have an important role to play. So, it is generally reasonable for officers to use deadly force when they are defending themselves against threats of death or severe bodily harm posed by the person seized. Likewise, it is generally reasonable for officers to use deadly force when defending innocent persons or the public at large from threats of death or severe bodily harm posed by the person seized.

Rules governing the use of deadly force under the Fourth Amendment trace to *Tennessee v. Garner*, 471 U.S. 1 (1985). In that case, officers were in pursuit of Edward Garner, who was suspected in a residential burglary. The officers caught up to Garner as he was approaching a fence. The officers ordered Garner to stop. Garner did not comply, but instead started to climb the fence. Despite the fact that the officers had a clear view of Garner's empty hands, and were otherwise fairly certain he was unarmed, they shot him in order to prevent his escape. Garner died of his wounds. Writing for the Court, Justice Byron White held that it is unreasonable for officers to use deadly force solely to prevent the escape of a suspected criminal. Instead, officers may only use deadly force where there is "probable cause to believe that the suspect poses a significant threat of death or serious physical injury to the officer or others." Whether such probable cause exists is determined by looking at the totality of the circumstances. Among the factors courts can consider are the nature of the crime, which may inform assessments of dangerousness, other indicators of dangerousness, such as possession of a weapon, and whether the suspect is resisting arrest or merely fleeing from officers. *See* Graham v. Connor, 490 U.S. 386 (1989). In *Garner*, those factors showed that the officers' use of deadly force was unreasonable. After all, Garner was relatively slight of build, unarmed, actively trying to escape, fleeing on foot, suspected of a non-violent crime, and did not otherwise pose an immediate threat to the officers or others.

Although the Fourth Amendment governs the use of force to effect seizures of persons, courts are cautious in second-guessing the judgments of officers on the scene, who often must make split-second decisions in a moment of crisis. Courts therefore assess reasonableness of the use of force "from the perspective of a reasonable officer on the scene." Plumhoff v. Rickard, 134 S.Ct. 2012 (2014). In *Plumhoff*, Rickard led officers on a high-speed chase until he was cornered in a parking lot. In an effort to escape, Rickard drove into a patrol car and then toward officers, nearly hitting them. During this stage of the encounter, officers shot into Rickard's car, striking him and causing him to crash. Rickard died on the scene. In a subsequent civil action brought by Rickard's heir the Court held that, judged from the perspective of a reasonable officer on the scene, the use of deadly force was not unreasonable given the extreme nature of Rickard's reckless driving and the immediate threat he posed to officers. The Court further held that it was not unreasonable for officers to continue shooting into Rickard's car until the threat had terminated.

Cases like *Rickard* raise the question whether officers act unreasonably when they use more than the minimum amount of force sufficient to effect a seizure. It is tempting to think that, if officers could have engaged in a lesser use of force, then the use of greater force is by definition unreasonable. As the Court made clear in *Harris*, however, the availability of less forceful alternatives does not necessarily mean that the force actually used was unreasonable. In that case, Victor Harris led officers on a sustained high-speed chase after being caught speeding and refusing to stop. In an effort to seize Harris, Deputy Timothy Scott tapped the rear fender of Harris's car with the front bumper of his patrol car. This maneuver caused Harris's car to swerve out of control and crash. Harris was seriously injured in the crash and became a quadriplegic. In a subsequent civil action, Harris argued that the more reasonable alternative would have been for officers to terminate the chase, noting that they had his license plate number and therefore knew where to find him. Writing for the Court, Justice Antonin Scalia refused to "lay down a rule requiring the police to allow fleeing suspects to get away whenever they drive so *recklessly* that the put other people's lives in danger." He instead focused on whether, under the rules set forth in *Garner* and *Graham*, the officers acted reasonably in light of the threat to officers and the public posed by Harris's reckless driving. Taking into account the totality of the circumstances, Justice Scalia had no difficulty holding that the officers did not act unreasonably by using force in an "attempt to terminate a dangerous high-speed car chase that threatens the lives of innocent bystanders."

The need to use deadly force may sometimes arise in part due to the unconstitutional conduct of officers. For example, in *City of Los Angeles, California v. Mendez*, 137 S.Ct. 1539 (2017), officers effected an illegal entry of Mendez's home. Mendez was asleep when they entered and rose from his bed with a BB gun, which he used to shoot rats. Seeing the gun, officers shot Mendez, injuring him severely. In a subsequent civil action, Mendez alleged that the officers' illegal entry provoked his response, rendering unreasonable their subsequent use of force. The Supreme Court rejected the notion that prior illegal action always renders unreasonable law enforcement's use of force as an encounter evolves, preferring instead to focus on the circumstances facing officers at the time they engage in the use of force.

What You Need to Know:

1. The use of force to effect a search or seizure is governed by the Fourth Amendment.

2. When assessing the reasonableness of force used to effect a search or seizure, courts ask whether, on a totality of the circumstances, the officers' conduct struck a reasonable balance between the individual's Fourth Amendment interests and the interests of officers and the public.

3. The use of deadly force to effect a seizure is governed by the same principles limiting the use of deadly force in cases of self-defense and defense of others. Under these rules, officers may only use deadly force where there is "probable cause to

believe that the suspect poses a significant threat of death or serious physical injury to the officer or others."

4. When assessing the reasonableness of an officer's use of force, courts view the situation from the point of view of a reasonable officer on the scene at the time of the incident, taking into account the fact that officers in such situations often must make split-second decisions.
5. The availability of less forceful alternatives does not necessarily render an officer's use of force unreasonable.

LESSON 19: STOPS & FRISKS

As the Court has made clear time and again, the "touchstone" of the Fourth Amendment is reasonableness. Reasonableness is achieved by striking a balance between the privacy and security interests of those who are searched and seized and government interests, including public safety, law enforcement safety, and preventing, detecting, and prosecuting crime. Although the Court has expressed a preference for prior review by a magistrate, it has also recognized that requiring judicial approval before every search and seizure can unreasonably compromise government interests. For example, it has granted law enforcement officers broad license to effect arrests in public when they have probable cause to believe that the arrestee is committing or has committed a crime. In *Terry v. Ohio*, 392 U.S. 1 (1968), the Court relied on this balancing of interests approach to justify the use of stops and frisks.

In *Terry*, Detective Martin McFadden was patrolling downtown Cleveland in plainclothes when he observed two men, John Terry and Richard Chilton, as they appeared to reconnoiter a store. At some point, they were joined by a third man, Carl Katz. Based on their behavior and over forty years of law enforcement experience, Detective McFadden believed that the men were preparing to rob the store. He therefore approached the three suspects, identified himself, and asked for their names. When they mumbled a response, McFadden grabbed Terry, spun him around, and patted down his outer clothing in order to determine whether he was armed. During that pat down, McFadden found a pistol in Terry's overcoat. Terry subsequently was convicted on charges of carrying a concealed firearm.

Before the Supreme Court, Terry argued that McFadden did not have the probable cause necessary to justify seizing him and searching him. Although the Court agreed that McFadden had seized and searched Terry, it disagreed that the seizure and search in question required probable cause. Citing government interests in crime control and the need to provide officers with the tools they need to deal effectively with "the rapidly unfolding and often dangerous situations on city streets," the Court held that officers may stop suspects based on reasonable suspicion of criminal wrongdoing. During a stop, the Court held, officers may take investigative steps reasonably calculated to confirm or dispel their suspicions. The Court further held that, in the course of a stop, officers may frisk suspects and their personal effects based on reasonable suspicion that the suspect is armed and poses a potential danger. These frisks are limited to pat downs of a suspect's outer clothing and cursory examination of their effects to search for weapons.

The *Terry* Court endorsed the power of law enforcement officers to conduct limited seizures and limited searches on less than probable cause in order to address the demands and threats of circumstances as they develop during evolving encounters on the street. That holding raised some definitional questions. For example, what is necessary to establish "reasonable suspicion"? What marks the line between casual encounters, which are not subject to Fourth Amendment regulation, and stops, which are? Where, in turn, should we mark the line between stops, which are justified on reasonable suspicion, and arrests, which require probable cause? Similarly, what marks the line between visual inspections not governed by the Fourth Amendment and frisks? And what is the line between frisks, which are justified on reasonable suspicion, and searches that require probable cause?

Reasonable suspicion for a stop exists when, on a totality of the circumstances, there exists objective basis to suspect that a person has engaged, is engaging, or is about to engage in a crime. *See* United States v. Cortez, 449 U.S. 411 (1981). Similarly, reasonable suspicion for a frisk exists when, on a totality of the circumstances, there exists objective basis to suspect that a person is armed and poses a danger. Officers "must be able to articulate something more than an inchoate and unparticularized suspicion or hunch," but the level of certainty required for a stop or frisk is "less demanding than that for probable cause." United States v. Sokolow, 490 U.S. 1 (1989).

Although the level of certainty demanded by reasonable suspicion is less than for probable cause, the two standards often implicate the same considerations. For example, the uncorroborated statements of an anonymous informant absent a sufficient showing of credibility and basis of knowledge are not enough to establish reasonable suspicion for a stop. *See* Florida v. J.L., 529 U.S. 266 (2000). But the Court appeared to relax this rule somewhat in *Navarette v. California*, 134 S.Ct. 1683 (2014), holding that law enforcement may stop a motorist based on an anonymous tip reporting reckless and potentially impaired driving in light of the serious public safety concerns relating to drunk driving. Avoiding contact with law enforcement, even to the point of running away when police appear on the scene, may not, by itself, be sufficient to show reasonable suspicion. Nevertheless, "Headlong flight—wherever it occurs—is the consummate act of evasion." Illinois v. Wardlow, 528 U.S. 119 (2000). Although "it is not necessarily indicative of wrongdoing . . . it is certainly suggestive of such." Thus, attempting to flee from law enforcement may, in combination with other facts and circumstances, demonstrate reasonable suspicion.

Stops are seizures. As the Supreme Court held in *United States v. Mendenhall*, 446 U.S. 544 (1980), a person is seized whenever, "in view of all the circumstances surrounding the incident, a reasonable person would have believed that he was not free to leave." Applying that test in *Florida v. Royer*, 460 U.S. 491 (1983), the Court held that, when officers confronted Royer in the airport, told him he was under suspicion for transporting drugs, took possession of his identification and tickets, and then asked him to accompany them to a back room, he was "seized" for purposes of the Fourth Amendment. By contrast, the Court held in *Immigration and Naturalization Service v. Delgado*, 466 U.S. 210 (1984), that workers in a factory were not seized during an immigration raid because the agents were careful to leave open pathways of egress. Similarly, the Court held in *United States v. Drayton*, 536 U.S. 194 (2002), that two passengers on a bus were not seized when officers got on to ask questions about drug trafficking because, again, the officers were careful to leave an open path of egress.

As the Court held in *California v. Hodari D.*, 499 U.S. 621 (1991), a seizure is not a seizure until the person targeted is seized. In particular, a suspect who flees attempts by officers to stop him is not "seized" while he is still in flight.

The line between stops and arrests is less clear, but nevertheless important. Arrests require probable cause and also provide additional powers, including the authority to conduct a search incident to arrest. On the other hand, authority to conduct searches incident to arrest of cars are somewhat limited by *Arizona v. Gant*, 556 U.S. 332 (2009) (discussed in Lesson 12), but those limits may not apply to car frisks conducted during traffic stops under *Michigan v. Long*, 463 U.S. 1032 (1983). Although there is no clear line between stops and arrests, *see* United States v. Sharpe, 470 U.S. 675 (1985), the Court held in *Dunaway v. New York*, 442 U.S. 200 (1979), that taking custody of a suspect and transporting him to a stationhouse for interrogation bears all the hallmarks of a full custodial arrest. But the Court has held that asking for identification does not convert a stop into an arrest. *See* Hiibel v. Sixth Judicial District Court of Nevada, Humboldt City, 542 U.S. 177 (2004). In *Davis v. Mississippi*, 394 U.S. 721 (1969), the Court held that taking fingerprints, while the hallmark of custody, does not necessarily convert a stop into an arrest. Some courts have also held that a show-up identification at or near the scene of a stop does not convert the seizure into an arrest. *See, e.g.*, People v. Hicks, 68 N.Y.2d 234 (1986).

Frisks are searches. The line between conduct that is not a search and frisks is therefore marked by physical intrusion test from *United States v. Jones*, 565 U.S. 400 (2012), and the reasonable expectation of privacy test from *Katz v. United States*, 389 U.S. 347 (1967). The line between frisks and searches that require probable cause is determined by the objective purpose of the search. If the objective purpose of a search is to identify weapons, such as patting down outer clothing, then it is a frisk. If the objective purpose is to discover evidence, then it requires probable cause. For example, in *Minnesota v. Dickerson*, 508 U.S. 366 (1993), the Court held that opening a cigarette pack discovered during a frisk and investigating its contents for drugs was a search for evidence, and therefore could not be justified under *Terry*.

What You Need to Know:

1. *Terry v. Ohio,* 392 U.S. 1 (1968), established the authority of officers to conduct stops and frisks.
2. To justify stops, officers must point to specific facts and circumstances providing reasonable suspicion that the person stopped is engaged in criminal activity.
3. To justify frisks, officers must point to specific facts and circumstances providing reasonable suspicion that the person frisked is armed and poses a threat.
4. During stops, officers may take reasonable investigative steps to confirm or dispel their suspicions.
5. During frisks, officers may conduct a cursory inspection to determine the presence of weapons, but cannot engage in conduct objectively calculated to discover evidence.

LESSON 20: THE FOURTH AMENDMENT EXCLUSIONARY RULE

Those who have suffered violations of their Fourth Amendment rights have a number of options in terms of remedies. They may seek monetary compensation or injunctive relief in a civil action under 42 U.S.C. § 1983, which allows suits against agents of states, under *Bivens v. Six Unknown Named Agents of Federal Bureau of Narcotics*, 403 U.S. 388 (1971), which allows suits against federal agents, or under *Monell v. Department of Social Services of City of New York*, 436 U.S. 658 (1978), which allows suits against municipalities. The substantive and procedural law governing these actions is complex and beyond the scope of criminal procedure courses (these are civil actions, after all)—although you will often see Fourth Amendment issues decided in the context of civil actions. In the criminal procedure context, the sole remedy for violations of Fourth Amendment rights is the exclusion of evidence at trial from a prosecutor's case-in-chief.

The Fourth Amendment exclusionary rule traces to *Boyd v. United States*, 116 U.S. 616 (1886). There, the Court held that a law compelling the production of documents in revenue cases was unconstitutional under the Fourth and Fifth Amendments. The Court reasoned that compelling someone to produce documents containing incriminating information was tantamount to compelling that person to bear witness against himself, which violates the Fifth Amendment, and is also contrary to the "spirit and meaning" of the Fourth Amendment. The only way to remedy the unreasonable seizure and to prevent potential self-incrimination was, in the *Boyd* Court's view, to require that the government return the documents and to prohibit them from using at trial the contents of those documents or any knowledge gained by reviewing those documents.

Exclusion in *Boyd* was premised on the proposition that, on the facts there, "the Fourth and Fifth Amendments run almost into each other." In *Weeks v. United States*, 232 U.S. 383 (1914), the Court held that the exclusion of evidence is required even where government action violates only the Fourth Amendment. There, the Court held that evidence secured as a result of a Fourth Amendment violation must be suppressed as a matter of principle in order to give full "force and effect" to Fourth Amendment rights. As Justice Oliver Wendell Holmes would later put it, allowing the government to use illegally seized evidence at trial would reduce the Fourth Amendment to "a form of words." Silverthorne Lumber Co. v. United States, 251 U.S. 385 (1920). The *Weeks* Court was also concerned with basic fairness and worried about the government's ability to profit from its agents' wrongdoing. Finally, the Court in *Weeks* worried about judicial integrity and the possibility that, by admitting evidence seized in violation of the Fourth Amendment, courts might be seen as endorsing unconstitutional actions by executive agents.

In *Weeks*, the Court seemed to suggest that exclusion of illegally seized evidence is a personal remedy to which defendants who have suffered violations of their Fourth Amendment rights are entitled. It amplified that view in *Agnello v. United States*, 269 U.S. 20 (1925), suggesting that the admission of illegally seized evidence is itself "prejudicial" to substantial Fourth Amendment rights. Soon thereafter, the Court's reasoning in support of the exclusionary rule began to shift. For example, in *Byars v. United States*, 273 U.S. 28 (1927), the Court noted that it "must be vigilant to scrutinize the attendant facts [of police actions] with an eye to detect and a hand to prevent violations of the Constitution by circuitous and indirect methods." Exclusion and the threat of exclusion served that goal by deterring officers from engaging in unreasonable searches and seizures. This deterrence rationale reappeared in *Wolf v. Colorado*, 338 U.S. 25 (1949). There, the Court held that the Fourth Amendment is incorporated to the states through the Fourteenth Amendment. It nevertheless declined to hold that state courts are required to exclude evidence seized in violation of the Fourth Amendment, preferring to preserve space for state courts and legislatures to develop their own strategies for preventing state law enforcement agents from perpetrating Fourth Amendment violations.

The deterrence rationale assumed a more prominent place in *Elkins v. United States*, 364 U.S. 206 (1960). In that case, the Court eliminated the "silver platter doctrine," which allowed federal courts to admit evidence seized in violation of the Fourth Amendment by state law enforcement officials. Writing for the Court, Justice Potter Stewart argued that the "exclusionary rule is calculated to prevent, not to repair." At that time, many states had elected not to adopt the exclusionary rule, but others had. Justice Stewart reasoned that preserving the silver platter doctrine would compromise efforts by state courts that had adopted the exclusionary rule to supervise, discipline, and deter violations by law enforcement officers under their supervision. And, as Justice Stewart noted, those state efforts had been quite successful. For example, California courts had long refused to adopt the exclusionary rule as a remedy for Fourth Amendment violations. The California Supreme Court changed directions in *People v. Cahan*, 44 Cal.2d 434 (1955). According to Justice Stewart, the Attorney General of California reported soon after *Cahan* that the exclusionary rule had succeeded in reducing Fourth Amendment violations, in part by promoting cooperation between police and prosecutors.

The Court finally incorporated the exclusionary rule in *Mapp v. Ohio*, 367 U.S. 643 (1961). In that case, Justice Thomas Clark invoked both constitutional principle and deterrence as grounds for holding that state courts are obliged to exclude from a prosecutor's case-in-chief at trial evidence seized in violation of the Fourth Amendment. That was the last time the Court would invoke constitutional principle as a justification for the exclusionary rule. In the years after *Mapp* the Court has been consistent in holding that the sole justification for the exclusionary rule is its ability to deter officers from engaging in violations of the Fourth Amendment. *See, e.g.*, United States v. Calandra, 414 U.S. 338 (1974). As we shall see, that decision has been critical in limiting the scope and application of the exclusionary rule. The Court now measures the potential deterrence value of exclusion in particular classes of cases against the costs to society when relevant and reliable evidence is suppressed, compromising the truth-seeking function of trials and the ability of the criminal justice system to hold guilty parties responsible for their conduct.

What You Need to Know:

1. Those who suffer violations of their Fourth Amendment rights may seek compensatory and equitable relief through civil actions.
2. In the criminal context, the sole remedy for Fourth Amendment violations is the exclusionary rule.
3. The Fourth Amendment exclusionary rule was first justified by appeal to constitutional principle and the integrity of the courts.
4. In later years, the Court abandoned the principled rationale in favor of deterrence as the sole ground for exclusion in Fourth Amendment cases.

5. The Fourth Amendment exclusionary rule was made applicable to the states in *Mapp v. Ohio*, 367 U.S. 643 (1961).

LESSON 21: WHO CAN SEEK EXCLUSION AND WHEN?

The exclusionary rule is subject to a number of restraints. Among the most important are rules governing who can seek exclusion and in what contexts. Rules governing both of these questions trace to the Court's focus on deterrence as the sole justification of exclusion.

Fourth Amendment "Standing"

In *Rakas v. Illinois*, 439 U.S. 128 (1978), the Court held that only those who have suffered a violation of their *personal* Fourth Amendment rights may seek suppression of evidence. Rakas alleged that he was the target of an illegal search when officers searched a car in which he was a passenger. On that basis, he argued that he had standing under Article III of the Constitution to seek suppression of evidence seized during that search. Writing for the Court, Justice William Rehnquist clarified that the relevant question was not whether Rakas had Article III standing to seek suppression, but, rather, whether he had suffered a personal violation of his Fourth Amendment rights leading to discovery of the evidence to be suppressed. To answer that question, Justice Rehnquist turned to the definition of Fourth Amendment "search" advanced in *Katz v. United States*, 389 U.S. 347 (1967). Applying that standard, he held that Rakas could only seek suppression if the evidence was seized pursuant to a search that intruded on *his* person, *his* house, *his* papers, or *his* effects, or that otherwise violated *his* reasonable expectations of privacy. Because the car subject to search did not belong to Rakas, and because he could not otherwise establish that the search violated his reasonable expectations of privacy, the Court held that he could not seek exclusion of the evidence.

The Court's holding in *Rakas* is tied to its narrowing approach to exclusion generally. By the time it decided *Rakas*, the Court had made clear that there is no individual right to exclusion. Rather, exclusion is justified only by its potential to deter future Fourth Amendment violations. As the Court pointed out in *Rakas*, those who suffer violations of their personal Fourth Amendment rights are able to seek suppression of evidence seized as a result of those violations. In the Court's view, that threat is enough to deter officers from violating the Fourth Amendment. Any potential additional deterrence benefit that might be gained by allowing targets or others to also seek exclusion is not significant enough to justify the additional social costs in terms of the truth-seeking function of trials and the ability of the criminal justice system to hold offenders responsible for their conduct. Applying this same basic rationale, the Court has also rejected efforts by co-conspirators to seek exclusion of evidence, *Alderman v. United States*, 394 U.S. 165 (1968), and by those charged with possession crimes who argue that the possession charge itself confers automatic "standing" to seek exclusion, *United States v. Salvucci*, 448 U.S. 83 (1980). In all these cases, the Court has required those seeking to exclude evidence to show that it was seized in violation of their personal Fourth Amendment rights.

The Court's commitment to the rule promoted in *Alderman*, *Rakas*, and *Salvucci* was tested in *United States v. Payner*, 447 U.S. 727 (1980). There, agents of the Internal Revenue Service conspired amongst themselves and with civilian agents to steal bank documents in order to advance their investigation of tax avoidance schemes involving offshore banks. When a representative of one of the suspect banks was visiting the United States on business the agents arranged for him to go on a date. While he was out, a private detective working with the agents stole the banker's briefcase, took it to a locksmith, who picked the lock, and then met with agents to copy documents found in the briefcase. Some of these documents showed that Payner had been secreting funds offshore to avoid paying income taxes.

Faced with this conscious, planned violation of the Fourth Amendment, the district court granted Payner's motion to suppress the stolen documents. In granting that motion, the district court emphasized the intentional, flagrant nature of the violation and the important role of courts in deterring this sort of conduct in the future. Writing for the Supreme Court on appeal, Justice Byron White reversed. Although there was no doubt that federal agents engaged in flagrantly unconstitutional conduct, it was the banker, not Payner, whose reasonable expectations of privacy were violated when the agents searched his briefcase. Despite the fact that the documents reported on Payner's financial transactions, he had no reasonable expectation of privacy in those papers pursuant to the third party doctrine. *See* California Bankers Ass'n. v. Shultz, 416 U.S. 21 (1974).

Rules governing who can seek exclusion of evidence put a premium on determining whose reasonable expectations of privacy have been violated. Certainly, anyone whose person, house, paper, or effect is subject to unlawful search can seek exclusion. So too can people who have significant and sustained personal connections to a house, paper, or effect. For example, in *Minnesota v. Olson*, 495 U.S. 91 (1990), the Court held that an overnight social guest has a reasonable expectation of privacy in the home. Contrariwise, the Court held in *Minnesota v. Carter*, 525 U.S. 83 (1998), that individuals who were only in a home for a couple of hours and solely for business purposes (specifically, packaging cocaine for sale) could not establish a personal expectation of privacy in the premises. Together, these cases suggest that duration and purpose are key factors in determining whether someone has a reasonable expectation of privacy in a home. Visitors who stay overnight or come-by frequently are more likely to have established a reasonable expectation of privacy than short-term visitors who are merely present at the time of a search. Likewise, those on a premises for social purposes are more likely to have a reasonable expectation of privacy than those present for business purposes—particularly when the business in question is criminal in nature.

Ownership is neither necessary nor sufficient to establish a reasonable expectation of privacy in a premises or effect. For example, the lawful tenant of a rental apartment has a reasonable expectation of privacy in that apartment, which is regarded as her "house." By contrast, the landlord who owns her apartment does not. Similarly, the lawful occupant of a hotel room has a reasonable expectation of privacy in that hotel room. *See* Johnson v. United States, 333 U.S. 10 (1948). But the hotelier whose owns the facility probably does not. And the lawful possessor of a rental car would have a reasonable expectation of privacy in that car, even if he is not listed on the rental agreement, while the company that owned and rented the car probably would not. *See* Byrd v. United States, 138 S.Ct. 1518 (2018).

What You Need to Know:

1. In order to seek exclusion of evidence, a defendant must establish that the agents conducted an unconstitutional search of her person, house, paper, or effect, or that the search otherwise violated her personal expectations of privacy.
2. Being the target of a search or present on the scene of a search does not automatically confer "standing" to challenge the constitutionality of a search or to seek the exclusion of evidence.
3. Overnight guests and other long-term social guests may have sufficient connections to establish a reasonable expectation of privacy in a home.
4. Ownership of a house or effect is neither necessary nor sufficient to establish a reasonable expectation of privacy.

LESSON 22: THE FRUIT OF THE POISONOUS TREE DOCTRINE AND THE CAUSE REQUIREMENT

The exclusionary rule extends not only to the evidence discovered and seized during an unlawful search, but also to evidence discovered as a result of that illegality. *See* Wong Sun v. United States, 371 U.S. 471 (1963). This is sometimes described as the fruit of the poisonous tree doctrine. When determining whether evidence is fruit of the poisonous tree courts ask whether it has been secured "by exploitation" of an illegal search. Brown v. Illinois, 422 U.S. 590 (1975). To determine whether evidence has been found by exploitation of an illegal search courts consider many of the same factors relevant to determining cause in the criminal law and torts contexts, including whether the illegal search **in fact** led to discovery of the evidence, **temporal proximity** between the illegal search and discovery of the evidence, and any **intervening events or actors**. Consistent with its focus on exclusion as a tool for deterring future violations, courts also consider how **flagrantly** government agents exploited the illegal search or seizure to advance their investigation.

In *Hudson v. Michigan*, 547 U.S. 586 (2006), the Court relied in part on the cause in fact requirement to hold that the exclusionary rule is not available to remedy knock and announce violations. There, officers were serving a lawful warrant to search Hudson's home for drugs and firearms. Although they knocked and announced their presence, they effected a forceful entry before providing sufficient time for those on the premises to collect themselves and answer the door. Lower courts found that this premature entry violated Hudson's Fourth Amendment rights but, pursuant to a state-court appellate rule, denied his motion to suppress evidence discovered in his home. Writing for the Supreme Court, Justice Antonin Scalia affirmed. Among other considerations, Justice Scalia highlighted the fact that the officers had a lawful warrant and therefore the right to enter and search Hudson's home. Although they may have entered a few moments earlier than the Fourth Amendment allowed, that violation in no way caused the discovery and seizure of the evidence.

Wong Sun shows the role of time and intervening agents in determining the causal connection between a Fourth Amendment violation and the discovery of evidence. There, law enforcement agents illegally seized and arrested Wong Sun. Wong Sun was then arraigned and released. Several days later, he returned to the police station on his own initiative and made incriminating statements. At trial, Wong Sun sought to exclude those statements as fruits of his illegal arrest. "On the evidence that Wong Sun had been released on his own recognizance after a lawful arraignment, and had returned voluntarily several days later to make the statement," the Court held that "the connection between the arrest and the statement had become so attenuated as to dissipate the taint." Of course time was not the only factor at issue in *Wong Sun*. He also voluntarily returned to the police station after having been released from custody. In the Court's view that free-willed act broke the causal chain, removing the taint of the initial violation. By contrast, in *Dunaway v. New York*, 442 U.S. 200 (1979), the Court held that a confession given after a period of continuous custody should be suppressed, even though the suspect had been given his *Miranda* warnings.

In line with the rule that the independent acts of free willed agents will break the causal chain between an illegal search or seizure and the discovery of evidence, courts are often loath to suppress the testimony of third party witnesses. *See* United States v. Ceccolini, 435 U.S. 268 (1978). Even where law enforcement only discovered the witness as the result of an illegal search or seizure, the decision of the witness to testify usually breaks the causal chain.

The Court elaborated on the role of intervening events in assessing the causal connection between a Fourth Amendment violation and the discovery of evidence in *Utah v. Strieff*, 136 S.Ct. 2056 (2016). There, officers observed Strieff leaving a suspected drug house. Based solely on that evidence, an officer stopped Strieff. During the course of that stop, the officer asked for his identification and discovered that there was an outstanding warrant for his arrest. Relying on that warrant, the officer arrested Strieff and, pursuant to a search incident to that arrest, discovered drugs and paraphernalia on his person. At trial, Strieff argued that the initial stop was not supported by reasonable suspicion and that the drugs and paraphernalia should be suppressed as fruits of that poisonous tree. The trial court denied his motion but the Utah Supreme Court later reversed. Writing for the United States Supreme Court, Justice Clarence Thomas held that the existence of the outstanding warrant, which was in no way related to the illegal stop, served as an intervening event that broke the causal chain initiated by the illegal stop.

Prosecutors may also seek to avoid the exclusion of evidence by showing that officers did not exploit an illegal search or seizure in order to advance their investigation. This is often accomplished by showing that the officers inevitably would have discovered the evidence in question regardless of their illegal conduct or by showing that the officers gained access to the evidence through an independent path untainted by illegal conduct.

Nix v. Williams, 467 U.S. 431 (1984), is the standard case cited for the inevitable discovery doctrine. There, Williams was suspected in the disappearance of a 10-year-old girl. After he was arraigned and had asserted his right to counsel, officers cajoled Williams into revealing the location of the missing girl's body. That questioning violated Williams's Fifth and Sixth Amendment rights to counsel, potentially triggering an exclusionary rule that would have barred admission of the victim's body from evidence at trial. Writing for the Court, Chief Justice Warren Burger held that the body need not be suppressed. Investigators had already undertaken a careful search of areas where Williams was likely to have disposed of his victim's body. Following their search protocols, the searchers inevitably would have found her body in short order. Although it was relatively clear that the officers acted in bad faith when they questioned Williams, Chief Justice Burger held that the fact of inevitable discovery cleansed the taint of their offense by showing that they did not ultimately exploit their unconstitutional conduct to find the girl's body.

Murray v. United States, 487 U.S. 533 (1988), provides a useful example of the independent source doctrine in action. There, officers effected an illegal entry of a warehouse they suspected was the hub of a drug operation. Once inside, they observed several bales of marijuana. Rather than immediately seize the drugs, the officers withdrew and applied for a warrant to search the premises. The officers were careful not to cite any evidence in their warrant application gained as a result of their illegal entry. That warrant application was granted, providing officers lawful authority to reenter the building, where they rediscovered the marijuana. Writing for the Court, Justice Antonin Scalia held that the warranted search, which in no way exploited the illegal entry, provided an independent source of discovery, thereby erasing any taint from the initial Fourth Amendment violation.

What You Need to Know:

1. Under the fruit of the poisonous tree doctrine, the exclusionary rule extends to all evidence discovered and seized as the result of a Fourth Amendment violation.
2. Evidence is not regarded as fruit of the poisonous tree unless it would not have been discovered or seized "but for" the illegality.
3. Evidence is not regarded as fruit of the poisonous tree if the passage of time, intervening events, or intervening agents break the causal chain between an illegal search and the discovery and seizure of evidence.
4. Evidence is not regarded as fruit of the poisonous tree if officers do not exploit an illegal search to discover and seize evidence.

LESSON 23: GOOD FAITH AND PROCEDURAL CONSTRAINTS ON THE EXCLUSIONARY RULE

The warrant process provides important substantive and procedural constraints on the discretion of law enforcement agents to conduct searches and seizures. By design, searches conducted pursuant to a warrant should be justified by probable cause and the warrant itself should conform to the formalities dictated by the particularity requirement. Sometimes, however, mistakes are made. Warrants sometimes are issued on evidence insufficient to establish probable cause. Some warrants are defective due to ministerial or clerical errors. Searches conducted pursuant to deficient warrants may, by virtue of those deficiencies, be unlawful. But should evidence discovered and seized as a result of these illegal searches be suppressed?

In *United States v. Leon*, 468 U.S. 897 (1984), the Court held that exclusion serves no purpose where officers have acted in good faith by securing a warrant and scrupulously respecting that warrant. Writing for the Court, Justice Byron White pointed out that there is no deterrence to be achieved by punishing officers who engage in good faith efforts to respect the warrant process. After all, these are officers who, by virtue of their good faith efforts, have demonstrated their respect for the substantive and procedural demands of the Fourth Amendment. Moreover, because they are acting in good faith, they have no reason to feel the threat of potential suppression as a modifying force. Threats of punishment do not deter those who honestly and reasonably believe they are not doing anything wrong.

In *Herring v. United States*, 555 U.S. 135 (2009), the Court extended its reasoning in *Leon* to hold that exclusion is only appropriate in cases where officers have engaged in an intentional, knowing, or reckless violation of the Fourth Amendment. Writing for the Court, Chief Justice John Roberts reasoned that we can only expect the threat of exclusion to modify behavior in cases where the officers have engaged in some level of culpable misconduct. Although imposing exclusion without regard to culpability might enhance the overall deterrent effect of the exclusionary rule, the Chief Justice concluded that these marginal gains would not outweigh the considerable additional costs to truth-seeking. The only potential exception might be cases of systemic negligence, where exclusion can motivate policy changes necessary to minimize the future risk of Fourth Amendment violations.

The Court has applied this reasoning to withhold exclusion in cases where officers rely on arrest warrants that later turn out to have been vacated, *see* Herring v. United States, 555 U.S. 135 (2009) and Arizona v. Evans, 514 U.S. 1 (1995), legislation that is later held to be unconstitutional, *see* Illinois v. Krull, 480 U.S. 340 (1987), and established appellate court decisions, *see* Davis v. United States, 564 U.S. 229 (2011). The Court has also withheld exclusion in cases of searches conducted pursuant to warrants that contain ministerial errors, such as failures to properly incorporate an underlying affidavit, *see* Massachusetts v. Sheppard, 468 U.S. 981 (1984), entering a description of the place to be searched in the area of the warrant reserved for descriptions of the evidence to be seized, *see* Groh v. Ramirez, 540 U.S. 551 (2004), and where a warrant is too general as to the place to be searched (so long as the officers took all reasonable steps to meet the requirements of the Fourth Amendment), *see* Maryland v. Garrison, 480 U.S. 79 (1987).

Consistent with the deterrence rationale for the exclusionary rule, officers cannot claim good faith where they have engaged in culpable manipulations of the warrant process. For example, if officers lie by commission or omission when applying for a warrant, then they have not acted in good faith. *See, e.g.*, United States v. Vigeant, 176 F.3d 565 (1st Cir. 1999). Similarly, officers cannot claim good faith if they execute a warrant so insufficient when measured by well-established Supreme Court precedent that no reasonable officer would have relied on it. The Court has also been reluctant to accept a claim of good faith where the issuing magistrate was demonstrably not neutral, such as when the judge joins in the search. *See* Lo-Ji Sales, Inc. v. New York, 442 U.S. 319 (1979).

In keeping with its view of the exclusionary rule as a deterrent, the Court has also limited the procedural contexts in which it applies. In general, the exclusionary rule applies only to the prosecutor's case-in-chief. In the Court's view, the threat of excluding evidence from a prosecutor's case-in-chief at a criminal trial is sufficient to deter officers from engaging in culpable violations of the Fourth Amendment. Extending the reach of exclusion does not generate sufficient additional deterrence to justify the added costs to truth-seeking. For example, barring a prosecutor from using illegally seized evidence to cross-examine a defendant who chooses to testify at trial would issue a license to lie without adding much in terms of deterrent threat. *See* United States v. Havens, 446 U.S. 620 (1980); Walder v. United States, 347 U.S. 62 (1954).

Applying this same reasoning, the Court has held that illegally seized evidence is admissible in grand jury proceedings, *see* United States v. Calandra, 414 U.S. 338 (1974), civil tax proceedings, *see* United States v. Janis, 428 U.S. 433 (1976), civil deportation proceedings, *see* Immigration and Naturalization Service v. Lopez-Mendoza, 468 U.S. 1032 (1984), habeas and other collateral review proceedings, *see* Stone v. Powell, 428 U.S. 465 (1976), parole revocation and enforcement hearings, *see* Parole Board v. Scott, 524 U.S. 357 (1998), and sentencing proceedings, *see* United States v. Tejada, 956 F.2d 1256 (2d Cir. 1992).

What You Need to Know:

1. The exclusionary rule does not apply where officers have acted in "good faith."
2. The good faith exception applies when officers rely on a warrant issued by a detached and neutral magistrate that turns out to be defective or improvidently granted.
3. Courts generally will not exclude evidence unless the officers in question acted intentionally, knowingly, or recklessly, or where there is evidence of systemic negligence.
4. The exclusionary rule extends only to a prosecutor's case-in-chief. Illegally seized evidence is generally admissible for impeachment purposes and in collateral proceedings such as immigration enforcement and parole hearings.

LESSON 24: THE FIFTH AMENDMENT AND INTERROGATIONS

Two clauses of the Fifth Amendment regulate interrogations, the command that "No person shall . . . be compelled in any criminal case to be a witness against himself" and the guarantee that "No person shall . . . be deprived of life, liberty, or property, without due process of law." The limits on interrogations imposed by the Fifth Amendment have their roots in historical abuses of incommunicado interrogation by the Star Chamber and the use of torture during The Inquisition.

Due Process

In the early decades of the twentieth century, the Court struggled with how to deal with cases documenting brutal interrogation tactics by law enforcement. For example, in *Brown v. Mississippi*, 297 U.S. 278 (1936), officers repeatedly beat, whipped, and lynched suspects until they confessed. It was clear to the Court that these confessions were coerced. "It would be difficult to conceive of methods more revolting to the sense of justice than those taken to procure the confessions of these petitioners," Chief Justice Evan Hughes wrote for the Court. Rather than deciding the case based on the Fifth Amendment prohibition on compelled witnessing, however, the Court held that "the use of the confessions thus obtained as the basis for conviction and sentence was a clear denial of due process" because the tactics used by the officers produced an **involuntary confession**.

Although the Fifth Amendment prohibition on compelled witnessing has taken a more prominent role in regulating interrogations since *Miranda v. Arizona*, 384 U.S. 436 (1966), the due process clauses of the Fifth and Fourteenth Amendments remain as critical restraints on coercive interrogation tactics. For due process purposes, the question is whether, on the totality of the circumstances, the means and methods used by law enforcement in a particular case have resulted in an involuntary confession.

The Privilege Against Self-Incrimination

When applying the Fifth Amendment privilege against compelled witnessing it is necessary to determine when an utterance or other form of communication constitutes being "a witness." In *Schmerber v. California*, 384 U.S. 757 (1966), the Court held that to witness is to give "evidence of a testimonial or communicative nature." The Court narrowed that definition somewhat in *Pennsylvania v. Muniz*, 496 U.S. 582 (1990), concluding that witnessing is the product of a mental process. In that case, officers suspected Muniz of drunk driving. In order to confirm their suspicions, they asked him the date of his sixth birthday. Muniz struggled to answer, eventually responding incorrectly. The Court held that Muniz's answer to the question communicated the result of a mental process and therefore constituted being "a witness" for purposes of the Fifth Amendment. By contrast, his demeanor when attempting to answer the question, including his slurring while speaking, did not communicate the results of a mental process, and therefore was not witnessing. Applying these standards, suspects can be compelled to participate in a line-up, to provide fingerprints, and even to give a voice sample, writing sample, or to sign a records release because none of these activities communicate the product of a mental process.

The *Muniz* definition of witnessing likely excludes from Fifth Amendment protection the use of biometric identification to unlock or decrypt electronic devices such as smartphones and tablets because presenting a thumb for fingerprint recognition or a face for facial recognition does not report the results of a mental process. By contrast, compelling someone to enter a password likely is a form of witnessing.

The Fifth Amendment does not stand as an impediment to the compelled disclosure of documents that were voluntarily created. Even though documents may contain the products of mental processes, that witnessing is not "compelled" if the document was created voluntarily. *See* Fisher v. United States, 425 U.S. 391 (1976). In some cases, however, the act of producing documents can reflect the results of a mental process if, for example, it demonstrates knowledge of the documents' existence, knowledge of possession or control, or serves to authenticate the documents. *See* United States v. Doe, 465 U.S. 605 (1984). Where this is the case, the government must either immunize the act of production or seek production through another party, such as a corporate custodian or counsel. *See* Braswell v. United States, 487 U.S. 99 (1988). As the Court held in *United States v. Hubbell*, 530 U.S. 27 (2000), immunizing production is not a license to go on a fishing expedition. In order to give full effect to a grant of immunity in these circumstances, law enforcement must show prior knowledge of the documents or the criminal acts they disclose.

Fifth Amendment limits on interrogation apply only to natural persons. Corporations cannot claim a Fifth Amendment privilege against compelled witnessing. *See* Bellis v. United States, 417 U.S. 85 (1974). Of course, there are times when compelling the production of corporate documents may implicate the Fifth Amendment rights of individuals within the corporation. Where this is the case, those persons may refuse to participate in the production of documents on Fifth Amendment grounds. *See* Curcio v. United States, 354 U.S. 118 (1957).

There are some cases where individuals are required to keep records under an administrative or regulatory regime, but doing so will reveal their involvement in criminal wrongdoing. For example, in *Marchetti v. United States*, 390 U.S. 39 (1968), the defendant was engaged in illegal bookmaking, but was also required by law to pay a special tax on illegal bookmaking and to create associated documents. The Court held that putting Marchetti in this kind of catch-22 violated his Fifth Amendment privilege against compelled witnessing. This does not mean, however, that requiring someone to keep documents that might reveal criminal conduct necessarily runs afoul of the Fifth Amendment. Under the **required records rule**, an administrative or regulatory regime can require the creation of documents that may reveal criminal conduct if non-criminal participation in the scheme is possible. For example, in *Haynes v. United States*, 390 U.S. 85 (1968), the Court held that a regulation requiring the registration of sawed-off shotguns violated the Fifth Amendment because the possession of these shotguns was illegal. That result probably would have been different if the regulation required the registration of all shotguns, including those legal to possess.

What You Need to Know:

1. The Fifth Amendment prohibition on compelled witnessing and the Fifth Amendment guarantee of due process regulate law enforcement conduct during interrogations.
2. Due process bars law enforcement officers from engaging in conduct that produces involuntary confessions.
3. The Fifth Amendment privilege against compelled witnessing applies only to natural persons. It does not protect corporations.
4. To be a "witness" for purposes of the Fifth Amendment privilege against compelled witnessing is to report the result of a mental process.
5. The Fifth Amendment privilege against compelled witnessing does not apply to documents voluntarily created unless the act of production constitutes a form of witnessing.

LESSON 25: *MIRANDA V. ARIZONA*

Through the first half of the twentieth century, the Supreme Court continued to regulate police interrogations using the due process clauses of the Fifth and Fourteenth Amendments. Despite these efforts, reports persisted of police abuses in the context of interrogations. For example, the 1931 National Commission on Law Observance and Enforcement Report on Lawlessness in Law Enforcement documented the pervasive use of "third degree" type interrogation tactics and a 1961 Civil Rights Commission report showed that many officers still resorted to physical abuse and torture to secure confessions. By mid-century, the Court had become concerned as well with more broadly sanctioned psychological methods. As the Court reported in *Miranda v. Arizona*, 384 U.S. 436 (1966), "coercion can be mental as well as physical . . . the blood of the accused is not the only hallmark of an unconstitutional inquisition."

Writing for the Court in *Miranda*, Chief Justice Earl Warren described the basic stratagems that had become common currency in custodial interrogations. Relying on interrogation manuals widely used by law enforcement, Chief Justice Warren identified seclusion as the "principal psychological factor contributing to a successful interrogation." Officers were encouraged by these manuals to control when and where interrogations take place, to deprive subjects of "every psychological advantage," and to deny access to family, friends, and other sources of "moral support." Officers were instructed to project absolute control and "to display an air of confidence in the suspect's guilt and, from outward appearance, to maintain only an interest in confirming certain details." Officers were further instructed to offer possible excuses that might "minimize the moral seriousness of the offense" in order to "put the subject in a psychological state where his story is but an elaboration of what the police purport to know already—that he is guilty. Explanations to the contrary are dismissed and discouraged." Where these tactics failed, officers were instructed to resort to trickery or simply to wear suspects down by relying "on an oppressive atmosphere of dogged persistence." Interrogators were encouraged to pursue confessions "steadily and without relent, leaving the subject no prospect of surcease . . . [to]

dominate his subject and overwhelm him with his inexorable will to obtain the truth." These manuals imagined interrogations that could continue this way "for days," with minimal attention to the requirements of due process, "but with no respite from the atmosphere of domination." "It is possible in this way," officers were told, "to induce the subject to talk without resorting to duress or coercion." If a suspect indicated that he did not want to talk, interrogators were instructed to advise him that declining to answer questions indicated guilt. If a suspect asked to speak with an attorney, officers were told to opine on the expense such a request would entail to the suspect and his family and to point out that involving an attorney would just complicate the pursuit of truth.

Summarizing its findings, the *Miranda* Court identified the "essence" of police interrogation tactics: seclusion and control.

> [T]o be alone with the subject is essential to prevent distraction and to deprive him of any outside support. The aura of confidence in his guilt undermines his will to resist. He merely confirms the preconceived story the police seek to have him describe. Patience and persistence, at times relentless questioning, are employed. To obtain a confession, the interrogator must "patiently maneuver himself or his quarry into a position from which the desired objective may be attained." When normal procedures fail to produce the needed result, the police may resort to deceptive stratagems such as giving false legal advice. It is important to keep the subject off balance, for example, by trading on his insecurity about himself or his surroundings. The police then persuade, trick, or cajole him out of exercising his constitutional rights.

Even "without employing brutality, the 'third degree' or the[se] specific stratagems," the *Miranda* Court worried that "the very fact of custodial interrogation exacts a heavy toll on individual liberty, and trades on the weakness of individuals." It therefore held that custodial interrogations, by their very nature, raise concerns that suspects may be compelled to make statements that could later be admitted against them at trial. Faced with credible concerns of pervasive violations of the Fifth

Amendment privilege against compelled witnessing, the Court had a choice. It could either bar custodial interrogations altogether or it could prescribe a prophylactic means to dispel the inherently coercive atmosphere inherent to custodial interrogations. Famously, it chose the latter course.

After *Miranda*, statements taken from a suspect during a custodial interrogation are assumed to be "compelled." In order to avoid violations of the Fifth Amendment privilege against compelled witnessing, a prosecutor cannot use those statements against a suspect during her case-in-chief at trial. In order to avoid that presumption of compulsion, interrogators must advise suspects that they have the right to remain silent, that anything they say can and will be used against them at trial, that they have a right to consult with counsel before and during police questioning, and that an attorney will be provided for suspects who do not have or cannot afford one. If a suspect invokes his right to remain silent or his right to an attorney, then all questioning must stop. But, if a suspect voluntarily, knowingly, and intelligently waives his right to remain silent and his right to an attorney, then the presumption of compulsion is lifted.

If police interrogators fail to inform a suspect of his rights under *Miranda* before commencing with custodial questioning, then any statements made will be suppressed at trial. Officers may seek to "cure" such a situation by advising a suspect of his rights and seeking a waiver. *See* Missouri v. Seibert, 542 U.S. 600 (2004). Such attempts to cure may be deemed insufficient, however, if there is evidence that the violation reflects a practice or policy, or if there is other evidence that the officers violated the suspect's *Miranda* rights in bad faith.

The *Miranda* opinion was highly controversial in 1966. Law enforcement officers worried that it would mark an end to their ability to secure confessions, dramatically compromising crime control and public safety. Critics also denied the Court's claimed constitutional authority to impose procedures on law enforcement. In response to these complaints, Congress passed what would become 18 U.S.C. § 3501 in 1968 with the expressed purpose of overruling *Miranda* and reverting to the same test of voluntariness based on a totality of the circumstances elaborated by the Court in its due process cases. That set up a constitutional showdown, which eventually came to pass in *Dickerson v. United States*, 530 U.S. 428 (2000). Writing for the Court in that case, Chief Justice William Rehnquist made clear that *Miranda* is a constitutional decision, and therefore immune from legislative override. With respect to the prophylactic measures prescribed in *Miranda*, Chief Justice Rehnquist pointed out that they are minimal measures designed to resolve the Fifth Amendment concerns that inhere to custodial interrogations. The invitation remains open for Congress or a state legislature to come forward with alternative means sufficient to dispel the inherently coercive atmosphere of custodial interrogations. Absent such an alternative, the *Dickerson* Court maintained that officers seeking to admit in a prosecutor's case-in-chief at trial statements made during a custodial interrogation must abide by the Court's directions in *Miranda*.

In *Arizona v. Fulminate*, 499 U.S. 279 (1991), the Court held that due process remains as an independent source of constraint on police interrogations. Abiding the *Miranda* prophylaxis is a factor that suggests voluntariness, but it is not determinative of the due process question. Likewise, failing to abide the *Miranda* prophylaxis might raise concerns with regard to voluntariness, but falls well short of deciding the due process question.

What You Need to Know:

1. In *Miranda v. Arizona*, the Court held that custodial interrogations create an inherently coercive atmosphere that implicates the Fifth Amendment privilege against compelled witnessing.
2. In order to dispel that inherently coercive atmosphere, the *Miranda* Court prescribed a prophylactic procedure in which suspects are advised of their right to remain silent, that any statements will be used against them at trial, that they have a right to consult an attorney before and during questioning, and that an attorney will be provided to them if they cannot afford one.

3. If a suspect invokes his right to silence or his right to counsel, then all questioning must stop.
4. If a suspect voluntarily, knowingly, and intelligently waives his right to remain silent and his right to counsel, then any statements he makes during a custodial interrogation are admissible at trial so long as they are made voluntarily.
5. As the Court made clear in *Dickerson v. United States*, its holding in *Miranda* was grounded in the Fifth Amendment, and therefore cannot be overturned by statute; but the invitation remains open for legislatures and law enforcement to adopt alternative prophylactic means sufficient to meet the Court's constitutional concerns.

LESSON 26: CUSTODY, INTERROGATION, AND PUBLIC SAFETY

The protections afforded under *Miranda v. Arizona* apply only in the context of custodial interrogations. Statements not made in custodial circumstances or in response to interrogation do not implicate the Fifth Amendment privilege against compelled witnessing. Likewise, officers have no obligation to advise a suspect of his *Miranda* rights unless the suspect is being subjected to interrogation while in custody. Given these limits, it is important to provide clear guidance for officers on what constitutes "custody" and "interrogation" for Fifth Amendment purposes.

Miranda Custody

The *Miranda* Court defined "custodial interrogation" as "questioning initiated by law enforcement officers after a person has been taken into custody or otherwise deprived of his freedom of action in any significant way." That definition of custody is quite close to the "free to leave" test for Fourth Amendment "seizures" of persons discussed in Lesson 19. But, as the Court made clear in *Berkemer v. McCarty*, 468 U.S. 420 (1984), *Terry* stops fall short of "custody" for purposes of *Miranda*. *Terry* stops do not generate the kind of "inherently coercive atmosphere" characteristic of the incommunicado interrogations at issue in

Miranda. In addition, the nature of questioning during a *Terry* stop is more limited. Together, these considerations suggest that seizure combined with seclusion and investigative questioning are the hallmarks of "custodial interrogation."

Whether a suspect is in "custody" for purposes of *Miranda* is determined from an objective point of view. In general, the subjective perceptions of a suspect and his peculiar characteristics are not relevant. For example, in *Colorado v. Connelly*, 479 U.S. 157 (1986), the Court held that a suspect's mental disease was not relevant to assessing his custodial status, at least where those conditions were not known by or obvious to the officers on the scene. But, as the Court held in *J.D.B. v. North Carolina*, 564 U.S. 261 (2011), conditions affecting a suspect's perceptions may be relevant to assessing custodial status where those conditions are known to officers or are otherwise obvious. In that case, officers questioned a 13-year-old burglary suspect at his school in the company of a uniformed school security officer and members of the school's administrative staff. Although an adult in similar circumstances may not have been in "custody" for *Miranda* purposes, Justice Sonia Sotomayor held for the Court that children are different, and "to ignore the very real differences between children and adults would be to deny children the full scope of the procedural safeguards that *Miranda* guarantees to adults."

The paradigm for *Miranda* custody is arrest and seclusion in a police station. That does not mean that all questioning occurring in a police station is "custodial," however. In particular, if a suspect comes to a police station voluntarily in order to answer questions, then the Court has been reluctant to find that he is in "custody" for Miranda purposes. *See* California v. Beheler, 463 U.S. 1121 (1983). Similarly, if a suspect is told that he is not under arrest and is therefore free to leave at any time, then he is likely not in "custody." *See* Oregon v. Mathiason, 429 U.S. 492 (1977). The situation may be complicated somewhat if the suspect in question is on parole or supervised release, and therefore may believe that he is required to cooperate with police requests for an interview. But, as the Court held in *Minnesota v. Murphy*, 465 U.S. 420 (1984), parolee status is but one factor to consider when assessing whether a suspect is in "custody."

One might assume that someone who is in prison is by definition in "custody" for purposes of *Miranda*. But, as the Court held in *Howes v. Fields*, 565 U.S. 499 (2012), someone who lives in custodial circumstances is not necessarily in "custody" for *Miranda*. In that case, Randall Fields was serving a jail sentence when he was escorted by corrections officers from his cell to a conference room where police officers asked him questions about an offense separate from his crime of incarceration. Although there was no doubt that Fields's incarceration deprived him of freedom of action, the Court held that he was not in Miranda custody because he was told by the officers that he was free to return to his cell at any time. *See also* Maryland v. Shatzer, 559 U.S. 98 (2010).

Miranda Interrogation

The Court defined "interrogation" for *Miranda* purposes in *Rhode Island v. Innis*, 446 U.S. 291 (1980). There, officers arrested Innis soon after he perpetrated a robbery with a sawed-off shotgun. Innis was unarmed when he was arrested, so officers were keen to find his gun. Officers on the scene advised Innis of his *Miranda* rights several times. Innis asked to speak with a lawyer, at which point the supervising police captain on the scene instructed two officers to transport Innis back to the station, but not to question him in any way. During the trip, one of the officers opined to the other on how the missing firearm posed a danger to the public, and in particular to students at a nearby school for "handicapped children" who "might hurt themselves" if they found Innis's gun. Hearing this conversation, Innis asked to return to the scene so he could show officers where to find his gun. Innis was again advised of his rights under *Miranda*, but he stated that he "wanted to get the gun out of the way because of the kids in the area in the school."

Although there was little doubt that these officers engaged in conduct they hoped might generate an incriminating response, Justice Potter Stewart, writing for the Court, held that their conduct did not constitute "interrogation" for purposes of *Miranda*. Reviewing the *Miranda* opinion, Justice Stewart emphasized the Court's concerns with officers' exploiting the inherently coercive atmosphere of custodial interrogation. In light of these concerns, Justice Stewart held that "Interrogation . . . must reflect a measure of compulsion above and beyond that inherent in custody itself." In particular, "interrogation" occurs when "a person in custody is subjected either to express questioning or its functional equivalent," including "any words or actions on the part of the police (other than those normally attendant to arrest and custody) that the police should know are reasonably likely to elicit an incriminating response from the suspect." Because the officers did not directly question Innis, and because they had no reason to think that their brief dialogue would produce an incriminating statement, Justice Stewart held that Innis had not been subjected to "interrogation" for purposes of *Miranda*.

Applying the rule from *Innis*, the Court has held that putting a husband and wife, both of whom were under arrest and had invoked their right to counsel, into the same room and recording their conversation was not "interrogation" for purposes of *Miranda*. That is because neither suspect was acting as a police agent, and therefore could not engage in an "interrogation." Similarly, in *Illinois v. Perkins*, 496 U.S. 292 (1990), the Court held that questioning performed by an undercover officer posing as a fellow prisoner does not constitute "custodial interrogation" under *Miranda* because such questioning does not generate the inherently coercive atmosphere characteristic of custodial interrogation.

The Public Safety Exception

Although *Miranda* governs most instances of custodial interrogation, the Court carved out a narrow public safety exception in *New York v. Quarles*, 467 U.S. 649 (1984). In that case, officers arrested Quarles and discovered an empty gun holster on his person during a subsequent search incident to arrest. Concerned about the potential presence of an unsecured firearm, the arresting officer asked Quarles for the location of the gun. Quarles told the officer where to find the gun, but later sought to suppress those statements because he had not been informed of his rights under *Miranda*. Writing for the Court, Chief Justice William Rehnquist held that questions narrowly tailored to address concerns for public safety in the context of a potential emergency are not prohibited by *Miranda*.

What You Need to Know:

1. *Miranda* applies only where a suspect is subject to custodial interrogation.
2. "Custody" for purposes of *Miranda* occurs when a suspect is "deprived of his freedom of action in any significant way."
3. Arrest and seclusion in a police station usually constitutes "custody" for Miranda purposes but *Terry* stops do not.
4. "Interrogation" for purposes of *Miranda* occurs when a suspect is "subjected either to express questioning or its functional equivalent."
5. *Miranda* does not apply in cases where officers ask questions narrowly calculated to address public safety concerns in the context of a potential emergency.

LESSON 27: INVOCATION AND WAIVER

Fifth Amendment due process rights governing police interrogations need not be invoked and cannot be waived. They stand as immovable restraints on government action. Suspects cannot consent to be tortured as a method of interrogation. By contrast, the Fifth Amendment privilege against compelled witnessing guaranteed to suspects who are subject to custodial interrogation under *Miranda v. Arizona* must be invoked and can be waived. Suspects can submit themselves to custodial interrogation.

Invocation

Any invocation of the right to remain silent or the right to counsel during a custodial interrogation must be "scrupulously honored," and all questioning must stop. *See* Michigan v. Mosley, 423 U.S. 96 (1975). To be effective, however, that invocation must be clear, affirmative, and unequivocal. Mere silence in the face of Miranda warnings is not enough to invoke the right to remain silent. *See* Berghuis v. Thompkins, 560 U.S. 370 (2010). Instead, a suspect must speak in order to invoke his right to silence.

Invocations must be clear and unequivocal. Musings and ambiguous meanderings do not constitute invocations. For example, the Court held in *Davis v. United States*, 512 U.S. 452 (1994), that a suspect's declaration that "[m]aybe I should get a lawyer" is not an invocation, and therefore does not trigger a duty on the part of officers to inquire further in order to clarify a suspect's wishes.

Waiver

Waivers of *Miranda* rights must be affirmative, voluntary, knowing, and intelligent. Best practice is for officers to secure a clear, unequivocal, and affirmative waiver before commencing a custodial interrogation. Usually this is accomplished using a standard written form. Suspects initial next to each of the *Miranda* rights printed on the form and then sign a waiver at the end if they decide to speak. Such clarity is not required, however. *See* North Carolina v. Butler, 441 U.S. 369 (1979). As the Court held in *Berghuis*, waiver can be implied if, having been apprised of his rights, a suspect engages with officers and answers questions.

Voluntariness in the context of *Miranda* waivers is determined by whether, on a totality of the circumstances, a suspect's waiver "was the product of a free and deliberate choice rather than intimidation, coercion, or deception." Berghuis v. Thompkins, 560 U.S. 370 (2010).

For a waiver to be knowing and intelligent it must be "made with a full awareness of both the nature of the right being abandoned and the consequences of the decision to abandon it." Moran v. Burbine, 475 U.S. 412 (1986). This does not mean that the defendant needs to understand all the procedural and substantive law governing his situation or the nature of law enforcement's interests or investigation. *See* Colorado v. Spring, 479 U.S. 564 (1987). Rather, what is necessary is an actual understanding of the rights and consequences described in the *Miranda* warnings.

Knowledge and intelligence are independent of voluntariness. The voluntariness requirement is aimed at constraining officers' conduct. For example, in *Colorado v. Connelly*, 479 U.S. 157 (1986), Chief Justice Rehnquist held that an officer who questioned a mentally ill suspect did not engage in conduct sufficiently coercive to raise concerns about the voluntariness of that suspect's waiver and confession. But, the Court held, that same mental illness was relevant to determining whether the suspect *actually* understood his rights and the consequences of his waiver.

If an attorney has been retained to represent a suspect, then must he be apprised of this fact for a waiver of his right to counsel under *Miranda* to be knowing and intelligent? The answer is "no." As the Court held in *Moran*, it is not necessary to inform a suspect that he actually has an attorney so long as he understands that he has the right to consult an attorney and have one present during questioning. Notably, the situation might be different if the Sixth Amendment right to counsel is at issue.

Scope of Waivers and Invocations

A suspect may partially waive or partially invoke his rights under *Miranda*. For example, in *Connecticut v. Barrett*, 479 U.S. 523 (1987), the suspect agreed to speak with officers but refused to give a written statement. The officers scrupulously respected those limits, but, of course, his oral statements were used against him at trial.

A suspect who invokes either his right to remain silent or his right to counsel does so with respect to all potential crimes. *See* Arizona v. Roberson, 486 U.S. 675 (1988). That is because *Miranda* rights govern custodial interrogations generally, without reference to any specific criminal investigation or process. By contrast, as we shall see in Lesson 28, invocations of the Sixth Amendment right to counsel are crime specific, tied as they are to a particular prosecution.

Reinitiating Questioning

Invocations of both the *Miranda* right to remain silent and the *Miranda* right to counsel are not permanent. If a suspect invokes his right to remain silent, then officers may reengage after a reasonable cooling off period by again advising the suspect of his rights and again seeking a voluntary, knowing, and intelligent waiver. *See* Michigan v. Mosley, 423 U.S. 96 (1975).

If a suspect invokes his *Miranda* right to counsel, then officers may not reengage to seek a waiver unless:

1. the suspect has had the opportunity to consult with counsel, *see* Edwards v. Arizona, 451 U.S. 477 (1981), and any waiver occurs in the presence of counsel, *see* Minnick v. Mississippi, 498 U.S. 146 (1990); ***or***
2. the suspect has been released from *Miranda* custody and officers wait at least fourteen days before reengaging, *see* Maryland v. Shatzer, 559 U.S. 98 (2010).

As the Court held in *Shatzer*, release from *Miranda* custody does not require release from law enforcement custody. In that case, Shatzer was incarcerated while serving his sentence on a separate conviction, but was released from *Miranda* custody when he returned to the general prison population.

Regardless of whether he has invoked his right to remain silent or his right to counsel under *Miranda*, a suspect is always free to reconsider, reinitiate his engagement with officers, and waive his rights. For example, in *Oregon v. Bradshaw*, 462 U.S. 1039 (1983), the suspect in a motor vehicle homicide invoked his right to counsel. Later, while being transferred from the police station to jail, the suspect asked officers "what is going to happen to me now?" Writing for the Court, Justice Lewis Powell held that this provided sufficient grounds for the officers to engage with the suspect and seek a waiver.

What You Need to Know:

1. Invocations of *Miranda* rights must be clear, affirmative, and unequivocal.
2. Waivers of *Miranda* rights must be affirmative, voluntary, knowing, and intelligent.

3. Invocations of either the right to remain silent or the right to counsel under *Miranda* must be scrupulously honored and all questioning must stop.
4. Suspects may reinitiate their engagements with law enforcement any time after invoking either the *Miranda* right to remain silent or the *Miranda* right to counsel.
5. After an invocation of the right to remain silent, officers may reinitiate their engagement with a suspect and seek a waiver after a reasonable cooling off period.
6. After invocation of the *Miranda* right to counsel, officers may only reinitiate their engagement with a suspect and seek a waiver in the presence of counsel or after the suspect has been released from *Miranda* custody for at least fourteen days.

LESSON 28: SIXTH AMENDMENT RIGHT TO COUNSEL

The Sixth Amendment to the United States Constitution guarantees that "In all criminal prosecutions, the accused shall . . . have the Assistance of Counsel for his defence." The Sixth Amendment right to counsel traditionally was understood as a trial right. That interpretation made sense in eras when there were no professionalized paramilitary police forces charged with investigating crimes. As law enforcement agencies with investigative authority and powers emerged and expanded through the late nineteenth and twentieth century, so too did the Court's understanding of the scope of protections afforded by the Sixth Amendment right to counsel. For example, in *Powell v. Alabama*, 287 U.S. 45 (1932), the Court held that criminal defendants have a right to counsel during "the most critical proceedings against [them]," including "the time of their arraignment until the beginning of their trial, when consultation, thoroughgoing investigation and preparation [are] vitally important."

Two years before *Miranda v. Arizona*, the Court decided *Massiah v. United States*, 377 U.S. 201 (1964). There, the defendant was indicted, arraigned, and released on bail after being charged with attempting to import cocaine into the United States. In order to cement their case against Massiah, law enforcement recruited a co-conspirator named Colson to wear a wire and meet with Massiah in an effort to elicit incriminating statements. The scheme succeeded and evidence of statements made by Massiah to Colson were introduced at trial. Massiah was convicted. He appealed on Fourth, Fifth, and Sixth Amendment grounds. Writing for the Court, Justice Potter Stewart held that Massiah's Sixth Amendment right to counsel was violated "when there was used against him at his trial evidence of his own incriminating words, which federal agents had deliberately elicited from him after he had been indicted and in the absence of his counsel." In so holding, the Court brought the Sixth Amendment to bear on investigative efforts constituting "deliberate elicitation" at all stages of investigation after the Sixth Amendment right to counsel has "attached."

In *Massiah*, Colson, acting as a state agent, directly engaged Massiah in an effort to secure incriminating statements. But, as the Court held in *Brewer v. Williams*, 430 U.S. 387 (1977), more subtle measures may also constitute "deliberate elicitation." There, Robert Williams was arrested in Davenport, Iowa, pursuant to a warrant issued in Des Moines, Iowa, charging him with the Christmas Eve abduction of a young girl, whom police suspected he had murdered. He was represented by counsel, who instructed him not to speak with law enforcement officers. Williams was then arraigned in Davenport and scheduled for transfer to Des Moines in the company of two Des Moines police officers. Prior to his transfer, Williams's attorney again instructed him not to speak with the officers. The attorney also instructed the officers not to interrogate Williams.

During the trip back to Des Moines, the officers engaged in a conversation among themselves leading to what has famously been referred to as the "Christian burial speech." During this monologue, the officer opined that inclement weather was coming through the area, which would make finding the victim's body very difficult. He also lamented the fact that the girl's parents were unable to give their daughter a proper Christian burial. As the officers knew, Williams was deeply religious and suffered from mental problems. They therefore hoped that presenting the situation to Williams in these terms might make him consider cooperating with their efforts to find his victim's body. Their ploy worked. Williams led them to his victim's body.

At trial, Williams sought to suppress both the statements he made to the officers and his victim's body. Writing for the Court, Justice Stewart held that Williams's Sixth Amendment right to counsel had attached because "judicial proceedings" had been initiated against him at the arraignment. The Court then noted that Williams had clearly invoked his Sixth Amendment right to counsel and had not waived that right when he responded to the officer's speech. Finally, Justice Stewart held that the "Christian burial speech" was a deliberate effort to elicit an incriminating response from Williams.

Given the factual similarities between *Brewer* and *Rhode Island v. Innis*, 446 U.S. 291 (1980) (discussed in Lesson 26), it might be inferred that "deliberate elicitation" sets a different standard than "express questioning or its functional equivalent," perhaps by considering the objective purposes of officers. *See* Fellers v. United States, 540 U.S. 519 (2004).

Although *Miranda* governs only custodial interrogations, the Sixth Amendment right to counsel governs all efforts by state agents deliberately to elicit incriminating statements. As the *Massiah* Court held, that includes confidential informants. It also governs the use of jailhouse snitches. For example, in *United States v. Henry*, 447 U.S. 264 (1980), the Court held that the Sixth Amendment right to counsel is violated if a jailhouse informant actively engages a defendant in conversation leading to incriminating statements. By contrast, the Sixth Amendment right to counsel is not implicated if the informant simply acts as a "listening post." *See* Kuhlmann v. Wilson, 477 U.S. 436 (1986).

Unlike invocations of the *Miranda* right to counsel, which are general, the Sixth Amendment right to counsel is crime specific. *See* Maine v. Moulton, 474 U.S. 159 (1985). This means that law enforcement officers may question defendants who have invoked their Sixth Amendment right to counsel about uncharged crimes. *See* McNeil v. Wisconsin, 501 U.S. 171 (1991).

As the Court held in *Texas v. Cobb*, 532 U.S. 162 (2001), however, the scope of Sixth Amendment rights is not limited to "the four corners of the charging document," but also extends to any uncharged crimes that would be regarded as the same offense for purposes of the Fifth Amendment Double Jeopardy Clause under *Blockburger v. United States*, 284 U.S. 299 (1932).

In *Michigan v. Jackson*, 475 U.S. 625 (1986), the Court held that, just as in the *Miranda* context, if a defendant has asserted his Sixth Amendment right to counsel, then law enforcement officers may not reinitiate contact to pursue a waiver outside the presence of counsel. The Court's concern in *Jackson* was that, absent such a rule, officers might badger defendants until they waive their rights. Writing for the Court, Justice Antonin Scalia overturned *Michigan v. Jackson* in *Montejo v. Louisiana*, 556 U.S. 778 (2009). In the Court's view, the prophylactic measures built up around *Miranda* are sufficient to guard against efforts by law enforcement officers to badger a defendant into waiving his Sixth Amendment right to counsel. This means, however, that officers have virtually free rein to pursue a waiver of a defendant's Sixth Amendment right to counsel so long as they do not do so in the context of a custodial interrogation.

The remedy for violations of the Sixth Amendment right to counsel is to exclude statements elicited from the prosecution's case-in-chief at trial. But, as the Court held in *Kansas v. Ventris*, 556 U.S. 586 (2009), those statements can be used to impeach a defendant should he choose to testify at trial. The Court has not had occasion to consider whether the fruit of the poisonous tree doctrine applies to violations of the Sixth Amendment right to counsel.

What You Need to Know:

1. The Sixth Amendment right to counsel protects defendants from efforts by government agents deliberately to elicit statements in the absence of counsel.
2. The Sixth Amendment right to counsel "attaches" when judicial proceedings have been initiated, "whether by way of formal charge, preliminary hearing, indictment, information, or arraignment."

3. The Sixth Amendment right to counsel applies even when a defendant is not subject to custodial interrogation. It therefore bars efforts to elicit statements that involve subterfuge.
4. The Sixth Amendment right to counsel is crime specific, and does not bar efforts by law enforcement agents deliberately to elicit statements relating to crimes that are uncharged and unrelated.
5. The Sixth Amendment right to counsel can be knowingly, voluntarily, and intelligently waived. For purposes of law enforcement interrogation, *Miranda* warnings are sufficient to apprise defendants of their Sixth Amendment right to counsel and a waiver of the *Miranda* right to counsel will effectively waive the Sixth Amendment right to counsel as well.

LESSON 29: REMEDIES FOR FIFTH AND SIXTH AMENDMENT VIOLATIONS

Given the complexity and close relationships between due process protections, *Miranda*, and the Sixth Amendment right to counsel, it is worth aggregating the various consequences of invocation violations.

Under the Fifth and Fourteenth Amendment due process clauses, all suspects have a right not to be subjected to interrogations and interrogation methods that produce involuntary statements.

- Due process constraints on interrogations apply in all circumstances, regardless of whether a suspect is in custody.
- Due process constraints on interrogations cannot be waived. A suspect cannot consent to being tortured.
- Statements deemed involuntary are excluded from the prosecution's case-in-chief at trial.
- Statements deemed involuntary are also excluded for impeachment purposes.

- All investigative fruits discovered using statements deemed involuntary are excluded from trial unless the prosecution can establish an independent source or that discovery was inevitable.
- A suspect subjected to interrogation methods that produce an involuntary confession may also have a civil cause of action under 42 U.S.C. § 1983.

Under *Miranda*, anyone subjected to a custodial interrogation has the right to remain silent, the right to consult counsel, and the right to have counsel present during questioning. Statements made in the context of the inherently coercive atmosphere of custodial interrogations are presumed to be compelled for purposes of the Fifth Amendment unless the suspect has been apprised of his right to remain silent and his right to counsel and has voluntarily, knowingly, and intelligently waived those rights.

- Statements made outside the context of a custodial interrogation are not governed by *Miranda*.
- Both the right to remain silent and the *Miranda* right to counsel can be voluntarily, knowingly, and intelligently waived.
- Statements taken during a custodial interrogation in the absence of *Miranda* warnings are excluded from the prosecution's case-in-chief, but may be used to impeach the suspect if he chooses to testify at trial.
- Statements taken during a custodial interrogation after a suspect has invoked his right to remain silent or his right to counsel are excluded from the prosecution's case in chief, but may be used to impeach the suspect if he chooses to testify at trial.
- Investigative fruits in the form of witnesses and physical evidence discovered using statements made in violation of *Miranda* are admissible at trial.
- Investigative fruits in the form of second confessions taken after an effort to "cure" a

Miranda violation may not be admissible if they are taken pursuant to a policy designed to circumnavigate the protections afforded by *Miranda* or the officers otherwise showed bad faith.

- If a statement taken in violation of *Miranda* is not admitted at trial, then there is no residual constitutional harm. Victims of *Miranda* violations therefore probably do not have a civil cause of action under 42 U.S.C. § 1983.

The Sixth Amendment guarantees the right of defendants to the assistance of counsel at all critical stages of a prosecution.

- Once the Sixth Amendment right to counsel has attached, a defendant has the right to have counsel present any time government agents try to deliberately elicit an incriminating response.
- The Sixth Amendment right to counsel can be waived. With respect to police questioning during the investigative stage of a criminal trial, waiver of the right to counsel described in *Miranda* warnings is sufficient to show a waiver of the Sixth Amendment right to counsel.
- Statements taken in violation of the Sixth Amendment right to counsel are excluded from the prosecution's case-in-chief, but may be used to impeach the suspect if he chooses to testify at trial.
- The Court has not squarely addressed whether the investigative fruits of statements taken in violation of the Sixth Amendment right to counsel are excluded at trial.

LESSON 30: WITNESS IDENTIFICATION PROCEDURES

The gold standards for evidence at criminal trials, at least in the eyes of juries, are confessions and eyewitness identifications. Prosecutors are far more likely to achieve a conviction if they have a confession or the testimony of an eyewitness who identifies a defendant as the perpetrator. As studies and experience have shown, however, confessions and eyewitness identifications between strangers are among the least reliable forms of evidence. Together, false confessions and erroneous witness identifications account for the majority of mistaken convictions.

We have already seen how confessions may be unreliable, particularly when taken in the "inherently coercive atmosphere" of a custodial interrogation. The Court has responded to these concerns by introducing limits on custodial interrogations via due process, the Fifth Amendment privilege against compelled witnessing, and the Sixth Amendment right to counsel. Starting with *United States v. Wade*, 388 U.S. 218 (1967), the Court has also attempted to impose constitutional constraints on eyewitness identification procedures.

In *Wade* itself, the Court held that a corporeal line-up identification procedure is a "critical stage" of a criminal proceeding. The Court therefore held that defendants have a Sixth Amendment right to advice of counsel during corporeal line-up procedures occurring at any point after the Sixth Amendment right to counsel has attached. Thus, after the formal commencement of adversarial proceedings, officers must either arrange for the presence of counsel at a corporeal identification procedure or secure a valid waiver of the Sixth Amendment right to counsel from the defendant. Failure to abide the rule announced in *Wade* will result in the suppression of any results from the procedure and may even prohibit a prosecutor from pursuing an in-court identification during trial unless the prosecutor can show by clear and convincing evidence that an in-court identification would not be fruit of the tainted line-up.

In *Kirby v. Illinois*, 406 U.S. 682 (1972), the Court declined to extend the *Wade* rule to identification procedures conducted prior to the commencement of adversarial proceedings. There is, therefore, no Sixth Amendment right to the presence of counsel during a corporeal identification procedure if the Sixth Amendment right to counsel has not yet attached.

In *United States v. Ash*, 413 U.S. 300 (1973), the Court likewise declined to extend *Wade* to non-corporeal identification procedures such as photographic arrays. Thus, there is no Sixth

Amendment right to have defense counsel present if the defendant himself is not present—regardless of whether formal adversarial proceedings have commenced.

The same day the Court decided *Wade*, it also decided *Stovall v. Denno*, 388 U.S. 293 (1967). There, the Court held that due process requires the suppression of evidence from a pre-trial identification procedure if that procedure is unnecessarily suggestive, conducive to mistaken identification, and infected by improper police influence.[13] In *Stovall*, the defendant was alleged to have stabbed his victim eleven times during a home invasion. Officers brought him, in handcuffs, to the hospital where the victim was about to undergo surgery to repair her wounds from the attack. Officers asked her if Stovall was the man who attacked her. Despite the highly suggestive nature of this "show-up" identification procedure, Justice William Brennan, writing for the Court, held that it was necessary under the circumstances given the precarious situation of the victim. Thus, although the procedure was suggestive, it was not *unnecessarily* suggestive, and therefore did not violate due process.

Applying *Stovall*, courts have granted officers considerable leeway to conduct all manner of often highly suggestive identification procedures. For example, "show-up" street identification procedures conducted in the immediate wake of a crime are routinely upheld as appropriate both because they allow officers to arrest perpetrators who might get away and because they allow innocent persons to go free rather than suffer the indignity of arrest. The Court drew a line in *Foster v. California*, 394 U.S. 440 (1969), holding that due process was violated when Foster was placed in a line-up wearing a unique jacket next to two men substantially shorter than him. The witness nevertheless failed to identify Foster as the perpetrator. The witness again failed to identify Foster as the perpetrator during a subsequent show-up identification procedure. It was only in the context of yet another line-up, where Foster was the only person to reappear from the prior line-up, that the witness finally identified him as the perpetrator. On these facts, the

[13] This last requirement was made explicit in *Perry v. New Hampshire*, 565 U.S. 228 (2012).

Court held that, by their persistent manipulation of multiple identification procedures, and in light of the witness's multiple failures to identify Foster, the officers had engaged in a process of witness identification that was unnecessarily suggestive and that raised serious questions about reliability.

As the Court would later make clear in *Manson v. Brathwaite*, 432 U.S. 98 (1977), "reliability is the linchpin in determining the admissibility of identification testimony in both pre- and post-*Stovall* confrontations." Thus, even identifications taken during unnecessarily suggestive procedures may still be admissible absent significant indicia of unreliability. When making these assessments, *Manson* requires that courts take into account the witness's opportunity to observe a perpetrator during the crime, the degree of attention the witness gave to the perpetrator during the crime, the accuracy of any descriptions the witness may have given of the perpetrator prior to viewing the suspect, the witness's level of certainty in her identification, and the time that passed between the crime and the identification procedure.

Social scientists have invested considerable resources in developing a set of "best practices" for identification procedures. Among their recommendations are "double-blinding," which means that the officers conducting the identification procedure do not know who is the suspect among the persons or pictures used during the procedure, advising witnesses that the perpetrator may not be among the individuals presented, and presenting persons or pictures serially rather than together in an array. Although these and other methods have been shown to reduce significantly the risk of erroneous witness identifications, failure to abide best practices does not, by itself, constitute a violation of due process.

What You Need to Know:

1. Defendants have a Sixth Amendment right to have counsel present during any corporeal identification procedures conducted after the Sixth Amendment right to counsel has attached.

2. There is no Sixth Amendment right to have counsel present during identification procedures that do not

involve the presence of a defendant, such as procedures using photographs.

3. The Sixth Amendment does not govern identification procedures conducted before the Sixth Amendment right to counsel has attached.
4. Identifications taken in violation of the Sixth Amendment are not admissible at trial. In-court identifications that are the fruits of identifications taken in violation of the Sixth Amendment are likewise inadmissible.
5. Due process prohibits the admission of identifications made during procedures that are unnecessarily suggestive, conducive to mistaken identification, and infected by improper police influence.

CHAPTER 5

EVIDENCE

LESSON 1: INTRODUCTION

Students are often anxious when faced with learning the law of evidence. Many students only take evidence because it is a required course on the bar. A few more think it might be useful in their legal career. Even fewer—those who will ply their trade as trial lawyers—will make use of evidence day in and day out. Nonetheless, there are a few things to remember that might make the prospect of learning evidence a little less onerous.

The first and most important thing is that a course on evidence is just another course on procedure, like civil procedure or criminal procedure. That means that evidence is (like civil procedure and unlike criminal procedure) heavily statutory. For the most part, you will be reading the Federal Rules of Evidence (perhaps with some California Evidence Code rules thrown in for good measure) and the annotations prepared by the Advisory Committee on the rules of evidence, which are often quite useful in explaining what the rules mean. Because evidence law is statutory, the rules and annotations are the first place you should turn when trying to solve a problem in the law of evidence. If you do not read (and then pause and think about) the relevant rule *and* its annotation, you cannot understand what is going on.

The Federal Rules of Evidence offer some general guidance to thinking about the purpose of the evidence code. Rule 102 describes three values that the rules promote: fairness, efficiency, and accuracy (or trustworthiness). These values reappear throughout the Federal Rules, often repeated in the negative (for example, in Rule 403 which encourages judges to avoid unfair prejudice, wasting time, or confusing the issues). By far the most important value is accuracy or trustworthiness: the idea that the evidence admitted at trial be useful in establishing whether or not some fact is the case, or some witness is to be believed. Nonetheless, ensuring trials are efficient and preserving adversarial fairness in the presentation of evidence are each important values in their own right.

The Federal Rules of Evidence have a different scope than the Federal Rules of Civil or Criminal Procedure. The Civil and Criminal Procedure Codes for the most part cover what happens before or after or in the alternative to a civil or criminal trial: they are rules of pretrial practice, for summary judgment or plea bargaining, or for appeal. The Federal Rules of Evidence (with the exception of the rules that apply to certain types of privileged communication) *only apply to trials*. With the exception of the privilege rules, they do not apply to depositions, plea bargains, grand jury proceedings, sentencing, and so on.

Formally, the scope of the rules is laid out in Rule1101. That rule basically says, first, that the rules are *federal* rules and so only apply in *federal* court (Rule1101(a))—although many states have adopted something similar or identical to the federal rules. Second, Rule1101(c) says the privilege rules apply to *all* federal proceedings, but that the other rules mostly apply only to trials (Rule1101(b)), not to other parts of the criminal or civil process (Rule1101(d)).

We are studying the law of evidence. But what *is* evidence? *Evidence* is simply some piece of information that can be used to establish a fact. And a *fact* is something that is the case. Statements about facts can be true or false. The statement, "The traffic light was red when the car entered the intersection," is either true or false. It's true if, in fact, it was the case that the traffic light was red at the appropriate time. And we can *prove* that it was the case using different items of evidence: the testimony of some eyewitness; a video recording from a red-light CCTV camera; a live tweet from someone at the scene; the contents of an accident report; tire rubber collected from the scene of the accident; the testimony of an expert as to the cause of the accident; a scale diorama representing the accident scene; and so on.

It's also worth distinguishing between evidence *in general*, that is, anything that might support some fact, versus evidence that *has been admitted* for use at trial. Not all evidence is admissible, that is, not all evidence goes before the jury. And it is important to keep these two meanings of evidence separate, especially when we come to Rule 104(a).

One type of evidence is worth special comment: live witnesses testimony at trial. Witnesses tell us what happened: they testify, under oath (Rule 603), about what they personally perceived (Rule 602). While lawyers usually say that the evidence here is what the witness *says*—their *testimony*, to use the technical term—what we are really interested in are the *perceptions* contained in their *memory*. Live witnesses tell us about what they remember seeing, hearing, smelling, tasting, or touching, and part of the job of the attorneys is to determine whether what they remember is accurate: what the rules often refer to as *reliable* or *trustworthy*.

What You Need to Know:

1. *Evidence* is a piece of information that can be used to establish whether it is more or less likely that some fact is the case, or some statement about the fact is true or false.
2. Evidence *law* is a form of procedure. Like civil procedure, it is heavily statutory, and the statute is annotated. You need to read the statute and the notes to really grasp what is going on.
3. Evidence law serves three primary values: accuracy, efficiency, and fairness.
4. Evidence law is limited in scope. Under Rule 1101, most of the rules apply only to the trial part of the legal process. If the proceeding occurs before or after the actual trial, the rules do not usually apply.
5. The one exception is privilege rules. We will discuss these rules later on: for now, we only need to know that privilege rules can apply more broadly than most evidence rules, both before and after the trial itself.

LESSON 2: THE TRIAL STRUCTURE

Since the Rules of Evidence are the rules of procedure for trials, we can understand the rules of evidence as a little like the rules of a game. The goal of the game is persuading the factfinder at trial to find in your favor. There are two sides to the game, plaintiff (or prosecution) and defendant. To obtain a judgment in her favor, the attorney will need to satisfy the ultimate burden of proof, by making a winning argument that some factfinder (whether judge or jury) will think is sufficiently believable to render a verdict in that party's favor. Attorneys' winning arguments depend upon introducing items of evidence for consideration by the factfinder (often a jury). If evidence is *admitted*, it becomes part of the trial record, and the attorney can then argue that the factfinder ought to draw certain conclusions from the evidence; if the item is excluded, it is not part of the record, and the attorneys cannot make these sorts of arguments.

For example, in a traffic case, the plaintiff may want to argue that a driver negligently hit a pedestrian in the crosswalk. She will want to show that the driver entered the crosswalk when the light was red, and the "Walk" sign directed the victim to cross the intersection. One item of evidence could be the statement of a bystander, who could say that the light was, indeed, red. If this evidence is admissible, then the plaintiff can make her argument and (hopefully) satisfy her burden of proof; if the evidence is inadmissible and excluded, then she needs some other item of evidence if she is to make this argument. If she can't find another item of evidence to make the "light was red" argument, then she needs to make *some other argument*. If she can't make some other argument, she loses.

The rules of evidence define the relevant pieces—witness, judge, attorney—by telling us their roles in the game—the trial. Witnesses play an important role in this process. Attorneys introduce evidence primarily through the live testimony of witnesses at trial. The most important role of witnesses is to tell the court what they perceived, to establish some fact relevant to the attorney's story. However, the trial process relies on witnesses for a variety of other functions: to confirm documents or other tangible items of evidence are what the proponent claims them to be; to discuss the credibility of other witnesses; to report statements made by people who are not available to testify at trial; and so on.

Trials are structured, in part, to enable juries or judges to assess whether live witnesses are trustworthy or not. American trials do this in a particular way: they are adversarial battles that allow lawyers to present competing stories about what happened. In a typical trial, first, a jury is selected, and then each side gets to present opening statements to the jury. The plaintiff or prosecution, bearing the burden of proof, goes first. The defendant goes second. Opening statements recite the facts each side plans to introduce at trial, giving the jury a roadmap of what to expect. They are not supposed to try to persuade the jury that the statements are true or false.

After opening statements are over, the plaintiff or prosecution puts on its case. It does so by calling witnesses and asking them questions, as well as introducing other items of evidence. After the attorney finishes questioning her witness on what is called a *direct*, the defendant gets a turn to question, or *cross-examine* the witness. The plaintiff may decide to ask more questions to clear up issues raised by the defense counsel: this is called *redirect*. The parties can continue questioning the same witness, back and forth, until their questions are exhausted or the judge calls a halt, and then move onto the next witness.

Each side can also make short motions arguing that certain items of evidence not be admitted: for example, that certain questions not be asked, because the answer would be inadmissible; or that some document or other item be kept from the jury. These short, oral motions are traditionally signaled by the attorney *objecting* to the introduction of the evidence; the judge then calls the attorneys to the bench, hears arguments from both sides out of earshot of the jury, and rules on whether the evidence is admissible.

After the plaintiff or prosecution presents all its evidence, it rests its case. If it has presented enough evidence, then the defendant gets a chance to disprove that case. The defendant puts on her case in the same way: by calling witnesses and questioning them on direct; and allowing the plaintiff or prosecutor to cross-examine them. At the end of this process, both sides have an opportunity to make *closing arguments*, which are persuasive stories, supported by the evidence that each side has managed to introduce. At closing, each party reminds the jury of the evidence they have heard and tries to show the jury how that evidence supports the story they want to tell. The parties will argue that some evidence is particularly trustworthy, while other evidence ought to be discounted. After that, the judge reads the jury *instructions*, telling them what laws they must apply, and then the jurors *deliberate* and render their verdict.

What You Need to Know:

1. Evidence law regulates an adversarial battle between two sides: each side uses admissible evidence, usually introduced through the testimony of some live witness, to satisfy the relevant burden of proof.
2. The trial begins with opening statements; then the plaintiff or prosecution put on their case; at the end of which the defendant can put on its case.
3. To prove its case, each side can use witnesses. The party calling the witness engages in *direct* questioning of the witness; after which the opposing party can *cross-examine* the witness.
4. An item is *admitted* into evidence if the court or other tribunal makes it part of the official record. In a jury trial, the jury can only consider and examine admitted evidence; it cannot consider excluded evidence.
5. Attorneys may object to the introduction of evidence by making an oral motion to exclude the evidence. These motions are heard by the judge, out of earshot of the jury, at the bench. The judge permits both sides to argue, and then rules on the admissibility of the evidence.
6. After all the evidence has been presented, the parties make closing arguments. These closing arguments are persuasive stories that tell the jury how to understand the evidence they have heard, and what weight to assign to it.

LESSON 3: PROCEDURAL RULES GOVERNING THE ROLES OF THE LAWYER AND JUDGE

Apart from witnesses (whose role we will return to later when we look at Article VI), the other two major roles governed by the Rules of Evidence are those of the attorney and the trial judge. Lawyers play a major role in determining what evidence the jury (or judge, in a bench trial) gets to hear. As an organizational matter, the attorneys amass the evidence for use in the case (the Civil Procedure or Criminal Procedure rules on discovery govern a lot of this process) and determine what evidence best supports the story they wish to tell at trial (and what evidence most threatens the success of that story). The rules of evidence really kick in at trial, where the attorneys are primarily responsible for objecting to evidence to keep it out.

A few features of this structure are worth emphasizing. First, the adversarial structure of the trial process renders judges, as an initial matter, *passive*. They do not rule upon the inclusion or exclusion of evidence until called upon to do so by a lawyer making a motion objecting to the introduction of an opponent's evidence. Judicial passivity raises a couple of structural features of the use of evidence at trial: first, evidence is admitted unless an opposing party objects. The default is just to let in all the evidence. Because of this default, the law of evidence operates primarily to exclude evidence at trial. Nonetheless, whenever a question of admissibility *is* raised by one of the parties, the *judge*, not the jury, determines the admissibility of evidence.

Two sets of procedural rules govern the role of the judge at trial. Rule 104(a) identifies how judges are to establish whether some item of evidence is admissible or not. These questions of admissibility are called *preliminary questions*. Here, it is worth remembering the distinction between *general evidence* and *admitted evidence*. Rule 104(a) allows the judge, when ruling on the admissibility of a particular item of evidence, to consider any *general* evidence the parties might use to support their claims, including *unadmitted* or inadmissible evidence. She will then determine, based on the *preponderance of the evidence* whether some item of evidence is admissible.

Imagine the plaintiff wants to introduce a tweet stating "the traffic light was red when the car entered an intersection." That testimony is only admissible if the tweet was made by some identifiable person who could see the traffic light and the defendant's car at the time of the accident. These other facts necessary to establish the tweet is admissible are called *preliminary facts*. The judge, in ruling on admissibility, gets to consider all the available preliminary facts and evidence. She can consider, not only the fact stated in the tweet—that the light was red when the car entered the intersection—but other evidence as well, necessary to establish the other facts (the tweeter's identity, location, and ability to discern cars and colors) that support or undermine the tweet's admissibility.

Making decisions on the fly, often without advance warning, can be difficult for a judge. Sometimes, judges' decisions turn on the demeanor of witnesses at trial. So appellate courts apply the *abuse of discretion* standard in reviewing trial courts' rulings, meaning the ruling stands unless it bears no rational relationship to the evidence supporting it. That rule gives trial judges lots of discretion when ruling on the admissibility of evidence.

Another set of rules, governing procedure on appeal, force the trial attorneys to help out the trial judge. The best time to raise a motion objecting to the introduction of some item of evidence is when the issue is fresh: when the evidence is introduced at trial. Judges are most likely to rule correctly when alerted to the rule they are supposed to apply. These features—that the motion be *timely* and *specific*; and that the judge has *broad discretion* in making her rulings—are covered by Rule 103, governing the standards courts use on appeal. That rule entrenches judicial discretion and rewards timely and specific objections (while punishing the failure to object at the appropriate time in the appropriate way).

Rule 103 is also an indirect way of regulating the roles of attorneys at trial. It specifies a two-track system for appellate review. The first track applies the more forgiving "harmless error" standard of Rule 103(a). There are two situations in which the harmless error standard applies. First, an attorney may seek to *exclude* evidence. If she wants to preserve her right to appeal under the harmless error standard, she must *object* in a *timely fashion* when her opponent seeks to enter the evidence at trial, and state the *specific reason* for her objection (the rule of evidence or constitutional rule that would exclude the evidence). On the other hand, if the attorney is trying to *admit* the evidence, over the objection of another attorney, she must offer to show the judge why that evidence is admissible.

In either case, the standard on appeal is deferential to the trial judge's ruling: her decision on admissibility is reversible only if it affects a *substantial right of the party*. The phrase is vague, but means that no error will be reversed unless it had some significant effect on the jury's deliberations (for non-constitutional errors, which are the majority of errors) or the outcome of the trial (for constitutional errors); the rest are considered "harmless." However, if the attorney *does not object or does not state her reasons*, the rules mandate a much harsher standard. Under Rule 103(e) the court applies a *plain error* standard, which means that the appellate court will only reverse if there has been a *miscarriage of justice.*

What You Need to Know:

1. Judges, not juries, rule on the admissibility of evidence.
2. Judges are have lots of discretion in making their rulings on the admissibility of evidence.
3. Rule 104(a) allows judges to consider *any evidence* when ruling on admissibility; the judge applies the preponderance of the evidence standard.
4. Rule 103(a) requires that attorneys make a *timely* and *specific* objection if a court is to apply the harmless error standard; if not, the attorney waives her objection and the *plain error* standard applies on appeal.

LESSON 4: RELEVANCE, IRRELEVANCE, AND CONDITIONAL RELEVANCE

So far, we've considered what evidence is, how trials are structured, and the procedure for determining admissibility. We now turn to the substantive rules of evidence. In evidence law, there is a broad structure to the rules. Generally, the rules start out by restricting the use of some item of evidence at trial by excluding them from going before the factfinder. For the most part, the rules follow the same pattern: a global rule tells you that some category of evidence is inadmissible. However, the rules then usually follow up with a series of specific rules that tell you the exceptions to the global rule. It is this back-and-forth structure that makes the rules of evidence so disorientating: they say, "You can't do this, except when you can do it, except when you actually can't do it."

The relevance rule broadly follows this structure: Rule 402 says all irrelevant evidence is inadmissible; but relevant evidence *is* admissible; unless that relevant evidence is nonetheless excluded by any of the other rules in the evidence code, or some other statute, or the constitution.

Rule 402 is, however, a little deceptive. Superficially, it seems to excludes lots of evidence: *all* evidence that is irrelevant, without exception. While that's true as a formal matter, it turns out that the relevance standard is an easy one to satisfy. In effect, the demand that evidence be relevant or else it's inadmissible simply tracks the rule, first established by one of the major American writers on evidence law, James Bradley Theyer, that evidence law be rational. Remember, evidence is simply some piece of information that can be used to support some fact. According to Thayer (and under Rule 401(a)) if the item of evidence has *any rational* tendency to support (or undermine) the existence of some fact, then it is *relevant*, so long as (under Rule 401(b)) that fact is related to some claim or defense, or to the credibility of some witness.

Relevance thus has two distinctive features. One is called *logical relevance*. When considering the logical relevance of an item of evidence, we only consider whether some item of evidence can be linked, by a chain of rational arguments, to some claim or defense or credibility issue. Sometimes these chains of inference are quite lengthy and seem pretty weak. Thus, in a famous case, *Knapp v. State*, 79 N.E. 1076 (Ind. 1907), a defendant charged with murdering the local sheriff claimed self-defense. Here there are at least two facts that, in the words of Rule 401(b), "determine the action." If Knapp deliberately killed the sheriff without justification, then that fact establishes that he was guilty of murder. However, if Knapp killed the sheriff in self-defense—that is, if Knapp reasonably believed that he had to kill or be seriously injured—then *that* fact shows that he was *not* guilty of murder.

Knapp claimed that some unidentified person told him that the sheriff had brutally beaten an old man to death. This claim, if true, would be logically relevant for his self-defense claim. The defense's evidence (his testimony about the rumor he heard) makes it more probable than it would be without the evidence that someone *did* tell him that the sheriff beat and killed a man; which makes it more probable that the sheriff killed the man; which makes it more probable that Knapp had reason to be worried; which makes it more probable that Knapp had reason to defend himself. On the other hand, the prosecution introduced medical testimony to prove that the man the sheriff was supposed to have killed actually died from illness caused by alcoholism, and not any actions of the sheriff. The court held that the medical testimony was also logically relevant. The medical testimony was evidence that the man died from an illness not a beating, which justified an inference that Knapp had not heard the rumor he claimed to have heard, which made it less probable that had reason to fear the sheriff, which made it less probable he acted in self-defense (and more probable he was guilty of murder).

All that is required to establish logical relevance is a chain of common-sense inferences that tie the evidence, through some set of facts, to some logically plausible story that tends to prove a claim or defense. The relevant item of evidence need not stand on its own, but can gain support from other relevant items of evidence to form an interlocking narrative. In McCormick's famous phrase, "A brick is not a wall." So long as the link can be made, no matter how elongated the chain of inferences, then the evidence is logically relevant.

For evidence to be relevant under Rule 401 it need only be *logically relevant*. Rule 401 does not focus on the weight of the evidence. The evidence need only fit within a common-sense narrative directed towards some claim, defense, or the credibility of a witness. The practical effect of Rule 402's categorical exclusion of irrelevant evidence is therefore quite weak. For the most part, the problem is usually not that evidence is irrelevant, but that, though relevant, it is misused.

The most important irrelevance objection occurs when one item of evidence is relevant only if some other, yet-to-be-admitted item of evidence is too. Suppose, in the *Knapp* case, that the sheriff *had* beaten the old man to death when taking him into custody. That item is relevant to Knapp's self-defense claim only on condition that Knapp *knows that* the sheriff killed the old man. If Knapp did *not* know about the beating it cannot be the basis for his fearing the sheriff.

This sort of irrelevance objection is relatively easy to overcome. Under Rule 104(b), the proponent must simply show that she has sufficient admissible evidence to admit the second, linked item of evidence. The proponent must then, at some point before resting her case, admit the second item of evidence, or the court will strike the first item from the record (effectively un-admitting it). Rule 104(b) differs from Rule 104(a) in two ways. First, Rule 104(b) limits the judge to considering only *admissible* evidence when making her ruling. Second, Rule 104(b) applies a lower, sufficiency-of-the-evidence standard. Under the sufficiency standard, the judge is required to find only that, based on the proponent's evidence, a reasonable juror could believe the fact is the case.

The sufficiency standard is an important one. It will reappear in Rules (404)(b) (prior specific act evidence), 602 (personal knowledge of a percipient witness) and 901 (authentication of physical evidence) in which the admissibility of one item of evidence depends upon the admissibility of some other item.

What You Need to Know:

1. Evidence rules usually work by stating some broad rule excluding evidence, then some set of exceptions to the broad rule, then an exception to the exception, and so on.

2. The first major broad rule excluding evidence is Rule 402's categorical exclusion of all irrelevant evidence.
3. Under Rule 401, evidence is relevant if it has *any tendency* to make more or less likely some fact necessary to prove a claim or defense, or which goes to witness credibility.
4. So long as the evidence is logically relevant, its weight (or probative value) does not matter under Rule 401.
5. For any item of evidence, that item need not bear the whole weight of proving the case: it operates with other facts and evidence as part of an interlocking narrative of the case.
6. If the relevance of two items of evidence is interlinked, so that the admissibility of the first item is conditioned upon the second, then under Rule 104(b), the evidence is admissible if the proponent produces sufficient evidence for a reasonable juror to believe the fact is the case.
7. The proponent must introduce both items of evidence before resting her case; if she fails to introduce the second item, the first item will be struck from the record.

LESSON 5: PROBATIVE VALUE

Items of evidence can be more or less weighty or important dependent upon their probative value: how strongly they support or undermine some fact and how central is that fact to the case. A brick is not a wall, but some bricks are bigger or more important than others.

Each item of evidence is only as weighty as the weakest link in the chain of inferences we make from one argument to the next. In the *Knapp* case, both the evidence that Knapp did hear the rumor that the sheriff beat the old man, and the evidence that the old man died of alcoholism, and so Knapp *could not* have heard the rumor, are quite weak. In the language of evidence law, its probative value is quite low. The Advisory Committee Note mentions two features that affect the probative value or *weight* of some item of evidence: first, the availability of a limiting instruction telling a fact-finder to consider the evidence only for a particular purpose; and second, the availability of other means of proving the fact; and the importance of the fact to the rest of the case. This list is by no means exhaustive, and many other factors may affect the persuasiveness, or weight, of the evidence.

Some items of evidence have problematic side-effects, called *probative dangers*. For example, the prosecution might try to introduce a photograph of a crime scene for a particular purpose: to show how the victim died, proving death was intentional rather than a mistake. Nonetheless, the picture might be so gruesome that anyone who sees it would feel an irrational and extreme rush of emotion against anyone accused of the crime. That's bad: we don't want factfinders deciding cases based on emotion rather than reason. Rule 403 calls this probative danger *unfair prejudice*.

It's worth being careful here. Rule 403 is a rule that is tipped in favor of admitting evidence, in two ways. First, the rule permits a court to exclude evidence *only* if it fits one of three enumerated *probative dangers*: unfair prejudice (judging on the basis of emotion rather than reason); inaccuracy (confusing the issues or misleading the jury); or inefficiency (delay, timewasting, or needlessly repeating evidence). These three types of probative danger or evidentiary vice are the mirror image of the evidentiary virtues of fairness, accuracy, and efficiency set out in Rule 102.

Rule 403 tips in favor of inclusion in a second way: by requiring the court to assign a weight to both the evidence's probative value *and* the probative danger, and then to determine whether the probative danger *substantially outweighs* its probative value. Imagine a set of scales: if the probative value and the probative danger are of *equal weight*, the evidence is *admissible*; if the scales tip only *a little* towards the probative danger, the evidence is *still admissible*. Only if the scales tip *heavily* towards the probative danger, so the danger *substantially outweighs* the value, should the evidence be *excluded.*

Talk of probative value and probative danger often leads to confusion. For example, the crime scene photograph may have a lot of evidentiary value. It may be the only evidence showing how the crime was committed, and may clearly demonstrate that the killing was intentional. In that case, it is devastating for the defendant's case. Nonetheless, although we often say this evidence is *prejudicial* towards the defendant's case—even strongly prejudicial—it is not *unfairly* prejudicial so long as allows the jury to determine *rationally* how the crime was committed.

Rule 403 is something of a catch-all rule. Even if evidence is admissible by some other route, courts are usually obliged to engage in a Rule 403 balancing test just to make sure the evidence does not produce one of the prohibited probative dangers. Sometimes the rules of evidence vary the standard, to protect criminal defendants or as party of the law of hearsay. Nonetheless, unless the rules say otherwise, it is usually a good idea to undertake a Rule 403 balancing test before declaring the evidence admissible.

One final feature of the rules of evidence is worth mentioning: they are often purpose-specific, not item-specific. The rules often exclude an item of evidence when it is used for some specific purpose, yet admit it when it is used for some other purpose. An important Rule 403 case, *Old Chief v. United States*, 519 U.S. 172 (1997), exemplifies this purpose-specific feature. The case is a little long and complicated, but in essence, Old Chief had been convicted, a few years previously, for the crime of *assault causing bodily injury*, a felony. He was later arrested and charged with, among other things, assault with a dangerous weapon and being a felon in possession of a firearm. The prosecution wished to prove the felon-in-possession charge by introducing the judgment of the prior conviction, and in particular the title of the crime charged, assault causing bodily injury. Old Chief offered to stipulate that he had committed a prior felony crime, and thereby preclude the jury from hearing the title of the prior charge.

The prosecution objected, arguing that it should get to prove its case using any relevant evidence it saw fit. The Supreme Court recognized that attorneys use evidence to craft a story that has rational and narrative persuasiveness. Attorneys also face the challenge of satisfying the factfinder's expectations about the types of evidence it will see or hear at trial. Here, however, there was a problem: the title of the prior crime could unfairly prejudice the jury, because they might convict him based on the similarity between the current assault charge and the title of the prior crime, or decide he should be punished because he is a bad man, whether or not he committed the current crime.

Normally, where there is a problem about the factfinder's misuse of evidence, then the judge will give an instruction, under Rule 105, telling the jury to consider the evidence only for the permissible purpose and not the impermissible one. And usually, this sort of instruction under Rule 105 is sufficient. No one really believes the jury will ignore the impermissible purpose, but evidence law could not work without the fiction that they do. In *Old Chief*, however, the Court thought the probative danger of the title of the prior felony charge was so weighty that it substantially outweighed its probative value, and the curative instruction was insufficient. *Old Chief*, however, is an outlier: usually defendants are not permitted to stipulate in this way.

What You Need to Know:

1. *Probative value* describes an item of evidence's weight or importance. An item's weight can vary from case to case, depending upon how it fits with the other admissible evidence.

2. Probative danger comes in three categories: undue prejudice, confusing the issues or misleading the jury; and undue delay, wasting time, or repeatedly presenting the same evidence.

3. Rule 403 excludes evidence only if the probative danger *substantially* outweighs the probative value. It thus favors admissibility.

4. Evidence is used for some purpose. Rule 105 instructs the jury about the purpose for which to

consider the evidence, and to ignore the impermissible purposes.

5. Under *Old Chief*, in very rare, exceptional circumstances, Rule 105 may be insufficient to avoid the relevant probative danger, and so the trial court should permit stipulations, or exclude the evidence.

LESSON 6: CHARACTER EVIDENCE

Character evidence is a specific instance of the sort of probative danger identified in Rule 403. The problem with evidence about a person's character is not that it is irrelevant: on the contrary, whether someone has a good character or a bad character—whether they are careful or reckless, even-tempered or short-tempered, honest or dishonest—may be very relevant to proving some element of a claim or defense. The problem with character evidence is instead that the jury may use it for the wrong purpose: they may think that the case is about some prior incident and so confuse the current issues with the prior ones; or they may decide that some party is so bad that they ought be punished whatever the merits of the instant case. To avoid these misuses, the Federal Rules significantly limit the availability of character evidence at trial.

Rule 404 follows the traditional structure: it first excludes broad categories of evidence by defines some prohibited uses, for which the evidence is inadmissible, then creates some exceptions for which the evidence is allowed. The rule prohibits drawing a specific inference: that based on some *general tendency*, some person acted on a *specific occasion* in accordance with that tendency. The impermissible move is from general to specific: to say that because someone is reckless, then they acted recklessly on this occasion; or because someone is short-tempered, they acted angrily on this occasion; or because someone is peaceful, they acted non-violently on this occasion.

Three features of Rule 404 are worth emphasizing. First, it applies differently to civil and criminal cases. Second, it operates in conjunction with Rule 405. Third, a special set of rules, carved off by Rule 404(a)(3), apply to the use of character evidence to attack or support the credibility of witnesses. We will consider the credibility uses when we turn to Article VI.

In civil cases, character evidence is *broadly excluded.* However, in some civil cases, a person's character trait is an essential element of a claim or defense. Rule 404(a) doesn't really apply, because the evidence is used to infer a *general trait* not some specific act. In a defamation case, where the defendant is accused of maligning the plaintiff's character, the affirmative defense of truth requires the defendant to discuss the plaintiff's character. In a negligent hiring case, where the claim is that the employer should have known the employee had a bad character, both sides must discuss the employees character traits. And in a child custody case, the character of the parents is an important issue when determining the best interests of the child. In these sorts of cases, where character is an essential element of a claim or defense, we say that *character is in issue.* Under Rule 405(b), the normal rules of evidence apply to permit proof of character.

In criminal cases, Rule 404(a)(2) places the admissibility of character evidence in the hands of the defendant. Only the defendant can lead with character evidence. The prosecution *cannot* be the first party to introduce character evidence. But the *defendant* can, either by introducing evidence of the *defendant's* relevant *good character* under Rule 404(a)(2)(A), or evidence of the *victim's* relevant *bad character* under Rule 404(a)(2)(B). This is often referring to the defendant *opening the door* to character evidence. It does not matter whether the defendant *intends* to open the door: immediately she introduces character evidence, the prosecutor can introduce the same sort of evidence to rebut the defendant's character-based claims.

If the defendant does open the door, Rule 404(a) and Rule 405 entail a sort of mini-trial, with its own special rules. First, criminal defendants can only introduce character evidence if it is relevant to prove the elements of a claim or defense. If the defendant is charged with assault, she can only introduce evidence to show that she is peaceful, not that she is generous, or enterprising, or honest. And if the defendant does introduce evidence of a relevant character trait, the prosecution is limited to evidence rebutting that same trait.

Moreover, Rule 405(a) provides a weirdly limited procedure for proving or disproving character. The proponent can *only* introduce character in a particular way: by having someone (including the defendant herself) testify that *in her opinion* the defendant or the victim has that trait, or that the defendant or the victim has a *reputation* for possessing that trait. Totally *impermissible* under Rule 405(a) is the proponent introducing evidence of some specific prior instance in which the person acted in conformity with that trait.

When the witness testifies on direct about some person's character (including her own), she is required to assert that she has sufficient knowledge about that person to form an opinion about their character, or knows their reputation in the community. The only time specific act evidence is admissible under Rule 405(a) is when the *opponent*, on *cross-examination*, asks the witness what she knows about instances in which the person acted out of character, thereby testing how well the witness knows the person's character. For example, if the witness claims the on direct that, in her opinion, Defendant is peaceful, then the prosecution may ask whether the witness was aware that Defendant had assaulted her daughter. If the witness testifies as to Defendant's reputation for law-abidingness, the cross-examiner may ask whether Defendant had been arrested for shoplifting.

Confusingly, the cross-examiner is *not* allowed to introduce independent evidence to support her question, but must rest satisfied with the witness answer, even if she knows the witness lied. And the witness cannot introduce specific act evidence to rehabilitate herself, but must simply reassert her opinion or her understanding of the person's reputation in the community. Finally, to get to ask the question, the questioner must have a reasonable, good faith belief that the person did the bad act.

If the defendant opens the door by bolstering her own character or denigrating the victim's, the prosecution may rebut defendant's character evidence by offering character witnesses of her own. Rule 405(a) applies to the prosecution's witnesses too: they may only provide opinion or reputation evidence.

The prosecution's evidence is primarily limited to rebutting defendant's good character evidence or introducing evidence to show the good character of the victim. However, Rule 404(a)(2)(C) creates a special rule for homicide cases. If the defendant argues that the victim was the first aggressor, the prosecution can introduce evidence of the victim's character for peacefulness. The rule makes up for the fact that the victim is dead and cannot speak for herself.

What You Need to Know:

1. Under Rule 404(a), character evidence is generally impermissible when used to infer that, based on some general trait, a person committed a specific act.

2. Character evidence is totally impermissible in a civil case, unless a person's character is *in issue*, which means that it is an essential element of a claim or defense. In that case, the usual rules of proof apply. Rule 405(b).

3. Character evidence is only permissible in a criminal case if the defendant first *opens the door* with evidence of a relevant good character trait or the victim's relevant bad character trait. Rule 404(a)(2). If the defendant opens the door, the prosecutor may rebut with evidence of the same character trait (defendant's bad character; victim's good character).

4. Rule 405(a) allows this sort of character trait to be proved in two ways. On direct, the witness must testify only to her opinion of the general character trait or the victim's reputation in the community for possessing that trait. On cross-examination, the opponent can question the defendant about the basis of her knowledge, including her knowledge of specific instances that could undermine her opinion, or show that she is not fully aware of the person's reputation.

5. The prosecution can use the same process to rebut the defendant's character evidence either by of introducing opinion or reputation testimony

showing the defendant's bad character, or showing the victim's good character.

6. In homicide cases, if a defendant claims to be the first aggressor, Rule 404(a)(2)(C) permits the prosecutor to introduce evidence of the victim's character for peacefulness.

LESSON 7: SPECIFIC CONDUCT USED TO PROVE SOMETHING OTHER THAN A GENERAL TRAIT

Rule 404(a) prohibits a particular use of character evidence: to infer specific conduct in conformity with some more general trait. Rule 404(b) then gives a non-exhaustive list of uses that do not make that inference from general trait to particular act. Instead, the evidence is admissible introduced for some other purpose; to prove *motive, opportunity, intent, preparation, plan, knowledge, identity, absence of mistake, or lack of accident.*

The problem Rule 404(b) addresses is similar to Rule 403: an item of evidence may be useful for a specific purpose, but could have some bad effects. In *Old Chief*, the title of the prior felony charge, *assault causing bodily injury*, was relevant to the current felon in possession charge, but also permitted the jury to make an inference about the defendant's bad character as a convicted criminal. The title-of-offense evidence was ambivalent as between these two purposes.

In criminal cases, especially, the circumstantial evidence necessary to prove the relevant mental state may be ambivalent in this way. The prosecution may try to prove the defendant entered the building with the intent to commit a felony by introducing evidence showing the defendant had gambling debts she needed to pay off, or that she had broken into the house before, or that she had obtained tools that were characteristically used by burglars. In each case, the evidence points to a bad character trait precluded under Rule 404(a): that the defendant is a gambler, in the first instance, that she has burgled in the past, and so is likely to be a burglar, in the second; or that she is the sort of person who possesses burglary tools, and so is likely to be a burglar, in the third instance.

However, in each case, there is a permissible use that does not go through the impermissible inference that the defendant has the bad character of a gambler or burglar. In the first instance, the claim is that the defendant's *motive* is to obtain money to pay off debts; in the second, that she has *knowledge* of how to break into the house; and in the third, that she had *prepared* to break in by amassing the relevant tools. Each of these uses refers to evidence that, on this occasion, she had a specific motive, had specific knowledge, or had engaged in a specific act of preparation. In fact, in making these Rule 404(b) inferences, the proponent would ask for a Rule 105 instruction asking the jury to disregard the impermissible Rule 404(a) inferences they might otherwise draw.

One class of non-propensity evidence is worth mentioning: evidence of identity. Often, prosecutors want to introduce evidence of prior crimes to establish the defendant's identity as the person who committed the present crime. Quite often, such evidence is inadmissible: the claim that defendant had committed three prior similar crimes, and so must have committed this crime, invokes the propensity inference Rule (404) prohibits. However, suppose the police attempt to arrest two people during a drug deal. The dealer is arrested, but the buyer escapes. Later, the police arrest the buyer, but he denies being present at the deal, or knowing the buyer. Dealer's testimony that he has sold drugs to Buyer on *a number* of prior occasions *is* permissible evidence of identity. The evidence shows that Dealer had the ability to recognize Buyer again, given their prior interactions.

Also admissible is evidence that the defendant commits her crimes in a unique or signature manner. The features marking out the crimes must be sufficiently unusual to operate as unique identifier marking out the defendant from other people committing the same class of crimes. For example, the evidence could demonstrate that the person has a unique disguise, such as always wearing a Richard Nixon mask and a superman cape when robbing a bank; or some unusual and distinctive way of doing things.

The Advisory Committee notes that, having determined that the evidence is admissible under 404(b), courts should not forget to apply rule 403 to determine whether the probative danger of the evidence substantially outweighs its probative value. Thus, even if Rule 404(a) does not exclude the specific at evidence, Rule 403 may.

Rule 404(b) sometimes throws up a conditional relevance problem. Suppose the defendant is charged with selling stolen goods. His defense is lack of concurrence of the elements of the crime. He acknowledges committing the *actus reus*—selling stolen goods—but denies he had the appropriate *mens rea*—knowledge that the goods were stolen. The prosecution seeks to introduce evidence that defendant had been arrested on a prior occasion for selling stolen goods from the same source. That evidence is relevant if it tends to show that the defendant *knows* the goods sold in the *current* crime are contraband.

The standard of proof necessary to introduce prior bad act evidence is rather low. For example, to introduce prior act evidence to prove *knowledge*, under Rule 404(b), that the *current* activity was criminal, there had to have been a crime in the past. If the defendant committed a crime in the past, then he knew that he was committing a crime in the present. The problem is: who gets to determine whether there was a prior crime? The judge, under Rule 104(a), applying the *preponderance of the evidence* standard; or the jury, under Rule 104(b), applying the much lower, *sufficiency of the evidence* standard? Or some other, even higher standard? If defendant can exclude the Rule 404(b) evidence of knowledge, he wins the case. If he cannot, he loses.

That was the issue in *Huddleston v. United States*, 485 U.S. 681 (1988). Defendant's prior activity was never prosecuted, so *someone* must determine whether that activity amounts to guilt of a crime. The Court treated the 404(b) issue as one of *conditional relevance*. The defendant only *knew* he was committing a crime in the present on condition that he was guilty of doing so in the past. Under the conditional relevance analysis, the Rule 104(b) sufficiency standard applies.

The consequences of applying the sufficiency standard are harsh for a criminal defendant. The only issue in *Huddleston* was the defendant's mental state (knowledge), and so commission of the past crime was determinative of guilt for the present crime. In Huddleston, it looks, functionally, like the defendant is convicted on the *sufficiency* standard rather than the much higher *beyond a reasonable doubt* standard required for criminal conviction. That problem would remain, however, even if the Court used the 104(a) preponderance of the evidence standard: there would still be a disparity between the functional standard (the one for admitting the evidence) and the formal standard (the one for criminal guilt). In fact, the defendant seems to be arguing for an extra-high standard for admissibility, to avoid this gap. Here, the problem is not really the rules of evidence, but rather the *conclusive nature* of the evidence: it has really high probative value, once admitted. If the worry is that the jury will misuse the prior act evidence by finding it too convincing, the solution is to exclude it under Rule 403.

The habit evidence rule contained in Rule 406 permits using evidence that a person or organization does something *habitually* to prove that the person or organization acted in conformity with that habit on a particular occasion. The rule looks a lot like the Character Evidence Rule, but reaches the opposite conclusion. How so?

To prove that some person has a habit, the proponent must show, at the very least, that the person acts the same way over and over again on lots of occasions. In the words of the Advisory Committee Note, a habit is a *regular response to a repeated specific situation*. The Advisory Committee, however, includes a distinctive sort of response in its definition of habitual behavior: a *semi-automatic* or non-volitional response. Often, the two sorts of responses, regular and semi-automatic, run together. Every time Jenny stands in line in the coffee shop, she reaches for her smartphone, and does so without thinking. Every time Jorge takes the stairs down from the library, he descends two steps at a time, and does so without giving it any attention. Nonetheless, some behavior may be semi-automatic without being regularly repeated, for example when Jenny withdraws her hand from a too-hot cup of tea; and some behavior may be regularly repeated without being semi-automatic; for example, when Jorge gives the same, well-practiced handshake to his teammate every time she scores a goal. Which test we use—the regular response test or the semi-automatic response test—can thus produce different results when determining the admissibility of habit evidence.

What You Need to Know:

1. There are a variety of permissible *non-propensity*, meaning non-character evidence uses of past specific act evidence. The non-propensity use is permissible so long as it does not make the prohibited inference from general trait to specific act.

2. Instead, the propensity use is used to prove something more specific: a particular opportunity presented itself to the defendant; or that she knew some specific thing relevant to a claim or defense; or that she entertained some particular motive that drove her to commit the crime, and so on.

3. This specificity is important when considering one type of *identity* (modus operandi) evidence. If the evidence is the peculiar identifying features of some prior crime that are present in the current crime, then those identifying features must be so unique as to act as a sort of signature.

4. *Huddleston* determines what standard governs admissibility of prior bad act evidence: the sufficiency standard of Rule 104(b). The Court treats the issue as a version of conditional relevance: only if the defendant committed a prior crime did he knew that he was committing a crime in the present. While from the defendant's perspective that seems to lower the functional standard for conviction from beyond a reasonable doubt to sufficiency, the proper way of thinking about it is that, *once admitted*, the evidence of prior criminal activity has really strong probative value in *Huddleston*-type cases. It's not the rule of admission that's the problem, but the nature of the evidence.

4. Habit evidence is different from character evidence: it is not governed by Rule 405's limitations on the methods of proving character evidence, for a start. Habit evidence is either a regular response to a

repeated activity, or an semi-automatic response to some stimulus.

5. For the most part, these two tests pull in the same direction, but sometimes they pull apart, as when the regular response is conscious, rather than semi-automatic; or when we would expect the response to be semi-automatic, even though the stimulus was a one-off.

LESSON 8: VICTIMS AND PERPETRATORS OF SEXUAL VIOLENCE

The rest of Article IV of the Federal Rules of Evidence contains a set of rules discussing when evidence will be treated as presenting probative danger. The first set of rules we shall cover are expressly referenced in Rule 404(a)(2)(B). They apply to cases where the some claim of criminal or civil sexual assault, either on an adult or a minor.

Rule 412 is a *rape shield law*. It precludes the defendant in a criminal case introducing evidence about the victim's past sexual behavior which may be some logical relevance to establishing consent. Remember, Rule 404(a)(2) permits the defendant to open the door to a relevant character trait of himself or the victim: either his good character trait or the victim's bad character trait. Rule 412 takes one type of bad character trait—in the language of old-style earlier cases, the victim's *character for chastity*—off the table.

Rule 412 can be justified as addressing two distinct worries. The first is misusing the evidence of the victim's past sexual conduct by creating a trial-within-a-trial about the victim's moral character, as revealed through her past sexual activities. If the factfinder thinks the victim is of low moral character because she has participated in prior sexual activity, then the factfinder may be tempted to treat the victim as someone who was "asking" for sex, whether or not she consented to sex on this occasion. The second is overvaluing evidence of past sexual activity based on an inference from past consent to present consent.

Furthermore, stereotypical assumptions about male and female sexuality provide incentives for the defendant to open the door to evidence sexual conduct evidence in sexual assault cases. Under Rule 404(a)(2), when the defendant leads with evidence of the *victim's* bad character, the prosecution may rebut with evidence of the *same* bad character trait for the *defendant*. Our culture does not treat the sexual conduct of men and women equally. Men who have lots of sex are admired; women who have lots of sex are shamed. Accordingly, an attack on a woman's sexual character will likely devalue her character (and so her testimony); using similar evidence against a man will likely bolster his sexual character.

Rule 412(a) thus bans the use of for the purposes of proving the victim's past sexual conduct ("other sexual behavior") or her "predisposition" to engage in sexual activity. Such evidence clearly includes sexual activity, but it also includes behavior from which a factfinder might infer a willingness to engage in sexual activity, such as prior *offers* to engage in sexual intercourse. The Advisory Committee Note suggests the prohibition extends to the victim's sexual fantasies and mode of dress or lifestyle, if used to suggest her sexual character.

There are a number of exceptions to Rule 412(a)'s prohibition, however. In a criminal case, a defendant may introduce evidence of a victim's past sexual conduct to prove that someone other than he was the source of semen or whatever physical injuries the victim may have incurred. Such evidence becomes relevant when the prosecutor alleges that the defendant had sex with the victim, and the defendant denies it. The prosecutor might then introduce evidence that the victim had semen in or on her person, or her clothing or sheets; or that she had sustained bruising suggesting sexual intercourse. In that case, the defendant could rebut with evidence that someone else was the source of the semen or the injuries.

In a *civil* case, relevant evidence *is* admissible to prove a victim's past sexual conduct or predisposition. However, the presumption is that such evidence is to be excluded. The relevant standard in a criminal case is that the evidence is admissible only if its probative *value substantially outweighs* its probative danger. Notice that this is the inverse of the Rule 403 standard. Rule 403 is weighted in favor of admissibility; Rule 412 in favor of excludability. Rule 412 also requires the proponent to make a motion to submit the evidence, providing 14 days' notice and informing all the parties and the victim or her guardian. The court then holds an in-camera hearing, and provide the victim and the parties the opportunity to attend and explain why the evidence should be excluded.

The three other rules, Rule 413, Rule 414, and Rule 415, govern the admissibility of evidence used to show the sexual character of the *defendant* or a party in a civil case. Under Rule 413, if a criminal defendant is accused of sexual assault, then evidence of his prior sexual assaults are admissible: no ifs, ands, or buts. Sexual assault includes most forms of offensive sexual touching; and the defendant need not have been accused of a crime for the assault to count. Sexual assault does not, however, usually include lewd conversation, emails, texts and so on.

Rule 414 applies much the same procedure to criminal defendants charged with child sexual molestation: evidence of other child molestations are admissible (children are defined as individuals under the age of 14). Rule 415 applies to civil cases in which the claim depends upon a party's act of child molestation. Evidence of a defendant's other acts of molestation is admissible as character evidence. In each case, the idea is that factfinders tend to undervalue the testimony of people who are sexually assaulted, and especially children. All three rules, impose a 15-day notice requirement before the evidence can be admitted.

What You Need to Know:

1. Rule 412 places a categorical limit on a criminal defendant's general prerogative to use character evidence to prove a *witness's* past sexual behavior or her predisposition to engage in sexual conduct. The definition of sexual behavior or conduct is quite broad.

2. There are some limited exceptions to these prohibitions: to prove that someone other than the defendant was the source of semen or physical injuries.

3. In a civil case, evidence of a witness's sexual conduct or predisposition is not categorically excluded, but the standard of admissibility tilts strongly in favor of exclusion. The evidence may only be admitted if its probative value substantially outweighs its probative danger.
4. Rules 413–15 govern the character of the *defendant* in sexual misconduct cases. In cases of sexual assault on an adult, or molestation of a minor, evidence of the defendant's prior acts of molestation are generally admissible, so long as the defendant is given sufficient notice.

LESSON 9: OTHER POLICY PROHIBITIONS

The other Article IV rules follow the pattern established by Rule 404, and establish that items of evidence are inadmissible for some purposes, but admissible for others. Rule 407 prohibits introducing evidence that a party took steps, after some person has sustained harm or injury, to make future injuries or harm less likely to occur. These steps are generally referred to as *subsequent remedial measures*. Evidence is excluded dependent upon the sequence of events happening in a particular order: first, some harmful or injurious event, and after that, the remedial measures. Furthermore, the subsequent measures must have been taken in order to *prevent the harm or injury from recurring*, rather than for some other purpose, such as making the product or property look better.

Rule 407 promotes two policies. The more important is to encourage parties to take safety measures without having them worry that doing so could be admissible against them in a court of law. The less important is to block the inference that making safety improvements after an injury shows that a party was culpable in not taking action sooner. These policies apply only to *parties*: evidence that *someone other than the parties* took the remedial measures is generally admissible.

Under Rule 407, evidence of subsequent remedial measures is inadmissible to prove fault: that is, negligence, culpable conduct, a defect in some product, or the need for a warning.

Such evidence is permissible for other purposes, for example, resolving certain types of issues in contention at trial. Without some dispute, the evidence is inadmissible. One sort of dispute concerns ownership or control. For example, Defendant denies that the property or product was hers, so Plaintiff introduces evidence of subsequent improvements to show that she could make the changes because had *title or control.*

Another sort of dispute concerns the feasibility of taking safety precautions. If the defendant denies that improvements could be made, evidence of subsequent remedial measures is admissible to show that they could have been made. There is a Rule 403 worry here: if the product was manufactured a long time ago, then evidence of current safety improvements may have low probative value but a high danger of confusing the issues.

In a somewhat similar vein, Rule 409 seeks to encourage "good Samaritans" who help the injured by paying their medical expenses. The rule precludes using the payment of such expenses for the purpose of demonstrating liability for the injury. However, it is only *payments* that are excluded: conversations about why the party paid the medical expenses are admissible.

Rule 408 precludes evidence that a party attempted to engage in civil settlement offers, or evidence about the substance of those offers. The core case is where plaintiff offers to settle a case with defendant for a certain amount. If the defendant agrees but settlement breaks down, defendant cannot later offer the agreement as evidence of plaintiff's liability. Similarly, if defendant offers to settle for a lower amount than plaintiff claims at trial, defendant cannot offer the settlement offer to show plaintiff's damages claim is excessive.

The rule is broader than Rules 407 and 409, because it extends, not only to exclude the offer to pay some amount to settle or drop some claim, but also the *communications* and any other conduct between the parties during the negotiation process.

For Rule 408 to apply, however, there must be some dispute over liability or the amount to be paid in settlement. The rule only applies to offers to compromise, not to *admissions* of liability, where a party concedes fault, rather than disputing it.

Rule 408 precludes using such communications or conduct to attack a witness's credibility in two specific ways: as a prior inconsistent statement or by contradicting something they assert during their testimony. It does not preclude other forms of impeachment, such as a witness's bias or prejudice. Evidence of settlement negotiations is also admissible to demonstrate the witness sought to obstruct a criminal investigation or prosecution, for example, by buying someone off as a means of avoiding criminal liability. Finally, evidence of settlement negotiations is admissible to prove lack of undue delay.

While Rule 408 prevents evidence of *civil* settlement negotiations being admitted at trial, whether civil or criminal, the rule does not apply to *criminal* settlement negotiations between a party and a state official. Rule 410 governs those sorts of negotiations.

Rule 410 is the criminal settlement equivalent of Rule 408. It applies to what are colloquially called *plea bargains*. The rule makes certain evidence inadmissible in a criminal or civil trial against the defendant making the plea: the plea itself if it was later withdrawn; a plea of "no contest" (*nolo contendere*); any statements made during the plea allocution process (what the defendant says to the judge when pleading guilty), or any statements made during the negotiation process. As with Rule 408, the rule applies only to negotiations, not admissions. So the contents of a criminal defendant's uncontested *confession* made during the plea process are admissible at trial.

Rule 410 is now largely irrelevant thanks to *United States v. Mezzanatto*, 513 U.S. 196 (1995). In that case, the prosecutor demanded that the defendant waive Rule 410 as a condition of entering plea negotiations. Such waivers, the Supreme Court held, are permissible. Since defendants generally want the lower sentence offered in a plea rather than the protections of the rules of evidence, prosecutors now standardly require such waivers, and defendants agree to them.

The final policy rule is Rule 411, which precludes evidence of liability insurance to prove fault. The general idea is that, just because someone obtains insurance does not mean she is engaged in risky behavior. As in Rule 407, the evidence is admissible to prove ownership or control; and as in Rule 408, evidence of insurance is permissible to prove bias or prejudice. The rule has been construed quite narrowly, to permit evidence of other purposes that are not limited to whether carefully or carelessly, such as their *motive* in a criminal case (that is, to show the defendant acted criminally to obtain an insurance payout).

What You Need to Know:

1. The policy rules are basically more specific applications of Rule 403. Each of them is justified based on the danger of misleading or confusing the jury, or unfair prejudice. Each rule gives a series of specific uses that are prohibited, and then an open-ended list of permitted uses.

2. Rule 407, prohibits admitting evidence of later repairs or other remedial measures when offered to prove that the defendant is at fault; however the evidence is permissible to prove ownership, control, and feasibility.

3. Rule 408 prohibits admitting evidence of or from settlement efforts to prove liability. The scope of the prohibition is broad: any aspect of the settlement negotiation is excluded. However, there must be a dispute. If a party simply caved and confessed liability, there is no dispute, and the concession evidence is inadmissible. Settlement negotiation evidence *is* permissible, however, to prove bias of witness, and (lack of) delay, when, for example, a question of mitigating damages arises.

4. Rule 409 prohibits admitting evidence of payment or offers to pay medical expenses to prove liability. This rule is a narrow one. It is only the actual payment or offer that is excluded; anything else the witness says or does may be admitted.

5. Rule 410 prohibits admitting evidence of the substance of criminal plea negotiations that do not

result in a guilty conviction. Such evidence is permissible for purposes of clarification or for use in a perjury proceeding. But the rule has been largely gutted by *Mezzanatto*, which allows prosecutors to condition guilty pleas on the defendant's waiver of Rule 410.

6. Rule 411 prohibits admitting evidence of the presence or absence of an insurance policy to prove liability. However, the rule is quite narrow, and evidence of insurance is admissible for a number of other uses, including to prove ownership or control of some object.

LESSON 10: WITNESSES AND TRIAL CONDUCT

In our ordinary, non-legal, language, a *witness* is someone who perceives something. Under the Federal Rules of Evidence, the term *witness* has a more restricted meaning, one that is vitally important for understanding, not only the first three rules in Article VI, but also the meaning of *expert witness* in Article VII, and the meaning of *hearsay* in Article VIII.

Under the Rules of Evidence, a witness is someone who appears at the current *formal legal proceeding*, usually one in which the witness can be subject to cross-examination, and most centrally, a trial. She gives evidence (*testimony*) about things that she has *personally perceived*, and does so under *oath and penalty of perjury*. These features of witness testimony provide certain *evidentiary guarantees* for the factfinder, who can assess the live witness's *demeanor* when giving her evidence under *oath* and responding to *cross-examination*. The evidentiary guarantees in turn allow the factfinder to assess four *credibility factors*: the witness's *perception* of the events; her *memory* of what she perceived; the *sincerity* or honesty of her testimony; and whether there are gaps or inconsistencies in her story or *narration*.

Rule 601 allows anyone to be a witness. Unusually, for the law of evidence, it is a broadly *inclusionary* rule: it starts by *admitting* evidence, before providing for exceptions allowing for its exclusion. One reason is that historically, competence to testify was extremely limited. Legislators and judges were the gatekeepers of witness testimony, mostly preventing people from testifying under various common law rules and statutes. Rule 601 sweeps away this historical baggage, and renders *everyone* presumptively competent to testify.

Three categories of witnesses are often challenged as incompetent: children, people with mental illnesses, and people addicted to drugs. However, such individuals are *not* categorically excluded from serving as witnesses: the question is whether they can recall what they claim to have perceived, can communicate what they recall, and understand their duty to tell the truth. These factors are best assessed under Rules 602 and 603.

Rule 602 characterizes testimony as statements made from *personal knowledge*. Rule 602 requires that the witness have personally perceived what she claims to have seen, heard, touched, smelled, or tasted. This raises a question of conditional relevance similar to Rule 104(b): in fact, the Advisory Committee suggests that Rule 602 just is a "specialized application of the provisions of FRE 104(b)." The witness claims to have perceived some fact; that claim is relevant only on condition she *did or could have* perceived it. Accordingly, the rule requires that the proponent introduce foundation evidence under the sufficiency standard contained in Rule 104(b), to establish she could have perceived what she claims to have seen, heard, etc. So long as there are sufficient grounds to believe that a reasonable juror could find the witness had personal knowledge, the jury will get to evaluate that question for themselves.

Rule 603 requires that witnesses make some formal statement that they understand their obligation to tell the truth, when they testify. What matters is that the witness understand the importance of telling the truth: their *oath or affirmation* need not take any particular form, so long as it establishes the witness's commitment to truth-telling.

When presenting their case, the attorneys normally get to determine when to call witnesses and to cross examine them. However, under Rule 611, the trial court can change things up to make the procedures *effective for determining the truth*; avoid *time wasting*; and *protect witnesses from harassment or undue embarrassment.* So long as the court does not abuse its discretion, it can tinker with the order of calling witnesses and other aspects relating to the presentation of evidence.

Rule 106 provides one limit on the trial court's power over the order of presenting evidence. Where one party introduces only *part* of a *document or other recorded statement*, and the writing or recording presents a partial and misleading picture of what went on, the *opposing party* may demand that the rest of the recording or writing be introduced *at the time* the proponent introduced the originals. The rule *only* applies to written or recorded statements: it does *not* apply to live witness testimony. The Supreme Court affirmed this procedure in *Beech Aircraft v. Rainey*, 488 U.S. 153 (1988).

Rule 611(c) regulates some important aspects of questioning witnesses. On direct, the proponent usually *cannot* ask *leading questions*: that is, questions designed to elicit some specific answer by suggesting some answer to the witness. Exceptions to this rule permit leading questions when the witness is an *adverse party* or *associated with* one, or when the witness is *hostile*. It is usually easy to determine which parties are adverse; individuals associated with adverse parties may be co-conspirators, or the party's relatives, friends, or co-workers. Hostile witnesses are ones who make it clear they are unwilling to answer counsel's direct questions, for whatever reason. Hostility is often manifested by claimed lapses in memory, failures to understand, meandering answers to direct questions, or some bias against of one of the parties. As opposed to hostility, some witnesses may simply find it difficult, through an inability easily to comprehend or articulate their answers. These types of witness include: children, the infirm, or the excessively timid. Confronted with these witnesses, the court has discretion to allow leading questions.

Leading questions are always permissible on cross examination. However, Rule 611(b) requires that cross examination usually not exceed the scope of direct examination. A cross-examiner can ask questions that go to witness credibility, or matters already raised on direct examination. However, the rule effectively permits the proponent to set the scope of witness testimony unless the court finds reasons of fairness or efficiency justify going beyond the scope of direct. Otherwise, the opponent must wait to recall the witness during her case in chief or rebuttal case if she wants to go beyond the scope of the direct.

What You Need to Know:

1. Under Rule 601, all witnesses are presumed competent. That means that the question of competence is up to the jury to determine. Only if the witness cannot remember what happened or cannot communicate will she be declared incompetent.

2. Some witnesses raise competency red flags. The primary ones are children, the insane and people addicted to narcotics or alcohol. However, even these groups are competent to serve as witnesses unless they *categorically could not* perceive what they claim to have perceived, or are incapable of communicating what they saw to the jury or are currently intoxicated. Again, it is up to the jury to determine how much credibility to afford their testimony.

3. Under Rule 602, all witnesses must have *personal knowledge* of the matters about which they testify. Personal knowledge just means that they perceived the thing about which they are testifying. The issue is essentially one of conditional relevance; they could only testify about some matter if they actually perceived it. Accordingly, personal knowledge is assessed under the sufficiency standard.

4. Rule 603 requires all witnesses to affirm that they will tell the truth, and to demonstrate that they understand the importance of truth telling. Together, Rules 601–603 establish what it means to be a witness at a trial.

5. Normally, the attorneys get to determine how to present their evidence. But Rule 611 permits the judge to step in to alter the way evidence is

presented, to make the trial fairer, more efficient, or less confusing to the jury. One limit on this judicial power is Rule 106's process for clearing up unfairly misleading uses of *documentary* or recorded evidence: if a proponent offers part of a document or recording, and it would be unfair not to introduce some other portion of it, Rule 106 allows the opposing part to introduce the rest right away, if she so choose.

6. Rule 611 also regulates the manner of cross-examining witnesses. Leading questions—ones that suggest a particular answer—are usually prohibited on direct examination. The exception is when a witness is hostile or is (or is associated with) an adverse party. Leading questions *are* permitted on cross-examination, but cross-examination itself is usually restricted to questions about the witness's credibility and matters already raised on direct.

LESSON 11: WITNESS CREDIBILITY: CHARACTER FOR HONESTY AND DISHONESTY

The point of live witness testimony is to assess the credibility of witnesses: their perception, memory, sincerity and narrative reliability. The rules of evidence, however, set out a structure for assessing credibility. In general terms, that structure requires a party first to introduce evidence *attacking* a witness's credibility before an opponent may introduce evidence *supporting* the witness's credibility.

The order of credibility evidence—impeachment first, rehabilitation second—reflects the Federal Rule's belief that evidence that the witness is honest has the potential to mislead the jury if used at the wrong time. Clever attorneys can use the evidence to vouch for the witness, taking the all-important credibility determination out of the hands of the jury, who overvalue claims that the witness is honest if they hear it before hearing evidence that the witness is dishonest.

Rule 607 permits any party, including the proponent who called the witness, to attack the witness's credibility. Rule 607 thus sweeps away some historically restrictive rules that prevented certain witnesses from being impeached. But the Rules of Evidence are less specific about the permissible *modes of impeachment*: ways to attack *the witness* directly as unreliable because of failing to perceive or remember accurately, or as insincere of having gaps in their story. There are five such ways to impeach a witness: dishonesty (that is, their character for untruthfulness), inconsistency, incapacity, bias, and contradiction. Other evidence may call a witness's testimony into question *indirectly*, by presenting a different narrative of the events at issue. So long as that evidence is not introduced *for the purpose of impugning the witness's credibility*, then it does not count as impeachment evidence.

The rules expressly mention evidence introduced to illustrate the witness's character for truthfulness or to prove inconsistency between the witness's current testimony and prior statements about some matter. And Rule 601 presumes everyone has the capacity to be a witness. But the rules are silent on proving that a witness is biased, or the scope of evidence used to contradict testimony expressly. In these last two cases, common law practices remain especially important to discern what evidence is admissible or inadmissible.

Impeaching a witness by questioning their character for honesty is governed by three sets of rules. Rule 404(a), the character evidence rule, sets aside a witness's character for honesty as a special type of character evidence (Rule 404(a)(3)), and directs us to Rules 608 and 609. Rule 609 governs the use of *criminal convictions* used to impeach a witness's character for honesty; Rule 608 governs all other witness character evidence.

Under Rule 404(a), parties are usually precluded from introducing character traits, with a limited exception in criminal trials for the relevant trait of a defendant or victim. However, Rule 404(a)(3) directs us to Rule 608; which in turn establishes that it is permissible to introduce evidence about the character of a *witness* for the trait of honesty or dishonesty. Just by taking the stand, the witness puts her character for truthfulness in issue. However, Rule 608 preserves Rule 405's weird mini-trial process for proving character, along with some other limitations.

Impeachment always precedes rehabilitation: accordingly, Rule 608 states that evidence of the witness's good character—truthfulness—can only be introduced *after* her character for truthfulness has been attacked. Once on the stand, however, the witness can be impeached with her character for truthfulness. Suppose the plaintiff, in her case-in-chief, calls Wendy to testify that the light was red when the defendant entered the intersection and hit the plaintiff. Defendant could confront Wendy, on cross-examination, with questions about her character for honesty. Or the defendant could wait until its case-in chief, and call another witness, Xander, to testify about Wendy's bad character for telling the truth. Plaintiff could *then*, in its rebuttal case, call Yasmine to attest to Wendy's character for truthfulness. Plaintiff *could not*, however, call Yasmine before Xander impugned Wendy's character for honesty.

Rule 608 requires the party *introducing* evidence of the witness's character for honesty or dishonesty to use *reputation* or *opinion* evidence. Thus, Xander would testify that in his opinion, Wendy is dishonest; or he could testify that to his knowledge, she has a bad reputation in the community for honesty. Similarly, Yasmine could testify that in *her* opinion, Wendy is honest or has a good reputation in the community for honesty. But a party may only introduce *specific act* evidence to prove honesty or dishonesty *on cross examination* of the witness or someone else testifying to that witness's character for honesty. In our example, the defendant *could* ask *either* Wendy or Yasmine if Wendy had failed a lie detector test or been charged, though not convicted, of perjury. Remember, just by testifying, Wendy put her character for honesty in issue, and Yasmine has just testified, on direct, in general terms (reputation or opinion evidence) about Wendy's character for *honesty*. She may then be cross-examined by the defendant, who can ask her about the specific instances evidencing Wendy's dishonesty.

The final oddity Rule 608 shares with Rule 405 is that the questioner cannot use *extrinsic evidence* to prove specific acts of honesty or dishonesty. The cross-examiner must take the answer the witness gives: she cannot rebut it by calling another witness to introduce the specific act evidence on direct. Thus, if Wendy lied about having failed the lie detector test, defendant *could not* ask Xander if Wendy failed the test, because Xander's testimony is *extrinsic evidence* about Wendy's character for honesty, not in the form of opinion or reputation evidence. Nor could defendant introduce the lie detector printout into evidence because, once again, that evidence is extrinsic evidence of the specific act.

What You Need to Know:

1. Impeachment and rehabilitation concern a specific mode of relevance: the witness's credibility. A party may impeach a witness *either* on direct *or* on cross-examination; and parties may now impeach their *own* witnesses, under Rule 607. However, impeachment must *precede* rehabilitation: a party cannot bolster the credibility of a witness unless that witness's credibility has first been attacked.
2. The process for impeaching or rehabilitating a witness's character for truthfulness, under rule 608, tracks the process under Rules 404(a) and 405. If the party attacks or bolsters a witness's character for untruthfulness on *direct*, she must do so using *opinion or reputation* testimony; if the party attacks a witness's character for honesty on cross-examination, she must elicit *intrinsic* evidence of specific acts of dishonesty.

LESSON 12: CHARACTER FOR DISHONESTY: USING PRIOR CONVICTIONS TO IMPEACH

One category of witness evidence is excepted both from Rule 404's prohibition on the use of character evidence to prove conformity with some trait *and* Rule 608's weird procedure, which prohibits extrinsic of specific past acts. That is certain evidence of prior *criminal convictions*, admissible to prove a witness's character for dishonesty. As with Rule 608, simply testifying is enough to put the witness's character in issue.

However, unlike Rule 608, if the evidence falls within certain well-defined categories, it is admissible, even though that evidence is extrinsic evidence of past specific acts.

Rule 609 requires that the defendant have been *convicted* of some crime. It is not enough that the defendant have been merely arrested or charged. Civil judgments obviously do not count as a criminal conviction; neither do criminal acts that *might* lead to prosecution, nor indictments nor deferred criminal judgments. Some kind of final judgment at trial is necessary for a conviction. Furthermore, Rule 609 prioritizes relatively recent convictions over older ones. There is a special rule for any conviction more than ten years old, dated from the time of final release or the entry of final judgment on the conviction whichever is later. *All* convictions dated earlier than this ten-year period are much harder to admit, as the rules apply the *mirror image of Rule 403* standard: the probative *value* of admitting the evidence must *substantially* outweigh the probative dangers of excluding it.

For crimes less than ten years old, Rule 609 provides two routes to inadmissibility. Under Rule 609(a)(2), evidence of crimes of dishonesty or *crimen falsi* are *automatically* admissible to prove character for dishonesty. So long as the crime involves some element of falsification, it does not matter whether the crime for which the defendant was convicted is a felony or a misdemeanor. Even misdemeanors are admissible to prove dishonesty.

Crimen falsi include a narrow range crimes whose elements require misrepresentation: so crimes that involve fraud, such as embezzlement or perjury or forgery do fit. Crimes that are *not crimen falsi* include assault, drug offenses, kidnapping, and the like. Other crimes are sometimes committed using deception or misrepresentation, though their elements do not specify fraud as an element of the offense. Theft crimes fall in this category, and have caused a lot of confusion: ordinarily, theft does not involve active deception by the thief, but sometimes thieves do operate in this manner. Rule 609(a)(2) now makes it clear that only if the statute makes deception an element of the offense, or it can be *readily determined* from the judgment that the offense was committed by deception or a false statement, will the crime count as a *crimen falsi*.

For all other convictions, if the crime is a misdemeanor, it is likely *inadmissible*. That is because the other route to admissibility under Rule 609(a)(1) requires the conviction to be a *felony*. Any felony is admissible to impeach under Rule 609(a)(1) (so felony *crimen falsi* are admissible under both routes, Rule 609(a)(1) *and* (2)). However, felony convictions less than ten years old are not automatically admissible, and there are different standards dependent upon the status of the witness.

In a *civil case* or a *criminal case* where the witness is *not the defendant*, the ordinary balancing test from Rule 403 applies (Rule 609(a)(1)(A)). However, in a *criminal case* where the witness *is* the defendant, the rules adopt an ambivalent stance towards the admission of evidence: Rule 609(a)(1)(B) requires that the probative value outweigh the probative danger. Note that there is a word missing here that is included in Rule 403 or its mirror image (e.g., Rule 609(b)(2)): that word is *substantially*. Where the evidence is a felony conviction of the defendant-witness in a criminal trial, the rule does not tip heavily towards admission *or* exclusion.

Many people find admitting of evidence of a felony conviction to prove character for dishonesty quite weird. After all, a crime of violence is not probative of *dishonesty*, though it may be probative of other criminal traits. Or consider what happens if there is evidence of criminal activity but *no* conviction: the evidence is inadmissible under Rule 609 and the evidence of criminal activity is only admissible under Rule 608 if it demonstrates a character for dishonesty. While criminal activity amounting to a *crimen falsi* would be admissible under Rule 608, other criminal activity amounting to a felony likely would not, unless there was evidence of deceit or false statement.

The obscure relation between dishonesty and non-deceitful felony convictions makes the weighting requirement imposed by Rule 609(a)(1) somewhat random. Some judges believe that felons are bad people or disregard rules, and so likely dishonest; others refuse to make this inference. So for some judges, a felony conviction has high probative value; for others it has low probative value. Probative value should decrease the more time has elapsed between the crime and the testimony: Rule 609(b) codifies that view of probative value. Where the witness is a criminal defendant in a criminal trial, and the felony conviction is similar to the crime charged, then courts sometimes find the Rule 609(a)(1)(B) danger of misuse is very high, and so exclude the evidence; other courts find the probative value high and so admit the evidence.

Finally, Rule 610 precludes evidence of a witness's religious beliefs or opinions to impeach their credibility. However, the evidence may be used for other purposes, such as to prove bias.

What You Need to Know:

1. The rules for impeaching a witness's character for truthfulness using one category of prior bad acts—crimes—are very different from the standard character evidence rules. Evidence of a witness's prior crimes are often admissible to prove their character for dishonesty. The usual character evidence methods-of-proof rules do not apply to this sort of evidence.
2. Timing matters. Where the crime is older than ten years, usually measured since the date the criminal finished her sentence, then the crime is admissible only if the probative value of the crime *substantially outweighs* the probative danger.
3. If the crime is less than ten years old, there are two different routes to admissibility. The easiest, under Rule 609(a)(1), is where the prior crime is a *crimen falsi* (a crime requiring element of misrepresentation or fraud). All *crimen falsi*, whether felonies or misdemeanors, are admissible. Otherwise, Rule 609(a)(2) requires the prior crime be a felony. If the witness is the defendant, then the felony is admissible only if the probative value outweighs the probative danger. For all other witnesses, the evidence of a prior crime is admissible to impeach so long as the probative

danger does not substantially outweigh the probative value.

LESSON 13: CREDIBILITY: PRIOR INCONSISTENT STATEMENTS

Sometimes a witness changes her story at trial. Upon witnessing the accident, Wendy told the plaintiff and a policeman that the defendant's car entered the intersection when the traffic light was red. At trial, however, Wendy denies making the statement, or says that the light was green, or says that she cannot remember. There are two possible reasons the plaintiff may seek to introduce the original statement: to prove that Wendy's original story is the *true* one; or to prove that Wendy is *not credible* as a witness (or both). The first use—to prove the *prior inconsistent statement* is the *true* one—is covered by the *hearsay* rule. We'll cover that use in Lesson 21. However, the second use, to impeach Wendy as unreliable or untrustworthy, is admissible as *impeachment* evidence to undermine her credibility.

Prior inconsistent statements impeach because they *contradict* the witness's testimony on the stand. The statement is useful, not because it is true, but because it shows that one or both of the statements is false. What matters is that it cannot *both* be the case that the traffic light was red *and* the traffic light was green when the defendant's car entered the intersection. The witness is uncertain or mistaken about what she percieved.

Prior statements must be inconsistent to be admissible for impeachment purposes. But how inconsistent? The prior statement need not *directly* contradict current testimony, although that is the core scenario; so long as the prior statement conveys a *significantly different picture of events* than the current testimony, it is inadmissible. Current testimony may be inconsistent with prior statements when it leaves out material facts, or when the witness claims not to remember what happened in ways that indicate the witness has not forgotten, but simply does not want to testify about the subject she is questioned about. Current testimony is *not* inconsistent just because it is less thorough than the prior statement.

Prior inconsistent statements may be proved either by questioning the witness about her statement or by introducing *extrinsic evidence*: either another witness testifying to the content of the statement, or some document or recording that has memorialized the prior statement. Rule 613 provides a gloss the process of admitting this sort of evidence. Start with questioning the witness. If the prior inconsistent statement is memorialized in some writing or recording, the proponent need not disclose the contents of the statement to the witness.

However, if an opposing counsel requests, the proponent must show the contents of the statement to the opponent's lawyer. If the proponent seeks to introduce extrinsic evidence of the prior inconsistent statement, the witness must, at some point, have a chance to explain or deny the statement; and the opponent must be given an opportunity to examine the witness about the prior inconsistent statement, so as to have a chance of rehabilitating her.

In our example, if the plaintiff impeaches Wendy with her prior inconsistent statement on cross-examination, plaintiff's counsel need not introduce extrinsic evidence of the statement (for example, a police report of the accident). She can simply ask Wendy to repeat the prior statement memorialized by the police in the report. If defense counsel asks to see the report, plaintiff must show it to her. If plaintiff seeks to introduce the portions of the report containing Wendy's statement into evidence, or to have the police officer testify about Wendy's prior inconsistent statement, defendant must have a chance to examine Wendy and Wendy must have an opportunity, at some point, to explain the inconsistency.

Rule 613 does not expressly cover prior *consistent* statements, which may be offered to *bolster* an inconsistent witness's testimony. The general rule that proof of honesty is admissible *only after* impeachment for dishonesty applies to prior consistent statements as well. Furthermore, these statements have *very low probative value*: remember, the impeaching claim is that the inconsistency between a witness's prior position and her present one undermines her credibility. Adding a consistent statement does not remove the inconsistency: it does not cancel the inconsistent statement, nor add anything new to the present position. Thus, prior *consistent* statements are usually precluded for credibility purposes.

There are two exceptions to this general rule. The first exception permits using a prior consistent statement to rebut a charge of recent fabrication: that the witness made up her story for purposes of testifying at trial. In *Tome v. United States*, 513 U.S. 150 (1995), the Court interpreted Rule 801(d)(1)(B) to limit the *hearsay* use of prior consistent statements to prove the *truth* of statement. The Court imposed two limits on admissibility: first the prior statement is only admissible to rebut an opponent's claim that the witness had recently changed her story; and second, the *prior consistent* statement must have been made *before* witness developed her motive to lie. Many federal circuits extend the *Tome* rule to impeachment statements as well. More controversially, some Circuits allow proof of prior consistent statements if the statement was made close in time to the inconsistent one, to prove the *inconsistent* statement was never made.

What You Need to Know:

1. Prior inconsistent statements may be used for two purposes: to impeach a witness's credibility or to prove that the prior statement is the true one. The second, substantive use is covered by Rule 801(d)(1)(A).

2. The impeachment use, which is covered by Rule 613, does not require *either* the prior statement or current testimony to be true. The method of impeachment simply shows that the statements cannot *both* be true. At least one (and perhaps both) is false.

3. A witness may be impeached with a prior inconsistent statement using *either* intrinsic or extrinsic evidence. The only limitation on impeachment is that, if extrinsic evidence is used, such as a document or testimony by someone else, then the witness must be given an opportunity to explain the statement and cross-examine the witness. Furthermore, if some document is used for

impeachment, then opposing counsel must be given an opportunity to examine the document on request.

LESSON 14: CREDIBILITY AND SPECIFIC CONTRADICTION

Witnesses may also be impeached for *bias*: the claim that the witness has some motivation to lie, based on a relationship with one of the parties or some stake in the litigation. The relationship may be personal or professional; and the stake in the case could extend to emotional, moral, or religious issues. Remember, Rule 610 *permits* introducing evidence of religion to show bias. Thus, evidence that an expert is paid by one of the parties is admissible; as is evidence that the witness is a friend or relative of a party or another witness; or evidence that the witness has feelings, stemming from moral or religious beliefs, that predispose them against a party or another witness.

There is no Federal Rule regulating the use of bias evidence. Nonetheless, in *United States v. Abel*, 469 U.S. 45 (1984), the Supreme Court endorsed bias as a permissible method of impeachment. Bias evidence is always relevant, and may be proved using extrinsic evidence, subject to Rule 401 and Rule 403's balancing scheme. A witness impeached for bias may be rehabilitated with evidence that she was not biased, but such evidence is *only* admissible *after* she has been impeached.

Witnesses may also be impeached for *incapacity*: the claim that the witness lacks the physical inability to perceive what she claimed to perceive; or that the witness lacks the mental ability to remember what she claimed to remember. Rule 601 precludes *judges* from excluding witnesses for lack of capacity. And Rule 602's sufficiency standard creates a *low bar* to admissibility. The Rules of Evidence leave capacity determinations up to the factfinder, who is supposed to determine how well the witness could perceive or remember what she claims to have seen, heard, touched, etc. As with bias, evidence about the witness's capacity is always relevant, and is governed by Rules 401 and 403. If the witness is impeached for lack of capacity, she may be rehabilitated with evidence demonstrating capacity: either her ability to perceive accurately, or her ability to remember what happened.

Finally, witnesses may be impeached using a process called *specific contradiction*. This process can lead to some confusion. First, specific contraction looks a lot like impeachment through prior inconsistent statements. But it is importantly different. The purpose of specific contradiction is to claim that the witness's testimony is *untrue* in some respect, not simply that it is inconsistent. The testimony fails to match the *world* not some prior statement. Second, specific contradiction is often confused with introducing evidence that undermines some party's case. But the purpose of specific contradiction is to *directly impeach* the witness's testimony. It claims that the witness is not credible because wrong about some matter of fact. Lots of relevant evidence could conflict with the witness's testimony: but only some of it will be directed towards demonstrating that some particular witness is mistaken and so not to be trusted.

Perhaps the most famous case turning on specific contradiction is Abraham Lincoln's defense of William "Duff" Armstrong in 1858, who was accused of murdering his victim by striking him with a "slung shot," which killed him. The key prosecution witness claimed to see the fatal blow from some distance away, because the full and bright. Lincoln impeached the witness using an almanac which showed the phases of the moon, suggesting that the moon would not have provided much illumination. Here, there is no prior statement, just testimony at trial and the fact that the moon's light was weak, undermining the witness's credibility.

Once again, the Federal Rules do not govern the use of specific contradiction. However, the common law *collateral evidence rule* prohibits introducing *extrinsic evidence* to prove some matter that is *not material* to some claim or defense, or to the credibility of some *other* witness.

Thus, if Wendy testifies that the light was red when Defendant's car entered the intersection, striking plaintiff, her credibility may be impeached by *specifically contradicting* two facts: first, that the light was red at the relevant time; and second, that the defendant's coat was blue. The first fact is relevant to prove some matter affecting the outcome of the case:

whether the defendant was culpable or not. Defendant can introduce extrinsic evidence of this material fact to prove Wendy was mistaken: for example a CCTV footage showing the light was green; or the testimony of a police-officer who saw the accident.

Defendant might also try to prove that Wendy was mistaken by introducing evidence that Defendant's coat was orange, not blue. However, the outcome of the case does not turn on whether or not Defendant's coat was blue. That matter is thus *collateral* rather than material. The probative danger of focusing too heavily on this sort of evidence is to confuse the jury, so that they are no longer sure what the trial is about. Or the collateral issue may encourage the jury to overvalue the evidence or waste time focusing on a minor issue. The probative value is to show the witness is mistaken about one aspect of the accident, and so may be mistaken about others. The collateral evidence rule deals with this evidence by allowing the proponent (here, the defendant) to ask the witness about the collateral evidence (the color of the coat); but requires the proponent to take the witness's answer, and prohibits introducing extrinsic evidence on the collateral matter. The process is identical to that contemplated in Rule 405 and rule 608(b).

What You Need to Know:

1. There are no specific rules for impeachment for *bias* or *incapacity*. That means that the proponent can impeach the witness using any method, intrinsic or extrinsic. Bias requires that the witness have some stake in the litigation or relationship with a party that would motivate her to lie. Incapacity means that the witness could not have perceived what she claimed to have seen, heard, touched, tasted, or smelled.

2. Impeachment through *specific contradiction* requires the proponent to prove that a witness's claim that some fact was the case it *is not true*. The conflict is between the witness's testimony and a fact (not between two statements, one at trial, one before trial).

3. The manner of proving a specific contradiction depends upon whether the fact is *material* or *collateral*. A collateral matter is one that goes only to credibility through contradiction, rather than to some fact used to prove a claim or defense. For collateral matters, the common law *collateral evidence rule* applies to limit impeachment to *intrinsic* evidence. For material contradictions, the proponent can impeach the witness using any method, intrinsic or extrinsic.

LESSON 15: LAY OPINION EVIDENCE

The rules of evidence distinguish between two major types of opinion evidence: lay opinion and expert opinion. Expert opinion need not be based on inferences derived from the witness's personal perceptions. Instead expert opinion may appeal to specialized, scientific, or technical knowledge, of the type specifically excluded from lay opinion under Rule 701(c). As the Advisory Committee notes, the difference is not between types of witness, but types of *evidence*, each deriving from a different source of knowledge.

Both types of opinion evidence, should, in turn, be distinguished from testimony that recounts a witness's *personal knowledge* about some set of facts. Fact testimony provides particular details about what the witness *directly perceived*. Lay opinion testimony, because not about what the witness directly perceived, flunks the personal knowledge requirement. But lay opinions are really closely related to personal knowledge: they are ordinary inferences derived from what the witness saw, heard, smelled, and so on. So Rule 701(a) makes it relatively easy to admit lay opinion testimony. It carves out an exception for lay opinion testimony so long as the inference is *rationally derived* from the witness's perceptions and is *helpful* to the trier of fact (Rule 701(b)).

For example, if Wendy personally perceives the defendant run a red light, she might form the opinion that defendant was driving negligently or recklessly, or that defendant was driving too fast. These opinions are rationally based on what she perceived: the speed of the car, the time it took the car to stop, the driver's posture or expression, and so on. But the claim that the defendant was driving negligently is not a fact, in the technical meaning of the rules. It is an opinion based on the witness's evaluation of the underlying facts. Each of these factual observations could be extracted from the witness one by one, but they need not add up to the whole: the conclusion that the driver was negligent. Rule 701 permits the witness, rather than just the factfinder, to infer from the mass of individual facts that the driver was negligent and state that opinion to the factfinder.

An important limit on the admissibility of opinion evidence is the requirement that the evidence be *helpful* to the factfinder. One way of understanding the helpfulness requirement is as promoting the Rule 102 value of *accuracy*: the opinion is helpful if it makes it easier for the factfinder to understand some issue in the trial. However, the testimony is *unhelpful* and so should not be admitted when the opinion simply takes sides, or the factfinder has all the necessary information to draw some conclusion in its possession.

Difficulties can arise when the opinion testimony is based upon some relevant experience that enables the witness to give her opinion of something she has perceived. Perhaps the witness has experience driving, and so knows what a car going through a red light at forty miles per hour looks like. Or perhaps a witness has smoked marijuana, and so knows what it smells like; or is familiar with the consumption of alcohol, and so can tell when someone is drunk. However, if the witness's knowledge of background facts necessary to give her opinion is *too specialized*, then her opinion, even if helpful, becomes that of an expert. Thus, opinion testimony based on special training or education tends to qualify the witness as an expert, whereas opinion testimony gained through ordinary experience, or familiarity with some aspect of a trade or institution, need not. Thus, a police officer need not qualify as an expert to testify about how heroin is sold on street corners, because anyone in the neighborhood could observe these facts. But an officer may need to qualify as an expert to testify about special features of drug distribution that go beyond her personal perception and depend upon her training as a narcotics officer.

For the most part, the opinion testimony rules do not preclude testimony on any subject matter, including the *ultimate issues* in the case. An ultimate issue is one that is determinative of some claim or defense, without any intervening inferences. For example, if Wendy observed the defendant's car enter the intersection and strike the plaintiff, Rule 704 permits her to testify that, in her opinion, the defendant was driving negligently or carefully. Or a witness in a criminal case could testify that a defendant struck the victim intentionally or accidentally.

There are two major limits on testimony about ultimate issues. First, in a *criminal cases*, Rule 704(b) precludes expert witness opinion as to the defendant's mental state or condition. This limitation was introduced after John Hinkley attempted to murder President Reagan, and was found not guilty by virtue of insanity following expert testimony on his behalf. The second limitation is Rule 403, which operates to exclude the evidence if the opinion as to the ultimate fact is likely to supplant the factfinder's role in drawing that conclusion.

What You Need to Know:

1. *Fact* and *opinion* testimony are technical terms. Facts are those things a witness perceives; opinions are *rational inferences* drawn from facts. The distinction between the two is fuzzy, so the rules of evidence permit any witness to testify about both facts and opinions.
2. However, Rule 702 places some limits on the admissibility of opinion testimony: lay opinion testimony must be based on personal knowledge and must be rationally derived from those facts, and must be helpful to the factfinder.
3. If the opinion lacks any of these three elements, then the witness must be qualified as an expert to testify about the opinion. Rule 701(c) bolsters this approach, and prohibits witnesses from smuggling in expert testimony under the guise of lay testimony.

4. Rule 704 permits certain types of opinion testimony that goes to the ultimate issue in the case. Permissible topics include whether the defendant is guilty or innocent, or some party is liable or not. The exception is in criminal cases, where experts are precluded from testifying about the defendant's mental state if that constitutes an element of the crime or a defense.

LESSON 16: EXPERT OPINION TESTIMONY

Sometimes a party wishes to prove some fact that depends upon specialized technical or scientific or other knowledge. For example, having observed the car enter the intersection, Wendy, as a lay person, would be able to give her opinion as to just how fast the car was going. However, if she was asked about the braking distance for that make or model of car given the speed it was going, she would rely, not upon personal observation, but *specialized knowledge* about the car. Rule 702 governs the admissibility of these sorts of expert opinions.

Rule 702 contains a threshold question regarding the admissibility of expert testimony: is the witness really an expert on this subject? The Rule takes a broad approach to what counts as expertise: the rule treats experts as any person qualified by "knowledge, skill, experience, training, or education." A *formal education* or *professional license* often provide sufficient evidence of expertise: the stereotypical expert may be qualified because of her Ph.D. in physics or chemistry, or her advanced medical degree. Nonetheless, a degree or license is not required to qualify as an expert. Experts *also* include individuals whose *experience* in a particular industry or occupation gives them special insight to testify about the industry's or corporation's specialized practices or procedures. For example, police officers who work investigating narcotics cases could qualify as experts on the practice of drug dealing and drug trafficking, supposing that a sufficient basis could be laid to demonstrate they had enough familiarity with the drug trade.

While these types of qualification are important, they are only a sufficient basis to qualify the expert if relevant to the subject-matter of her testimony. Each case requires a fact-specific inquiry to ensure the expert's qualifications are relevant to the issues presented in the case. A neurosurgeon might be qualified to testify about skull fractures but *not* about the causes of cancer in some patient. A police officer experienced in narcotics trafficking is usually *not* qualified to discuss the chemical composition of the drugs trafficked.

The major portion of Rule 702, however, concerns the requirements that an expert's testimony be sufficiently *helpful* and *reliable* to aid the factfinder's understanding of the issues. Expert testimony can be helpful in a variety of ways. Sometimes understanding the evidence requires esoteric knowledge well beyond a laypersons' ordinary experience. Specialized scientific knowledge is the core example of this sort of specialized knowledge; but experts may prove helpful in valuing antiques; assessing the causes of accidents; calculating liability; identifying drugs; analyzing D.N.A. samples; and so on.

Rule 702 requires judges to be active gatekeepers when determining whether the substance of expert testimony is sufficiently *reliable* to help the factfinder. Rule 702 thus incorporates the Supreme Court's decision in *Daubert v. Merrill Dow Pharmaceuticals, Inc.*, 509 U.S. 579 (1993), which makes courts responsible for evaluating the relevance and reliability of expert opinion. The prior standard, derived from the D.C. Circuit case, *Frye v. United States*, 293 F. 1013 (D.C. Cir. 1923) (and which is still applied in some states), required a court to determine whether the expert's testimony was based on standards that were "*generally accepted*" in the scientific community at the time. The *Frye* test tended to exclude cutting edge scientific opinion; worse, by deferring to the scientific community to determine the reliability of the evidence, the scientific community, not the judge, was effectively responsible for determining which expert testimony was reliable and which was not.

The *Daubert* test places responsibility for determining reliability squarely on the shoulders of the trial judge. The *Daubert* standard rests on the "assumption that the expert's opinion will have a reliable basis in the knowledge and experience of his discipline." The expert's opinion will usually derive from some principles or methods she used to in developing her conclusions. Daubert requires the court to assure itself that these underlying principles or methods are trustworthy: rational, objective, and so on. The Supreme Court announced a five-factor test to assess reliability: (1) whether the expert's reasoning or methodology can be or has been tested (and so verified or falsified); (2) whether it has been peer-reviewed or submitted for publication; (3) what is the error-rate in applying the methodology; (4) whether there are some standards that practitioners in the field apply when developing their conclusions (and whether the expert applied those standards); and finally (5) whether the theory or methodology has general acceptance within the scientific community (the *Frye* standard). None of these factors is, on its own, dispositive; and the list is not exhaustive.

Reliability is a lower standard than correctness. The 2000 Advisory Committee Note points out that expert opinions can conflict, and that conflict alone is not a bar to admissibility. *Multiple* conflicting expert opinions may be reliable, though only one (or neither) may be correct. It is up to counsel to establish whether the opinion, once found to be reliable, is credible or not.

In two later cases, the Supreme Court expanded *Daubert* to cover the reliability of scientific *conclusions*, not just scientific *methodology* (General Electric Co. v. Joiner, 522 U.S. 136 (1997)); and then in *Kumho Tire Company, Ltd. v. Carmichael*, 526 U.S. 137 (1999), the Court held that the *Daubert* test applied to *all* expert testimony, not merely scientific testimony. In *Kumho Tire*, the plaintiff's expert was an expert in tire failure analysis. He proposed to testify that the cause of a fatal car crash was a defect in the tire, and claimed his long experience in analyzing defective tires enabled him to recognize certain problems simply through observing the tire. Though his testimony was based on experiential, rather than scientific knowledge, the Court applied *Daubert* and rejected his testimony as unreliable because based on too many subjective factors.

What You Need to Know:

1. Rule 702 governs the testimony of experts as to matters within their expertise. The rule takes a broad view of what constitutes an expert: anyone

can be an expert so long as they have the relevant knowledge, skill, experience, training, or education. The first obligation of the court is to determine that the expert has the sort of specialized knowledge that will help the trier of fact to determine some matter in the case. Often, this simply requires reviewing the expert's professional or educational qualifications.

2. If the expert is properly qualified, then the court must consider whether her testimony is *reliable.* The Federal Rules require judges to act as *active gatekeepers*, determining reliability for themselves. Unlike some state jurisdictions, federal judges cannot simply admit expert testimony because it is of the sort relied upon by others in the field. Instead, they must determine that the *principles and methods* upon which the testimony is based are *reasoned* than speculative, *objective* rather than subjective.

3. To assess whether the testimony is rational and objective, courts apply what are called *Daubert* factors to determine the reliability of the underlying principles and methods used to arrive at the proffered opinion. The *Daubert* opinion requires the judge to consider additional indicia of reliability: (1) whether the expert's technique or theory can be tested; (2) whether it has been scrutinized in a peer-reviewed publication; (3) what is the error-rate of the theory; (4) what are the standards usually applied in the field; and (5) what is the general acceptance of the reasoning or methodology in the relevant scientific field.

4. While the five factors enumerated in *Daubert* apply to scientific research, including both methodology and conclusions, the Daubert factors comprise an open-ended list, and these factors and others apply to all expert opinions, including non-scientific testimony. Non-scientific testimony includes testimony based on skill or experience: the judge

must ensure that this sort of testimony is reliable, too.

LESSON 17: THE BASES OF AN EXPERT'S TESTIMONY

One major difference between expert and lay testimony resides in the *basis* of their opinion. Lay opinion testimony *must* be rationally derived from the witness's perceptions; expert testimony need not. Experts may testify about matters other than those they have personally observed. But this creates a problem: under Rule 602 and 701 (and, as we shall discover, Rules 801 and 802), the stuff upon which the expert bases her opinion may *inadmissible.*

The Advisory Committee Note to Rule 703 identifies three separate sources for expert testimony. The first matches Rule 701: information derived from *personal perception*; what the Advisory Committee calls the *firsthand observations of the witness.* For the most part, this sort of information is obtained before trial. For example, a medical witness might base her testimony upon an earlier examination of the injured party. Here, the witness has had the opportunity, before trial, personally to observe the injury that forms the subject-matter of her testimony.

The second source is *matters presented at trial*: either from *observing a witness* or from *hypothetical questions* summarizing the evidence that counsel could pose to the witness. These questions might take the form of asking the expert witness to assume certain facts: for example, that a certain amount of asbestos, a dangerous carcinogen, was found in the air that plaintiff breathed over a certain amount of time. The expert would then give an opinion of the medical consequences of ingesting the asbestos. It is worth noting that the questions themselves are not evidence, only the answers.

The final source of expert opinion is information gleaned from data *outside the courtroom, and other than by the expert's own personal observation.* To return to the medical example, the physician may base her opinion about the nature and cause of an injury upon statements made by third parties or through reading medical reports prepared by other people. This is where the problem arises: these other materials may be evidence that has not been admitted at trial or may be inadmissible. Nonetheless, Rule 703 permits experts to testify about such facts or data *if it is the sort that the expert would reasonably rely on* when reaching an opinion in her field.

The basic idea in contained in Rule 703 is that people who work in the relevant field generally have some standard sources of information that they rely upon in forming an opinion. So long as the expert's testimony relies on the sorts of sources people in the field would ordinarily rely upon, Rule 703 permits the expert to offer opinion evidence even if the information upon which she bases her testimony is *inadmissible*. Doctors rely on notes and X-rays prepared by other doctors; accountants rely on tax returns prepared by other people; economists rely on predictions of the value of property prepared by others. These documents and other information may not be admissible directly. So long as the information is of this, industry-standard, *quality* and so long as there is *an adequate amount* of information for the expert to form an opinion, then she may reasonably give her opinion based upon that information. The underlying information, however, ordinarily may not be admitted into evidence as part of her opinion.

Otherwise inadmissible information forming the basis of an expert's opinion *can* find its way into evidence under Rule 703 if it would "help the factfinder understand the expert's thought process and determine what weight to give to the expert's opinion." Williams v. Illinois, 567 U.S. 50 (2012). Under this rule, evidence that is otherwise inadmissible (for example, under the hearsay rules if offered substantively) may nonetheless be offered for the limited purpose of helping the factfinder assess the expert's reasoning. Because this evidence would normally be inadmissible, Rule 703 requires the proponent to satisfy a relatively heavy burden: the probative value of the evidence must *substantially* outweigh the probative danger to be admissible for the purpose of supporting the expert's testimony. This is the *mirror image* of the Rule 403 standard, and tips the balance in favor of exclusion.

Rule 705 liberalizes the manner in which expert opinion evidence is presented at trial. Under the rule, an expert can state her opinion without first testifying about the facts or data which underlie her testimony. The expert can go straight into presenting her opinion, for example, that the injury was caused by being struck by an automobile traveling above the posted speed limit; or that the drugs were of a sufficiently high purity to result in death, without having to first state the basis for that opinion. The rule does not guarantee that the expert be able to testify in this manner: it vests discretion with the court to require the expert to state the grounds for her opinion first. Furthermore, if an opponent wishes to challenge the expert's testimony, Rule 705 requires the witness to disclose the basis of her opinion on cross examination.

What You Need to Know:

1. Sometimes, a proponent wishes an expert to testify, not only about her opinions, but about the reasons she formed those opinions. Rule 703 considers three separate bases for expert testimony, and determines their relative admissibility.

2. The first basis of expert opinion is those matters that the expert has *personally observed*. In that case, the expert's opinion is most like lay opinion testimony: she has personal knowledge of the underlying facts, and Rule 703 renders this sort of testimony broadly admissible.

3. The second basis for expert testimony are hypothetical questions or the testimony of *other* witnesses that the expert has heard while observing them testify. These sources are also broadly admissible: attorney's questions do not count as evidence; testimony has already been admitted; and so the jury gets to hear both.

4. The real issue is the third basis for expert opinion testimony: evidence that would be otherwise inadmissible, perhaps because it is hearsay, or because authentication would be too hard or lengthy for the trial. In that case, the evidence is

admissible for the limited purpose of assessing the expert's reasoning. Even so, the proponent can only enter this sort of information into evidence if the probative *value substantially outweighs* probative *danger*. This standard is the reverse of Rule 403, and so favors exclusion as the default standard.

5. Rule 705 resolves questions about the order of presentation of expert opinions versus basis-of-opinion evidence. Essentially, the court gets to decide; however, the rule expressly permits the expert to state her opinion without first having to state the basis for it, so long as she discloses it, if required, on cross-examination.

LESSON 18: HEARSAY

The hearsay doctrine is a corollary of Rule 601–603's definition of a witness, and the Federal Rules' preference for live witness testimony. The basic idea is that any statement that is *not* live witness testimony (in the special sense defined by Rules 602 and 603) is presumptively *inadmissible*. Live witness testimony gives the factfinder three great assurances of trustworthiness—it is offered under *oath*; subject to *cross examination*; and the factfinder can observe the witness's *demeanor*. These three *evidentiary guarantees* help resolve doubts about the four *credibility factors* surrounding any witness's testimony: their *perception* and *memory* of the events, and their ability to *narrate* what they perceived without gaps or ambiguity and *sincerely*, that is, honestly.

Hearsay is basically *not-testimony*. It is canonically defined as *an out of court statement offered to prove the truth of the matter asserted* (Rule 801(c) is substantially the same as this canonical definition). Rule 802 follows the familiar pattern of presumptively excluding all hearsay statements, unless they can be fitted into one of the eight exemptions or twenty-nine exceptions contained in Rules 801, 803, 804, or 807. The Advisory Committee explains that the hearsay exceptions are series of categorical rules. Unlike the process we have examined up to this point, the hearsay rules determine their application: if a statement is *admissible* under one of the exemptions or exceptions contained in hearsay rules, then there is no further case-specific balancing of the probative value against the probative danger, as in Rule 403. The rules themselves accomplish this sort of balancing function.

The good news is that there is *some* rhyme and reason to the exemptions and exceptions, and remembering the sorts of evidence they track can make life a lot easier.

Why exclude hearsay? Take the famous trial of Sir Walter Raleigh, charged with treason because accused of planning to kill the King. The prosecution's case is based on evidence that Portuguese made the following statement to Raleigh's alleged co-conspirator, Cobham: "Raleigh plans to kill the King." The prosecution wishes to introduce the statement to help prove the treason. Cobham could testify as a witness—at trial, under-oath, subject to cross-examination—that some person called Portuguese made the statement to him. But Portuguese is nowhere to be found.

What we really want to do is to put *Portuguese* on the stand, under oath, to see if he really did *perceive* Raleigh planning to kill the King; and whether he accurately *remembers* what he saw; and if, under oath and penalty of perjury, Portuguese is still *sincere* about making the statement, or whether he would retract it; and whether there are any gaps or ambiguities in his *narration* of what he claims he perceived. But because Portuguese is unavailable, he cannot be put under oath and cross-examined while the factfinder observes his demeanor. Cobham's testimony would provide a poor, second-hand version of this evidence. Lacking the usual guarantees of reliability, the default position is to exclude it.

It is worth noting four factors of the standard hearsay definition here. First, the statement must be *out of court* to qualify as hearsay. All this means is that the *statement* is *not testimony*. Remember, *testimony* is the utterances of the witness while on the stand at the current legal proceeding, made under oath. That is why we call people who speak hearsay *declarants* and their utterances *statements*: it helps to distinguish them from *witnesses* who given *testimony*. Suppose Portuguese was in the courtroom with Cobham just before Cobham was called to testify. Portuguese's statement would *still* be *out of court* for purposes of the hearsay rule, because it is not live witness testimony, subject to the evidentiary guarantees that ensure its reliability. It is the *statement* of an out-of-court *declarant.*

Second, there must be some *statement.* We will return to statements at a little more length, but Rule 801 defines a statement as an utterance or non-verbal act intended to communicate something. If there is no statement, there is no hearsay. Third, and relatedly, the statement must assert some *matter* or, more accurately, a *fact.* It must, in other words, make an assertion about the world that can be true or false. In *Raleigh's Case*, Portuguese's statement is "Raleigh plans to kill the King." The fact that Portuguese asserts *just is* that Raleigh does plan or intend to kill the King. This may look like a trick, but it's not. Often the fact (the matter) asserted by a statement is perfectly described in the statement itself. Just as often, the statement needs little translation. Suppose the defendant, after hitting a pedestrian in a crosswalk, told a passerby, "My brakes were acting funky." The fact asserted by the statement is that defendant's brakes were malfunctioning. A little translation makes it clear. Or suppose plaintiff sues defendant, a doctor, for medical malpractice, claiming the defendant botched plaintiff's plastic surgery. If plaintiff told a partygoer just after the surgery, "I'm the hottest one here!" then a natural interpretation would be that plaintiff meant to assert that she was the best looking person at the party. Of course, the statement is ambiguous; she might have been wearing a thick hoodie to a pool party precisely to cover her scarred face: that is one of the reasons why it would be preferable to have live testimony from the plaintiff, rather than the second-hand account of the partygoer.

The fourth and final issue is what is meant by offering the statement to *prove the truth* of the matter asserted. Here, the question is for what purpose the statement is offered. Remember, statements may be admissible for one purpose, and not for another. The hearsay rule only excludes statements whose relevance (which is to say, whose purpose) depends upon their *truth.*

Working out whether a statement is offered to prove its truth can be a little tricky. First, we need to work out what fact the statement is supposed to assert. In Raleigh's Case, it was that Raleigh intended to kill the King. The statement is materially relevant to prove an element of treason: intent. And it only helps prove that element if it is true. So the idea is to work out what fact the statement asserts, and independently of that, what fact the proponent wants to prove using that statement. If they match, that is, if the fact must be true to support what the proponent wants to prove, then the statement is offered to prove the truth of the matter asserted.

Consider the statement, "I'm the hottest one here!" That statement asserts (on at least one interpretation) that the plaintiff is the best-looking person at the party. But the statement could be offered to prove two separate things. First, that the plaintiff is, in fact, the best-looking person at the party. Or second, that the plaintiff *thinks* he is the best-looking person at the party. However, the fact asserted by the statement is *not* what the plaintiff thinks: he doesn't say, "I *think* I'm the hottest. . ." He says he *is* the hottest. If defendant offers the statement to prove that defendant was the best-looking person (to show that the operation was not botched, but was a tremendous success), then it is offered for its truth. If defendant offers the statement to prove that the defendant *thought* he was the best looking, the matter asserted (the fact that plaintiff *is* the best looking) does not match what it is offered to prove (the fact that plaintiff *thought* he was the best looking), and so was *not* offered to prove the truth of the matter asserted. We will return to some more of these examples in the next section, when we discuss *non-hearsay*.

What You Need to Know:

1. Hearsay is *an out of court statement offered to prove the truth of the matter asserted.* Rule 801(c) essentially adopts this definition, with a few minor differences.

2. Hearsay can be understood as any utterance that is *not testimony*. To help distinguish out-of-court speakers from witnesses, and their utterances from testimony, the out-of-court speaker is called the *declarant* and the out-of-court utterance is called a *statement*.

3. *Out-of-court* means not given by a witness, under oath, on the stand, as testimony at the current legal proceeding. A *statement* is an utterance intended to communicate something.

4. The *matter asserted* is some fact, capable of being true or false, that the declarant intends to communicate through her statement.

5. Statements are hearsay only if they are offered to *prove the truth* of the fact that they communicate. So we need to know the proponent's purpose in offering the statement. Often, the proponent will offer the statement to prove something other than that the fact it asserts is true; she may offer the statement, for example, to prove the fact it asserts is false, or as circumstantial evidence to prove what the declarant was thinking, whether or not what the declarant was thinking is true or false. Identifying these non-hearsay purposes can be really tricky, and requires some care.

LESSON 19: NON-HEARSAY

Hearsay is generally any statement that fits the canonical definition: an *out of court statement offered to prove the truth of the matter asserted*. Any statement that doesn't fit the definition, isn't hearsay. But the Federal Rules of Evidence do not observe this simple dichotomy between statements that are hearsay and those that are not. Frustratingly, Rule 801 adds a class of statements that *fit* the hearsay definition, but which the Rule nonetheless labels *not hearsay*. For that reason, we have to come up with a different name for all those statements that don't fit the canonical definition, and so aren't hearsay. I will call statements that aren't hearsay *non hearsay*.

An important class of non hearsay statements include those that *are* uttered out of court, and do communicate some fact, but the purpose for introducing the statement is something other than proving the truth of the fact communicated. We have already covered one major set of non hearsay statements: prior inconsistent statements used to *impeach* a witness. When offered for impeachment purposes, we do not claim that the prior statement is *true*; merely that it contradicts the testimony at trial.

Sometimes hearsay requires us to be careful about what evidence is being offered. For example, sometimes the reason for introducing a statement is not to prove the *content* of the statement, but simply the fact that a statement was made: that someone uttered something. Suppose the question is one of identity: whether the plaintiff was at a party after his plastic surgery. Defendant offers evidence that a partygoer heard the plaintiff at the party say "I'm the hottest person at the party." What is the evidence the proponent wishes to enter into evidence? The fact that someone utters something (and their voice is sufficiently distinctive that a partygoer could identify them); or the something that she said (that she was at the party)? Only the communicative content of the statement—the something the declarant said (I'm. . .at the party")—can be hearsay. In this case, the defendant can introduce the fact that the plaintiff said something—that it was distinctively plaintiff's voice—as evidence that he was at the party. *What* she said (the fact communicated by the statement) is irrelevant to the type of voice-identification proof the proponent wants to make, even though it proves the same thing.

Some statements are offered, not to prove they are true, but to prove they are false. This sort of use is important for plaintiffs claiming harm in defamation cases. In a libel case, plaintiff's claim just is that defendant's statement, "Plaintiff is a drunk and terrible at evidence," is false. Plaintiff cares about the content of the statement—what it communicates—but not because it is true.

There are three *other* types of core non-hearsay statements: those that tell us something about the *declarant's* state of mind; those that tell us about the *listener's* state of mind; and those that do not state a fact, but are used to *do* something, such as transfer property or threaten a victim.

The first two types of statement are typically used to provide *circumstantial evidence of some person's mental state*, where their mental state is important to some issue in the case. The mental state could be *intent,* or *knowledge* or *lack of recklessness* in a criminal case; or *confusion* in a trademark case; or lack of sanity, or some other mental state. For the most part, people do not state that they are *thinking* something: they simply communicate the content of their thought. There is a difference between the fact communicated by the statement, "I *believe* this is really sore," and the fact communicated by the statement, "This is really sore." The first refers directly to the declarant's mental state—what she believes. If the proponent seeks to prove the declarant's mental state, then it matters whether it is true that she believes what she says she believes. The second statement describes the effect of some action. In the second statement, it does not matter whether the declarant was right or wrong about the fact. Her act may or may not have caused pain. The statement is not offered because it is *true* but because it is circumstantial evidence of what was in the declarant's mind at the time.

The lack-of-sanity statements operate in a similar way. If a declarant says, "I am a dolphin, and I need a fish tank to swim in," and the statement is offered to prove she is insane, then the statement is non hearsay *both* because the statement offered is *false* (the defendant is not a dolphin); *and* because it is circumstantial evidence of the declarant's mental state (it shows he is insane). The fact the statement communicates is that the declarant is a dolphin; that is not the fact that it is offered to prove.

The second type of statement depends for its relevance on its *effect on the listener*. These statements are circumstantial evidence of the *listener*'s mental state when reacting to something the declarant said. In the Knapp case, remember, some Declarant told Knapp, "The Sheriff beat an old man to death." The out-of-court statement was admissible as circumstantial evidence of Knapp's mental state: the reasonable *fear* the statement engendered necessary to mount his self-defense claim. It does not matter whether it was *true* that the Sheriff beat the old man; all that matters is the effect of the statement on Knapp: that it caused him fear. Sometimes statements are offered to show that some responsible person—an employer or official—had notice of some wrongdoing. So a declarant's statement to her employer that, "Supervisor is harassing me," is admissible in an employment discrimination case if offered to prove that the employer *knew* or was *on notice* that declarant claims harassments. Whether or not the statement is true, the employer is now under a duty to investigate.

The third type of statement is one that is sometimes hard to wrap one's head around. The general idea is that some utterances do not state *facts* that are true or false, but are used to *do* things, like order people about, ask questions, transfer property, and so on. The utterance, "Shut the door!" is neither true nor false, and so cannot be offered for the purpose of proving the *truth* of the matter asserted (there is no fact asserted). Similarly, "I name this ship the Seven Rings" does not describe the ship's name: it *gives* the ship a name. Before the naming ceremony, the ship had no name. The purpose of the ceremony is to accomplish something: to name the ship. The law uses verbal ceremonies to do things quite a lot. "We hereby enact the following law. . ." is an activity. We can transfer property using words, such as "Jane conveys her property to John." These verbal acts do not (only) describe the transfer, they *are* the act of transferring the property. Because the words are offered to prove the *act*, and not to state some fact describing some event, they are not offered for their truth.

What You Need to Know:

1. It pays to be really literal when thinking about hearsay and non-hearsay. First, the goal is to identify some matter of fact that the hearsay statement asserts. The next step is to identify the proponent's purpose in offering the statement into evidence—why it is relevant. If the purpose does not require proving that the statement is true, then the statement is not offered for a hearsay purpose, and so is non-hearsay.

2. Separating hearsay from non-hearsay is one of the trickiest aspects of using the hearsay rules. However, there are three broad categories of non-hearsay: if you can spot them, then that should help a lot.

3. The first two types of non-hearsay involve circumstantial evidence of someone's mental state: either (1) the declarant's (i.e., the speaker's) or (2) the listener's. So the goal is to separate out what counts as direct and circumstantial evidence of a mental state. If the statement is direct evidence of a mental state, then the statement will contain some reference to the mental state. That is, words indicating a mental state—*think; know; remember; feel; etc.*—will appear in the statement itself. These sorts of statement *are hearsay* when offered to prove a mental state: they assert that the declarant is thinking something specific, they are offered to prove that the declarant was, in fact, thinking what she claimed to be thinking; and so they can only be admitted if covered by some exception (usually Rule 803(3)).

4. Circumstantial evidence of declarant or listener's state of mind *lacks* any mention of a mental state. The statement is not offered to prove that what said is true; only that what the declarant said, or what the listener heard, correlated with some relevant mental state in the case. So if the statement is offered to prove [lack of] *knowledge* or [lack of] *intent* or [lack of] *confusion*, and the statement does not mention a mental state, but circumstantially helps to illustrate it, then it *is* admissible as *non-hearsay*. A frequently-tested set of non-hearsay statements are the utterances of insane people used to prove their insanity, e.g., "I am the King of Mars."

5. The third category of non-hearsay utterances are statements that are not capable of being true or false. Only statements that describe or assert some fact can be true or false. But there is another category of statements that *do* something just by saying something. These are often called "verbal acts." "Shut the door;" or "Welcome!" are acts of this sort. The most important verbal acts are probably

those that are used to accomplish some legal act, such as transferring property from one person to another, or pronouncing a couple married, and so on. These are often called *legally operative* facts.

LESSON 20: STATEMENTS AS VERBAL AND NON-VERBAL CONDUCT; MULTIPLE HEARSAY

Rule 801(a) defines a statement, for purposes of the hearsay rule. Statements are communications intended to assert some fact. We can communicate in a variety of ways: by speaking (orally) or writing; or even non-verbally, through sign-language, or by nodding assent, or giving a thumbs-up to show we are okay. For the most part, *silence* does not count as a statement, although we will consider one important exception in Rule 801(d)(2)(B).

Rule 801(a) places an important limit upon the sorts of communications that count as statements: they must *intend* to assert some fact. The limit works in two distinct ways. First, only utterances or conduct that the declarant means to communicate some fact counts. If I walk around the supermarket and pick up a tomato, squeeze it, and put it back on the shelf, that set of actions provides circumstantial evidence from which others may *infer* that I think the tomato is bruised or too ripe; but I do not mean to *imply* that fact, I do not intend to communicate it to some audience. In a famous example, from the case Wright v. Tatham, 7 Ad. & E. 313, 112 Eng. Rep. 488 (1837), a ship captain inspects his ship before sailing off in it; upon finishing his inspection, he escorts his wife and children aboard. It is reasonable to *infer* from the fact that the captain allowed his family to sail on the ship the further fact that he thinks the ship is seaworthy; but he makes no statement to that effect.

I could, nonetheless, make a statement if my actions *were* intended to communicate something to an audience. Suppose Defendant wanted to convince people that her hamburgers were safe to eat and produced a poster with a picture of Defendant and her daughter eating the hamburger. In a subsequent tort case for food poisoning, the activity depicted in the poster would count as a statement, because it intends to assert that the meat is safe for consumption.

Non-humans cannot make statements: they do not intend to assert anything. Clocks may tell us the time, but they do not make a statement. A dog may bark at a stranger: it does not make a statement. A parrot may say, "Mistress killed the victim!" Its utterance does not count as a statement. License plates do not state the driver's license number. Photographs to not state the scene they depict (though they may contain statements). If a freeway sign flashes, "10 minutes to downtown," the sign is *not* a statement *so long as* the sign operates automatically. If there is some person sitting at a remote computer somewhere typing the message to be displayed on the sign, then the writing *is* a statement: the computer operator intends to communicate the time (the machine does not).

The second limit applies to the scope of an utterance. Just like the ship captain's inspection, some utterances imply other facts not contained in the original utterance. For example, if Defendant calls a telephone number and says to the person who answers, "I'd like to buy a $10 bag of marijuana," that statement intends to communicate a verbal act: it is an offer to buy some drugs. It also implies a fact, that the person who answered the telephone is a drug dealer. However, the declarant does not intend to assert the fact, *the person who answers this phone is a drug dealer*. The declarant just wishes to buy some drugs. Her statement is admissible as a non-hearsay verbal act; the inference from her statement is admissible because *it is not a statement* Defendant intended to assert.

The approach I have just sketched out is the one followed by the Federal Rules of Evidence. Some jurisdictions take the broader approach to statements: they include, not only what the declarant directly intended to communicate, but any fact that can be reasonably implied by the declarant's utterance or conduct. Because these state evidence rules include more acts and utterances as statements, they exclude more items of evidence as hearsay.

Sometimes, acts are *both* assertive conduct *and* direct evidence of the fact they assert. Suppose Willa testifies, in a tort case claiming faulty repair of a bicycle, that she asked John whether he could ride a bike, and instead of answering, John jumped on a nearby bicycle and started riding around. Here, John's conduct is both an act intended to assert some fact—that he can ride the bike. But John's conduct *is also* the act of riding the bike. Willa has personal knowledge of John's bike-riding abilities; she directly perceived them for herself. *John's* assertion is hearsay; Willa's testimony about what she saw need not include that assertion.

A further feature of hearsay statements is worth mentioning: one statement can include *another* hearsay statement, which can include *yet another* hearsay statement, and so on. This feature of hearsay is called *hearsay within hearsay* or sometimes *multiple hearsay*. For each statement there is an associated declarant, the person who made the statement (Rule 801(b)). Thus, John might testify that, "Jill told me she overheard Jane say that she saw a blue car running a red light just before the accident." Here, we have one witness, John, and two declarants, Jill and Jane. Jill's statement is often referred to as the *external statement* and Jane's as the *internal statement*. If there are more than two statements, we often talk of multiple *levels* of hearsay, with the levels number from the external statement (level 1) to the most internal statement. Rule 805 tells us that *each* statement (each level of hearsay) must fit an exception or exemption to the hearsay rule to be admissible.

What You Need to Know:

1. In the Federal Rules, "statement" means something quite specific. A statement is an utterance made by a speaker, where the speaker intends to communicate some information.

2. The Federal Rules thus preclude many non-humans from making statements: neither machines nor animals can make statements.

3. A statement can be expressed in words or implied in through certain actions. Some obvious non-verbal statements are the act of nodding one's head, or giving a thumbs down. Only matters *intended* to be directly communicated by the statement are part

of the statement itself; other inferences, even ones directly implied by the statement, are not.

4. A statement may have other statements contained within it. Where the included statements are also hearsay, then we have the problem of hearsay within hearsay, or multiple hearsay. If the whole statement is to be admissible, then every statement it contains must be admissible too. Each statement may be admissible under the same, or under some different exception to the hearsay rule. So long as they are covered by some exception or exemption (or the internal statements are non-hearsay), then the statement is admissible. But if one of the statements is inadmissible, then the full statement is too.

LESSON 21: NOT HEARSAY: PRIOR INCONSISTENT STATEMENTS; IDENTIFICATION

The Federal Rules create three general exemptions and exceptions to statements that fit the definition of hearsay. The first are exemptions under Rule FRE 801(d) that require the declarant to be available to testify at trial as a witness; the second are exceptions that require the declarant to be affirmatively *unavailable* as a witness at trial; and the third are exceptions in which the declarant's availability as a witness is *immaterial*, that is, *does not matter*.

One way to approach hearsay is to distinguish two broad types of statement. First, those that do *not* fit the definition of hearsay, and so just aren't hearsay. We have already covered these types of statements, and call them *non-hearsay*. Second, those that fit the definition of hearsay and so are presumptively excluded; some exception may apply to allow them to be admitted later on. But the Federal Rules carve out a *third* set; those statements that fit the definition of hearsay but are called "*not hearsay*."

To organize this third set of not hearsay statements, Rule 801(d) distinguishes two broad categories of not hearsay statements: those in which admissibility depends upon the *declarant being available at trial as a witness*; and those offered against the *opposing party*. The first category has a substantial guarantee of trustworthiness: having the witness present at trial to be questioned about the statements certainly makes such statements more reliable. For example, there are three types of prior statements by declarant-witness evidence covered by Rule 801(d)(1), each of which comes with a different level of trustworthiness: prior *inconsistent* statements; prior *consistent* statements; and prior statements of *identification*.

We have seen that *prior inconsistent statements* may be offered for purposes of impeachment, that is, not because they are true, but because they conflict with the witness's current trial testimony. When offered for *credibility purposes*, prior inconsistent statements are *non hearsay*. If, however, the prior inconsistent statement is offered for *substantive purposes*, that is, to prove that the *prior* statement is *true*, then it fits the description of hearsay: an out of court statement offered to prove the truth of the matter asserted. The rule characterizes prior inconsistent statements offered to prove the truth of the matter asserted as *not hearsay* on condition that they meet two further guarantees of reliability: (1) the prior statement is *inconsistent* with current testimony; and (2) the out-of-court statement was *also* given at a formal hearing under oath.

The second condition imposed by Rule 801(d)(1)(A) limits the sorts of prior inconsistent statements to those given in a deposition, or a previous trial, or some other formal legal hearing. While most of these hearings will allow for cross-examination of the declarant under oath, the Rule does not require it. The Rule is drafted to include inconsistent statements given before a *grand jury*, where the declarant-witness might not be subject to cross examination.

Prior *consistent* statements are covered by Rule 801(d)(1)(B); they too may be used both for credibility purposes and substantive purposes. The rule does *not* condition admissibility upon some prior formal process. These statements are treated as having low reliability, whatever their purpose, and are difficult to admit. Nonetheless, a Supreme Court Case, *Tome v. United States*, 513 U.S. 150 (1995), established that prior consistent statements are admissible if the declarant is a witness, and the statement is offered as a response to a charge that the witness testimony at the current trial was recently fabricated, or is a response to some improper influence or motive, such as coercion or bribery. Even if these triggering conditions, contained in the text of Rule 801(d)(1)(B), are met, however, the Court imposed a further temporal condition upon admissibility. The declarant must have uttered the prior consistent statement *before* developing a reason to fabricate, or before the existence of the improper influence or motive. So the proponent is required to identify just when the declarant-witness had a reason to lie, and then demonstrate that declarant-witness uttered the prior consistent statement *before* developing the reason to lie.

The third type of declarant-witness statement is perhaps the simplest one, and treated by the rules as the most reliable. Under Rule 801(d)(1)(C), a *prior statement of identification*, made before testifying at the current trial, is admissible to prove identity, so long as the declarant-witness was able to perceive the person they identified at the time they claim to have seen (or heard, etc.) that person. The earlier statement is admissible both for impeachment purposes, as a prior inconsistent statement, and for its substantive use, to show identity. For example, a victim of domestic abuse may have told the police that the abuser is her partner. She may later recant, and refuse to identify him at trial. The prosecutor can use the earlier statement of identity both for impeachment purposes, to undermine her credibility, or substantively, to prove that the person who assaulted the victim was her partner.

The justification for admitting such statements is that the earlier statement was made closer in time to the event, and under less suggestive conditions than the courtroom testimony, so is likely to be more accurate than an in-court identification. In *United States v. Owens*, 484 U.S. 554 (1999), the Supreme Court held that being available as a witness means being able to answer questions, on cross-examination, about the circumstances surrounding the earlier identification. In that case, the defendant was charged with assaulting the victim, causing a serious head injury resulting in memory loss. While recuperating in hospital, a police officer showed the victim a photo array: the victim identified his assailant as the defendant. At trial, the victim could no longer identify who had assaulted him. Prosecution offered evidence of his prior identification under Rule 801(d)(1)(C). Defendant claimed that the victim was not really a *witness* because, when cross-examined, he could not remember much detail about identifying the defendant to the police officer. The Court held that the victim was, nonetheless available as a witness, as he was willing to answer questions. The Court did suggest that a total inability to answer questions could count as a failure to qualify as a witness if that failure precluded evaluating the witness-declarant's credibility.

What You Need to Know:

1. The Federal Rules categorize certain statements as "not hearsay" even though these statements meet Rule 801(c)'s definition of hearsay. Rule 801(d)(1) not-hearsay statements are the out-of-court utterances of someone who is currently available to testify as a witness, and so is *both* a declarant and a witnesses. She can thus be questioned about these out-of-court statements on the stand, which is why the Rules call the statements "not hearsay."

2. However, Rule 801(d)(1) *only* apples *if* the declarant is available as a witness. Witnesses are considered available even if they cannot remember the circumstances in which they made the prior statement, so long as they are broadly able to be cross-examined and their credibility undermined.

3. There are three categories of declarant-witness statements under Rule 801(d)(1).

4. Rule 801(d)(1)(A) *prior inconsistent statements* are out-of-court statements that contradict or undermine the witness's testimony on the stand. Accordingly, the witness must testify for the statement to be admissible. Furthermore, the statement *must* have been made at a prior hearing, under oath.

5. Rule 801(d)(1)(B) *prior consistent statements* are out-of-court statements that bolster or support the

witness's testimony on the stand. They have little probative value, and so the Supreme Court, in *Tome*, restricted their admissibility for their truth by requiring the witness (1) testify; (2) be impeached on the basis of recent fabrication or improper influence or motivation; and (3) that the prior consistent statement have been made *before* the declarant-witness developed the illicit motivation.

6. Rule 801(d)(1)(C) *statements of prior identification* are out-of-court statements that identify someone. They are broadly admissible for that purpose.

LESSON 22: OPPOSING PARTY'S STATEMENTS

Rule 801(d)(2) carves out another class of statements that fit the definition of hearsay, but are *not hearsay* for purposes of the Federal Rules. These are *statements of party opponents*. So long as the statement is one that is made by the opposing party, or is fairly attributable to that party—as described in Rules 801(d)(2)(B)–(E)—then the statement is admissible, without any further qualifications. The rationale for the rule is an unusual one, given that hearsay rules usually appeal to the value of *accuracy*, that is, trustworthiness or reliability. Here, the value is *efficiency*—really necessity. For the adversarial system to work, we need the statements of the parties in order to litigate the case. Note that the rule does *not* require that the party opponent be available to testify: all that matters is the statement be made by a party (or reasonably attributable to the party) and that that statement be offered by that party's opponent.

As a preliminary matter, where there are multiple parties, the party opponent rule allows the proponent to use the statement against *only the party* who *made the statement*. Imagine Jack sues Jane and Jill for personal injury because each drove through an intersection at the same time, hitting Jack as he is crossing the street. If Jane blurted out, "It was my fault," Jane's statement is admissible, under Rule 801(d)(2)(A), against Jane *just because* she is an opposing party and she made the statement. That's all that is needed to satisfy the rule. But the statement is admissible against Jane *only*, *not* against Jill, because Jane is the party opponent, and Jill is not.

If the statement is made in a *representative capacity*, then it is admissible against the declarant and the entity she represents. So if Jane was the employee of Taxi Co., and she makes the statement in her capacity as one of Taxi Co.'s drivers, then the statement is admissible *both* against the company *and* against Jane (though still not against Jill).

Rule 801(d)(2) does *not* require a showing that the declarant is *trustworthy* or that the declarant perceived the event. This lack of trustworthiness is pretty much unique in the context of the hearsay rule. Consider the famous case, *Mahlandt v. Wild Canid Survival & Research Center, Inc.*, 588 F. 2d 626 (8th Cir. 1978). An employee of Washington University's biology department kept one of the University's wolves (along with two dogs) in his fenced-in back yard. A young child managed to enter the back yard: Employee's son discovered the boy, injured, with the wolf standing over him. The son told Employee that the "Wolf bit the child." This evidence was inadmissible hearsay: the son was not a party to the lawsuit, and his statement did not fit under an exception to the hearsay rule. In addition, because the son did not witness which animal did the biting, the son lacked the sort of first-hand knowledge necessary to render his statement reliable. Nonetheless, based on his son's statement, Employee told Washington University, his employer, that "Wolf bit the child." At a meeting to discuss the incident, the University's board members noted that the "Wolf bit the child." The child sued both Employee and the University for personal injury. At that point, both Employee and University became child's party opponents, and their statements, though based on son's unreliable evidence, became admissible against each of them under Rule 801(d)(2).

The harder cases come when some other person has made a statement, and the proponent claims that statement is reasonably attributable to the opposing party. Rule 801(d)(2)(B) covers adoptive admissions, where the party opponent does *not* make the statement, but through their actions endorses the statement as if it were their own. For example, forwarding an email with a "see below" annotation, or retweeting a tweet, could count as an adoptive admission. However, silence or a failure to respond is usually insufficient to adopt a statement unless there is some duty to respond: remember, silence does not count as a *statement* under Rule 801(a). One place in which courts often impose a duty to respond is when someone is directly accused of criminal activity in circumstances that would reasonably call for a denial.

Some people are employed to speak on others' behalf. Under Rule 801(d)(2)(C), these statements of an opposing party's spokesperson are treated as statements of the party. It is worth noting that *attorneys* are often authorized to speak on behalf of some party: accordingly, an attorneys statements can fall under the Rule 801(d)(2)(C) exemption. Similarly, in the *Malhandt* case, the University's board were authorized to speak on behalf of the University. So their statements were admissible under Rule 801(d)(2)(C).

A hugely important category of statements are those made by an opposing party's agents or employees. To be admissible under Rule 801(d)(2)(D), the statements must be made within the scope of the agency or employment relation, and while the person is working for the party opponent as their agent or employee. For example, in the *Malhandt* case, worked for the University, and his statements about his care of the University's wolf were about a matter concerning his employment while he was employed by the University. So whatever Employee said about the wolf was admissible, not only directly against him as a party opponent under Rule 801(d)(2)(A), but *also* against the University, under Rule 801(d)(2)(D).

Finally, under Rule 801(d)(2)(E), a criminal coconspirator's statement is admissible against a party so long as the coconspirator's statement was made *during the criminal conspiracy* and was a statement *in furtherance of* the conspiracy. This second requirement limits the range of available statements: the statement cannot simply amount to idle bragging, personal reminiscences, and the like. The statement must be one that advances the conspiracy in some way. But statements that engage in planning, allocate responsibility, or discuss payment, and so on, can satisfy this requirement.

The first element requires that proponent prove that there is a conspiracy. Often, the only evidence of a conspiracy are the statements between the opposing party and a coconspirator in furtherance of the conspiracy. In such circumstances a proponent may seek to rely in whole or in part upon the statement she seeks to introduce as evidence of the conspiracy: a practice often called *bootstrapping.* In *Bourjaily v. United States*, 483 U.S. 171 (1987), the Supreme Court held that Rule 801(d)(2)(E) permitted using the coconspirator's statement as *part* of the evidence of a conspiracy: the rules were later amended to make clear that Rule 801(d)(2)(E) requires *in addition,* some circumstantial evidence to demonstrate the conspiracy, in addition to the statement offered into evidence.

In *Bruton v. United States*, 391 U.S. 123 (1968), a co-conspirator confession implicated *both* defendants, but was admissible only against one, but not against the other. The Court held that such confessions cannot be admitted in a joint trial of both defendants, even with a limiting instruction, where there was a substantial risk that the factfinder would use the confession against *both* defendants. The options are to sever the trials or to redact the confession in such a manner that it does not directly implicate the co-defendant. It may be permissible to circumstantially link the co-defendant with the events described in the confession; but simply redacting the co-defendant's name is likely not enough.

What You Need to Know:

1. Rule 801(d)(2) exempts from the federal definition of hearsay those statements made by or attributable to a party, if offered against that party. The basic justification for exempting these sorts of statements is necessity: without them, trials could not function as part of an adversarial system. The opposing party need *not* be available to testify as a witness for the statement to be admissible.

2. There are five types of opposing party statement. In *none* of these five cases need the opposing party have personal knowledge of the facts asserted by her statement—another unique feature of these sorts of statements. The statements do not need to

be *trustworthy*: it is enough that opposing party adopts the underlying facts and asserts them for herself. But the statements are admissible only against the *party* making the statement. They are not admissible against other parties, such as co-defendants, to whom the statements are not attributable.

3. The easiest of the five cases is a direct admission out of mouth of the party opponent whether in an individual or representative capacity. If in a representative capacity, the statement is admissible against the declarant and the entity she represents. The second sort of case is one in which the party adopts or otherwise acquiesces in the statements of some other person. Usually, the party manifests her adoption of the statement; but in exceptional cases, silence is enough where there is some expectation that the party would speak to dispel some serious inference, such as criminal activity.

4. The last three cases are ones in which some sort of relationship must be established. Rule 801(d)(2)(C) admits statements made by a party's authorized delegate; Rule 801(d)(2)(D) admits statements made by the party's agent or employee in the course of their agency or employment. Finally, Rule 801(d)(2)(E) admits the statements of co-conspirators so long as the statement is made during the course of and in furtherance of the conspiracy, so long as there is some circumstantial evidence *in addition to the statement* that some criminal conspiracy was afoot.

5. Under *Bruton*, if there is a substantial likelihood that a defendant's confession, though inadmissible against a codefendant, will be nonetheless be considered by the factfinder despite a limiting instruction, then the trial must be severed or the statement sufficiently redacted to remove the taint.

LESSON 23: SPONTANEOUS STATEMENTS, STATE OF MIND & THE *HILLMON* DOCTRINE

The next set of rules are covered by Rule 803, which stipulates that the availability of the declarant as a witness are immaterial (unlike rule 801(d)(1)) but requires the declarant to have perceived whatever facts she makes statements about (unlike Rule 801(D)(2)). There are lots of exceptions in Rule 803: of the twenty-eight exceptions, the vast majority state conditions under which certain types of documents are admissible to prove their contents: such as marriage certificates; property deeds; court judgments; and the like. The first few rules govern certain types of statements that are more traditionally verbal: for example, spontaneous utterances asserting some fact relevant to an issue in the case.

The first two types of spontaneous statements are *present sense impressions* and *excited utterances*. Spontaneity guarantees reliability: the brevity of the time lapse between the declarant's perception of the event and her response to it leaves no time for the declarant to lie about what she saw. The circumstances giving rise to these two sorts of statements often overlap. But the rules provide distinct criteria of admissibility. A present sense impression is a statement that describes some event *as it happens or immediately after*. Thus, if Dede saw a blue car drive through a red light and hit a pedestrian in the intersection, and immediately tweeted, "Saw a car run a red light and hit someone," the statement is admissible under rule 803(1) as a present sense impression. However, if Dede waited until an hour later, and posted the same statement on her Facebook page, the statement would be *inadmissible*, as too much time would have passed.

Only the *descriptive* parts of a present sense impression are admissible. The rule requires a tight connection between the statement and the event. If Donny, Defendant's son, tweeted within a few minutes of the accident, "Dad just ran a red light *because he was late picking me up from school*!" that italicized part of the statement, though made within the time frame contemplated by Rule 803, is outside its scope. The statement does not describe or explain the running of the red light, but places blame.

Rule 803(2) applies to *excited utterances.* These are statements reliable because made *in response to* and *under the stress of* some exciting stimulus. The scope of the statements captured under the exited utterance Rule is broader than the present sense impression rule: the excited utterance must merely *relate to* the event it discusses. The Rule thus proposes a looser connection between the statement and the event, so including statements that mention the cause of the event, rather than simply describing what happened. So long as Donny *was excited* when he posted his tweet, his *whole statement* comes in under the excited utterance doctrine, because the italicized part refers to the cause of the accident. Furthermore, the amount of time that can lapse between the exciting event and the statement may be longer than under the present sense impression rule. What matters is that the declarant *is still excited* when she makes the statement: it is the stress of excitement that, in part, ensures reliability.

Rule 803(3) really includes four separate rules. All of them depend upon the fact that the declarant is testifying about something she perceives about herself: what she is thinking; what she is feeling; what she plans to do; and what she remembers doing. All but the last are admissible in evidence.

The first two categories of statement refer to what the declarant is thinking or feeling. If the plaintiff, after being hit by a car driving through the intersection, says, "My whole left side is in agony," then the statement will be admissible as a *present sense impression* to prove the extent of his injuries. Or remember the *Knapp* case: suppose Knapp told a friend, "I *think* the Sheriff is out to get me." That statement would be admissible as *direct evidence* to show that his fear of the Sheriff to prove self-defense. (If Knapp just told the friend, "The Sheriff is out to get me," that statement would be admissible as *non hearsay, circumstantial* evidence of his state of mind.)

One of the most famous of all evidence cases, *Mutual Life Insurance Co. v. Hillmon*, 145 U.S. 285 (1892), introduced the next doctrine: a declarant's statement that she *plans* to do something or *intends to do it* in the future, is admissible to prove that the declarant *did* do it. In its strongest form, the doctrine applies, not only to the declarant, but to people the declarant mentions in her statement. If Knapp said, "I'm going to meet the Sheriff at the local bar in an hour," then that statement is admissible to prove *both* that Knapp went to the local bar *and* that the Sheriff did too.

Rule 803 permits evidence of what someone is *currently* thinking or feeling; however it excludes statements about some previous state of mind. Thus, if Knapp told a friend after the shooting, "I now remember that, just before I killed him, the Sheriff looked like he wanted to harm me," it is not a statement of Knapp's *then existing* state of mind. Instead, it describes some *prior* event. The Advisory Committee Note singles out a similar sort of statement, one that asserts something the declarant remembers *now* about something they did in the *past*. These types of statement are a direct substitute for witness testimony: statements in which the witness testifies under oath in front of a factfinder about something they remember happening in the past, out of court. If a *declarant's* statements discuss what happened *in the past* (rather than something that is happening *now* or *will happen in the future*) then these backward-looking statements would directly undermine the need for live witness testimony. If Knapp told his friend, "I remember now! The sheriff threatened to shoot me," that current statement of memory is inadmissible to prove the prior event.

What You Need to Know:

1. Rule 803 does not require a declarant to be either available or unavailable. Availability is immaterial. The first three hearsay exceptions under Rule 803 are all spontaneous utterances. While there are some differences between each type of statement, they are considered reliable because spontaneity inhibits the declarant's ability to fabricate or mislead. All three statements require the declarant to have personal knowledge of the event witnessed.

2. A present sense impression describes an event as it is happening or right after. While some minor time lapse is permissible, it must be brief. The scope of the exception is fairly narrow: only the parts of the

statement that describe or explain the event are admissible. An excited utterance is admissible so long as there was an exciting event, and the declarant was speaking under the stress of excitement. Excitement may last longer than the time period contemplated by the present sense impression exception. And the scope of the excited utterance exception is broader: it includes matters relating to the startling event, not merely those that describe or explain it.

3. The third type of spontaneous statement is one that describes a *then existing mental, emotional, or physical condition*. Such statements include utterances about being in pain or other bodily feelings. But they also include direct evidence of the declarant's state of mind, such as what they are thinking, confused about, or intending or planning to do.

4. These last sorts of statements about the declarant's current intention to do something in the future are admissible to prove that declarant did what she said she would under the *Hillmon doctrine*. The declarant's statement of her plan or intent is admissible substantively to prove her conduct in accordance with plan. Under *Hillmon*, such statements are also admissible to prove that a third party acted in accordance with the plan. So if the statement is that defendant planned to meet the victim at some secluded spot, the statement is admissible to prove that *both* defendant *and* victim went to that spot.

5. However, a declarant's statement of their current state of mind memorializing some *past act* is inadmissible to prove that fact. So statements of the form, "I currently believe that I remember something that happened in the past," or their equivalent, are inadmissible under Rule 803(3).

LESSON 24: INJURY REPORTS; RECORDED RECOLLECTION

Some statements characteristically appear in various sorts of documents: medical reports, transcripts of depositions or prior hearings; business and public records, and the like.

Rule 803(4) admits statements, often contained in medical reports, that describe *past* physical conditions *if made to a physician* or related to certain other people *for the purposes of medical diagnosis*. The idea is that, if someone is injured, they have an interest in accurately reporting their medical history to a physician or other medical personnel to ensure appropriate treatment. So the requirement of medical diagnosis minimizes the chances of lying. Statements that do *not* report an injury, but simply cast blame or assert fault, are inadmissible under the Rule.

Though statements for purposes of medical diagnosis are inadmissible to prove fault, these statements can include the cause of the injury. Furthermore, the statement may be made to some intermediary—a parent, if the declarant is a child; or a nurse or other medical professional—so long as it is for the purposes of diagnosis.

Rule 803(5) permits an attorney to use documents, not only to jog the memory of forgetful witnesses, but to substitute for their memory, if the document shows sufficient signs of reliability. Rule 803(5) applies only if the declarant-witness once had personal knowledge of the event memorialized in the document *and* she memorialized the facts relating to that event *when fresh in her mind*. Furthermore, the proponent must show the statement accurately reflects the event memorialized.

Rule 803(5) is triggered only if the declarant-witness *cannot now recall* the event memorialized in the document. The proponent must first try to jog her memory to show that she cannot testify from (present) memory, rather than a document recording her *past recollection*. The process of attempting to jog, revive, or *refresh* a witness's *present memory* is covered by Rule 612. The goal is to elicit testimony: a witness's statement, at trial and under oath, about what she personally perceived. Anything can be used to jog her memory: the smell of perfume; a beach ball; a document containing her past statement. But none of this stuff is evidence: the evidence is the witness's testimony about her memory, not the stuff that jogs her memory.

Under Rule 612, If the *proponent* uses a *document*—often the transcript of a deposition or prior hearing—then the *opponent* must have a chance to inspect it, cross-examine the witness about it, and introduce those bits of the document that relate to the witness's testimony. Under Rule 612, the *proponent* does *not* get to introduce the document if she successfully jogs the witness's testimony. If, however, she fails to jog the witness's memory, she can use Rule 803(5) to introduce the document if it was made when the events were fresh in the declarant's mind and accurately memorializes them.

There is, however, one oddity about the rule: while the declarant-witness can *read* the contents of the document into evidence, the *document itself* is inadmissible by the proponent. Only the *adverse party* can introduce the document into evidence.

What You Need to Know:

1. Rule 803(4) primarily covers statements made *to* medical personnel, and has a relatively broad scope. The statement's reliability derives from the theory that people are likely to accurately report their medical condition to facilitate treatment. So the rule does not require that the statement be made at the same time as the injury: statements made for medical diagnosis can be made a long time after the injury or incident that precipitated the treatment.
2. Statements admissible under the medical diagnosis exception include, not only statements referencing the injury, but also statements that are reasonably necessary for treatment or diagnosis. The sorts of statements that are particularly excluded are ones that place blame or fault, or otherwise anticipate litigation.
3. Recorded recollections, under Rule 803(5), can be contrasted with Rule 612's process for refreshing

memories. Under Rule 612, a writing or other means of *restoring* ("refreshing") witness's memory aim to get the witness to testify from their *present memory*, on the stand, of what she perceived in the past. Only if that attempt fails can the proponent turn to Rule 803(5), and use some writing (or other recording) as a *substitute* for the witness's memory on the stand. The writing *replaces* the witness's current and failed memory with some out of court writing that was made on some subject the witness *once knew about*, that was made *contemporaneously* with the incident it records, and which *accurately* records her memory.

4. The proponent does not get to enter the document into evidence: the witness must read out the contents of the document. Only the *opponent* gets to enter the document recording the writing into evidence under Rule 803(5).

LESSON 25: BUSINESS RECORDS AND PUBLIC RECORDS

The next set of hearsay rules pertain to documents made by some person or official when conducting their business. For business records, the idea is that the record-keeper has a self-interested financial stake in maintaining accurate records: they (or their employers) rely on the records to inform their business decisions. In the case of official records, the idea is that the record-keeper is under an official duty to keep accurate records. A subsidiary justification for admitting these types of records is based on habit: these are the sorts of documents regularly recorded by the businessperson or official again and again over a significant period of time. They are thus less likely to be shaded in anticipation of litigation or otherwise reflect an inaccurate picture of the events they record.

Business records are covered by Rule 803(6) and Rule 803(7). The rule covers *all* types of business activity, whether legal or illegal. The defining characteristic of business activity is simply having a financial stake in the activity, whether running a multinational corporation or selling single cigarettes illegally on a street corner. The business need not be run for profit—charitable and other non-profit institutions are considered businesses for purposes of the rule. And the rule covers *all* types of business records, from formal documents to marginal notations.

The problem for many business records is that the business cannot identify precisely who made the recording, either because they have no way of identifying that person, or because multiple people may have been involved in the recording process. For example, when a large online store conducts its inventory process, thousands of people may be involved, and the company may not take care to identify each one. What matters, however, is that the company knows, given its inventory practices, that *someone* is responsible for preparing inventory, and that this person would report the information accurately, that is, from personal knowledge. Furthermore, the business must demonstrate that maintaining a record was a routine part of the business's operation: that the record was made in the course of a "regularly conducted activity of the business" *and* that it was a regular practice to make the recording.

To prove all this, the business need not identify all the participants in the chain of making the business record. Instead, the business can simply identify the person ultimately responsible for keeping its business records—the *custodian of records*—who then testifies as to the conditions identified in Rule 803(6)(a)–(c): that the record was made close to the time of the activity, by someone with knowledge, during the course of a regular business activity, in which making the record was a regular part of that activity. This part of the business record rule looks a lot like the past recollection recorded rule: whomever made the note must have personal knowledge of the event. The business record will then be admitted *unless* the *opponent* can show that the person making the record or the manner of preparing the record are *untrustworthy*, that is, inaccurate or unreliable.

Sometimes, there is a chain of statements made in the course of business from one declarant to another. The stock keeper could report the inventory to a supervisor, who reports it to her manager. So long as all of these declarants work for and report in the course of the business, Rule 806 treats these statements as part of a single recording process: there is no hearsay within hearsay. Multiple hearsay arises only from the statement of some "outsider" to some business insider, who then reports it as part of a business record.

Rule 803(7) is just a version of the rule that silence is not a "statement" as defined by Rule 801(a). Evidence of the *absence* of a business record of some activity is admissible to show that the activity did not happen, so long as the *opponent* does not show that the failure to record the activity was *untrustworthy*.

The public record rule does not quite track the business record rule. Instead, Rule 803(8) carves out three separate exceptions to the hearsay rule. Nonetheless, the rule has a broad scope as to the type of record at issue: it includes any public entity, municipal, state, or federal, domestic or foreign; as well as any form of recording, One difference between business records and public records relates to contemporaneity: a public record (unlike a business record) need not be made at or near the time of the event it records.

The first public record exception, under Rule 803(8)(A)(i) are statements that report some public office's activities. For example, the booking record of a local jail may be admissible to show that the jail had placed that person in custody on some particular date; or a government agency's "received" stamp to show that claim was filed on a certain date. The record memorializes that the government agency or official has dome some act.

The next two exceptions, under Rule 803(8)(A)(ii) and (iii) can be hard to tell apart. Rule 803(8)(A)(ii) covers facts *personally observed* by a *public official*, and which they were under a duty both to *observe* and to *report*. A classic example is the weather at a particular time on a particular day, reported by a meteorological official (a weather person) whose job it is to observe and record the weather. The person must be a public official, and must have personal knowledge.

Excluded from these types of reports are matters observed by some lay person which are *then* reported on to the public official. In such circumstances, the layperson has personal knowledge, but the public official does not. Rule 803(8)(A)(ii) also specifically excludes police investigative reports when offered by the government against a defendant in a criminal trial: what the rule calls a "matter observed by law-enforcement personnel." Instead, the officer herself must testify—a procedure which is also required by the Confrontation Clause contained in the Sixth Amendment to the United States Constitution.

Rule 803(8)(A)(iii) renders admissible reports filed by a government agency after it has conducted an official investigation of some matter. A Supreme Court Case, *Beech Aircraft Corp. v. Rainey*, 488 U.S. 153 (1988), explained that both the factual findings *and* the opinions of the investigators were admissible. In that case, a military aircraft crashed, killing both pilots. Their surviving spouses brought suit, alleging a manufacturing defect caused the crash. They sought to admit a part of an accident report, contained in a section entitled "opinions," that included the possibility that the alleged defect caused the crash. The Court held that such opinions, so long as based on factual investigation.

Unlike the other official record exceptions—or even the business record exception—Rule 803(8)(A)(iii) allows into evidence statements made by some "outsider" that are adopted by the investigator and form the basis of her report. Here, the idea is that the investigator is a government expert, able to assess the trustworthiness of the statement and determine whether to rely upon it or not in conducting her investigation.

As with Rule 803(8)(A)(ii), Rule 803(8)(A)(iii) prohibits the admission into evidence of criminal investigative reports offered by the prosecution against a defendant in a criminal trial. Taken together, both rules operate as a blanket prohibition against using police reports against a criminal defendant under *any* of the hearsay rules: whether the business record exception or the past recollection recorded exception. This feature of police records—that they may not be used by the prosecution against a criminal defendant in a criminal case, even if they fit some other hearsay rule—is highly unusual. It violates the normal rule that an item of evidence inadmissible for one purpose may nonetheless be admissible for another purpose.

Rule 803(8)(B) contains a similar requirement to Rule 803(6) that the evidence be *trustworthy*, assessed if an opponent objects to the admissibility of evidence on this ground.

What You Need to Know:

1. Business records gain their trustworthiness from the financial interest business people have in keeping accurate accounts of their business activities. Business records are presumed trustworthy so long as the record is the sort that regularly made during the ordinary activities of the business by someone with knowledge of the event recorded contemporaneous with that event.
2. Rule 803(6) takes a broad view of what counts as a business: it includes almost any commercial activity, including the activity of non-profit institutions. The business activity need not be legal to count.
3. Business records must be authenticated, under the rule, by someone with knowledge of the making or keeping of such records, such as a custodian of records. Finally, the record is admissible so long as the opponent does not raise a significant concern about its trustworthiness.
4. Under Rule 803(7), the absence of a business record is admissible to show the non-occurrence of some event, so long as the business would normally record that kind of event.
5. Public records fall into three types. The first are records of what the public agency or official *did*: issued a notice to appear; processed a passport at the border, and so on. The second is are matters observed by some public official and that she was under a legal duty to record. Such records require personal knowledge of the event on the part of the official. The third are the factual findings, including opinions, from some legally authorized official investigation.

6. The scope of the admissible evidence is much broader under the official-investigations rule than under the rule admitting matters observed under a duty to record. The former permits the introduction into evidence of statements of "outsiders" who were not public officials, but whose statements the officials relied on in compiling their report; such outsider statements are inadmissible if part of a public report of a matter observed by a public official.
7. Police reports, if offered by the state against a criminal defendant, *are not admissible* as public records, whether matters observed or public investigations; nor can they be admitted as business records.

LESSON 26: FORMER TESTIMONY

The next set of exceptions cover rule 804, which *requires* that a declarant be *unavailable as a witness* if the evidence is to be admissible. The declarant may be present in the courtroom: however, mere presence does not make someone a witness. They must, in addition, be available to take the stand and testify under oath subject to cross-examination. If, for some reason, some person cannot fulfil this role, they are unavailable to testify as a witness. Demonstrating that a declarant is unavailable under Rule 804(a) is a necessary preliminary step before determining whether one of the exceptions under Rule 804(b) applies.

Rule 804(a) lists five different ways in which a declarant is unavailable as a witness. Of the five ways in which a witness may be unavailable, two involve physical non-presence. One type of unavailability, covered by Rule 804(a)(4), is due to illness or death. The second, covered by Rule 804(a)(5) occurs when the proponent cannot procure the declarant's physical attendance at trial after serving a subpoena or some other legal process upon them *and, in addition, after taking other reasonable steps* to ensure the declarant appears at the trial. Under Rule 804(a)(5), simply serving process is not enough. The proponent must demonstrate to the court that she has made a reasonable effort to contact and persuade the witness to attend, including by paying expert witnesses for their testimony, or other travel costs, and so on.

The three other types of unavailability do not refer to physical non-presence: they instead contemplate that a physically available declarant has some legal or other impediment exempting her from testifying as a witness. Rule 804(a)(1) categorizes as unavailable a declarant who exercises a privilege and so decline to testify. Such privileges include the privilege against self-incrimination and the spousal privilege. Rule 804(a)(2) covers situations in which the declarant has no privilege to claim, but simply refuses to testify even after the court orders the declarant to testify. The final form of unavailability is where the declarant fails to act as a witness by simply not remembering anything about the subject of her testimony. In this last case, the declarant must be sworn in as a witness and cross-examined to demonstrate that she can no longer remember the matter about which she was called to testify; only then may her statement be admitted under one of the exceptions in Rule 804(b).

Rule 804(b) creates five hearsay exceptions for unavailable declarants. The first exception is the former testimony rule, Rule 804(b)(1), which rests upon the idea that if a declarant testified as a witness at a prior hearing, and was (or was available to be) cross-examined about some information relevant to the instant trial, then that information has (or could have) satisfied the normal evidentiary guarantees of trustworthiness in the current case too, and so is likely sufficiently accurate. The requirement that the witness be available for cross-examination rules out one type of hearing: grand jury hearings. The Rule requires the declarant to have testified under oath at a prior hearing, to have been available for cross examination at that hearing, and for the prior cross-examiner to have the *right relationship* to the current opponent and share a *similar motive* in developing the testimony.

What sort of relationship is the right one depends upon whether the *current* trial is criminal or civil. If the *current* trial is a *criminal* one, then the prior cross-examiner must be the *same party* as the current opponent. So if a criminal defendant, on trial for murder, seeks to introduce the prior testimony of a currently unavailable witness at a previous trial, the prosecutor in the current case must represent the same party as the prosecutor in the previous case. In addition, that previous prosecutor must have had a *similar motive* to cross examine the witness. If the prosecutor at the instant trial represents the federal government, but at the prior trial the prosecutor represented the State of California, then these are different parties, and the evidence is inadmissible. Similarly, if the prosecutor at the prior trial sought to cross examine the declarant about defendant's alibi, and at the instant trial, the evidence would be used to support a self-defense claim, the motive in cross-examining the declarant would be different, and so the evidence would be excluded.

If the current trial is a civil trial, the relationship between the prior cross-examiner and the current opponent need not be so tight. Instead, what matters is that the prior cross-examiner be a *predecessor in interest.* This is usually taken to mean that the current and prior cross-examiner and the current one share the *same reason* for cross-examining the witness. A minority of jurisdictions demand that the current and prior cross-examiner be in *privity* with each other, which means that they share the same right, title, interest, or obligation with regard to the case and the subject of cross examination.

What You Need to Know:

1. Rule 804 requires that a declarant be *unavailable* to testify as a witness at trial for the evidence to be admissible. There are five grounds of unavailability: privilege; refusal to testify; absolute failure of memory; unable to attend the trial because of physical injury or death; and unavailable because the proponent has been unable, after making a reasonable effort, to secure the declarant's attendance.

2. To show inability to secure attendance, under Rule 804(a)(5), the proponent must do more than serve a subpoena upon the declarant: she must make *reasonable* efforts, such as paying an expert or the transportation costs of the witness. Failure to take

reasonable efforts means the statement will be excluded.

3. Rule 804(b)(1) applies to prior testimony given by the declarant as a witness at an earlier legal proceeding. The statement is reliable because given under oath and subjected to appropriate cross examination. What counts as appropriate cross-examination varies depending upon whether the *current* trial is a *criminal* or *civil* trial. If the current trial is a criminal one, then the prior cross-examination must have been conducted by the same party and with a similar reason to question the witness. In a civil case, the cross-examiner must be a *predecessor in interest*, which usually means someone with a similar interest in questioning the witness. In a minority of jurisdictions, it means someone who has privity with current opponent, which means some sort of property interest.

LESSON 27: DYING DECLARATIONS; DECLARATIONS AGAINST INTEREST, FORFEITURE; RESIDUAL EXCEPTION

The most final way to be absent from a trial is because of death. Rule 804(b)(2) treats some statements by people who think they are at death's door as having special salience. The rule makes admissible statements by people who think they are on the brink of death about the cause or circumstances that brought about that belief. The first thing to note is that, under the Federal Rules (as opposed to some state rules of evidence) the declarant *need not actually die*. What matters is that they think they are about to die. The second feature is that they must think they are about to die *now*. A person who has been given six months to live, or even six weeks or six days, does not believe that death is immanent. The idea is that (as the Advisory Committee notes) "powerful psychological pressures" operate at the time of death, so that someone believing that death is immanent will want to get especially serious matters off her chest. The only statements that are admissible, however, pertain to who or what caused death, and under what circumstances.

Dying declarations are admissible in any civil trial. However, a somewhat persnickety rule applies to criminal trials: dying declarations are only admissible in a *criminal trial* if that trial is for *homicide*. Dying declarations are *inadmissible* for other types of criminal prosecution (rape, robbery, theft, drug crime, etc.).

Rule 804(b)(3) provides an exception where the absent declarant's statement places them at risk of taking a financial hit, or puts them in criminal or civil legal jeopardy. It is not enough that the declarant be subjected to social ridicule or hatred. The guarantee of trustworthiness comes from the legal risk assumed by the declarant when making the statement: self-interest would normally prevent someone from making such a statement unless it was true. Thus, for example, if there was a dispute about paternity, and Anakin tells Luke, "I am your father," Anakin opens himself up to a possible civil lawsuit. Or if a declarant in a car accident states that they suffered no physical injury, thus forgoing one grounds of civil suit, such a statement falls under the exceptions for statements against interest. However, such statements are only admissible if it a reasonable declarant would have thought she might be exposed to legal liability. Thus, statements made in confidence to friends may not count; nor statements made just before the declarant committed suicide (thus avoiding legal liability). Finally, in a criminal case, if the statement exposes the declarant to *criminal* liability, then some corroborating evidence, other than the statement itself, is required.

Rule 804(b)(4) makes admissible statements by declarants about certain matters peculiarly concerning themselves or their families: their birth, marriage, divorce, and so on, even though they may lack personal knowledge about some of these facts. For example, a declarant lacks personal knowledge of their date of birth: although they were there, they were too young to know or remember what was going on, and must have been told by a parent or found out from some other record. Rule 804(b)(4)(b) extends admissibility of evidence of this sort if the declarant is an intimate of the person whose details they are giving.

Rule 804(b)(6) is essentially an estoppel rule. A party is precluded from objecting to the evidence of a declarant if they have wrongfully procured the declarant's absence as a witness, and did so with the purpose of preventing their testimony. The mental state limitation is an important one: the party may have, for example, killed the witness in a bar fight. In killing the witness, the party might have *known* that the witness could not testify against the party; but the party need not have killed the witness *for the purpose of* preventing that testimony. This narrow reading was endorsed by the Supreme Court in *Giles v. California*, 554 U.S. 353 (2008).

Finally, there is the residual exception, contained in Rule 807. If you are relying on the residual exception in an exam, then you are almost certainly wrong. If the residual exception applied broadly, the other hearsay rules would be redundant. The residual exception applies to circumstances *not covered by* Rules 803 or 804. On one interpretation (the better one), the residual exception simply suggests that the rules are open-ended: if there is some hearsay exception that the drafters did not identify, but which is nonetheless particularly trustworthy, then we ought to recognize the exception without waiting for the drafters. This, however, is the minority view. The majority view is that if one element of some hearsay exception has not been fulfilled, then, so long as the other circumstances are sufficiently trustworthy, and there is a strong showing of necessity, then the evidence may be admissible. So if a business record appears trustworthy, but the business is illegal drug dealing, and there is no custodian of records available to testify as to the trustworthiness of the record-keeping, then equally or more trustworthy expert testimony about the record-keeping may make the record admissible, so long as there was no other way to get the evidence in, and the evidence is central to the case.

What You Need to Know:

1. Death is the ultimate form of absence from trial. However, under Rule 804(b)(2), a declarant need not actually die for her statement to count as a dying declaration. Instead, the statement is regarded as trustworthy because the declarant believes death is immanent, and that belief prompts her to tell the truth. To count as a dying

declaration, her statement must concern the cause or circumstances of the declarant's death.

2. In a civil case, a dying declaration is fully admissible. However, a dying declaration is admissible in a criminal case only if the crime charged is homicide. So care must be taken in specifying the crime charged.

3. Declarations against interest are trustworthy because of the legal or financial jeopardy in which they place the declarant. The theory is that a declarant would not make the statement, given the legal and financial risk to which she exposes herself, unless the statement were true.

4. The proponent must show that a reasonable person who made the statement would have believed it to be true; and that the statement is, in fact, contrary to some pecuniary, proprietary, or penal interest. If the interest is penal, and the case is a criminal one, the proponent must *also* provide corroborating evidence of the claim.

5. Rule 804(b)(6)'s forfeiture by wrongdoing exception to is a form of estoppel that prohibits an opponent complaining when she wrongfully prevented a witness from testifying. The rule is narrowly construed to require the proponent to prove that the opponent's *purpose* was to exclude the declarant's testimony at trial.

6. Rule 807, the residual exception, is only exceptionally applied. While the rule was adopted to leave the federal rules open-ended, and so to encourage the development of new rules, it is generally not interpreted that way. The rule is applied if there is exceptional need for the evidence in circumstances evincing a high degree of trustworthiness, where admitting the statement will serve the interests of justice.

LESSON 28: CONSTITUTIONAL ISSUES: DUE PROCESS AND CONFRONTATION

The Constitution applies to the Rules of Evidence, as to all federal statutes. Where the rules conflict with the Constitution, the Constitution wins out. Two clauses of the Constitution are of special interest for the law of evidence: the Fifth Amendment's Due Process Clause (for state evidence codes, the Fourteenth Amendment substitutes in); and the Sixth Amendment's Confrontation Clause.

Of the two, the Due Process Clause has garnered much less attention recently. The Clause requires that the defendant be afforded a fair opportunity to defend herself against the state. However, the Federal Rules of Evidence were adopted after the Warren Court's rights revolution. For the most part, the Rules attempted to simplify and rationalize the law of evidence, by updating the common law to drop the bits that conflicted with due process, as well as adopting the due process values of fairness and justice in the text of Rule 102 (and mirroring those values throughout the Rules). For the most part, states have followed suit. In *Chambers v. Mississippi*, 410 U.S. 284 (1973), for example, the state did not call a key witness, and a now-outdated common law rule—the *voucher rule*—precluded the defendant from cross-examining his own witness. The Supreme Court ruled that the Due Process Clause of the Fourteenth Amendment (it was a state case) permitted cross-examination. The voucher rule was superseded by Rule 607, which permits impeaching one's own witness. Other unfair or unjust rules have similarly fallen out of favor.

By far the more currently controversial rule is the Sixth Amendment's Confrontation Clause. The Clause guarantees the right of a *criminal defendant* to *confront* the prosecution's witnesses against her. That Clause enjoyed a renaissance in the mid-2000s, sponsored by Justice Scalia's originalist arguments in its favor. Up until that point, there were not a lot of Supreme Court Confrontation Clause cases, but the major one, *Ohio v. Roberts*, 448 U.S. 56 (1980), interpreted the Confrontation Clause to track the most well-established hearsay exceptions. In *Crawford v. Washington*, 541 U.S. 36 (2004), the Supreme Court changed tack.

Now, the Confrontation Clause applies *in a criminal trial* to exclude *testimonial hearsay statements* introduced by the *prosecution* from a declarant who is *unavailable to testify*. The rationale is that the Sixth Amendment creates an independent and important right for criminal defendants to *cross-examine* their accusers in a criminal trial—where accuser means any witness for the state.

The clause does *not* apply to three large categories of hearsay: (1) hearsay in *civil* cases; (2) hearsay introduced by the defendant *against the prosecution* in criminal cases; and (3) hearsay declarations from *someone who winds up testifying* in open court (at the current or a prior trial), *subject to cross-examination*.

The Confrontation Clause only applies to *testimonial statements*: statements given to some government agent—whether a law enforcement agent or some substitute or delegate—as part of an interrogation or its *functional equivalent* during a criminal investigation. Statements given outside the interrogation context, whether spontaneously, or to someone who is not a state agent—a friend, a bystander, tweeted out to the world in general, or addressed to oneself in a diary—do not count as testimonial statements. However, certain statements to law enforcement *delegates* such as medical officials acting under a duty to report domestic violence or child abuse to the criminal authorities, could count as testimonial. They would count as testimonial if the circumstances suggested that the law enforcement delegate was interrogating the witness as part of a criminal prosecution.

The clearest class of non-testimonial statements are ones where the *primary purpose* of the statement is to report an *ongoing emergency*. Davis v. Washington, 547 U.S. 813 (2006). Emergencies include the need to ensure that a victim is safe or to determine where a violent person is located. Michigan v. Bryant, 562 U.S. 344 (2011). In *Ohio v. Clark*, 576 U.S. ___, 135 S.Ct. 2173 (2015), the Court held that questioning by state teachers to determine whether a child was being abused, and whether that abuse was ongoing, fell under the emergency exception. The child abuse had been going on for some time, so the permissible duration of the emergency, during which the primary purpose of questioning remains non-testimonial, may vary considerably depending on the nature of the emergency.

All this means that the Confrontation Clause can be a major hurdle to admissibility of the hearsay statements in a criminal case of an unavailable prosecution witness *against* the defendant *if the statements are testimonial.* One major way to admit the hearsay statements, then, is to show they are non-testimonial, either because the primary purpose was to remediate some emergency, or because the statements were not part of an interrogation or were given to someone other than a state official. And another is simply to have the declarant testify as a witness at trial.

What You Need to Know:

1. The Federal Rules establish that relevant evidence is admissible unless the Constitution provides otherwise. One of the major constitutional exceptions is the Sixth Amendment's Confrontation Clause.

2. The Confrontation Clause applies only to *criminal cases* and prohibits the admission of hearsay evidence offered by the State *against a criminal defendant* without the opportunity for the defendant to *cross-examine* the witness.

3. The Confrontation Clause provides a limited protection for criminal defendants. It protects against hearsay only if the declarant is *unavailable* and her statement is *testimonial.* A statement is testimonial only if made to some law-enforcement official or their surrogate during a custodial interrogation or its functional equivalent, with the primary purpose of creating evidence for a criminal prosecution.

4. The confrontation clause does not apply to statements responding to an *ongoing emergency*, where law enforcement officers need information to respond to some dangerous situation. Also, two types of hearsay are traditionally admissible even under the Confrontation Clause: dying declarations

(Rule 804(2)), and statements of witnesses that the defendant wrongfully and intentionally prevented from testifying (Rule 804(6)).

5. The clause does not apply to three large categories of hearsay: (1) hearsay in *civil* cases; (2) hearsay introduced by the defendant *against the prosecution* in criminal cases; and (3) hearsay declarations from *someone who winds up testifying* in open court (at the current or a prior trial) or is otherwise *subject to cross-examination* by the defendant.

6. The *Due Process Clause* of the Fifth and Fourteenth Amendments also prohibits the introduction of evidence if it would unfairly prejudice some party, usually a criminal defendant. However, because the Federal Rules were designed to promote fairness, one of the values incorporated in Rule 102; and because the Rules did away with many of the more problematic provisions of the common law, the Due Process Clause now rarely (if ever) conflicts with the Federal Rules.

LESSON 29: AUTHENTICATION AND THE BEST EVIDENCE RULE

In addition to witness testimony, trials often involve various items of evidence, including documentary and physical evidence, that must be authenticated to be admissible. Authentication simply means demonstrating, with sufficient certainty, that the item is what its proponent claims it to be.

Authentication presents a conditional relevance problem. The document is relevant to prove that the contract existed; or the gun is relevant to prove that the defendant used the weapon to kill the victim; but each item is relevant only on condition that it was the document the parties signed or the gun that was used in the crime. Under Rule 901, the standard for authenticating evidence is the same as Rule 104(b): sufficiency of the evidence. The idea is to make it relatively easy to admit the evidence, and then allow the parties to dispute the authenticity of the item.

There are essentially two types of items that fall under Rule 901(a): those that are unique and those that are generic. Unique items are relatively easy to authenticate: some person with knowledge of the item testifies that the item is what the proponent claims it to be. One of the witnesses to the contract testifies that the document is indeed the contract made between the parties; a ballistics expert testifies that the bullet that killed the victim was fired by the gun introduced into evidence at trial. Other items of evidence are generic: one gun looks like any other gun. To establish that *this* gun, the one offered at trial and which fired the bullet, was the one taken from the defendant, we need to establish a *chain of custody* tracing the movement of the item from where it was seized to trial.

Where there are gaps in the chain of custody, we simply ask whether there is sufficient evidence to believe that the item is what the proponent claims it is. If the gun was seized by the police, and stored in an evidence locker, there may be a dispute over the authenticity of the gun if multiple officers had access to the locker, or multiple guns were stored there. Nonetheless, so long as a reasonable juror could believe that the gun that was stored in the locker is the gun offered into evidence at trial, then the evidence is admissible.

These general principles explain the non-exhaustive list of ten examples contained in Rule 901(b). Of the first five items on the list, the opening example states the general rule: someone who is able to identify some particular item testifies that it is what they claim it is. The next four examples are unique items: someone's handwriting; an expert's testimony that the item matches some sample; that the item can be identified by its distinctive characteristics; and that a recording can be identified as some specific person's voice. The other things are more generic items: telephone calls to particular numbers; public records; old documents and data; and so on.

Not all types of physical evidence require a witness to authenticate them. Certain especially trustworthy *documents* are authentic on their face. Rule 902 provides a list of these *self-authenticating* documents. These include various public documents, certified documents, and notarized documents.

Sometimes the question is whether the original document must be produced at all, or whether witness testimony or some other version of the document is admissible in its stead. The *Best Evidence Rule*, contained in Rules 1001–1104, answers that question. The general idea is if a witness has personal knowledge of some conversation or event, then the witness's testimony is enough; the proponent need not provide any document or other recording that memorializes the conversation or event. Here, the content of the document is not in issue; the underlying event is what we want to know about, and the witness is someone with personal knowledge of it. However, if the *content* of the *document* or recording is in issue, then Rule 1002 (the Best Evidence Rule) requires the proponent produce an original or a copy. The content of a document is in issue if there is *some dispute about what the document or recording says*; or because the witnesses *lacks* personal knowledge of the event it memorializes, and so is testifying about the event *in reliance* on the document or recording; or some claim or defense requires proof using the document or recording.

For example, imagine an FBI agent listens to a tape recording an incriminating conversation between the defendant and a co-conspirator. The proponent wants to get the *conversation* into evidence, not the document. If the co-conspirator is available to testify about that conversation, then the Best Evidence Rule does not apply to exclude the co-conspirator's statement. Because the co-conspirator was present at the conversation, and so has personal knowledge of it, then *either* the co-conspirator's testimony or the recording are admissible. Imagine, however, that the co-conspirator is unavailable. The FBI agent does *not* have personal knowledge of the conversation: she was not present at the conversation, and gained all her information from the tape. Now the Best Evidence Rule does apply, and the recording *or a copy* must be produced to satisfy the rule.

Two further features of the Best Evidence Rule, however, make it incredibly easy to satisfy. First, under Rule 1003, copies ("duplicates") are just as admissible as the original. The definition of *both* originals *and* copies under Rule 1001 is extremely broad: *original* includes printouts, photographic negatives, and so on; *duplicate* includes photocopies, for example. The major exclusions are typed or handwritten copies of the original (see the Advisory Committee Note to Rule 1001).

The second feature is also useful: under Rule 1004, if the original is destroyed then, so long as the proponent did not destroy the original *in bad faith*, the proponent may offer a substitute, whether oral, typed, handwritten or whatever. The same rule applies if the proponent requests a copy of the document from her opposing party, and the opponent fails to provide it. As the Advisory Committee Note suggests, "if failure to produce the original is satisfactorily explained, secondary evidence is admissible."

What You Need to Know:

1. Usually, physical evidence must be authenticated by producing a witness to testify that the item is what it's proponent claims it to be. Rule 901, which governs authentication, is simply more specific application of the Rule 104(b); it applies the *sufficiency* standard to admit physical evidence if a reasonable juror could believe it is what its proponent claims it to be.
2. For purposes of Rule 901, physical evidence falls into two broad categories: unique and generic. Unique evidence may be authenticated by a witness with personal knowledge of the item; generic evidence may be authenticated by a witness with personal knowledge of the process of maintaining the item separate from others of its type and producing it at trial.
3. Some *documents* are *self-authenticating* and so *do not* require a witness to authenticate them. Self-authenticating documents defined by Rule 902, fall into three categories: public records; certified documents, and notarized documents.
4. The Best Evidence Rule contained in Rule 1001–1004 only applies if the issues at trial present some question that requires proof of the *content* of a document or other recording, rather than the

underlying event the document or recording memorializes.

5. If the content is in issue, Rule 1002 requires the proponent to produce an *original* or a *duplicate*. The Rule is easy to satisfy, given Rule 1001's definition of original or duplicate. If the original cannot be obtained by the proponent, because lost, destroyed, or otherwise unobtainable, oral, written, or typed evidence is admissible to prove the content of the document.

LESSON 30: PRIVILEGES

The Federal Rules delegate the law of privileges to the States. Rule 501 originally contemplated a broad law of privileges, but it proved so controversial that the rule, as it stood, could not pass Congress. Different States protect different privileges. However, one uniform privilege—the one we'll focus on—is the attorney-client privilege.

The attorney client privilege is an unusual evidence rule. It applies, not only during trial, but also before and after. Once a client attempts to hire an attorney, their confidential communications are sacrosanct unless the *client*, or her attorney acting as the client's agent, discloses them.

The justification for the rule is that non-disclosure of confidential communications between attorney and client encourages free and frank communications between these two, so that the attorney can offer candid and fully-informed legal advice. There is no assumption that the communications cover matters that are unlawful: instead, whether out of embarrassment, or privacy concerns, or for a variety of other reasons, clients may seek to shelter certain conversations from the scrutiny of their family, friends, the public, or even the state. To enable this sharing of information, the content of the conversations is not discoverable, not only before trial, but *in perpetuity*, even *after* the client has died!

The attorney-client privilege attaches to: (1) a *communication* made (2) in *confidence* (3) between a *lawyer and client* (4) in the course of the *provision of legal services.* Some of these elements overlap.

The first element requires there to be some communication, defined in the same manner as a statement in Rule 801(a): some utterance the speaker intended to make to the attorney. The speaker must intend to communicate some information to the attorney. For example, physical appearances are not communications. If the client slurs her speech because drunk, the fact that her speech was slurred was not the communication; only the content of what she said counts. Accordingly, the fact that her speech was slurred is not covered by the privilege. Similarly, handing over a package usually does not count as a communication. If a client gives her diary to an attorney, the giving of the diary is not a communication covered by the privilege.

Second, the communication must be made *in confidence.* That means that the client and the attorney must take reasonable steps to ensure that their communications are not disclosed to anyone else. If the conversation can be heard by some third party, then it is not confidential. So if the client knows someone is monitoring her phone calls, because, for example, she is a jail inmate, then the call is not confidential, and the communication is not privileged.

Third, the conversation must be between a *lawyer* and a *client.* Suppose the client keeps a diary: the diary is a conversation between the client *and herself.* The information in a diary is not usually prepared at the behest of the lawyer or for the purposes of communicating to the lawyer. So this sort of communication, prepared for oneself, or a doctor, and so on, is not privileged.

Sometimes, this provision overlaps with the confidentiality element: if the client speaks to someone other than a lawyer, the conversation is not confidential either. For example, the client may speak to an accountant, and then the accountant passes the information on to the lawyer. Accountants are generally not lawyers; so there is no attorney-client privilege that applies to the accountant-client conversation. Sometimes, however, a lawyer will direct a client to speak to someone who is not a lawyer, but who acts on the lawyer's behalf: a paralegal, an intern, but also a translator or an accountant. So long as these third parties are acting *under the lawyer's direction*, then they count as a "lawyer" for purposes of the privilege.

In the corporate context, the nature of a "client" can be quite complex. Are all the corporation's employees the corporate counsel's clients? Or only the corporation's decision-makers. In *Upjohn Co. v. United States*, 449 U.S. 383 (1981), the Court held that employees *could* count as clients in certain circumstances, so long as the communications made by employees to corporate counsel were made at the direction of corporate superiors for the purpose of obtaining legal advice regarding matters within the employees' duties, and the employees knew the purpose of the communications.

Finally, the conversation must be in the course of *providing legal services*. If the conversation is between a lawyer and a client, but for some *other* purpose, such as gossiping about friends, then it is not a privileged conversation. Similarly, if the lawyer is acting *as an accountant* in helping file taxes, or is acting *as a postal worker* in transferring a box of incriminating evidence from the client to the police, these non-lawyerly activities are not protected by the privilege.

Some types of legal activity look a lot like non-legal activity. Many states think that preparing tax information is not legal activity. But if there is a significant amount of legal work that intermingled with the non-legal work, then the activity is likely protected. In *Upjohn*, the Supreme Court held that privilege extended to those associates a law firm used to engage in investigatory activities as part of the fact-finding part of the process of representing the client. Fact-finding of this sort, the Court held, was a legal activity, even though it is the sorts of thing also done by private investigators or the police.

Clients, and lawyers acting on behalf of clients, can waive the attorney-client privilege, thereby allowing third parties to discover the contents of their communications. The rule is usually stated by asserting that only the client can waive the privilege. Waiver occurs when the client engages in conduct inconsistent with confidentiality. For example, a client who files a lawsuit claiming her attorney was incompetent waives the privilege. But attorneys can *also* waive the privilege, so long as that attorney has implied authority to waive the privilege on behalf of the client, and client ratifies her attorney's waiver by failing to stop it. Waiver requires voluntary disclosure: if a court mistakenly orders a client or attorney to disclose the information, for example, the client or attorney does not waive privilege by complying with the court's demand for disclosure. However, an attorney may accidentally waive a privilege by disclosing confidential information to a third party. If an attorney inadvertently discloses privileged material, she may seek to maintain its privilege status by claiming she took reasonable steps to prevent disclosure and also took reasonably prompt measures to retrieve the inadvertently disclosed information.

The *scope* of the waiver can vary: the relevant unit of waiver may be the communication or the subject matter. Some courts hold that disclosure of *part* of a communication waives the privilege as to the *whole* communication. Some courts hold that disclosure of *a particular subject matter* waives the privilege as to the *same or related* subject matters.

Finally, there is an important exception to the privilege that applies to criminal matters. Under the *crime-fraud exception* to the attorney-client privilege. Sometimes clients seek legal services to further some criminal enterprise or fraudulent objective. The exception *only* refers to communications concerning current or future criminal or fraudulent activities; the privilege still covers communications about past criminal or fraudulent acts. For the exception to apply, extinguishing the privilege, the client must intentionally solicit the attorney's advice in order to engage or seek to engage in present or future criminal or fraudulent activity; and the attorney must give advice which furthers the activity.

What You Need to Know:

1. Privileges are unique in that they often apply outside the trial, and so have a more extensive application than the other rules of evidence. For example, the attorney-client privilege begins immediately the client seeks to retain some counsel, and lasts for ever, even after the client's death, unless the client, or counsel acting on behalf

of the client, waives the privilege. The privilege is justified based on the need for open and frank communication between the attorney and her client, for example, when sharing embarrassing or secret information that the client may wish to keep from the public or their family members.

2. The attorney-client privileged has four features: it applies to a (1) communication, made (2) in confidence, (3) between an attorney and client, (4) in the course of the provision of legal services. A communication is the sort of intentional utterance covered by Rule 801(c); and the communication is made *in confidence* if there is a reasonable effort to ensure that third parties are excluded from the communication process. The communication must be made to the attorney: a diary that communicates information to oneself is not covered by the privilege, nor are communications that are initially made to a third party. However, if the communication is made to a third party at the direction of the attorney, to help the attorney understand the issues raised by the client, then the communication may still be privileged.

3. A privilege exists only when the attorney providing distinctively legal service. Accounting services, or transporting goods from the client to some third party are generally not considered legal services. However, investigation is considered a distinctively legal service, so long as it is part of the fact-gathering process for some case.

4. Only the client can waive the attorney-client privilege. However, an attorney *can* waive the privilege if acting as an agent for client. The scope of the waiver depends upon whether waiver is intentional or accidental; and when intentional waiver occurs. Pretrial intentional waivers may not require full disclosure of communications on related subject matters.

5. The crime-fraud exception to the privilege entails that the privilege does not apply when the client seeks an attorney's advice to commit a *current or future* crime or fraud. The crime-fraud exception does *not* apply to communications concerning *prior* criminal acts. Those backwards looking communications are still within the privilege.

CHAPTER 6

INCOME TAX

LESSON 1: INTRODUCTION

The Income Tax course typically covers the federal income tax consequences of individuals who are U.S. citizens or residents. Other advanced tax courses, such as corporate tax, partnership tax, and international tax, cover the federal income tax consequences of business entities, such as corporations and LLCs, and of nonresident alien individuals and foreign corporations.

Income Tax is perhaps the quintessential statutory course. There are no significant constitutional issues, and many of the answers can be determined by carefully reading the relevant **statutes**. These statutes are embodied in the Internal Revenue Code (the "Code"), which is found in Title 26 of the United States Code. All references to "section" in this Chapter refer to the Code. The Code is huge, as it deals with all matters relating to the raising of federal revenues. Take a look at the Table of Contents at the front of your Code & Regulations supplement. Subtitle A covers income taxes, a portion of which is the focus of this course. Subtitle B deals with estate and gift taxes, subtitle C employment taxes, and so on. The Table of Contents can be a useful resource to see the forest as you are studying particular trees (statutes).

While the primary sources of federal income tax law are the statutes, sometimes the statute does not provide clear answers. In those cases, the Treasury Department can resolve these ambiguities by issuing **regulations**. The regulation number corresponds to the statute to which it relates. Thus, Treas. Reg. section 1.61–1 interprets Code section 61. Treasury regulations are accorded tremendous deference by courts unless the regulation is inconsistent with the underlying statute, in which case the statute controls. This means that if a taxpayer is faced with a regulation that she doesn't like, she nevertheless will usually be required to comply with it.

In addition, the Internal Revenue Service (IRS) sometimes issues **revenue rulings**, which explain the IRS's view of how a statute applies to a set of hypothetical facts. Courts give revenue rulings significantly less deference than regulations, which means that taxpayers may be able to take positions contrary to a revenue ruling and still prevail in court.

Another source of law is case law. Taxpayers can challenge IRS determinations in the Tax Court or, if they pay the asserted tax and then claim a refund, in Federal District Court or the Court of Federal Claims. After trial, taxpayers or the government can appeal in federal Circuit Courts and, if granted certiorari, the U.S. Supreme Court. Given the statutory nature of federal income tax law, these cases nearly always are focused on the question of how the relevant statutes apply to the facts of the case. Sometimes the facts are disputed, but more commonly the only question is how the statute should be interpreted. In situations where Treasury Regulations or revenue rulings have been issued, the government's interpretation is granted some degree of deference, so the thumb is on the scale of the government side. Absent such guidance, a reviewing court engages in straightforward statutory interpretation to determine the meaning of the relevant statutes.

Thus, the hierarchy of authority in Income Tax is as follows:

1. **Statute**. If the statute is clear, end of story.
2. **Regulations**. Where the statute is unclear, regulations will be respected except in unusual circumstances.
3. **Revenue rulings & case law**. Where the statute is unclear and there are no relevant regulations, revenue rulings and case law would be determinative subject to a few caveats. First, revenue rulings are not granted significant deference by courts and therefore may not be determinative. Second, interpretations by courts may not represent binding precedent on other courts. For example, an interpretation by the Ninth Circuit Court of Appeals is not binding on other

circuits (and in fact is generally not binding on the Tax Court).

The federal income tax on individuals—the subject of this chapter—is just one source, albeit the largest, of federal revenues, generating nearly 50 percent of total federal revenues. The federal corporate income tax generates roughly 10 percent of federal revenues. A surprisingly large amount of federal revenues, about 35 percent, are generated by employment taxes (also known as wage taxes). These taxes only tax income from services, and they fund Medicare and the Social Security system. The estate and gift tax taxes gratuitous transfers by extremely wealthy individuals and generates only a tiny portion of federal revenues, less than one percent. Finally, excise taxes (e.g., on tobacco and gasoline) raise about three percent of federal revenues.

What You Need to Know:

1. Income Tax covers the federal income tax consequences of individuals who are U.S. citizens or residents.
2. Income Tax is a statutory course. The primary source of law is the body of statutes known as the Code.
3. Treasury regulations help fill in the gaps if a statute is unclear. They are granted significant deference by reviewing courts.

LESSON 2: OVERVIEW OF FEDERAL INCOME TAX

This lesson provides a very general bird's eye perspective of how an individual's federal income tax liability is calculated. First, an individual's **gross income** is determined. Gross income includes payments received for personal services, interest received from bonds, dividends received from shares of stock, gains on the sale of property, and other similar types of receipts. Next, the individual's **deductions** are determined. Deductions include business expenses, such as office rent, and certain personal deductions, such as payments of mortgage interest and charitable contributions.

The excess of total gross income over total deductions equals **taxable income**. Taxable income is applied to the tax rates in section 1. Those tax rates are **progressive**, meaning that as taxable income rises, the tax rate that is applied to the income increases. An example of a simple progressive rate structure is:

First $10,000 of taxable income taxed at 10%

Next $40,000 of taxable income taxed at 20%

Next $50,000 of taxable income taxed at 25%

All remaining taxable income taxed at 30%

Notice that as taxable income rises, the applicable tax rate rises. One important thing to remember is that the higher rates are applied only to the income in the particular bracket, not to all of the taxpayer's income. Thus, a taxpayer who earns $120,000 of taxable income would owe $27,500 ($1,000 on the 1st $10,000; $8,000 on the next $40,000; $12,500 on the next $50,000; and $6,000 on the remaining $20,000). One somewhat common fallacy is that moving into the next tax bracket increases the tax rate on all income. In the example, this fallacy would result in the taxpayer owing $36,000 ($120,000 × 30%). This is not the case. Even the highest income taxpayers get to "ride the rates" and take advantage of the income tax rates in the lower brackets.

This discussion illustrates the difference between marginal tax rates and effective tax rates. A taxpayer's **marginal tax rate** is the rate that applies to the last dollar of income earned. In the example above, the taxpayer's marginal tax rate is 30%, because the taxpayer's last dollar (in fact, the last 20,000 dollars) was taxed at that rate. A taxpayer's **effective tax rate** is the average rate of tax, which equals the total amount of tax paid divided by her taxable income. Here the taxpayer pays tax of $27,500 on taxable income of $120,000, resulting in an effective tax rate of 23%. In progressive tax systems, a taxpayer's effective tax rate will never exceed and will typically be lower than the taxpayer's marginal rate.

As you will soon see, this overview of the federal income tax is tremendously simplified. There are tons of nuances and complexities that have been glossed over. Nevertheless, it is useful to keep the big picture in mind as you work through these nuances and complexities. One nuance worth mentioning now involves character. There are special flavors of gross income and deduction that cause certain items to be taxed either more favorably or less favorably than ordinary income or ordinary deductions. For instance, certain capital gains and dividends are subject to special lower rates, as discussed in Lesson 21. Another nuance involves the timing of income or deduction realization—when are items of income or deduction recognized? Yet another deals with the issue of attributing items of income or deduction among two or more taxpayers—who is the proper taxpayer?

Thus, the lessons that follow ask the following questions:

1. What items are included in gross income?
2. What items are deductible?
3. When are items of gross income and deduction realized?
4. What is the character of items of gross income and deduction?
5. Which taxpayer must report items of gross income and deduction?

What You Need to Know:

1. Taxable income equals the amount of a taxpayer's total gross income minus the taxpayer's total allowable deductions.
2. Taxable income is applied to the progressive tax rates in section 1 of the Code.
3. In a progressive tax system, a taxpayer's marginal tax rate, which is the rate that applies to the last dollar of income earned, is typically higher than the taxpayer's effective tax rate, which is the average rate of tax.

LESSON 3: WHAT IS GROSS INCOME?

Gross income is defined in section 61(a) to include a number of common types of gross income items, including

1. Compensation for personal services, such as salaries and bonuses (section 61(a)(1));
2. Gains from the sale of property (61(a)(3));
3. Interest received on bonds and other debt instruments (61(a)(4));
4. Rents and royalties received for allowing others to use property (61(a)(5) & (6)); and
5. Dividends received on shares of corporation stock (61(a)(7)).

If an item is on the list in section 61(a), it is included in gross income unless another Code section specifically excludes it. But the section 61(a) list is explicitly not exhaustive. The parenthetical "(but not limited to)" means that other items may be included in gross income. The Supreme Court, in *Commissioner v. Glenshaw Glass*, 348 U.S. 426 (1955), held that windfalls, such as the receipt of punitive damages, are included in gross income. The Court explained that "undeniable accessions to wealth, clearly realized, and over which the taxpayers have complete dominion" constitute items of gross income.

Thus, all accessions to wealth that are realized result in gross income. This is an extremely broad interpretation. However, there are some items that could reasonably be considered accessions to wealth that are nevertheless not considered gross income.

1. **Unrealized gains**. When property appreciates in value, the owner becomes wealthier. Thus, mere appreciation is an accession to wealth. But the tax law has always imposed a realization requirement before gains are treated as gross income (and before losses are deductible). The **realization rule** requires that the taxpayer dispose of the property—through a sale or exchange or other realization event—before the appreciation (or, as tax lawyers commonly call it, the built-in gain) is taxed. Thus, if I buy stock for $10 and it appreciates to $100, I have no gross income, even though I am obviously

$90 richer because of the appreciation. But if I *sell* the stock for $100, then I realize the $90 of gain, which is included in gross income. The realization rule is grounded in concerns about valuation (taxing built-in gains as they accrue would require annual valuations) and liquidity (taxes resulting from mere appreciation would have to be paid in cash). Some tax policy experts rightfully question whether these concerns justify the realization rule, because the rule encourages tax-motivated behavior (such as holding on to highly appreciated property instead of selling it) and requires other tax rules to mitigate this effect (these will be discussed in Lesson 21). In fact, the realization rule is so problematic that it has been called the Achilles' heel of the federal income tax. Nevertheless, it is unlikely to go away anytime soon.

2. **Imputed income**. Imputed income constitutes the economic benefit that one receives from performing services for oneself or from using one's own property. In theory, these benefits should be included in gross income. A taxpayer has the same accession to wealth regardless of whether the taxpayer earns $500 of income and uses the income to pay for someone to landscape her yard or whether she does the landscaping herself—in each case, she ends up with the same landscaped yard. Likewise, if the taxpayer earns money to pay rent or instead lives in her own house "rent-free"—in each case, she is living in the same house. However, the tax law does not treat this sort of "self-help" income as gross income. Like the realization rule, the exclusion of imputed income is grounded in concerns about valuation and liquidity.

3. **Borrowing proceeds**. When a taxpayer borrows money, it might appear that she has an accession to wealth. After all, the taxpayer has new cash that she can use to buy goods or services. But borrowing simultaneously creates an obligation of the

taxpayer to repay the cash at some point. Thus, borrowing is not considered gross income. This is known as the **borrowing exclusion**. Borrowing does not result in gross income and, correspondingly, the repayment of the principal amount of borrowed funds is not deductible. (The payment of *interest* on the borrowed funds—which is the "rent" paid for using the principal—may be deductible, as discussed in Lesson 15.)

What You Need to Know:

1. Gross income includes the items listed in section 61(a).
2. Gross income generally includes other items that constitute accessions to wealth, such as prizes and windfalls.
3. Gross income does not include unrealized appreciation (also known as "built-in gains") due to the realization rule, which requires that a realization event occur before the appreciation is taxed.
4. Gross income does not include imputed income, which constitutes the benefits that a taxpayer receives from providing services to herself or from using her own property.
5. The realization rule and the exclusion of imputed income are both grounded in concerns over valuation and liquidity.
6. When a taxpayer borrows, she has no gross income because there is no accession to wealth due to the obligation to repay the borrowed funds.

LESSON 4: GROSS INCOME IN THE FORM OF PROPERTY, SERVICES, OR DEBT RELIEF

Most commonly gross income is received in the form of cash. (In addition to actual currency, "cash" includes checks and money orders.) For instance, salaries are almost always paid in cash. But what if a taxpayer receives an accession to wealth in the form of property or services? Treas. Reg. section 1.61–1(a) explains that gross income may be realized in any form, whether in money, property, or services. Thus, whether an employer pays an employee $100 of cash, $100 worth of property (such as stock), or $100 worth of services (such as a free massage), the employee generally realizes $100 of gross income regardless. This rule makes sense because if gross income were avoidable simply by avoiding the use of cash, parties would be encouraged to arrange for in-kind payments to lessen tax burdens. This would be far less efficient as employers would be forced to speculate as to what property and services an employee desires. Paying employees in cash allows employers to not have to worry about that; employees can use the cash to buy whatever their hearts desire. Discouraging cash as a medium of payment would be terrible policy.

While receipts in the form of property and services are taxed the same as receipts of cash, they result in some additional complications. While the value of cash is obvious, the **fair market value** (FMV) of property or services may be debatable. Under the tax law, FMV is the price that would be agreed upon by a willing buyer and a willing seller, with neither being compelled to buy or sell, and both having reasonable knowledge of the relevant facts. This standard can be easy to apply in some circumstances, such as in the case of publicly traded stock, but in many other situations the determination of FMV may require an appraisal, and appraisals can be more art than science. In light of this, it is not surprising that the IRS often disagrees with taxpayers' FMV determinations.

To illustrate these concepts, assume that an employee receives 100 shares of employer stock as a year-end bonus. The stock clearly represents gross income; the only question is how much. The amount of gross income depends on the FMV of the 100 shares. If the company is a public company, such as Microsoft Corporation, determining that FMV is easy. As I am writing this sentence, Google Finance tells me that Microsoft shares are trading at $71.92 per share, so 100 shares have a FMV of $7,192 right now.

If the company is a private company, determining the FMV of shares can be quite difficult, especially if (as is common for private companies) there have been no recent sales of the company's stock. Assume that a recent appraisal determines that the FMV of each private company share is $1,000, so the FMV of 100 shares is $100,000. In that case, an employee who received 100 shares as compensation would have $100,000 of gross income.

What if, instead of giving the employee the stock for free, the company gives the employee stock at a discount? For instance, in the private company example, assume that the employee pays $200 per share, while the FMV is $1,000 per share. This $800 per share discount represents compensation and, accordingly, it is included gross income. Thus, the employee realizes $80,000 of gross income ($800 per share discount times 100 shares). In the earlier case, where the employee paid $0 for the stock, the discount was $100,000; here, the discount is only $80,000 because the employee is paying $20,000 cash for the stock.

In either case, whether the employee is granted the shares for free or pays some amount for the shares, the employee's *subsequent* gain upon the sale of those shares will be determined by reference to $100,000. Consider the case where the employee was granted the shares free of charge, and assume that one year after the grant the employee sells the shares for $150,000. As noted above, the employee realizes $100,000 of gross income when she receives the shares. When she sells the shares she would realize $50,000 of gain, because the $150,000 of sales proceeds exceeds the $100,000 she already included in gross income (this $100,000 will be her "basis" in the stock; basis is discussed in Lesson 5). This makes perfect sense as she ends up with $150,000 of cash: she paid tax on $100,000 when she received the shares and she pays tax on the remaining $50,000 when she sells the shares.

This **compensatory discount** situation must be contrasted with a **bargain purchase**. A bargain purchase occurs when, in an arm's length transaction, a purchaser buys property or services for less than the FMV of the property or services. Assume that a valuable antique is (unbeknownst to the seller) underpriced by $500 in a garage sale. When a buyer purchases the antique, the buyer does not have gross income even though the buyer has an accession to wealth of $500. This is known as the bargain purchase rule, and it is related to the realization rule. The $500 built-in gain is treated as unrealized appreciation.

The compensatory discount rule and the bargain purchase rule may appear difficult to reconcile. In both cases, the taxpayer is richer by the amount of the discount/bargain. But only the discount is immediately taxed. This inconsistency however is justified by practicality. We can't encourage employers to pay employees in the form of discounts, so we tax these discounts just like they are cash. We also can't scrutinize every single arm's length transaction that occurs to see if one side somehow got the better of the other side. Context matters.

One final point: a taxpayer is benefitted when she receives cash, property, or services. A taxpayer can be benefitted in yet another way: when someone pays her debts for her. In *Old Colony Trust Company v. Commissioner*, 279 U.S. 716 (1929), the taxpayer's employer paid the taxpayer's federal income tax liabilities on his behalf. The issue was whether this payment resulted in gross income to the taxpayer, and the Supreme Court held that it did. Again, this makes perfect sense as $100 of debt relief is as valuable as $100 of cash.

What You Need to Know:

1. Gross income may be realized in any form, including cash, property, services, and debt relief.
2. Gross income items in the form of property or services must be valued, and their FMV is the amount that is included in gross income.
3. Gross income also includes discounted purchases of property or services by employees or other service providers. The discount to FMV is the amount that is included in gross income.
4. The bargain purchase rule provides that no gross income is realized when property or services are purchased in an arm's length transaction; any

bargain element is treated as unrealized appreciation.

5. The compensatory discount rule and bargain purchase rule are conceptually inconsistent, but practical considerations justify the different outcomes.

LESSON 5: GAINS ON DISPOSITIONS OF PROPERTY

Gains are included in gross income. Under the realization rule, gains are only included in gross income when there is a realization event, such as a sale for cash or an exchange for other property or for services. Under section 1001(a), upon such a realization event, the taxpayer realizes gain to the extent the taxpayer's **amount realized** exceeds her **adjusted basis** in the property. Amount realized and adjusted basis are terms of art that are very important.

Amount Realized

Amount realized is defined in section 1001(b) as the sum of any cash and the FMV of any property received upon the disposition of the property. While not explicitly stated in the statute, the FMV of any services received in exchange for the property is also included in the amount realized. And, as Treas. Reg. section 1.1001–2(a)(1) makes clear, the amount realized also generally includes the amount of any debt relief that the taxpayer receives in the transaction. Thus, if a buyer of property assumes the seller's mortgage debt, the amount of that debt is included in the seller's amount realized.

For example, assume that a taxpayer sells property for $50,000 of cash and $40,000 of stock and the buyer assumes the seller's mortgage, which has a balance of $110,000. The seller's amount realized is $200,000.

Adjusted Basis

Conceptually, a taxpayer's basis is a scorecard that keeps track of dollars that have already been taxed so that those dollars are not taxed again later. Consider a very simple set of facts: a taxpayer earns $100 cash of compensation, pays tax on that compensation using other dollars, and buys corporate stock with the $100 cash. The taxpayer eventually sells the stock for $120 cash. The sale is a realization event, and the taxpayer's amount realized is $120. Without any offset for basis, the taxpayer would have $120 of gain and therefore would be taxed on all $120. This double taxes $100 of that $120, because the taxpayer was taxed on $100 when he earned the compensation and now he's taxed on it again when he sells the stock. Thus, while the taxpayer at the end of the day is only $120 richer (he started with zero cash and ends up with $120 cash), he would have been taxed on $220 ($100 at the outset and another $120 upon the sale). The whole purpose of basis is to prevent this nonsensical result. The taxpayer has $100 of basis in the stock when he purchases it for $100 cash. There are no adjustments to basis under these facts, so the taxpayer's gain realized on the sale is only $20, which is the right answer, as he already paid tax on $100.

Turning now to the technical mechanics, a taxpayer's adjusted basis equals the taxpayer's initial basis plus or minus certain adjustments specified in section 1016(a). Initial basis is generally determined under section 1012, which provides that the taxpayer's initial basis in property is the property's cost. If a taxpayer pays cash for property, the cost is obviously the amount of cash paid. But if the taxpayer paid for property by transferring other property, by providing services, or by incurring debt, the value of that property, services, or debt is included in the taxpayer's initial basis.

For example, assume that a taxpayer buys property by paying the seller $20,000 in cash and giving the seller a promissory note for $180,000. The seller's initial basis is $200,000. The same would be true if the taxpayer, instead of "borrowing" $180,000 from the seller (by giving the seller a promissory note), had borrowed the $180,000 from a third-party bank (by giving the bank a promissory note and then giving the borrowed cash to the seller). Borrowed cash (whether borrowed from the seller or from a third party lender) that is used to purchase property is included in basis, just like cash that comes from the taxpayer's own pocket.

In many situations, the initial basis is adjusted for certain items. The rules for adjusting basis are found in section 1016(a). A common upward adjustment to basis occurs when amounts are spent to improve the property. Improvements increase the amount of already taxed dollars invested in the property and therefore they need to be included in the adjusted basis to prevent those dollars from being taxed again upon the disposition of the property. A common downward adjustment is for depreciation deductions, which are discussed in Lesson 13.

Realization Versus Recognition

Gain that is realized is generally **recognized**, and recognized gain is included in gross income under section 61(a)(3). The general recognition rule is found in section 1001(c). However, there are certain nonrecognition rules that apply in some specific situations. For example, realized gains in so-called like-kind exchanges of real property are not recognized under section 1031 and are therefore not included in gross income. But absent the application of such a special rule, the default rule is that realized gains are recognized and included in gross income (unless a specific exclusion applies).

What You Need to Know:

1. Gain realized equals the excess of amount realized over adjusted basis.
2. Amount realized includes the amount of cash, the FMV of property or services, and the amount of debt relief received by the taxpayer upon disposition of property.
3. Basis represents a scorecard of already taxed dollars and its purpose is to prevent the double taxation of those dollars.
4. Adjusted basis equals the initial basis plus or minus the adjustments found in section 1016(a).
5. Initial basis is generally the cost of property, and it includes the amount of cash paid, the FMV of property or services transferred, and the amount of debt incurred in acquiring the property.

6. The default rule is that realized gains are recognized. Recognized gains are included in gross income unless a specific exclusion applies.

LESSON 6: GIFTS

The Code specifically excludes some items from gross income. These **exclusions** are found in sections 101 through 139G. A significant exclusion relates to **gifts**. Under section 102(a), gifts (whether inter vivos or testamentary) are excluded from gross income. Accordingly, if a taxpayer receives cash, property, services, or debt relief as a gift, the taxpayer does not realize gross income. While gifts are not subject to *income* tax, they may be subject to the federal *gift* tax, though the gift tax only applies to fairly large gifts by extremely wealthy donors.

Definition of "Gift"

Because of the gift exclusion, it is beneficial for transferees to claim that transfers to them are gifts and not compensation or other types of gross income. The Supreme Court in *Commissioner v. Duberstein*, 363 U.S. 278 (1960), defined the term "gift" for section 102 purposes as a transfer that "proceeds from detached and disinterested generosity. . . out of affection, respect, admiration, charity, and like impulses" and explained that "the most critical consideration" in characterizing the transfer as a gift "is the transferor's intention." Under this definition, quid pro quo arrangements and compensatory payments (even voluntary ones, such as bonuses and tips) cannot qualify as gifts.

While transferees prefer to characterize transfers as gifts, transferors may not because gifts are not deductible, whereas compensation and other forms of gross income often give rise to a deduction for the transferor.

Gifts of Property

Gifts are not realization events, so when a gift is in the form of property, the donor does not realize gain or loss. The donee's initial basis in the gifted property is determined by section 1015 (in the case of inter vivos gifts) or section 1014 (in the case of testamentary transfers).

Under section 1015, inter vivos gifts generally result in a **carryover basis**—the transferor's adjusted basis in the gifted property simply carries over to the transferee. But if the gifted property has a built-in loss (meaning that the property's adjusted basis is higher than its FMV) at the time of the gift, the transferee takes what is known as a **split basis**. Under the rule for split basis, if the donee subsequently sells the property for a *loss*, the basis that is used to calculate the loss is the lower FMV. If the donee subsequently sells the property for a *gain*, the basis that is used to calculate the gain is the transferor's adjusted basis.

For example, assume that stock with a FMV of $30 and an adjusted basis of $50 is gifted to Taxpayer. Taxpayer receives a split basis: $30 for calculating loss and $50 for calculating gain. If Taxpayer eventually sells the stock for $25, then Taxpayer realizes a $5 loss. If Taxpayer instead sells the stock for $52, Taxpayer has $2 of gain. If Taxpayer sells the stock for an amount realized between $30 and $50 (inclusive), Treas. Reg. section 1.1015–1(a)(2) explains that Taxpayer realizes neither gain nor loss.

While the general carryover basis allows taxpayers to shift the tax burden of built-in gains between taxpayers (from donor to donee), the split basis rule effectively prevents taxpayers from shifting the tax benefit of built-in losses. Congress was apparently more worried about the shifting of losses than the shifting of gains.

For testamentary gifts, the basis rules are simpler. Under section 1014, the donee typically takes a basis equal to the FMV on the date of death. For property with a built-in gain, this is referred to as a **stepped-up basis**, as the basis of the property is increased from the decedent's adjusted basis to the higher FMV. If the property has a built-in loss, then the transferee receives a **stepped-down basis**.

Notice that the realization rule combined with the stepped-up basis rule allows unrealized appreciation to go completely untaxed. If a taxpayer buys stock for $100 and it appreciates to $1,000,000 at the time of her death, her heirs will take the stock with a $1,000,000 basis, meaning that no one will ever pay income tax on that $999,900 of built-in gain. Imagine what the stepped-up basis rule will do for Mark Zuckerberg's heirs!

What You Need to Know:

1. Gifts are excluded from gross income.
2. Gifts are transfers that proceed from the transferor's detached and disinterested generosity out of affection, respect, admiration, charity, and like impulses.
3. Quid pro quo arrangements and compensatory payments are *not* gifts.
4. Gifts are not deductible by transferors.
5. Inter vivos gifts of property with a built-in gain result in a carryover basis for the donee.
6. Inter vivos gifts of property with a built-in loss result in a split basis for the donee.
7. Where there is a split basis, the lower FMV at the time of gift is used to calculate losses, while the higher adjusted basis of the transferor is used to calculate gains.
8. Testamentary gifts result in a basis equal to the FMV on the date of death.

LESSON 7: CANCELLATION OF DEBT INCOME

In Lesson 3 we learned that borrowing does not result in gross income, because the borrower has an offsetting obligation to repay the borrowed funds. Accordingly, there is no accession to wealth. The same is true if one "borrows" property or services by receiving the property or services in advance of payment. If a taxpayer receives $500 of landscaping services on day 1 but doesn't make payment until day 30, the borrowing exclusion applies just as if the taxpayer receives $500 of cash on day 1 and repays the amount on day 30. The flip side of the borrowing exclusion is that the taxpayer does not receive any deduction when borrowed funds are repaid.

The borrowing exclusion is premised on the assumption that the borrowed amounts will in fact eventually be repaid. But what if they are not repaid? In that case, there generally will be gross income, known as **cancellation of debt** (COD) income (or discharge of indebtedness income). COD income is justified because, once the obligation to repay ceases, the taxpayer has received an accession to wealth by virtue of the original transfer of cash (or property or services) to him. Section 61(a)(12) provides the rule that COD income is generally gross income.

The following chart summarizes the tax consequences from borrowing:

Borrowing	Repayment	Cancellation of Debt
No gross income (borrowing exclusion)	No deduction for repayment of principal (though interest payments may be deductible)	Generally gross income

Bona Fide Versus Spurious Discharges

Some transactions that might appear at first glance to result in COD income in fact do not. Reduction (or elimination) of a taxpayer's debt may instead be a form of payment. An employer may compensate her employee by reducing the amount of debt owed by the employee to her. This is not a cancellation of debt; rather the employee has used his services to pay the debt. Thus, the income here is compensation income (which is gross income under section 61(a)(1)). Likewise, a father may make a gift to his son by reducing the son's debt to the father. In that case, the reduction is a gift, which is excluded from gross income under section 102(a). These transactions have been called spurious discharges of debt, because they might appear to result in COD income, but instead the reduction of the debt is simply a form of payment.

Bona fide debt discharges arise when debts are reduced or canceled because the debt has gone down in value. Why do debts go down in value? Often because the borrower's ability to repay the debt in full has been impaired. In extreme cases, lenders write off the entire amount of a debt because they understand that the costs of trying to enforce the debt are greater than what they can reasonably expect to receive from these efforts. Debts can also go down in value due to a change in prevailing interest rates. If interest rates have gone up, lenders will often accept a payment of less than the amount of the debt instrument so that they can relend the money at the new higher rates.

Exclusions of Certain COD Income

If a taxpayer has received a bona fide discharge of part or all of a debt, the reduction results in COD income under section 61(a)(12) equal to the amount of the debt reduction. Section 108 is an exclusion provision that excludes some kinds of COD income. Section 108 is one reason why it is important to distinguish between bona fide and spurious discharges. Only bona fide discharges result in COD income, and only COD income is eligible for potential exclusion under section 108. A compensatory discharge represents compensation income under section 61(a)(1) and therefore is not eligible for exclusion under section 108.

Section 108 has a wide variety of exclusions. One important one is the **insolvency exclusion**, found in section 108(a)(1)(B). If, at the time of the COD income, the taxpayer is insolvent, any COD income is excluded up to the amount of the taxpayer's insolvency. A taxpayer is insolvent to the extent the FMV of all of the taxpayer's assets exceed the amount of all of the taxpayer's debt, determined immediately before the discharge that gave rise to the COD income. For example, assume that the taxpayer realizes $50,000 of COD income and, immediately before the discharge, the taxpayer owned $250,000 of assets and had $280,000 of liabilities. The taxpayer is insolvent to the extent of $30,000, and that amount of COD income is excluded from gross income. The taxpayer therefore must include only $20,000 of COD income in gross income.

The insolvency exclusion, like many of the other section 108 exclusions, does not come free. Under section 108(b), the taxpayer must reduce certain **tax attributes**, such as basis in property, by the amount of the excluded COD income. In the example above, the taxpayer may have to reduce her basis in property by the $30,000 of excluded COD income. Because basis reduces future tax liabilities (by, for example, reducing future gains), the taxpayer will have more gross income in the future as a result of the basis reduction. In effect, the insolvency exclusion is not really an exclusion but instead a deferral provision. It reduces the taxpayer's immediate tax burden when she is insolvent but increases the tax burden in later years.

What You Need to Know:

1. The borrowing exclusion is premised on the assumption that borrowed amounts will eventually be repaid. COD income is generally realized when that assumption proves erroneous.
2. Some debt discharges are merely forms of payments of compensation, gifts, or other transfers. Those spurious debt discharges do not result in COD income, but may result in other types of gross income.
3. Bona fide debt discharges arise because the debt has gone down in value due to doubts about the borrower's ability to repay or because of interest rate fluctuations.
4. Bona fide debt discharges give rise to COD income, which is eligible for exclusion under section 108. Section 108 does not apply to spurious debt discharges.
5. An important exclusion in section 108 is the insolvency exclusion, which excludes COD income to the extent of the taxpayer's insolvency.

LESSON 8: PERSONAL INJURY RECOVERIES

Under the general definition of gross income, personal injury awards or settlements would typically constitute gross income in their entirety. This is because there would be no basis available to offset the amounts received. Taxpayers have no basis in their body parts nor in their physical or emotional well-being.

Physical Injury Claims

Perhaps because this seems harsh, Congress enacted section 104(a)(2), which excludes certain personal injury recoveries from gross income. That provision excludes all damages received as a result of personal *physical* injury except to the extent of the portions (if any) of the damages that represent punitive damages, reimbursement of previously deducted medical expenses, or pre- or post-judgment interest. Thus, so long as the claim involves a physical injury (such as car accident, slip-and-fall, and medical malpractice cases), all other components of damages, like lost past and future wages, future medical expenses, and physical and emotional pain and suffering are excluded from gross income.

Punitive damages, on the other hand, are always taxable. Previously deducted medical expenses likewise are taxable, on the ground that the taxpayer received the benefit of the prior deduction but now no longer bears the economic burden of those expenses. The exception for previously deducted medical expenses is not as significant as it may appear because, as we will see in Lesson 17, taxpayers often are unable to claim deductions for their medical expenses. Thus, in most physical injury cases, all or nearly all of the recovery is tax-free by virtue of section 104(a)(2).

Non-Physical Injury Claims

In *non-physical* personal injury cases, such as employment discrimination, defamation, and intentional infliction of emotional distress claims, the entire recovery is included in gross income except to the extent the recovery represents reimbursement for prior medical expenses that had not been deducted. In the typical non-physical injury case, this means that except for the reimbursement of out-of-pocket mental-health-related medical bills, the entire recovery is taxable.

Given the drastically different tax treatment between physical injury and non-physical injury recoveries, it is not surprising that the IRS and taxpayers often disagree about how claims ought to be characterized, with taxpayers emphasizing their physical aspects. It is important to note that the IRS and the courts have determined that physical symptoms of emotional distress, such as stomach disorders, do not on their own cause a claim to constitute a physical injury claim, based on language to that effect in section 104(a)(2)'s legislative history.

Structured Settlements

The exclusion for personal physical injury awards applies to lump sum payments as well as so-called **structured settlements**. In a structured settlement, the plaintiff receives his award in installments over time. A portion of each installment represents a portion of the damages and the remainder represents interest that the plaintiff receives for delaying his receipt of the damages. The section 104(a)(2) exclusion applies to both components. In other words, the exclusion is effectively extended from personal injury damages to interest on personal injury damages.

To illustrate, assume that Taxpayer A receives a $100,000 lump sum cash settlement for damages from a car accident and that all of it is excluded under section 104(a)(2). Taxpayer A invests the $100,000 in annuity which pays him $12,000 every year for ten years. Under the rules for taxing annuities, Taxpayer A will realize $2,000 of interest income each year and, assuming his marginal tax rate is 25 percent, would owe $500 in additional tax annually.

Taxpayer B, also injured in a car accident, instead receives a structured settlement that will pay him $12,000 per year for ten years. Because the recovery qualifies for complete exclusion under section 104(a)(2) and because the exclusion extends to structured settlements, all of Taxpayer's B payments are tax-free. This leaves Taxpayer B $500 richer (on an after-tax basis) than Taxpayer A during each of the ten years even though they are in precisely the same economic situations.

What You Need to Know:

1. In personal *physical* injury cases, recoveries are excluded from gross income except for any portions that represent punitive damages, reimbursements

of previously deducted medical expenses, or interest.

2. In personal *non-physical* injury cases, recoveries are included in gross income except for the portion of the recovery that represents the reimbursement of prior medical expenses that were not deducted.
3. In a structured settlement of a personal physical injury claim, all of the payments are excluded from gross income even though a portion of each payment represents interest.

LESSON 9: FRINGE BENEFITS

Employers, in addition to paying their employees cash salaries and bonuses, also often give their employees valuable services or property, such as meals, health insurance, and parking. These ancillary benefits are known as **fringe benefits**. As we learned in Lesson 4, gross income can be realized in any form including property and services. Thus, fringe benefits are taxable unless a specific exclusion that applies.

Health Insurance and Qualified Retirement Plans

The largest fringe benefit exclusion, in terms of revenue losses to the government, is the exclusion in section 106 for employer-provided health insurance. When an employer pays for all or part of an employee's health insurance, section 106 applies to exclude that benefit from the employee's gross income. This exclusion costs the government over $200 billion annually in foregone federal taxes (both income taxes and employment taxes).

The second largest exclusion applies to retirement plans. When an employer contributes money to a "qualified plan," such as a 401(k) plan, for the benefit of an employee, the amount is excluded from the employee's gross income. In order for a retirement plan to be qualified, it must be available to all employees, not just executives, and it must meet a number of other technical requirements. This exclusion costs the government approximately $140 billion each year.

Section 119

Section 119 excludes the value of lodging and meals provided on the employer's business premises if they are provided **for the convenience of the employer**. To satisfy this standard, the employee must show that the lodging and meals were provided principally to allow the employee to better perform her job responsibilities, rather than for a compensatory purpose. In addition, in the case of lodging, the employee's contract also must require that the employee accept such lodging. For example, emergency room doctors who are on overnight call can exclude the value of the sleeping facilities provided by a hospital.

Section 132

Section 132 provides a host of different fringe benefit exclusions. The **no-additional-cost service exclusion** generally covers services provided by an employer to an employee where the employer does not incur a substantial cost (including foregone revenue) in providing those services. The classic example is free standby air travel for airline employees. Because the standby seat would otherwise have been empty, the airline incurs no substantial additional cost in giving an employee the seat. The **qualified employee discount exclusion** applies to exclude certain discounts on goods and services that the employee sells to customers. The **de minimis exclusion** applies to items of very small value such as coffee and doughnuts. Other exclusions apply to free or discounted parking, transit passes, and the use of employer fitness centers.

Section 132(a)(3) excludes **working condition fringes**. Working condition fringes are property and services provided by an employer to an employee where, if the employee had paid for them herself, she would have received a deduction. Thus, when an employer provides an employee with the use of an office, computer, and phone or pays to fly the employee to work temporarily at another work location, these benefits are excludible working condition fringes.

What You Need to Know:

1. Fringe benefits are included in gross income at their FMV unless a specific exclusion applies.
2. The two largest fringe benefit exclusions, in terms of the cost to the government, are those for employer-provided healthcare and qualified retirement plans.
3. Section 119 excludes from gross income the value of on-premises lodging and meals that are provided for the convenience of the employer.
4. Section 132 provides a variety of different exclusions, including exclusions for no-additional-cost services, qualified employee discounts, and de minimis fringes.
5. Section 132(a)(3) excludes working condition fringes, such as the use of office space, computers, phones, and supplies.

LESSON 10: PERSONAL RESIDENCE GAINS, LIFE INSURANCE PROCEEDS, AND MUNICIPAL BOND INTEREST

This final lesson on exclusions from gross income covers three exclusions: for certain personal residence gains, life insurance recoveries, and interest on state and local bonds.

Personal Residence Gains

When a taxpayer sells her personal residence for an amount realized greater than her adjusted basis, she realizes and recognizes a gain to the extent of that excess. Generally gains recognized are included in gross income under section 61(a)(3). But section 121 often will exclude some or all of the gain recognized on the sale of a personal residence. Whatever gain that section 121 does not cover remains gross income.

In general, section 121 excludes from the gross income the gain recognized on the sale of a home if the taxpayer has used the home as principal residence for at least two out of the past five years. The exclusion is limited to the first $250,000 of gains

($500,000 for married taxpayers filing joint returns). The two year use-as-a-principal-residence requirement does not require continuous use for two years. To illustrate the application of section 121, assume that an unmarried taxpayer buys a residence for $200,000 and uses it as a principal residence for 6 months. She then moves to another state but continues to use the residence as a vacation home for 3 years. Then she moves back and uses the residence as a personal residence for 1.5 years and thereafter sells the residence for $480,000. She has an amount realized of $480,000, an adjusted basis in the home of $200,000, and a gain realized and recognized of $280,000. Because she used the home as a principal residence for a total of two years (six months at the beginning and 18 months at the end) out of the five years preceding the sale, she may exclude $250,000 of the gain recognized from gross income. The remaining $30,000 of gain recognized constitutes gross income.

If a taxpayer is, due to circumstances beyond her control (such as a change in employment), unable to meet the two year condition, section 121(c) provides some relief. For example, if a taxpayer is forced to sell after using the home as a residence for only one year, then she may exclude up to $125,000 (or $250,000 if married filing jointly) of gain.

Life Insurance Proceeds

Under section 101(a), the proceeds of life insurance policies are generally excluded from gross income. This rule applies to both term policies, which are effectively a pure "bet" on the insured's mortality, and cash value policies, which combine such bets with a savings component. The tax law carefully defines insurance to ensure that, in cash value policies, the mortality features constitute a relatively significant piece of the economics of the instrument.

Municipal Bond Interest

Interest income is generally included in gross income under section 61(a)(4). However, one category of interest, interest received on certain state and local bonds, is excluded from gross income under section 103. These bonds are known as municipal bonds. The exclusion for municipal bond interest is intended to benefit the municipalities even though the nominal beneficiary of the tax benefits is the holder of the bond. The exclusion allows municipalities, when they borrow, to pay lower interest rates than non-municipal bond issuers. Assuming a marginal tax rate of 40 percent, a taxpayer would prefer a municipal bond paying 3.01 percent in tax-free interest over an otherwise economically identical non-municipal bond paying 5.00 percent interest. This is because, on an after-tax basis, the former yields 3.01 percent while the latter yields 3.00 percent (5 percent less 40% of 5 percent).

The municipal bond exclusion is one clear example of a situation where the nominal beneficiary of a tax break—here, the holder of the municipal bond—is not its intended economic beneficiary—here, the municipal bond issuer, who can now borrow at significantly lower interest rates. The same is true with tax burdens. Tax burdens can be shifted from the taxpayer who formally pays the tax to other parties in the transaction through, for example, higher prices.

What You Need to Know:

1. Section 121 generally excludes from gross income gains on the sales of homes that have been used as principal residences for at least 2 out of the past 5 years, up to a cap of $250,000 ($500,000 for married couples filing jointly).
2. Section 101 generally excludes life insurance recoveries from gross income.
3. Section 103 generally excludes from gross income interest received on certain municipal bonds. The exclusion is designed to benefit municipalities by allowing them to borrow at lower interest rates.

LESSON 11: ORDINARY AND NECESSARY BUSINESS EXPENSES

We turn now to deductions. Deductions offset gross income, reducing taxable income. Taxable income is what is applied to the tax rates.

While gross income may be realized even if the item in question is not specifically identified as an item of gross income in section 61, deductions may be claimed only if there is a statutory provision that explicitly grants the deduction.

Deductions fall into one of two main categories: **business/ investment deductions** and **personal deductions**. Business/ investment deductions are justified on the ground that expenses incurred in generating gross income must be deductible so that only *net* income is taxed. Congress has also granted personal deductions in certain contexts so as to encourage certain behaviors, such as homeownership and charitable giving.

Section 162

Section 162 grants deductions for **ordinary and necessary expenses** paid in connection with an ongoing trade or business. This covers expenses like office rents and salaries for workers. The term "ordinary" seems to suggest that an expense must be typical or regular and recurring, but that is not the case. If a delivery business pays damages because one of its drivers ran someone over, those damages are still ordinary under the statute even though they are not (we hope) typical. While courts sometimes discuss the typicality of the expense, the better view, expressed by the Supreme Court in *Commissioner v. Tellier*, 383 U.S. 687 (1966), is that the "ordinary" condition is intended to distinguish **immediately deductible expenses** from **capital expenditures**, which are not immediately deductible. Capital expenditures are discussed in the next lesson.

The "necessary" component is intended to distinguish between **legitimate business expenses** and **disguised personal consumption expenses**, which are not deductible. Taxpayers have an incentive to claim personal consumption expenses as business expenses to reduce their tax liabilities. To prevent this, claimed business expenses that look suspiciously like personal consumption must be scrutinized to determine their legitimacy. A classic example is *Henry v. Commissioner*, 36 T.C. 879 (1961), where a tax lawyer and accountant claimed yacht maintenance expenses as business deductions because the yacht flew a pennant with the number "1040" on it. As you might expect, the court held that these expenses were not necessary.

In addition, to be deductible under section 162, an expense must be incurred in carrying on a **trade or business**. The term "trade or business" is an important term of art in tax. It describes a profit-seeking activity in which the taxpayer's activity is continuous and regular. It is distinct from mere investment activities, which involves less continuous and regular activity. A taxpayer who practices law for 40 hours per week and spends another couple of hours per month managing a house that he rents out is engaged in a trade or business (of law practice) and in an investment activity (managing the rental house).

The "carrying on" requirement means that **pre-operating expenses** are not deductible under section 162. Thus, if a taxpayer is going to open up a restaurant, expenses incurred before the restaurant actually opens (such as employee training expenses) are not immediately deductible under section 162. But section 195 generally allows for 1/60th of the aggregate of these pre-operating expenses to be deducted each month for the first 60 months of operation.

Section 212

Section 212 is similar to section 162 except that it applies not to trade or business expenses but rather to expenses attributable to investment activities that generate rents or royalties. Thus, in the example above involving the lawyer, he would be able to deduct his ordinary and necessary expenses incurred in managing his rental house under section 212.

Reasonable Compensation

Section 162(a)(1) specifically allows a deduction for reasonable compensation of employees. Allowing deductions for salaries makes sense; after all, the employer is paying the compensation to earn gross income. What then is the purpose of the reasonableness condition? It generally applies only in the context of related parties to prevent nondeductible gifts (or nondeductible dividends by closely held corporations) from being disguised as deductible compensation. If a father employs his son, he might try to overpay the son. If successful, the father would effectively be deducting a gift equal to the amount of the overpayment. As we've seen, payments of gifts are nondeductible. While the son would realize additional income, if the son's marginal tax rate were lower than the father's, this strategy would lower the father's and son's aggregate tax liability. To prevent this, the reasonableness condition requires an evaluation of whether the son's salary is consistent with what one would expect to see in an **arm's length transaction**. In actual arm's length transactions (such as between a public company and its CEO), the reasonableness condition should not be at issue because by definition the salary was negotiated at arm's length.

What You Need to Know:

1. Deductions may be claimed only if there is a statutory provision that explicitly grants the deduction.
2. Section 162 provides that ordinary and necessary expense incurred in a carrying on a trade or business are deductible.
3. The "ordinary" condition in section 162 is intended to distinguish between immediately deductible expenses and capital expenditures.
4. The "necessary" condition in section 162 is intended to distinguish between legitimate business expenses and disguised personal consumption expenses.
5. A trade or business is a profit-seeking activity in which the taxpayer's activity is continuous and regular.
6. Pre-operating expenses are not deductible under section 162 because the taxpayer is not yet carrying on the trade or business.
7. Section 212 provides that ordinary and necessary expenses incurred in connection with investment activities are deductible.
8. Reasonable compensation is deductible under section 162. Unreasonable compensation is

generally found only in non-arm's-length situations.

LESSON 12: CAPITAL EXPENDITURES

Certain expenditures, even if related to business or investment activity, are not immediately deductible; instead these expenditures create basis in an asset. This rule is known as the **capitalization doctrine**, and it is codified in section 263 of the Code. The capitalization doctrine is also implied by the "ordinary" condition found in sections 162 and 212. Expenditures that give rise to basis are known as **capital expenditures**. In tax lawyer language, outlays that relate to business or investment activity are either **immediately deductible** (e.g., under sections 162 or 212) or are **capitalized** (under section 263).

Capitalization Theory

The theory behind the capitalization doctrine is that expenses incurred in generating gross income items should generally be matched timing-wise with those items. Thus, when a taxpayer purchases a building that is expected to generate rents for many years, the capitalization rule (and the related concept of **depreciation**, discussed in the next lesson) prevents the building's cost from being deducted entirely in the year of purchase and instead spreads the cost over the building's anticipated useful life. The matching issue arises whenever the taxpayer incurs a cost that is expected to help generate income beyond the current taxable year.

Asset Purchase Costs

Some capital expenditures are obvious. When a taxpayer purchases an asset that is expected to have value beyond the taxable year, the cost of that asset is capitalized. For example, the costs of equipment, machinery, computers, land, buildings, stocks, bonds, patents, and trademarks are all capitalized and create basis in those assets.

Repairs Versus Improvements

Other capital expenditures are more subtle. The costs of improvements to property must be capitalized and added to the basis of the property. On the other hand, the cost of repairs are not capitalized. Sometimes distinguishing between repairs and improvements is easy. Replacing one shingle on a roof is clearly a repair, while replacing the entire roof is an improvement. Other times the issue is far less clear. Treasury recently finalized an extensive regulation (Treas. Reg. section 1.263(a)–3) that attempts to differentiate between repairs and improvements.

Repairs to business or investment property are immediately deductible under section 162 or 212, while repairs to personal-use property (such as the taxpayer's home) are treated as non-deductible personal expenses. Improvements to property, whether used for business, investment, or personal purposes, are capitalized and added to basis in all instances.

Transaction Costs

When a taxpayer buys a long-lived asset, any transaction costs incurred in acquiring the property are capitalized in addition to the purchase price paid by the taxpayer. Therefore, if a taxpayer buys 100 shares of Microsoft stock for $7,000 and pays her stock broker $100 to effectuate the purchase, both amounts are capitalized, resulting in $7,100 of basis in the stock.

Intangible Benefits

While the cost of intangible *assets*, such as stocks, bonds, promissory notes, patents, and trademarks, are clearly capitalized, there historically was some uncertainty about how outlays that created intangible *benefits* (that were not normally considered assets) would be treated. Advertising is the classic example. If a taxpayer spends millions of dollars on an advertising campaign that is expected to result in enhanced consumer recognition for many years, is the cost capitalized? As a matter of pure theory, the answer is "yes." However, taxpayers historically deducted those costs. Then, in *INDOPCO, Inc. v. Commissioner*, 503 U.S. 79 (1992), the Supreme Court arguably implied to the contrary. Eventually, Treasury issued an extensive regulation dealing with intangibles (Treas. Reg. section 1.263(a)–2) that generally allows taxpayers to immediately deduct the cost of intangible benefits that are not normally considered assets. This taxpayer-friendly regulation covers advertising costs, as well as employee training costs and business downsizing costs.

Self-Created Assets

Sometimes, instead of buying an asset on the market, a taxpayer will build or create it itself. Section 263A generally requires the self-creation costs to be capitalized. For example, General Motors must capitalize the salaries of its assembly-line workers who build its cars. This puts taxpayers who self-create assets on the same tax footing as taxpayer who buy assets from third parties.

What You Need to Know:

1. Capital expenditures are not immediately deductible; instead they result in basis.
2. The purpose of the capitalization doctrine is to better match items of gross income with their related costs.
3. The purchase price of an asset that is expected to have value beyond the taxable year is capitalized.
4. If the purchase price of an asset is capitalized, the transaction costs in consummating the purchase are also generally capitalized.
5. Improvements to property are capitalized, while repairs are not.
6. In general, the costs of acquiring intangible *assets* are capitalized, while costs incurred to generate intangible *benefits* (such as advertising costs) are not.

LESSON 13: DEPRECIATION

Most tangible assets (such as equipment and machinery) wear down over time. Some intangible assets (like patents) likewise lose value over time due to obsolescence or exhaustion.

When these **wasting assets** are used in a trade or business or in an investment activity, section 167 allows the taxpayer to claim annual **depreciation deductions** to reflect this diminishing utility over time. Depreciation deductions are known as **cost recovery**, because the cost of the property is "recovered" through tax deductions over time. Immediate deduction is also a type of cost recovery, but the recovery is accomplished all at once through an immediate 100 percent deduction.

Tax lawyers typically use the term depreciation to refer to cost recovery attributable to tangible assets and **amortization** for intangible assets. Despite the different terminology, they refer to the same concept: the spreading of the taxpayer's cost of wasting assets over the assets' useful lives. For the remainder of these lessons, the term depreciation will be used to reflect this concept, regardless of whether the asset in question is tangible or intangible.

Depreciable Assets

For an asset to be depreciable, section 167 requires that the asset be (i) a wasting asset and (ii) used in the taxpayer's trade or business or investment activities. The first condition, that the asset be a wasting asset, requires the asset to be of a character that it is subject to wear and tear, exhaustion, or obsolescence. Most assets will qualify as wasting, so it is easier to identity the relatively few types of non-wasting assets. Common non-wasting assets include raw land (as opposed to any improvements on such land, such as buildings and other structures, which are wasting assets), works of art, antiques, stocks, bonds, and promissory notes. Because land is non-depreciable, a building's purchase price must be split between the underlying land, which is non-depreciable, and the cost of the building itself, which is depreciable. In addition, items in a taxpayer's inventory are not depreciable.

The second condition requires that the property be used in a profit-seeking activity, either in a trade or business or investment activity. This means that personal-use assets, such as homes and personal-use cars, are not depreciable.

Depreciation Calculations

Depreciation deductions are formulaic, meaning that taxpayers do not determine the amount of any actual annual diminution in value. Instead the calculations are made via predetermined schedules. In fact, taxpayers receive depreciation deductions even if the actual value of the property goes *up* in value. The schedules are mechanically applied regardless of what happens with respect to actual value.

The starting point for depreciation calculations is the initial basis of the property, which generally is the cost of the property plus any transaction costs in acquiring the property. Thus, if a taxpayer buys equipment for $100,000 and pays his lawyer $5,000 to review the purchase contract, the taxpayer's initial basis is $105,000, which will be the amount subject to the depreciation schedule.

For tangible assets, the depreciation schedules are set forth in section 168. Depending on the type of asset, the depreciation schedules are as short as 3 years or as long as 39 years. Useful lives for all different types of tangible assets have been listed by the IRS in Rev. Proc. 87–56.

For intangible property, there are two different rules. When intangible property is acquired in connection with the purchase of a trade or business, section 197 provides that the cost of the intangible is depreciated on a straight-line (i.e., pro rata) basis over fifteen years (or 180 months). Thus, if a taxpayer buys $1.8 million of depreciable intangible assets in connection with her purchase of a trade or business, the taxpayer would be allowed to claim $10,000 of deductions each month for the next 180 months.

Other "stand-alone" wasting intangibles (such as prepaid expenses like insurance or rent) are depreciated on a straight-line basis over their expected useful lives. Thus, if a taxpayer on January 1 of Year 1 pays $300,000 for three years of business casualty insurance, the taxpayer would claim $100,000 of depreciation deductions in each of Year 1, Year 2, and Year 3.

Effect on Adjusted Basis

Depreciation deductions reduce the adjusted basis of property under section 1016(a)(2). This is consistent with the fact that these deductions represent cost recovery. Thus, if property with an initial basis of $100,000 has given rise to $75,000 of depreciation deductions, the adjusted basis will be $25,000, which is the amount of its unrecovered cost.

Section 179 Elections & Bonus Depreciation

Section 179 allows small businesses to elect to immediately deduct the cost of certain purchased property, subject to various limitations. A taxpayer who receives a section 179 deduction forgoes basis equal to that amount. This again is consistent with cost recovery—the section 179 deduction represents a 100% immediate deduction of that cost, so it is not eligible for additional cost recovery through depreciation.

Congress periodically has allowed taxpayers to elect to immediately deduct all or a portion of the cost of certain types of depreciable property placed service during a specified period of time. This is referred to as bonus depreciation and is codified in section 168(k). The 2017 Tax Act allows for 100% bonus depreciation for depreciable tangible personal property placed in service before 2023. This means that the entire cost of such property may be deducted immediately, resulting in a zero adjusted basis for the property.

What You Need to Know:

1. Section 167 allows a taxpayer to claim depreciation deductions with respect to wasting assets that are used in a trade or business or in an investment activity.
2. Common non-wasting assets include raw land, artworks, antiques, stocks, bonds, and promissory notes.
3. Depreciation deductions are formulaic.
4. Section 168 provides the depreciation schedules for *tangible* wasting assets.

5. Section 197 provides for straight-line depreciation over fifteen years for wasting intangible assets acquired in connection with the purchase of a trade or business.
6. Other stand-alone wasting intangible assets are depreciated straight-line over their expected useful lives.
7. Depreciation deductions reduce basis under section 1016(a)(2).
8. Small businesses may elect under section 179 to immediately deduct the cost of certain purchased property, subject to various limitations.

LESSON 14: LOSSES

Thus far, we have seen a variety of ways that taxpayers can recover their costs. When property is sold for a gain, the offset of adjusted basis against the amount realized constitutes a recovery of the unrecovered costs (these uncovered costs are represented by the amount of adjusted basis). When a deduction is claimed, the deduction represents an immediate 100 percent cost recovery. And depreciation deductions represent a formulaic recovery of costs over time.

Loss Calculation

Losses recognized on the disposition of property are another cost recovery mechanism. Under section 1001(a), upon a realization event, a loss is realized to the extent the adjusted basis of the property exceeds the amount realized. Note that this is simply the inverse of the gain realized formula. Under section 1001(c), losses realized (just like gains realized) are recognized unless a specific Code section says otherwise. But while gains recognized result in gross income under section 61(a)(3) unless an exclusion applies, losses recognized are deductible only where section 165 allows a deduction.

Business/Investment Losses

Under section 165(c), losses recognized by individuals are generally deductible only if they are attributable to a trade or business or investment activity. Thus, for example, losses recognized on the sale of business equipment or shares of stock are deductible.

For example, assume that I buy business equipment for $100,000. For the period before I sell the property, I had properly claimed $60,000 of depreciation deductions with respect to the equipment. Accordingly, my adjusted basis in the equipment immediately before the sale is $40,000. If I sell the property for $10,000, my loss realized is $30,000. The loss is recognized under section 1001(c), and it is deductible under section 165(c)(1). I received $60,000 of cost recovery through depreciation deductions and $30,000 through my loss deduction, for a total of $90,000 of deductions. This equals the $90,000 of my "cost" of using the equipment; I bought it for $100,000 and sold it for $10,000.

What if, instead of selling the business equipment, the equipment was stolen or destroyed and I had no insurance on it. Theft and destruction are realization events, albeit unhappy ones. Thus, in this situation, my loss is the amount of my adjusted basis in the property immediately before the theft or destruction, which here was $40,000. Thus, my loss deduction is $40,000. This is true regardless of the equipment's actual fair market value. Loss deductions on business- or investment-related assets are always determined with respect to adjusted basis, not the current FMV. This makes sense as the adjusted basis represents the amount of unrecovered cost, which has nothing do with current FMV.

What You Need to Know:

1. A loss is realized to the extent the adjusted basis of property exceeds the amount realized.
2. Losses realized are recognized, unless a specific non-recognition rule applies.
3. Losses recognized are only deductible if section 165 allows the deduction.
4. Under section 165(c), recognized business- or investment-related losses are deductible.

5. Losses on the disposition of personal-use assets (such as a taxpayer's personal residence) are non-deductible.

LESSON 15: INTEREST

In Lesson 7, we learned that the repayment of borrowed funds does not give rise to a deduction. On the other hand, **interest** payments may be deductible under section 163(h). In other words, while repayments of loan *principal* are never deductible, payments of *interest* sometimes are.

For individuals, the following categories of interest are generally deductible: (i) interest attributable to a trade or business; (ii) interest attributable to investment activities; (iii) interest attributable to a taxpayer's passive activities (passive activities are discussed in Lesson 26); (iv) qualified residence interest; and (v) student loan interest. Interest payments by individuals that are not on this list are non-deductible. Thus, non-deductible interest includes interest on loans to purchase personal-use cars as well as interest on personal credit cards.

Trade or Business Interest

It is not surprising that trade or business interest is deductible because interest is an ordinary and necessary expense in carrying on a trade or business. The only conceptual issue is how to determine when interest is allocable to a trade or business or to some other activity. The tax law generally traces debts (and the corresponding interest payments) to the uses of the debt proceeds under Treas. Reg. section 1.163–8T. Thus, if a taxpayer borrows money to buy business equipment or to pay employee salaries, the interest on the loan is allocated to the trade or business and therefore is generally deductible.

Investment Interest

Investment interest is interest paid on loans used to acquire investment assets, such as stocks, bonds, options, and other financial instruments. While this type of interest is deductible, it is subject to a significant limitation found in section 163(d)(1). For any taxable year, the amount of investment interest paid that is deductible is limited to the amount of the taxpayer's **net**

investment income for that year. Any amount of investment interest expense that exceeds the taxpayer's net investment income carries over to the following year, where the limitation would be applied again to see how much, if any, of the investment interest expense is deductible. The carrying over continues until all of the taxpayer's investment interest expense has been deducted or the taxpayer dies, whichever comes first. Net investment income generally means the amount of interest income realized by the taxpayer net of any expenses attributable to that interest income.

For example, assume that in Year 1 the taxpayer pays $20,000 of investment interest and realizes $16,000 of interest income (with no expenses attributable to the interest income). In Year 2, the taxpayer pays another $5,000 of investment interest and realizes $8,000 of interest income. The tax consequences are as follows. In Year 1, the taxpayer may deduct $16,000 (of the total $20,000) of investment interest expense, with the remaining $4,000 carrying over to Year 2. In Year 2, the taxpayer may deduct $8,000 (of the total $9,000) of investment interest expense, with the remaining $1,000 carrying over to Year 3.

Home Mortgage Interest

Interest paid on certain home mortgage loans are deductible. In order to be deductible, the loan proceeds must have been used to purchase, construct, or substantially improve a residence of the taxpayer. However, interest deductions are allowed only with respect to the first $750,000 of mortgage loans. Thus, if a taxpayer borrows $1,000,000 to purchase a residence, only interest on $750,000 of the loan would be deductible.

For purposes of the home mortgage interest deduction, residence is defined to include the taxpayer's principal residence and, if the taxpayer has more than one residence, another residence of the taxpayer's choice. This rule allows taxpayers to claim deductible interest on mortgages with respect to a vacation home, subject to the $750,000 cap described above. The cap applies to the aggregate of all mortgage loans so that a taxpayer who borrows $500,000 to buy a principal residence and another $250,000 to buy a vacation home may deduct all of the interest on both loans.

Student Loan Interest

Section 221(a) allows taxpayers to deduct interest paid with respect to student loans used to pay higher education expenses. However, the deduction gradually phases out at higher income levels. Thus, for example, unmarried taxpayers who earned at least $80,000 of adjusted gross income (the concept of adjusted gross income is covered in Lesson 18) in 2017 would not be able to claim any student loan interest deductions.

What You Need to Know:

1. While loan principal payments are never deductible, interest payments may be deductible under section 163(h).
2. Interest is allocated to activities or assets based on how the associated debt proceeds are used.
3. Interest attributable to a trade or business of the taxpayer is deductible.
4. Investment interest is deductible, but it is subject to a significant limitation in section 163(d)(1).
5. Mortgage interest deductions are allowed with respect to loans used to purchase, construct, or substantially improve a residence of the taxpayer.
6. The mortgage interest deduction is available only with respect to the first $750,000 of qualifying mortgage loans.
7. Student loan interest is deductible, subject to a phase-out that gradually eliminates the deduction at higher income levels.

LESSON 16: CHARITABLE CONTRIBUTIONS

Under section 170, a taxpayer can deduct contributions of cash or property (but not services) to certain religious, charitable, scientific, literary, and educational organizations, collectively referred to as **501(c)(3) organizations** (after the Code section that exempts these organizations from paying tax). This deduction is known as the **charitable deduction**.

Adjusted Gross Income Limitations

The charitable deduction is subject to limitations based on the donor's adjusted gross income (AGI). As we will see in Lesson 18, AGI generally equals a taxpayer's gross income reduced by her business deductions. The precise limitations depend on the nature of the charitable donee and whether the contribution is in the form of cash or property. Charitable organizations that receive donations from a large number of donors, as well as religious and educational organizations, are known as **public charities**, while the remainder of charitable organizations are known as **private foundations**. In general, for *cash* contributions to the *public charities*, the AGI limit is 60 percent, meaning that these contributions can only be deducted to the extent that they in the aggregate do not exceed 60 percent of the donor's AGI. For cash contributions to private foundations, the AGI limit is 30 percent. For *property* contributions, the AGI limit for *public charities* is 30 percent, and for *private foundations* it is 20 percent. Any deduction disallowed under these rules may be carried forward up to five years, subject to the same limitations.

Property Contributions

As we learned in Lesson 6, the gifting of property is not a realization event for the donor. Thus, a charitable donor who gives property with a built-in gain (i.e., where the FMV of the property exceeds its adjusted basis) does not realize that gain. At the same time, the donor generally receives a deduction equal to the FMV of the donated property. This combination—of unrealized gain and a FMV deduction—is a particularly favorable tax result for charitable donors. Charitable donees technically receive a carryover basis in the donated property but because they are tax-exempt they won't pay tax on the built-in gain when they sell it.

However, while the general rule is that a charitable donor of appreciated property can take a FMV deduction, section

170(e)(1) limits the deduction to the amount of the property's adjusted basis in certain situations. First, if the built-in gain in the property is not long-term capital gain (long-term capital gains are discussed in Lesson 21), the deduction is generally limited to adjusted basis. Second, in the case of a contribution of *tangible* personal property, the deduction is limited to adjusted basis if the donated property is unrelated to the donee's charitable purpose. Thus, while a donation of an appreciated painting can result in a FMV deduction if donated to an art museum, it will not if donated to a hospital. Third, charitable deductions for property donated to private foundations (as opposed to public charities) are limited to adjusted basis, except if the donation is in the form of public company stock.

While these limitations may seem onerous, they are often pretty easy to navigate around. In general, contributions of appreciated public company stock to any charitable donee result in a FMV deduction. Likewise, contributions of *real* property held for investment will generally result in a FMV deduction if donated to a public charity.

Because gifts are not realization events, contributions of built-in loss property do not generate realized losses. The amount of the deduction is the FMV of the property. This combination—of unrealized losses and FMV deductions—can cause valuable tax deductions to effectively evaporate into thin air. If the built-in loss property is business or investment property, the better strategy would be for the donor to sell the property for cash (resulting in a loss deduction for the donor under section 165(c)) and then donate the resulting cash proceeds. An even better strategy would be for the donor to instead contribute *appreciated* property of equivalent value that qualifies for a FMV deduction.

What You Need to Know:

1. Taxpayers generally can take a charitable deduction equal to the amount of cash or the FMV of property that they contribute to 501(c)(3) organizations.

2. Very large charitable deductions relative to the taxpayer's AGI are limited to a percentage of that

AGI. The precise percentage limit depends on whether the donee is a public charity or private foundation and whether the donation is in the form of cash or property.

3. Contributions of property to charities are not realization events, and they therefore do not result in realized gains (or losses).
4. Contributions of built-in gain property generally result in FMV deductions. However, section 170(e)(1) limits the deduction to the property's adjusted basis in certain situations.
5. Contributions of built-in loss property result in FMV deductions. This can cause valuable tax deductions to go to waste.

LESSON 17: STATE AND LOCAL TAXES AND MEDICAL EXPENSES

Although most of the deductions we have covered thus far relate to business or investment activity, some are **personal deductions**. Home mortgage interest deductions and charitable contribution deductions are personal deductions. This lesson describes two additional personal deductions: deductions for state and local taxes and for medical expenses.

The repeal of some or all personal deductions is often mentioned in tax reform discussions. While business/investment deductions are critical parts of an income tax, personal deductions (and personal exclusions, such as the exclusion for employer-provided healthcare) instead represent government spending accomplished through the tax code. For this reason, these deductions and exclusions are known as **tax expenditures**. Tax reformers often call for repealing (or limiting) personal deductions and using the resulting additional government revenue to pay for lower tax rates. One practical problem with this approach is that two of the largest categories of personal deductions (in terms of revenue cost), the home mortgage interest deduction and the charitable contribution deduction (each costing in excess of $50 billion annually), are political "sacred cows" that appear to be more or less untouchable.

State and Local Taxes

Section 164 generally allows taxpayers to deduct up to $10,000 of property taxes and income taxes paid to state or local governments. However, a taxpayer may choose to deduct (up to the $10,000 cap) state and local *sales* taxes in lieu of state and local *income* taxes (state and local *property* taxes are always deductible regardless of the choice). This choice is particularly beneficial to taxpayers who reside in states that do not impose an income tax, such as Florida and Texas. If a taxpayer chooses to deduct sales tax, she does not have to retain receipts for every purchase. The IRS allows taxpayers to use an optional table that estimates the amount of sales tax paid based on their income levels, state of residence, and other factors. Taxpayers that use the optional table can also deduct actual sales tax paid on certain big-ticket items like cars and boats that are substantiated by a receipt.

Medical Expenses

Section 213(a) allows a deduction for out-of-pocket medical expenses, but only to the extent the aggregate of those expenses during the year exceeds 7.5 percent (in 2018) or 10 percent (in later tax years) of the taxpayer's adjusted gross income (AGI is discussed in the next lesson). This effectively means that only very large medical costs (relative to the taxpayer's income for the year) result in a deduction, and even then a significant portion of the expenses will not be deductible. For example, assume that a taxpayer with $100,000 of AGI incurs medical expenses of $10,000 during 2018. Only $2,500 of the medical expenses will be deductible under section 213(a) after application of the 7.5 percent AGI floor.

What You Need to Know:

1. Personal deductions, such as the home mortgage interest deduction and charitable contribution deduction, and personal exclusions, such as the exclusion for employer-provided healthcare, are known as tax expenditures, because they represent

government spending accomplished through the Code.

2. Tax reformers often advocate for eliminating or reducing tax expenditures and using the additional government revenue to reduce tax rates.
3. Two of the most significant personal deductions, in terms of revenue cost, are the charitable contribution deduction and the home mortgage interest deduction.
4. Section 164(a) allows a deduction for state and local property taxes and income taxes, up to an aggregate $10,000 cap. However, taxpayers may choose to deduct state and local sales taxes in lieu of income taxes.
5. Section 213 allows a deduction for out-of-pocket medical expenses to the extent that the aggregate of those expenses exceed 7.5 percent (10 percent beginning in 2019) of the taxpayer's adjusted gross income.

LESSON 18: AGI, THE STANDARD DEDUCTION, AND THE DEDUCTION FOR QUALIFIED BUSINESS INCOME

In general, taxable income is equal to the excess of gross income over allowable deductions. But (as you might expect by now) the Code adds some complications. Allowable deductions, which were covered in Lessons 11 through 17, are divided into different categories, which affects their utilization in reducing taxable income.

Above-the-Line Deductions

Adjusted gross income (AGI) is a term of art that is very important. AGI is defined in section 62(a) as gross income minus the deductions listed in section 62(a)(1) through (21). These deductions are known as above-the-line deductions, and they are the best type of deductions for the taxpayer. Of the deductions we've studied, the following are above-the-line deductions: deductions attributable to most trades or businesses (62(a)(1));

deductions attributable to losses recognized on the sale or exchange of property (62(a)(3)); deductions attributable to investment activities that generate rents or royalties (62(a)(4)); and student loan interest deductions (62(a)(18)). Any allowable deduction that is not an above-the-line deduction is called an **itemized deduction** (also known as a **below-the-line deduction**).

Itemized Deductions

Itemized deductions are those deductions that are not listed in section 62(a) (other than the new deduction for qualified business income, which is described below). Taxpayers can only deduct their itemized deductions if they elect to forgo the **standard deduction**. The standard deduction is a flat amount set by Congress that is adjusted annually for inflation. In 2018, the standard deduction is $12,000 for an unmarried taxpayer. Thus, if the aggregate of the taxpayer's itemized deductions exceeds $12,000, the taxpayer would choose to itemize her deductions. If the aggregate was less than $12,000, the taxpayer would claim the standard deduction.

Of the deductions that we have studied, the following are itemized deductions: (1) home mortgage interest deductions; (2) charitable deductions; (3) state and local tax deductions; and (4) medical expense deductions.

Above-the-line deductions are better for taxpayers than itemized deductions for two main reasons. First, while taxpayers can simultaneously claim above-the-line deductions *and* the standard deduction, itemized deductions are allowed only *in lieu of* the standard deduction. Second, some personal deductions are phased out using formulas that are based on AGI, and only above-the-line deductions reduce AGI. For example, medical expense deductions are only allowed to the extent that they in the aggregate exceed a floor based on AGI, and student loan interest deductions phase out as the taxpayer's AGI grows.

New Deduction for Qualified Business Income

The 2017 Tax Act created a brand new deduction for certain "qualified business income" that is neither an above-the-line nor a below-the-line deduction. This means that it does not reduce

AGI but can be claimed in addition to (and not just in lieu of) the standard deduction. Qualified business income generally means trade or business taxable income earned by the taxpayer directly (i.e., in a sole proprietorship) or through so-called pass-through business entities (such as LLCs, partnerships, and S corporations). Pass-through entities do not pay taxes themselves (unlike regular corporations, which pay the corporate tax) but instead pass their gross income and deductions through to their owners, who report the items on their own tax returns. Qualified business income does not include wages earned by employees. There are a number of technical limitations on the definition of qualified business income that are intended to prevent taxpayers from characterizing services income as qualified business income, but it is not clear how effective these limitations will prove to be.

New section 199A generally allows taxpayers to deduct 20 percent of their qualified business income. This effectively exempts 20 percent of a taxpayer's qualified business income from tax. For example, if a taxpayer earns $100,000 of qualified business income, the taxpayer would generally receive a $20,000 deduction. On a net basis, this means that only $80,000 of the qualified business income will end up being subject to tax. This is true even if the taxpayer claims the standard deduction because the new deduction is allowed to taxpayers whether or not they itemize their deductions.

What You Need to Know:

1. Adjusted gross income equals gross income less the deductions listed in section 62(a)(1) through (21).
2. These deductions are known as above-the-line deductions.
3. Allowed deductions other than above-the-line deductions (and other than the deduction for qualified business income) are known as itemized deductions or below-the-line deductions.
4. While above-the-line deductions may be claimed *in addition* to the standard deduction, itemized deductions may be claimed only *in lieu of* the standard deduction.

5. Under new section 199A, a taxpayer may generally deduct 20 percent of the amount of qualified business income that the taxpayer realizes. This deduction does not reduce AGI, but it can be claimed in addition to the standard deduction.

LESSON 19: TIMING OF GROSS INCOME AND DEDUCTIONS

We turn now to issues of **timing**. When are items of gross income or deduction realized? We have already studied a couple of timing rules relating to *property* transactions. Under the realization rule, gains or losses are generally only realized when property is sold or exchanged. And, under the depreciation rules, "wasting" deductions for property used in a trade or business or in an investment activity are realized according to formulaic depreciation schedules.

Timing issues with respect to other transactions, such as compensation for services, are governed by the taxpayer's **method of accounting**. Individual taxpayers typically use the **cash method of accounting**. The other major method of accounting is the **accrual method**.

Income Under the Cash Method

A cash method taxpayer realizes income when the taxpayer receives cash, property, or services. Receipt can be actual (e.g., the taxpayer receives a check in her mailbox) or constructive. Under Treas. Reg. section 1.451–2(a), the **constructive receipt doctrine** provides that a taxpayer realizes income when (i) cash or property is made available to the taxpayer, and (ii) the taxpayer may receive the cash or property without substantial restrictions or limitations. The purpose of the doctrine is to prevent taxpayers from "turning their backs on income" to defer the income until a later year. For example, if a taxpayer is legally entitled to an immediate payment and if the counterparty is ready, willing, and able to give the taxpayer a check, the taxpayer is in constructive receipt of the payment if the taxpayer asks the counterparty to delay payment until the following year.

Under *Revenue Ruling 60–31*, if a service contract explicitly calls for a delayed payment, the constructive receipt doctrine is not triggered, as long as the contract is entered into before any services have been performed. For example, if a contract executed in Year 0 calls for the taxpayer to perform services in Year 1, but to be paid on January 15 of Year 2, there will be no constructive receipt in Year 1.

Cash Equivalency & Economic Benefit Doctrines

In general, a contractual obligation of a counterparty to pay the taxpayer is not "cash" or "property" under the cash method. Thus, for example, an account receivable for services rendered is neither cash nor property, and therefore the mere generation of such a contractual right to payment does not result in income realization. Instead, gross income is realized when the account receivable is paid.

However, certain contractual rights are treated like cash or property. Under the **cash equivalency doctrine**, promissory notes of extremely creditworthy obligors are treated like cash in certain situations. The specific conditions for cash equivalency are set forth in the case of *Cowden v. Commissioner*, 289 F.2d 20 (5th Cir. 1961).

Under the **economic benefit doctrine**, contractual rights that are backed by a security interest in property or by an escrow account or other similar device are treated as property and therefore immediately taxed under the cash method. Accordingly, to avoid the economic benefit doctrine, the payee must remain a general unsecured creditor of the payor.

Deductions Under the Cash Method

Deductions under the cash method are generally allowed when payment is *actually* made in the form of a delivery of cash, property or services. There is no "constructive payment" doctrine.

Accrual Method

As noted above, individuals rarely use the accrual method. Under the accrual method, gross income is generally realized as the right to the income is earned. Thus, while a cash method taxpayer generally realizes gross income generally when a bill is *paid by* the client, an accrual method taxpayer generally realizes gross income when the bill is *delivered to* the client. On the deduction side, an accrual method taxpayer generally realizes a deduction when the obligation to make the payment is incurred. Accordingly, while a cash method taxpayer would deduct business expenses as accounts payable *are paid*, an accrual method taxpayer would deduct them when the taxpayer *receives the bill.*

What You Need to Know:

1. The realization and depreciation rules are timing rules that relate to property transactions.
2. Most other transactions are governed by the particular method of accounting used by the taxpayer.
3. Most individual taxpayers use the cash method of accounting, which focuses on the receipt or payment of cash, property, or services.
4. The constructive receipt doctrine treats the taxpayer as having received income prior to actual receipt in cases where the taxpayer attempts to turn her back on income.
5. While contractual rights to payment are generally *not* considered cash or property under the cash method, the cash equivalency and economic benefit doctrines treat contractual rights as cash or property in certain situations.
6. Under the accrual method of accounting, income and deductions are realized when income is earned or when expenses are incurred.

LESSON 20: THE ANNUAL ACCOUNTING PERIOD

Taxpayers report their gross income and deductions for a yearlong period, known as the **taxable year**. For individuals, the taxable year is generally the calendar year, beginning on January 1 and ending on December 31, and their income tax returns are due on April 15 of the following year. The tax return generally incorporates relevant information that the taxpayer possesses as of December 31. Thus, an event or transaction that occurs on or after January 1 typically has no impact on the tax return for the previous year. This general rule can sometimes be quite harsh, and therefore Congress has given taxpayers some relief in certain circumstances.

Claim of Right Doctrine and Section 1341

In *North American Oil Consolidated v. Burnet*, 286 U.S. 417 (1932), the Supreme Court held that if a taxpayer receives an item of income under a **claim of right**, the taxpayer realizes gross income even if the possibility exists that the taxpayer may eventually have to return part or all of the item. To illustrate, assume that a taxpayer receives on December 31 of Year 1 a royalty check for $50,000, but in Year 2, the taxpayer is required to repay $5,000 of the amount due to sales that were canceled in Year 2. The claim of right doctrine applies, and the taxpayer must report $50,000 in gross income in Year 1. Instead of reducing the Year 1 gross income, the repayment would result in a $5,000 deduction (as an ordinary or necessary business expense) in Year 2.

This result would be an unhappy one for the taxpayer if her marginal tax rate is higher in Year 1 than in Year 2. Congress enacted section 1341 to provide relief in these types of situations. Under section 1341, if a claim of right in excess of $3,000 is repaid by the taxpayer in a later tax year, the taxpayer may choose to take a tax *credit* on her Year 2 tax return equal to the increase of her tax in Year 1 as a result of the claim of right (in lieu of claiming a Year 2 *deduction* in the amount of the repayment). (Credits reduce tax liability on a dollar-for-dollar basis, while deductions reduce the amount of taxable income that is applied to the tax rates in section 1.) Thus, in the example above, if the taxpayer's Year 1 marginal tax rate was 40 percent and Year 2 marginal rate was 30 percent, the taxpayer would take a credit in Year 2 equal to $2,000 ($5,000 claim of right times the taxpayer's Year 1 marginal rate). This would be a better result than simply taking a deduction of $5,000 in Year 2. The deduction would shelter $5,000 of taxable income, and because her marginal tax rate is only 30 percent in Year 2, the sheltering of $5,000 of taxable income would save her only $1,500 of tax. Thus, electing the credit in lieu of the deduction under section 1341 saves her $500 in Year 2 taxes. If the marginal tax rates for the years were reversed, so that her Year 1 rate was 30 percent and her Year 2 rate 40 percent, the taxpayer would be better off simply claiming the deduction in Year 2.

Tax Benefit Rule

What if a taxpayer claims a deduction for a payment in Year 1 but then receives a refund of the payment in Year 2? As long as the deduction was proper based on facts known to the taxpayer on December 31, the deduction is allowed in Year 1, consistent with the general principle discussed in the first paragraph above. Section 111(a), known as the **tax benefit rule**, deals with the tax consequences of the receipt of the refund. In general, the refund is gross income; after all, the taxpayer has received cash and the taxpayer has no basis to offset the cash. But, if the extra deduction in Year 1 did not result in any tax benefit to the taxpayer (in the form of a reduction in tax owed in Year 1), then the refund is excluded from gross income.

For example, assume that a taxpayer pays $4,000 in estimated state income tax payments in Year 1. In Year 2, the taxpayer receives a refund of $400 of these state income tax payments. She would claim a $4,000 state income tax deduction under section 164 in Year 1. Assuming the extra $400 deduction reduced her Year 1 tax burden, the $400 refund is included in gross income. But if the extra deduction was in fact irrelevant in determining the Year 1 federal tax liability, then the $400 refund would be *excluded* from gross income. Thus, if in Year 1 the taxpayer claimed the standard deduction in lieu of her itemized deductions (which include section 164 deductions), then the $400 refund would be excluded from gross income in Year 2.

Net Operating Losses

If a taxpayer incurs an overall loss for a taxable year, the taxpayer does not owe any federal income taxes for that year because she has no positive taxable income to which the tax rates would be applied. Under section 172, business losses, known as a **net operating losses**, may be carried forward to later taxable years. Due to the carryforward, the taxpayer's future taxable income will be at least partially sheltered.

What You Need to Know:

1. In general, every tax year stands alone. This means that whatever happens in Year 2 generally does not have any impact on what goes on the taxpayer's Year 1 tax return and vice versa.
2. When a taxpayer receives an item of income under a claim of right, the item is gross income in the taxable year of receipt, even if the taxpayer repays the item in a later tax year.
3. Under section 1341, when a taxpayer repays an item that has been received under a claim of right, the taxpayer may claim, in the year of repayment, a credit equal to the amount of excess tax paid in the earlier year or may claim a deduction equal to the amount of the repayment.
4. Under the tax benefit rule in section 111(a), refunds of previously deducted expenses are included in gross income except to the extent that the prior deduction did not result in any tax benefit.
5. Net operating losses may be carried forward to later taxable years.

LESSON 21: CAPITAL GAINS, CAPITAL LOSSES, AND QUALIFIED DIVIDEND INCOME

We turn now to the issue of **character**. The default rule is that an item of income is ordinary income and an item of deduction is an ordinary deduction. Ordinary income and ordinary deductions are netted against one another (after taking into account any exclusions or limitations that might apply), and the net ordinary income amount is applied to the tax rate schedules in section 1.

There are some special "flavors" or characters of income and deduction that are treated differently. **Long-term capital gains** and **qualified dividend income** are taxed at preferential rates, currently maxing out at a top rate of 20 percent (compared to the current regular top rate of 37 percent). In addition, **capital losses** are subject to significant limitations.

Long-Term Capital Gains and Qualified Dividend Income

Under section 1222(3), a long-term capital gain is generally a recognized gain from the sale or exchange of a capital asset that has been held by the taxpayer for more than one year.

Capital assets generally include all property held by the taxpayer that is *not* excluded from capital asset treatment by section 1221(a)(1) through (8). The most significant exclusions from capital asset treatment are the ones for inventory (1221(a)(1)), business property (1221(a)(2)), intellectual property created by the taxpayer (1221(a)(3)(A)), and accounts receivable for services provided by the taxpayer or for inventory sold by the taxpayer (1221(a)(4)).

Qualified dividend income generally includes dividends received from a corporation organized in the United States or from a foreign corporation that is organized in a country that has a comprehensive income tax treaty with the United States.

Short-term capital gains (recognized gains from the sale or exchange of a capital asset that has been held for one year or less) are taxed as ordinary income, as is dividend income that is not qualified dividend income.

Defenders of the preference for long-term capital gains justify it with a variety of arguments. Some argue that the preference is designed to encourage investment or to counteract the effect of taxing gains that represent inflation or the "bunching" of multiple-years' worth of appreciation into a single year. The best argument in favor of the capital gains preference is that it mitigates the **lock-in effect** that results from the realization rule, thereby facilitating the flow of capital from one investment to another. High tax rates on capital gains can discourage sales of current investments even when other more attractive investment opportunities exist, simply because sales (and other realizations) trigger an immediate tax burden while merely holding onto the current investment does not. Lower rates on long-term capital gains mitigate, but do not eliminate, this problem.

Defenders of the qualified dividend income preference point to the fact that income realized by a corporation is taxed twice: once at the corporate level when the income is earned by the corporation and again at the shareholder level when the income is distributed as a dividend. The qualified dividend income preference ameliorates the effect of this double taxation by reducing the burden of the shareholder-level tax.

Capital Losses

Capital losses are recognized losses from the sale or exchange of a capital asset, but only if those losses are deductible under section 165. If losses are nondeductible (because, e.g., the property sold is a personal-use asset), the loss is not a capital loss; instead, the loss is simply ignored in calculating the taxpayer's tax liability.

Capital losses offset capital gains. Short-term capital losses first offset short-term capital gains, and long-term capital losses first offset long-term capital gains. Then, any "excess" short-term capital losses (i.e., those in excess of short-term capital gains) offset net long-term capital gains, and any excess long-term capital losses offset net short-term capital gains. To the extent any net long-term capital gains remain after this process, they are taxed at preferential rates and, to the extent any net short-term capital gains remain, they are taxed as ordinary income.

If the aggregate amount of capital losses (regardless of whether they are short-term or long-term) equal or exceed the aggregate amount of capital gains (regardless of short-term or long-term status), all of the capital gains will be fully offset. In addition, any excess of capital losses over capital gains is deductible as an ordinary deduction up to a maximum $3,000 under section 1211(b). Any net capital loss in excess of $3,000 creates a **capital loss carryforward**, which is treated as a capital loss in the following taxable year.

It is important to note that qualified dividend income, while subject to the same preferential tax rates as long-term capital gains, cannot be offset by capital losses.

Special Sub-Categories of Long-Term Capital Gains

Normally, the current top marginal rate for long-term capital gains is 20 percent. However, a higher maximum rate applies to certain types of long-term capital gains. For long-term capital gains on **collectibles** (such as works of art), the maximum rate is 28 percent. In Lesson 23, we will see that **unrecaptured section 1250 gains** are taxed at a maximum rate of 25 percent.

What You Need to Know:

1. Absent a special rule, items of income are ordinary income and items of deduction are ordinary deductions.
2. Net ordinary income (i.e., ordinary income less ordinary deductions) is subject to the tax rate schedules in section 1.
3. Long-term capital gains and qualified dividend income are preferentially taxed relative to ordinary income.
4. Long-term capital gains are recognized gains from the sale or exchange of a capital asset that has been held by the taxpayer for more than one year.
5. Short-term capital gains and nonqualified dividend income are taxed as ordinary income.
6. Capital losses are recognized losses from the sale or exchange of a capital asset, but only if those losses are deductible under section 165.
7. Capital losses first soak up capital gains (with short-term capital losses first netted against short-term gains and long-term against long-term gains). Any excess capital loss is deductible as an ordinary deduction up to $3,000, and any remaining capital loss is treated as a capital loss carryforward.

LESSON 22: QUASI-CAPITAL GAINS AND LOSSES

There is another category of character that applies to property that has been used by the taxpayer in a trade or business. Gains and losses from this property are initially characterized as **section 1231 gains and losses**, though they will ultimately be characterized as either long-term capital or ordinary.

Section 1231 Assets

We learned in Lesson 21 that assets used in a trade or business are *not* capital assets under section 1221(a)(2). Instead, most of these assets are **section 1231 assets**. Section 1231 assets include land and depreciable property that have been used in the taxpayer's trade or business for more than one year. If these assets have been used in a trade or business for one year or less, they are neither capital assets nor section 1231 assets; therefore, gains or losses from these assets are characterized as ordinary income or ordinary deductions by default.

Netting of 1231 Gains and Losses

Once section 1231 assets have been identified, the next step is to determine the total amount of gains or losses recognized on those assets during the taxable year. If the aggregate amount of section 1231 gains during the year exceeds the aggregate amount of section 1231 losses, then all of the section 1231 gains are treated as long-term capital gains and all of the section 1231 losses are treated as long-term capital losses. On the other hand, if the aggregate amount of section 1231 losses equals or exceeds the aggregate of section 1231 gains, then all of the section 1231 losses are treated as ordinary deductions and all of the section 1231 gains are treated as ordinary income.

For example, assume that a taxpayer realizes $100,000 of section 1231 gains and $75,000 of section 1231 losses during the taxable year. Because the section 1231 gains exceed the section 1231 losses, all of the gains and losses are treated as long-term capital. Thus, the taxpayer ends up with $100,000 of long-term capital gains and $75,000 of long-term capital losses. If the taxpayer has no other capital gains or losses, the $75,000 of long-term capital losses would offset $75,000 of long-term capital gains, and the remaining $25,000 of net long-term capital gains would be taxed at preferential rates.

What if the gains and losses were reversed, so that the taxpayer realized $75,000 of section 1231 gains and $100,000 of section 1231 losses? In that case, the section 1231 losses exceed the section 1231 gains and, therefore, all of the losses and gains are treated as ordinary. Thus, the taxpayer ends up with $100,000 of ordinary deductions and $75,000 of ordinary income, netting to a $25,000 ordinary deduction. This ordinary deduction can be used to offset the taxpayer's other ordinary income.

These examples show that the section 1231 rules are taxpayer friendly. If there is a net 1231 gain, the net gain is taxed at preferential rates. If there is a net 1231 loss, the net loss is characterized as an ordinary deduction, which can absorb high-rate ordinary income and is not subject to the limitations on capital losses. It's a win-win for the taxpayer. Congress has provided this win-win situation to encourage taxpayers to make investments in their businesses.

Special Rules

The discussion thus far has described the operation of section 1231 in the typical case. As with much of tax law, the details can get far more complicated in certain situations. If one or more section 1231 assets is subject to a casualty, theft, or condemnation, a special rule in section 1231(a)(4)(C) must be applied before performing the general netting process described above. In addition, if a taxpayer has recognized a net section 1231 loss during the previous five taxable years, a special recapture rule in section 1231(c) must be applied after the netting process and may re-characterize a net section 1231 gain for the current year (which would otherwise be taxed as a net long-term capital gain) as ordinary income.

What You Need to Know:

1. Section 1231 gains/losses are initial characterizations that will ultimately be characterized either as long-term capital gains/losses or as ordinary income/deductions.

2. Section 1231 assets include land and depreciable property that have been used in a trade or business for more than one year.
3. If gains recognized on section 1231 assets during the taxable year exceed losses recognized on section 1231 assets, then all of the gains and losses are treated as long-term capital gains/losses.
4. If losses recognized on section 1231 assets during the taxable year equal or exceed gains recognized on section 1231 assets, then all of the losses and gains are treated as ordinary deductions/income.
5. A special rule applies where one or more section 1231 assets is subject to a casualty, theft, or condemnation during the taxable year. In that case, section 1231(a)(4)(C) must be applied before the general section 1231 netting process.
6. Another special rule, found in section 1231(c), may apply if the taxpayer has recognized a net section 1231 loss during the previous five taxable years.

LESSON 23: DEPRECIATION RECAPTURE

In Lesson 13, we learned that taxpayers are allowed to claim depreciation deductions with respect to wasting assets that are either used in a trade or business or held for investment. These deductions reduce the adjusted basis of the asset pursuant to section 1016(a)(2). This lesson covers the character of any gain that represents the recapture of prior depreciation deductions. For example, assume that an asset with an initial cost of $100,000 is subject to $60,000 of depreciation before it is sold for $120,000. The $60,000 of depreciation reduces the asset's adjusted basis from $100,000 to $40,000, and, accordingly, the gain recognized is $80,000 ($120,000 less $40,000). However, the property actually appreciated by only $20,000, from $100,000 to $120,000. The other $60,000 of gain represents **depreciation recapture**. Depreciation recapture will occur whenever the formulaic tax depreciation schedules turn out to be more generous than the actual economic depreciation. In this example, there was no economic depreciation at all, as the asset actually went *up* in value, so all of the depreciation was recaptured.

Section 1245 Recapture

In general, depreciation recapture with respect to property other than real property is taxed as ordinary income under section 1245. The rationale is that the prior depreciation deductions constituted ordinary deductions that reduced ordinary income, so any recapture should be taxed as ordinary income. Importantly, characterization under section 1245 trumps all other characterization provisions.

To illustrate, assume that, in the example above, the asset sold was not real property, so section 1245 applies. Under section 1245(a), $60,000 of the $80,000 gain would be characterized as ordinary income. The remaining $20,000 of gain (the amount of "true" economic gain) is characterized under other characterization rules. If the asset is a capital asset under section 1221(a), the $20,000 gain would be a capital gain. If the asset is a section 1231 asset, the $20,000 gain would be a section 1231 gain that would go into the section 1231 netting process; in that case, the $60,000 gain that is characterized as ordinary under section 1245 is *not* a section 1231 gain and therefore does not go into the section 1231 netting process. If the asset is neither a capital asset nor a section 1231 asset, the $20,000 gain would be taxed as ordinary income under the default rule.

If the asset in the example were sold for $100,000 or less, all of any gain that is recognized would be characterized as ordinary income because all of the gain represents depreciation recapture. Thus, if the asset were sold for $75,000, all $35,000 of gain recognized would be ordinary income under section 1245, and none would be capital gain or section 1231 gain.

Unrecaptured Section 1250 Gain

Section 1245 generally only applies to depreciable property that is not real property. In the case of depreciable real property, such as a building (but not the land on which it sits, which is non-depreciable), section 1250 technically could apply to recapture some depreciation as ordinary income. But section 1250 only applies to depreciation deductions in excess of straight-line depreciation, and since 1986 straight-line depreciation is generally required for real property. This means that, in most modern contexts, section 1250 has no continuing relevance.

Accordingly, if depreciable real property which is a capital asset (because it was held for investment) is sold for a gain, all of the gain is generally taxed as a long-term capital gain. If depreciable real property which is a section 1231 asset (because it was held in connection with the taxpayer's trade or business) is sold for a gain, all of the gain is generally initially characterized as a section 1231 gain, and, if the taxpayer's section 1231 gains exceed her section 1231 losses, the gain will ultimately be treated as a long-term capital gain.

Congress has provided a slightly less preferential tax rate for long-term capital gains that represent depreciation recapture with respect to real property. These so-called **unrecaptured section 1250 gains** are taxed at a maximum gain of 25 percent, rather than the normal preferential rate of 20 percent.

To illustrate these rules, assume that a building, which was purchased by the taxpayer for use in her trade or business, was acquired for $200,000 and sold many years later for $225,000. The taxpayer properly claims $100,000 of depreciation deductions on the building before it is sold. The taxpayer's gain recognized is $125,000 ($225,000 amount realized less $100,000 of adjusted basis). Section 1245 does not apply because the building is *real* property, and section 1250 does not apply because the property was placed in service after 1986. Therefore, all of the gain recognized is section 1231 gain. Assuming the taxpayer's section 1231 gains (including the gain on the building) exceed the taxpayer's section 1231 losses, the $125,000 is characterized as a long-term capital gain. $100,000 of the gain is further classified as unrecaptured section 1250 gain, so it is subject to a special 25 percent maximum tax rate. The $25,000 of true economic gain is "plain vanilla" long-term capital gain, taxable at the typical maximum rate of 20 percent. Therefore, the total maximum tax attributable to the sale is $30,000 (25 percent of $100,000 plus 20 percent of $25,000).

These recapture rules for real property are more generous to the taxpayer than the corresponding rules under section 1245 for non-real property. Defenders of the generous treatment justify it by arguing that encouraging greater real estate investment is good economic policy.

What You Need to Know:

1. Depreciation recapture is the amount of gain that represents prior depreciation deductions. In contrast, true gain is the amount of economic appreciation that accrues while holding an asset.
2. Section 1245 provides that depreciation recapture with respect to non-real property is characterized as ordinary income.
3. Section 1245 trumps all other characterization provisions. Any gain that is not characterized as ordinary income under section 1245 is characterized under the other characterization rules, such as section 1231.
4. Gain that is characterized as ordinary income under section 1245 does not go into the section 1231 netting process.
5. In general, depreciation recapture with respect to depreciable real property is not characterized as ordinary income. Instead, if that gain is characterized as a long-term capital gain, a special 25 percent maximum tax rate applies (rather than the 20 percent maximum rate for plain vanilla long-term capital gains).

LESSON 24: WHO IS THE PROPER TAXPAYER?

We turn now to the issue of the proper taxpayer. In general, all individuals who are U.S. citizens or residents are required to file a federal income tax return reporting their taxable income and to pay the corresponding tax liability.

Joint Returns

Individuals who are married are allowed to, and typically do, file a **joint tax return**. Both taxpayers include their individual tax items on the joint return, and a special tax rate structure in section 1(b) applies to their aggregate taxable income. In addition, the standard deduction amount and other amounts and limitations in the Code are typically higher for taxpayers filing joint returns.

In situations where one spouse earns a very large percentage of the couple's aggregate income, a couple will often pay *less* in tax than if they were unmarried and filed two individual tax returns. This phenomenon is known as the **marriage bonus**. On the other hand, in situations where couples earn more equal amounts of income, they often pay *more* in tax than if they were unmarried. This is known as the **marriage penalty**. The tipping point has historically been roughly 70 percent, though it can vary depending on the couple's taxable income and other tax characteristics, and the 2017 Tax Act will affect the tipping point going forward. Under the historic tipping point, as the higher earning spouse earned greater than 70 percent of the couple's aggregate income, the marriage bonus would grow. As the lower earning spouse earned more than 30 percent of the aggregate income up to 50 percent, the marriage penalty would grow.

Married couples can choose to file two separate individual tax returns, in which case each return would be subject to the special **married-filing-separately** tax rate structure in section 1(d). However, the special rates in section 1(d) (as well as other special rules that apply to married couples filing separately) almost always result in the couple owing *more* in total federal income tax than if they had filed jointly, so the married-filing-separately option is rarely exercised.

Shifting of Income

Because of the progressive rate structure, families have a strong incentive to shift income from higher-income members to lower-income members. Simple gifts will not do the trick, because gifts are not deductible by donor. In other words, gifts are made in *after-tax* dollars. Income shifting only occurs if there is a transfer of *pre-tax* dollars.

The IRS and courts are aware of the incentive to shift income, and they have created doctrines to police such behavior.

In *Lucas v. Earl*, 281 U.S. 111 (1930), the Supreme Court held that income from services is taxed to the individual who performs the services even if payment for the services is deflected to another taxpayer. Likewise, in *Helvering v. Horst*, 311 U.S. 112 (1940), the Court held that interest income is taxed to the owner of the bond even where the rights to interest payments from the bond had previously been gifted to another taxpayer. These cases, and others along the same lines, make up what is known as the **assignment of income doctrine**. When triggered, the assignment of income doctrine attributes income items formally earned by a transferee back to the transferor.

Another income-shifting strategy involves the payment of excessive "compensation" to family members who work for a business owned by another family member. If the excessive portion of the compensation were deductible, the result would be a transfer of pre-tax dollars from the transferor (who gets to deduct them) to the transferee (who would include them in gross income). But as we learned in Lesson 11, the IRS and courts will scrutinize these familial compensation arrangements to ensure that they are consistent with arm's length results. To the extent the purported compensation is unreasonably high (relative to an arm's length standard), the transferor's deduction will be disallowed under section 162(a)(1), thereby preventing the income shift.

Nevertheless, there remains some viable income shifting strategies. If an item of property is gifted outright (unlike in the *Horst* case where only the interest rights were gifted), all future income streams from that property, such future interest and dividend payments, will be recognized by the donee rather than the donor. And if property with a built-in gain is gifted, the basis rules discussed in Lesson 6 allow the gain to be shifted to the donee.

Kiddie Tax

Even if an income shift is successful, section 1(g), known as the **kiddie tax**, may reduce or eliminate the desired tax benefits. Under the kiddie tax, the *unearned* income of a dependent child, while still reported by the child on the child's own tax return, is nevertheless taxed at the *parents'* marginal tax rate (if that rate is higher than the child's normal rate). In general, a dependent child is defined as a child who is under the age of 18, a child who is 18 years old and who receives more than half of his support from their parents, or a child who is between the ages of 19 and 23 who receives more than half of their support from their parents and who is also a full-time student.

What You Need to Know:

1. In general, every individual must file his or her own tax return.
2. Married couples can, and typically do, file joint tax returns.
3. Joint returns can result in a marriage bonus in some cases and in a marriage penalty in others.
4. While married individuals can file separately, this would usually increase their collective tax liability and, therefore, this option is rarely exercised.
5. The assignment of income doctrine taxes compensation for services to the individual who performs those services and income from property to the owner of the property, regardless of who formally receive these income items.
6. Familial compensation can be an income-shifting strategy, but section 162(a)(1) prevents the deduction of unreasonably high compensation.
7. Gifts of property shift future income from the property to the donee, and the basis rules in section 1015 allow built-in gains to be shifted as well.
8. The kiddie tax generally taxes unearned income of a dependent child at the parents' marginal tax rate.

LESSON 25: TAX SHELTERS AND NONRECOURSE DEBT

The final two lessons deal with certain **tax shelters** that were very popular before 1986 and the rules that were enacted in that year to shut them down. These tax shelters generated lots of "phantom" deductions in the early years of the shelter, followed by an equal amount of phantom income in the later years. Because of the time-value of money and potential favorable character swaps (i.e., where the early deductions were ordinary while the later income was long-term capital gain), these tax shelters produced extremely favorable after-tax results even where they made no sense apart from tax effects. These tax shelters were problematic for a number of reasons. They reduced government revenues, which had to be made up in other ways, such as through higher tax rates on legitimate transactions. They distorted the economy by causing taxpayers to pursue tax-motivated transactions rather than transactions that were justifiable on their non-tax economics. They also hurt taxpayer morale, by allowing wealthy taxpayers to avoid tax through sophisticated tax planning.

Nonrecourse Debt

A key ingredient in many of these tax shelters was the use of **nonrecourse debt**. If the borrower defaults on a nonrecourse debt, the lender's recourse is limited to the property that secures the debt. For example, if a borrower incurs nonrecourse debt in acquiring a property and subsequently defaults on the loan, the lender's only recourse is to foreclose on the property. If the amount recovered by the lender through the foreclosure sale is less than the amount of the debt, the non-recourse borrower is not responsible for the difference. If the loan were recourse, the borrower would be personally responsible for the difference.

For example, assume that I buy property by paying $20,000 cash and borrowing $180,000 on a *nonrecourse* basis. Later on, when the property is worth $150,000 and the nonrecourse loan principal is still $180,000, I default on the loan and the lender forecloses on the property. Because the loan is nonrecourse, I am not personally responsible for the $30,000 difference between the amount of the loan and the value of the property. If the loan were *recourse*, then the lender could sue me for the $30,000 **deficiency**.

As this example illustrates, the economics of nonrecourse lending are such that the lender, rather than the borrower, incurs the risk of the property value dropping below the amount of the debt. When the property value dropped below $180,000, the lender alone suffers the loss. Whether the property drops to $180,000, $150,000, or even zero, my loss is always limited to my $20,000 down payment.

Tax Treatment of Nonrecourse Debt upon Borrowing

For tax purposes, the incurrence of nonrecourse debt is treated the same the incurrence of recourse debt. Thus, just as a recourse borrower realizes no gross income upon borrowing (as we learned in Lesson 3), so does a nonrecourse borrower. And, just as a recourse borrower who incurs the debt in acquiring property receives basis credit in the property for the debt (as we learned in Lesson 5), so does a nonrecourse borrower.

Tax Consequences upon Disposition of Leveraged Property

When property subject to a debt (whether recourse or nonrecourse) is sold or exchanged, the general rule is that the amount of the debt is included in the seller's amount realized. For example, assume that I buy land for $200,000, using $180,000 of debt proceeds, and sell the land when it is worth $210,000 and the outstanding loan balance remains $180,000. If the loan is recourse, the seller pays me $30,000 cash and assumes the recourse debt. If the loan is nonrecourse, the seller pays me $30,000 cash and simply takes the property subject to the nonrecourse debt. In either case, my amount realized is $210,000 ($30,000 of cash and $180,000 of debt relief) and my gain is $10,000 ($210,000 of amount realized minus my $200,000 adjusted basis).

If the land is "under water" (meaning that its value is less than the amount of outstanding debt) upon disposition, things get trickier. Assume that the land above is worth only $150,000 and I give the land back to the lender. If the debt is *recourse*, my amount realized is $150,000, the value of the land at the time of the transfer, and I recognize a loss of $50,000. Since the loan is recourse, I am liable to the lender for another $30,000. If I fail to pay the $30,000, I would realize cancellation of debt income (potentially excludible under section 108, as discussed in Lesson 7).

On the other hand, if the loan was *nonrecourse* and I transferred the land back to the lender, the result is completely different. In two famous (at least in the world of tax) cases, *Crane v. Commissioner*, 331 U.S. 1 (1947) and *Commissioner v. Tufts*, 461 U.S. 300 (1983), the Supreme Court held that my amount realized would be $180,000 (the amount of the outstanding nonrecourse debt) even though the property is worth only $150,000. Thus, I would recognize a $20,000 loss and zero cancellation of debt income.

What You Need to Know:

1. A nonrecourse loan is a loan where the lender's recourse in the event of default is limited to foreclosing on the property that secures the loan. A recourse loan is one where the lender can sue the borrower if the collateral is not sufficient to satisfy the outstanding loan balance.
2. A nonrecourse lender bears the risk that the value of the property that secures the loan may drop below the amount of the outstanding loan balance.
3. When debt proceeds are used to acquire property, the borrower receives basis credit in the property for the debt regardless of whether the debt is recourse or nonrecourse.
4. In general, when property that is subject to a debt is sold, the amount of the debt is included in the seller's amount realized.
5. If underwater property is transferred to a *recourse* lender, the seller's amount realized equals the fair market value of the property.
6. If underwater property is transferred to a *nonrecourse* lender, the seller's amount realized equals the amount of the nonrecourse debt, pursuant to the *Crane* and *Tufts* cases.

LESSON 26: AT-RISK AND PASSIVE ACTIVITY RULES

The pre-1986 tax shelters mentioned in the previous lesson typically involved a leveraged purchase of real estate at a high valuation. The purchase was financed by large amounts of nonrecourse debt, with only a relatively small cash down payment. The use of nonrecourse loans meant that all the buyer could lose was the small cash down payment. Large debt and high valuations resulted in large interest and depreciation deductions in the early years of the shelter. These deductions could be used to offset the taxpayer's compensation and investment income in those early years. In later years, the tax shelter would eventually kick off income (because interest deductions would get smaller as the loan was repaid and depreciation schedules would be ending) and, upon disposition there would be gain (under the *Crane* and *Tufts* cases), but the taxpayer could just invest in another tax shelter to shelter that income when it was realized.

The Tax Reform Act of 1986 (the "1986 Act") effectively shut down these shelters and other similar ones through three main mechanisms. First, the 1986 Act substantially lengthened the depreciation schedules of real estate. Second, the act extended the **at-risk rules** to certain real property transactions. Third, it enacted the **passive activity rules**.

At-Risk Rules

In Lesson 25, we learned that nonrecourse borrowing gives rise to basis in purchased property, even though the borrower is not personally liable on the loan. If the property is depreciable, the basis gives rise to depreciation deductions. The 1986 Act extended the at-risk rules in section 465 to certain real property transactions. Prior to that, the at-risk rules applied only to non-real property transactions.

Section 465 generally limits the amount of losses that a taxpayer may claim with respect to an investment to the amount the taxpayer has at risk. At-risk amounts include cash and property contributions and the amount of *recourse* borrowing. Nonrecourse borrowing is generally not considered at risk.

While the 1986 generally extended these rules to real property transactions, it allowed nonrecourse borrowing from traditional lenders (e.g., banks) to be considered at risk if the borrowing was made with respect to real property. Thus, the 1986 at-risk rule extension to real property effectively applies only to *seller-financed* nonrecourse purchases.

Passive Activity Rules

The 1986 Act created the passive activity rules in section 469. In effect, these rules create three separate baskets of activities: (1) **active activities**, (2) **portfolio activities**, and (3) **passive activities**. Active activities are those in which the taxpayer **materially participates**. Portfolio activities are activities relating to the buying, holding, and selling of stocks, bonds, and other similar financial instruments for investment. Passive activities are all other activities.

Section 469 limits deductions from all passive activities (i.e., non-portfolio activities in which the taxpayer does not materially participate) to the amount of income from all passive activities. The limitation applies on an annual basis. Any passive deductions in excess of passive income in a taxable year are carried over to subsequent tax years, while retaining their status as passive activity deductions.

Passive activity losses are therefore effectively quarantined from other sources of income. Passive activity losses may be used *only* against passive activity income. This effectively eliminates the time-value of money benefits sought by the pre-1986 tax shelters because they defer the losses generated in the early years until the recognition of income and gains in the later years.

The passive activity rules are complex and the subject of lengthy regulations. A critical issue is the definition of material participation. If a taxpayer materially participates in an activity, any losses from the activity are unaffected by section 469. Treas. Reg. section 1.469–5T intricately defines material participation. A common method for satisfying the material participation standard in that regulation is for the taxpayer to spend more than five hundred hours on the activity during the taxable year.

What You Need to Know:

1. The pre-1986 tax shelters often involved nonrecourse-debt-financed purchases of real property at high valuations. These purchases resulted in large early deductions, comprising of interest and depreciation deductions.
2. The 1986 Act attacked these shelters by lengthening the depreciation schedules for real property, extending the at-risk rules to seller-financed acquisitions of real estate, and enacting the passive activity rules.
3. As applied to real estate, the at-risk rules limit losses on seller-financed non-recourse acquisitions of real estate to the amount of cash or property invested in the project by an investor.
4. The passive activity rules limit passive activity deductions to the amount of passive activity income, with any excess carrying over as passive activity loss carryovers to the subsequent year.
5. Passive activities are activities in which the taxpayer does not materially participate and that are not portfolio activities.
6. Material participation is defined in Treas. Reg. 1.469–5T. A common way to satisfy the material participation standard is to spend more than five hundred hours per year on the activity.

CHAPTER 7

PROFESSIONAL RESPONSIBILITY

LESSON 1: INTRODUCTION

One of the few required upper-class courses at most U.S. law schools has to do with the duties and liabilities of lawyers. Your law school, or an individual professor, may call this course any number of things: "Professional Responsibility" (inevitably abbreviated "PR"), "Legal Ethics," and "Legal Profession" are the most common names. For several years I have called my class "The Law Governing Lawyers" to emphasize a seemingly obvious, but often misunderstood point. This class is about *law*. There is an extremely interesting academic discipline—a branch of applied ethics—that deals with the relationship between the duties of lawyers and morality more generally. For the most, however, part your required law school course about lawyers' responsibilities will focus on their legal obligations.

You may hear experienced lawyers tell you to consult your moral compass if you encounter an ethical dilemma in practice. With all due respect, that is terrible advice if you are looking to avoid professional discipline or civil liability. While you should of course strive to act as an ordinarily decent person would, you will encounter issues in practice (and in law school!) that demand the same kind of legal research and analysis that you would presumably supply to a client facing an issue of antitrust or securities law. Sometimes the law imposes requirements that differ or add to the reasons that an ordinarily decent person would rely upon. Judicial opinions in disciplinary and civil liability cases are full of lawyers who did the right thing in moral terms, but messed up the law somehow. In no way do I mean to slight the perspective of "real ethics" or "ethics beyond the rules." In fact, it is my primary area of concentration as a scholar. In your required professional responsibility class, however, you will mostly be focusing on the legal duties of lawyers.

Students often experience additional anxiety about this class because it is the first subject tested on the bar exam. It is possible to take the Multistate Professional Responsibility Exam (MPRE) during law school, and all but a handful of states require a passing score on the MPRE for admission to practice law. As a result, students may be taking the MPRE during or immediately after taking Professional Responsibility. This timing understandably adds to the stakes of the class. Yes, there are bar review classes that help you prepare for the MPRE, but it is a fairly sophisticated exam and you'll be better off if you've encountered the material in a class.

Curious about the coverage of the MPRE? Go to the "Preparing for the MPRE" page on the National Conference of Bar Examiners' website:

http://www.ncbex.org/exams/mpre/preparing/

Click the link for "Subject Matter Outline." The specifications for each administration of the MPRE include subject-matter coverage. You can see, for example, that 12–18% of the questions on each test form will pertain to conflicts of interest, 6–12% to competence and malpractice, and so on. If your PR class is light on coverage in some subject area, make sure to focus your MPRE preparation on that area.

PR is the only class you'll have in law school that you are almost guaranteed to use in your practice. If you're a transactional lawyer, you may never use your knowledge of civil procedure. If you do criminal defense work for individuals, it is unlikely that business organizations will come in handy. But it is a near certainty that, no matter what you end up doing, you will have to deal with confidentiality and privilege, conflicts of interest, the allocation of authority in the attorney-client relationship, the duties of competence, diligence, and communication, attorneys' fees, unauthorized practice of law and multijurisdictional practice rules, or other PR doctrines.

Relatedly, one of the challenges for you is to see how legal issues for lawyers can emerge from the work lawyers are performing for clients. At most law schools PR is a 2L or 3L class, and the reason is that the specific PR issues arise out of the lawyer's representation of a client in a litigated matter, deal, or some other work. If you didn't know, for example, that statutes of limitation can be asserted as a defense to a claim not filed within a prescribed period of time, then you may not perceive that a lawyer may be negligent for failing to create and follow an office calendaring system that would provide an alert when a client's case is approaching the expiration of the limitations period. Or, if you're not thinking of the elements of a cause of action for fraud, you may not notice that sending an opinion letter to a lender, knowing that it contains a material misrepresentation of fact, would expose a lawyer to liability. Much of the fun of this class (and yes, I think it's actually a lot of fun, despite the griping you may have heard from other students) comes from the intersection of PR-specific issues with the law and facts of the underlying representation.

LESSON 2: SOURCES OF LAW

You will spend a great deal of time reading and applying state **rules of professional conduct** or, as they will be referred to here, **disciplinary rules**. (Lawyers often refer to the state rules of professional conduct as "ethics rules" but, as discussed in Section 1, you should understand that they are binding law, not summaries of what decent people would do.) Lawyers like to say the legal profession is self-regulating, but that is not entirely accurate. The practice of law in any given state is regulated by rules adopted by state courts—generally the state's highest court, although in always-quirky New York it is the four appellate divisions of the supreme (trial) court. While lawyers (along with judges and law professors) have a significant role in drafting these rules, the profession isn't really self-regulated. Instead, lawyers who violate the rules are subject to discipline by official entities constituted by their state's judiciary. These entities may be called something like "Attorney Regulatory Committee" (Colorado), "Attorney Registration and Disciplinary Commission" (Illinois), or "Office of Disciplinary Counsel" (Washington State). Sometimes they are referred to as the "state bar," but even in those states the ultimate authority to discipline lawyers rests with state courts. Whatever an entity is called in your state, it will be referred to here as the **state disciplinary authority**.

By the way, the MPRE uses certain key words and phrases, and you should get in the habit of using them too. They can be found under the "Preparing the MPRE" tab on the National Conference of Bar Examiners' website:

http://www.ncbex.org/exams/mpre/preparing/

Click the "MPRE Key Words and Phrases" link. For example: "When a question refers to discipline by the 'bar,' 'state bar,' or 'state disciplinary authority,' it refers to the appropriate agency in the jurisdiction with authority to administer the standards for admission to practice and for maintenance of professional competence and integrity."

A lawyer is **subject to discipline** for violating the state disciplinary rules. The MPRE tests the American Bar Association (ABA) **Model Rules of Professional Conduct**. When you are out there in the real world, however, you will be subject to the disciplinary rules of at least the jurisdiction in which you are admitted to practice, and possibly the rules of other jurisdictions as well. See Model Rule 8.5(a), which states that a lawyer is subject to discipline in her admitting jurisdiction as well as any other jurisdiction in which she provides or offers to provide legal services. These state rules may differ from the ABA Model Rules. The Model Rules are, as the name suggests, nothing more than suggestions that may be adopted by state courts. As it happens, they are the product of a great deal of experience. The ABA has been in the business of drafting model standards for professional regulation at least since the promulgation in 1969 of the Model Code of Professional Responsibility. States therefore generally follow the Model Rules pretty closely. (The only exception is California; in substance its law is not far off that of other states, but the language and structure of the rules is very different.) This chapter will cite and discuss the Model Rules, and your instructor probably will as well. Even where state rules generally track the Model Rules, however, there may be important differences in detail, so when you're out in practice, make sure to refer to your state's version of the disciplinary rules.

The Model Rules have black-letter **rules** which state the conditions under which a lawyer will be subject to discipline. They also feature **comments**, which elaborate on the text of the rules. Strictly speaking, the comments are not binding on a disciplinary authority. In some cases, however, the comments are extremely important. For example, Rule 1.9(a) on successive-representation conflicts prohibits taking on a new client where the interests of the new client are materially adverse to the interests of a former client, where the matters are the same or substantially related. When are matters substantially related? Unfortunately, there's no answer in the text of the rule, so you'll have to look to Comment [3] for guidance. The comment says matters are deemed substantially related if the lawyer may have learned confidential information of the former client that could be used to the detriment of the former client in the representation of the new client. That's pretty important, and you wouldn't have known the definition of substantially related matters without reading the comments. If your instructor assigns a particular comment, make sure to pay particular attention to it.

Being disbarred, suspended from practice, or even publicly or privately reprimanded is a bummer. However, it is not the only bad thing that can happen to a lawyer. Lawyers in practice may in fact be much more concerned about **non-disciplinary remedies**. The two most significant are (1) **civil liability** to clients or third parties and (2) **disqualification** from representing a client in pending litigation. The most common instance of civil liability is for malpractice—i.e. negligence in the representation of a client—breach of fiduciary duty, or breach of fiduciary duty. The most common context for disqualification is the representation of a client where the lawyer is burdened with a conflict of interest. There are also other downsides that lawyers worry about, such as contempt of court, fee forfeiture, loss of the protection of the attorney-client privilege, or procedural sanctions such as striking a claim or defense. In all of these cases, sanctions are imposed not by the state disciplinary authority, but by another entity such as the trial court (in the case of disqualification for conflicts of interest) or a court in a separate action for malpractice or some other cause of action asserted by a client or third party.

Lawyers may also be **criminally** liable, to the same extent as non-lawyers, if they engage in the *actus reus* of a crime with the requisite *mens rea*. For example, imagine that a state statute makes it a crime to "knowingly, intentionally and corruptly persuade . . . other persons with intent to cause them to withhold documents from, and alter documents for use in, official proceedings." (That language is taken from a federal obstruction-of-justice statute at issue in *Arthur Andersen LLP v. United States*, 544 U.S. 696 (2005).) A lawyer is representing a health-care company under investigation by the state Attorney General's office for fraud on the state's public benefits program. If the lawyer advises the client to shred a bunch of documents lest they fall into the hands of the Attorney General, that lawyer may be liable under the state statute, just as a non-lawyer would be. *There is no "acting in a legal capacity" defense to criminal liability.*

The relationship between the disciplinary rules and non-disciplinary remedies is a bit complicated. The drafters of the ABA Model Rules disclaim the intent to create a private right of action for violation of the disciplinary rules: "Violation of a Rule should not itself give rise to a cause of action against a lawyer nor should it create any presumption in such a case that a legal duty has been breached." Model Rules Scope ¶ [20]. Of course, the drafters can say that until they're blue in the face, but if a court decides, for example, that it will allow a jury in a lawsuit for breach of fiduciary duty to consider expert testimony that a reasonable lawyer would comply with Rule 1.8(a) when entering into a business transaction with a client, then the rule in effect becomes incorporated into the standard of care. Or, as happens frequently in conflict of interest cases, a court may order disqualification of counsel as a remedy for the prejudice to the adversarial process that might result from a lawyer (or law firm) simultaneously representing parties with adverse interests.

There's nothing mysterious about the incorporation of disciplinary rules into remedies grounded in other areas of law. If you like the analogy, it is no different than consideration of custom in an ordinary negligence case. It can be confusing, however, to see the disciplinary rules cited in non-disciplinary contexts. You'll see a lot of this in conflicts of interest cases. Technically speaking, the authority to disqualify a lawyer from a representation is part of the court's **inherent power** to regulate the conduct of proceedings before it. It is not acting as a disciplinary authority when it considers a motion to disqualify a lawyer. It may, however, refer to the disciplinary rules to determine whether the representation constitutes a conflict of interest under applicable standards. It may cite Rule 1.7 or 1.9 of State X, but strictly speaking it is not bound to follow those rules. As a result, you will sometimes see subtle differences in the standards applied in disciplinary and disqualification cases. Some courts, for example, have permitted law firms to employ screens to cure imputed conflicts caused by newly hired lawyers joining the firm, even though the state version of Rule 1.10(a) did not permit screening. What's the deal with that? A lawyer may be subject to discipline for violating Rule 1.10(a), but would not be subject to disqualification by the trial court for continuing the representation with the screen in place. (See below, Lesson 14, for more on the screening issue.)

This kind of split result does not happen frequently, but it is not unheard of. Pay close attention to the procedural setting of cases you read. If they're disciplinary actions (often captioned something like "*In re Jones*" or "*Attorney Grievance Committee v. Smith*"), then the disciplinary rules supply the governing law. If they're something else, like a negligence lawsuit or a motion to disqualify, then the law is given by the underlying state law of torts, agency, contracts, fiduciary duty, or the trial court's inherent power. Those standards may, in turn, incorporate the disciplinary rules by reference, but they need not. Most of the time the applicable law is clear, but please get in the habit of noting it.

Some of this complexity is reflected in the **Restatement (Third) of the Law Governing Lawyers**. Your instructor may or may not want you to refer to provisions of the Restatement along with the Model Rules. (For what it's worth, it is used as authority by the drafters of the MPRE.) The Restatement takes into consideration not only the disciplinary rules, but also the applicable law of torts, contracts, agency, evidence, procedure, and criminal and constitutional law. Like all Restatements, it does not merely summarize the law, but represents the best view of the American Law Institute on what the law is and what it should be. In most cases, the Model Rules and Restatement are consistent, but there may be differences. For example, the definition of confidential information in Model Rule 1.6(a) is "information relating to the representation of a client." Confidential information is defined in Restatement § 59 as "information relating to the representation of a client, *other than information that is generally known*." Most of the time this distinction won't make a difference, since if information is publicly known, the client is unlikely to gripe to a disciplinary authority about the lawyer's disclosure of it. But there may be a case in which it matters, so make sure you notice any differences between the Restatement and the Model Rules.

There are some issues in which no Model Rule exists. Remember, the Model Rules and their state equivalents are all about professional discipline. A lawyer may be disciplined, for example, for disclosing confidential client information. But if you want to know whether, in those circumstances, the attorney also caused a waiver of the attorney-client privilege, you won't find the answer in the Model Rules. The reason is that the attorney-client privilege is governed by the law of evidence. The Restatement does take evidence law into account, however, and you will find many provisions (starting with Section 68) dealing with the attorney-client privilege. Similarly, because the Model Rules presuppose the existence of an attorney-client relationship, there is no provision in the Model Rules governing the formation of an attorney-client relationship. You will have to look to Restatement § 14 for that standard. Unauthorized practice of law (UPL) rules, similarly, regulate the activities of non-lawyers, so you wouldn't expect them to be in the Model Rules (although there is a rule prohibiting lawyers from *assisting* non-lawyers in the authorized practice of law, or from practicing law in a jurisdiction in which they are not authorized—see Model Rule 5.5(a)). You must look to state law for rules on UPL.

What You Need to Know:

1. State rules of professional conduct, or disciplinary rules, are adopted by state appellate courts and form the basis for professional discipline, such as disbarment, suspension, or reprimand.

2. Lawyers are also subject to civil liability under agency, tort, and contract law, as well as criminal

liability. They are also subject to regulation by the courts in which they practice, under the court's inherent authority.

3. The disciplinary rules may be relevant to other law, but other law need not follow the disciplinary rules exactly. Sorting out the sources and content of all law bearing on the activities of lawyers is one of the major challenges of this course.

LESSON 3: OVERARCHING POLICIES

Think back to your first-year classes. The material probably started to make more sense once you could see the effect of the policy goals the law was aiming at. For example, in very general terms, tort law seeks to provide people with a measure of protection for their physical and emotional security by creating incentives to take reasonable care, while not unduly driving up the cost of useful goods and services like consumer products and health care. That means, for example, that a defendant is not legally responsible for all accidents that can be causally traced back to its actions, but only those that are reasonably foreseeable. Why the foreseeability limitation? Because the law is supposed to influence behavior, to create incentives to take reasonable care, and if a consequence is impossible to foresee, there is nothing that the defendant could have done to safeguard against it.

You get the point: Keeping policies in mind will help make sense of legal doctrines and guide you in applying them. What are those general policies in Professional Responsibility? Here's a list of some of the most important ones:

The lawyer-client relationship is highly **fiduciary** in nature. That means the lawyer must always ensure that the client's interests come first, and that the lawyer is not being influenced by some personal interest, or the interest of other clients. An implication of the fiduciary nature of the relationship is that it is not the client's responsibility to ensure that she is not being taken advantage of by the lawyer. *Caveat emptor* may be a principle of commercial relationships, but it does not apply to the lawyer-client relationship. A lawyer must, for example, ensure that a client fully understands the terms of a fee agreement or any other contractual provision affecting the client's interests. If the client doesn't understand some bit of legalese like "retaining lien," the lawyer must explain it. Another implication of the fiduciary relationship is that the client gets to define the objectives of the representation. See Restatement § 16(1). The lawyer then provides competent and diligent assistance in accomplishing those objectives.

Lawyers owe clients some fairly demanding **duties**. These include competence, diligence, communication, candid advice, and absolute discretion with respect to confidential information (no blabbing secrets, no self-dealing with confidential information, and no using confidences to help other clients). Some of these duties may be modified, or the client may waive compliance with them, but only if the lawyer provides the client will full information about the risks and benefits of modifying the background duties. Any change from the default duties stated in the rules of professional conduct requires **informed consent**. This is a defined term in the rules and an extremely important concept in this area. It means full disclosure, full information, and full appreciation of the risks.

Generally speaking, the client comes first. See the first two points about the fiduciary, demanding nature of the attorney-client relationship. However, a lawyer is an officer of the court, and that means certain duties are also owed to the tribunal. (Tribunals include not only courts but arbitrators and administrative agencies acting in an adjudicative capacity—think of something like the Board of Immigration Appeals. See Rule 1.0(m) for this definition.) The most important duty owed to the tribunal is **candor**. A lawyer may not participate in the introduction of false testimony or evidence into a court record and, in some cases, may even be required to take steps to correct false evidence that got into the record without the lawyer's participation. The details get a bit tricky here (see Lesson 16, below), but as a rough guide, if duties to the client and duties to the court conflict, the latter win out.

Lawyers also owe some duties to non-clients and non-tribunals, generally referred to as **third parties**. Lawyers don't owe much to a litigation adversary, but there are still rules imposing certain standards of fairness in litigation. The situation is more complicated in transactional practice, where the duties owed to other parties to a deal are largely a matter of applicable tort (i.e. fraud) and contract law. For example, a lawyer representing a borrower who provides an opinion letter to a lender, certifying the borrower's compliance with certain legal requirements, may be liable to the lender for negligence in the preparation of the opinion (e.g. failing to investigate other liens on the client property used by the lender as security for the loan). Lawyers sometimes see this as a kind of divided-loyalty problem, but it's not technically a conflict. There may be cases in which the problem for lawyers is to harmonize the duties they owe to clients and to third parties. There's no absolute priority of client duties over others.

A final policy issue, which some teachers may spend time on in class, is the relationship between the rules of professional conduct and more general principles of ethics. Presumably all decent, well-intentioned people recognize reasons to be trustworthy, keep their promises, avoid lying and related forms of trickery and deception, refrain from humiliating and harassing others, and so on. These are principles of ordinary morality or ethics (some philosophers distinguish these two words, but most don't) which apply to all people simply by virtue of being moral agents. These duties persist even when people act in professional roles. Lawyers are people, too! Sometimes it may happen, however, that the *legal* duties that arise from the lawyer's professional role and the lawyer-client relationship require a lawyer to do something that appears to be a violation of ordinary-person moral requirements. A common example is, in the course of representing a criminal defendant, cross-examining a witness the lawyer knows (or at least has very good reasons to believe) is telling the truth, in an effort to discredit the witness's testimony. This may have the effect of humiliating the witness, who has been made to look unreliable or untruthful in front of the jury. Despite the general background moral duty not to humiliate others, most lawyers would believe themselves to be permitted or required by their professional duties to engage in the cross-examination (assuming it is in the client's best interests, the lawyer believes it won't backfire by making the lawyer look like a jerk, and so on). You may also read cases like

Spaulding v. Zimmerman, 116 N.W.2d 704 (Minn. 1962), which present a conflict between the professional duty of confidentiality and the possibility of avoiding harm to others by disclosing protected confidential information.

This general problem, known as **role-differentiated morality**, is interesting as a theoretical matter and may be important to your professional responsibility teacher. (Shameless plug: I have an introductory book on the subject, called *Ethics and Law: An Introduction*, published by Cambridge University Press—check it out!) There are a number of law review articles and books considering role morality in depth. In an overview like this, perhaps the most that can be said is that the law, including the law prescribing duties for lawyers, does not purport to exhaust the content of morality. Even if there is a legal obligation to do X, someone may ask whether a decent, ethically conscientious person would do X. (X might be something like cross-examining a witness known to be telling the truth, in an effort to make the witness appear mistaken or unreliable.) Maybe the answer is yes, but if X is the sort of thing that decent, ethically conscientious people generally do not do, there had better be a good reason for doing what the law requires. Giving these sorts of reasons is the task of theoretical legal ethics, which may be within your professional responsibility teacher's learning objectives.

What You Need to Know:

1. The lawyer-client relationship is a highly fiduciary one. The lawyer's most basic duty is to act with reasonable competence and diligence to further the client's lawful objectives, as the client defines them.
2. Lawyers owe strict duties of candor to tribunals. These duties make take precedence over obligations owed to the client, such as confidentiality.
3. In addition to duties to clients and courts, lawyers also owe some duties to third parties under background law such as the law of fraud.
4. Role-differentiated morality is the potential divergence between the duties that apply to the occupant of a professional role, such as a lawyer,

and the moral considerations that apply generally to all moral agents.

LESSON 4: FORMATION AND TERMINATION OF AN ATTORNEY-CLIENT RELATIONSHIP

You may have heard that British barristers follow what is called the "cab-rank" rule. In this system, lawyers are like taxicabs waiting at the airport to pick up riders. They take clients in the order they come, and have no discretion to reject clients. The only grounds for refusing to represent a client are conflicts of interest or lack of competence in the relevant field of law. That's not exactly how it works in practice in the U.K., since barristers get clients through solicitors, not directly, and solicitors and barristers' clerks can work together to steer clients to the right barrister. But I mention this system because it represents an ideal that is respected in the American legal profession. That is the ideal that all clients deserve representation and lawyers should not refuse to represent a client due to disagreement with the client's goals or values.

Lawyers in the United States have almost unlimited **discretion** in selecting clients. They can decline to represent a client because they're too busy, don't have expertise in the area, think the client won't pay its fees or may be a pain in the tuches, or really any reason at all. (There was a decision from a state human rights agency in the early 2000's holding that lawyers are subject to state anti-discrimination laws in client selection. It's called *Stropnicky v. Nathanson* if you want to hunt for it on Westlaw. As far as I know it's the only decision so holding.) The only exception is for lawyers who have agreed to accept court appointments to represent indigent parties. Those lawyers may not decline appointment without good cause. See Model Rule 6.2.

Lawyers aren't conscripted into service. They agree to represent clients. True, sometimes lawyers can be appointed by a court to represent an indigent client, but for the most part, the lawyer-client relationship is entirely voluntary. In the usual case, there is an **expressly** formed attorney-client relationship, with disclosure of its terms, maybe some negotiation, perhaps a signed retention agreement and payment of fees. The usual case is fairly uninteresting. The more interesting cases involve **implied** attorney-client relationships. In these cases, the required intent to form a relationship is implied from the conduct of the parties.

In a famous case called *Togstad v. Vesely, Otto, Miller & Keefe*, 291 N.W.2d 686 (Minn. 1980), which will be in PR casebooks until the end of time, a prospective client came to a lawyer's office. Mrs. Togstad's husband had been seriously injured in what may have been an episode of medical malpractice, and she wanted to know—as she put it—whether she had a case. She explained the facts to the lawyer who later recalled saying, "I don't think you have a case *that we'd be interested in taking*." Medical malpractice cases are expensive, risky propositions, and the firm simply may not have wanted to commit its resources in that way. The problem was, the prospective client heard something different. She heard the lawyer say, "I don't think you have a case." In other words, she thought he had listened to her description of the event and formed a legal opinion that there was no medical malpractice. She didn't bring a lawsuit against the doctor and the statute of limitations ran on her medical malpractice claim.

When she later found out her medical malpractice claim would have likely been a winner, she sued the lawyer for giving her bad advice. The lawyer responded by saying, in effect, "Who are you to me?" There was no attorney-client relationship, the lawyer argued, and thus no duty to use reasonable care when giving advice to Mrs. Togstad. But the trial court allowed the jury to resolve a factual issue underlying the duty determination: What would a reasonable person in Mrs. Togstad's position believe, based on what she testified the lawyer had said to her? The jury found that she could have believed the lawyer had considered the facts of her case and rendered an opinion.

In a footnote the court stated that it doesn't really matter whether the professional duties owed by the lawyer to Mrs. Togstad arose as a matter of tort or contract law. On a tort theory, Mrs. Togstad would have to show that the lawyer rendered advice in circumstances in which it was reasonably foreseeable that, if the lawyer did so negligently, Mrs. Togstad would be injured. Under a contract theory, the question would be whether there was either an agreement or promissory estoppel. The Restatement now summarizes the formation rule in Section 14. This isn't the best-drafted provision in the Restatement. Here's my summary of the formation rule: An attorney-client relationship is formed either if:

1. Both sides expressly agree, or
2. The would-be client does something that a reasonable lawyer would understand as a manifestation of intent that the lawyer provide legal services and either
   a. The lawyer does something that manifests the lawyer's agreement to provide legal services or
   b. The lawyer fails to clearly manifest failure to agree (i.e. "I'm not representing you") in circumstances in which a reasonable person would rely on the lawyer to provide legal services.

Pretty ugly, I know. Maybe it's best to give an example. This is adapted from Illustration 4 to Restatement § 14. Defendant receives a summons from the state Department of Natural Resources, stating that his factory is out of compliance with an emissions permit and, if no answer is received in 30 days, Defendant will be subject to substantial civil penalties. Defendant calls Lawyer, who practices environmental litigation. Lawyer tells Defendant, "Bring a copy of the summons to my office and I'll get back to you and let you know whether we can take your case." Defendant hears nothing from Lawyer until a day before the answer is due, when Lawyer calls and says, "Mmm, yeah, I don't think this is a case we're interested in handling." As the Restatement rightly concludes, there was an attorney-client relationship formed here. Defendant relied on Lawyer by not hiring other counsel, and to do so was reasonable given Lawyer's practice specialization and what he communicated to Defendant.

Termination of the attorney-client relationship is subject to Model Rule 1.16. There are a couple of features of that rule to notice. First, pay attention to the distinction between mandatory and permissive withdrawal, in Rules 1.16(a) and (b). There aren't many grounds for mandatory withdrawal, but be sure you know what they are. The permissive-withdrawal section is quite broad. As long as withdrawal can be accomplished without material adverse effect on the client, or one of the enumerated grounds in Rule 1.16(b)(2)–(7) is satisfied, the lawyer can withdraw. One qualification on withdrawal is that, if the lawyer is representing the client in a litigated matter, the lawyer must obtain the court's permission to withdraw. See Rule 1.16(c). Suppose a lawyer is representing a client on an hourly fee arrangement in a breach of contract lawsuit. The client stops paying the lawyer. The lawyer concludes, reasonably, that continuing to represent the client would be an unreasonable financial burden, and therefore the lawyer may withdraw under Rule 1.16(b)(6). The lawyer files a motion to withdraw as counsel with the court before whom the litigation is proceeding. The judge says, "Cry me a river, counsel—you agreed to represent this client, and you took the risk of not getting paid. I'm ordering you to stay in. Motion denied." Despite having permission under Rule 1.16(b) to *seek* to withdraw, the lawyer is stuck in the representation due to the trial court's refusal to grant permission to withdraw. (This happens all the time, by the way.)

What You Need to Know:

1. For lawyers not accepting court-appointed representation, there is no legal requirement to represent any given client, and no legal constraints on reasons for turning down a representation.
2. An attorney-client relationship may be formed expressly or by implication from the conduct of the parties. Implied attorney-client relationship can be formed in circumstances in which a reasonable person would believe that an attorney has agreed to provide legal services.
3. Withdrawal from representation can be mandatory or permissive. The grounds for permissive withdrawal are fairly broad. In any case in which the attorney is representing the client in litigation, however, the attorney must obtain the permission of the court to withdraw.

LESSON 5: ALLOCATION OF DECISION-MAKING AUTHORITY WITHIN THE RELATIONSHIP

The attorney-client relationship is an **agency** relationship. In any principal-agent relationship, one party (the principal) appoints another (the agent) to act on her behalf and subject to her control. It is a voluntary relationship, so the parties have a great deal of latitude to specify the terms of their relationship. I like the term used by English solicitors: The client *instructs* the lawyer. That's a good way to think about it. The client hires the lawyer and instructs her to pursue certain objectives. But the client, as someone who presumably is not an expert in the law, cannot instruct the lawyer on how to pursue the client's objectives. That is within the expertise of the lawyer, so the lawyer should have substantial discretion to select the means through which the lawyer will pursue the client's ends.

That division of labor is recognized by Model Rule 1.2(a). The client gets to make decisions about the **objectives** of the representation. Certain decisions are so important that they are, by definition, included within the objectives of the representation and are solely for the client to make. In civil litigation, a lawyer is required (note the "shall abide" language) to respect her client's decision to accept or reject a settlement offer. In criminal defense representation, the client has certain fundamental constitutional rights, such as deciding whether to plead guilty, waive a jury trial, or to take the stand, and the lawyer must abide by the client's decision regarding these matters. Note that these decisions are not the only ones that are within the client's exclusive authority to decide. *Any* decision that goes to the objectives of the representation is for the client alone to make.

Regarding the **means** of representation, it's true that lawyers have expertise that many clients do not, but the rules still contemplate that the lawyer and client will deliberate about how the representation will be carried out. See the language in Rule 1.2(a) directing the lawyer to consult with the client about the means, and see Rule 1.14(a)(2) requiring the lawyer to *reasonably* consult with the client about means. The key word here is "reasonably." It would drive the client crazy, and be pointless, to consult about every minor procedural decision that the lawyer must make—how broadly should we write this request for production? should we take the deposition of that witness, or is it enough to interview him? should we raise that evidentiary issue in a motion *in limine* or just deal with it if it comes up at trial? Unless the client is a lawyer, or represented by in-house counsel, there is no need to raise technical issues with the client. But some "means" issues may be important enough to warrant discussing with the client. Adding a claim or defense, joining a party, or pursuing a line of discovery may affect the cost of the representation and may also potentially have a sufficiently impact on the outcome that client deserves to be involved in the decision-making process. What if the lawyer and client disagree? See Comment [2] to Rule 1.2, which basically says, "work it out." If the disagreement becomes so intractable that it rises to the level of a *fundamental* disagreement, the lawyer can withdraw from the representation. See Rule 1.16(b)(4). Otherwise, like the characters in Sartre's *No Exit*, the lawyer and client are stuck dealing with each other forever.

The Model Rules do not attempt to restate general agency law, but agency principles are extremely important in the law governing lawyers. The Restatement of Agency goes into much more detail, but for the purposes of a professional responsibility class the treatment of agency law in Sections 20–33 should be sufficient. A couple of highlights: Authority (or power) in an agency relationship may be conferred expressly or by implication, it may be inherent in the role of principal or agent, and the agent may be apparent authority due to acts of the principal. These agency-law principles are often invoked when there is a question about the authorization of one of the parties to do an act that binds the other. As an example of **express** authorization, recall that the client has the exclusive authority to make decisions regarding settlement. That's true, but the client can also authorize the lawyer to make or accept a settlement offer. Let's say a lawyer representing the defendant is going to a mediation. The client may say, "I authorize you to offer up to $75,000, but no more, to settle the case." If the defendant's lawyer offers $50,000 and the plaintiff accepts, the agreement to settle is binding. If, on the other hand, the client had not authorized the lawyer to make a settlement offer, the settlement would not be binding. Wise lawyers obtain verification that the lawyer in fact has authorization to settle. See Restatement § 27, cmt. d.

Implied authorization flows from the overall purpose of the representation. Suppose a client retains a lawyer to negotiate the sale of her business. The lawyer is required to proceed in a manner reasonably calculated to advance the client's objective of selling her business, at a reasonable price, and subject to reasonable terms. See Restatement § 16(1). Along the way, the lawyer has to a whole bunch of different things, including making representations and disclosure to potential buyers. The client should be deemed to have authorized these various acts, which are means to the ultimate end of selling her business. The lawyer therefore has implied authorization to do things that further the client's objective. Implied authorization frequently arises in connection with the duty of confidentiality. Ordinarily a lawyer would be required to refrain from disclosing any information relating to the representation of the client. See Model Rule 1.6(a). That includes details about the seller's business. To the extent this information must be disclosed in order to permit prospective buyers to evaluate the business, however, the client has impliedly authorized (by directing the lawyer to obtain a buyer for her business) the lawyer to disclose some information that would otherwise be confidential. See the reference in Rule 1.6(a) to implied authorization.

The tricky category is **apparent** authority. The key to understanding apparent authority is that it arises when the principal does something that a third party would reasonably understand as conferring the power on the agent to do something that would otherwise be within the principal's power. See Restatement § 27, cmt. b. Many apparent authority cases involve some kind of limitation on the lawyer's authority that is known to the lawyer but not to third parties with whom the lawyer is dealing. See the illustrations in Restatement § 27, cmt. c.

Finally we have **inherent** authority, which is simply authority that cannot be waived or modified by agreement of the parties. The most important area of inherent authority for lawyers is the power (and indeed the duty) to refuse to "perform, counsel, or assist future or ongoing acts in the representation that the lawyer reasonably believes to be unlawful." Restatement § 23(1).

What You Need to Know:

1. Generally speaking, the client makes decisions concerning the **objectives** of representation, while the lawyer has discretion with respect to the **means** by which the representation is carried out. Certain important decisions, such as whether to settle a civil matter, are presumptively for the client to make.
2. Lawyers must communicate with their clients regarding the means of representation.
3. A lawyer is an agent for the client (called the "principal" in agency law). As an agent, the lawyer's power to act depends on lawful delegation from the principal. This grant of authority can be express, implied, or apparent. Lawyers retain the inherent authority to refuse to perform unlawful acts.

LESSON 6: ATTORNEYS' FEES, TRANSACTIONS WITH CLIENTS, AND HANDLING CLIENT FUNDS

An attorney's fee, and any charges for expenses, must not be **unreasonable**. See Model Rule 1.5(a). Notice the double-negative. "Not unreasonable" is not the same as "reasonable," is it? This wording suggests a fairly deferential approach by disciplinary authorities to attorneys' fees. However, discipline isn't everything. A court may deem an attorney's fee unreasonable as a matter of contract law. (My colleagues who teach contracts tell me the fee term of the engagement agreement may be deemed unconscionable, but more likely to violate an implied term of reasonableness in the contract.) As for discipline, the rule includes an eight-factor test for the reasonableness. The Restatement has a simpler three-factor test that I think does a better job of capturing the factors that influence courts in determining whether a fee is unreasonable as a matter of contract law. See Restatement § 34 cmt. c. Both Model Rule 1.5(a)(3) and the Restatement comment mention the fee customarily charged in the community for similar legal services. That seems to be the most important factor in many fee disputes and disciplinary proceedings.

There is a well-known case in many casebooks called *In re Fordham*, 668 N.E.2d 816 (Mass. 1996). It involved a highly experienced civil litigator who offered to represent a defendant in a relatively straightforward criminal case alleging driving under the influence. The lawyer had never handled a criminal defense matter, nor appeared in this court. He and his associates spent an inordinate amount of time working on the case, but obtained a good result for the client. The final bill was in the neighborhood of $50,000, while most criminal defense lawyers in the community charged around $4,000–$5,000 for that type of representation. The good result and the lawyer's experience would appear to count in favor of the fee, under Model Rule 1.5(a)(4) and (a)(7). But what sunk the lawyer in this case was that he was essentially charging to client to educate himself on how to practice criminal law in state court. Also, the client probably did not appreciate the significance of the specialization of law practice. The lawyer was in fact a highly accomplished antitrust litigator, but the client likely did not realize that he was no more suited to doing criminal defense work than a recent law school graduate. (Okay, maybe that's a bit of an overstatement—the lawyer was smart and experienced and trainable, but still, he would have had to learn a lot of local rules, procedures, and substantive law to represent the client competently.) On the Restatement analysis, it's clearer that the lawyer's fee is unreasonable. Restatement § 34, cmt. c note that the client should make a free and informed choice, and that the fee should fall "within the range commonly charged by other lawyers in similar representations." In practice I tend to see professional **custom** as the most important factor bearing on the reasonableness of an attorney's fee.

The reasonableness requirement in Model Rule 1.5(a) pertains to all fee arrangements, whether hourly, contingent, flat, reverse-contingent, hybrid, or whatever. Remember that when analyzing contingent fee agreements under Model Rule

1.5(c). It's easy to get caught up in the specific disclosure requirement of that rule and forget to ask the reasonableness question.

Contingent fees are those in which the amount of the lawyer's fee depends on the result obtained for the client. The most familiar are the "no recovery, no fee" arrangements customary in plaintiffs' personal-injury representation. A lawyer may charge one-third of the client's recovery, by way of judgment or settlement. The lawyer may also advance the expenses of representation (sometimes called "hard costs"), including things like filing fees, charges for court reporters, and expert witness fees. Under Model Rule 1.5(c), a lawyer must inform the client of whether the fee calculation will be on the gross amount of recovery, or will be net of the cost of expenses advanced by the lawyer. Read Rule 1.5(c) carefully and make sure to follow all the disclosure requirements, including that the agreement be in a writing signed by the client.

When thinking about contingent fees, remember that they compensate a lawyer for three things: (1) *services*, i.e. the value of her time; (2) *financing*, i.e. advancing the value of her time and the hard costs of representation; and (3) *insurance*, i.e. bearing the risk of non-recovery. Because of the risk-bearing or insurance function performed by contingent fee financing, in some cases it may appear that the attorney is receiving an unjustified windfall. In other cases, however, the attorney may be stuck working away for many months or years on a case that does not produce much of a payoff, and of course some cases lose at trial or on a dispositive motion. The reasonableness analysis of contingent fees has to take all three of these functions into account.

Lawyers may not charge contingent fees for representing criminal defendants, or for work on a matrimonial matter in which the fee is contingent upon securing a divorce or upon the amount of a property or support judgment. Model Rule 1.5(d). The idea is to avoid creating a severe misalignment of interests with the client. In a criminal defense matter, for example, if the lawyer gets paid only if the client is acquitted at trial, the lawyer may have an incentive to talk to client out of accepting a favorable plea offer. Note, however, that an attorney may accept a contingent fee for representing a client seeking to recover on an existing judgment requiring the payment of alimony or child support. See Model Rule 1.5, cmt. [6].

Lawyers may share fees with other lawyers, provided that either the division is proportional to the work they perform for the client or the lawyers retain joint responsibility (i.e. continue to be liable to the client for malpractice). Model Rule 1.5(e). This type of fee division is commonly encountered in referral arrangements in plaintiffs'-side tort litigation. Many lawyers who advertise widely are basically operating referral services. They accept the representation of clients, try to settle many of the cases quickly, and refer out the cases they are unable to settle. They will seek to retain some portion of the judgment or settlement eventually obtained by the other lawyer. That's fine as long as the referring firm retains joint responsibility for the representation. (Generally the amount of recovery exceeds the value of the services provided by the referring firm.) In addition, the client must be fully informed of the details of the fee-sharing arrangement and provide informed consent, confirmed in writing. Note that this rule pertains only to sharing fees with another lawyer. Sharing fees with non-lawyers is absolutely prohibited. See Model Rule 5.4(a).

If a fee arrangement with a client includes any "ownership, possessor, security, or other pecuniary interest adverse to a client," it is subject to the **business-transaction** conflicts rule. See Model Rule 1.8(a). That rule has demanding disclosure and written consent requirements, and also insists that the transaction be substantively fair and reasonable from the client's point of view. An example of a fee provision triggering this rule in an individual-client representation would be a promissory note given by the client to secure payment of the fee, or a second mortgage on the client's house. A more "business-y" version of that transaction would be a lawyer representing a startup company who agrees to provide legal services in exchange for some percentage of the client's stock. It is permissible to do this, hoping the client will be the next Google and the lawyer will be a zillionaire, but the transaction must satisfy the requirements of Model Rule 1.8(a). The reasonableness requirement of Rule 1.5(a) applies to stock-for-fee arrangements, just as it does to any other type of fee.

Lawyers must use extreme care with client **funds** or tangible property. If they hold valuable property for clients (jewelry, art, antiques, etc.) it must be appropriately safeguarded and held separately from the lawyer's own property. Model Rule 1.15(a). The more common situation involves client funds. Suppose a lawyer agrees to represent a client in a divorce proceeding, charging her usual hourly rate of \$250/hr. In order to secure the payment of the fee, the lawyer asks the client to deposit \$5,000 as a retainer. The term "retainer" has a variety of meanings—see Restatement § 34, cmt. e—but in this case it is an advance against future work to be performed by the lawyer. As such, it does not yet belong to the lawyer. It is the client's property until earned, and therefore must be kept separate from the lawyer's property. This separation occurs through the use of trust accounts. See Model Rule 1.15(c). As the fees are earned, the funds may be transferred from the trust account to the lawyer's office account. Often this occurs monthly, with the lawyer sending the client a summary of tasks performed and time spent.

Another situation in which lawyers must carefully separate client funds from their own occurs when a lawyer receives the proceeds of a **settlement**. Suppose the lawyer has a 1/3 contingent fee agreement, and receives \$30,000 in settlement proceeds from the defendant. The proper course of action is for the lawyer to deposit the entire \$30,000 in her trust account, write a check from the trust account to her office account for the \$10,000 attorneys' fees portion, and write a check for \$20,000 to the client. The lawyer must also promptly notify anyone who has an interest in funds received by the lawyer. See Model Rule 1.15(d).

For the purposes of your PR course you probably just need to know the basics of trust-accounting rules and practices, most importantly that client funds must be held separately. In practice, however, this is a huge disciplinary and liability risk for lawyers, who must be extremely careful to comply *exactly* with state trust-accounting rules (which vary quite a bit in detail).

What You Need to Know:

1. The requirement of reasonableness applies to all fee arrangements.
2. There are a lot of detailed disclosure and consent requirements in the fee rules, all for the protection of clients. Lawyers must use extreme care in establishing fee arrangements and disclosing their terms. If an agreement involves a financial interest adverse to a client, such as a promissory note or an ownership interest in the client's business, it also must comply with Rule 1.8(a).
3. Client property and funds must be separated scrupulously from the lawyer's own property. Money belonging to a client stays in a trust account until it's earned.

LESSON 7: COMPETENCE AND MALPRACTICE

Lawyers owe duties of **reasonable care** to their clients. More precisely, they owe the care that a reasonable *professional* would provide in similar circumstances. The cause of action for legal malpractice is very similar to what you probably learned about in first-year torts as the cause of action for medical malpractice. Many lawsuits brought under the general umbrella term "legal malpractice" can be classified as claims for **negligence** or breach of **fiduciary duty**. In most cases it doesn't really make any substantive difference, although in some states it may affect the applicable statute of limitations. See Restatement § 49, cmt. c. For the purposes of your Professional Responsibility class, however, you can probably treat a legal malpractice claim as one for negligence.

In any negligence action, the plaintiff must show four elements: Duty, Breach (that is, failure to comply with the applicable Standard of Care); Causation; and Damages. Organizing your thinking around these elements and you will pick up all the issues that might arise in a legal malpractice case.

The element of **duty** differs a bit from most other areas of negligence liability, in that in most cases a duty of care runs only to those with whom the lawyer is in **privity** of contract. Remember the *MacPherson v. Buick* case in torts, where Judge Cardozo made a big deal of expanding liability for defective products beyond privity of contract? Well, for the most part that's not the case in legal malpractice. In most cases a duty requires an attorney-client relationship. Remember from the discussion of the *Togstad* case that it can be a question of fact whether there is an attorney-client relationship. If not, a lawyer owes no duties of reasonable care with two narrow exceptions: (1) A lawyer who invites a non-client to rely on the lawyer's opinion or provision of legal services, and (2) the intended beneficiaries of the lawyer's service to the client. An example of (1) would be a lawyer who provides an opinion letter to a lender, certifying that the lawyer has checked and found no liens or encumbrances on the property the client (the borrower) is using as collateral for a loan. See the well-known case of *Greycas, Inc. v. Proud*, 826 F.2d 1560 (7th Cir. 1987). Typical cases falling within exception (2) involve a lawyer who prepares a will or trust instrument for a testator, with the intention of conveying property to certain beneficiaries. If the lawyer messes up somehow—e.g. by blowing the Rule Against Perpetuities—the beneficiaries may sue the lawyer for negligence, even though they weren't the lawyer's client. The idea is that allowing the beneficiaries to bring the action reinforces the duty that the lawyer owed to the now deceased testator. The somewhat notorious case of *Lucas v. Hamm*, 56 Cal.2d 583 (1961), was one of the first judicial decisions recognizing lawyer liability to non-clients. It is frequently mocked for its additional holding that the Rule Against Perpetuities is a "pitfall for the unwary" and a reasonable lawyer might still mess it up. That aspect of the case has been distinguished away, and now a competent lawyer will be expected to comply with the Rule.

Speaking of reasonable care, let's move on to the element of **breach** of duty or the applicable **standard of care**. Just as in medical malpractice, the standard isn't what an ordinary reasonable person would do, but what a reasonable *professional* would do. The Restatement says lawyers must act with the "competence and diligence normally exercised by lawyers in similar circumstances." Restatement § 52(1). In other words, *custom* is dispositive of the standard of care. (Compare the result in conventional negligence cases, including Learned Hand's famous *T.J. Hooper* opinion.) Because this is the standard, the plaintiff in a legal malpractice case must generally introduce expert testimony to establish the standard and the defendant's failure to comply with it. The standard of care is generally determined on a statewide basis, so a lawyer in Buffalo could testify that a lawyer in Schenectady had been negligent. A lawyer who holds herself out as a specialist—for example, claiming to be "an expert in international taxation issues"—may be held to the heightened standard of care of lawyers who are also experts in that field. Rules of professional conduct may be relevant to the standard of care, but courts generally do not give them *per se* effect, comparable to safety statutes in ordinary negligence cases.

The biggest barrier to recovery for most plaintiffs in legal malpractice cases is the element of **causation**. Remember that to show cause in fact, a plaintiff must prove that it is more likely than not that, but for the defendant's negligence, the outcome would have been different. That means a client must show not only that the lawyer's conduct departed from the standard of care of other professionals in similar circumstances, but that if the lawyer hadn't been negligent, she would not have experienced the loss. To show how difficult it can be for plaintiffs to prove causation, think back to the *Togstad* case referred to in the lesson on formation of the attorney-client relationship. Remember that Mrs. Togstad thought she was hiring the lawyer to pursue a medical malpractice case against a neurosurgeon, whose allegedly negligent treatment injured Mrs. Togstad's husband. Assuming there is an attorney-client relationship, and therefore a duty of care, the causation element of Mrs. Togstad's legal malpractice claim would go like this:

> If the lawyer hadn't been negligent (by advising me that I didn't have a viable medical malpractice case), I would have brought the medical malpractice case and recovered against the neurosurgeon.

But in order to prove she would have recovered against the neurosurgeon, Mrs. Togstad would, in effect, have to prove the underlying medical malpractice case. That means that, as part of her legal malpractice case, she would need to introduce all of the expert testimony that would be required to prove the underlying claim in the medical malpractice case. Otherwise she would be unable to show that the lawyer's negligence deprived her of something of value. This is known as the "case within a case" analysis. *See* Restatement § 53, cmt. b.

The same analysis of causation applies to transactional cases: A client must prove that, but for the lawyer's negligence, she would have gotten a better deal. *See, e.g.*, Viner v. Sweet, 70 P.3d 1046 (Cal. 2003). It also applies to civil lawsuits against criminal defense lawyers. Proving causation in criminal defense cases is a real bear. Courts generally require the client to either obtain exoneration through direct appeal or collateral review, or to prove actual innocence of the charged offense. Otherwise, they reason, the cause of the bad result of which the client is complaining is the client's crime, not the lawyer's negligence.

If the plaintiff can show duty, breach, and causation, recoverable **damages** in a legal malpractice case can be significant. You may be surprised to learn that there is no requirement in any state, except Oregon, that lawyers carry malpractice insurance. Many states don't even require that lawyers disclose to clients whether they have malpractice insurance.

What You Need to Know:

1. You can think of medical malpractice as basically a tuned-up negligence case, with a few distinctive features, such as the privity requirement for duty and the necessity of introducing expert testimony to establish the standard of care.
2. The causation element is a significant impediment to clients' recovery for negligence.

LESSON 8: SIXTH AMENDMENT INEFFECTIVE ASSISTANCE OF COUNSEL

The duties of a criminal defense lawyer are given by the same tort and agency-law principles that apply to civil litigators. However, as a matter of malpractice law—specifically, the requirement of showing but-for causation, it is difficult to establish the liability of a criminal defense lawyer for damages.

Practically speaking, therefore, the most important source of guidance for criminal defense lawyers is the client's right, under the Sixth Amendment to the U.S. Constitution, to the effective assistance of counsel.

The Supreme Court defined the standard for showing ineffective assistance of counsel in *Strickland v. Washington*, 466 U.S. 668 (1984). On direct appeal, state post-conviction review, or in a federal habeas corpus proceeding, the client must make two showings: (1) deficient **performance** by the attorney and (2) resulting **prejudice**.

A court will evaluate the performance of an attorney using a reasonableness standard, under "prevailing professional norms." The rules of professional conduct may be relevant to establishing prevailing professional norms, but reviewing courts are really applying an objective standards reasonableness, as determined by practices in the relevant professional community. For example, suppose a lawyer advises a client to plead guilty without also advising the client that the guilty plea would subject him to deportation under federal immigration law. Was the lawyer's performance deficient? In a case raising this issue, the Supreme Court considered the weight of prevailing professional norms and concluded that the attorney's advice fell below the constitutionally required standard. Padilla v. Kentucky, 559 U.S. 356 (2010).

To show prejudice under the second prong of *Strickland*, the client must show a reasonable probability that, but for the lawyer's deficient performance, the result of the proceeding would have been different. The Court in *Strickland* reminded lower courts that they need not consider performance, the first prong, if the evidence was overwhelming on prejudice. In other words, if it is reasonably likely that the result of the proceedings would have been the same, even if the lawyer's performance hadn't been deficient, the case can be resolved on prejudice. If the evidence of guilt against the defendant is overwhelming and the defense lawyer made only a few relatively minor mistakes, the prejudice prong will be decisive. Although the prejudice standard makes reference to the result in a hypothetically fair trial, a defendant may obtain relief if the lawyer's erroneous advice leads to the defendant rejecting a plea bargain that would have been advantageous. Lafler v. Cooper, 566 U.S. 156 (2012).

In a few cases prejudice may be **presumed**. If a lawyer objects that it is impossible to provide adequate representation to co-defendants and the trial court does not investigate the conflict, prejudice will be presumed. Holloway v. Arkansas, 435 U.S. 475 (1978). In the absence of a timely objection, a defendant whose lawyer simultaneously represented a co-defendant must show that "an actual conflict of interest adversely affected" the representation. Cuyler v. Sullivan, 446 U.S. 335 (1980). "Adverse effect" here does *not* refer to *Strickland* prejudice. That is, the defendant need not show a substantial likelihood that the outcome of the trial would have been different. Rather, it means a showing that defense counsel was influenced or limited in the strategic decisions she made, due to the interests of the other client. These conflicts are rare outside the context of simultaneous representation of co-defendants, and indeed the Supreme Court has suggested (in dicta) that the presumption of prejudice in *Cuyler* may be limited to such cases. Mickens v. Taylor, 535 U.S. 162 (2002).

The remedy for a finding of deficient performance that caused the defendant to suffer constitutional prejudice is generally a new trial with substitute—and hopefully competent—counsel. Because this is a fairly intrusive remedy, courts tend to bend over backwards to find that the lawyer's performance was not deficient, or that any errors did not cause prejudice to the defendant. The Court in *Strickland* specifically warned lower courts not to second-guess decisions of trial counsel that fall within a broad zone of reasonable performance. Suppose the lawyer did not call an alibi witness, and the defendant later claims this was constitutionally deficient performance. The lawyer may respond that she believed the witness would not be credible, or that some other defense was more likely than the client's alibi to be successful. Those are the sorts of tactical judgments that courts will very rarely find on review to have been deficient on the first prong of *Strickland*. Similarly, courts may conclude that even fairly lousy representation was unlikely to have resulted in prejudice, under the second prong of *Strickland*, in light of the weight of the state's evidence of guilt.

What You Need to Know:

1. The Sixth Amendment guarantees the effective assistance of counsel. The two-part *Strickland* test is used to determine when counsel's performance was deficient, and when deficient performance resulted in prejudice to the defendant.
2. Reviewing courts tend to be deferential to counsel's performance and reluctant to disturb the results of proceedings.
3. In a few cases, the most important of which is concurrent representation of co-defendants with a conflict of interest, prejudice may be presumed.

LESSON 9: CONFIDENTIALITY-RELATED DOCTRINES: INTRODUCTION, AND DISTINGUISHING BETWEEN RULE OF CONFIDENTIALITY, ATTORNEY-CLIENT PRIVILEGE, AND WORK PRODUCT

If I had a nickel for every time a lawyer or court mixed up the duty of confidentiality and attorney-client privilege . . . I'd have a lot of nickels. There is an fundamental, extremely important distinction between (1) privileges or immunities that can be asserted in opposition to an official demand for information, such as a subpoena or a question at a deposition, and (2) the duty an agent owes to the principal not to disclose or make adverse use of confidential information. The attorney-client privilege and work product doctrine are part of the law of evidence and procedure, respectively, and as such can be used to block disclosure of otherwise admissible or discoverable evidence. The duty of confidentiality, on the other hand, arises from the law of agency and the rules of professional conduct. It limits the disclosure of confidential information, or its use against the interests of a client.

A *demand* for information, as I'm using that term here, *excludes* a situation in which an attorney is in a pickle and would very much like to be able to disclose confidential information. In an actual criminal defense case with harrowing facts, an attorney was representing a defendant charged with murdering his wife and kidnapping, and possibly killing, his children. It was unclear whether the kids were still alive, but the attorney believed they might be. The client made a statement which suggested they might be found—possibly alive—at a remote location in the wilderness. As a legal matter, what may or must the attorney do? The answer is given by the applicable rule of confidentiality, *not* the attorney-client privilege. The understandable desire the attorney felt to disclose the location of the children, possibly saving their lives, is not the kind of official demand for information that invokes the law of evidence and procedure. The case is purely a matter of the duties owed by the lawyer to the client. If the lawyer disclosed in violation of the duty of confidentiality established in the state rules of professional conduct, he would potentially have provided ineffective assistance of counsel. *See* McClure v. Thompson, 323 F.3d 1233 (9th Cir. 2003) (because district court made findings that lawyer reasonably believed the children may still be alive, reviewing court concluded that disclosure was within bodily-harm exception to duty of confidentiality).

It may help to think of confidentiality-related doctrines as establishing overlapping zones of protection. The attorney-client privilege is located entirely within the duty of confidentiality. In other words, the professional duty, under Rule 1.6(a) extends to all communications protected by the attorney-client privilege, and to much else besides. The work-product doctrine overlaps somewhat with the attorney-client privilege. Some documents may be protected work product and may memorialize attorney-client privileged communications. Other work product may not be protected by the attorney-client privilege, as when it contains information learned from third parties. But it will almost certainly also be within the protection of the duty of confidentiality under Rule 1.6(a).

The **attorney-client privilege** protects (1) communications, (2) made between lawyers and clients, (3) in confidence, (4) for the purpose of providing legal assistance to the client. Restatement § 68. (You may see an eight-part test from the influential treatise on evidence law by John Henry Wigmore. It is the same in substance as the Restatement test.) It *excludes* information learned in communications with non-clients (such as witnesses); observations or facts that do not reveal the content of confidential communications; communications not made in confidence; and communications that pertain to matters other than the client's legal interests. Watch out for fact patterns that test each of the elements of the privilege. For example:

- An attorney is talking with her client on the subway on the way to a court hearing. The communication was not made in confidence, so it is not protected by the privilege.
- A client brings her best friend along to a meeting with her lawyer, thinking the friend will be useful for moral support. The communication is not solely between lawyer and client; the presence of the friend destroys the confidentiality necessary for a privileged communication. (There are some exceptions to this rule for third parties whose presence is necessary to facilitate the communication, such as translators.)
- The President of a non-profit corporation talks to the corporation's attorney about two competing proposals for a new fund-raising campaign. The President is not looking for legal advice about the proposals, but for the attorney's judgment about which will be more effective. The communication is not for the purpose of obtaining legal assistance, and therefore not privileged.

The **work product** doctrine has its source in common law, in a case called *Hickman v. Taylor*, 329 U.S. 495 (1947). The basic idea is to prevent adversaries in litigation from free-riding off the other side's preparation. If an attorney goes to the trouble of investigating, interviewing witnesses, and reaching conclusions about the likely legal significance of the facts that have been discovered, it would be unfair to allow the adversary to swoop in and make use of all of this information. Particularly troublesome would be invading the zone of privacy around the attorney's mental impressions. The work-product doctrine therefore exempts from discovery "documents and tangible things that are prepared in anticipation of litigation . . . by or for another party or its representative." Fed. R. Civ. P. 26(b)(3)(A). (There are differences between the work-product doctrine as codified in the Federal Rules of Civil and Criminal Procedure and common-law work-product under *Hickman* and *U.S. v. Nobles*, 422 U.S. 225 (1975). You probably won't get that deep in the weeds in your Professional Responsibility class, but the differences may come up in Evidence, Criminal Procedure, or a similar course.) Because of its foundation in the adversary system, work product protection extends only to materials prepared for litigation or in anticipation of litigation. If you see documents prepared in the ordinary course of business, they are not protected as work product. Ordinary work product, which is mostly factual information learned from witness interviews or other investigation, can sometimes be discovered by the adversary on a showing of substantial need for the information and inability to obtain the equivalent information without undue hardship. Fed. R. Civ. P. 26(b)(3)(A)(ii). But the "mental impressions, conclusions, opinions, or legal theories" of an attorney—so-called opinion work product—is protected almost absolutely from discovery (with a few exceptions you probably won't get into in your PR class). Fed. R. Civ. P. 26(b)(3)(B).

The attorney-client privilege and work-product doctrine are subject to the **crime-fraud exception**. Otherwise protected communications or information may be subject to discovery if the client's purpose in retaining the lawyer was to obtain assistance in committing a crime or fraud. Restatement § 82. It is important to see that the lawyer need not share the client's purpose. The lawyer may be entirely innocent, but if the client used her services to commit a crime or fraud, then communications between the parties may be discoverable. A number of fairly technical waiver doctrines can apply to destroy the protection of the privilege or work-product doctrine. If your teacher wants you to be familiar with waiver, read the rules and comments carefully in Restatement §§ 78–80, 91–92.

What You Need to Know:

1. Only legal protections rooted in the law of evidence or procedure may be used to resist discovery or disclosure in response to an official demand such as a subpoena, request for production of documents, or question at trial or a deposition.
2. The duty of confidentiality is broader than the attorney-client privilege and work-product doctrine; that is, an attorney may be required to keep information confidential that is not protected from discovery by the law of evidence and procedure.
3. The attorney-client privilege protects confidential attorney-client communications made for the purpose of providing legal assistance.
4. The work product doctrine applies to documents prepared in anticipation of litigation, and can be divided into ordinary (sometimes discoverable) and opinion (almost never discoverable) work product.

LESSON 10: RULE OF CONFIDENTIALITY AND EXCEPTIONS

Attorneys have demanding duties which prohibit the disclosure or adverse use of confidential information. The **scope** of protected confidential information is very broad. Rule 1.6(a) defines it as all "information relating to the representation of a client." That covers quite a bit more than attorney-client privileged communications or documents protected as work product. It includes things like information learned from sources other than the client; observations and facts that would not be considered "communications" for the purposes of the attorney-client privilege; and documents prepared in the ordinary course of business, and thus not protected as work product.

When reading older cases you may encounter a distinction between "confidences" and "secrets." This is terminology from the old Model Code of Professional Conduct, but it has been preserved in the rules of several states, including important jurisdictions like New York and the District of Columbia. On

Model-Code-influenced terminology, the lawyer's duty of confidentiality generally covers all information that is "likely to be embarrassing or detrimental to the client if disclosed, or [that] the client has requested be kept confidential." (That language is from the New York rule.) In practice there is unlikely to be much of a difference between information covered by this version of the rule and by the more modern definition in Model Rule 1.6(a).

Once we know the scope of protected confidential information, we can ask the question: What duties does an attorney have with respect to it. Most obviously, not to **disclose** it, without the informed consent of the client, implied authorization, or an applicable exception in Rule 1.6(b). In addition, however, lawyers must also refrain from making **adverse use** of confidential information. See Model Rule 1.8(b). Suppose a lawyer is representing Company A, which is considering making an effort to acquire Company B. Company A very much wants to keep this plan secret, because it worries that the stock price of Company B will go up if its plans are discovered. The lawyer is also representing Investor, a wealthy individual. May the lawyer tip off Investor about Company A's takeover plans, so that Investor can buy stock in Company B and make a killing? Apart from any question of whether this would be insider trading in violation of federal law, the lawyer's disclosure of the contemplated takeover would be a violation of the duty owed under Rule 1.8(b) to Company A.

As we will see, the prohibition on making adverse use of confidential information underlies many of the specific rules on conflicts of interest. In the example above, could the lawyer also represent Company B, given the existing representation of Company A and knowledge of its planned takeover attempt? Not without the consent of both clients, because duties of communication and reasonable care, owed to Company B, may require the lawyer to communicate any information about possible takeover bids, possibly to allow Company B to prepare takeover defenses. But this would be a clear violation of the duty of confidentiality owed to Company A. When there is a risk that a lawyer will violate a duty owed to one client because of a relationship with another, there is *by definition* a conflict of interest under Rule 1.7(a). We'll talk about conflicts soon, but for now it is extremely important to flag the relationship between duties of confidentiality and conflicts of interest.

You will probably see a lot of talk about the rule of confidentiality as very strict, almost absolute. That may have once been true, and still is in California, but in most states the duty not to disclose confidential client information is subject to a number of exceptions. Before we get to enumerated exceptions in Rule 1.6(b), however, note that Rule 1.6(a) contemplates two situations in which the lawyer may disclose confidential information: (i) with the client's **informed consent**, and (ii) where disclosure is **impliedly authorized**. (It would be nice if the drafters of the rules had enumerated these cases—you may want to write little numbers (i) and (ii) in your rule book to remind yourself that disclosure is permitted under these circumstances.) Informed consent requires full disclosure to the client of the risks of disclosing confidential information. See Rule 1.0(e). Implied authorization is a concept from agency law. Remember that the client determines the objectives of the representation after consultation with the lawyer, and the lawyer then proceeds in a manner reasonably calculated to advance the client's lawful objectives. Restatement § 16(1). Suppose a landowner retains a lawyer to negotiate the sale of a parcel of land. If the lawyer finds a potential buyer, she has to disclose something like "this land is for sale." That information would be protected by the duty of confidentiality, but since the client's objective is to sell the land, disclosing to the prospective buyer that the land is for sale is pretty clearly calculated to advance the client's objectives. Thus, the disclosure is impliedly authorized.

Now on to the enumerated **exceptions**. In most states, and in the Model Rules, the exceptions in Rule 1.6(b) are permissive, not mandatory. That means an attorney may disclose, but need not, and *either way* will not be subject to discipline. Briefly summarizing the exceptions, they are: (b)(1) prevent reasonably certain bodily harm; (b)(2) and (b)(3) prevent, rectify, or mitigate future frauds and the consequences of past and ongoing frauds, for which the lawyer's services were used; (b)(4) obtain advice on compliance with rules of professional conduct; (b)(5); self-defense; (b)(6) comply with law or court order; and (b)(7) detect and resolve conflicts of interest. In all of these cases, disclosure is permitted only to the extent reasonably necessary to carry out the purpose of the exception. For example, consider the self-defense exception, Rule 1.6(b)(5). A lawyer who is accused of having participated in the client's securities fraud may, if necessary, disclose the fraud to investors, but would not be permitted to report the fraud to the *Wall Street Journal*. A lawyer who disclosed the fraud to the media would be potentially subject to discipline, even if more modest disclosure would have been permissible in self-defense. With all of the exceptions, please read the rules carefully and make sure all the elements are satisfied.

What You Need to Know:

1. The duty of confidentiality is very broad in scope, and protects more than attorney-client privileged communications or attorney work-product.
2. Lawyers may not disclose or make adverse use of confidential information without the client's informed consent, implied authorization, or under one of several enumerated exceptions.
3. The extent of disclosure under the exceptions to confidentiality is limited to that which the lawyer reasonably believes necessary to accomplish the purpose of the exception. Over-disclosure can subject a lawyer to discipline.

LESSON 11: CONCURRENT CONFLICTS OF INTEREST

Conflicts of interest is a technical, occasionally mysterious-looking subject, but at its heart it's actually about something fairly easy to understand: Conflicts rules prevent lawyers from getting into positions in which there is a significant risk that they will compromise the duties they owe to clients. Because the rules aim at the **risk** of harm, not actual harm to clients, there is no such thing as a "potential" conflict. Getting into a situation in which another client relationship or a personal interest of the lawyer risks harm to a client is, by definition, a conflict of interest. Similarly, "no harm, no foul" is not a principle of legal ethics, and certainly has no application to conflicts of interest. A lawyer may be subject to discipline for representing conflicting interests even if no harm to the client results.

What kind of risks are we talking about? I always tell students to think **functionally** when looking for conflicts. That means, first, think about the duties a lawyer owes to her client. The most important ones are: (1) **confidentiality**—keeping secrets and not using confidential information against the interests of the client to whom it pertains; (2) **competence**—using reasonable care to pursue the client's objectives; (3) **loyalty**—acting first and foremost in the client's interests, and not being influenced by the interests of other clients, prospective clients, the lawyer's own interests, and so on; (4) **independence**—being able to advise the client based only on considerations that pertain to the client's legal situation. Now, the second step in the analysis is to identify other client relationships (with current or former clients), the interests of third parties, or the lawyer's own interests. Might any of those considerations create a significant risk that the lawyer will not perform all the duties owed to the client? If yes, then there is a conflict of interest *by definition*. Remember, conflicts rules regulate the risk of harm to clients; they do not apply only when there is a showing of actual harm. The risk has to be significant—far-fetched possibilities of harm do not create conflicts—but if you could imagine a dishonest, lazy, or careless lawyer failing to carry out a duty owed to Client A because of the representation of Client B, the former representation of Client C, the desire to win business from Client D, or a personal interest of the lawyer, then there is a conflict.

Rule 1.7(a) defines "concurrent conflict of interest" as either the representation of one client **directly adverse** to another client (Rule 1.7(a)(1)) or a **material limitation** on the representation of a client created by another interest or relationship (Rule 1.7(a)(2)). Notice that for "directly adverse" representation, it is immaterial whether the two matters on which the lawyer is representing the clients are related. Suppose a lawyer represents Earl's Rooter, a company that clears tree roots out of drain pipes. The lawyer provides general business advice to Earl's Rooter but does not represent the company in litigation. Along comes a prospective client who was injured when his car collided with a truck owned by Earl's Rooter and driven by its employee. The lawyer thinks it might be fun to take on a personal injury case. Is it permissible? No, because the representation of the plaintiff would be directly adverse to his current client, Earl's Rooter. As we will see below, the test for non-consentable conflicts does ask whether the lawyer is representing parties on opposite sides of the litigation. For the purposes of the "is there a conflict?" question, however, relatedness is immaterial. For examples of what constitutes a direct adversity and material limitation conflict, see Rule 1.7, comments [6] and [8], respectively.

Notice that *nothing turns on how a concurrent conflict of interest is characterized.* The rest of the analysis is the same. A lawyer is prohibiting from representing a client if the representation creates a concurrent conflict of interest unless the conflict is consentable (or waivable—it means the same thing) and each affected client gives informed consent. Some material limitation conflicts may be so severe that the interests of the clients are, in effect, directly adverse. For example, imagine the simultaneous representation of a company and a manager in defense of a Title VII sexual harassment lawsuit. The company may want to claim that the manager was a rogue employee who disregarded the company's anti-discrimination policies, while the manager may want to claim that higher-level managers tacitly condoned his behavior. The different litigation positions that would favor each client certainly creates a material limitation, as described in Rule 1.7, cmt. [8]: There is a significant risk that the lawyer would be unable to "consider, recommend or carry out an appropriate course of action" for each of the two co-clients. If the positions are so much in tension, however, one might describe the representation of the co-defendant as the representation of one client directly adverse to another client. That's okay—nothing turns on whether you put this situation into the direct adversity box or the material limitation box.

The analysis of consentability in given by Rule 1.7(b). A conflict is consentable if it does not fall within the three categories of cases set out in the rule. Most of the time you can ignore Rule 1.7(b)(2), representation prohibited by law. That exception is intended to refer to other law such as statutory or regulatory prohibitions on former government lawyers representing clients in private practice. See Rule 1.7, cmt. [16]. The clearest category is Rule 1.7(b)(3)—representing both sides in the same litigation. As noted above, representing the plaintiff in the personal injury case, while representing the defendant, Earl's Rooter, in general business matters, is a direct adversity conflict under Rule 1.7(a)(1). But it is consentable, because the law firm is not representing Earl's Rooter in the personal-injury litigation. The third category, Rule 1.7(b)(1) is the most difficult to define precisely. A conflict is not consentable if a reasonable lawyer would not believe that it is possible to provide competent and diligent representation to both clients, even if they consent. These cases arise where the adversity of interests is so severe that there is really no way to represent one client effectively without creating a substantial risk of harming the other. Imagine trying to represent both the buyer and the seller in a complex commercial real estate transaction. Many terms of the sales contract would create risk for one of the parties. Could a lawyer effectively represent both, and seek to obtain a deal that is in both parties' interests? Probably not, in a complicated transaction with many terms that require negotiation. For this reason, it is likely to be a non-consentable conflict. *See*, *e.g.*, Baldasarre v. Butler, 625 A.2d 458 (N.J. 1993) (holding that simultaneous representation of buyers and sellers in commercial real estate transactions creates a conflict that is *per se* non-consentable).

Assuming a conflict is consentable, the next question is whether the lawyer obtained the informed consent from each affected client. **Informed consent** is one of the most important concepts in all of the law of lawyering. (It is a defined term in the Model Rules—see Rule 1.0(e) for the definition.) Start with the idea that the lawyer-client relationship is highly **fiduciary** in nature. That means the lawyer is obligated to act in the client's best interests, notwithstanding any competing interests. But the law also recognizes the principle of client autonomy. The client define for itself what its "best interests" are, and if it wishes to modify or relax some of the duties owed to it by a lawyer, that should be its prerogative. However—and this is extremely important—any modification or waiver of what would otherwise be duties owed by a lawyer must follow full disclosure by the lawyer of the material risks the client thereby incurs, and any alternative courses of action. Only then will the client's consent be deemed informed. Without informed consent the modification of duties will be ineffective and the lawyer will be held to the default duty.

Under the Model Rules, informed consent must be "confirmed in writing." This means that the lawyer can explain the risks to a client and obtain the client's oral consent, but it must subsequently be memorialized in a writing to the client. A typical example would be a phone call in which the client agrees, followed by an email from the lawyer reciting that the client agreed to permit the lawyer to represent the other client notwithstanding those risks. That would be informed consent confirmed in writing.

Finally, although stated separately in Rule 1.10(a), please note that the conflicts of one lawyer in a "firm" (also a defined term in the Model Rules—see Rule 1.0(c)) are **imputed** to other lawyers in the same firm. That establishes a principle of "all for one, and one for all," and reflects the reality that lawyers in a firm share confidential information about all clients of the firm. If Lawyer A in the firm would be prohibited from representing a prospective client, because of Lawyer A's representation of another client, the same would be true of Lawyer B in the same firm. We will return to the subject of imputation in Lesson 14, on migratory lawyers, where it becomes extremely important in the analysis. For now, it is important to know that isolation mechanisms—sometimes called firewalls or screens—will not avoid the imputation of concurrent conflicts of interest.

What You Need to Know:

1. Conflicts rules regulate risk, not harm to clients. A lawyer may be subject to discipline for representing conflicting interests even if no harm to the client results.

2. Conflicts should be understood functionally, but are defined in terms of whether the representation of

another client is directly adverse to a lawyer's client, or whether the lawyer's representation of a client will be materially limited by some other relationship (often, but not always, another client).

3. Most concurrent conflicts are consentable, but some area not; the most important category of non-consentable conflicts are those multiple representations in which it is impossible to represent one client effectively without risking harm to the other.
4. Conflicts of interest are imputed to other lawyers working in the same firm.

LESSON 12: PERSONAL-INTEREST CONFLICTS

Rule 1.8 enumerates several common situations in which the lawyer's representation of a client would be limited, or prohibited outright, because of a personal interest of the lawyer. Rule 1.7(a)(2) states that there is a conflict of interest if the lawyer's representation of a client would be materially limited by a personal interest of the lawyer. You may therefore be wondering why Rule 1.8 isn't redundant. The answer is twofold: First, Rule 1.8 reminds lawyers of cases in which a personal-interest conflict is likely to arise. Second, the rule sometimes establishes **consentability** or **disclosure** requirements that differ from those in the general material limitation conflicts rule. For example, if a lawyer wishes to enter into a business transaction with a client, she must provide extensive disclosure, as described in Rule 1.8(a), and obtain the client's informed consent, in a writing signed by the client, to the terms of the transaction and the lawyer's role in it. All of that disclosure and documentation would probably be a good idea when obtaining informed consent to *any* conflict, but it is specifically required under Rule 1.8(a). By the way, note that the business-transactions rule applies whenever a lawyer knowingly acquires an "ownership, possessory, security, or other pecuniary interest adverse to a client." A lawyer representing a start-up company in exchange for some shares of the company's stock is required to comply with Rule 1.8(a).

Elsewhere Rule 1.8 sets out specific information that must be disclosed to clients as part of the process of obtaining consent. Consider the aggregate-settlement rule, Rule 1.8(g). Suppose a lawyer represents multiple plaintiffs in a mass-accident case, like a bus crash. The bus company may offer to settle with all the lawyer's clients at once, in exchange for a lump sum payment to be divvied up among the clients by the lawyer. This is not prohibited, but the lawyer must obtain each client's informed consent after the disclosure specified in the rule. Similarly, Rule 1.8(h)(2) prohibits a lawyer settling a malpractice claim with an unrepresented client or former client without first informing the client in writing of the desirability of obtaining separate legal representation.

Rule 1.8(f) might be called a "consent-plus" provision. A lawyer may accept payment for representation from a third party, such as a liability insurer or a family member, as long as the lawyer obtains the client's informed consent *and* assures herself that there will be no interference with her professional judgment as a result of the third-party payment *and* undertakes to protect client confidences from disclosure. Rule 1.8(a) is also a consent-plus rule, because it requires that the terms of the transaction be fair and reasonable to the client. Other provisions of Rule 1.8 establish non-consentable conflicts. Look at Rule 1.8(c) on gifts from clients (including testamentary gifts—i.e. being named in a client's will), Rule 1.8(d) on obtaining media rights in the client's story, Rule 1.8(e) on providing financial assistance to a client in litigation, and Rule 1.8(i) on acquiring a proprietary interest in the subject of the representation.

Finally, Rule 1.8(j) on sexual relationships with clients was added to the Model Rules both to protect vulnerable clients from abuse and to ensure that the lawyer's independent judgment would not be compromised by feelings for the client. In the case of an organizational client, it applies to a client constituent who "supervises, directs, or regularly consults with" the lawyer. Rule 1.8, cmt. [19]. The sex-with-clients rule is also non-consentable, but it does not apply to sexual relationships that pre-date the formation of the attorney-client relationship. It is also unusual in that the conflicts it recognizes are not **imputed** to other lawyers in the same firm.

What You Need to Know:

1. The personal-interest conflicts rule mostly overlaps with the prohibition in Rule 1.7(a)(2) on representing a client when a lawyer's personal interests would materially limit the lawyer's competent and diligent performance of professional duties. But it does specify particular recurring situations that demand attention.
2. The disclosure, consent, and imputation requirements in Rule 1.8 may vary from the usual requirements of Rule 1.7(a)(2)—pay close attention to them!

LESSON 13: SUCCESSIVE CONFLICTS

Some duties owed by a lawyer terminate when the lawyer-client relationship is over. After the representation is concluded, a lawyer no longer owes a duty of reasonable care to pursue the client's objectives, for example. Some duties, however, persist beyond the termination of the relationship. The most important of these is to protect the confidential information of former clients from disclosure (Rule 1.6(a)) or adverse use (Rule 1.8(b)). In addition, a client should not have to worry that her lawyer will turn around and attack work the lawyer performed for the client, while representing a new client. Both of these duties—to protect confidential information from disclosure or misuse, and not to attack the lawyer's own work—underlie Rule 1.9, the successive representation conflicts rule. Note, for example, how Rule 1.9(c) creates an ongoing duty, surviving termination of the attorney-client relationship, not to use confidential information to the disadvantage of a former client.

Rule 1.9(a) prohibits the representation of New Client, whose interests are materially adverse to those of Old Client, in the same or a substantially related matter, unless Old Client gives informed consent. The element in this analysis that is the most frequently litigated, and the cause of the most confusion, is the requirement that the matters be **substantially related**. It doesn't help that the text of the rule does not define substantially related matters, but leaves it to Comment [3]. Restatement § 132 does a better job here, by including both loyalty-based and confidentiality-based tests for substantially related matters in the text. But I'm burying the lede . . . when are matters substantially related?

By far the most common fact pattern involves access by the lawyer to **confidential information** of Old Client that might "materially advance the [New Client's] position in the subsequent matter." Rule 1.9, cmt. [3]. Comment [3] has a helpful illustration, which I will embellish a bit and turn into an MPRE-style question:

> Lawyer, a general practitioner, represented Husband in various business and tax matters for several years. Lawyer knew that Husband employed an extremely aggressive tax-avoidance strategy involving a partnership in the Cayman Islands. Lawyer had advised Husband on several occasions that the structure and the tax treatment claimed by Husband was "just on this side of the fine line between lawful and unlawful," and attempted to dissuade Husband from exempting income derived from the Cayman Islands partnership. After the last such warning, Husband angrily said, "If I wanted to do something good for my soul, I'd go to church. I'm sick of your goody-two-shoes advice. You're fired!"

Six months later, Wife made an appointment to see Lawyer. She told Lawyer that she was tired of trying to make her marriage work and was determined to seek a divorce from Husband. Lawyer informed Wife that he had formerly represented Husband in business and tax matters. "I know," replied Wife, "so you know what a jerk he is." Wife then said, "Seriously, I am aware of those facts, and I consent to you representing me regardless." Lawyer then filed a petition for divorce on behalf of Wife.

Is Lawyer subject to discipline?

A. Yes, because the former representation of Husband created a non-waivable conflict of interest.

B. Yes, because the former representation of Husband was substantially related to the representation of Wife.

C. No, because the business and tax matters are not substantially related to the divorce representation.

D. No, because Wife gave her informed consent to the representation.

The answer, according to Rule 1.9, cmt. [3], is (B). One might have the intuition that the business and tax matters are not substantially related to a subsequent divorce, but Lawyer here had access to confidential information that might "materially advance the [new] client's position in the subsequent matter"—i.e. Wife's position in the divorce. Maybe Wife has no idea about the Cayman Islands entity. She may be entitled to conduct discovery to find out whether her Husband has any offshore accounts, but the information is still "confidential factual information" obtained by Lawyer in the previous representation, and for that reason, the divorce is substantially related to Lawyer's former representation of Husband. See also Restatement § 132, cmt. d(iii).

By the way, Option (A) is incorrect because all successive-representation conflicts are waivable. Option (D) is incorrect because it is the former client, Husband, who must give informed consent to the representation.

Whether two matters are substantially related turns, in the great majority of cases, on this type of access to confidential information. There are a few cases, however, in which the lawyer does not have access to confidential information of a former client, often because the former client had agreed to share it with another. In the well-known case of *Brennan's, Inc. v. Brennan's Restaurants, Inc.*, 590 F.2d 168 (5th Cir. 1978), a lawyer represented a family restaurant business in New Orleans. The family's business was structured as a complicated agglomeration of entities. During the time of family harmony, on behalf of the business, Lawyer obtained trademark protection on a cheery rooster design, promoting "Breakfast at Brennan's." As sometimes happens, the family business became embroiled in strife. The family split up the entities into two competing businesses. Lawyer continued to represent one set of entities. A disagreement arose concerning the use of the rooster trademark. In the ensuing trademark infringement litigation, Lawyer argued that the trademark was invalid. The opposing family group replied, "Wait a second—when you used to work for us, you obtained protection for the trademark!" The court held that by attacking the work he had previously performed for the former client (i.e. the previously unified family business), the lawyer breached a duty of **loyalty** to the former client. The case did not involve a threat to confidential information, because all the family members and their entities had shared information during the time of harmony. The only basis for disqualifying Lawyer from the subsequent representation was therefore his attack upon the trademark he had previously obtained. This result is now recognized in Restatement § 132(1) & cmt. d(ii).

In addition to the substantial relationship test, make sure to analyze whether the representation of the new client is **materially adverse** to the interests of the past client in the matter on which the lawyer represented the past client. See Rule 1.9, cmt. [2]. Also, make sure the past client really is in the past—that is, check to see whether the representation is ongoing. The attorney-client relationship generally terminates upon the completion of agreed-upon work. But what if the client didn't retain the lawyer for only one matter, but there was an ongoing professional relationship? In that case it can be hard to determine when the client becomes a "former" client for conflicts purposes. Maybe not until there's a clean break, with the lawyer sending a letter saying, "I'm no longer representing you." Or maybe, after a period of time, the relationship just kind of peters out. This is a factual question that may arise in some cases, so make sure to look at the terms of the initial engagement agreement between the attorney and client. For an interesting recent case involving this and many other conflicts issues, see Western Sugar Coop. v. Archer-Daniels-Midland Co., 98 F.Supp.3d 1074 (C.D. Cal. 2015).

What You Need to Know:

1. The successive conflicts rule is narrower than the concurrent conflicts rule. It prohibits only materially adverse representation of the new client

in a matter that is the same as, or substantially related to, the lawyer's work for the old client.

2. The precise formulation of the substantial relationship test varies by jurisdiction. The Model Rules look to the acquisition of confidential information of the old client. The Restatement adds a prohibition on a lawyer attacking work performed for the former client. Most substantial relationship cases involve the confidentiality interest of the former client.

LESSON 14: MIGRATORY LAWYERS

You're very unlikely to work at the same law firm, corporate legal department, government office, or other organization at which you started right after law school. Most lawyers change jobs several times over the course of a career. When a lawyer moves from one employer to another, conflicts issues may arise not only from the lawyer's personal representation of clients at the previous firm, but also from the work performed by other lawyers in the firm. In other words, the **imputation** of conflicts of all lawyers working in the same firm may create complications for moving lawyers. The principles governing the imputation of conflicts in moving-lawyer cases rely on two presumptions about confidential information. This analysis developed in judicial decisions on motions to disqualify law firms for conflicts of interest. The best known case is *Silver Chrysler Plymouth v. Chrysler Motors Corp.*, 518 F.2d 751 (2d Cir. 1975), and this is sometimes called the *Silver Chrysler* analysis. It is now contained in the Model Rules and Restatement, but you have to read the rules and comments carefully. See Rule 1.9(b) & cmt. [6]; Restatement § 124 cmt. c(ii); Restatement § 132 cmt. h. The analysis proceeds in two steps.

Step 1: A moving lawyer is **presumed** to have acquired confidential information of all clients of the former law firm. However, that presumption is rebuttable as it pertains to the confidential information of any given client of the prior firm. The moving lawyer may be able to show, usually by submitting an affidavit, that she did no work for a client of the old firm, or did not work on a particular matter. The idea is to show that the lawyer could not have learned any confidential information pertaining to that client. If the lawyer makes this showing, the lawyer escapes personal disqualification. She can now work on a matter at the new law firm that is materially adverse and substantially related to the old law firm's representation of its client.

Step 2: If the moving lawyer cannot rebut the presumption of having acquired confidential information of a client, the moving lawyer will be presumed to share that confidential information with other lawyers at the new firm. That presumption may be rebutted if (and only if) the jurisdiction recognizes **screening** to block the imputation of conflicts in such a situation, and the screen is established in a timely manner. See Rule 1.10(a)(2) for the Model Rules position on screening, but understand that this is a controversial topic and not all states allow screens in these cases. If permitted, a screen instructs the newly hired lawyer not to discuss the representation of the former client with lawyers at the new firm. The idea is to prevent the incoming lawyer from blabbing confidential information about the former client. You'll find some screening cases that seem to emphasize keeping information about the clients of the hiring firm extra-double confidential, with separate locks on filing cabinets, passwords for electronic files, and so on. That doesn't really make sense, given that the client to be protected is the client of the old firm and the moving lawyer.

Here is an example of the presumptions at work. The law firm of White & Pinkman represented, among other clients, a local businessman in negotiations to acquire a commercial laundry facility. The businessman, Fring, revealed confidential information to the law firm about his financial dealings, including debts he owed to several banks. The negotiations concerning the laundry business were handled by corporate lawyers at White & Pinkman. An associate at the firm, Goodman, represented Fring in personal-injury cases arising out of minor slip and fall incidents at a local chain of restaurants owned by Fring. Goodman had no involvement with the laundry negotiations and learned very little information about Fring's business interests, since it was almost never relevant to the defense of the slip-and-fall cases.

Goodman recently accepted an offer to join a different law firm, Hamlin & McGill. Unbeknownst to Goodman, Hamlin & McGill was representing the seller of the laundry business in contentious negotiations with Fring. After Goodman joined Hamlin & McGill, Fring became furious and demanded that the firm cease representing the seller. "My lawyer betrayed me!" he said in an angry letter describing Goodman's departure from White & Pinkman. How should this case be analyzed under the successive conflicts rule?

First, notice that interests of the new client, the seller of the business, are materially adverse to the interests of the former client, Fring. The two firms are representing the seller and Fring in the same matter—i.e. the negotiations over the transaction. If Goodman is deemed to have "represented" Fring in the matter, he will be personally conflicted out of representing the seller and—far worse for the firm—his conflict will be imputed to other lawyers in the firm under Rule 1.10(a). This is where Rule 1.9(b) and *Silver Chrysler* come in. Goodman did not represent Fring in the business negotiations, but only in minor personal-injury matters. So he's not conflicted out on that basis. He may be disqualified under Rule 1.9(b), however, if the firm the lawyer had previously been associated with (White & Pinkman) had represented Fring *and* if Goodman had acquired confidential information pertaining to Fring that is material to the new matter (i.e. the representation of the seller in the laundry negotiations). Goodman is presumed to have acquired confidential information, but he may rebut the presumption by showing that the only work he did for Fring was on personal-injury matters and thus he would not have acquired the information that could be used against Fring in the representation of the seller.

If the facts had been different, and Goodman had done a bit of work on the laundry transaction—not extensive involvement, but enough to where he would be unable to rebut the presumption of having acquired confidential information—then he would be carrying a "taint" of the previous representation. This means he would be personally conflicted out of representing the seller *and* that conflict would be imputed to other lawyers in the new firm, Hamlin & McGill. The new firm would have to withdraw from representing the seller, which would be a real bummer for the firm. In a jurisdiction that allows screening, it can protect itself by establishing a screening mechanism before the moving lawyer, Goodman, joins the firm.

What You Need to Know:

1. The key to analyzing moving-lawyer conflicts cases is identifying the matters on which the lawyer worked at the prior law firm, and determining whether the lawyer likely acquired confidential information in the course of that representation which could be used adversely on behalf of a client of the new firm.
2. Moving-lawyer conflicts cases are a subset of successive-representation conflicts generally, and so you also have to determine whether the interests of the old and new clients are materially adverse, and whether the matters are the same or substantially related.

LESSON 15: REPRESENTING ORGANIZATIONS

Not all clients are natural persons. Many are corporations, partnerships, unions, trade associations, government agencies, and other organizations. Rule 1.13 sets out a number of principles for lawyers representing organizational clients. These principles can also be found in agency and corporate law, but it's handy to have them collected together in Rule 1.13.

The first principle of organizational representation is that the organization itself is the client—not any of the individual directors, officers, or agents (often referred to as the "**constituents**" of an organization) who act on its behalf. See Rule 1.13(a). If the President of a corporation works with the corporation's outside law firm to evaluate a merger opportunity or defend against a lawsuit, both the President and the lawyer are acting as agents of the corporation. That seems obvious, and it's clear enough in theory, but in practice it is very easy for lawyers to get mixed up and act as though the client is the individual with whom they deal on a daily basis. This can be disastrous when the individual constituent is not acting in the best interests of the organization. A lawyer may choose to represent a constituent in addition to the organization, thus having two clients. See Rule 1.13(g). In that case, however, the concurrent representation must pass muster under Rule 1.7. When dealing with an organizational constituent, if the lawyer knows or should know that the constituent's interests are adverse to those of the organization, the lawyer must give what is sometimes called a "corporate *Miranda*" warning. Rule 1.13(f). This warning reminds the constituent that the lawyer is acting in the best interests of the organization, which may not be in the individual's best interests.

Speaking of wrongdoing by constituents, one of the major issues for lawyers representing organizations is what to do when they discover evidence that some officer or employee is up to no good. Rule 1.13(b) states that when a lawyer *knows*—and remember, knowledge is a defined term, and means actual knowledge—that an officer, employee, or other person is acting in a way that is a violation of a legal obligation to the organization (e.g. by engaging in some kind of self-dealing) or is doing something that will result in legal liability that will be imputed to the organization, the lawyer must act in the best interests of the client. Well, no kidding! A lawyer always has a duty to act in the best interests of her client. But the rule goes on to prescribe a specific course of action that the lawyer must pursue, known as "**up the ladder**" reporting. The lawyer must refer the matter to a higher authority, such as the general counsel or the CEO and, if necessary, all the way to the board of directors in a corporation. The report to a higher authority is intended to give someone in charge the opportunity to take corrective action to address the wrongdoing discovered by the lawyer.

Lawyers sometimes get tripped up by this, so be careful: If a lawyer for the corporation reports evidence of wrongdoing to the board of directors, has the lawyer violated her duty of confidentiality under Rule 1.6? No, because the client is the organization (Rule 1.13(a)), the duty of **confidentiality** is owed to the client, and the board of directors is the highest authority that can act for the client. The lawyer has never disclosed information outside the organization by reporting to the board.

That's not to say lawyers may not want to disclose, in appropriate circumstances. Suppose a lawyer learns that the Chief Financial Officer of a corporation is engaging in massive securities fraud, which will lead to substantial financial losses for investors. The lawyer has reported this to the board, but it took no action. Now what? Rule 1.13(c) says that, in these limited circumstances, the lawyer may disclose confidential information, but only if and to the extent the lawyer reasonably believes necessary to prevent harm to the organization. This is the only sense in which a lawyer for an organization can be said to be acting as a whistleblower. This permission to disclose does not apply if the lawyer has been retained to investigate possible wrongdoing or to defend the organization in litigation. Rule 1.13(d).

The reporting up (Rule 1.13(b)) and reporting out (Rule 1.13(c)) procedures have much in common with the regulations issued by the Securities and Exchange Commission under the Sarbanes-Oxley Act, prescribing duties for lawyers "appearing and practicing before" the SEC. If your Professional Responsibility teacher wants you to know about the Sarbanes-Oxley regulations, note carefully the similarities with Rule 1.13 and differences.

If a lawyer reports up evidence of wrongdoing or discloses confidential information as allowed by Rule 1.13(c) and is fired for doing so must inform the board of directors about the firing and the reason for it. Rule 1.13(e). Again, the idea is to give the board a chance to rectify the wrongdoing discovered by the lawyer.

What You Need to Know:

1. The organization is the client, the organization is the client, the organization is the client. Pretty much everything you need to know follows from that proposition. The lawyer's duties are owed to the client, not to any individual constituents.

2. If the lawyer knows that a constituent is engaged in wrongdoing, she must proceed in the best interests of the organization. This may involve reporting "up the ladder" and may, in certain very limited circumstances, permit disclosing confidential information.

LESSON 16: WITNESS PERJURY AND CANDOR TO THE TRIBUNAL

You may get tired of hearing the little motto that lawyers are supposed to be "zealous advocates" for their clients. It's a harmless enough phrase, as long as you remember that the full principle is "zealous advocacy within the bounds of the law." The right to advocate for one's client is not unlimited, and the most important limitation on advocacy is that the lawyer must never knowingly present false evidence, including witness testimony to a tribunal. (**Tribunal** is a defined term—see Rule 1.0(m).) In addition to the criminal law of perjury and obstruction of justice, and the common-law power of courts to punish contemptuous conduct, the prohibition on presenting false evidence is contained in Rule 3.3. There are several things to notice about this rule.

First, notice the division between Rule 3.3(a)(1) and (a)(3). The first provision, (a)(1), applies to the attorney's own statements. The second, (a)(3), applies to evidence offered by the lawyer. When would a lawyer make a false statement of fact under Rule 3.3(a)(1)? Imagine that the lawyer sends a letter to the judge (copied to opposing counsel, of course—see Rule 3.5(b)), falsely stating that her client is in the hospital and requesting a continuance of the scheduled trial date. That would be a violation of Rule 3.3(a)(1). The more common scenario involves a false statement made by a witness called by the lawyer, and that would be handled by Rule 3.3(a)(3).

Something that may not immediately be clear from the structure of the rules is the division into what I call **prospective** and **retrospective** duties. In other words, with respect to both the attorney's own statement and evidence offered by the attorney, the rule specifies both what should be done before the statement or evidence is offered—don't knowingly make false statements or offer false evidence—and what should be done if the lawyer subsequently discovers that a false statement was made or false evidence was introduced. Both Rule 3.3(a)(1) and (a)(3) begin with a statement of the prospective duty, and continue with the retrospective duty. Notice one difference: The retrospective duties apply only to **material** false statement or evidence. Also, the retrospective obligation with respect to false statements by the attorney is to correct the statement. With respect to false evidence it is to take "reasonable remedial measures." What does that mean? Look at Comment [10]. The idea here is that the lawyer should begin with less intrusive measures, relying on the client or witness to correct the false statement. That's what is meant by the suggestion to "remonstrate" with the client or witness. If that doesn't work, however, the lawyer may have to do more, including disclosing to the tribunal. Rule 3.3(c) makes clear that these remedial obligations may include disclosing confidential information protected by Rule 1.6.

All of these duties are subject to a *mens rea* requirement. They apply only when the lawyer *knows* the statement or evidence is false. See Rule 1.0(f) for the definition of knowledge. It means actual (that is, subjective) knowledge, but it does say that knowledge may be inferred from the circumstances. This doesn't mean that the standard is what a reasonable lawyer should have known, but it does mean that a lawyer cannot ignore an obvious falsehood. See Rule 3.3, cmt. [8]. An important qualification on the knowledge requirement is that sometimes in criminal defense cases, a court will bend over backwards to find that a lawyer did not know a client's proposed testimony was false, even though any rational human being would conclude the client is lying. *See, e.g.*, State v. McDowell, 681 N.W.2d 500 (Wis. 2004). This is because of the special problem facing a lawyer representing a criminal defendant. The accused in a criminal proceeding has a number of constitutional rights, including the right to take the stand (even if the lawyer thinks it would be a really bad idea), the privilege against self-incrimination, and the right of self-representation. There is a risk that a defense lawyer too concerned about her obligations of candor to the tribunal might interfere with those rights. That' was basis of the defendant/petitioner's argument in an important U.S. Supreme Court case, *Nix v. Whiteside*, 475 U.S. 157 (1986).

In *Nix*, the defendant was accused of murder during a drug deal that went sour. The defendant testified that he believed the victim was reaching for a gun, and stabbed him in self-defense. The defendant initially said he did not see a gun, but had reason to believe that's what the victim was doing, based on having seen the victim around town with a gun, and having heard the victim ask his girlfriend to bring his "piece." Later, however, the defendant changed his story and said he saw "something metallic" in the victim's hand. The defense lawyer warned the defendant that he could not testify falsely at trial, and that if he insisted on telling the "something metallic" version of the story, the lawyer would inform the court of his belief that the client was intending to testify falsely. Assuming the lawyer knew the client's story was a lie—and one might question whether the lawyer in fact had this knowledge, but the Supreme Court assumed he did—then what the lawyer did was within the range of acceptable professional responses to the possibility of client perjury. Thus, it did not constitute deficient performance under the first prong of *Strickland v. Washington*, 466 U.S. 668 (1984), the decision that established the test for ineffective assistance of counsel. It is extremely important to keep in mind, however, that the Court in *Nix* did ***not*** say a defense lawyer had to do what that lawyer did. If something else is within the range of professional responses in the relevant community, it would be consistent with the lawyer's obligation under the Sixth Amendment to follow those procedures.

An example of a procedure followed in some states is the so-called "free **narrative**" approach. Rather than question the client directly, a criminal defense lawyer might simply say, "Mr. Whiteside, why don't you tell the jury what happened on that day," and allow the defendant to tell his version of the story. The idea is to avoid the lawyer having to elicit testimony the lawyer knows is false. The problem with the narrative approach is that it pretty clearly flags for the jury—who probably have watched as much *Law and Order* as you have—that the defense lawyer knows the client's story is false.

For more on the dilemma for criminal defense lawyers presented by client perjury, see one of the all-time classic law review articles in this area, Monroe H. Freedman, *Professional Responsibility of the Criminal Defense Lawyer: The Three Hardest Questions*, 64 Mich. L. Rev. 1469 (1966). There's a good chance your teacher will talk about Freedman's "trilemma," in which a lawyer has to compromise on either duties owed to the client or candor to the tribunal.

Rule 3.3 is all about candor to the tribunal. Lawyers are also prohibited from lying to regular ol' non-tribunal parties. Rule 4.1(a). Rule 4.1(b) also prohibits lying by omission; a lawyer may not fail to disclose a material fact where disclosure would be necessary to avoid assisting the client's criminal or fraudulent act. Importantly, Rule 4.1(b) is qualified by the duty of confidentiality—a lawyer need not disclose to prevent a client's crime or fraud if disclosure is prohibited by Rule 1.6. Be careful! Now that Rule 1.b(b)(2) and (b)(3) permits disclosure of confidential information to prevent, rectify, or mitigate the consequences of a client's fraud, disclosure of material facts may be mandatory in order to avoid discipline under Rule 4.1(b).

What You Need to Know:

1. The duty to prevent false evidence from entering the record is quite stringent, requires the lawyer to take remedial action if the falsity is subsequently discovered, and may require the disclosure of information otherwise protected by the rule of confidentiality.
2. All of these duties, however, kick in only when the lawyer knows of the falsity.
3. The criminal defense setting presents a particular challenge due to the constitutional entitlements of the defendant. States vary in their approaches to criminal defense perjury.

LESSON 17: ANTI-CONTACT RULE AND OTHER LITIGATION MISCONDUCT

From the client's point of view, one of the advantages of hiring a lawyer is not having to deal with other lawyers—they have to deal through your lawyer. That principle is enforced by Rule 4.2, called the *ex parte* contact rule or the anti-contact rule. The rule prohibits lawyers from communicating about the subject matter of the representation with anyone else the lawyer knows to be represented by counsel in the matter, without the consent of the other lawyer. Notice that term "knows" again. As in the perjury rule, Rule 3.3, the requirement of knowledge means actual, subjective knowledge that the other person is represented in the matter. Comment [8] to Rule 4.2 does warn, however, that a lawyer may not close her eyes to the obvious. Still, the rule is actual knowledge, so watch for facts on an exam that test whether the lawyer communicating with another person knows they are represented.

Interestingly, the prohibition on contacting a represented person can be waived, but it must be waived by that person's lawyer. See Rule 4.2, cmt. [3]. Watch out for a fact pattern in which the other person says the communication is okay, but the lawyer does not have the consent of that person's lawyer.

Notice that I'm using the word "person" here and not "party." An older version of the rule said lawyers are prohibited from contacting other *parties*, but this made it sounds like the prohibition only applied after there was filed litigation. (Plaintiffs and defendants are "parties," but one becomes a plaintiff or defendant only by being involved in a lawsuit.) The language of the rule was changed from party to person, to clarify that the prohibition applies to contact prior to the filing of a lawsuit. In fact, there is no limitation in the rule to litigation—it applies also to represented parties to a deal. There is no requirement that the positions or interests of the persons be adverse. Thus, the rule applies to contact with a represented co-party, or another person aligned in interests in a transactional matter.

When the other "person" is an entity, such as a corporation, the anti-contact rule still applies. The question then is, which natural-person agents (often called "constituents" of the entity) are out of bounds for communication. Comment [7] states three categories: (1) those who supervise, direct, or regularly consult with the organization's lawyer regarding the matter; (2) those who can make decisions on behalf of the entity with respect to the matter; and (3) those whose acts and omissions can be imputed to the organization for the purposes of vicarious liability. Older versions of the rule made a confusing reference to "admissions" by agents of the organization, and several state supreme court cases have had to clarify the scope of that language. *See, e.g.*, Messing, Rudavsky & Weliky, P.C. v. President and Fellows of Harvard College, 764 N.E.2d 825 (Mass. 2002); Palmer v. Pioneer Inn, 59 P.3d 1237 (Nev. 2002). The word "admission" is not part of the current version of Rule 4.2, and so hopefully this confusion is a thing of the past.

The most common application of this rule is to pre-filing **investigations**. Imagine, for example, that there was an accident at a construction site, and the lawyer for an injured worker wants to determine which of several subcontractors was responsible for the accident. The lawyer might want to send out an investigator to talk to witnesses. If the attorney knows that one of the witnesses is covered by the anti-contact rule—perhaps because his or her actions could be imputed to a represented party for purposes of civil liability—can the lawyer instruct a non-lawyer investigator to have this communication? On their face the Model Rules apply only to lawyers, but there are a couple of provisions that deal with a lawyer's responsibility for the acts of a non-lawyer. One is Rule 5.3(c)(1), which makes a lawyer responsible for the conduct of another if the lawyer orders the conduct. The other is Rule 8.4(a), which states that a lawyer may not violate the rules "through the acts of another."

That brings us to a significant controversy surrounding the application of this rule to the activities of law-enforcement agents. Suppose an Assistant United States Attorney (AUSA) directs an FBI agent to interview the target of an investigation. Suppose further that the target has not yet been indicted. After indictment, the Sixth Amendment would prohibit the FBI agent from communicating with the target in the absence of the target's lawyer. Massiah v. U.S., 377 U.S. 201 (1964). What about pre-indictment? Would that communication be "**authorized by law**" and therefore permitted by Rule 4.2? Look carefully at Comment [5]. It says that a communication is not necessarily authorized by law just because it does not violate a federal or state constitutional right. In a case called *U.S. v.*

Hammad, 858 F.2d 834 (2d Cir. 1988), a federal court held that the AUSA had engaged in misconduct by, among other things, directing contact with someone known to be represented by counsel in the matter (an investigation of Medicare fraud). However, the AUSA also engaged in other wrongdoing, including preparing a fake subpoena to scare the target into talking. In the years since *Hammad* was decided, it was largely distinguished down to its facts. In theory, however, there is still a gap between conduct that does not violate the Sixth Amendment (or another constitutional right) and that which is authorized by law.

There are numerous other rules regarding litigation misconduct in the 3-series rules, most of which are fairly self-explanatory. Rule 3.1, on frivolous claims and contentions, largely duplicates Rule 11 of the Federal Rules of Civil Procedure. It does make clear, however, that a lawyer may be subject to professional discipline, as well as litigation sanctions, for bringing groundless claims. The rule also notes that nothing in the rule prohibits a criminal defense lawyer from "putting the state to its proof"—that is, requiring the state to prove its case beyond a reasonable doubt, even if the lawyer is convinced with perfect certainty that the defendant is guilty of the charged offense. Rule 3.2 states that a lawyer must make reasonable efforts to move along a proceeding, but then takes away that prohibition in the last clause—"consistent with the interests of the client." If the client seeks delay, when would it not be consistent with the interests of the client to seek delay? The rule is widely regarded as toothless, but again, a lawyer may be subject to litigation sanctions for engaging in unjustified delaying tactics.

Rules 3.4 and 3.5 contain numerous provisions pertaining to pretrial litigation, discovery, and the trial process. Some provisions are redundant with other law, including rules of evidence and procedure, and rules of specific tribunals. For example, some allusions to inadmissible evidence or vouching for the justness of a cause or credibility of a witness (Rule 3.4(e)) may be grounds for ordering a new trial. Falsifying evidence or counseling a witness to testify falsely (Rule 3.4(b)) may subject a lawyer to criminal liability for obstruction of justice. A difficult and complicated area of law pertains to unlawfully obstructing access to evidence or concealing an item with potential evidentiary value (Rule 3.4(a)). Several well-known cases deal with lawyers possessing evidence of a crime, fruits of a crime (such as a bag of money from a bank robbery), instrumentalities of a crime (such as a murder weapon), or contraband—i.e. materials that are unlawful to possess, such as drugs or child pornography. Seeking to influence a judge or juror by prohibited means (Rule 3.5(a)) can also subject the lawyer to criminal liability. Engaging in conduct intended to disrupt a tribunal (Rule 3.(5(d)) can expose a lawyer to sanctions for contempt of court. All of these rules are important, but the rules of professional conduct add little to other legal constraints on what lawyers may do while representing a client in a litigated matter.

The perennial issue of "trying a case in the media" is the subject of Rule 3.6. The rule has been amended in response to the Supreme Court's decision in *Gentile v. State Bar of Nevada*, 501 U.S. 1030 (1991). That case held that state rules of professional conduct prohibiting extrajudicial statements by lawyers that have a "substantial likelihood of materially prejudicing an adjudicative proceeding" do not violate the First Amendment. The current version of Rule 3.6(b) contains a number of "safe harbors"—statements a lawyer may make without worrying about being subject to discipline.

Rule 3.7 is the advocate-witness rule. It prohibits a lawyer from serving as an advocate *at a trial* (note—not in pretrial proceedings) in which the lawyer is likely to be a necessary witness. The rationale is to avoid the possibility that the jury might be confused by the lawyer's dual role. Is the lawyer testifying as a witness or serving as an advocate? A common scenario in which the advocate-witness rule might be implicated is where a lawyer had a hand in drafting a contract and was a witness to a conversation that might shed light on the interpretation of a crucial contract term. If there is subsequent litigation about the meaning of the term in the contract, the lawyer would not be able to serve as an advocate at trial, if the lawyer's testimony would be necessary. This disqualification is not imputed to other lawyers in the firm, Rule 3.7(b), so a partner of the lawyer could serve as an advocate.

Rule 3.8 contains a number of rules pertaining specifically to **prosecutors**. Some of them are similar to constitutional doctrines, but they may differ in subtle ways. For example, Rule 3.8(d) resembles the rule of *Brady v. Maryland*, 373 U.S. 83 (1963) and *Giglio v. United States*, 405 U.S. 150 (1972), which require disclosure of evidence known to the prosecutor that tends to exculpate the defendant or which may be useful in impeaching a prosecution witness. Some rules go beyond the requirements of the constitution. For example, Rule 3.8(a) prohibits a prosecutor from prosecuting a charge that the prosecutor knows is not supported by probable cause. That rule applies even if a grand jury returned an indictment against the defendant, because as everyone knows, a skilled prosecutor could get a grand jury to indict a ham sandwich. Rule 3.8(f) adds to the prohibitions in Rule 3.6 on making extrajudicial statements that have a substantial likelihood of materially prejudicing an adjudicative proceeding; Rule 3.8(f) also prohibits making a statement that has a substantial likelihood of heightening public condemnation of the accused. A couple of relatively new provisions, Rule 3.8(g) and (h) set out duties to rectify wrongful convictions. These have not yet been adopted by many states.

What You Need to Know:

1. The anti-contact rule protects the attorney-client relationship from interferences. It applies when a lawyer knows another person is represented by counsel in the matter. It is not limited to litigated matters; nor is it limited to persons who interests are adverse to the client's.

2. Many provisions in these rules duplicate principles from the law of evidence, procedure, or constitutional law. However, there may be differences in detail, so be careful to differentiate the disciplinary rules from other applicable legal constraints.

LESSON 18: UNAUTHORIZED PRACTICE OF LAW (UPL)

You may wonder why you should care about restrictions on the practice of law by non-lawyers. After all, you are going to be a lawyer, licensed to practice law in your jurisdiction. There are several reasons you should care about this subject. The first is simply that it's interesting as a window into what the legal profession sees as distinctive about itself. Lawyers claim to be different from ordinary businesspeople because they belong to a **profession**, and restrictions on the unauthorized practice of law are the practical means by which lawyers block competition from competing service providers such as accountants, real estate brokers, bank trust officers and, more recently, on-line sellers of legal documents like LegalZoom and RocketLawyer. Another reason to care about unauthorized practice of law (UPL) limitations is that in the United States these are enforced on a state-by-state basis. A lawyer admitted to practice in New York is just as much subject to New Jersey UPL limitations as a non-lawyer would be. (We'll see in the next section that there are some exceptions permitting temporary practice by an out-of-state lawyer.) Finally, lawyers must not assist another—whether an out-of-state lawyer or a non-lawyer—in the unauthorized practice of law. Rule 5.5(a). Lawyers thus need to understand the scope of UPL restrictions on those they employ or retain for a particular purpose.

The rationale for maintaining UPL restrictions is to protect the public. However, one may question whether these regulations are overly broad. A famous study in the 1990's found that there was no greater rate of error in residential real estate closings handled by real estate brokers or title companies, which was permitted in South New Jersey, as compared with those closing handed by lawyers, which was required in North Jersey. *See* In re Opinion No. 26, 654 A.2d 1344, 1359 (N.J. 1995). What did vary, however, is cost. Closings in North Jersey were, on average, $800 more expensive than in South Jersey. There is no doubt that some tasks can only be performed by those with specialized legal training, but there is reason to believe that the preparation of routine documents such as residential leases, simple wills, and uncontested divorce petitions where no children are involved could be handled competently by non-lawyers. Some lawyers bristle at this suggestion. "There's no such thing as a 'routine' representation," they say. "And how would a non-lawyer know if there's some subtle complication that would be apparent only to a lawyer?" Those are fair questions, but shouldn't consumers have a right to decide whether they wish to pay extra for the additional protection they get from hiring a lawyer?

In a recent case called *North Carolina Board of Dental Examiners v. Federal Trade Commission*, 135 S.Ct. 1101 (2015), the Supreme Court held that a state board regulating the practice of dentistry was not immune from antitrust liability because it was not a state actor or actively supervised by the state. The dental board sought to keep non-dentists from offering tooth-whitening services, reasoning that whitening teeth was within the scope of the practice of dentistry. The Court upheld the determination by the Federal Trade Commission that this restriction restricted competition in violation of antitrust laws. This ruling will not likely have that much of an impact on UPL enforcement, to the extent UPL regulations are promulgated by state courts. But it does show the anti-competitive impact of legal restrictions limiting the provision of certain types of services to one professional group.

If whitening teeth can be deemed the "practice of dentistry," what is the definition of the "practice of law"? One thing you have be clear about it that the practice of law is ***not*** limited to entering an appearance on a litigated matter. In some other legal systems, a subset of the legal profession has the exclusive authority to appear in courts of general jurisdiction. The *bengoshi* profession in Japan has this right, and until recent reforms access to the High Courts was limited to barristers in the United Kingdom (solicitors drafted pleadings and dealt with pretrial matters). But the United States has always had a **unified** profession, in the sense that lawyers perform a wide variety of tasks, including drafting pleadings for litigation, drafting documents such as wills and trust instruments, advising clients on compliance with legal obligations, negotiating the terms of transactions and preparing contracts memorializing these terms, and of course pleading and arguing cases in courts, administrative tribunals, and before arbitrators. All of these activities can potentially be considered the practice of law. There's a good bit of state variation on specific questions, such as whether real estate brokers or title company employees can select and fill in the blanks of form documents such as deeds. But generally there's a decent likelihood that if an activity requires knowledge and experience in law, and involves the application of this knowledge to the specific rights and obligations of another person, it may be the practice of law. Please don't make the mistake of thinking that if someone's activities do not include entering an appearance in a litigated matter, they are not the practice of law.

Note, however, that the definition of the practice of law *excludes* the provision of general, non-tailored information. (If it did not, state UPL commissions would find themselves answering a lot of complaints alleging violations of the First Amendment.) A non-lawyer can write a book about defamation law. What a non-lawyer cannot do is advise someone whether she has a viable cause of action for defamation against someone who said something nasty about her.

Some activities may constitute the practice of law, under the broad definition adopted in most states, but are nevertheless *authorized.* All citizens are permitted to act *pro se*—that is, to research the applicability of law to their own situation, draft legal documents, and represent themselves in court. State and federal administrative agency regulations sometimes authorize non-lawyers to serve as representatives. For example, the Board of Immigration Appeals authorizes representation by "[a]ny reputable individual of good moral character." 8 C.F.R. § 1292.1(a)(3). Certain professions also enjoy the right to provide limited types of legal services. For example, certified public accountants (CPAs) may represent taxpayers in practice before the IRS. Finally, alternative dispute resolution forums, such as the American Arbitration Association, may authorize non-lawyer representatives to appear on behalf of the parties.

What You Need to Know:

1. Restrictions on the unauthorized practice of law are intended to protect the public from incompetent or unethical providers of legal services. They do so by

excluding competition by non-lawyers and thus may result in higher prices for consumers.

2. The practice of law is defined quite broadly, to include drafting documents, providing advice, and serving as a representative in negotiations, litigation, or alternative dispute resolution proceedings. It is not limited to in-court representation.

LESSON 19: MULTIJURISDICTIONAL PRACTICE (MJP)

The issue of multijurisdictional practice (MJP) is really nothing more than UPL for lawyers. Despite some interest during the ABA Ethics 20/20 Commission debates in a so-called "driver's license" model, authorization to practice law remains a state-by-state affair. A Missouri driver's license allows you to drive in Illinois, but without an Illinois *law* license, a Missouri-licensed lawyer would not be permitted to practice law in that state.

Suppose Lily is a lawyer who is admitted to practice only in New York. She prepares a will for a client in Florida, or negotiates the settlement of a civil lawsuit on behalf of a client in Florida. She has violated Florida unauthorized practice of law regulations to the same extent as a non-lawyer would for doing the same things. That was the holding of an important case that really focused the attention of the legal profession on the UPL issues created by cross-state practice. *See* Birbrower, Montalbano, Condon & Frank, P.C. v. Superior Court, 949 P.2d 1 (Cal. 1998). In that case a New York law firm represented a California client in a dispute over a software licensing agreement. The agreement was governed by California law, and negotiations and ultimately an arbitration proceeding under the agreement took place in California. The New York lawyers provided competent representation, but they violated the California statutory prohibition on the unauthorized practice of law. As a result, the fee agreement between the law firm and its client was illegal and against public policy, and therefore unenforceable—ouch.

Based on the discussion in the previous lesson, you should be able to analyze the issue of whether the law firm's services included "the practice of law." It provided advice on the interpretation of the software licensing agreement, negotiated with the other party, represented the client in an arbitration, and negotiated and drafted a settlement agreement. Those activities all fall within the definition of the practice of law. It's a bit weird and counterintuitive, but even though a non-lawyer would have been authorized to appear as a representative in the arbitration proceeding, an out-of-state lawyer still needed to be authorized to practice in California before appearing in the arbitration.

We know the firm was practicing law, but how do we know it was practicing "in California"? What if no firm lawyers had ever flown out to California? What if the licensing agreement was governed by New York law but the client was still in California? Can a New York lawyer advise a New York client on California law governing a licensing agreement? What if the client was from Nevada but the other party was in California and the agreement was governed by California law? The *Birbrower* court said that the test for whether the firm practiced law *in California* is "whether the unlicensed lawyer engaged in sufficient activities in the state, or created a continuing relationship with the California client that included legal duties and obligations." *Birbrower*, 949 P.2d at 5. It does not matter whether the lawyer was ever physically present in the state. "[O]ne may practice law in the state . . . although not physically present here by advising a California client on California law in connection with a California legal dispute by telephone, fax, computer, or other modern technological means." *Id.* at 5–6. The most important factor, in my view, is the provision of legal services to a California client. Remember that the primary purpose of UPL regulations is to protect citizens of a state from incompetent or unethical service providers. It follows that the principal reason to enforce California UPL regulations against out-of-state lawyers is to protect California citizens. If a New York law firm bungles the interpretation of California law while representing a New York client, that's a problem for New York. But providing incompetent services to California clients? That's California's problem.

If the New York law firm had been representing the California client in a litigation proceeding in California, it would have had a readily available solution. Out-of-state lawyers may apply for admission *pro hac vice* (that is, for the purpose of a single matter) and represent a party in litigation. The court supervising the litigation has the authority to authorize the limited-purpose representation. In *Birbrower*, however, the law firm was engaged exclusively in non-litigation representation—negotiations, arbitration, and drafting documents. Without a supervising court, there was no authority to whom the firm could appeal for *pro hac vice* admission. One of the lessons of *Birbrower* is, therefore, that cross-state practice of law is a real headache for transactional lawyers. Litigators can always seek *pro hac vice* admission, but there is no comparable mechanism for business lawyers.

The ABA responded to *Birbrower* and similar cases by amending Model Rule 5.5(c) to add several "safe harbors" for the temporary practice of law by out-of-state lawyers. As long as a state has adopted these rules, an out-of-state lawyer may provide legal services on a temporary basis . . .

1. In association with local counsel who actively participate in the matter. (Note that under Rule 1.5(e) the out-of-state lawyer and local counsel may share fees only if both lawyers assume responsibility for the representation—that is, they are on the hook for potential malpractice liability—or the division of fees is proportional to the work performed.)
2. If admitted *pro hac vice* or with a reasonable expectation of being so admitted.
3. In an arbitration or other ADR proceeding (remember, the arbitral tribunal has no authority to grant effective *pro hac vice* admission) if related to the lawyer's practice in a state in which the lawyer is admitted.
4. Otherwise reasonably related to the lawyer's practice in a state in which the lawyer is admitted.

It is extremely important to see that these exceptions are only for the practice of law on a temporary basis. However, temporary practice may include practice on a recurring basis or for an extended period of time, for example if related to a single negotiation or litigated matter. See Model Rule 5.5, cmt. [6]. The line that cannot be crossed is the establishment of an office or other "systematic and continuous presence" in the state. Model Rule 5.5(b). There is no safe harbor for that type of representation. The exceptions in Rule 5.5(c) are aimed at occasional, episodic practice in another state that is related to the lawyer's activities in her admitting jurisdiction. For example, if litigation is proceeding in South Dakota and it is necessary to travel to Minnesota to take a deposition, a lawyer admitted only in South Dakota would not be subject to discipline for the unauthorized practice of law in Minnesota.

What You Need to Know:

1. Lawyers, just like non-lawyers, can engage in the unauthorized practice of law in a state if they are not admitted to practice in that state.
2. Limited safe harbors may exist for the temporary practice in a state, as long as it is reasonably related to practice in the lawyer's admitting jurisdiction.
3. Establishing a systematic and continuous presence in a state, without being admitted to practice in that state, is a violation of Rule 5.5 and state unauthorized practice of law regulations.

LESSON 20: ADMISSION TO PRACTICE

While we're on the subject of admission to practice in a state, we should talk about how an attorney goes about being admitted to practice. As discussed in connection with multijurisdictional practice, lawyers are admitted by individual states, and permitted to practice only in the state of their admission. The Supreme Court has held that the Privileges and Immunities Clause applies to admission to practice, and so a state may not discriminate against non-residents without a substantial reason. New Hampshire Supreme Court v. Piper, 470 U.S. 274

(1985). An examples of a state restriction that might violate the Privileges and Immunities Clause is a New York statute requiring non-resident attorneys admitted to practice in New York to maintain a physical "office for the transaction of law business" within the state. A federal court recently held that the statute did not violate the Privileges and Immunities Clause because it did not have a "protectionist purpose"; rather, it was intended to ensure that non-resident lawyers maintained sufficient physical presence for service-of-process purposes. Schoenfeld v. Schneiderman, 821 F.3d 273 (2nd Cir. 2016). In addition, any requirement imposed by a state for admission to practice must meet the basic rational-basis requirement of the Due Process Clause. Schware v. Board of Bar Examiners, 353 U.S. 232 (1957).

Most states require an applicant for admission to have graduated from a law school approved by the American Bar Association. A few states permit graduates of non-ABA-approved law schools to apply for admission. All states other than Wisconsin require applicants to pass a **bar examination**. An large and increasing number of jurisdictions use multi-state examinations prepared by the National Conference of Bar Examiners. Attorneys already admitted in one jurisdiction may apply for admission on motion—that is, without taking another bar exam—but generally only if they have practiced for a certain number of years.

All states require an applicant to make a showing of good **moral character** and fitness to practice law. The attempt by states to use this standard to bar suspected members of the Communist Party from becoming lawyers led to numerous constitutional challenges and Supreme Court decisions. *See, e.g.*, Konigsberg v. California State Bar, 353 U.S. 252 (1957); In re Anastaplo, 366 U.S. 82 (1960); Baird v. Arizona State Bar, 401 U.S. 1 (1971); In re Stolar, 401 U.S. 23 (1971); Law Students Civil Rights Research Council v. Wadmond, 401 U.S. 154 (1971). From time to time cases still arise in which an applicant's political beliefs or activities are a ground for denial of admission. *See, e.g.*, In re Roots, 762 A.2d 1161 (R.I. 2000) (denying admission to applicant who had denounced the federal government and supported placing fake liens on the property of federal officials); In re Hale, 723 N.E.2d 206 (Ill. 1999) (denying admission to leader of white supremacist organization).

The vast majority of character and fitness denials involve more mundane misconduct. Grounds for **denial** of admission include:

- Conviction of a crime, particularly one involving dishonesty or abuse of a position of trust.
- Academic misconduct.
- Termination of employment for reasons such as embezzlement or dishonesty.
- Neglect of financial responsibilities, including defaulting on student loans and failing to make child support payments.
- Abuse of legal processes, such as a pattern of filing frivolous or harassing lawsuits.
- Dishonesty in the application process, including failure to disclose information, even if the information by itself would not have justified denial of admission.

Misconduct that would justify a denial of admission must be reasonably related to the applicant's fitness to practice law. For example, in a state case from the 1970's, the applicant conceded that non-marital cohabitation would be considered morally wrongful by the people of her state; nevertheless, the Virginia Supreme Court held that the applicant's then-unconventional living arrangement could not support a denial of admission because it was not relevant to her conduct as a lawyer. Cord v. Gibb, 254 S.E.2d 71 (Va. 1979). However, it is *not* the case that an application for admission may be denied only for reasons that would justify discipline of a lawyer already licensed to practice. Admissions committees can take a more proactive approach and seek to keep potential wrongdoers out of the bar entirely. Of course, this goal assumes that it is possible to predict future wrongdoing on the basis of past misconduct.

Applicants may not make a false statement of material fact on an application for admission, and they are also prohibited from disclosing a fact where it would be necessary to correct a misapprehension the applicant knew has arisen in connection with an application for admission. *See* Model Rule 8.1. If dishonesty on an application is discovered after the applicant is admitted, discipline may be imposed on the lawyer for misconduct in connection with the application. These requirements of **candor** in the application process also apply to lawyers who may be asked to certify that they believe the applicant to possess the requisite good moral character required for admission to the bar.

What You Need to Know:

1. Admission to the bar generally requires a degree from an approved law school, passing a written bar examination, and demonstrating good moral character.
2. The Constitution sets limits on the restrictions states may place on applicants for admission to practice.

LESSON 21: ADVERTISING AND SOLICITATION

At the risk of exaggerating a little, I find it helpful to think about this subject as a tug-of-war between the First Amendment and the desire by state regulators to keep a tight leash on attorney advertising to further the ideal of law as a profession, not a mere business. Since the Supreme Court's holding in *Baird v. Arizona State Bar*, 433 U.S. 350 (1977), that attorney advertising is commercial speech protected by the First Amendment, the Court has only given increasing protection to commercial speech. *See, e.g.*, Zauderer v. Office of Disciplinary Counsel, 471 U.S. 626 (1985) (overturning discipline against lawyer who published truthful newspaper advertisement for plaintiffs in products liability case). Clients have a right to know about the availability of legal services and about specific legal rights they may have. Under the Court's *Central Hudson* test, a restriction on commercial speech can survive constitutional scrutiny only if it materially advances a substantial state interest and is narrowly drawn. *See* Central Hudson Gas & Elec. Corp. v. Pub. Serv. Comm'n of N.Y., 447 U.S. 557 (1980).

Protecting the public from deceptive advertising counts as a substantial interest under *Central Hudson*, so states have the right to regulate attorney advertising that is false or misleading. Beyond that, however, restrictions that are aimed at preventing tacky or undignified advertising, or which are drawn too broadly, are likely to be challenged under the First Amendment. For a well-reasoned case written by Judge Calabresi, applying the *Central Hudson* framework to state restrictions on advertising, see Alexander v. Cahill, 598 F.3d 79 (2nd Cir. 2010).

As a result of the back-and-forth between state regulators and courts, you will find quite a bit of variation in state rules on attorney advertising. Some states are quite keen to push the constitutional limits and regulate advertising to the greatest extent possible. Others take a more laissez-faire approach. As always, this discussion will focus on the ABA Model Rules, but if your instructor asks you to pay attention to your own state's rules, you can bet that advertising is one area in which there will be some differences from the Model Rules.

Model Rule 7.1 states the overarching standard that applies to all regulations of attorney advertising and solicitation: A lawyer may not make a false or misleading communication about the lawyer or the lawyer's services. Illustrating the tug-of-war theme, you will find many cases in which the issue was whether the particular communication by the lawyer was false or misleading when it falls in the gray zone between truth and falsity. For example . . .

- A television advertisement showing a simulated jury trial by a recent law school graduate is misleading because the lawyer had never actually tried a case to a jury. In re Zang, 741 P.2d 267 (Ariz. 1987).
- A lawyer who advertised that he was a "lawyer with 20 years of United States Marine Corps experience" was disciplined because he had been a ROTC instructor, not a Marine Corps lawyer. In re Huelskamp, 740 N.E.2d 846 (Ind. 2000).
- Advertisement stating "we speak Spanish" was misleading when only a non-lawyer assistant spoke

Spanish. In re Kaszynski, 620 N.W.2d 708 (Minn. 2001).

None of these cases involves an out-and-out lie, but courts nevertheless will impose discipline against lawyers to communications that get too clever with the truth.

Comment [3] to Rule 7.1 states that an advertisement may be deemed misleading when it truthfully reports a lawyer's achievements, but does so in a way that may cause a reasonable person to form an unjustified expectation about the results the lawyer may be able to obtain. For example, in *Farrin v. Thigpen*, 173 F. Supp. 2d 427 (M.D.N.C. 2001), a dramatization was found misleading where it showed an insurance company settling when it found out the identity of the plaintiff's lawyer. Advertisements announcing big verdicts are sometimes considered misleading, because a prospective client may believe that they implicitly promise similar results. Lawyers who call themselves one of the top lawyers in the state may also be found to have created unjustified expectations on the part of prospective clients. *See, e.g.*, In re Peters, 474 N.W.2d 164 (Minn. 1991). Perhaps the most extreme example of this phenomenon, involving the blandest imaginable statement by a lawyer, is *Medina County Bar Ass'n v. Grieselhuber*, 678 N.E.2d 535 (Ohio 1997), which actually found the motto "We Do It Well" to be false and misleading because it is unverifiable—how would a prospective client know if the lawyer really did it well? If *that* is the kind of statement that a grievance committee may find false or misleading, you can see that Rule 7.1 is sometimes interpreted quite broadly.

Rule 7.2(a) states a general permission to **advertise** in written, recorded, or electronic media. It is important to distinguish advertising from **solicitation**, which is treated very differently as a matter of constitutional law and also under the Model Rules. The Supreme Court has held that advertisement is protected by the First Amendment as commercial speech, but in-person solicitation may be regulated much more tightly, in light of the risk that a trained advocate might persuade a prospective client to hire the lawyer, against the prospective client's interests. *See* Ohralik v. Ohio State Bar Ass'n, 436 U.S. 447 (1978). Accordingly, Model Rule 7.3, to which we'll return momentarily, prohibits most in-person and other live communications which are an attempt to obtain business from a prospective client. However, if a communication is not "in-person, live telephone or real-time electronic contact," then it is considered advertising and is presumptively permitted by Rule 7.2(a), as long as it is not false or misleading—that is, as long as it does not violate Rule 7.1. Lawyers may not, however, give anything of value to another person for recommending the lawyer's services. *See* Rule 7.2(b). A common example of a practice that would violate this rule is giving a pair of tickets to a basketball game to a chiropractor for every referral of a patient to a personal-injury lawyer. There are some exceptions in Rule 7.2(b), and you should look carefully at Comment [5], which deals with electronic marketing.

As mentioned, Rule 7.3(a) establishes a categorical ban on in-person, live, or real-time electronic communications aimed at soliciting employment for pecuniary gain. Notice the latter qualification. Lawyers may use an in-person communication to obtain clients if they are not motivated by pecuniary gain—for example, if they are public interest advocates seeking clients to challenge a discriminatory practice by some institution. First Amendment freedom-of-association cases, including *NAACP v. Button*, 371 U.S. 415 (1963), are an impediment to any effort by a state court to adopt rules banning *all* in-person solicitation, including seeking clients to pursue civil rights claims. *See also* In re Primus, 436 U.S. 412 (1978). Another exception to the prohibition on solicitation covers family members, former clients, or prospective clients who themselves are lawyers (e.g. in-house counsel for a potential corporate client). Notwithstanding these exceptions, solicitation is prohibited if it involves coercion, duress, or harassment, or if the target of the solicitation has made it known that he or she does not wish to be solicited by the lawyer. *See* Rule 7.3(b).

A couple of miscellaneous provisions are no big deal, but you should know them. Rule 7.4 governs communication of the fact that an attorney **specializes** in a particular area of practice. That's okay. *See* Rule 7.4(a), which conforms to *Peel v. Illinois Atty. Reg. & Discip. Comm'n*, 496 U.S. 91 (1990). Of course, like all other communications about a lawyer's services, the fact of specializing in some field of law must be truthful. If a lawyer wants to state that he or she is *certified* as a specialist, however, there must be some approved organization in the state to do the certifying. *See* Rule 7.4(d). Rule 7.5 is concerned with firm names. Trade names, such as "Texas Law Hawk," are permitted by Model Rule 7.5(a), but are prohibited in many states.

What You Need to Know:

1. Attorney advertising is mostly permissible and fairly strongly protected by the First Amendment. Solicitation is mostly prohibited and lacks constitutional protection. The difference is that solicitation involves live, in-person, or real-time electronic contact with a prospective client.
2. The most important principle in the regulation of otherwise permissible advertising is that it not be false or misleading. Courts tend to interpret the prohibition on false communications broadly.

LESSON 22: REPORTING PROFESSIONAL MISCONDUCT—THE "RAT RULE"

One of the hallmarks of a profession—as distinguished from an ordinary business or trade—is that it aspires to be **self-regulating**. The American legal profession is regulated by rules of conduct promulgated by state courts, potential civil liability for negligence, breach of fiduciary duty, and fraud, and legislation and administrative agency regulations. However, an aspect of self-regulation is recognized in Rule 8.3, and that is the duty to report the misconduct of other lawyers.

A case called *In re Himmel*, 533 N.E.2d 790 (Ill. 1988), got everyone's attention when a lawyer was disciplined for failing to report the misconduct of another lawyer. A client retained Himmel to represent her in a lawsuit against her former attorney who had converted the client's settlement proceeds. Himmel and the former lawyer negotiated a settlement providing that the former lawyer would repay the client, and that Himmel would not report him to state disciplinary authorities. Applying the Model Code version of the duty to report, the Illinois Supreme Court suspended Himmel for one year for failing to report the former lawyer.

Notice something important about Model Rule 8.3(c): The Model Rules do not require reporting of information protected by Rule 1.6—that is, "information relating to the representation of a client." The old Model Code provision at issue in *Himmel*, on the other hand, stated that "[a] lawyer possessing unprivileged knowledge" of wrongdoing must report. *See* Model Code, DR 1–103(A). If you do not *immediately* see the difference between these rules, go back and review Lesson 9 on the distinction between the duty of **confidentiality** (i.e. Rule 1.6(a), "information relating to representation") and the **attorney-client privilege**. The Model Code version of the reporting rule exempts communications covered by the attorney-client privilege. Do you see why Himmel would have had to report the settlement negotiations and the content of the settlement agreement? By contrast, Model Rule 8.3 does not require reporting of information relating to the representation. A modern-day Himmel, in a Model Rules jurisdiction, would not have to report. Please make sure you understand this. The duty of confidentiality supersedes the reporting obligation. Since a great deal of information learned about another lawyer's misconduct is likely to be "information relating to the representation of a client," in practice the reporting obligation does not often arise. One context in which it does arise, however, is when a lawyer learns about misconduct by another lawyer in the same firm. *See, e.g.*, Board of Overseers v. Warren, 34 A.3d 1103 (Me. 2011).

Rule 8.3(a) requires reporting only of a violation that raises a substantial question as to the lawyer's honesty, trustworthiness, or fitness to practice in some other respect. As Comment [3] puts it, the reporting obligation is limited to misconduct "that a self-regulating profession must vigorously endeavor to prevent." So there's no violation of Rule 8.3 if a lawyer knows of some minor violation of a professional duty.

What You Need to Know:

1. The duty to report professional misconduct is qualified by the duty of confidentiality.

2. The reporting obligation applies only to misconduct indicating another lawyer's unfitness to practice.

TABLE OF CASES

INDEX

References are to Pages